Lecture Notes in Computer Science 14046

Founding Editors

Gerhard Goos
Juris Hartmanis

The series Lecture Notes in Computer Science (LNCS), including its subseries Lecture Notes in Artificial Intelligence (LNAI) and Lecture Notes in Bioinformatics (LNBI), has established itself as a medium for the publication of new developments in computer science and information technology research, teaching, and education.

LNCS enjoys close cooperation with the computer science R & D community, the series counts many renowned academics among its volume editors and paper authors, and collaborates with prestigious societies. Its mission is to serve this international community by providing an invaluable service, mainly focused on the publication of conference and workshop proceedings and postproceedings. LNCS commenced publication in 1973.

Xiaowen Fang

Editor

HCI in Games

5th International Conference, HCI-Games 2023
Held as Part of the 25th HCI International Conference, HCII 2023
Copenhagen, Denmark, July 23–28, 2023
Proceedings, Part I

 Springer

Editor
Xiaowen Fang
DePaul University
Chicago, IL, USA

ISSN 0302-9743   ISSN 1611-3349 (electronic)
Lecture Notes in Computer Science
ISBN 978-3-031-35929-3   ISBN 978-3-031-35930-9 (eBook)
https://doi.org/10.1007/978-3-031-35930-9

This Springer imprint is published by the registered company Springer Nature Switzerland AG
The registered company address is: Gewerbestrasse 11, 6330 Cham, Switzerland

Foreword

Human-computer interaction (HCI) is acquiring an ever-increasing scientific and industrial importance, as well as having more impact on people's everyday lives, as an ever-growing number of human activities are progressively moving from the physical to the digital world. This process, which has been ongoing for some time now, was further accelerated during the acute period of the COVID-19 pandemic. The HCI International (HCII) conference series, held annually, aims to respond to the compelling need to advance the exchange of knowledge and research and development efforts on the human aspects of design and use of computing systems.

The 25th International Conference on Human-Computer Interaction, HCI International 2023 (HCII 2023), was held in the emerging post-pandemic era as a 'hybrid' event at the AC Bella Sky Hotel and Bella Center, Copenhagen, Denmark, during July 23–28, 2023. It incorporated the 21 thematic areas and affiliated conferences listed below.

A total of 7472 individuals from academia, research institutes, industry, and government agencies from 85 countries submitted contributions, and 1578 papers and 396 posters were included in the volumes of the proceedings that were published just before the start of the conference, these are listed below. The contributions thoroughly cover the entire field of human-computer interaction, addressing major advances in knowledge and effective use of computers in a variety of application areas. These papers provide academics, researchers, engineers, scientists, practitioners and students with state-of-the-art information on the most recent advances in HCI.

The HCI International (HCII) conference also offers the option of presenting 'Late Breaking Work', and this applies both for papers and posters, with corresponding volumes of proceedings that will be published after the conference. Full papers will be included in the 'HCII 2023 - Late Breaking Work - Papers' volumes of the proceedings to be published in the Springer LNCS series, while 'Poster Extended Abstracts' will be included as short research papers in the 'HCII 2023 - Late Breaking Work - Posters' volumes to be published in the Springer CCIS series.

I would like to thank the Program Board Chairs and the members of the Program Boards of all thematic areas and affiliated conferences for their contribution towards the high scientific quality and overall success of the HCI International 2023 conference. Their manifold support in terms of paper reviewing (single-blind review process, with a minimum of two reviews per submission), session organization and their willingness to act as goodwill ambassadors for the conference is most highly appreciated.

This conference would not have been possible without the continuous and unwavering support and advice of Gavriel Salvendy, founder, General Chair Emeritus, and Scientific Advisor. For his outstanding efforts, I would like to express my sincere appreciation to Abbas Moallem, Communications Chair and Editor of HCI International News.

July 2023   Constantine Stephanidis

HCI International 2023 Thematic Areas and Affiliated Conferences

Thematic Areas

- HCI: Human-Computer Interaction
- HIMI: Human Interface and the Management of Information

Affiliated Conferences

- EPCE: 20th International Conference on Engineering Psychology and Cognitive Ergonomics
- AC: 17th International Conference on Augmented Cognition
- UAHCI: 17th International Conference on Universal Access in Human-Computer Interaction
- CCD: 15th International Conference on Cross-Cultural Design
- SCSM: 15th International Conference on Social Computing and Social Media
- VAMR: 15th International Conference on Virtual, Augmented and Mixed Reality
- DHM: 14th International Conference on Digital Human Modeling and Applications in Health, Safety, Ergonomics and Risk Management
- DUXU: 12th International Conference on Design, User Experience and Usability
- C&C: 11th International Conference on Culture and Computing
- DAPI: 11th International Conference on Distributed, Ambient and Pervasive Interactions
- HCIBGO: 10th International Conference on HCI in Business, Government and Organizations
- LCT: 10th International Conference on Learning and Collaboration Technologies
- ITAP: 9th International Conference on Human Aspects of IT for the Aged Population
- AIS: 5th International Conference on Adaptive Instructional Systems
- HCI-CPT: 5th International Conference on HCI for Cybersecurity, Privacy and Trust
- HCI-Games: 5th International Conference on HCI in Games
- MobiTAS: 5th International Conference on HCI in Mobility, Transport and Automotive Systems
- AI-HCI: 4th International Conference on Artificial Intelligence in HCI
- MOBILE: 4th International Conference on Design, Operation and Evaluation of Mobile Communications

List of Conference Proceedings Volumes Appearing Before the Conference

1. LNCS 14011, Human-Computer Interaction: Part I, edited by Masaaki Kurosu and Ayako Hashizume
2. LNCS 14012, Human-Computer Interaction: Part II, edited by Masaaki Kurosu and Ayako Hashizume
3. LNCS 14013, Human-Computer Interaction: Part III, edited by Masaaki Kurosu and Ayako Hashizume
4. LNCS 14014, Human-Computer Interaction: Part IV, edited by Masaaki Kurosu and Ayako Hashizume
5. LNCS 14015, Human Interface and the Management of Information: Part I, edited by Hirohiko Mori and Yumi Asahi
6. LNCS 14016, Human Interface and the Management of Information: Part II, edited by Hirohiko Mori and Yumi Asahi
7. LNAI 14017, Engineering Psychology and Cognitive Ergonomics: Part I, edited by Don Harris and Wen-Chin Li
8. LNAI 14018, Engineering Psychology and Cognitive Ergonomics: Part II, edited by Don Harris and Wen-Chin Li
9. LNAI 14019, Augmented Cognition, edited by Dylan D. Schmorrow and Cali M. Fidopiastis
10. LNCS 14020, Universal Access in Human-Computer Interaction: Part I, edited by Margherita Antona and Constantine Stephanidis
11. LNCS 14021, Universal Access in Human-Computer Interaction: Part II, edited by Margherita Antona and Constantine Stephanidis
12. LNCS 14022, Cross-Cultural Design: Part I, edited by Pei-Luen Patrick Rau
13. LNCS 14023, Cross-Cultural Design: Part II, edited by Pei-Luen Patrick Rau
14. LNCS 14024, Cross-Cultural Design: Part III, edited by Pei-Luen Patrick Rau
15. LNCS 14025, Social Computing and Social Media: Part I, edited by Adela Coman and Simona Vasilache
16. LNCS 14026, Social Computing and Social Media: Part II, edited by Adela Coman and Simona Vasilache
17. LNCS 14027, Virtual, Augmented and Mixed Reality, edited by Jessie Y. C. Chen and Gino Fragomeni
18. LNCS 14028, Digital Human Modeling and Applications in Health, Safety, Ergonomics and Risk Management: Part I, edited by Vincent G. Duffy
19. LNCS 14029, Digital Human Modeling and Applications in Health, Safety, Ergonomics and Risk Management: Part II, edited by Vincent G. Duffy
20. LNCS 14030, Design, User Experience, and Usability: Part I, edited by Aaron Marcus, Elizabeth Rosenzweig and Marcelo Soares
21. LNCS 14031, Design, User Experience, and Usability: Part II, edited by Aaron Marcus, Elizabeth Rosenzweig and Marcelo Soares

22. LNCS 14032, Design, User Experience, and Usability: Part III, edited by Aaron Marcus, Elizabeth Rosenzweig and Marcelo Soares
23. LNCS 14033, Design, User Experience, and Usability: Part IV, edited by Aaron Marcus, Elizabeth Rosenzweig and Marcelo Soares
24. LNCS 14034, Design, User Experience, and Usability: Part V, edited by Aaron Marcus, Elizabeth Rosenzweig and Marcelo Soares
25. LNCS 14035, Culture and Computing, edited by Matthias Rauterberg
26. LNCS 14036, Distributed, Ambient and Pervasive Interactions: Part I, edited by Norbert Streitz and Shin'ichi Konomi
27. LNCS 14037, Distributed, Ambient and Pervasive Interactions: Part II, edited by Norbert Streitz and Shin'ichi Konomi
28. LNCS 14038, HCI in Business, Government and Organizations: Part I, edited by Fiona Fui-Hoon Nah and Keng Siau
29. LNCS 14039, HCI in Business, Government and Organizations: Part II, edited by Fiona Fui-Hoon Nah and Keng Siau
30. LNCS 14040, Learning and Collaboration Technologies: Part I, edited by Panayiotis Zaphiris and Andri Ioannou
31. LNCS 14041, Learning and Collaboration Technologies: Part II, edited by Panayiotis Zaphiris and Andri Ioannou
32. LNCS 14042, Human Aspects of IT for the Aged Population: Part I, edited by Qin Gao and Jia Zhou
33. LNCS 14043, Human Aspects of IT for the Aged Population: Part II, edited by Qin Gao and Jia Zhou
34. LNCS 14044, Adaptive Instructional Systems, edited by Robert A. Sottilare and Jessica Schwarz
35. LNCS 14045, HCI for Cybersecurity, Privacy and Trust, edited by Abbas Moallem
36. LNCS 14046, HCI in Games: Part I, edited by Xiaowen Fang
37. LNCS 14047, HCI in Games: Part II, edited by Xiaowen Fang
38. LNCS 14048, HCI in Mobility, Transport and Automotive Systems: Part I, edited by Heidi Krömker
39. LNCS 14049, HCI in Mobility, Transport and Automotive Systems: Part II, edited by Heidi Krömker
40. LNAI 14050, Artificial Intelligence in HCI: Part I, edited by Helmut Degen and Stavroula Ntoa
41. LNAI 14051, Artificial Intelligence in HCI: Part II, edited by Helmut Degen and Stavroula Ntoa
42. LNCS 14052, Design, Operation and Evaluation of Mobile Communications, edited by Gavriel Salvendy and June Wei
43. CCIS 1832, HCI International 2023 Posters - Part I, edited by Constantine Stephanidis, Margherita Antona, Stavroula Ntoa and Gavriel Salvendy
44. CCIS 1833, HCI International 2023 Posters - Part II, edited by Constantine Stephanidis, Margherita Antona, Stavroula Ntoa and Gavriel Salvendy
45. CCIS 1834, HCI International 2023 Posters - Part III, edited by Constantine Stephanidis, Margherita Antona, Stavroula Ntoa and Gavriel Salvendy
46. CCIS 1835, HCI International 2023 Posters - Part IV, edited by Constantine Stephanidis, Margherita Antona, Stavroula Ntoa and Gavriel Salvendy

47. CCIS 1836, HCI International 2023 Posters - Part V, edited by Constantine Stephanidis, Margherita Antona, Stavroula Ntoa and Gavriel Salvendy

https://2023.hci.international/proceedings

Preface

Computer games have grown beyond simple entertainment activities. Researchers and practitioners have attempted to utilize games in many innovative ways, such as educational games, therapeutic games, simulation games, and gamification of utilitarian applications. Although a lot of attention has been given to investigate the positive impact of games in recent years, prior research has only studied isolated fragments of a game system. More research on games is needed to develop and utilize games for the benefit of society.

At a high level, a game system has three basic elements: system input, process, and system output. System input concerns the external factors impacting the game system. It may include, but is not limited to, player personalities and motivations to play games. The process is about game mechanism and play experience. System output includes the effects of game play. There is no doubt that users are involved in all three elements. Human Computer Interaction (HCI) plays a critical role in the study of games. By examining player characteristics, interactions during game play, and behavioral implications of game play, HCI professionals can help design and develop better games for society.

The 5th International Conference on HCI in Games (HCI-Games 2023), an affiliated conference of the HCI International Conference, intended to help, promote, and encourage research in this field by providing a forum for interaction and exchanges among researchers, academics, and practitioners in the fields of HCI and games. The Conference addressed HCI principles, methods, and tools for better games.

This year, researchers from around the world contributed significant amounts of work in multiple themes. Regarding game design and development, researchers reported their continuous efforts in addressing game design from both system and user/player perspectives. It is noteworthy that a major portion of the papers are related to research work dedicated to improving our society through gamification, serious games, and learning games. The papers included in the proceedings represent the professionalism and commitment to society of the HCI in Games community.

Two volumes of the HCII 2023 proceedings are dedicated to this year's edition of the HCI-Games Conference. The first volume focuses on topics related to game design and development, as well as gamification and serious games. The second volume focuses on topics related to games for learning, as well as understanding players and the player experience.

The papers in these volumes were included for publication after a minimum of two single–blind reviews from the members of the HCI-Games Program Board or, in some cases, from members of the Program Boards of other affiliated conferences. I would like to thank all of them for their invaluable contribution, support, and efforts.

July 2023   Xiaowen Fang

5th International Conference on HCI in Games
(HCI-Games 2023)

Program Board Chair: **Xiaowen Fang,** *DePaul University, USA*

Program Board:

- Amir Zaib Abbasi, *King Fahd University of Petroleum and Minerals, Saudi Arabia*
- Dena Al-Thani, *HBKU, Qatar*
- Abdullah Azhari, *King Abdulaziz University, Saudi Arabia*
- Barbara Caci, *University of Palermo, Italy*
- Ben Cowley, *University of Helsinki, Finland*
- Khaldoon Dhou, *Texas A&M University-Central Texas, USA*
- Kevin Keeker, *Sony Interactive Entertainment, USA*
- Daniel Riha, *Charles University, Czech Republic*
- Owen Schaffer, *Bradley University, USA*
- Jason Schklar, *UX is Fine!, USA*
- Fan Zhao, *Florida Gulf Coast University, USA*
- Miaoqi Zhu, *Sony Pictures Entertainment, USA*

The full list with the Program Board Chairs and the members of the Program Boards of all thematic areas and affiliated conferences of HCII2023 is available online at:

http://www.hci.international/board-members-2023.php

HCI International 2024 Conference

The 26th International Conference on Human-Computer Interaction, HCI International 2024, will be held jointly with the affiliated conferences at the Washington Hilton Hotel, Washington, DC, USA, June 29 – July 4, 2024. It will cover a broad spectrum of themes related to Human-Computer Interaction, including theoretical issues, methods, tools, processes, and case studies in HCI design, as well as novel interaction techniques, interfaces, and applications. The proceedings will be published by Springer. More information will be made available on the conference website: http://2024.hci.international/.

General Chair
Prof. Constantine Stephanidis
University of Crete and ICS-FORTH
Heraklion, Crete, Greece
Email: general_chair@hcii2024.org

https://2024.hci.international/

Contents – Part I

Gamification and Serious Games

Contents – Part II

Game Design and Development

Stocks Investment Decision-Making: A Theoretical Model

Saeed Abo-oleet[1]($\boxtimes$), Fan Zhao[2], and Xiaowen Fang[1]

[1] DePaul University, Chicago, IL 60604, USA
Abo.oleet@gmail.com, Xfang@cdm.depaul.edu
[2] Florida Gulf Coast University, Fort Myers, FL 33965, USA
fzhao@fgcu.edu

Abstract. With the proliferation of technology, equity investors have more access to financial information that enables them to make investment decisions independently. However, this decision-making process is mostly ignored by the HCI and IS literature. Therefore, this study seeks to address this gap by investigating individual users' intention to invest in stocks by developing a Value-Cost model. The model is based on the Transaction Cost Economics Theory (TCE) and the concept of perceived value. The study model argues that as long as the users' perceptions of benefits are higher than the endured costs, users will perceive stocks investment as a valuable endeavor, forming positive intentions towards investment. The model is presented, and hypotheses are proposed.

Keywords: Equity Investment · Decision-Making · Transaction Cost · Investors Behavior · Perceived Value

1 Introduction

Technology has transformed how the financial industry functions. Banks and stock brokerage firms have shifted from serving customers face-to-face or over the phone to serving them virtually through their online presence. With the proliferation of technology, retail investors have more access to financial information that can help them plan their financial activities, such as tracking real-time stock price, portfolio management, market liquidity etc. [1]. Technological advances have also enabled retail investors to fully control their investment decisions where they can buy and sell stocks without the need for intermediaries such as brokers (e.g., Robinhood). Such a shift has attracted information systems researchers to investigate the role of technology in individuals' investment decisions [2–4].

However, most IS research has focused on the e-financial adoption and acceptance side while overlooking other issues related to the investment decision-making process. Investment decision-making is categorized as complex behavior in nature [5, 6]. Retail investors are considered less able to objectively evaluate an investment's risks and returns since they tend to be emotionally biased [7]. The vast abundance of information resulting from the widespread use of technology (e.g., social media) further complicates investment decision-making, especially equity investments. For instance, it has been validated that stock markets overreact to information [8]. Another example is the drastic price increase in Game Stop stocks in 2020 due to an organized movement led by individual investors on Reddit [9].

A decision regarding investing in equities is reached by evaluating various choices, such as the suitability of investing at a certain point in an investor's life, taking into account several factors such as wealth, years until retirement, risk appetite etc. In a recent paper, Choi and Robertson assert that regardless of having many theories that investigate investors' motivations and beliefs, the difficulty resides in testing these theories with observational data [10]. There are a notable amount of papers that used methodology surveys to explore how investment decisions are made based on pure market variables and demographics in different contexts such as corporate finance [11, 12], professionals investors [13–15], and households [10]. Also, other studies have employed behavioral theories such as the theory of planned behavior (TPB), the theory of reason actions (TRA), and prospect theory to explain individual investors' decision-making process [16–19]. Long-term capital growth, dividends and a hedge against the inflationary erosion of purchasing power are among the factors impacting people to invest in stocks.

Nevertheless, a comprehensive model that explains retail investors' decision-making process, especially those who do not have much experience, is yet to be developed. Thus, in this paper, we rely on the IS practices of conducting research by building a theoretical model that explains what motivates individual users to invest in equities. We argue that inexperienced retail investors make their decisions by weighing the benefits gained against the costs endured, resulting in their overall perceived value. People vary in their assessment of costs and benefits, highlighting the unique differences between people. By relying on the Transaction Cost Economics Theory (TCE) and the concept of perceived value, we propose a theoretical model that considers these differences regarding investors' valuation process and how it influences their intentions to invest in stocks. This model hypothesizes that investment intentions are explained by investors' assessment of perceived benefits against perceived transaction costs. Higher overall perceived benefits lead to a higher perception of value, positively impacting their investment intentions.

The perceived transaction costs are considered a dynamic factor that differs among different users and for the same user based on the situation and circumstances that they are currently experiencing. For instance, when a current investor doubts future regulations regarding some industries they have invested in, the investment cost will increase regardless of the current investment stage. Consequently, this leads to performing a reassessment of the value. If they feel the value is still greater, they are assumed to continue investing in stocks.

Zuravicky argues that individuals' investment in a company's equity is the most effective channel for raising capital [20]. Therefore, organizations ought to understand what drives individual users to invest in stocks because these individual investors might be what save them from vanishing (e.g., GameStop). Also, this model can help service providers such as online trading companies identify individual users' perceived costs and aim to minimize them. Thus, the proposed model could explain how to reduce stock investing costs by accounting for individual differences, which will help practitioners and policymakers understand what constitutes the investment, making them capable of shaping future strategies related to development and marketing.

The remainder of the paper proceeds as follows. Section 2 reviews the literature. Section 3 presents our theoretical model. Section 4 discusses the proposed model and concludes.

2 Background

2.1 Investment Motivations

There has been a wide range of factors explaining investment motivation derived from various sources. First, heuristic factors are the rule of thumb that aids the decision-making process in complex and uncertain environments [21]. Heuristics are helpful whenever there is a time constraint. Heuristics factors that affect investors' decisions include representativeness, availability bias, anchoring, gamblers fallacy, and overconfidence [22]. Second, factors based on the prospect theory assume that individuals may make a decision that does not necessarily maximize their utility because they place other considerations above utility. Factors related to the prospect theory include loss aversion, regret aversion, and mental accounting [23]. Third, investors might invest based on pure market factors such as price changes or past trends etc. [8, 22, 24]. Finally, investors might base their decisions on how others invest, herding factors [25].

Other researchers focus on employing theories that explain individuals' behavior (e.g., TPB) and salient factors rooted in the IS and Psychology literature (e.g., self-efficacy, perceived risk, information asymmetry). In these studies, researchers try to understand the motivations behind individuals' involvement in the investment process. For instance, Sondari and Sudarsono utilize the TPB, where attitudes toward investment and subjective norms have significantly influenced the intention to invest [26]. Also, Qureshi has conducted a study to measure the main determinants of investment decision-making and concludes that risk propensity, framing of the problem, information asymmetry, and perceived risk are the main determinants [27]. Others state that external factors consisting of regulation and information technology positively affect investment decisions [28].

2.2 Transaction Cost Economics (TCE)

A transaction is a process by which a good or service is transferred across a technologically separable interface [29]. Coase questions the existence of firms without the help of the market in providing them with the agents they need [30]. He argues that acquiring such agents constitutes several costs, such as finding those agents, the costs of drafting contracts, etc. Coase explains that reducing these costs is due to the power of command and control exercised from top to bottom. He argues that the firm helps settle disputes and consequently reduces costs related to the management of contracts and agreements.

The core proposition of TCE is to help organizations in selecting the best governance (market, hybrid, or hierarchy) while conducting a transaction [31]. In classical economics, it is assumed that information is symmetric in the market, where buyers and sellers are assumed to have the same amount of information, meaning that the transaction can be completed without any cost. In reality, however, such transactions involve various costs, such as the costs associated with searching, negotiating, contracting, and maintaining a relationship with a business partner while completing the transaction.

TCE has two critical assumptions: bounded rationality and opportunism. Bounded rationality refers to humans' limited memories and processing capacity, making them unable to fully process all information simultaneously. Indeed, they cannot accurately forecast the consequences of this information [32]. Opportunism refers to how people might act in their self-interest, where some might not always act honestly [33, 34]. Accordingly, TCE identifies three dimensions affecting transaction costs: uncertainty, asset specificity, and transaction frequency.

Reaching an optimal decision may be difficult, where TCE views bounded rationality as an issue with many uncertainties. Moreover, when transaction costs include asset-specific investments, this raises the possibility that people will behave opportunistically, thus increasing the chance of being exploited. Overall, the combination of uncertainties and asset specificity will result in information asymmetry, eventually raising transaction costs. Finally, transaction frequency refers to the frequency that a particular transaction is repeated [29]. Transaction costs are minimized when making a renewal or another contract with the same counterparty because the established relationship reduces the perceived risk of opportunism [35]. Hence, the lower the transaction costs, the more likely the transaction will be conducted.

Previous behavioral-related research utilization of TCE primarily explains the monetary cost associated with completing a specific activity, such as adopting new technology or buying products online. Such utilization excludes the subcomponents of this construct (e.g., searching cost, negotiation cost) and its antecedents, uncertainty, asset specificity and transaction frequency. This limits the power of TCE in explaining the overall costs associated with making a particular decision. In this paper, TCE is adopted to explain the overall transaction cost associated with making an equity investment. This paper also extends the TCE by incorporating the perceived value that is reviewed next.

2.3 Valuation Process

Perceived value is not a new concept that is rooted in diverse fields and theoretical perspectives [36]. It has been connected to psychology and social psychology [37] and marketing research [38], which contribute to strong terminological heterogeneity. Initial perceived value research focuses on the quality-price relationship [36]. This, in a way, brought forward the definition of value as the "cognitive trade-off between perceptions of quality and sacrifice" [39]. Zeithaml proposes four definitions that are based on customers' perceptions: (1) "value is low price," (2) "value is whatever I want in a product," (3) "value is the quality I get for the price I pay," and (4) "value is what I get for what I give" [38]. A widely adopted definition that represents these four perspectives is hence proposed as: "the consumer's overall assessment of the utility of a product based on what is received and what is given" [38]. As a result, the perceived value was conceptualized as this unidimensional construct, even though Zeithaml has suggested that value is a higher-level abstraction, and a difference exists between the (objective) attributes of a product or service and the (subjective) outcomes or perceptions of those attributes [36]. Therefore, the customer's perceived value is a subjective (or personal) concept; indeed, it is perceived by the consumer rather than the seller's objective.

Users' value perceptions involve some sort of cost-benefit analysis [36]. It is broadly defined as the trade-off between benefits and sacrifices (i.e., costs) associated with a specific service or product. But, the broad definition of perceived value simplifies the multi-dimensionality of decision-making [40]. Consequently, the value-based adoption model (VAM) is introduced, where benefits and sacrifice are modeled as antecedents of the perceived value. In terms of the consequences, previous literature suggests that customer value leads ultimately to actual behavior [41]. Hence, customer value is a significant predictor of a user's choice [36]. Behavioral outcomes associated with value include technology adoption, purchase intention [42], repurchase and loyalty [43]), and customer satisfaction [44, 45].

3   Theoretical Model

According to Zeithaml, perceived value is the result of the overall assessment of the utility of a product or service based on what is received and what is given. Yet, researchers argue that the broad interpretation of costs and benefits ignores the multi-dimensionality of decision-making and does not fully represent perceived benefits and sacrifices [40]. The TCE argues that people will attempt to minimize their transaction costs. Consequently, value maximization is the common assumption when evaluating consumer behavior. Therefore, users' evaluation of the trade-off between the benefits and sacrifices (i.e., costs) of investing in stocks will result in their overall perception of its value, which eventually will impact their behavior towards it.

If the proposed Value-Cost model in Fig. 1 is valid, then the more uncertainties users have regarding investing in stocks, the more transaction costs they experience. These uncertainties can be related to environmental risks_ such as rare disaster risks and new governmental policies, or uncertainties related to the market_ such as the ambiguity of the returns compared to the risks. Also, when users invest unique investments (e.g., time and effort) in learning how to trade stocks, the overall transaction costs increase due to the difficulty of redeploying knowledge to other areas (e.g., real estate investment).

The Value-Cost model argues that users who perceive stocks as valuable are more likely to invest in them. However, the valuation process is complicated due to different aspects. Therefore, the authors operationalize perceived benefits as a multidimensional construct that involves two sub-constructs: liquidity and prospect of growth (discussed further later). Simply, when individual investors believe that stock investment can be liquidated in a timely manner and they can grow in value, they would perceive the investment in stocks as beneficial, resulting in a higher perception of value. As long as this perception of benefits is high, the costs of investing in stocks are regarded as unnecessary since benefits surpass them, thus leading to positive intentions to invest.

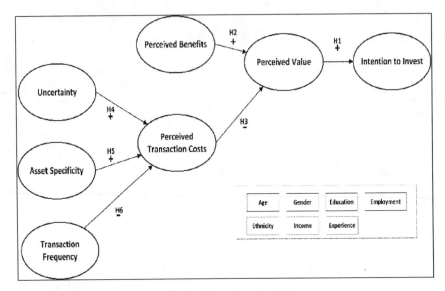

Fig. 1. Value-Cost Model

3.1 Perceived Value

The premise of VAM is that sacrifices and benefits should constitute more meanings than the general operationalization that is limited to quality versus price [40]. Some researchers adopt the TCE to account for the costs of using sharing platforms while perceived benefits assess the possible gains [46]. Similarly, the authors utilize the TCE to explain the sacrifices/costs of stocks investment and both perceived benefits to describe the gains of making such an investment. Consequently, we define perceived value as investors' overall assessment of stock investment based on the considerations of its benefits and sacrifices (i.e., costs).

Behavioral intention is argued to have the same determinants of actual behavior [47] while it is the immediate determinant of actual behavior [48]. The theory of reasoned action (TRA) and the theory of planned behavior (TPB) highlight the intention to perform a given behavior [48]. Intentions are presumed to capture the factors that impact the behavior, indicating how users are willing to try and how much effort they are willing to wield to perform the behavior. The stranger the intention to be a part of specific behavior, the more likely its performance should be [48].

Previous research indicates that users' perception of value leads to positive behavioral intentions such as_ the continuous use of smartwatches and e-government, the purchase intention in social commerce and free-to-play games, the adoption of mobile internet, wearable devices and mobile payment [40, 49–54].

Based on the above discussion, the authors argue that investors' investment intentions in stocks are explained by their assessment of overall perceived value. For instance, for users who believe that investing in stocks is valuable, the perceived benefits (e.g., exchangeable for cash at any time) must be greater than the costs associated with it. Consequently, the authors debate that as long as the perceived value of the investment is high, investors will have positive intentions to invest. Therefore, the proposed model (Fig. 1) hypothesizes the following:

H1: Perceived value is positively associated with the intention to invest.

3.2 Perceived Benefits

Perceived benefits can be intrinsic or extrinsic [40, 46]. The economic benefits are attributed to extrinsic motivations where users expect tangible rewards while investing in stocks, which creates value in them. Stock's ability to be easily liquidated coupled with the possibility of increased price create value in them.

First, liquidity is the ease with which an asset is traded while offering the lowest possible price concession [55, 56]. In simpler terms, liquidity means the efficiency or ease with which an asset or security can be converted into ready cash without affecting its market price. Liquidity is a multidimensional factor that encompasses quantity, cost, and time [57]. Due to these three dimensions, Holden et al. assert the equal importance of liquidity for both liquidity demanders and suppliers. *"Liquidity matters because it represents the cost, quantity, and time of a trade to the liquidity demander. Equivalently, it represents the profit, quantity, and time of a trade to the liquidity supplier"* [57]. For an investor who wants out, liquidity is the extent to which she can sell her exact offered stocks for the price she requires and the in a timely manner she has anticipated. Liquidity has been identified as an essential factor impacting investors' decision-making. For instance, Ng and Wu examine the stock preference of Chinese retail investors, concluding that liquidity is a significant factor that affects their investment decisions [58]. Therefore, when individual investors believe they can liquidate their stocks at any time, they perceive them as valuable.

Second, stocks' ability to grow in value in the future makes them appealing to investors since the return on investment will increase. For instance, it has been concluded that individual Chinese investors prefer low-priced stocks with growth potential [58]. Additionally, domestic fund managers lean towards investing in stocks that pay significant dividends and have high growth potential [59]. Thus, the extent to which investors believe that stocks might be worth more in the future creates value in them, which explains some users' motivation behind obtaining them. For investors, there should be a level of belief that their stocks will grow in value as time goes on. Without this growth, it would not be logical to risk losing their investment due to market volatility instead of locking it in saving accounts.

Hence, liquidity and the prospect of growth create value in stocks, generating positive outcomes for investment intentions. Eventually, the more value stocks investors perceive, the more positive intentions they have to invest in them. However, this belief is subjective, where different users have different views, thus emphasizing the role of individual differences in users' perceptions of stock value. As a result, the authors define liquidity as stocks' ability to be exchanged for cash promptly without decreasing in value. The prospect of growth is defined as a stock's capability to grow in value in the future. Therefore, perceived benefits are defined as users' belief that stocks can be liquidated at any time and that they have the potential to grow in value in the future. Therefore, the proposed model (Fig. 1) hypothesizes the following:

H2: Perceived benefits are positively associated with perceived value.

3.3 Perceived Transaction Costs

According to the TCE, it is expected to have different transaction costs while making an economic exchange, such as the costs related to searching for information about the exchange, negotiating the transaction terms and policy, and policing and enforcing these terms [29]. So, processing such costs is difficult since people who conduct the exchange have limited memory and cognitive processing capacity. Moreover, some of the exchange parties might act in their own best interests.

Thus, the authors define the perceived transaction costs as investors' perception of the time and cognitive effort needed to invest in stocks. Perceived transaction costs might represent different facets, such as the cost of staying up to date on the market (i.e., searching for information costs) compared to other types of investments (e.g., real estate). This includes the time and effort expended in the evaluation process that investors go through before investing, such as comparing the prices of assets and fees. Another facet would include the cost of monitoring a particular exchange (i.e., transaction), which is related to the time and effort spent to ensure that a transaction is executed successfully (e.g., buy order status). Finally, the adapting cost represents the costs endured to adapt some exceptions after the transaction implementation, such as making changes to a transaction.

Users' assessment of the perceived transaction costs of investing in stocks impacts their investment decision. High perceived transaction costs will have a negative effect on the perceived value of stocks. However, if users' perceived benefits exceed the costs, they will have positive intentions to invest due to the minimized transaction costs. Perceived transaction cost is a dynamic attribute that might change over time due to the effect of its antecedents. Therefore, the proposed model (Fig. 1) hypothesizes the following:

H3: Perceived transaction costs are negatively associated with perceived value.

3.4 Uncertainty

It is assumed that all transactions are conducted under a level of uncertainty [60]. Williamson explains that uncertainty arises from imperfect foresight and humans' inability to solve complex problems associated with transactions, which can be regarded as the cost associated with unexpected outcomes and information asymmetry [29]. In the stock market, retail investors are faced with many uncertainties that can be attributed to different sources, such as uncertainty related to the market itself or uncertainties related to the environments of that market. The authors argue that the uncertainty construct can be explained by three sub-constructs_ perceived environmental uncertainty, perceived risk and perceived regulatory uncertainty.

First, environmental uncertainty has long been rooted in the IS literature [61]–[63]. For example, in the organizational context, environmental uncertainty refers to the inability to forecast the effect of external factors on the failure or success of a decision-making process inside a specific organization [64, 65]. Although environmental uncertainty has been viewed as an objective construct, it is generally considered a perceptual construct [66]. Therefore, in this paper, perceived environmental uncertainty refers to external factors that make retail investors unable to fully predict the success of their investment decisions (e.g., global health issues, wars, elections, economic disasters etc.). For instance, Choi and Robertson study the motivations behind retail investors' stock market participation. They conclude that 45.5% of the participants and non-participants are concerned about rare economic disasters such as the great depression, which might result in less returns on their investments in stocks [10]. Also, they demonstrate that 30% of the participants are concerned that the stock market might drop in value if bad news arrives that the US's material standard of living will change in the next year or five years.

Second, perceived risk refers to the extent users believe investing in the stock market is risky. It has been argued to be a multidimensional construct that can lead to financial losses due to security and privacy threats, along with non-financial ones, such as risks related to psychological pressure [67]. The authors argue that users' overall perception of risk matters the most since perceiving something as risky regardless of the risk's cause or source would make users doubt it. Hence, users' perceptions of the transaction costs associated with investing in stocks will increase. Perceived risk has been excessively employed in the IS literature [67–71].

Third, perceived regulatory uncertainty is defined as users' inability to predict the future state of the regulatory environment [72]. Regulations are constantly changing, presenting new challenges for every industry. Consequently, the authors argue that new regulations might disrupt the stock market, leading users to develop a sense of uncertainty around it, eventually resulting in higher transaction costs.

Overall, the authors define uncertainty as the extent to which users believe investing in stocks involves the possibility of exposure to threats and harm. The authors hypothesize that the more uncertain investors are about the stock market, the more transaction costs they perceive. For instance, new governmental policies on a certain industry will negatively affect its affiliated companies, and their stocks value, eventually increasing the transaction costs since investors had not anticipated such laws when they first began investing in them. Therefore, the proposed model (Fig. 1) hypothesizes the following:

H4: Uncertainty is positively associated with perceived transaction costs.

3.5 Asset Specificity

Williamson defines asset specificity as durable investments undertaken to support particular transactions [29]. The redeployment of such investments will entail switching costs [73]. A specific asset is more valuable in a particular exchange than another, resulting in a lock-in effect that causes hold-up problems [29, 34]. Therefore, highly asset-specific investments pose potential costs because of their lower value outside the exchange relationship. Asset specificity takes many forms: a physical asset, a monetary asset, the body of knowledge, a personal relationship, a specific skill, etc. [31].

Researchers explain the asset of procedural learning as the amount of time and effort related to initiating a relationship and acquiring the skills needed to use a new service effectively [74]. Gao and Waechter use the construct asset specificity to explain how first mobile payment adopters spend time and effort learning to use and install the required software [75]. Abooleet and Fang conclude that asset specificity increases the perceived transaction costs of mobile payment technology [76]. Therefore, Asset specificity can be captured through two sub-constructs: perceived complexity and perceived access barriers.

First, perceived complexity is defined as the degree to which investing in stocks is difficult to understand. In the IS literature, perceived complexity and its effects have been extensively investigated under different labels (i.e., perceived ease of use, perceived trial-ability, effort expectancy, etc.) in various contexts. The more complexity users perceive, the more transaction costs they will endure. For instance, users who spend a significant amount of time and effort learning how to navigate an online trading platform or educating themselves on how to invest might experience high transaction costs since this learning procedure cannot be redeployed to another context, such as real estate or crypto investment. Indeed, the lack of knowledge about how to invest is concluded to be one of the major factors affecting investment decisions, where 39% of the non-participants in the stock market regard it as an inhibitor of participation, while 33% of the current participants think so [10].

Second, perceived access barriers refer to what extent investors believe that the stock market is expensive and difficult to access. The authors argue that users might have to overcome some barriers, such as reaching a certain amount of wealth, having low consumption commitments, and can spare some cash. For instance, to invest in and trade stocks, investors must have bank accounts, which are not available to everyone. These barriers increase the transaction cost that retail investors endure, negatively influencing their intentions to invest.

Therefore, asset specificity represents investors' belief that investing in stocks is difficult to learn and associated with access barriers. The authors argue that users might invest in many forms of assets, such as learning how to invest in stocks, installing a specific tool/app (e.g., Robinhood), or overcoming entry barriers such as having a bank account. Therefore, the more assets are invested in being involved in the stock market; the more investors perceive more transaction costs since these assets might not be redeployed. Thus, the proposed model (Fig. 1) hypothesizes the following:

H5: Asset specificity is positively associated with perceived transaction costs.

3.6 Transaction Frequency

Transaction frequency refers to the frequency that a particular transaction is repeated [29]. It is assumed that higher transaction frequency motivates companies to employ hierarchical governance structures since these structures make it easier to recover large transactions of a recurring kind [29, 77]. It has been argued that researchers have failed to empirically confirm this relationship [73]. Kim and Li state that various transaction costs are endured when entering into an agreement, such as gathering information, evaluating options and negotiating costs [35]. However, these costs are minimized when making a renewal or another contract with the same counterparty because the established relationship reduces the perceived risk of opportunism.

A handful of studies in IS and consumer behavior have adopted the construct and concluded its negative effect on transaction costs. For example, Teo and Yu conclude that the more consumers shop online, the less they perceive online shopping costs [33], which has also been confirmed by Gao [60]. Similarly, some show that transaction frequency negatively impacts users' perceived transaction costs while using Airbnb [78]. Also, it has been concluded that transaction costs of online travel products are negatively affected by the number of purchase times [35]. Finally, researchers further confirm this relationship by investigating online bidders' repurchase intentions [79].

Although the transaction frequency factor has not been strongly emphasized compared to uncertainty and asset specificity dimensions, the authors decide to employ it in this study to adapt the TCE as a whole. Transaction frequency represents how frequently investors invest in a given period. Based on the TCE assumption, the more users interact with stocks, the fewer transaction costs they perceive since they already have enough information about the transaction. For example, for a retail investor to learn how to navigate and keep up with the stock market, they would have to collect a lot of information and conduct thorough research, which increases the overall cost of that investment. Nevertheless, if they are routinely involved in the market, their perception of costs decreases. Hence, the proposed model (Fig. 1) hypothesizes the following:

H6: Transaction frequency is negatively associated with perceived transaction costs.

4 Discussion and Conclusion

This paper proposes a fresh, comprehensive model explaining the decision-making process that retail investors go through to invest in the stock market. The transaction cost economics theory (TCE) and perceived value are adapted to develop it.

Several financial-related studies have published surveys to investigate investors' motivations behind investments by asking participants about certain factors associated with the stock market. However, these factors are usually represented by one observational variable (i.e., one question/item), which might produce some inconsistency. In the IS literature and social science field, defining constructs and developing measurements must be conducted systematically and robustly, followed by a statistical analysis that ensures their validity and reliability. In this paper, we rely on the IS methods of conducting research by building the theory based on the previous findings in the field, which might introduce some new insights into how individual investors make their decisions. As Choi and Robertson argue, "*a model based on assumptions that are closer to the truth may be more likely to successfully predict behavior out of sample.*" They argue that understanding users' perceptions, although they might provide no complete insights about their actual decisions, is beneficial.

An online survey will be developed and utilized to test the study's hypotheses. Exploratory factor analysis (EFA), followed by confirmatory factor analysis (CFA), will be performed first to assess the measurement model. Structural Equation Modeling (SEM) will be utilized to test and validate the hypothesized relationships in the Value-Cost Model (Fig. 1). SEM is selected because it allows for testing the entire model while accounting for the measurement error. Previous papers in this domain have not relied heavily on SEM but focused on analyses that do not consider measurement errors, such as linear regression and correlation.

Previous application of perceived value suggests that users process information rationally where cost is considered when deciding whether something is valuable. Nonetheless, the authors argue that the valuation process is more complex, requiring investigating both perceived value and cost independently. Consequently, this research will add to the body of knowledge by presenting a model that explains retail investors' intentions to invest and extending a well-respected and sound theory.

References

1. Fernández-López, S., Rey-Ares, L., Vivel-Búa, M.: The role of internet in stock market participation: just a matter of habit? Inf. Technol. People **31**(3), 869–885 (2018). https://doi.org/10.1108/ITP-06-2017-0191
2. Lee, M.-C.: Predicting and explaining the adoption of online trading: an empirical study in Taiwan. Decis. Support Syst. **47**(2), 133–142 (2009). https://doi.org/10.1016/j.dss.2009.02.003
3. Liao, Z., Cheung, M.T.: Internet-based e-banking and consumer attitudes: an empirical study. Inf. Manage. **39**(4), 283–295 (2002). https://doi.org/10.1016/S0378-7206(01)00097-0
4. Rotchanakitumnuai, S., Speece, M.: Modeling electronic service acceptance of an e-securities trading system. Ind. Manag. Data Syst. **109**(8), 1069–1084 (2009). https://doi.org/10.1108/02635570910991300
5. Hirschey, M., Nofsinger, J.: Investments: analysis and behavior (2009)
6. Shanmugham, R., Ramya, K.: Impact of social factors on individual investors' trading behaviour. Procedia Econ. Finance **2**, 237–246 (2012). https://doi.org/10.1016/S2212-5671(12)00084-6
7. Ali, A.: Predicting individual investors' intention to invest: an experimental analysis of attitude as a mediator. World Acad. Sci. Eng. Technol. **50**, 994–1001 (2011). https://www.researchgate.net/publication/269168739
8. de Bondt, W.F.M., Thaler, R.: Does the stock market overreact? J Finance **40**(3), 793–805 (1985). https://doi.org/10.1111/j.1540-6261.1985.tb05004.x
9. Malz, A.M.: The GameStop episode: what happened and what does it mean? J. Appl. Corp. Financ. **33**(4), 87–97 (2021). https://doi.org/10.1111/jacf.12481
10. Choi, J.J., Robertson, A.Z.: What matters to individual investors? Evidence from the horse's mouth. J. Finance **75**(4), 1965–2020 (2020). https://doi.org/10.1111/jofi.12895
11. Gompers, P., Kaplan, S.N., Mukharlyamov, V.: What do private equity firms say they do? J. Financ. Econ. **121**(3), 449–476 (2016). https://doi.org/10.1016/j.jfineco.2016.06.003
12. Graham, J.R., Harvey, C.R.: The theory and practice of corporate finance: evidence from the field. J. Financ. Econ. **60**(2–3), 187–243 (2001). https://doi.org/10.1016/S0304-405X(01)00044-7
13. Cheung, Y.-W., Chinn, M.D., Marsh, I.W.: How do UK-based foreign exchange dealers think their market operates? Int. J. Financ. Econ. **9**(4), 289–306 (2004). https://doi.org/10.1002/ijfe.252
14. Cheung, Y.-W., Chinn, M.D.: Currency traders and exchange rate dynamics: a survey of the US market. J. Int. Money Financ. **20**(4), 439–471 (2001). https://doi.org/10.1016/S0261-5606(01)00002-X
15. Gompers, P.A., Gornall, W., Kaplan, S.N., Strebulaev, I.A.: How do venture capitalists make decisions? J financ econ **135**(1), 169–190 (2020). https://doi.org/10.1016/j.jfineco.2019.06.011
16. Akhtar, F., Das, N.: Predictors of investment intention in Indian stock markets: extending the theory of planned behaviour. Int. J. Bank Market. **37**(1), 97–119 (2019). https://doi.org/10.1108/IJBM-08-2017-0167
17. Hasan, N., Bao, Y., Chiong, R.: A multi-method analytical approach to predicting young adults' intention to invest in mHealth during the COVID-19 pandemic. Telemat. Inf., **68** (2022). https://doi.org/10.1016/j.tele.2021.101765
18. Nugraha, B.A., Rahadi, R.A.: Analysis of young generations toward stock investment intention: a preliminary study in an emerging market. J. Account. Invest. **22**(1), 80–103 (2021). https://doi.org/10.18196/jai.v22i1.9606

19. Ramya, K., Kalpana, M.: Relationship between personality related factors and individual investors trading behaviour. J. Contemp. Res. Manage. **12**(3), 27–41 (2017)
20. Zuravicky, O.: The Stock Market: understanding and applying ratios, decimals, fractions, and percentages. Rosen Publishing Group, Incorporated (2005). https://books.google.com/books?id=tIKSswEACAAJ
21. Ritter, J.R.: Behavioral finance. Pac. Basin Financ. J. **11**(4), 429–437 (2003). https://doi.org/10.1016/S0927-538X(03)00048-9
22. Waweru, N.M., Munyoki, E., Uliana, E.: The effects of behavioural factors in investment decision-making: a survey of institutional investors operating at the Nairobi stock exchange. Int. J. Bus. Emerg. Markets **1**(1), 24–41 (2008)
23. Kahneman, D., Tversky, A.: On the interpretation of intuitive probability: a reply to Jonathan Cohen. Cognition **7**(4), 409–411 (1979). https://doi.org/10.1016/0010-0277(79)90024-6
24. Lai, E.L.-C.: Competition for foreign direct investment in the product cycle. Japan World Econ. **13**(1), 61–81 (2001). https://doi.org/10.1016/S0922-1425(00)00044-X
25. Tan, L., Chiang, T.C., Mason, J.R., Nelling, E.: Herding behavior in Chinese stock markets: an examination of A and B shares. Pac. Basin Financ. J. **16**(1–2), 61–77 (2008). https://doi.org/10.1016/j.pacfin.2007.04.004
26. Sondari, M.C., Sudarsono, R.: Using theory of planned behavior in predicting intention to invest: case of Indonesia article information (2015)
27. Qureshi, S.A.: Psychological factors and investment decision making: a confirmatory factor analysis working on the financial reform and different industries analysis of Paksitan view project (2017). https://www.researchgate.net/publication/314284307
28. Putu, L., Hartini, Y., Suarmanayasa, N., Sinarwati, N.K.: The influence of internal and external factors on investment decisions with financial literature as moderate variables. Int. J. Soc. Sci. Bus. **6**, 91–102 (2022). https://doi.org/10.23887/ijssb.v6i1
29. Williamson, O.E.: The Economic Institutions of Capitalism: Firms, Markets, Relational Contracting. Free Press, New York (1985)
30. Coase, R.H.: The nature of the firm. Economica **4**(16), 386 (1937). https://doi.org/10.2307/2626876
31. Williamson, O.E.: Transaction-cost economics: the governance of contractual relations. J Law Econ **22**(2), 233–261 (1979). https://doi.org/10.1086/466942
32. Williamson, O.E.: Transaction cost economics. Handbook New Inst. Econ., pp. 41–65 (2005). https://doi.org/10.1007/0-387-25092-1_4
33. Teo, T.S.H., Yu, Y.: Online buying behavior: a transaction cost economics perspective. Omega (Westport) **33**(5), 451–465 (2005). https://doi.org/10.1016/j.omega.2004.06.002
34. Williamson, O., Ghani, T.: Transaction cost economics and its uses in marketing. J. Acad. Mark. Sci. **40**(1), 74–85 (2012). https://doi.org/10.1007/s11747-011-0268-z
35. Kim, Y.G., Li, G.: Customer satisfaction with and loyalty towards online travel products: a transaction cost economics perspective. Tour. Econ. **15**(4), 825–846 (2009). https://doi.org/10.5367/000000009789955125
36. Zauner, A., Koller, M., Hatak, I.: Customer perceived value—Conceptualization and avenues for future research. Cogent Psychol. **2**(1). Cogent OA, Dec. 31 (2015). https://doi.org/10.1080/23311908.2015.1061782
37. Holbrook, M.B., Schindler, R.M.: Age, Sex, and Attitude toward the past as predictors of consumers' aesthetic tastes for cultural products. J. Mark. Res. **31**(3), 412–422 (1994). https://doi.org/10.1177/002224379403100309
38. Zeithaml, V.A.: Consumer Perceptions of Price, Quality, and Value: A Means-End Model and Synthesis of Evidence (1988)
39. Dodds, W.B., Monroe, K.B., Grewal, D.: Effects of price, brand, and store information on buyers' product evaluations. J. Mark. Res. **28**(3), 307–319 (1991). https://doi.org/10.1177/002224379102800305

40. Kim, H.W., Chan, H.C., Gupta, S.: Value-based adoption of mobile internet: an empirical investigation. Decis. Support Syst. **43**(1), 111–126 (2007). https://doi.org/10.1016/j.dss.2005. 05.009

41. Bolton, R.N., Drew, J.H.: A multistage model of customers' assessments of service quality and value. J. Cons. Res. **17**(4), 375 (1991). https://doi.org/10.1086/208564

42. To, P.L., Liao, C., Lin, T.H.: Shopping motivations on internet: a study based on utilitarian and hedonic value. Technovation **27**(12), 774–787 (2007). https://doi.org/10.1016/j.techno vation.2007.01.001

43. Sanchez-Fernandez, R., Iniesta-Bonillo, M.Á.: Consumer perception of value: literature review and a new conceptual framework. J. Cons. Satisfaction, Dissatisfaction Comp. Behav. **19**(3), 40–58 (2006)

44. Pandža Bajs, I.: Tourist perceived value, relationship to satisfaction, and behavioral intentions. J. Travel Res. **54**(1), 122–134 (2015). https://doi.org/10.1177/0047287513513158

45. Slack, N., Singh, G., Sharma, S.: Impact of perceived value on the satisfaction of supermarket customers: developing country perspective. Int. J. Retail Distrib. Manage. **48**(11), 1235–1254 (2020). https://doi.org/10.1108/IJRDM-03-2019-0099

46. Liang, T.P., Lin, Y.L., Hou, H.C.: What drives consumers to adopt a sharing platform: an integrated model of value-based and transaction cost theories. Inf. Manage. **58**(4) (2021). https://doi.org/10.1016/j.im.2021.103471

47. Davis, F.D.: Perceived usefulness, perceived ease of use, and user acceptance of information technology. MIS Q. **13**(3), 319–339 (1989). https://doi.org/10.2307/249008

48. Ajzen, I.: The theory of planned behavior ICEK. Organ. Behav. Hum. Decis. Process. **50**, 179–211 (1991). https://doi.org/10.1080/10410236.2018.1493416

49. Hong, J.-C., Lin, P.-H., Hsieh, P.-C.: The effect of consumer innovativeness on perceived value and continuance intention to use smartwatch. Comput. Hum. Behav. **67**, 264–272 (2017). https://doi.org/10.1016/j.chb.2016.11.001

50. Li, Y., Shang, H.: Service quality, perceived value, and citizens' continuous-use intention regarding e-government: empirical evidence from China. Inf. Manage. **57**(3), 103197 (2020). https://doi.org/10.1016/j.im.2019.103197

51. Gan, C., Wang, W.: The influence of perceived value on purchase intention in social commerce context. Internet Res. **27**(4), 772–785 (2017). https://doi.org/10.1108/IntR-06-2016-0164

52. Hamari, J., Hanner, N., Koivisto, J.: 'Why pay premium in freemium services?' A study on perceived value, continued use and purchase intentions in free-to-play games. Int J Inf Manage. **51**, Apr. (2020). https://doi.org/10.1016/j.ijinfomgt.2019.102040

53. Lin, K.Y., Wang, Y.T., Huang, T.K.: Exploring the antecedents of mobile payment service usage: perspectives based on cost–benefit theory, perceived value, and social influences. Online Inf. Rev. **44**(1), 299–318 (2020). https://doi.org/10.1108/OIR-05-2018-0175

54. Yang, H., Yu, J., Zo, H., Choi, M.: User acceptance of wearable devices: An extended perspective of perceived value. Telematics Inform. **33**(2), 256–269 (2016). https://doi.org/10. 1016/j.tele.2015.08.007

55. Amihud, Y., Mendelson, H.: Asset pricing and the bid-ask spread. J. finance. Econ. **17**(2), 223–249 (1986). https://doi.org/10.1016/0304-405X(86)90065-6

56. Camilleri, S.J., Galea, F.: The determinants of securities trading activity: evidence from four European equity markets. J. Capital Market. Stud. **3**(1), 47–67 (2019). https://doi.org/10. 1108/jcms-02-2019-0007

57. Holden, C.W., Jacobsen, S.E., Subrahmanyam, A.: The empirical analysis of liquidity. SSRN Electron. J. (2014). https://doi.org/10.2139/ssrn.2402215

58. Ng, L., Wu, F.: Revealed stock preferences of individual investors: evidence from Chinese equity markets. Pacific Basin Finance J. **14**(2), 175–192 (2006). https://doi.org/10.1016/j.pac fin.2005.10.001

59. Covrig, V., Lau, S.T., Ng, L.: Do domestic and foreign fund managers have similar preferences for stock characteristics? A cross-country analysis. J. Int. Bus. Stud. **37**(3), 407–429 (2006). https://doi.org/10.1057/palgrave.jibs.8400195
60. Gao, L.: Understanding consumer online shopping behaviour from the perspective of transaction costs. EKP **13**(3), 1576–1580 (2015)
61. Duncan, R.B.: Characteristics of organizational environments and perceived environmental uncertainty. Adm. Sci. Q. **17**(3), 313 (1972). https://doi.org/10.2307/2392145
62. Gordon, L.A., Narayanan, V.K.: Management accounting systems, perceived environmental uncertainty and organization structure: an empirical investigation. Acc. Organ. Soc. **9**(1), 33–47 (1984). https://doi.org/10.1016/0361-3682(84)90028-X
63. Milliken, F.J.: Three types of perceived uncertainty about the environment: state, effect, and response uncertainty. Acad. Manag. Rev. **12**(1), 133–143 (1987). https://doi.org/10.5465/amr.1987.4306502
64. Ajibolade, S.O., Arowomole, S.S.A., Ojikutu, R.K.: Management accounting systems, perceived environmental uncertainty and companies' performance in Nigeria (2010)
65. Rasi, R.E., Abbasi, R., Hatami, D.: The effect of supply chain agility based on supplier innovation and environmental uncertainty. Int. J. Supply Oper. Manage. **6**(2), 94–109 (2019). www.ijsom.com
66. Chen, J.: Environmental uncertainty in encyclopedia of management theory, 2455 Teller Road, Thousand Oaks, California 91320: SAGE Publications, Ltd., (2013). https://doi.org/10.4135/9781452276090.n85
67. Featherman, M.S., Pavlou, P.A.: Predicting e-services adoption: a perceived risk facets perspective. Int. J. Hum. Comput. Stud. **59**(4), 451–474 (2003). https://doi.org/10.1016/S1071-5819(03)00111-3
68. Abramova, S., Böhme, R.: Perceived benefit and risk as multidimensional determinants of bitcoin use: a quantitative exploratory study. In: 2016 International Conference on Information Systems, ICIS 2016, no. Zohar 2015, pp. 1–20 (2016)
69. Huang, W.: The impact on people's holding intention of bitcoin by their perceived risk and value. Econ. Res.-Ekonomska Istrazivanja **32**(1), 3570–3585 (2019). https://doi.org/10.1080/1331677X.2019.1667257
70. Park, D.H.: Virtuality changes consumer preference: the effect of transaction virtuality as psychological distance on consumer purchase behavior. Sustainability (Switzerland) **11**(23) (2019). https://doi.org/10.3390/su11236618
71. Yang, Y., Liu, Y., Li, H., Yu, B.: Understanding perceived risks in mobile payment acceptance. Ind. Manag. Data Syst. **115**(2), 253–269 (2015). https://doi.org/10.1108/IMDS-08-2014-0243
72. Hoffmann, V.H., Trautmann, T., Hamprecht, J.: Regulatory uncertainty: a reason to postpone investments? Not necessarily. J. Manage. Stud. **46**(7), 1227–1253 (2009). https://doi.org/10.1111/j.1467-6486.2009.00866.x
73. Rindfleisch, A., Heide, J.B.: Transaction cost analysis: past, present, and future applications. J Mark **61**(4), 30–54 (1997). https://doi.org/10.2307/1252085
74. Wang, Y.S., Wu, S.C., Lin, H.H., Wang, Y.M., He, T.R.: Determinants of user adoption of web ATM: an integrated model of TCT and IDT. Serv. Ind. J. **32**(9), 1505–1525 (2012). https://doi.org/10.1080/02642069.2010.531271
75. Gao, L., Waechter, K.A.: Examining the role of initial trust in user adoption of mobile payment services: an empirical investigation. Inf. Syst. Front. **19**(3), 525–548 (2015). https://doi.org/10.1007/s10796-015-9611-0
76. Abooleet, S., Fang, X.: The role of transaction cost in the adoption of mobile payment technology. In: 27th Annual Americas Conference on Information Systems, AMCIS 2021, pp. 0–10 (2021)

77. Teo, T.S.H., Wang, P., Leong, C.H.: Understanding online shopping behaviour using a trans-action cost economics approach. Int. J. Internet Market. Adv. **1**(1), 62 (2004). https://doi.org/10.1504/IJIMA.2004.003690

78. Li, C.Y., Fang, Y.H.: The more we get together, the more we can save? A transaction cost perspective. Int. J. Inf. Manage. **62** (2022). https://doi.org/10.1016/j.ijinfomgt.2021.102434

79. Yen, C., Hsu, M.H., Chang, C.M.: Exploring the online bidder's repurchase intention: a cost and benefit perspective. ISEB **11**(2), 211–234 (2013). https://doi.org/10.1007/s10257-012-0201-0

Games as Cinematic Experiences: Discussing Filmic Modes and Ludic Elements in Video-Game Storytelling

Natalia Arsenopoulou[1]([⊠]) [iD], Anna Poupou[2] [iD], and Charalampos Rizopoulos[2] [iD]

[1] Department of Communication and Media Studies, National and Kapodistrian University of Athens, Athens, Greece
natarsen@media.uoa.gr

[2] Department of Digital Arts and Cinema, National and Kapodistrian University of Athens, Psachna, Greece
{annap,c_rizopoulos}@dcarts.uoa.gr

Abstract. This paper explores a wide range of questions regarding the synergies and interconnections between cinema and digital games in terms of narratives and aesthetics. After providing an overview of the shared features and overlaps between these two narrative forms from the early stages of video game production, this paper examines the cinematic features that can be traced in older and recent video games, focusing on issues of mise en scene, editing, genre and materiality. Furthermore, this paper continues by exploring the impact of video games on film narration, following what Buckland describes as "video game logic" and patterns of film narration on video games. Finally, the discussion of "ludonarrative disso-nance" is addressed, associated with a set of hypotheses for further development, proposing a taxonomy of game/players types and spectatorial/ludic practices in relation to cinematic modes.

Keywords: Video games · cinema · Filmic modes · transmedia storytelling · ludonarrative dissonance · film editing · cutscenes

1 Introduction

Almost thirty years after Lara Croft's first appearance in the 1996 eponymous video game published by Eidos Interactive, a TV series by Amazon Studio based on *Tomb Raider* is already in development stages in 2023. At the same time the studio has also announced a *Tomb Raider* feature film and a new video game, while an anime series will be featured on Netflix. This effort to create a Marvel-like multiverse by Amazon studios based on this franchise is only one of the many recent examples proving that the interconnections between narrative video games and cinematic/televisual storytelling in early 2020s appear stronger than ever before. This trend has been enhanced during the last ten years not only due to the rise of major streaming platforms but also due to the establishment of the superhero blockbusters as the most successful mainstream film genre of the decade, with multiple titles appearing also in the video game industry (e.g.

Batman, Avengers, Spider-Man etc.). Towards this convergence of cinematic and ludic narratives, tropes and mechanics point many recent case studies, such as the new version of *Cyberpunk 2077* that was released together with the anime *Cyberpunk: Edgerunners* (Netflix 2022), the three seasons of *The Witcher* (Netflix 2019 --) or the TV series *Last of Us* produced by HBO (2023), just to mention only a few adaptations that successfully migrated from one medium to another. According to the *Hollywood Reporter*, one of the main tendencies in video games of the 2010's was a mainstream turn towards more solid story-driven titles that "offer an opposite – and often more sanguine – experience to the many playful shoot-em-ups and death-defying first-person shooter titles that dominate the industry" (Beresford, 2019).

While academic discourse on the intrinsic relationship between video games and cinema is not new, in the last twenty years it is constantly revitalized with innovative scopes, transmedia approaches or critical views. A point of criticism, for example, was that scholars with a film theory background tended to underestimate the essential differences between video games and feature films (the lack of real-action footage, actors or continuity editing in video games), the constant compromise between efficiency in game control and visual complexity (Arsenault & Perron 2015: 34), or the rich intertextuality of non-cinematic environments in which video games relate to (e.g. role playing games, mapping technologies, literature, programming), producing insufficient cinema-centric approaches that highlight what has been called "the cinema envy" that has characterized many video game designers (Zimmerman 2002, Arsenault & Perron 2015: 32). Furthermore, as Fassone, Giordano and Girina (2015: 5) comment on Mark Wolf's seminal essay, the link between the two media goes beyond "characters and plotlines", or even aesthetics, visual codes, iconographies, practices and social spaces, but also these two forms share "production models, professional figures and [...] familiar consumption behaviors".

Following this debate on the relationship between films and video games as it has been developed in the last twenty years, we propose a loose categorization of eight (at least) major topics, referring to different or complementary approaches (adaptation, narration, aesthetics, and film theory).

1. Adaptation:
   i) Films/TV series based on video games.
   ii) Video games based on films (or audiovisual franchises).
2. Narration:
   iii) Films that are not video games adaptations but follow narrative structures that resemble video-game storytelling - or what Warren Buckland calls "the video-game logic" (2021: 105) (e.g. *The Fifth Element* [Besson 1997], *Fight Club* [Fincher 1999], *The Matrix* [The Wachowskis 1999], *Inception* [Nolan 2010], *Son of Saul* [Nemes 2015], *Tenet* [Nolan 2020], etc.) and films about videogames and virtual environments.
   iv) Cinematic storytelling in video games (e.g. *The Witcher 3 Wild Hunt* [CD Projekt Red 2015, *The Last of Us* [Naughty Dog 2013] etc.).
   v) Video games referring to film genre conventions (*Red Dead Redemption, L.A. Noire, Grand Theft Auto, Max Payne,* among others).
3. Aesthetics:

vi) Cinematic / animatic *mise-en-scène* and editing inside video games (cutscenes, acting, framing, camera movements, POV shots, camera angles, depth of field, transitions, soundscapes and music etc.).
vii) Cinematic tropes, motifs or materials inside video-games (use of found footage, film and video materiality, cameras, screenings, use of cctv, cameras, video tapes, video editors as game mechanics).
4. Theory.
viii) Narrative theory/film theory applied in video game analysis (e.g. ludonarrative dissonance, ludic/spectatorial practices etc.).

For the purposes of this presentation we will focus on the dialogue between cinema and video games, in terms of narration (iii, iv, v) and aesthetics (vi, vii) to specific case studies.

2 Video Games and Cinema: A Brief History and Current Trends

Early video games, like those developed for the coin-operated arcade machines, included narrative elements in the form of plain text, functioning as an introduction to the game-world and to the main storyline. Early games developed for home consoles and computers followed a similar trend. Narrative elements, such as skippable bits of exposition, were regarded as something out of the ordinary and were included in-between gameplay, as a reward for completing levels and as a way to promote the (often simplistic) story. This type of early cutscenes was clearly distinct from the action parts both in terms of aesthetics and function - resembling the opening titles of early cinema and the intertitles of silent films (c.f. Jenkings 2004: 9). Even though the majority of the aforementioned games did not feature significant narrative content, nor did they employ sophisticated cinematic elements, they still provided the affordances to form the basis for loose film adaptations - a minimal indication of the influence between the two entertainment industries [i.e. the arcade game *Street Fighter* (Capcom, 1987) and *Super Mario Bros* (NES, 1985) for home consoles and their homonymous movie adaptations in 1994 and 1993, respectively].

The advent of the first game engines (*Filmation* in 1984, *Freescape* and *SCUMM* in 1987, etc.), along with the affordability of consoles and personal computers with more powerful graphic cards and more storage capacity (particularly the advent of the CD-ROM) were factors that allowed game companies to develop more refined and advanced narrative and visual representation techniques. This was the turning point when pre-recorded videos, pre-rendered animation files and voice overs were introduced in cutscenes, substituting in some extent or in total the previews-used visuals and storytelling methods. It was also the time when the first Full Motion Video (FMV) games emerged; a genre which incorporated, in a more obvious manner, cinematic techniques in game design for action representation and as narrative means[1].

[1] In certain cases, the FMV was, due to its novelty, the key selling point for a game title, and gameplay was only a secondary consideration, as exemplified by numerous titles during that era. A notable example is Star Wars: Rebel Assault and its sequel, Star Wars: Rebel Assault II: The Hidden Empire (LucasArts, 1993 and 1995, respectively); a large part of both games is linear sequences consisting of shooting at moving sprites over an FMV background.

However, the combination of cinematic features with interactive elements can be traced a few decades back in interactive movies[2], an experimental/hybrid form of artistic expression in the style of choose-your-own-adventure. *Kinoautomat* (Radúz Činčera, 1967) is considered to be the first interactive movie. The release of Black Mirror's interactive episode *Bandersnatch* in 2018 brought the genre back to the fore, signaling the turn of the streaming platform to a provider of interactive movie experiences and gaming services. In the film industry, though, interactive movies did not gain as much popularity as the FMV games of the 80s-90s. The *7th Guest* (Trilobyte, 1993), a puzzle game set completely in first person perspective, features simple cinematic techniques with pre-recorded live-action video clips mostly used for narrative parts, pre-rendered (3D) animated sequences for character movement representation and closeups. The Myst series, starting with the eponymous *Myst* (Broderbund, 1993), adopted a similar tactic. *Phantasmagoria* (Sierra, 1995) features live-action clips and cinematic techniques such as closeups and transitions between first- and third-person perspective. Other games belonging to the point and click adventure genre, such as *The Beast Within: A Gabriel Knight Mystery* (Sierra, 1995), employed similar techniques, albeit not always to the same extent. The *Dragon's Lair* franchise falls in the same category, but features hand-drawn animated cutscenes and action sequences instead of live-action pre-recorded video fragments. Film adaptations of video games and the beginning of transmedia storytelling can be traced during the same period. A notable example is the *Wing Commander* series (Origin Systems, 1990 - 2007); it spans both the era of hand-drawn graphics (its first two instalments released in 1990 and 1991) and that of FMV (beginning with *Wing Commander III: Heart of the Tiger* in 1994), while a motion picture (featuring a completely different cast) was released in 1999.

Traditionally, cutscenes and actual gameplay were mostly distinct from each other, the former appearing mainly as an introduction to the game, during the finale, and sporadically throughout the game - usually at relatively few 'checkpoints', such as the end of a major battle (i.e. sequence of several missions) in *Star Wars: TIE Fighter* (LucasArts, 1994), or as the 'briefing' before a mission in the Thief series starting with *Thief: The Dark Project* (Looking Glass Studios, 1998). It started to be joined more organically with gameplay during the FMV era - for instance, all exposition in *Wing Commander IV: The Price of Freedom* (Origin Systems, 1996) is done through traditionally produced cinematic sequences featuring well-known actors; a similar trend is evident in point and click adventure games of the FMV era, such as the ones mentioned above (*Phantasmagoria, The Beast Within*), due to the nature of this particular game genre, which necessitates expository dialogue after each user action.

At a later stage, cutscenes became even more deeply intertwined with gameplay, following advances in technology that allow such seamless integration. Nowadays, actual gameplay graphics are used instead of a traditional set, actors, and crew; actors are still used in some capacity for the purposes of motion capture and combined with 3D

---

[2] In the game industry, the terms "Full-Motion Video" and "Interactive Movie" (or alternatively "Interactive Film") are used interchangeably to categorise games which incorporate extended cinematic live-action or animated sequences into gameplay or as a narrative technique. In this paper the term "Interactive Movie" refers to titles which are primarily cinematic in nature (films, TV series episodes or other works of art) and provide affordances for physical interaction.

scanning. Of course, the use of well-known actors for voice overs is a long-established practice that continues to the present day[3].

Procedural content generation and AI-assisted design of digital games in general may also encompass camera handling and the interchange between player- and computer-controlled actions, thereby interjecting cutscene-like sequences as dictated by plot elements and the individual characteristics of players. Virtual cameras, cinematography systems and tools developed as extensions for use with popular game engines, i.e. *DMM's Virtual Film Tools* for *Unity*, *Cinetracer* for *Unreal Engine*, allow game designers to produce titles with rich graphics and cinematics. The same tools and engines are used by the film industry, as well, in pre- and post-production to lower the cost and time spent and as assistant in film direction.

3 Film Aesthetics in Video Games

3.1 From the Long-Take *Mise En Scene* to Editing Techniques as Game Mechanics

Probably the most characteristic filming disposition used in video games is the extremely long, continuous take, frequently combined with the first-person-look in POV or over-the-shoulder view: if the action is not interrupted by a cutscene, by other visual elements controlled by the player (such as close-up shots to objects, inventory screens etc.) or by the failure of the player (leading to a loop), the action continues in a seemingly endless one-shot long take that follows the character into his quest. If the extreme long-take, the one-shot film, or even the pseudo-one-shot film (i.e. *Rope*, Hitchcock 1947) was considered until the 1990s as an experimental form, proving the directorial virtuosity of the few European highbrow auteurs that dare to master the 'sequence-shot' (such as Tarkovski, Angelopoulos, Jancso, Tarr etc.), in the last decade its use is much more frequent in both arthouse and mainstream films (*Victoria* [Schipper 2015], *Birdman* [Iñárritu, 2014], *1917* [2019 Mendes], *Boiling Point* [Barantini 2021]). However, this immersive disposition has been so intensely associated with the development of video games over the last twenty years, that even when it is currently used in contemporary films, it automatically raises critical questions about a "videogame aesthetics" that permeates through cinema. A significant example is the critically acclaimed film *Son of Saul* (Nemes, 2015), a disturbing film shot in first person perspective long takes following the main character in Auschwitz: the film provoked negative reactions during its competition in Cannes Festival about its immersive formal choices that were categorized as

---

[3] Indicative examples include: Mark Hamill as the Joker, Kevin Conroy as Batman, and John Noble as Scarecrow in the Batman: Arkham series of games (Rocksteady Studios, 2009 - 2015), Dennis Hopper as Steve Scott in Grand Theft Auto: Vice City (Rockstar Games, 2002), Samuel L. Jackson as Tenpenny in Grand Theft Auto: San Andreas (Rockstar Games, 2004), Dan Castellaneta as Nordom in Planescape: Torment (Black Isle Studios, 1999), Patrick Stewart as Uriel Septim VII in The Elder Scrolls IV: Oblivion (Bethesda Softworks, 2006), Christopher Plummer and Max von Sydow as Arngeir and Esbern, respectively, in The Elder Scrolls V: Skyrim (Bethesda Softworks, 2011), David Suchet reprising his role as Hercule Poirot in Agatha Christie: Murder on the Orient Express (The Adventure Company, 2006), Keanu Reeves as Johnny Silverhand in Cyberpunk 2077 (CD Projekt Red 2020), etc.

coming from the video game aesthetics (Peron 2015). What was disturbing for the film reviewers in this case was the particular use of video game aesthetics in this very bleak treatment of the Shoah, touching the issue of its unrepresentability, while the use of the same stylistic choices to more mainstream films and other audiovisual forms (music video, advertisement, web videos) have been firmly established since the implementation of digital cinematography in all audiovisual sectors. Furthermore, the continuous long take is currently the most used format in amateur recordings from mobile devices (smartphones, screen recordings, (endless) zoom meetings, vlogs, travelogues, go-pro action videos etc.), thus totally reversing its status from a revered and serious modernist expression to a trivial and easy practice of recording, frequently without any intervention by editing techniques.

This change in the way the long-take is being artistically perceived has pushed many game designers if not to abandon (yet) this disposition, at least to enrich the cinematic features in games by entering the realm of film editing. The idea of a primitive form of decoupage existed even in mid-90s, as the 'mouselook' (and its keyboard-based precursors) in 3D games offered to the player the chance to choose and control the frame - at a certain point at least. However, in recent game examples, creative ideas that are related to editing techniques appear more often and are not limited to foregrounding the cinematic aspect of the visuals (in cutscenes for example); editing tools are more often used as game mechanics to reinforce player interactivity and improving their competence, hence achieving a higher degree of immersion.

The most obvious example can be found in *Read Dead Redemption II*, in which the player / spectator has the freedom to choose between the standard gameplay view mode and the cinematic mode. When entering a cutscene or the cinematic mode the frame ratio changes from widescreen 16:9 to anamorphic widescreen 2.39:1: with the two black stripes appearing on the top and bottom this transition between the two modes is not concealed and integrated to gameplay, but on the contrary highlighted with a stylistic difference. The standard mode (that can be found in many similar recent games) is a 3rd person view with the camera following the character, with free roaming, alternate distance and mouselook, that allows the player to control on-screen and off screen space, or space organization through framing (in the same scene for example they can choose whether the frame shows a landscape in extreme long shot without human figures, a close up of the hero at the right corner of the frame in close up and the landscape in the background, a medium two-shot with little attention to space etc.). To this we can also add the 'dead-eye' mechanics in which the flow continues in slow motion and make visible sensory features such as the smell of humans and animals.

The cinematic mode however is the most impressive feature in terms of editing: entering the cinematic mode gives access to three cameras from different angles (named in the control scheme rather arbitrarily as cinematic camera, focus camera and cycle camera). The player has the freedom to alternate views from these three cameras in most parts of the game, during action scenes, dialogue scenes, free roaming, or long journeys. Interestingly the distance, angle, axis and movement of these three cameras are not stable (and predictable), but change accordingly to the particularities of the landscape and theme: so, from these three cameras we get a large variety of frames that range from extreme long shots with landscapes – where the human figures scarcely appear, aerial views, impressive tracking shots of the characters from above in extreme low angle medium framings (for example the feet of the horses and characters from bellow riding in steep paths), close-up to faces, lateral tracking shots framing the dialogue of two characters while riding their horses or eerie tilt shots that frame the characters riding away in the forests – without the camera following them. The framing also alternates the soundscape, so in a long shot we hear the dialogue from a long distance.

As players choose the camera they want to follow, and the exact moment to change the point of view, they are practically in a process of real-time editing (though closer to televisual editing than to cinematic). This practice also exposes the player/spectator to the harsh reality of classic old-school continuity editing: as the cuts are marked rather randomly by the player (as they don't exactly know the frame that follows) these scenes are full of continuity errors (jump cuts, repetitions, reverse of 180 axis etc.). This however does not reduce the cinematic feeling; it adds a ludic degree of defying the rules of continuity editing. Finally, the cinematic mode is not used as the typical game mechanism that could help in action scenes – by giving insights, by helping to aim, or by revealing invisible angles from the enemy side: on the contrary, entering the cinematic mode can totally plunge the players abilities and responsiveness in action scenes. Nevertheless, this can appear as the ultimate ludic challenge for the user, not only to play and complete the action scene, but most importantly to 'direct' and 'edit' it at the same time so as to create an artistically accomplished video that can be shared and admired online.

Equally resourceful uses of editing tools can be found in many recent games: in *Cyberpunk 2077* (CD Projekt Red 2020) for example, the 'Braindance' mechanics has been considered as the most successful feature of the game. Braindance (or BD) constitutes the most expanded form of entertainment in 2077, and it can range from its innocent legal forms that can be used for kids' entertainment to illegal forms of hard-core material that can lead to a drug addiction or 'cyberpsychosis'. Braindance sessions allow the main character/user/player to re-live recorded memories of another person, as experienced with all the five senses of the subject. This technology was originally used for the punishment, correction, and rehabilitation of criminals, but soon developed to a whole range of popular entertainment, including exploitation BDs, pornography, snuff material or the live experience of a subject at the moment of his death. As most of this material is considered too intense to re-live, a form of editing is necessary. During gameplay, "V", the main character, has on many occasions the opportunity to make use of an unedited, raw Braindance material. In these sessions a few minutes clip can be seen in viewing mode or in editing mode: the latter opens into a screen that looks like an editing tool, with a timeline featuring three different levels (visual, audio, thermal) that allows the user to apprehend different layers of that recording. In view mode, the user adopts a strictly first-person view – that is the view of the subjects that experienced the particular time-wrap. In editing mode we change into a third person camera view that can freely move into this limited space, giving to the player the freedom to explore objects, to define details and to overhear dialogues or sounds. The player is made to see the clip multiple times, going backwards and forwards, manipulating space, watching it closely frame by frame, and marking selected durations in the timeline, in order to discover evidence and information. In this way a classical whodunit and procedural strategy is here enriched by using editing tools as ludic mechanics and by putting the user at the place of a movie editor.

These examples show that if cinematic elements in gaming were primarily associated with impressive visuals, or identified as moments in which the player gives away the need to control and enters the state of a passive spectator, in latest examples we witness a more interactive and creative dimension of cinematic tools, techniques and modalities, through uses of camera framing and editing, that brings closer the ludic and filmic elements in gaming.

3.2   Film Genre as a Framework for Open-World Games: Cinephilia, Genre and Materiality

Apart from the obvious category of games that originated from specific films or audio-visual franchises, many recent games do not follow the path of adaptation but adhere to major film genres following their generic rules and conventions in terms of narratives and aesthetics. This strategy, successfully applied by publishers such as Rockstar Games, appears more efficient than the adaptation of a single film, series or even universe, as it gives the chance to game designers to multiply plots and subplots, characters, situations and iconographies, while renovating the formal aspects of the game in the multiple levels, spaces and populations that inhabit these openworlds. Games such as *Red Dead Redemption I* and *II* (Rockstar Games 2010, 2018), for example, can be considered as anthological references to the Western genre canon, including classical, modernist, post-classical examples, and at the same time aiming at a multidimensional cinephilic pleasure not only through impressive visuals and intertextuality but also by giving the player/spectator the chance to interact with the cinematic aspects of framing, camera angles, frame ratio and editing, as described above. While Pekinpah's film *Wild Bunch* (1969) stands as an overarching point of reference for the second title, inscribing the game in the revisionist phase of the genre, many other intertextual references to canonical western examples have been noted by reviewers and put forward during the promotion of the game; in many reviews, for example, we find lists about the films that were used as references, such as *The Assassination of Jesse James By the Coward Robert Ford* (Dominic 2007), *Butch Cassidy and The Sundance Kid* (Hill 1969), *A Fistfull of Dollars* (Leone 1964), *Django Unchained* (Tarantino 2012) and many others - some of them well hidden to be discovered as 'Easter eggs'. This excessive cinephilia, apart from being an ingenious promotional strategy and contributing to the critical appraise of the game, creates a ludo-cinephilic pleasure for those who are trying to identify the references, or could trigger a discovery of classic movie titles unknown by younger audiences.

Red Dead Redemption Begins with a clearly expository cutscene, introducing us to the main character and his world, that in 1911 is an already civilized West with no place for outlaws and gunslingers. The scene that takes place in the train, bringing John Marston to Armadillo, uses as a point of reference the introduction of *The Man Who Shot Liberty Valance* (Ford, 1962) in which the Senator Ransom Stoddard with his wife return to the small city of the West where all signs of "wilderness" have been eradicated due to the impact of modernity, the arrival of civilization and also the efforts of the main hero. This 1962 film is considered as an "epitaph" of the classical western as Ford revisits the founding myths of the genre, narrating the death of the West, and offering not only a self-referential, knowledgeable version of western, but also an alternative (and arguably open) ending that introduces a degree of non-linearity, complex storytelling, and ambiguity to the solid narrative construction of the Western. In terms of image, RDR opens with a well-lit, clearly structured, edited in continuity scene that presents a typical iconography of the genre's classical phase (establishing shots of the city and the train station, the three men walking down the Main Street shot in a typically Fordian low angle shot, discreet track-in, pan and tilt camera movements, fast paced editing and shot-reverse-shot modalities). In terms of the soundtrack the credits' main theme (harmonica, whistles and metal resonations) is a clear reference to the italo-american spaghetti phase and a tribute to Ennio Moricone. The dialogue of two upper-class elderly women overheard in the train by Marston introduces the theme of the exploitation of the land of the natives and the violent implementation of Eastern norms and laws in the Frontierland, a topic explored by the revisionist American westerns of the 1960s and 1970s. In general, this introductory cutscene has no surprises and presents a rather typical and conventional set of formal and thematic elements that refer to well-coded filmic and televisual conventions of the genre.

On the contrary, the credits and introductory cutscenes of *Red Dead Redemption II*, set in 1899 and thus constituting the prequel of the first game, put forward a much richer and more multilayered cinematic imagery. The opening of the introductory scene of RDR II, showing the wagon in the snowstorm and the arrival of the Van der Linden gang in the mining camp, is a clear reference to Tarantino's *Hateful Eight* (2015) in terms of *mise-en-scène* and lighting. This film constitutes an example of modernist return to the classical phase of the genre, while at the same time the director shots this movie with 70 mm celluloid, expressing an obsession with film materiality and analogical formats that will become one of the most important trends in art-house cinema in the late 2010s and early 2020s. In the same direction, one of the most impressive visual features of the game is the reference to pre-cinematic devices that form constitutive elements of the Western genres (daguerreotypes, tinetypes, photographs, cart-postals, dime-novels and biographies of Wild West living legends). While pausing during gameplay, the screengrab turns into a slowly developing b&w tinetype, interrupting in this way the visually cinematic flow with traces of a pre-cinematic materiality.

One of the major tropes in recent arthouse and mainstream cinema is the use of various analogue or digital forms for aesthetic and narrative purposes: found footage, home movies in Super 8 or home videos can be found in many works, while a few directors chose to shot directly in older VHS forms (e.g. *The Fablemans* [Spielberg, 2022], *Aftersun* [Welles 2022], *Magnetic Fields* [Gousis 2022], *Archive 81* [Netflix 2022]). In many cases this fixation to the analogue materiality can be related to topics of personal memory or auto-ethnography; Furthermore, found footage has been used for many decades as a strategy of horror films (from *Cannibal Holocaust* [Deodato 1980] to *Blair Witch Project* [Myrick & Santhez 1999] and many others) while the altered image quality of video has been associated with uncanny visions and metaphysical appearances (Ringu Nakata 1999). Found footage in various forms of video tapes has been used as a game mechanic since the 1980s, and has created the sub-genre of 'found footage horror games' (e.g. *Final Take* (Hush Interactive 2016), *Resident Evil 7: Biohazard* (Capcom

2017) and others). A good example of this convergence of cinematic plots, patterns and materials to a psychological horror video game is the *Blair Witch* (Bloober 2016). Based on the iconic mock-found footage film of 1999, the main character in first person's POV gets lost in the Blair Witch forest during the search for a lost boy. In his quest he finds a video camera and video tapes in consecutive stages: when the main characters plays, pauses and rewinds them in the camera, these tapes can alter reality and move between three temporal layers of this forest. The screen of the camera has the ability as well to reveal ghostly creatures that inhabit the forest that cannot be seen with bare eyes. So the player uses the video tape not only to gather information, but to navigate through space and time. The game uses a minimalistic overlook that imitates the display option of a 1990s simple handycam, highlighting in this way the material aspect of its grainy and poorly lit image.

In the same direction, but in a quite different mode that is based more on exaggeration than minimalism can be found in *Cyberpunk 2077*: despite the speculative and futuristic character of the "Braindance" sessions, we can trace in it a clear reference to *Blade Runner* (Scott 1982), and specifically to the enhancing device that Deckard uses to scan, augment and print a photogram, permitting at the same time to change a point of view inside this picture. The sound design in the game is also a clear reference to the iconic soundscape of this scene composed by Vangelis that can be found in the first title of the original soundtrack of the movie (main theme). Sound is another dimension that brings games closer to cinema. The evolution of sound in games mirrors that of graphics in that sound has transitioned from something simplistic or barely functional to an integral parameter of game immersion that is now seen as an independent artistic endeavour on par with other categories of music composition and sound design (the 2023 edition of the Grammy Awards featured the category 'Best Score Soundtrack for Video Games and Other Interactive Media' for the first time). Although sound was overlooked in the early days of video games due to an emphasis on visual elements, it quickly gained in importance and, in certain cases, even ended up overshadowing graphics - for instance, in the *Thief* series, as well as other stealth-based games, sound cues are at least as important as visual ones. They are woven into game mechanics to the point where it is impossible to play the game effectively without sound and a quiet environment. But even in other game genres, sound has increasingly gained in importance, as it was used as an avenue for conferring cinematic qualities to gameplay. A good example is the series of space simulators based on the Star Wars franchise released by LucasArts in the 1990s, starting with *X-Wing* (1993). Although early series titles featured a MIDI soundtrack, the fact that it reproduced the original Star Wars score composed by John Williams helped to increase player immersion. Furthermore, it dynamically adapted to changes that occurred during the mission, a quality that was lost when later games in the series (e.g. *X-Wing vs. TIE Fighter*, 1997) opted for a pre-recorded audio track. In recent story-driven titles, sound cues and clues that help the player navigate are a common element: the main character in *Blair Witch* for example who is lost in a forest without visual landmarks, can use sound landmarks in order to map this way into this maze.

Finally, another point of convergence between cinema, video and games, is the sub-genre called "screenlife" that includes crime or horror feature films using screen

recordings (computer and mobile phone screens, video calls, texting, surfing) as a narrative device: movies that are completely shot in screenlife mode appear more often after
2014 and Bekmambetov's Unfriended, while limited use of "screenlife" aesthetics can
be found even in recent arthouse films such as Haneke's Happy End (2017). Screenlife
elements, however, have been long used in video games, featuring a variety of screens,
pop-up windows, dialogue boxes, emails, chat devices and video calls, bringing the
aesthetics of everyday communication applications closer to video game aesthetics and
cinematic forms.

3.3   Point of View and Characterization: Restricted and Immutable vs. Restricted and Mutable vs. Free

Games that adopt a third-person perspective showcase one or more main characters
with whom players are supposed to identify, in a manner analogous to the protagonist
of a movie, in the sense that the main characters are fully exposed to the audience;
furthermore, avatar customization (in games in which the exact appearance of these
characters is not very important) can reinforce the players' sense of identification with
the main character(s). The degree of customizability depends largely on whether the
character(s) in question are deeply interwoven in the narrative, so much so that their
inherent traits and characteristics, including their appearance, needs to be set by the
game designers. Typical examples of this category are games that place the player in
control of specific and largely immutable characters, such as *Red Dead Redemption, The
Last of Us* and the *Witcher* series; here, players customize various aspects of the main
characters, but not the identity of the characters themselves.

In other cases, the focus is on the attributes of the narrative itself and what the
characters loosely represent; in this case, the player may be left with considerable room
for personalization when it comes to avatar appearance. Examples of this category are
games such as *The Elder Scrolls III: Skyrim* (Bethesda Softworks, 2011), *Baldur's Gate*
and its sequel, *Baldur's Gate II: Shadows of Amn* (Black Isle Studios, 1998 and 2000,
respectively), among others; players have a wide range of choices when it comes to
their characters' gender, attributes (e.g. race, class, etc.), and physical appearance (e.g.
hair, skin, and eye color), the plot will focus on other attributes of the main character
which are independent of the aforementioned characteristics and are not amenable to
customization by the player.

In the case of third-person games, there is a clear element of staging and direction
that has been interwoven in the action itself; the camera can move around, often not
controlled by the player, while the action (and the players' involvement in it) continues
to evolve. Games such as *Red Dead Redemption* and *God of War* (Santa Monica Studio,
2018) features a cinematic camera option that can be used during exposition.

In contrast to third-person games, there is a greater need for first-person games to
resort to constraining the field of view and camera controls in general; the player has no
visible body in the game world (with the exception of quasi-corporeal elements such as
hands, weapons, etc.), and thus the focus shifts to whatever the first person camera is
pointing at. This kind of point of view is considered less cinematic, as it is rarely used in
cinema - after the unsuccessful experiment of *Lady in the Lake* (Montgomery, 1947) that
first made use of the first person point of view throughout the film and the spectators only

see the main character when he looks himself in the mirror. During expository sequences, control is often wrested from the players, as the camera is focused on the characters and/or objects the exposition is about - sometimes along with changes in game camera properties, e.g. zooming, focus, etc. An example of this first-person's view can be found in *Cyberpunk 2077:* despite the fact that the character V is fully customizable by the player in terms of gender, voice, appearance and social background, these choices have no impact on the plot. The players have the chance to see V only when and if they decide to activate the mirrors that can be found in the game - so even accidental reflections of V's figure on surfaces do not occur. During dialogues or expository sequences, the players have total control of the camera properties. On the other hand, cinematic cutscenes with no control by the player in this game are rare, and they are all related to the second character, Johnny Silverhand - who is modelled after Keanu Reeves, so in this case the character is totally immutable in restricted cutscenes.

One can thus differentiate between two broad categories of camera control schemes during expository sequences, namely free and restricted; in the latter case, one can further distinguish between degrees of constraint (complete vs. partial).

4 Narrative and Storytelling Aspects of Films and Games

Theorists such as Aarseth (1997), Murray (2017), and Ryan (2006) support the view that games can be included in the category of narrative media, the characteristics of which can be studied and analyzed in a broader context based on established narrative theories. On the other hand, ludologists, like Juul (1998) and Eskelinen (2001), set the act of playing at the core of video-games and draw a line between interactive (gameplay) and non-interactive (narrative) elements of a game, setting stories as a secondary/supporting feature.

For Murray, this argument between ludologists and narratologists lies mainly in the interpretation of the term 'narrative' and the focus on the formal characteristics of games and literature (Murray, 2005), while Ryan (2006) observes that "the communicative model of classical narratology does not work for the mimetic mode of film and theatre", a field covered by the later formalist and structuralist narrative theories. She also regards narratology as an "unfinished project" suggesting that if the existing theories fail to support interactive storytelling, an expanded theoretical framework should be formed rather than rejecting the coexistence of interactive/ludic and narrative elements. To the defense of the ludologists' stance, not all kinds of games have narrative context, or as Jenkins (2004) notes, if they do, it is unlikely to follow exactly the same storytelling methods with other narrative media.

The conflict between narratologists and ludologists has become rather obsolete as both disciplines are continuously evolving and, respectively, their fields are broad enough to fit into narrow, binary framesets. What also seems not to be taken into consideration is the variety of games, their distinct features and the expectations of users as their targeted audiences. Thus, narratives may serve a different purpose depending on game genres, for instance in rule-based games narratives support gameplay by setting the rules, placing goals, and awarding players for their completion while those of make-believe rely on storytelling techniques for achieving the required suspension of disbelief and immersion in the game story world.

4.1 Categories of Games and Players

There have been various attempts to categorize games and players; some indicative ones are briefly described below. However, it is important to state that any such categories are not necessarily mutually exclusive; in most cases, games incorporate elements from various categories; at the same time, players derive enjoyment from various aspects of games, which could place them under various categories at the same time.

Roger Caillois (1958/2001) describes four broad categories/patterns of play: *Agôn*, which is about demonstrating skill and superiority over one's opponent; *Alea*, where the main determining factor of success or failure is chance; *Mimicry*, in which the player engages in roleplay, adopting alternate roles and identities, and *Ilinx*, which revolves around the sensory and physical aspects of play and the pleasure derived through them. Furthermore, Caillois makes the distinction between *ludus* and *paidia* depending on whether the playful activity is structured or not.

Lazzaro (2008) similarly distinguished four different categories of fun: hard fun, soft fun, serious fun, and people fun. *Hard fun* corresponds to the most 'traditional' view of games, that of overcoming challenges and demonstrating superiority over the computer or other players. *Easy fun*, on the other hand, focuses more on the acts of exploration and discovery, and interaction with the game world and its characters. *Serious fun* is more related to the practice of gamification, i.e. introducing game elements and mechanics to otherwise non-game-oriented applications. People fun is related to the social and/or interpersonal aspects of gaming and the pleasure that can be derived from them. Parallels between the two aforementioned frameworks may be postulated to an extent - most notably, strong associations may be posited between *agôn* and *hard fun*, and *mimicry* and *easy fun*.

With respect to player categories, Bateman & Boon (2005) distinguish four primary player types. The *Conqueror* type is highly competitive; players of this type seek to display their superior skill, thus highly correlating with the *agôn* game pattern and *hard fun*. On the other hand, the *Wanderer* type places more importance on exploration and new experiences; as a rule, players of this type are not very competitive; thus, they are good candidates for *easy fun*. The *Manager* type is primarily concerned with personal efficiency and 'mastering' the game mechanics. Finally, the *Participant* player type is mostly interested in the social aspects of play, and are thus more compatible with *people fun*. These are characteristics that describe players, and as such it is possible for said players to seek their particular type of fun (or enjoyment in general) outside of the stated aims of any particular game. For instance, wanderers may disregard 'optimal' game choices (e.g. in terms of score) for the opportunity to explore more of the game world, or may replay games in order to make different choices that may change the ending. The rise in popularity of open-world games partially fulfils the need to cater to different types of players - for instance, players who conform to the *Conqueror* archetype tend to appreciate more ludic elements, while players who conform to the *Wanderer* archetype are more willing to explore the game world, interact with NPCs in various ways, etc.

A similar categorization has been proposed earlier by Bartle (1996, 2003), who used two axes in order to represent player types: (i) preference for interacting with other players as opposed to exploring the game world, and (ii) preference for acting on things as opposed to interacting with them. Based on these axes, Bartle distinguished between the categories of *killers, achievers, explorers,* and *socialisers. Killers* are competitive players who aim to demonstrate their superiority to other players. Although similarly motivated, *achievers* place more emphasis on the accumulation of points. *Explorers*, as the word implies, aim to uncover as many aspects and inner workings of the game world as possible, potentially discovering exploits, "easter eggs", or other hidden content. *Socialisers* strive to understand other players and form relationships with them. Bartle (2003) later expanded this typology by adding a third axis "implicit" vs. "explicit", further breaking down each type.

Nacke, Bateman, & Mandryk (2014) have proposed the *BrainHex* framework, according to which players can be categorized in terms of seven broad archetypes based on neurological evidence: *Seekers, Survivors, Daredevils, Masterminds, Conquerors, Socialisers,* and *Achievers. Seekers* are after sensory stimulation; they exhibit curiosity and like to explore the game world - as such, they tend to opt for games that feature easy fun (according to Lazzaro's framework described above). *Survivors* enjoy the emotion of fear, for instance as featured in horror-themed movies or games, and the subsequent relief that is experienced upon the successful resolution of the plot. Nacke et al. note that this category may be regarded as a special case of Caillois' *ilinx* that is associated with the state of panic. *Daredevils* love playing a game to its limits, e.g. taking (in-game) risks, running around very quickly, and generally seeking gratification through high-intensity sensory cues. An association between this player category and Caillois' *ilinx* can also be identified in this case. *Masterminds* are more management- and strategically-oriented, drawing parallels with managers (as suggested by Bateman & Boon and described above) in their appreciation of efficiency and planning; Nacke et al. note that this player category can be linked to Lazzaro's hard fun and overcoming challenges. *Conquerors* try to achieve the best performance, whatever this may mean in the context of a particular game (e.g. high score, getting the best items, etc.). There is a direct association with Lazzaro's *hard fun* and the need to overcome challenges, ideally in an emphatic manner. *Socialisers* seek interaction and communication with other players and the affective connotations this behavior may entail (e.g. trusting others and being displeased when others break this trust). A link with Lazzaro's *people fun* can be easily postulated. Finally, *achievers* can be regarded as another aspect of the Conqueror in that they are more goal-oriented, whereas conquerors predominantly derive their fun from overcoming challenges, not fulfilling goals. Typically, achievers are completionists; they strive for ultimate completion of games.

4.2   Narrative Structures in Films and Video-Games

Non-linearity in non-physically interactive media (books, movies, theatrical plays - with the exception of participatory theatre), where present, applies mostly in the level of *syuzhet* (the order in which the events are presented) and does not affect the *fabula* (story). It is usually approached structurally by the reordering of temporal sequence of the events (*in medias res, mise en abyme* etc.), the entanglement of characters' storylines, loops and/or spatiotemporal shifts in storyworld, multiple or open endings, segmented and (semi)autonomous episodic formats. Visually, nonlinearity, in the notion of temporal or spatial simultaneity, is usually represented using the split-screen technique and multiple frames. Though as a medium, film generally does not afford interaction, in the narrow physical sense of the term at least, it still requires active participation on the part of the viewer, in the form of cognitive processes. The assembling of the events by the viewer for the interpretation of the story can be defined as a low-level interaction and a form of (latent) agency. Suspension of disbelief is also required in order for the viewer to experience the story, to be immersed in the imaginary world, to empathize with the characters etc.

Run Lola Run (Tom Tykwer, 1998) is a notable example of a multi-linear structured film with closed loops - a structure common in videogames consisting of separate levels such as platform games. In this case non-linearity is applied in multiple levels with the use of various techniques; on an overall *structural* level with the repetition of the central part of the story presented in three linear variations leading to different possible outcomes, on a *temporal* level with time shifts presented as intervening shots of future events and on a *spatial* level with the use of different camera takes and framing of the same event, split-screen technique and spatial montage offering a variation of PoVs within the same timeframe. Video game logic can also be traced throughout the movie. The opening sequence resembles the introductory cutscene of a game in which a goal is set to be accomplished in a given time, followed by story variations in analogy to game-rounds. Each of the first two "rounds" leads to an undesirable outcome and after a brief ending scene, in the style of a game ending cutscene, the story restarts from the same "save point" until the goal is achieved. In each "round" the protagonist is aware of her previous actions and their causal effects, as a game player would, but cannot fully control the outcome of the present actions.

Inception (Nolan, 2010) follows a similar logic presenting two levels of non-linearity. In overall, it uses open-ended structure with *mise-en-abyme* technique and self-referentiality traced in the closing scene with the closeup of the spinning top, creating a sense of ambiguity between the actual world and the dreamworlds. On a second level, within the dreamworlds, it follows a nested structure in the form of "Chinese-box" with foldbacks ("dream within a dream" transition analogous to a video-game level-to-level progression). The first act, as Buckland (2015) observes, resembles the first, tutorial-like, levels of a game introducing players to the game rules and how the game is played. He also notices other game conventions as repetitions of actions, the increasing level difficulty, the defiance of laws of nature. In addition, similarities with sandbox games can be drawn from characters' ability to (re)construct a priori or in "real time'" the environment within the dreams.

Compared to cinema, games require more activity on the part of the consumer ("player"); they have been described by Aarseth (1997) as 'ergodic' media, implying a different approach to that of the film viewer, adding to the already complex nature of involvement with games (e.g. Calleja, 2011). Game designers may indeed elect to give players the ability to shape the narrative in various ways. True non-linearity, in the form of emergent open-structured narratives, is comparatively rare due to the necessary technology largely not being up to the task; however, the illusion of non-linear narratives is a frequent feature in games, often by means of embedded narratives and branching storylines that may result in a single ending or a number of different, but pre-scripted, endings. In The *Witcher 3: Wild Hunt* (CD Projekt Red, 2015), choices made throughout the game, such as which quests to complete or not to complete, whom to favor, even what to say in dialogues with important NPCs, may lead to one of a limited number of different endings.

Interestingly, sometimes game designers choose to give players the ability to essentially derail the storyline, often to a breaking point - for instance, in *Ultima VII: The Black Gate* (Origin Systems, 1992), the player gains access to the *Armageddon* spell, which effectively destroys all life in the game world with the exception of the protagonist and a couple of NPCs, rendering the game unwinnable with immediate effect (the game world remains available for exploration, albeit devoid of life). In other cases, the effect of the player's actions become apparent later in the game, when it is too late for players to backtrack, leaving them no option but to restart the game or reload a saved game - for instance, in some games (e.g. *Legend of Kyrandia*, Westwood Studios, 1992), the player can unknowingly destroy essential items that must be used later in the narrative.

The above point to a compromise between freedom of action and the need to provide a consistent narrative, often with strange results that may, if examined closely, affect the players' suspension of disbelief. In *Red Dead Redemption 2* (Rockstar Games, 2018), player actions affect the in-game character's standing in the world by means of a Honour system; good or honourable actions increase honour, whereas evil or dishonourable actions decrease it. However, plot-critical missions may entail morally dubious, if not outright dishonourable, actions that the player must undertake, often without affecting honour. In *The Elder Scrolls V: Skyrim* (Bethesda Softworks, 2011), players can engage in morally questionable acts that can be written off by paying a fine, with no other consequences. Such issues are not related to morality (since a morally grey in-game universe is a common feature in games), but to consistency - in a cinematic context, these issues would conceivably be regarded as signs of a problematic script.

An additional device that is often leveraged as a means of increasing player engagement is the inability to save the game at various points. When used appropriately (and not excessively), it may indeed engage the player in a way that is similar to intense cinematic sequences that are characterised by tension and 'grip' the viewers' attention. In such cases, the player has no option but to carry on until that particular segment of the game is over. On the other hand, this practice may have an undesirable effect, for instance, if such segments are prolonged and are used more often than necessary. Doing so may dissuade prospective players, especially casual gamers or those who cannot afford to have their progress undone due to not being able to save the game. When used correctly, this practice can be regarded as imposing some sort of *episodic* structure in the game; after each 'episode', there are no short-term loose ends, and the game is in a state of denouement, or "cooling off" / lack of intensity that typically follows rising tension and the climax (a succession that is a typical device employed in staged productions even in ancient times).

4.3   A Discussion of Narrative Theories and Practices in Game Development and Movie Production

While the majority of games focus on providing interactive experiences (action-, strategy- or puzzle-oriented) with narrative having mostly a secondary, supportive role, recent technological advances have made possible a more holistic design approach in game development, applying techniques for seamless transition between narrative and ludic features and holding a promise for a more unified experience. Emergent narratives rather than embedded pre-structured (linear or not) stories, the use of drama managers and AI-driven NPCs are applied in order to develop systems that are able to create coherent narratives with satisfying plots and meaningful interaction. Respectively, over the last two decades, a shift has been made towards building a theoretical framework which places games on a continuum with traditional narrative media (Aarseth 2012, Caracciolo 2015).

Crawford acknowledges the importance of embedding fictional stories within gameplay, adding though that they do not constitute storytelling per se. He follows a user-centred approach, with the question of "what does the user do", as core for game development in order to design and provide meaningful choices within narrative context. He also focuses on the interaction of the player's game character with AI-driven NPCs and the competence of the latter to provide motivation for action and provoke emotional responses (Crawford, 2012).

In a more theoretical framework, Murray describes Holodeck (inspired by the TV series *Star Trek*), a computer-generated 3D simulation of a fictional world, as the ideal interactive storytelling system. The player is invited to step into this world, to impersonate a character, and to interact in a physical manner (language, body movements, gestures etc.) with intelligent agents which, in turn, are programmed to respond reasonably to the player's actions and at the same time are responsible for the building a satisfying narrative arc (following the Aristotelian model) and sustaining the story coherence (Murray, 2017).

Ryan departs from possible worlds theory in her analysis of the modal structures of storyworlds. She also takes into consideration the importance of private worlds (as a character's set of knowledge, obligations and wishes) for character development and story creation. These private worlds produce narratives of their own, justifying characters' behaviours and actions within the story and have the potential of weaving their own narrative strands, creating "a bundle of possible stories". This extends not only to main characters but to potential subagents, enriching the narrative (Ryan, 1991). While character development is a central aspect in filmmaking, it is largely overlooked in videogames. The issue of ludonarrative dissonance - when players actions and narrative collide - may be partially the result of poor character design or the inability of their actions to influence the story in a dynamic manner.

McDowell suggests an innovative approach in movie production and cinematic storytelling. He claims that as we enter the post-cinematic era, digital media, in particular XR, have much more to provide to the film industry than just a mere supporting technology; they are likely to reshape the process we conceive and tell stories. As he states, virtual reality, augmented reality and mixed reality "demand that we shift away from linear narrative, the fixed or controlled frame, into a new multi-dimensional narrative space. We now need to pay attention to the entire worldspace, the sphere of narrative opportunities around us". The film *Minority Report* (Spielberg, 2002) was based on the concept of world building as a design approach; starting with no script at all, the storyworld was conceived and designed and the story was built upon it - to state McDowell's actual words "world had become a container for narrative". Referring to the case of *Minority Report*, he concludes that "This design-driven, media-agnostic, multi-platform capability flips the twentieth century model on its head and paves the way for new story practices ahead" (McDowell, 2019).

Certain types of video-games, such as contemporary open world / sandbox games, are in part developed upon characteristics of the above concepts. Rather than applying fixed embedded narratives with multi-linear, branching structures or multiple strands, open world games appear to be closer to the type of emergent narratives, relying more on the design of the imaginary world, its rules and affordances and the story is shaped by the actions of the user and the interaction with (AI-driven) NPCs and world elements.

5   Concluding Remarks

In the past, narrative and plot elements were largely considered secondary to action sequences, often due to limitations in storage and processing power available on home consoles and computers. The latter suffered less from storage-related issues and featured an interaction model based on the keyboard and, later, the mouse; thus, it was more amenable to games featuring more complex narratives (comparatively speaking), and is part of the reasons why adventures, role playing, and strategy games flourished on the PC. Compared to the not so distant past, digital games as a media form have nowadays become more mainstream in various ways. A factor that may be seen both as an antecedent and a consequence of the rise of games to prominence as a 'normal' form of entertainment is the adoption of cinematic techniques in their presentation. The increase in the popularity of casual games, greatly encouraged by the ubiquity of smartphones (which now are equipped with hardware capable of supporting even graphics-heavy, technically demanding games), has been accompanied by an increase in the wider acceptance of games and gamer culture in general.

Games as a media form have become more cinematic, and may appeal to persons who do not belong to their originally intended audience; additionally, they may be consumed in a fashion reminiscent of more traditional media - e.g. as if they were movies watched by non-gamers or casual gamers during gameplay or in forms of walkthrough web videos. The development of lighter, user-friendly and easy editing applications, or even the 'gamification' of non-professional editing programs (such as Filmora) together with the practice of posting clips online in social media, has opened a space for a ludic approach to video creativity. This space has been capitalised in game design, creating a new creative playground by offering cinematic features in games that can be used, manipulated and shared by the players in the form of walkthroughs, video essays or clips. Whereas cinematic features in video games were primarily associated with pre-rendered cutscenes and were associated with the players' passivity and loss of control, in later examples we witness a more interactive and creative dimension of cinematic tools, techniques and modalities, through uses of camera framing and editing, that brings closer the ludic and filmic elements in gaming. Cinematic strategies such as a genre self-referentiality, intertextuality and cinephilia, together with high production values, stardom and promotional strategies contribute to the cultural acceptance and critical appraise of video games based on films productions.

The similarities and differences between cinema and games with respect to aesthetics and narrative that were highlighted in this paper indicate that the interplay between cinema and games in terms of narrative and expressive techniques is a complex subject, influenced by factors pertaining to the medium itself, its production process, and the 'end user' (the player or the viewer, for games and films respectively), and that it warrants more attention as the end product of a process that may give rise to a hybrid media form to occupy the (often not very well defined) space between cinema and games.

References

Aarseth, E. Cybertext: Perspectives on Ergodic Literature. Johns Hopkins University Press (1997)

Aarseth, E. A narrative theory of games. In: FDG '12: Proceedings of the International Conference on the Foundations of Digital Games (2012)

Arsenault D., Perron B. De-Framing Video Games in The Light of Cinema, Journal GAME - Games as Art, Media, Entertainment, Issue 4:Vol I, pp. 25–36 (2015)

Bartle, R.: Hearts, clubs, diamonds, spades: players who suit MUDs. J. Online Environ. 1 (1996)

Bartle, R.A.: Designing Virtual Worlds (2003), available at https://mud.co.uk/richard/Designing VirtualWorlds.pdf. Accessed 29 Jan 2023

Beresford, T.: How Gaming Changed in the 2010s. The Hollywood Reporter (2019/12/23). https://www.hollywoodreporter.com/lists/how-gaming-changed-2010s-1256603/introduction-of-twitch/. Accessed 15 Feb 2023

Buckland, W.: Narrative and Narration: Analyzing Cinematic Storytelling. Wallflower - Columbia University Press, New York (2021)

Buckland, W.: Inception's Video Game Logic. In: Furby, J. & Joy, S. (eds.) The Cinema of Christopher Nolan: Imagining the Impossible. Wallflower Press. (2015)

Caillois, R.: Man, Play, and Games. University of Illinois Press, Urbana and Chicago (1958/2001)

Calleja, G.: In-game: From Immersion to Incorporation. The MIT Press, Cambridge, MA (2011)

Caracciolo, M.: Playing, "home": videogame experiences between narrative and ludic interests. Narrative 23(3), 231–251 (2015)

Crawford, C.: Chris Crawford on Interactive Storytelling. 2nd edn. New Riders, Berkeley CA (2012)

Eskelinen, M.: The Gaming Situation. Game Studies. Int. J. Comput. Game Res. 1(1), (2001). https://www.gamestudies.org/0101/eskelinen/, Accessed 17 Feb 2023

Fassone, R, Giordano, F., Girina, I, Reframing Video Games in The Light of Cinema, Journal GAME - Games as Art, Media, Entertainment, Issue 4:Vol I, pp. 5–14 (2015)

Jenkins, H.: Game Design as Narrative Architecture. In: Wardrip, F. & Harrigan, P. (eds.), First Person. The MIT Press, Cambridge (2004)

Juul, J.A.: Clash between Game and Narrative (1998). www.jesperjuul.net/text/clash_between_game_and_narrative.html. Accessed 10 Feb 2023

Lazzaro, N.: Why We Play: Affect and the Fun of Games: Designing Emotions for Games, Entertainment Interfaces and Interactive Products. In: Sears, A. & Jacko, J.A. (eds.), The Human-Computer Interaction Handbook: Fundamentals, Evolving Technologies, and Emerging Applications (2nd ed.), pp. 679–700. Taylor & Francis, New York, NY (2008)

Murray, J. Hamlet on the Holodeck. Updated ed. eds. The MIT Press (2017)

McDowell, A.: Storytelling shapes the future. J. Futures Stud. 23(3), 105–112 (2019)

Murray, J.: The Last Word on Ludology v Narratology in Game Studies. (preface to keynote talk) DiGRA 2005 Conference: Changing Views - Worlds in Play. (2005). https://inventingthemedium.com/2013/06/28/the-last-word-on-ludology-v-narratology-2005/. Accessed 10 Feb 2023

Nacke, L.E., Bateman, C., Mandryk, R.L.: BrainHex: A neurobiological games typology survey. Entertainment Comput. 5(1), 55–62 (2014)

Peron, D.: Le fils de Saul": Auschwitz, caméra embarquée. Libération (2015/05/15) https://www.liberation.fr/cinema/2015/05/15/auschwitz-camera-embarquee_1310249/. Accessed 16 Jan 2023

Ryan, M.L.: Avatars of Story. University Of Minnesota Press (2006)

Ryan, M.L.: Possible Worlds, Artificial Intelligence, and Narrative Theory. Indiana University Press, Bloomington (1991)

Wolf, M.J.P.: Inventing space: toward a taxonomy of on- and off screen space in video games. Film Quart. **51**(1), 11–23 (1997)

A Survey on Application of Game Design Element in Edutainment

Souad Ahmad Baowidan[✉]

Information Technology Department, Faculty of Computing and Information Technology,
King Abdulaziz University, Jeddah, Saudi Arabia
Sbaawidan@kau.edu.sa

Abstract. The application of game design principles in several fields, including education, business, medicine, and leisure activities, has emerged as a highly effective method of imparting knowledge and providing entertainment. To boost engagement, gamification involves integrating game concepts into non-game settings, such as a webpage, online forum, learning control system, or company intranet. A game design method known as "edutainment" blends entertainment with teaching to speed up learning. Gamification, edutainment, and serious game design aspects can be utilized in various industries for various goals. These three gaming design approaches can be employed in education to give students common experiences. As an aspect of the gaming experience, games can teach new skills and knowledge for the student to pick up. Practice and reinforcement of current information and abilities are also developed through gaming. The idea of game design elements is applied in marketing, entrepreneurship, and working in business development. In gaming design, video games are employed in marketing and secret codes to capture the user's attention and transform them into devoted consumers. In the healthcare profession, the notions of the game in gamification, edutainment, and serious games are employed to assist patients, especially younger patients, in understanding healthcare principles, from managing chronic diseases to ensuring medication compliance.

Keywords: Gamification · Edutainments · Serious game · Medicine · Business · Education · Leisure

1 Introduction

The basic principle of game design and its influence on people's behavior has transformed the relationship with policies, products, services, and all the aspects that can transition into the game interphase. The game design's main element or basic framework is the deployment of technology in tracking human behavior [1]. The application of game design principles in several fields, including education, business, medicine, and leisure activities, has emerged as a highly effective method of imparting knowledge and providing entertainment [2]. A significant amount of literature focuses on the significance of how game design aspects are created, emphasizing the relevance of imparting learning via instructional game design and the critical skills needed for game designers [3].

© The Author(s), under exclusive license to Springer Nature Switzerland AG 2023
X. Fang (Ed.): HCII 2023, LNCS 14046, pp. 39–50, 2023.
https://doi.org/10.1007/978-3-031-35930-9_3

Designing educational games requires considering certain factors [4]. Governmental and business service providers and stored data can follow daily human actions and behavior. Such data is critical in designing the game algorithms and setting the appropriate rewards for the game goals. Using the principle is developing a progression by enabling humans to attain small achievements attached to extrinsic values [5], the game design can incorporate different kinds of rewards. For example, rewards for walking some kilometers every day may be rewarded by receiving tax breaks, and so on. Therefore a successful game design must incorporate a compressive dataset of human activities monitored over time. In recent times, apart from government bodies, different service providers in the fields of education, business, medicine, and leisure activities continued to monitor, record and store human behavior datasets to improve game design algorithms. Such datasets are not only instrumental in manipulating rewards for the game design but also in creating a sense of personal responsibility through subsequent reputation and fame. Such data are often attached to the person's legacy as it can outlive their source.

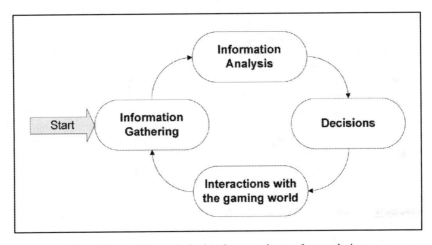

Fig. 1. Interactive cycle in the play experience of game design

One aspect that improves the play experience and player retention is the quality of the game design. Traditional marketing literature dictates that a good product from the service provider must meet the customer's expectations, preferences, and needs [6]. Therefore the basic framework of the digital game design must satisfy the player's choice. Applicable players' judgments and opinions often emanate from the play experience. Relevant players' views and conclusions always originate from the play experience. Participants interact with a virtual universe during a game session regardless of the type of game and the objective intended to achieve. The virtual universe receives input from the participants and gives feedback by changing its status and possibly interface. The participants then receive the information regarding the game session interaction outcome; the player decides the next course of action based on the received data (*See* Fig. 1. Interactive cycle in the play experience of game design) [7].

An interactive recurrent of the circle occurs until the participant loses or wins the game or may temporarily postpone their game session. This interactive circle of game design is the primary source of fun for the participants who win any gameplay session. On the other hand, in the case of a failure within the game session, the interactive circles can be the source of the participant's negative judgment, frustration, disappointments, and resentments. A complex topic still being researched is the vision of game design or the game creation procedure. Since gamification, edutainment, and serious game processes are designed for use in education and other sectors, this article will address new and well-known proposed game design components that show their significance.

2   Game Design Principles

2.1   Gamification

Gamification is deploying a game design interface and elements in a non-game context. Precisely, gamification is the concept deployed to motivate the performance of a specific task [8]. Gamification draws its blueprint from video games with a critical stirring influence by serving the psychological wants for relatedness, competence, and autonomy. Therefore this provocative influence of video games can be transferred to another non-game context via gamification [8]. To boost engagement, gamification involves integrating game concepts into non-game settings, such as a webpage, online forum, learning control system, or company intranet [9]. By adding game principles and gaming variables to digital sites, gamification provides viewers with proactive instructions and data that help them achieve company objectives and goals [10]. A powerful gamification experience engages the participant's feelings and clearly illustrates the best tasks the audience may carry out to contribute to shared objectives [2]. A gamification application provides immediate constructive criticism to users as they engage with it, guiding them toward essential milestones.

Various online platforms and applications have deployed game design elements to boost motivation and customer retention [11]. An excellent example of the deployment of the game design is a google map and the use of the local guide system. Different studies have revealed the motivating effect of gamification [12, 13]. In most cases, numerous research work simultaneously uses a combination of different game-designing interfaces. To assess the impact of gamification in various settings and situations.

Additionally, game design elements can produce different results [14]. However, not every gamification game design has successfully yielded the design results. Failure of specific gamification interfaces has been attributed to their intrusive nature. In other cases, such failures have been caused by the non-alignment to the existing system, apart from being below the original expectations [15]). Therefore it is evident that the success of the gamification interface cannon is guaranteed.

2.2   Edutainment

The popularity of incorporating entertainment in the education system has been increasing over the past few decades. The edutainment concept also referred to as "learning through play," is often considered to be the integration of learning and enjoyment. The ability of participants to shape their experiences and follows their passion can be achieved spontaneously through edutainment [16]. Walt Disney devised the term "edutainment" in 1954 [17]. A game design method known as "edutainment" blends entertainment with teaching to speed learning [18]. However, the global reception and endorsement of the introduction of edutainment endowments were picked in 1970 [19]. Media intended to entertain while educating viewers is alluded to as instructional entertainment (or edutainment) [2]. According to Sala [17], the purpose of edutainment game design purposes to educate and entertain learners by boosting their enthusiasm and excitement through casual educational settings that are instructional, flexible, and informative. Thus, video games, TV shows, and other entertaining programs are utilized in edutainment to communicate learning processes in business, school, and different settings.

2.3 Serious Game

Serious games are often designed to serve agendas other than entertainment [9]. In general, the word "serious" is added to describe video games utilized in the arts, politics, science, disaster response, education, security, and other fields of study and research [2]. Serious games have been employed in various industries, such as marketing healthcare and education, to promote behavioral change [20]. The main objective of serious games is to offer an opportunity for refining and practicing a new skill within a specific sphere. Serious games are designed to increase motivation, change behavior, create awareness, teach skills, and transfer knowledge. Studies have shown that serious games teach key attitudes and specific skills by combining structures, knowledge, and learning strategies. Serious games are referred to as a subgenre of significant storytelling when narrative techniques are used beyond the context of amusement, and the narrative advances as a series of high-caliber patterns that represent a thoughtful progression [3].

Serious games get popularity from their immersive, engaging, and entertaining nature. Therefore serious games have been designed to be used in learning and skill development to improve engagement and better outcomes. Research has linked the introduction of serious games in the work environment to increased productivity [21]. Additionally, gamified training programs have witnessed improved participation and engagement among the participants [22]. Although there is nothing wrong with the old method used in different work environments, serious games are increasingly being adopted as it comes with multiple advantages in transferring information and knowledge. Precisely, some of the features that guarantee the effectiveness of serious games are taps in the human psychology and philosophy of positive emotion improves learning. Moreover, human actions have consequences in the real world. Often, such consequences may cause hurt feelings and damage material. However, serious games present a safe virtual space for experiments, thus limiting the possibility of damage and hurt feelings. Finally, a noticeable advantage of serious games is the design incorporating higher engagement and immersion.

3 Application and Significance Game Design Components

The application of game design has been witnessed in different areas to solve challenges and problems. Most sectors that have employed the game design concept have been training consultancies, sustainability projects, healthcare, and education. Other sectors that have used serious game design have been the creation of social awareness platforms by government agencies, customer retention in business and marketing spheres, and military training and security intelligence simulations. This research paper will focus on the four application areas of the game design principle: education, business, medicine, and leisure.

3.1 Education

The introduction of the game design component has been anchored on the psychological finding that play has a significant role in a child's social, emotional, mental, and physical development [23]. Moreover, children can acquire experience and knowledge through play in the physical environment, apart from wellness and health from such settings [24]. Thus, designing the children's play environment is significant to guarantee holistic development. The rise in indoor play environments for children has been attributed to the parents' growing concern over safe play activities, among other factors [25]. This has caused the current generation of children to spend more time indoors than outdoors.

Gamification, edutainment, and serious game design aspects have been utilized in various industries for various goals [9]. These three gaming design approaches have been employed in education to give students everyday experiences which may be applied to subsequent active learning, such as class debates [18], which impart new information and abilities. As an aspect of the gaming experience, games can teach new skills and knowledge for the student to pick up [4]. Practice and reinforcement of current information and abilities are also developed through gaming. There have been multiple previous research works and meta-analyses on introducing the game design principle in the education environment (See Table 1. Past meta-analyses and some meta-syntheses that examined the impact of serious games on learning achievement). The general findings of this research prove that the introduction of game design principles positively influences the education outcome compared to the conventional approaches.

Interactive cities for learners, a new interface in the edutainment setting, sprung up by the end of the twenty-first century. One notable type of edutainment project is Kidzania [26]. Kidzania has been referred to as one of the most comprehensive educational interactive interfaces in the modern edutainment sphere [27]. Kidzania was designed by Xavier López Ancona and Luis Javier Larguesgoiti and was meant for kids up to 14 years. This edutainment platform further spread across the globe and has been adopted by many countries [27].

In summary, although teachers and instructors still use exercise and recreation to help learners remember lesson features, edutainment is equally on the rise in the digital age. Edutainment has served in bridging the gap and managing efficient learning. Edutainment has helped in the appearance of empirical classroom data. The success of edutainment has been attributed to emotions that directly influence learning. Additionally, such an

Table 1. Past meta-analyses and some meta-syntheses that examined the impact of serious games on learning achievement.

Year	Authors	Number ofo primary studies	Main conclusion with regard to learning achieved with serious games versus more conventional instruction
1981	Dekkers and Donatti	93	Games as effective as more conventional
1986	van Sickle	42	Games more effective to a small degree
1992	Randel, Morris, Wetzel and Whitehill	68	Games more effective for retention, but not for immediate learning gain
1999	Lee	19	Games combined with conventional more effective than games alone
2006	Vogel, Vogel, Cannon-Bowers, Bowers, Muse and Wright	32	Games more effective than conventional for cognitive gain outcomes
2011	Sitzmann and Ely	65	Games more effective than conventional for declarative and procedural knowledge acquisition and retention
2013	Wouters, van Nimwegen, van Oostendorp and van der Spek	38	Games more effective for knowledge learning and retention
2015	Clark, Tanner-Smith and Killingsworth	69	Games more effective for cognitive learning outcomes

achievement also stemmed from the fact that emotional desire and pleasure are critical elements in human psychology, thus attracting participants in the edutainment sphere.

3.2 Business

The game design concept has been modified, introduced, and applied in marketing, entrepreneurship, and business development. Since the blueprint of such algorithms has been predesigned, their incorporation in the business world is anchored on already existing business processes. Therefore, game design in business settings involves merging two systems—the game algorithm and business models—instead of building a new system from scratch. In gaming design, video games are employed in marketing and secret codes to capture the user's attention and transform them into devoted consumers [2]. They then can use these passionate fans to protect their wares and purchase new in-game goodies or games in the brand [4]. It's the goal of every organization or business setting for its employees to attain their full potential. Therefore, corporations are adapting the game design dynamics to drive their business performance. The game design models and blueprints have been used in the business world due to their engagement, ability to introduce new learning techniques, and adaptation to change.

According to Zubek [3], the game theory paradigm gives a mathematical framework for evaluating the most probable action to accomplish the desired results in a corporation or organization. This planning enables staff to make well-informed choices, from marketing, product, and pricing introductions to target market choices and promotional plans. There are various noticeable examples of game design in the business sector, including Hilton Garden Inn, Nike, and Starbucks. Another evident example of the adaptation of game design in the business world is Hilton Garden Inn. This game design technology has improved reception desk and housekeeping skills [28]. Apart from enhancing the guest experience, the video game introduced by the company boosts information retention and fun for the employees. The NikeFuel program implemented by Nike increased consumer engagement with the company's products. Successful participants are often given virtual prices and permeated to share their results [29]. The gamification algorithm in Nike ensures the customer still engages with the company, even after buying products from them; hence the company forms part of the customer's daily lives. Starbucks has introduced a loyalty app with gamification features that gift customer's free drinks and other kinds of presents [30]. The sole purpose of such an app is to promote customer retention and loyalty by rewarding customers who purchase coffee from them. Other noticeable game design applications in the business world include Fresh Desk, Hendrick Automotive Group, Topps Tiles, T-Mobile, and Deloitte Leadership Academy, among others.

In summary, the deployment of game design in the business sector has enhanced performance in various ways. When successfully programmed using reliable data, game design in the business world will increase employee experience, facilitate a meaningful learning experience and shorten onboarding. Either through a seamless adaptation towards organizational change or aligning the workforce with company-wide goals, corporations gain significant advantages from the elements and features of gamification.

3.3 Medicine

Like in other fields, the game design concept has been incorporated into healthcare. To improve clinical outcomes, healthcare gamification integrates game mechanics, game design techniques, and gaming principles with existing health systems [31]. In healthcare, game mechanics have majorly been introduced in wellness-related applications. There are various ways in which the game design concept manifests itself in such applications. In the healthcare profession, the notions of the game in gamification, edutainment, and serious games are employed to assist patients, especially younger patients, in understanding healthcare principles, from managing chronic diseases to ensuring medication compliance [4]. One of the notable scenarios is giving the participants virtual gifts to motivate them to continue the wellness or fitness challenge. The game design also allows the participants to share their results or progress with other people or users of the service to bring the element of competition and encourage more users of the service. Finally, using progress bars in such applications invokes progress-related psychological biases within the users, making them want to advance and continue the health-related challenge.

Interestingly, the game design principles have also been introduced in other illnesses such as back pain, elderly patients, and movement impairment. For such medical conditions, the game design must incorporate key algorithms specific to the type of illness. The healthcare app has been introduced to address other topics like kids' health care, emotional health, physical therapy and rehabilitation, chronic condition, and self-management medication [32]. Studies have proven that the introduction of the game design principle is beneficial not only to the patient users but also to healthcare providers [33, 34]. As the patients improve their health condition and wellness through such apps, the healthcare providers attain their desired patient satisfaction records and collect the necessary data to improve service provision. Thus this setup increases the number of App users while enhancing the status and reputation of the healthcare providers.

Using the game design principle in the healthcare sector has benefitted patients as it introduces digital engagement, thus making them think less about their ailments. Gamification further improves the user learning capacity, boosting the patients' understanding of their illness, and motivating them to continue their journey towards a healthy body and mindset [35]. The noticeable trend in healthcare gamification includes simulation games, telehealth, social connection, and attention to behavioral, mental, emotional, and cognitive health. Simulation games are often instrumental in upgrading medical procedures, monitoring, and the healthcare providers' technical know-how [36]. Extensive simulation techniques enable comprehensive patient health monitoring by visualizing the healthcare-related behavioral consequence. Equally, the success of long-distance clinical healthcare has been attributed to the introduction of electronic health information and telecommunication—also known as telehealth—among other factors. Such a trend was witnessed during the COVID-19 pandemic, where patients could be monitored remotely, reducing the workload of inpatient monitoring and improving patient flow and the general service provision [37]. The use of telehealth applications is most likely to increase in the coming years due to the rise in streamlining media and video conferencing.

Similarly, using the game design principle in the healthcare sector has benefitted healthcare providers by facilitating ease in healthcare training and education by boosting the use of healthcare applications and collecting data on patients and specific illnesses. Compared to the traditional approach of reading educational materials, gamification, and computerized simulations allow healthcare providers to learn and train in less time with a higher success rate [38]. Therefore the quality of healthcare provision can be improved by maintaining healthcare knowledge through advanced training. Equally, gamification allows the user to monitor the health journey with ease. This can involve the storage of medical records, booking appointments, and so on.

Interestingly, the self-service through the game design principle relieves the healthcare providers from routine paperwork as some of the services have been digitized, and the patients can undertake them independently [39]. This frees up more time for the healthcare providers to focus on other duties within the facilities and help more people. Deployment of the game design principle further helps the facilities collect patient data and their perception. Such algorithms enable users to give more feedback which can be instrumental in developing new healthcare trends [40]. Additionally, healthcare providers and product manufacturers can use such data to introduce products that address the target audience's desires.

Some of the widely used gamification Apps in the healthcare sector healthcare app for kids such as Yummilo, MyTeeth, and My PlayHome Hospital [41, 42]. Emotional gamification Apps in healthcare include Happify, Loóna, and Moodfit [43–45]. Examples of self-management medication and chronic condition apps include Flaredown, Manage My Pain, and Mango Health [46–48]. The game design principle and mechanics have been deployed in rehabilitation and physical therapy Apps such as Eye Workout, Prehab, and Physera. Fitness and nutrition Apps allow users to monitor various health conditions such as calories, menstrual cycles, hydration, heart rate, activity, and sleep.

3.4 Leisure Activities

Gamification and game design features have been introduced to traditional leisure activities to improve user enjoyment outcomes. In contemporary society, gamification has offered new ways for generation Z and millennials to engage. Game design features heavily rely on technology to perform well or be developed. Artificial intelligence (AI) is utilized in video games to provide intelligent, receptive, or adaptable behavior, particularly in NPCs (non-player characters) [3]. Designers frequently fake these NPCs' appearances of intelligence. One of the examples of the use of the game design principle in the leisure sector is the Wonderwall technology introduced by Bounce [49]. The technology introduces a giant computer game from a standard ping pong table through a projection mapping technique. In this game, the participants are awarded when they land in key designated areas. Another interesting newly introduced dimension of an old-age pub game is gamified types of playing darts, such as Killer and Shanghai, introduced by Flight club [50].

The introduction of game design algorithms in the leisure sector has been attributed to destination appeal and additional income since the new content resonates with the current generation, broadening the consumer base. The FSM algorithm is one of the most popular tricks [10]. The ability to communicate with other gamers via connection is one of the key benefits of IoT in the gaming sector [4]. However, there is no restriction on the number of participants because decentralized technology enables continuous real-time connection with any participant from any part of the globe. Therefore, gamified technology can add an income stream and destination appeal and be refreshed with new content, making for an all-around savvy investment. Game design in the leisure sector has equally been employed on a large-scale dynamic. One good example of this approach is the Sports Monster concept in Seoul, South Korea [51]. In this context, the game design technology is deployed in the digital, adventure, exciting and basic zones. These zones incorporate various activities that use VR simulators and interactive screens, enabling the user to enjoy an individualized experience of a diversity of entertainment.

The future of the game design element in the leisure sector is promising as most of the concept is increasingly being adopted in the field. Although different age groups are receptive to gaming and leisure, the incorporation of new technology in game design is heavily enjoyed by generation Z. The growing world of competitive socializing concepts continues to pump fresh air into the future of game design elements. Therefore gamification in the leisure sector has a greater potential for growth as it is a component of successful consumer interaction.

4 Conclusion

In conclusion, this article aimed to survey the application of game design elements in key sectors of human well-being. This article aimed to survey the application of game design elements in key sectors of human well-being. The basic principle of game design and its influence on people's behavior has transformed the relationship with policies, products, services, and all the aspects that can transition into the game interphase. The game design's main element or basic framework is the deployment of technology tracking human behavior. A complex topic still being researched is the vision of game design or the game creation procedure. Gamification, edutainment, and serious game processes continue to be deployed in various sectors such as education, business, healthcare, and leisure. The introduction of the game design component in the education sector has been anchored on the psychological finding that play has a significant role in a child's social, emotional, mental, and physical development. As an aspect of the gaming experience, games can teach new skills and knowledge for the student to pick up. Additionally, Practice and reinforcement of current information and abilities are also developed through gaming. Although teachers and instructors still use exercise and recreation to help learners remember lesson features, edutainment has served to bridge the gap and manage efficient learning. Edutainment has helped in the appearance of empirical classroom data.

The game design concept has been modified, introduced, and applied in marketing, entrepreneurship, and business development to increase employee experience, facilitate a meaningful learning experience and shorten onboarding. Like in other fields, the game design concept has been incorporated into healthcare and leisure. Using the game design principle in the healthcare sector has benefitted patients as it introduces digital engagement, thus making them think less about their ailments. Similarly, gamification in the leisure sector continues to be embraced due to its potential for growth as it is a component of successful interaction with consumers. Therefore the success of game design elements in these sectors is anchored on its principle is developing a progression by enabling humans to attain small achievements attached to extrinsic values.

References

1. Gauthier, A.: Manipulating interface design features affects children's stop-and-think behaviours in a counterintuitive-problem game. Assoc. Comput. Mach. **29**(2), 1–21 (2022)
2. Moreira, T., de Classe, R., De Araujo, M., Xexéo, G.B., Siqueira, S.: The play your process method for business process-based digital game design. Int. J. Serious Game. **6**(1), 27–48 (2019). https://doi.org/10.17083/ijsg.v6i1.269
3. Zubek, R.: Elements of game design. MIT Press, Cambridge (2020)
4. Martens, A., Wolfgang, M.: Gamification-a structured analysis. In: International Conference on Advanced Learning Technologies, Austin, TX, USA (2016)
5. Martela, F.: Expanding the map of intrinsic and extrinsic aspirations using network analysis and multidimensional scaling: examining four new aspirations. Front. Psychol. **10**(1), 1 (2019)
6. Fabricatore, C., Nussbaum, M., Rosas, R.: Playability in action videogames: a qualitative design model. Hum.-Comput. Interact. **7**(4), 1 (2002)
7. Victor, P.L.: The impact of marketing strategies in healthcare systems. J. Pentru Med. si viata s.r.l, **12**(2), 93–96 (2019)
8. Seaborn, K., Fels, D.I.: Gamification in theory and action: a survey. Int. J. Hum Comput Stud. **74**(1), 14–31 (2015)
9. Morganti, L., Federica, P., Elena, C., Antonio, C., Francesco, A., Fabrizia, M.: Gaming for earth: serious games and gamification to engage consumers in pro-environmental behaviours for energy efficiency. Energy Res. Soc. Sci. **29**(1), 95–102 (2017)
10. Ahmad, M.: Categorizing game design elements into educational game design fundamentals. Game Design Intell. Interact. **1**(1), 1–17 (2019)
11. Kalafatoglu, Y.: Gamification in business: a review of the studies. Eurasian Business Perspect. **1**(1), 53–73 (2020)

12. Dichev, C., Dicheva, D.: Gamifying education: what is known, what is believed and what remains uncertain: a critical review. Int. J. Educ. Technol. Higher Educ. **14**(1), 9 2017
13. Hamari, J.: Do Badges increase user activity? A field experiment on the effects of gamification. Comput. Hum. Behav. **71**(1), 469–478 (2017)
14. Koivisto, J., Juho, H.: The rise of motivational information systems: a review of gamification research. Int. J. Inf. Manage. **45**(1), 191–210 (2019)
15. Liu, D.: Toward meaningful engagement: a framework for design and research of gamified information systems. MIS Q. **41**(4), 1011–1034 (2017)
16. Wong, K.: Similarities and Differences Between 'Learn Through Play' and 'Edutainment'. Murdoch University Research Repository, Perth (2006)
17. Sala, N.: Virtual reality, augmented reality, and mixed reality in education". current and prospective applications of virtual reality in higher education. IGI Global **1**(1), 48–73 (2020)
18. Rabah, J., Cassidy, R., Beauchemin, R.: Gamification in education: Real benefits or edutainment. In: 17th European Conference on e-Learning, Athens, Greece (2018)
19. Aksakal, N.: Theoretical view to the approach of the edutainment. Procedia. Soc. Behav. Sci. **186**(1), 1232–1239 (2015)
20. Hammady, R., Arnab, S.: Serious gaming for behaviour change: a systematic review. Information **13**(3), 142 (2022)
21. Virtanen, A.: Growth Engineering (2023). www.growthengineering.co.uk/19-gamification-trends-for-2022-2025-top-stats-facts-examples. Accessed 1 Feb 2023
22. Growth Engineering (2022). www.growthengineering.co.uk/serious-games-that-changed-the-world. Accessed 1 Feb 2023
23. Babuc, Z.T.: Exploring parental perceptions and preferences about play: a case study in Erzurum. Procedia. Soc. Behav. Sci. **197**(1), 2417–2424 (2015)
24. Kroeker, J.: Indoor and outdoor play in preschool programs. Univ. J. Educ. Res. **1**(4), 641–647 (2017)
25. Song, J.H., Choi, K.R.: Kids color-design playground apparatus proposal. J. Korea Furniture Soc. **25**(4), 239–249 (2014)
26. Soto-Maciel, A.: International growth for the concept of children's edutainment: the case of kidZania. Reverse Entrepren. Latin Am. **1**(1), 121–133 (2018)
27. Laura, D.P.: A Scaling up framework for innovative service ecosystems: lessons from Eataly and kidZania. J. Serv. Manag. **29**(1), 146–75 (2018)
28. Stringam, B.B., Gerdes, J.H.: Hospitality and Tourism Information Technology. J. Serv. Sci. Manag. **1**(1), 1 (2021)
29. Mio, M.: Science in Our World (2013). https://sites.psu.edu/siowfa13/2013/12/06/nike-fuel-bands-the-new-fitness-tracking-technology/. Accessed 2 Feb 2023
30. Xin, O.W.: Gamification effect of loyalty program and its assessment using game refinement measure: case study on starbucks. In: Alfred, R., Iida, H., Ag. Ibrahim, A., Lim, Y. (eds.) Computational Science and Technology. ICCST 2017. Lecture Notes in Electrical Engineering, vol. 488. Springer, Singapore (2018). https://doi.org/10.1007/978-981-10-8276-4_16
31. Gentry, S.: Serious gaming and gamification interventions for health professional education. Cochrane Database Syst. Rev. **1**(1), 1 (2018)
32. Virella, P., Ilene, Y.: Mobile and web-based apps that support self-management and transition in young people with chronic illness: systematic review. J. Med. Internet Res. **21**(11), 13579 (2019)
33. Cao, L.: The association between mhealth app use and healthcare satisfaction among clients at outpatient clinics: a cross-sectional study in inner Mongolia, China. Int. J. Environ. Res. Public Health **19**(11), 6916 (2022)
34. Carlqvist, C.: Health care professionals' experiences of how an ehealth application can function as a value-creating resource - a qualitative interview study. BMC Health Serv. Res. **21**(1), 1 (2021)

35. Berglund, A.: Understanding and assessing gamification in digital healthcare interventions for patients with cardiovascular disease. Eur. J. Cardiovasc. Nurs. **21**(6), 630–638 (2022)
36. Haubruck, P.: Evaluation of app-based serious gaming as a training method in teaching chest tube insertion to medical students: randomized controlled trial. J. Med. Internet Res. **20**(5), 195 (2018)
37. Behar, J.A.: Remote health diagnosis and monitoring in the time of COVID-19. Physiol. Measur. **41**(10), 10TR01 (2020)
38. van Gaalen, A.E.J.: Gamification of health professions education: a systematic review. Adv. Health Sci. Educ. **26**(2), 683–711 (2020)
39. Sardi, L.: A systematic review of gamification in e-health. J. Biomed. Inform. **71**(1), 31–48 (2017)
40. Cheng, V.W.S.: Recommendations for implementing gamification for mental health and wellbeing. Front. Psychol. **11**(1), 1 (2020)
41. Google Play (2021). http://play.google.com/store/apps/details?id=com.playhome.hospital&pli=1. Accessed 2 Feb 2023
42. App Store (2013). http://apps.apple.com/us/app/myteeth/id715668236. Accessed 2 Feb 2023
43. Happify. https://www.happify.com/. Accessed 2 Feb 2023
44. Loóna (2022). https://loona.app/. Accessed 2 Feb 2023
45. Moodfit (2022). https://www.getmoodfit.com/. Accessed 2 Feb 2023
46. Flaredown (2023). http://flaredown.com/. Accessed 2 Feb 2023
47. Manage My Pain (2023). https://managemypainapp.com/. Accessed 2 Feb 2023
48. Maxey, R.: TrialCard (2022). https://corp.trialcard.com/capabilities/physician-education-and-awareness-3. Accessed 2 Feb 2023
49. Optoma (2023). http://www.optoma.co.uk/case-studies/586-wonderball-revolutionises-ping-pong-at-bounce. Accessed 2 Feb 2023
50. Thomas, T.: LPF - the Leisure Property Forum (2023). http://leisurepropertyforum.co.uk/. Accessed 2 Feb 2023
51. AMOS Sport Bussiness School (2022). http://www.amos-business-school.eu/actualite/discover-sports-monster-south-korea-study-trip. Accessed 2 Feb 2023

Level Flow Patterns in Game Design

Michael Brandse[✉]

Ochanomizu Sola City Academia 3F, Digital Hollywood University, 4–6 Kandasurugadai,
Chiyoda-ku, Tokyo 101–0062, Japan
michaelbrandse@dhw.co.jp

Abstract. Challenge within video games is a necessary component, one from which many players derive the majority of entertainment from. To understand challenge better, we looked at and defined challenge in prior research as obstacles that impede progress. Players then need to overcome these obstacles using a variety of skills in order to be able to continue playing the game. Since we looked primarily at how the objects contributing to the challenge were designed, we did not look at how the challenge were ordered within a given environment. Therefore, in order to expand on the research into challenge, we now also look at how challenge is ordered within a given environment, since the order in which challenge is encountered can have a significant impact on how the player experiences the challenges within the game. We analyzed a large variety of games, and found 5 common level flow patterns within games. Using these flows, it will be easier for developers to construct compelling levels in games.

Keywords: Kansei Engineering · Storytelling · User Experience Design · Video Game Design · Interaction Design

1 Introduction

Since the earliest games like the famous Pong from the 1970's, games have developed into a huge industry that is now catering to millions of people. Within this timeframe, the industry has gone through many transformations and innovations. Not just in the sense of scope, but also in how games are being designed. One element that has not changed is how challenge remains a core component to the majority of games. However, while the need for challenge has not diminished with the majority of modern games still containing competitive elements, the ways challenges are designed has. Back in the earliest renditions of games, game design knowledge was sparse. The result was a large variety of games that were too difficult to play, impossible even. Since many of those extremely difficult games were development for the Nintendo Entertainment System, these kind of difficult games became well known as "Nintendo Hard" games [1] in popular culture. Furthermore, during those days, games were often played in game arcades. Since games in arcades cost money to operate, designers would often make extremely difficult games to increase profit, since the more difficult a game was, the easier it was for the player to fail and have to retry. As the industry started to move away from game arcades and game designers gained more experience and more resources to work with, the difficulty issue largely remedied itself. This gave designers a large variety of ways to incorporate challenge into their games. However, despite the advances in game design, a formal definition of challenge was never established.

The primary focus of challenge is to supply obstacles that the players need to exert effort in order to overcome it. Players of games generally do not find this a hassle, and instead, consider this an important source of enjoyment. Suits B. referred to this as the lusory attitude [2]. The lusory attitude is the willing acceptance of rules within the game that may not be the most efficient means of achieving the goals given by the game. A relatively recent example of this would be in the game Spider-Man [3], where the titular Spider-Man will have to complete a number of challenges, one type of which involves following drones throughout Manhattan and intercepting them before the time limit. If this challenge is completed well before the allotted time has passed, players will receive bonus points increasing the rewards gained from completing the challenge. Players who are aware of where the drone will eventually land could potentially take a shortcut to intercept the drone well before it arrives. This would allow them to get a much shorter time than players who have yet to complete this challenge and thus gain much more bonus points. However, the game will actively interfere with this, by failing the challenge if the distance of the player and the drone exceeds a certain amount.

The importance of challenge is further confirmed by Cox, who argues that the Theory of Flow is important to the immersion of gamers, which includes challenge as one of its components [4] as well as Juul, J., who included player effort in his own definition of games.

> "Player effort is another way of stating that games are challenging, or that games contain a conflict, or that games are "interactive". It is a part of the rules of most games (except games of pure chance) that the players' actions can influence the game state and game outcome. The investment of player effort tends to lead to an attachment of the player to the outcome since the investment of energy into the game makes the player (partly) responsible for the outcome." [5].

1.1 Locked Door and Puzzle Model

In past research [6], we have modelled a definition of challenge by looking at how challenge is encountered within the game and found that all challenges follow the pattern of obstructing player progress until the player has completed one or a number of arbitrary tasks. We named this model the "locked door and puzzle" model, where the door is unlocked (i.e. player progress is resumed) after solving the puzzle (i.e. completing the arbitrary tasks set out by the game developers). A similar model was presented by Naughty Dog in 2018 at the Game Developers Conference [7], speaking to the validity of the model we proposed (Fig. 1).

- Challenge objects are the objects in the game world with which the player can interact. Challenge objects serve to help players solve the puzzles.
- Difficulty is to make challenge objects and their connections harder to overcome.
- Rewards are used to provide the player with incentives to clear the challenge, and are often required to resume player progress (i.e. to unlock the locked door).

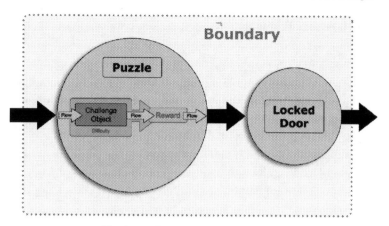

Fig. 1. Locked Door and Puzzle model

- Flow control is used to bind challenge objects together.
- Boundaries are the areas within each locked door and puzzle (as well as all the elements that make up the puzzle) are located.

1.2 Flow Within the Boundary

While we defined flow control in the model, we defined the role of flow control specifically as binding all the elements within a puzzle together, while also determining how the linked objects relate to one another. An example of this would be a timed challenge. In a timed challenge all the challenge objects will have to be cleared within a certain time in order for the player to solve the puzzle. Not clearing the challenge objects in time would then either cause the puzzle to reset partly or entirely, or even punish the player for failing the challenge.

However, one thing that also requires examination is the challenge object placement within each boundary, or the flow within the boundary itself. While the flow within the boundary does not necessarily have any direct effect on how challenge objects need to be cleared in order to proceed, the flow within the boundary directly affects in what order players may encounter challenge objects, which in turn can have significant effects on how the player experiences the game and approaches the challenges set forth by the game. Therefore, in this research we aim to examine the various manners of how the flow within boundaries is ordered. For the sake of brevity, we shall refer to this as level flow in this paper, which is also closer to how the term is used in level design in general. [8].

2 Research Method

2.1 Data Analysis

For this research, we observed a large number of games, in particular to how level flow was designed within each level. Any form of game-play was considered, including mini-games, small games within the game that generally follow different game rules than the main game does. We primarily focused on single player games.

2.2 Equipment

We analyzed the games, where possible, by playing them on the platforms they were originally released on. For games for which we either lacked the required hardware or the aptitude to reliably progress in the game, we used on-line video footage known as "let's plays," which are videos of players playing through games, often commenting on their progress. We primarily used let's play videos that documented the gameplay from the beginning to the end, without major omissions.

2.3 Protocol Design

For the initial research, we have attempted to analyze an as broad a selection of games as possible, across various genres, in order to get an as complete an understanding as possible about challenge design trends within games [Table 1].

Table 1. Selection of surveyed titles

Hardware	Survey Type	Surveyed Titles
Nintendo (Switch, 3DS, Wii)	Hardware and video	Xenoblade Chronicles Definite Edition, Xenoblade Chronicles 2, The Legend of Zelda a Breath of the Wild, The Legend of Zelda Skyward Sword, Kirby and the Forgotten Land, The Great Ace Attorney Chronicles, Tokyo Mirage Sessions #FE Encore, Crono Trigger, Terranigma, Zombies ate my Neighbours, Trials of Mana, Castlevania Portrait of Ruin, Final Fantasy Tactics A2: Grimoire of the Rift, La Mulana, La Mulana 2, Zack and Wiki: Quest for Barbaros Treasure, Octopath Traveller, Bravely Default 2

(continued)

Table 1. (*continued*)

Hardware	Survey Type	Surveyed Titles
Playstation (Playstation 3, 4, 5)	Hardware and video	Little Nightmares, Little Nightmares 2, Spider-Man, Spider-Man Miles Moralis, Ghost of Tsushima, Horizon Forbidden West, Ratchet and Clank: Rift Apart, Persona 5, Persona 5 Strikers, Secret of Mana, Ace Combat 7 Skies Unknown, Tales of Arise, Uncharted 4: a Thief's End, Uncharted: the Nathan Drake Chronicles, The Last of Us Part II, A Plague Tale Innocence, Scarlet Nexus, Breath of Fire Dragon Quarter, Puppeteer, Folklore, Final Fantasy XV
Personal Computer	Hardware and video	Mayhem in Single Valley, ENDER LILLIES, The Darkside Detective: a Fumble in the Dark, Omensight, Death's Door, Psychonauts, Psychonauts 2, Guacamelee 2, Ori and the Will of the Wisps, Eastward, Steamworld Dig 2, Momodora: Reverie Under the Moonlight, Final Fantasy XIII, The Witch's House MV, Mark of the Ninja Remastered, Record of Lodoss War –Deedlit in Wonder Labyrinth-, Persona 4, Elden Ring, Enter the Gungeon

3   Level Flow Patterns in Level Boundaries

To explain the various level flows we have observed in games, we will be using actual situations within games where we have encountered them as concrete examples. While these flows are commonly present in all games, we will be primarily be using The Legend of Zelda: Breath of the Wild [9] to illustrate our examples, as this title employs many different kind of level flows. Other games we will use to explain level flows in case The Legend of Zelda: Breath of the Wild proves insufficient are Castlevania: Symphony of the Night [10], Enter the Gungeon [11] and Death's Door [12].

3.1   Linear Level Flow

Within a linear flow, the player simply encounters and completes each challenge object in turn. Once all challenge objects have been completed, the player may receive a reward, after which the puzzle is considered completed and player progression is resumed (Fig. 2).

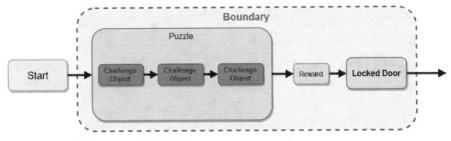

Fig. 2. Linear Flow

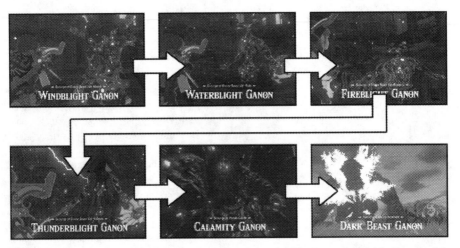

Fig. 3. Battle against Ganon Blights and Calamity Ganon in "The Legend of Zelda: Breath of the Wild"

In the game The Legend of Zelda: Breath of the Wild, the main narrative goal of the game is to defeat a creature by the name of "Calamity Ganon," which serves as the final challenge before the player sees the epilogue and end credits. In order to get sufficiently powerful to do this, the player is given the option of exploring the game world, gain access to dungeons by the name of "Divine Beasts" and defeat the boss monsters within each one. However, since the game is an open world game, the player can also immediately proceed towards the final boss instead of exploring the world first. If the player does this, the player will first have to defeat all the bosses the player would normally encounter within the Divine Beasts. Once the Ganon Blights have been defeated, the player will finally be able to fight the final boss, which has two separate phases; "Calamity Ganon" and "Dark Beast Ganon." The order in which the player has to defeat all of these bosses is always the same (see Fig. 3). It should be noted that if the player does choose to explore the world and clear every "Divine Beast," the final boss battle will be limited to just the final boss and its two phases.

While it is rare to have so many bosses to defeat as a final challenge[1], it's relatively common for a final boss in a game to have multiple phases, where the boss changes up its patterns and often changes its appearance too, like what happens in The Legend of Zelda: Breath of the Wild as well.

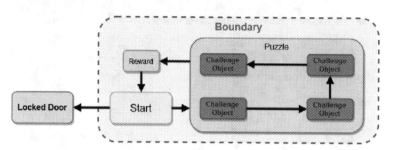

Fig. 4. Circular Flow

The circular flow is a variation on the linear flow. This flow is often used in small boundaries, where the player again completes each challenge object in sequence (Fig. 4). However, within a circular flow the start point is located right next to the goal of the puzzle (the reward which allows for resuming player progress). Initially, the passageway leading directly from the start to the reward is locked, with the means of unlocking this passageway being on the reward side. Once the player gets to the reward and unlocks the passageway, the passageway will become permanently accessible from both sides. This is done to provide a shortcut to the player, to make it so the player doesn't have to backtrack through the boundary to get to the locked door. It should be noted that we don't count flows where the player gets to the reward and is instantly teleported back to the start as a circular flow, unless said teleporting functionality goes both ways (i.e. the teleporting functionality becomes available from the start as well).

In the game Death's Door, the player will at one point come across a castle called "Castle Lockstone." In the very first room of this castle (see Fig. 5), the player enters from the bottom and has 3 passageways to choose from; a passageway to the top and passageways from both sides. However, the passageways from the sides are initially locked, with no direct way of unlocking them. Once the player progresses more through the castle, the player will eventually come to an enemy arena with a locked gate to the side. After the enemy arena is cleared and the player has claimed the reward, the locked gate will unlock and will lead right back to the first room of the castle. At this point, the previously locked gate will become permanently unlocked, thus creating a circular flow. The other locked sideway passage is unlocked in a similar manner.

---

[1] When the player encounters a large number of bosses in succession, this is often labeled a "boss rush.".

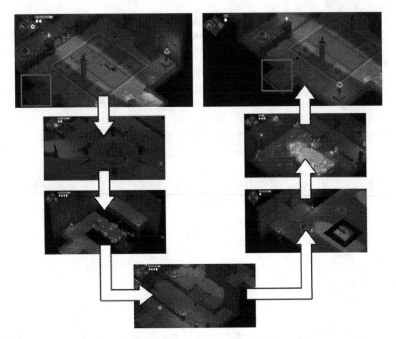

Fig. 5. Castle Lockstone in "Death's Door"

3.2 Open Level Flow

Open flow offers the player the choice in which order the player wishes to tackle each challenge object, by adding a number of challenge objects within an environment that all need to be cleared, but for which the order in which they are cleared is not of importance. The player is free to choose the order. Important to this flow is that the player is explicitly given the choice and that this choice will not impact the shape of the reward presented to the player (Fig. 6).

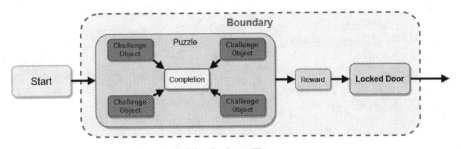

Fig. 6. Open Flow

Fig. 7. The Trial of the Sword quest in "The Legend of Zelda: Breath of the Wild"

In the game The Legend of Zelda: Breath of the Wild, there is a DLC[2] quest named "Trial of the Sword," where the player can strengthen a mythical sword upon completion of the trial. The trial consists of multiple floors and each floor functions as an enemy arena; the player has to defeat a number of enemies before passage to the next floor is unlocked. While the floors are encountered in a linear fashion, there is no set order in which the enemies on each floor have to be defeated, thus constituting as an open flow (Fig. 7).

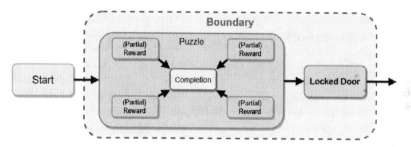

Fig. 8. Open Flow using Rewards

A variation on the open flow is one where the targets of the players are not the challenge objects, but rather rewards, either full rewards or partial. In this case, the player has to collect all of the rewards first in order to resume progress in the game. Oftentimes, this reward takes the form of a token where the token is part of a set (i.e. a partial reward). Once the player collects all the tokens required to complete the set, the player will be able to advance (Fig. 8).

---

[2] DLC, or downloadable content is additional content added after the game is released, often for a premium.

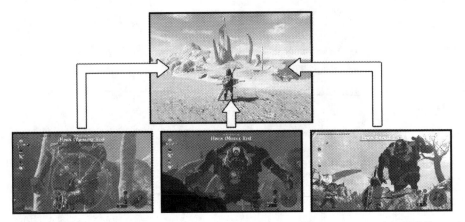

Fig. 9. The Three Giant Brothers quest in "The Legend of Zelda: Breath of the Wild"

In the game The Legend of Zelda: Breath of the Wild, the player can complete so called shrines, which reward the player with currency that allows for buying health or stamina upgrades. One of those shrines comes as a quest by the name of "The Three Giant Brothers (Fig. 9)." For this quest the player is required to collect three tokens (in the form of big glowing orbs) in order to open up the shrine. These orbs are held by three so-called Hinoxes. The player needs to either steal the orbs or defeat the Hinoxes in order to clear this quest. The order in which the player has to obtain the orbs is not set, nor is the order in which the player needs to fight the Hinoxes, if the player chooses to fight. While there is an implied order of strength, due to there being a significant difference in strength between each Hinox (with the "youngest kin" being the weakest and the "oldest kin" being the strongest), the player deviating from this implied order has no impact on the shape of the reward of this challenge.

3.3 Maze Level Flow

In a maze flow, the boundary itself is used as the main means of obstructing the player. Therefore, within a maze flow, the presence of challenge objects is not actually a necessity. Within a maze flow, the path to the goal or even the next challenge object is obscured through a variety of means. While obstructions tend to be visual in nature, we have observed a number of games using sound as well. Challenge objects, especially interactive ones, are sometimes used to provide the player with clues as how to proceed through the maze. Maze flows tend to have many dead ends to confuse the player, though this is not required. As long as the player cannot proceed through the puzzle using the usual observations as established through the core gameplay, the flow can be considered a maze flow (Fig. 10).

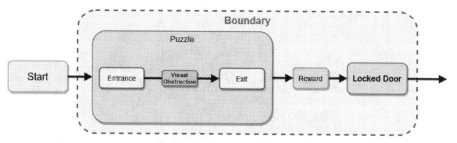

Fig. 10. Maze Flow

Fig. 11. Shrouded Shrine Quest in "The Legend of Zelda: Breath of the Wild"

In the game Breath of the Wild, the player will encounter a number of mazes. One of these mazes is encountered in the quest "Shrouded Shrine" in an area known as the "Typhlo Ruins." In these ruins, the player's visibility is obstructed through the use of pitch-black darkness the moment the player enters the area. The darkness is unaffected by the time of day. Scattered through the area are interactive challenge objects (torches) in the shape of bird statues, which can serve as beacons once lit, but also serve as hints where to go next. Each bird statue's beak is pointed in the direction of where the next bird statue is located guiding the player through the maze (see Fig. 11). While there are no explicit walls in this maze and the player can explore the area without ever relying on the bird statues, this is relatively difficult and relies a lot on chance. Therefore, the flow within this area can be considered a maze flow.

3.4 Random Level Flow

A random flow relies on the game randomly calculating and generating a boundary layout, generally through the means of a random number generator. Due to the random nature, a random flow also generally has randomly generated challenge objects. While some games completely randomize even whether certain challenge objects will appear, other games use a list of objects that need to be present within the boundary and randomizes their positions (Fig. 12).

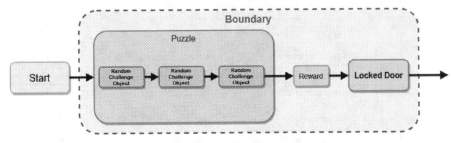

Fig. 12. Random Flow

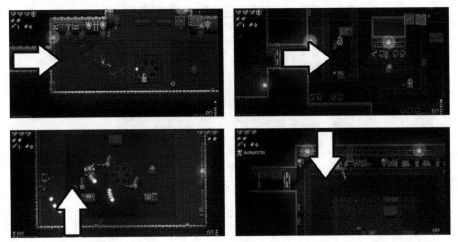

Fig. 13. Four different opening areas in "Enter the Gungeon," the direction of entry being randomized as indicated by the arrows.

In the game "Enter the Gungeon" the player needs to make their way through randomly generated environments fill with random enemy placement as well as random weapon pick-ups. While the map that is responsible for teaching the player the basics has very few random elements to it, once the player begins with the main game all levels become randomly generated. In Fig. 13 we show 4 environments that the player first encounters the moment the player starts the game, showing that each time the game is played again, the level layout completely changes. We have added arrow indicators to show where the player enters from, to show that it's not just the shape of the room, but the flow of the entire level that changes.

3.5 Backtrack Level Flow

Backtrack level flow involves setting up locked doors in early boundaries with no apparent means of clearing said boundaries at the time the player first encounters. Instead, it requires the player to remember these locked doors and return to them once the player has gained the required item or skill that allows the player to open the locked door and progress (Fig. 14). While certain genres use this type of flow relatively liberally, back-tracking is generally not considered an interesting flow by players, with some referring to the term as a derogatory term [13].

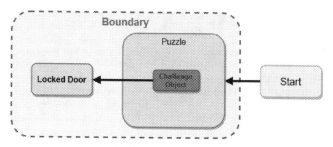

Fig. 14. Backtrack Flow

Fig. 15. Clock Room in Castlevania: Symphony of the Night

In the game Castlevania: Symphony of the Night, the player has to explore a giant castle but will be impeded at various points due to the player not having the required skills or items to proceed. These items and skills are acquired through the course of the game, thus requiring the player to go back to earlier areas of the castle that were previously inaccessible, i.e. backtrack, in order to advance the game. Once of those areas the player often needs to backtrack to is known as the "Clock Room" and is encountered fairly early on in the game. Initially, the player can only enter from the left or right, with the other potential entrances (entrance 1 through 4, see Fig. 15) being inaccessible. Once the player gains the ability to double-jump (a jump common in games where the player gains access to an additional jump while airborne), the player can enter entrance 1 and 3. Once the player gains the ability to fly, the player can enter entrance 2 as well. Finally, once the player procures two specific items within the game and wears them, the fourth entrance will open as well.

3.6 Mixing Flows

We have observed that puzzles in games don't necessarily use one single type of flow for each. Rather, oftentimes various types of flows are mixed together to create more compelling puzzles (Fig. 16).

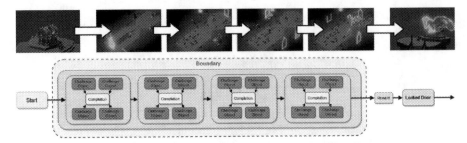

Fig. 16. Example of level flow mixing in "Death's Door"

One example of this can be found in the game "Death's Door." In this game the player will encounter so called "Avarice Chests" which will reward the player with a specific tool that allows further progression in the game. However, in order to get this item the player will first have to defeat four waves of enemies. The waves and the type as well as number of enemies encountered in each wave are fixed in a linear pattern. However, in each wave the player can choose by themselves in what order to defeat the enemies in that particular wave. In this example, the enemies in each way follow an open flow. However, each wave is encountered in a way that follows a linear flow. Were the player to fail the challenge, the player will have to start over again from the first wave, further reinforcing the linear nature of the waves.

4   Conclusion

Challenge is still a relatively misunderstood concept in games, despite it playing such a big role in how entertaining a game can be. While our locked door and puzzle model set out to define challenge not as a fuzzy concept, but rather as a tangible object that can be designed, our model was lacking in the sense that there was too big a focus on the challenge object and less on how this challenge object was placed within the world. The placement of challenge objects and the shape of the boundary both play an important role in how challenge is accessed, and should therefore be considered a key component of challenge.

Therefore, by also looking at level flow in games, we could define a number of common patterns of challenge object placement. In our observations we also found that level flow patterns are oftentimes mixed with other level flow patterns to create more compelling challenges. This knowledge will not only help us understand challenge more thoroughly, it will also help game designers and researchers alike create more effective game content. This will certainly be useful to a wide variety of fields, such as research into dynamic challenge or serious games and could even find a use in classroom instruction in game related courses, where students can be expected to have little to no game design experience. We hope that future work will be able to further validate and develop this model, as well as serve as a basis for challenge design research.

References

1. Enger, M.: What is "Nintendo hard"? (2012). https://www.giantbomb.com/profile/michaelen ger/blog/what-is-nintendo-hard/98057/. Accessed 30 Sept 2022
2. Suits, B.: The Grasshopper: Games. University of Toronto Press, Life and Utopia (1978)
3. Insomniac Games. Spider-Man (Software). Sony IntePOSFC ractive Entertainment, Japan (2018)
4. Cox, A., Cairns, P., Shah, P., Carrol, M.: Not doing but thinking: the role of challenge in the gaming experience. In: CHI '12 Proceedings of the SIGCHI Conference of Human Factors in Computing Systems, ACM New York, ACM, 79–88 (2012)
5. Juul, J.: The game, the player, the world: Looking for a heart of gameness. In: Copier, M., Raessens, J. (eds.) Level Up: Digital Games Research Conference Proceedings, Utrecht University, pp. 30–45. Utrecht University (2003)
6. Brandse, M.: The Shape of Challenge - Using Affordance Design to Create Challenge Within Games. HCI (2017)
7. Shaver, D., Yang, R.: Level design workshop: invisible intuition: blockmesh and lighting tips to guide players and set the mood. Game Developers Conference (2018). https://www. gdcvault.com/play/1025179/Level-Design-Workshop-Invisible-Intuition. Accessed 30 Sept 2022
8. The Level Design Book. Flow – How players move through the level (2022). https://book.lev eldesignbook.com/process/layout/flow. Accessed 30 Sept 2022
9. Nintendo EPD. The Legend of Zelda: Breath of the Wild (Software). Nintendo, Japan (2017)
10. Konami Computer Entertainment Tokyo. Castlevania: Symphony of the Night (Software). Konami, Japan (1997)
11. Dodge Roll. Enter the Gungeon (Software). Devolver Digital, United States (2016)
12. Acid Nerve. Death's Door (Software). Devolver Digital, United States (2021)
13. GiantBomb. Backtracking (Concept) (2020). https://www.giantbomb.com/backtracking/ 3015-239/. Accessed 03 Oct 2022

Making the Digital Tangible Through Analog Games: Design Retrospective of Digital Literacy Games

Scott DeJong[✉] 🆔

Concordia University, Montreal, QC, Canada
scottbdejong@gmail.com

Abstract. The digital is an inherently intangible place. Mediated through devices like smartphones, watches, and computers, our digital selves sit adjacent to, but are felt in, our reality. The benefits of these spaces are counteracted by issues like the disinformation and conspiracy which have been witnessed in recent protests, riots, and ideological divides. One response has been digital literacy education, where games have been one tool for raising awareness and teaching the skills of online participation. However, these approaches have prioritized videogames which remain in the abstract space of the digital. In trying to show the material impact of digital issues, this paper argues that analog games offer key affordances for making the digital tangible. Through a retrospective of two case studies on the design affordances of two digital literacy analog games – a board game and an escape room - this paper asks how analog games can reflect digital issues and, in doing so, help players untangle their realities with their digitally mediated selves. Its findings point to key affordances of analog games for grounding digital issues and provides insights for designers in how they think about game affordances whether making for digital or analog titles.

Keywords: Digital Literacy · Analog Games · Game Design

1 Introduction

Games and education seemingly go hand in hand. In younger grades, play-based curriculum encourages students to feel and manipulate the space around them to make sense of the world (Pyle & Danniels, 2017). As we get older, and develop more technical literacies, videogames emerge as a more efficient way to engage with larger audiences and distill concepts. However, games, and their educational efficacy, are not restricted to the classroom. They have been used to inform the general public with various initiatives demonstrating videogames as helpful digital literacy tools for discussing fake news (DeJong, 2023), misinformation (Roozenbeek & van der Linden, 2019), and relaying news stories (L. D. Grace & Huang, 2020). While videogames have been praised for their effectiveness, could the materiality and physicality of analog games offer a more effective means to make sense of these issues?

© The Author(s), under exclusive license to Springer Nature Switzerland AG 2023
X. Fang (Ed.): HCII 2023, LNCS 14046, pp. 66–80, 2023.
https://doi.org/10.1007/978-3-031-35930-9_5

Complimenting the work on digital games this paper explores the potential of analog games, or non-digital games more broadly, as tools for materializing digital issues to players. As calls for digital literacy tools increase, it becomes critical that we evaluate the various mediums and means through which we can make the public aware of the issues that impact us all. Digital problems like disinformation, conspiracy theories, and echo chambers have robust lineages that predate their digital lives. While people discuss them as online issues, these problems are felt today in misinformation fueled protests (Jeppesen et al., 2022) and growing distrust in journalism (De Maeyer, 2019). This suggests that we need tools to allow participants to feel how these digital spaces, and the issues within them, mingle. The social and cultural issues that emerge from our digital spaces are intangible, abstract, and challenging to make sense of. As this paper argues through its two case studies, analog games make systems tangible and grounded, which can encourage design to think beyond the intangibility of videogames towards material and affective focused design.

2 Literature Review

2.1 Digital Issues and Digital Literacy

The digital is an inherently intangible but embodied place. Mediated through devices and filtered, sorted, and categorized through platforms and algorithms (Bucher, 2018), our digital lives create digitized selves which refract back on our physical lives (Chan, 2022). Online connectivity extends and magnifies our identities (Belk, 2016) in ways that entangle our offline lives with the social, technical, and cultural spaces our online lives take up. Examples like the loss of personal privacy through the sale of user data (Sadowski, 2019), participation in streaming culture (Andrejevic, 2002), and politics of visibility (E. Kim, 2018) all illuminate a deeply interconnected and personal negotiation around one's private and public identity. Yet our digital-physical lives are made privy to an array of interactions which harm and help us. Marwick and boyd (2014) see these exchanges as networked where "technical mechanisms often drive normative sensibilities" (p. 1062). Yet as Taina Bucher (2018) notes these mechanisms are also black boxed, difficult to make sense of, but experienced in our lives. Our digital interactions remain ethereally bound, entangled in the code, cultures, and affordances of these technological spaces.

This intangibility becomes a concern when we look at the vast issues that are connected to and found online. In addition to privacy, issues like echo chambers (Sasahara et al., 2019), biased and racist filtering (Noble, 2018), fake news (Mohsin, 2020), conspiracy theory (Napolitano & Reuter, 2021), and disinformation (Freelon & Wells, 2020) are all exacerbated through digital infrastructure. Yet they extend offline in increasingly visible and felt ways that impact our lives. Moments like the Capitol Hill riots in the United States (Jeppesen et al., 2022), or the vaccine protests in Canada (Molas, 2022) raise questions among the public, governments, and academics on how to deal with these impacts.

For many, the solution has been education. Scholars like Barry Duncan (2006) constructed media and digital literacy programs and curriculum directions in the 1990s that focused on how users can participate and comprehend content online. These ideas still guide Canadian approaches today. Recently, the Canadian government re-solidified these in a recent digital Charter which pushes for a variety of educational initiatives from global education to particular forms of digital literacy approaches (Canada, 2022). However, digital literacy education has had more than a few problems to solve. Given the rapid rise of our technologically mediated lives, educational approaches have had to be open to adaptation. Unfortunately, this has been a slow and long process with older theories that could barely conceive of our modern landscape still being touted (Hoechsmann & DeWaard, 2015).

In fact, the label of digital literacy does a poor job at even recognizing all of the issues at play. Digital literacy is focused on comprehension and skills (Hadziristic, 2017), but struggles to think about the larger histories of many modern digital issues that extend beyond their online presence. Issues like disinformation and propaganda have histories that predate our modern technocultures (Tsfati et al., 2020), yet digital literacy initiatives remain focused on breaking down digital systems and not larger communication and cultural spaces. This allows issues to remain intangible, where discussing the particulars of an algorithm or "AI" end up becoming buzzwords with little definition and comprehension tied to them. This raises an alarming set of questions such as How do we help the public make sense of these spaces when they remain intangible to many researchers and educators? How do we teach about black-boxed systems when we struggle to comprehend them ourselves? Recognizing this, this paper particularly focuses on where analog games can be helpful as digital literacy interventions.

2.2   Digital Literacy Videogames

Whether digital or analog, games have long been tools for reflecting, simulating, and portraying aspects of our lives. Mary Flanagan (2009) points to ancient games like Senet for presenting farming practices or toys like dolls as tools for challenging and exploring gender expectations. Wargaming has a long lineage of simulation design (Caffrey, 2019), and influenced modern tabletop games like Dungeon's and Dragons (Lalone, 2019) which players have adapted to reflect social issues (Clarke et al., 2018; Kaylor, 2017). Similar to other media and artistic practice, games have always been a looking glass (Flanagan & Nissenbaum, 2014; Nicklin, 2022). Whether an imaginary space or our reality, play has long been a way that people engage with and understand the world around them (Bateson, 2006; Toh & Lim, 2021).

Games have been a part of the internet for some time but their adoption as educational tools for reflecting on the digital is more recent. Given the fact that media literacy initiatives did not really grow to prominence until the 2000s (Hoechsmann & DeWaard, 2015), it is no surprise that the turn for educational videogames about digital issues took some time. The earliest in Canada appeared in the 2000s by the nonprofit MediaSmarts. In the space of journalism, newsgames were an early genre of game used to breakdown media stories (Bogost et al., 2010) building from earlier claims of videogames as potential tools for consciousness raising around serious issues (Abt, 1987; Frasca, 2001). However, newsgames were less a teaching tool than an alternative way to tell a story (L. D. Grace & Huang, 2020). Many of these games quickly blossomed to a focus on digital citizenship (Raphael et al., 2010) which is embodied in Google's "Be Internet Awesome Campaign" which made the title Interland (2017). Other games like Factitious or Bad News Game emerged through partnerships between academia and designers and used simple quiz and narrative structures to discuss misleading content online (L. Grace & Hone, 2019; Roozenbeek & van der Linden, 2019). The popularity and visibility of videogames has somewhat placed them as defaults in the space of digital literacy games, subsequently obfuscating the potential that analog options might offer.

2.3 Digital Literacy Analog Games

There have been some analog counterparts. MediaSmarts in Canada has a print and play card game discussing algorithms (MediaSmarts, 2022), and the interest in Fake News and Alternative facts led to two commercial, but seemingly discontinued, card games being made (Breaking Games, 2017; Miller, 2017). The Media and Social Change lab at Columbia University designed *Lamboozled* a deck-building card game meant to help players understand that "some news stories just want to pull the wool over your eyes!" (Literat et al., 2020). However, just like the simplicity of the digital literacy videogames above, all these games are card games with a repetitive design of making media headlines and promoting particular types of content.

The lack of deep engagement and mechanics in these games suggests that analog games in the space of digital literacy have not been seriously considered. Wargaming and simulation design have shown how spaces can be modeled, and the growing spaces of foresight and cybergaming have begun to discuss digital issues (Havelin, 2021; "How Can We Credibly Wargame Cyber at an Unclassified Level?" 2018). In fact, despite wargaming trending towards digital games, designer, and scholar Rex Brynen (2020) urges wargaming to remember the distinct affordances of the tangibility of analog games. As Brynen writes, "In the age of digital war, digital expectations may sometimes hamper creative approaches" (p. 4) and, in fact, "manual games may often be preferable to digital ones precisely because they are better able to engage the players into thinking about these issues in a critical and innovative ways (p. 4). While discussing wargames, Brynen's arguments point to the potential affordances of analog games for offering new critical ways of discussing content, where the simplistic digital literacy card games struggle to engage in the affordances of analog games. Antero Garcia's (2020) work on tabletop role playing games point to the material and spatial practices of analog games to construct an array of literacies that occur in, at, and beyond the table. Promoted through the interactions between players and the system they begin to recognize the powerful learning affordances of non-digital options. Yet, analog games are still relatively understudied. In breaking down two digital literacy games, this paper contributes to this limited literature while providing key insights in how analog games can be actualized for digital literacy education.

3 Method

This paper engages in a case study analysis of two analog games which focus on digital issues. It prioritizes the affordances of the games and their genre for discussing digital literacy and uses the two relatively disparate projects to show the potential of the medium's materiality.

Given the intensity of these case studies on design and implementation affordances, this work focuses on two titles made by the author. First, an escape room titled *Reactile* focused on echo chambers and filter bubbles. Followed by *Lizards and Lies*, a board game about conspiracy theory on social media. As retrospective case studies, the author returned to the design notes, blogs, and recorded conversations from playtests for each of the games conducted (one in 2019 and the other from 2021–2022). The focus is on the distinct affordances of the analog titles, highlighting how they engaged in materiality, facilitation, and reflection to engage with digital literacy themes. Each analysis will begin with a summary and then focus on core aspects of the games, highlighting their use of physicality, their narratives, their gameplay, and how they presented digital issues.

4   Results

4.1   Cast Study 1: *Reactile*

Basic Overview. The first game, *Reactile*, was an escape room designed and implemented in 2019 as a Masters thesis project (DeJong, 2020). Escape rooms are team-based games where players work together to solve clues and puzzles in order to "escape" or get out of a room. This serious game used the "trapping" of players in a room to discuss content manipulation from echo chambers and filter bubbles. Players were placed "inside" an echo chamber where they solved puzzles, discussed content in the room, and navigated the space and non-player characters. The game was made publicly available and housed at Concordia University in Montreal for just under a month in the fall of 2019. In this time, the game had just over 20 players participate.

Physicality. *Reactile* localized play to a built environment and space. As part of a graduate research project, the longevity of the game was always going to be localized to the spaces available to me as a student and timing window for its implementation. Despite this, the environment of the game was central to relaying the analogy between the chamber of the game room and the echo chamber it was discussing.

Escape rooms naturally encourage players to look for clues in every mundane object. The space and nature of the game asks them to draw connections between objects, narrative, and theme; all of which is conveyed through the environment. Environmental storytelling is a key part of many mystery games, which escape rooms make deeper by allowing players to physically alter, navigate, and touch the space. In one case, players ripped things off walls, combined game pieces together, and attempted to remake the space as part of solving a clue. For *Reactile,* the space reoriented a graduate research office into a toy company's testing room through corporate logos, physical props of prototype games, and reviews of products on the walls. However, in play, this corporate office also became the very echo chamber the game was attempting to portray.

Narrative. Players were game play testers asked to play and review the company's (Reactile) newest products. They were welcomed and guided by non-player character, and Reactile Employee, Craig, who was tasked with having the players provide "unbiased" reviews for three of Reactile's newest toys. In time, players would find out that Reactile is manipulating them to offer positive reviews and as they uncover this manipulation, they work to expose it without raising suspicion from Craig.

Throughout the game, Craig would "check-in" on the players, provide them with other information, and bring in potential puzzle pieces. Craig functioned as a non-player character and game-facilitator where their surveillance of the room (through a camera hidden in the space) allowed them to monitor the players and game flow.

Gameplay. As players moved through this plot, they followed a sequential puzzle process with open moments for agency. At the start, players are highly directed in the space with one clue leading to one puzzle. However, as they begin to unlock containers and discover clues players are given an array of choices through which to reveal Reactile's nefarious scheme.

When they first enter the room, players are sat down at a table with three simple minigames setup - these are the "new" toys for them to review. After introducing each, Craig leaves them, and players will begin playing the games. In doing so, they quickly come across a note from a fired employee informing the players that something with Reactile is "not quite right".

In time, players begin to follow suggestions from the note and uncover a phone which gives them the ability to speak with this fired employee. Balancing conversation with Craig and the whistleblower through the "burner phone" creates conflicting dimensions that motivate play and provide affordances for the players to ask for help and remain skeptical of the information they were getting. In time, players come to see Craig as an antagonist, while the mysterious whistleblower is a skeptical ally they occasionally lean on.

Over time Connection to Content Manipulation. Throughout this time, the back and forth between players, space, and actors, allowed the game to reflect how personal information and digital communities can manipulate content and construct echo chambers and filter bubbles. Reflecting inputs and outputs of a system, each interaction with Craig was met with particular questions, and certain puzzles asked players to provide personal information through their play. Similar to signing up for social media and how content slowly builds an identity that can be categorized, as players offer this information Craig begins to adjust the space to their "preferences".

The room's atmosphere was "personalized" to the players. In the initial minigames, players were asked to share musical artists and colours they like and as they continued through the game the lighting and initial ambient playlist began to match what they had disclosed. Initially these changes were subtle but grew in intensity as the game went on leading to an endgame that filled the space with coloured light and personalized sounds that was almost overbearing to the players.

Similarly, puzzles and Craig's conversations with the players provided opportunity for hyper focused personalization. Some of the puzzles asked players to organize children's blocks with articles of clothing to make a "cool" avatar. Depending on what the players inputted, Craig would later appear in that outfit. Similarly, players would be provided with snacks and new materials that would reflect what they said in conversations with Craig.

The game's overall layout also hinted at the manipulation of content. The celebrity reviews on the wall, upon closer examination, were parodies or fake posts. This was furthered when players found a garbage bag filled with negative reviews which had been hidden and locked out of sight.

As players go through the game, they not only watch as the space and content get more personalized to what they disclosed, but also begin to find ways to manipulate that space by feeding Craig misleading information. Yet, in order to escape, they needed to challenge and break out of the filter bubble they ended up contributing to, where the ability to text the whistleblower employee provides them with chances to engage in information and content outside the space.

4.2   Case Study 2: *Lizards and Lies*

Basic Overview. The second game, *Lizards and Lies*, is a boardgame demonstrating how conspiracy theory moves through social media. The game was made publicly available to download, print, and play in the summer of 2022 in French, English, and Lithuanian. Designed over the course of a year and half, the game was influenced by wargaming and simulation design to playfully model how content moves. The game involved a mix of cards, a game board, and 4 playable characters. Using cards and character abilities players would work with one teammate against 2 other players to add or remove conspiracy theory from the social media network. The final and current iteration of the game includes a narrative that is impacted by the gameplay, where players witness how their management of conspiracy theory impacts a national election. The game has been showcased in art exhibitions, used as teaching tools in high school and university spaces (undergrad and graduate), as well as with various disinformation stakeholders (i.e., journalists, fact checkers).

Physicality. While *Reactile* had players move through the space to uncover a plot, *Lizards and Lies* seats them around a gameboard and play as one character on social media (Conspiracy theorist, Edgelord, Digital Literacy Educator, or Platform Moderator). Using character specific powers and cards players might add bird or lizard tokens to represent conspiracy theory, move meeples as moderators around the board, or place down "critically aware tokens" which look like brains to represent those who have become less susceptible to conspiratorial content.

All of this play occurs on a board, where players physically, add, move, and remove tokens to reflect its flow on social media. A typical gameboard (FIGURE) was designed around social media network graphs and contains communities as nodes and groups of connected nodes to form a network. As an abstraction of the digital, the game allows players to visualize and actualize their manipulation of social media as they add or remove content from different social media spaces.

Narrative. To further ground how the state of social media would reflect on our everyday, the game includes a narrative. Read in-between player rounds, the story follows a two-party election with one party leaning into the conspiracy theories, and another trying to discredit them. The two theories, represented by birds and lizards, are reflections of existing conspiracy theories. The birds allude to the Birds Aren't Real conspiracy, a now satirical movement which argued that many of the birds in America had been replaced by government drones that spy on the public (Birds Aren't Real, 2022). The lizards are in reference to a more problematic conspiracy theory which argues that world

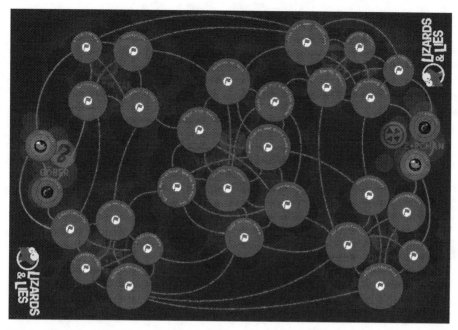

Fig. 1. The gameboard for *Lizards and Lies* showcasing the nodes, connections, and networks.

leaders are alien lizards, a rhetoric that was reinforced in science fiction and has roots in antisemitism (Parramore, 2021).

As gameplay continues, they revisit the story to reinforce how their actions on social media lead to real-world issues. In some cases, birds are being slaughtered throughout the nation, in others, politicians are attacked to try and have their "lizardness" revealed. These moments are dependent on player actions but also have a reciprocal effect on the board. For example, in the case of birds being murdered, the popularity of videos and posts discussing it leads to algorithms spreading messaging on social media and subsequently adds more conspiratorial content to the board.

Gameplay. *Lizards and Lies* is asymmetrical, where each player is doing something distinct to their character, making the game slightly more complex but providing space for them to see the skills, drawbacks, and benefits of each actor. Players participate as one of four characters split into two teams. Those who are spreading conspiracy theory are either Edgelords trying to stir the pot or conspiracy theorists trying to build up their community. They are resisted by platform moderators attempting to ban users and fact check content while digital literacy educators try to train users to be less susceptible to these theories.

Play occurs through the cards and character specific abilities. A player-character turn follows simple steps on a player board and character specific cards where the core decision space is how they choose to play their cards in relationship to the board space and opponents/teammate. Cards and actions typically focus on individual nodes on the board and have conditions for play (i.e., already having conspiracy there, or has a platform moderator there) which influences how players use their cards and think about the game.

Connection to Content Manipulation. The game functions as a model to social media and the movement of content on it. While the current iteration has a focus on conspiracy in how the players and narrative are designed, the game can be easily adapted to discuss other instances of content spreading through social media. Each player character is a social media actor and their distinct player cards are meant to reflect some of the challenges and benefits they provide. Platform moderators have to triage content and communities by deciding how to focus their actions which can cause management stress related to burnout that many moderators face (Schöpke-Gonzalez et al., 2022). Digital Literacy Educators take their time to impact the game and struggle to address conspiracy strongholds focusing instead on spaces that have yet to be targeted. Conspiracy theorists rely on having support to continually feed from and focus on building up communities who will proliferate their message. Finally, Edgelords, also referred to as Internet Trolls in the French version of the game, look for spaces to disrupt based on the potential susceptibility of the community there.

The game has a series of intricate references to the movement of content, the challenges of these actors, and the theories we have to understand them. This level of depth in the design allows the game's presentation to be modular for different audiences, where younger groups might focus on the references between social media and public discourse found in the narrative, and more knowledgeable groups might examine the particularities on how content ebbs and flows through the space. Critically, the game embodies Byun-Chun Han's (2017) notion of the "swarm" or the push and pull of digital movements where content like conspiracy or disinformation bubble up and recede. This back and forth becomes a concern when the waves compound on one another bubbling over into a space that harms the public. This is reflected in the turn order, where play jumps from a spreader to a stopper to a spreader, where removal of content is slightly weaker than the ability to add more. This creates a space where conspiracy begins to fill the board, is pushed back, and when the next spreader goes is able to gain further ground due to the lingering remnants of the past wave. While the particular mechanics that do this might take a more knowledgeable eye, even the observers to these games can notice the players filling the board up with colourful conspiracy and watching it get removed by other players, only to come back again.

The physicality of the game was critical to its learning success. Players have to follow the game's rules, manipulating them in their actions, and being forced to think about the logic behind them. Players physically add and move content around the board, helping them see how information can quickly spread from one social media space all the way to another. Players take the time to add content when they play a card, and in doing so can feel and visualize the impact of their actions. The need to win through control forces players to think about social media holistically, where single communities are seen as part of a larger ecology. These moments and aspects of the game ask players to question their own social media behaviours and reflect on larger events that spread through social media (i.e., elections, wars, pandemics).

5 Discussion

5.1 Materiality

Each of these case studies point to the distinct affordances of materiality and physical-ity for translating concepts to players. Both games placed players into the systems and themes they were trying to pursue. Materiality, or the ability to physically manipulate objects and the space, provided players with key narrative, mechanical, and environmen-tal effects which reflected the learning goals. Rather than the simple actions mediated through a computer clicks, or placement of cards into headlines, these games ask players to physically move around the space to "feel" the effects of the game.

This materiality of the games is what allows analog games to make the intangibility of digital issues felt. While digital games, especially through rising VR systems, have been referred to as immersive experiences (Dick, 2021), analog games have the potential to do so through a combination of mechanics and the space which places the system in the players hands. *Reactile* asked players to uncover the larger system driving content manipulation, while *Lizards and Lies* had players attempt to master the rules system in order to perform their character's actions in the digital ecosystem. The rules, procedures, and actions of the game are not bound or hidden in code but directly negotiated. These negotiations push players to witness, manipulate, and explore the boundaries of how these structures work. Rather than figuring out what the system is doing for them, players are part of what makes the game function. In short, players enact the rules.

From environment to story, the games could embed the issues into almost every aspect. Player cards in *Lizards and Lies* were a reflection of the actors they portrayed and had actions which forced the players to physically manipulate social media communities. The board and narrative set a stage to make the ephemeral and twisted digital networks something players can begin to conceptualize. *Reactile* immersed players in a space, where the notion of user outputs for system outputs was embedded in each puzzle and social interaction that players had to complete. These exchanges not only reinforce the process of turning data into tangible results but demonstrates their impact as the room overwhelmed players with sound and light.

Materiality goes beyond the bits and mechanical interactions, to the actual feel of these games. Critically, these digital issues while partially created through our online actions have embodied and felt impacts, something that design can think of in the affec-tive dimensions of the games. *Lizards and Lies* balance of collaboration and competition forced stoppers like platform moderators to feel pressure in dealing with what seemed like an endless barrage of conspiracy on the board. Alternatively, those spreading lies consistently referred to the satisfaction at being able to annoy and exacerbate the stop-pers, while also referencing frustration at people not always taking a liking to their theories. These experiences further entrenched players in the goals and challenges of the characters rather than have them rely on the party game tactics of the previously discussed Lamboozled or #Alternativefacts. Rather than laugh at the ridiculousness of headlines, players were actively thinking about the stresses, problems, and benefits of each role.

5.2 Reflection

Inherent to analog games is their sociality which creates unique affordances for reflection. Digital literacy videogames are often solitary experiences, played as a one-device to one-person interactions. This type of design typically restricts reflection to questions before the game, textual questions or worksheets provided during play, and a short review post the game. However, many analog games are group experiences. Whether collaborative or competitive, these games offer one system for a set of players. *Lizards and Lies* created a semi-collaborative and competitive space through teams. In doing so, players were pushed to think about their and their teammates abilities in relation to their opponents, and the need to strategize led to in-game reflection through conversation. Alternatively, *Reactile* was purely collaborative where players decoded clues and the space prompted a sharing of knowledge, ideas, and perspectives to succeed.

As social spaces, analog games create an opportunity for constant reflection before, during, and after play. However, to actualize this, the games still require facilitation. Unlike more simplistic titles, the nature of roleplay in *Reactile* and deep relationship between simulation mechanics and narrative in *Lizards and Lies* prompts facilitators to help players fully reflect on their experience. The complexity of the titles creates malleability for the product providing space for an instructor to further ground the game to the particular goals they are looking to get across. While digital titles might include questions during or after the game, a facilitator's presence allows them to prompt reflection based on the particular needs and objectives they are trying to get across. However, this need for a facilitator also points at a potential limitation of these case studies.

5.3 Limitations

While analog games offer powerful affordances, they still have drawbacks. The creation and distribution of these games is not able to match the potential reach and accessibility of a videogame. *Lizards and Lies* was made available online for the public to print and play themselves (needing to cut out the pieces) but those extra steps alone can demotivate potential educators and players from using the product. This is a problem even further exacerbated by *Reactile's* limited run and the difficulty of archiving escape rooms for recreation.

Analog games also take time. Even simple card games still require a set-up and gameplay loop that takes longer than the average fake news games time of 5–10 min (L. Grace & Hone, 2019; Moger et al., 2022). Both *Reactile* and *Lizards and Lies* required an hour or more to play, creating challenges for implementation in a typical classroom. While this time could be chunked up over a series of lessons, they still struggle to fit into the lessons already being taught.

Finally, these games are limited in their adaptability. While the visibility of the system creates powerful affordances for learning, these games are hard to adapt after release. In the short life of *Lizards and Lies* there have been requests to adapt the conspiracy theory narrative to the Ukraine war, something that requires a more robust response than some minor narrative changes. To compensate, the boardgame was released with a guide on how to alter the narrative to different issues, but this once again places labour on the user which can impact if the game actually sees use in a classroom.

6 Conclusion and Lingering Questions

Digital literacy requires a multiplicity of responses to help the public and key stakeholders make sense of the digital issues we face today. While on paper, videogames seem like a good fit, analog games can help players ground the impact and role of these issues through the materiality present in these games. The physicality of these games allows for powerful abstractions of relatively ephemeral issues, where play can create negotiations between players and systems that construct grounded learning.

This work is not to discount the videogames being done, but rather point to the use of tangible activities in making sense of the intangible. While educators and academics talk about the black-boxed nature of social media, it is critical we still recognize and show individuals how they are felt. When done right, analog games can be embodied, felt, and reflective experiences that engage with content in ways that video games struggle to do. *Reactile* and *Lizards and Lies* are just examples of the potential that analog games have and only hint at what could be created.

This work suggests that designers, educators, and scholars can actively consider how analog games can be fully used as digital literacy devices. This work is a start at looking at how analog games have powerful affordances for reflecting content and future work should continue to explore the use of analog and digital games for dealing with digital issues. There is a need to study the long-term effectiveness of these tools and consider how the goals of design can be optimally reflected in a game. Game makers should challenge the simple or easy designs they can make and think through the affective and felt dimensions of games to fully discuss these issues. While digital solutions might seem elegant and simple, thinking through their actual engagement with these issues and themes is critical when we talk about the actual goal: effectively informing our audiences.

Finally, and perhaps more critically, there is a need to interrogate if games are even the appropriate format for dealing with digital issues and digital literacy. The seriousness of these issues, and frivolity of games can sometimes obfuscate the intensity of the problems at hand. Games and play are received differently from various communities and cultures, where the fractured and targeted nature of digital issues like disinformation (Jaiswal et al., 2020) means that games might be an ineffective and inappropriate solution to intervene in some communities. With this in mind, it is critical to ask how designers and scholars in the space of games and education can consider their skill sets and knowledge for the audiences that require these interventions. Games are powerful tools, and analog games are powerful for conversation. Unlike digital options, the sociality and reflection inherent in analog games could be promising to further explore here. Thinking through what specific affordances they offer, who they can aid, and how they can be actualized for meaningful learning is critical to the success of an educational game no matter the medium.

References

Abt, C.C.: Serious Games. University Press of America (1987)

Andrejevic, M.: The work of being watched: interactive media and the exploitation of self-disclosure. Crit. Stud. Media Commun. **19**(2), 230–248 (2002). https://doi.org/10.1080/073 93180216561

Bateson, G. (2006). A theory of play and fantasy. In The game design reader: A rules of play anthology (pp. 314–328). MIT Press Cambridge, MA

Belk, R.: Extended self and the digital world. Curr. Opin. Psychol. **10**, 50–54 (2016). https://doi.org/10.1016/j.copsyc.2015.11.003

Benkler, Y., Faris, R., Roberts, H.: Network Propaganda: Manipulation, Disinformation, and Radicalization in American Politics. In Network Propaganda. Oxford University Press (2018). https://oxford.universitypressscholarship.com/view/10.1093/oso/978019 0923624.001.0001/oso-9780190923624

Birds Aren't Real. (2022). Birds aren't Real—History. Birds Aren't Real. https://birdsarentreal.com/pages/the-history

Bloom, M., Moskalenko, S.: Pastels and Pedophiles: Inside the Mind of QAnon. Stanford University Press (2021)

Bogost, I., Ferrari, S., Schweizer, B.: Newsgames: Journalism at Play. MIT Press (2010)

Boyd, D., Levy, K., Marwick, A.: The Networked Nature of Algorithmic Discrimination. New America, 5 (2014)

Breaking Games. Fake News. BoardGameGeek (2017). https://boardgamegeek.com/boardgame/239937/fake-news

Bruns, A.: Are Filter Bubbles Real? John Wiley & Sons (2019)

Brynen, R.: Virtual paradox: how digital war has reinvigorated analogue wargaming. Digital War **1**(1–3), 138–143 (2020). https://doi.org/10.1057/s42984-020-00004-z

Bucher, T.: If...Then: Algorithmic Power and Politics. Oxford University Press (2018)

Caffrey, M.: On Wargaming (Vol. 43). Newport Papers (2019). https://digital-commons.usnwc.edu/newport-papers/43

Canada, G.: Canada's Digital Charter: Trust in a digital world [Landing Pages]. Innovation, Science and Economic Development Canada (2022). https://ised-isde.canada.ca/site/innovation-better-canada/en/canadas-digital-charter-trust-digital-world

Chan, K.T.: Emergence of the digitalized self in the age of digitalization. Computers in Human Behavior Reports **6**, 100191 (2022). https://doi.org/10.1016/j.chbr.2022.100191

Clarke, S., Arnab, S., Morini, L., Heywood, L.: Remixing dungeons and dragons: a playful approach to student self-reflection. European Conference on Games Based Learning, 872–875, XI, XIV (2018). https://www.proquest.com/docview/2131784195/abstract/EA6097294 8354D5DPQ/1

De Maeyer, J.: Taking conspiracy culture seriously: journalism needs to face its epistemological trouble. Journalism **20**(1), 21–23 (2019). https://doi.org/10.1177/1464884918807037

DeJong, S.: Generational Controls: designing and implementing a serious intergenerational escape game that analogizes data personalization, filter bubbles and echo chambers [Masters, Concordia University] (2020). https://spectrum.library.concordia.ca/id/eprint/987068/

DeJong, S.: Playing with fake news: state of fake news video games. Int. J. Games Soc. Impact, 1(1), Article 1 (2023)

Dick, E.: The Promise of Immersive Learning: Augmented and Virtual Reality's Potential in Education | ITIF. Information Technology and Innovation Foundation (2021). https://itif.org/pub lications/2021/08/30/promise-immersive-learning-augmented-and-virtual-reality-potential/

Dubois, E., Blank, G.: The echo chamber is overstated: the moderating effect of political interest and diverse media. Inf. Commun. Soc. **21**(5), 729–745 (2018). https://doi.org/10.1080/136 9118X.2018.1428656

Duncan, B.: Media literacy: Essential survival skills for the new millennium. Sch. Libr. Can. **25**(4), 31–34 (2006)

Flanagan, M.: Critical Play: Radical Game Design. MIT Press (2009)

Flanagan, M., Nissenbaum, H.: Values at Play in Digital Games. MIT Press (2014)

Fletcher, R.: The truth behind filter bubbles: Bursting some myths. Reuters Institute for the Study of Journalism (2020). https://reutersinstitute.politics.ox.ac.uk/risj-review/truth-behind-filter-bub bles-bursting-some-myths

Frasca, G.: Rethinking agency and immersion: video games as a means of consciousness-raising. Digital Creativity 12(3), 167–174 (2001). https://doi.org/10.1076/digc.12.3.167.3225

Freelon, D., Wells, C.: Disinformation as political communication. Polit. Commun. 37(2), 145–156 (2020). https://doi.org/10.1080/10584609.2020.1723755

Garcia, A.: Gaming literacies: spatiality, materiality, and analog learning in a digital age. Read. Res. Q. 55(1), 9–27 (2020). https://doi.org/10.1002/rrq.260

Google. Play Interland—Be Internet Awesome. Play Interland - Be Internet Awesome (2017). https://beinternetawesome.withgoogle.com//en_us/interland/

Grace, L. D., Huang, K.: State of Newsgames 2020: a snapshot analysis of interactives, toys and games in journalism and allied industries (2020). https://doi.org/10.13140/RG.2.2.11165.74722

Grace, L., Hone, B.: Factitious: Large Scale Computer Game to Fight Fake News and Improve News Literacy. 1–8 (2019). https://doi.org/10.1145/3290607.3299046

Hadziristic, T.: The state of digital literacy in Canada: a literature review (2017). https://brookfiel dinstitute.ca/report/digital-literacy-in-a-digital-age

Hall, L.E.: Planning your escape: strategy secrets to make you an escape room superstar. Simon Element (2021)

Han, B.-C.: In the Swarm: Digital Prospects (E. Butler, Trans.). MIT Press (2017)

Havelin, M.: Misinformation & Disinformation in Canadian Society. A system analysis & futures study [MRP]. OCAD University (2021). http://openresearch.ocadu.ca/id/eprint/3505/

Hoechsmann, M., DeWaard, H.: Mapping digital literacy policy and practice in the Canadian education landscape (2015)

How can we credibly wargame cyber at an unclassified level?. PAXsims (2018). https://paxsims.wordpress.com/2018/08/06/how-can-we-credibly-wargame-cyber-at-an-unclassified-level/

Jaiswal, J., LoSchiavo, C., Perlman, D.C.: Disinformation, misinformation and inequality-driven mistrust in the time of COVID-19: lessons unlearned from AIDS denialism. AIDS Behav. 24(10), 2776–2780 (2020). https://doi.org/10.1007/s10461-020-02925-y

Jeppesen, S., Hoechsmann, M., ulthiin, iowyth hezel, McKee, M., VanDyke, D.: The Capitol Riots: Digital Media, Disinformation, and Democracy Under Attack (H. Giroux & C. Kumanyika, Trans.; 1st edition). Routledge (2022)

Kaylor, S.: Dungeons and Dragons and literacy: The role tabletop role-playing games can play in developing teenagers' literacy skills and reading interests. Graduate Research Papers (2017). https://scholarworks.uni.edu/grp/215

Kim, E.: The politics of visibility. In: Kim, D., Stommel, J., (Eds.), Disrupting the Digital Humanities (pp. 321–346). Punctum Books (2018). https://doi.org/10.2307/j.ctv19cwdqv.22

Lalone, N.: A Tale of Dungeons & Dragons and the Origins of the Game Platform | Analog Game Studies. Analog Game Studies, 4(3) (2019). https://analoggamestudies.org/2019/09/a-tale-of-dungeons-dragons-and-the-origins-of-the-game-platform/

Literat, I., Chang, Y. K.: The Media and Social Change Lab: LAMBOOZLED! | The Media Literacy Card Game | Teachers College Press (2020). https://www.tcpress.com/lamboozled

MediaSmarts: Digital Literacy Fundamentals. MediaSmarts (2012). https://mediasmarts.ca/dig ital-media-literacy/general-information/digital-media-literacy-fundamentals/digital-literacy-fundamentals

MediaSmarts: #ForYou: A Game About Algorithms. MediaSmarts (2022). https://mediasmarts.ca/digital-media-literacy/educational-games/foryou-game-about-algorithms

Miller, R.: #AlternativeFacts. Ultra Pro (2017). https://boardgamegeek.com/boardgame/226865/alternativefacts

Moger, A., Wagner, J., Phelps, A.: Fake news cycles: the repetitive design of disinformation games. Games Learning and Society Conference (2022)

Mohsin, K.: Defining "Fake News" (SSRN Scholarly Paper ID 3675768). Soc. Sci. Res. Netw. (2020). https://doi.org/10.2139/ssrn.3675768

Molas, B.: Barbara Molas: Understanding the Freedom Convoy and the Growth of Far-Right Movements in Canada | CDA Institute [Video] (2022). https://cdainstitute.ca/barbara-molas-understanding-the-freedom-convoy-and-the-growth-of-far-right-movements-in-canada/

Napolitano, M.G., Reuter, K.: What is a Conspiracy Theory? Erkenntnis , 1–28 (2021). https://doi.org/10.1007/s10670-021-00441-6

Nicklin, H.: Writing for Games: Theory and Practice (1st edition). CRC Press (2022)

Noble, S.U.: Algorithms of Oppression: How Search Engines Reinforce Racism. NYU Press (2018)

Parramore, L.: The far right's lizard conspiracy is bonkers. But it's definitely not harmless. NBC News (2021). https://www.nbcnews.com/think/opinion/qanon-s-capitol-rioters-nashville-bomber-s-lizard-people-theory-ncna1253819

Pyle, A., Danniels, E.: A continuum of play-based learning: the role of the teacher in play-based pedagogy and the fear of hijacking play. Early Educ. Dev. **28**(3), 274–289 (2017). https://doi.org/10.1080/10409289.2016.1220771

Raphael, C., Bachen, C., Lynn, K.-M., Baldwin-Philippi, J., McKee, K.A.: Games for civic learning: a conceptual framework and agenda for research and design. Games Culture **5**(2), 199–235 (2010). https://doi.org/10.1177/1555412009354728

Roozenbeek, J., van der Linden, S.: Fake news game confers psychological resistance against online misinformation. Palgrave Communications, 5(1), Article 1 (2019). https://doi.org/10.1057/s41599-019-0279-9

Sadowski, J.: When data is capital: datafication, accumulation, and extraction. Big Data Soc. **6**(1), 2053951718820549 (2019). https://doi.org/10.1177/2053951718820549

Sasahara, K., Chen, W., Peng, H., Ciampaglia, G. L., Flammini, A., Menczer, F.: On the Inevitability of Online Echo Chambers (2019). ArXiv:1905.03919 http://arxiv.org/abs/1905.03919

Schöpke-Gonzalez, A.M., Atreja, S., Shin, H.N., Ahmed, N., Hemphill, L.: Why do volunteer content moderators quit? Burnout, conflict, and harmful behaviors. New Media Soc., (2022). https://doi.org/10.1177/14614448221138529

Toh, W., Lim, F.V.: Let's play together: ways of parent–child digital co-play for learning. Interact. Learn. Environ. 1–11 (2021)

Tsfati, Y., Boomgaarden, H.G., Strömbäck, J., Vliegenthart, R., Damstra, A., Lindgren, E.: Causes and consequences of mainstream media dissemination of fake news: literature review and synthesis. Ann. Int. Commun. Assoc. **44**(2), 157–173 (2020). https://doi.org/10.1080/23808985.2020.1759443

Zelenkauskaite, A.: Creating chaos online: disinformation and subverted post-publics. Univ. Michigan Press (2022). https://doi.org/10.3998/mpub.12237294

GPU Based Position Based Dynamics
for Surgical Simulators

Doga Demirel[1]([✉]) [iD], Jason Smith[1], Sinan Kockara[2] [iD], and Tansel Halic[3] [iD]

[1] Department of Computer Science, Florida Polytechnic University, Lakeland, FL, USA
ddemirel@floridapoly.edu, jason@smith.software
[2] Department of Computer Science, Lamar University, Beaumont, TX, USA
skockara@lamar.edu
[3] Intuitive Surgical, Atlanta, Georgia
Tansel.halic@intusurg.com

Abstract. Position Based Dynamics is the most popular approach for simulating dynamic systems in computer graphics. However, volume rendering with linear deformation times is still a challenge in virtual scenes. In this work, we implemented Graphics Processing Unit (GPU)-based Position-Based Dynamics to iMSTK, an open-source toolkit for rapid prototyping interactive multi-modal surgical simulation. We utilized NVIDIA's CUDA toolkit for this implementation and carried out vector calculations on GPU kernels while ensuring that threads do not overwrite the data used in other calculations. We compared our results with an available GPU-based Position-Based Dynamics solver. We gathered results on two computers with different specifications using affordable GPUs. The vertex (959 vertices) and tetrahedral mesh element (2591 elements) counts were kept the same for all calculations. Our implementation was able to speed up physics calculations by nearly 10x. For the size of 128×128, the CPU implementation carried out physics calculations in 7900 ms while our implementation carried out the same physics calculations in 820 ms.

Keywords: Position Based Dynamics · GPU

1 Introduction

Position Based Dynamics (PBD) is the most popular approach for simulating dynamic systems in computer graphics [1]. Utilizing collision constraints to manipulate the positions of points in 3D space allows for simple physics calculations on large models [2]. Attempts to parallelize PBD saw specialized graphs and graph coloring to divide sets of constraints into independent sections, which can provide calculation time decreases of several orders of magnitude [3]. However, large and complex models are still computationally expensive, even with graph coloring. Reduced models can somewhat solve this problem by providing low dimensional copies of the model on which the PBD calculations are run and then projected back to the higher quality, displayed model [4]. As complex PBD models allow for complicated constraints, calculations can be slow on large models. In addition, specialized solvers can cause objects that would otherwise interact with one another to pass through. Utilizing a unified solver function on particle-based simulations allows many different substance types to interact [5].

Additionally, utilizing PBD provides excellent advantages when using volumetric models, such as VEG files. These files already contain information used by the PBD model, which allows modelers to define parameters for how the physics will affect their models, such as hardness and bend constraints [6].

We implemented GPU-based Position Based Dynamics (PBD) to iMSTK, an open-source toolkit for rapid prototyping interactive multi-modal surgical simulation, and compared it with available GPU-based PBD solvers. As iMSTK was formerly only able to do PBD calculations utilizing the CPU, it could not handle deforming large models in real-time [4]. Using the vast multithreading ability of the GPU allows us to efficiently manage significantly larger models with little to no performance impact.

Pan et al. [7] proposed a PBD-based Virtual Reality simulation framework for cholecystectomy in the paper. The authors used graph coloring to solve PBD constraints in parallel to satisfy organ deformations. For 22,650 tetrahedrons, they improved the time cost per step from 28.51 ms-29.10 ms (PBD on CPU) to 12.20 ms-12.35 ms (parallel PBD on GPU). Berndt et al. [8] proposed a PBD approach to simulate electrosurgery and interactive cutting. This study uses PBD to model the objects and their dynamics used in the surgery. Berndt et al. compared their PBD results with Pan et al. [9], where Pan et al. used extended PBD to simulate soft bodies. For 2,385 and 4,079 elements, simulation in [8] resulted in 4.2 ms and 5.3 ms, while [9] resulted in 8.1 ms and 19.3 ms, respectively.

In [3], a CUDA-based PBD is implemented using graph coloring for interactive deformable bodies. In [3], for 16,000 particles (only quantitative result with stretch, bend, and tetrahedral constraints), the average FPS for a single-core CPU was 15, while for a multi-core CPU and GPU, the reported results were 45 and 326, respectively. However, using graph coloring and solving with Gauss-Seidel [10] causes an imbalanced amount of work for each kernel due to the number of constraints for each color being different. Another work that utilizes Gauss-Seidel iteration with PBD is [12]. The study noted that a model with $\approx$3,000 vertices would run with 7-8FPS on the CPU while the FPS would increase to 42–43 on the GPU. In [11], authors introduced Vivace, a CUDA-based PBD is implemented using graph coloring for interactive deformable bodies. For 30,000 vertices, 52,000 elements, and 150,000 constraints, the solver could run at 15 ms per frame. Due to the limited number of iterations, Vivace provides approximate results, which leads to artifacts.

2   Methods

Utilizing NVIDIA's CUDA toolkit [13], we took the physics calculations that would otherwise have been done on the CPU and moved these calculations to the GPU. As the CUDA library does not support the standard library vectors, these values must be copied into individual arrays before being copied to the GPU. Once the data is on the GPU, the vector calculations can be carried out utilizing GPU kernels which behave similarly to the CPU calculations. However, special care was required to ensure that another thread did not overwrite the data used in one calculation. Graph coloring cannot be utilized because the GPU has much higher parallelization than the CPU. This was accomplished by allocating a second array and writing all the results into the second array.

Tasks sent to the GPU for calculation are split into blocks of threads. By adjusting how many threads we want per block, we can control how the tasks are divided on the GPU. As we are given access to the thread (T) and block number (B) in our kernels (functions that run on the GPU), we can treat these values similarly to indexing using 2D coordinates ($T + B * width$), where $width$ is the block dimension. In addition, we compare the mass of each point with DBL_{min} (the smallest number a double can represent that is greater than 0) to determine if we need to do any calculations.

In our velocity kernel (as seen in Table 1), we calculate the velocity by taking the current position (P_i) and subtracting the previous position (P_{i-1}), then dividing that vector by the delta time (Δt).

In the integration kernel (as seen in Table 2), we start by adding the gravity constant and acceleration multiplied by Δt. Then, we copy our coordinates for the next frame's velocity calculation (V_i). Finally, we update the position based on the velocity, delta time, and viscous damping coefficient *(VDC)*.

Table 1. GPU Velocity Kernel

$i \leftarrow T + B * width$	▶ Initialization
if $\lvert M_i \rvert > DBL_{min}$ **then**	
for all index $i \in M$ **do**	
$V_i \leftarrow (P_i - P_{i-1})/ \Delta t$	▶ Calculate Velocity

Table 2. GPU Integration Kernel

$i \leftarrow T + B * width$	▶ Initialization
if $\lvert M_i \rvert > DBL_{min}$ **then**	
for all index $i \in M$ **do**	
$V_i \leftarrow V_i + (A_i + g) * \Delta t$	▶ Calculate Velocity using Acceleration
$P_{i-1} \leftarrow P_i$	▶ Calculate Previous Position
$P_i \leftarrow P_i + (1 - VDC) * V_i * \Delta t$	▶ Update Position

3 Results

Our PBD implementation utilized NVIDIA's CUDA, a General-Purpose Graphics Processing Unit (GPGPU) library, which allows us to utilize graphical processing hardware to do general-purpose computing tasks, in this case, PBD physics calculations.

Utilizing two different computers, we tested each of the different settings with different-sized models to determine which were most optimal and which number of threads per block was optimal (as seen in Table 3 for hardware specifications).

Table 3. Hardware specifications for each computer

CPU: Intel i7 4790s RAM: 16GB DDR3 GPU: NVIDIA GTX 750	a. PC #1
CPU: Xeon E-2144G RAM: 16GB DDR4 GPU: NVIDIA Quadro P2000	b. PC #2

In addition to utilizing iMSTK, we tested using an open-source example project, setting the number of particles to the same number as the iMSTK simulation. We utilized Macklin et al.'s work [5] as a baseline for how fast we should expect our project to run, quickly identifying if the hardware or software is the cause for any perceived stutter or slowdown.

Time computation tests were performed first on PC #1, running CPU and GPU-based tests (as seen in Fig. 1) while comparing the computation time in microseconds (μs) with different sizes, ranging from 8×8 to 128×128. Tests utilizing the GPU were split into two categories, GPU with copy and GPU without a copy.

The results with copy included copying the data from the CPU to the GPU, doing the calculations, and then copying the results back from the GPU to the CPU. This shows the overhead of copying data through the PCIe interface to which the GPU is connected.

The results showed that the GPU without copy is faster than the CPU for larger sizes (32×32, 64×64, and 128×128) but is slower for smaller sizes (8×8 and 16×16). The GPU with copy is slower than the GPU without copy but still faster than the CPU for larger sizes (64×64 and 128×128). However, the computation time on the CPU increases much faster than GPU with data copy as the size increases.

For all sizes, our implementation on GPU with copy and GPU without copy showed at least 2x improvement over the performance in the Macklin et al. example. At 128×128, our GPU implementation with data copy showed a 2.7x improvement over Macklin et al.'s model and a 1.98x improvement over the CPU. For the same size, our GPU implementation without data copy showed a 4.66x improvement over Macklin et al.'s example and a 3.41x improvement over the CPU. When comparing GPU with and without data copy, data copy overhead decreased the GPU performance by 0.57x to 0.62x.

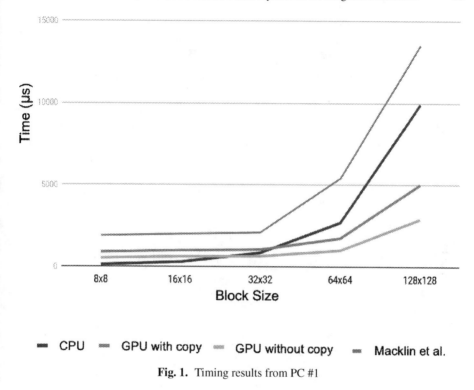

Fig. 1. Timing results from PC #1

Next, the same suite of time computation tests was performed on PC #2 (as seen in Fig. 2). Similar to the results from PC#1, for PC #2, smaller sizes (8 × 8 and 16 × 16) CPU outperformed the GPU with and without data copy, and Macklin et al.'s example. Comparable to PC #1, in PC#2, the CPU had the most significant increase in computation time from 64 × 64 to 128 × 128 with 3.16x.

For Macklin et al. and GPU with data copy, the increase was 2.6x, while for GPU without data copy, the increase was 2.65x. Unlike PC #1, in PC #2, Macklin et al.'s example outperformed CPU at 128 × 128 by 17.7%, while at 64 × 64, the time computation results were equal at 2500 microseconds. For PC #1, at 64 × 64, CPU computation results were 50% less than Macklin et al.'s example.

We tested our implementation (GPU without copy) with different block sizes and threads per block (TPB). The results showed that, generally, the time taken to perform the operation decreases as the block size and TPB increase. However, the differences between 32 and 64 TPB were all less than 10%. The most considerable difference between 32 and 64 TPB was recorded for 8 × 8 block size at 8.5%. For the 32 × 32 block size, 32 and 64 TPB performance was 240 μs.

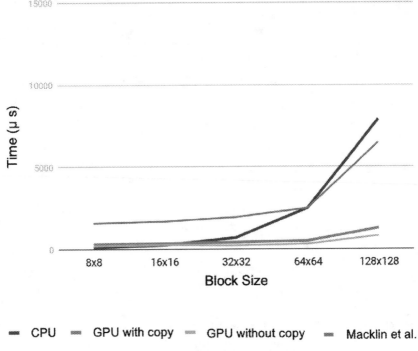

Fig. 2. Timing results from PC #2

For comparison of 8 and 16 TPB, block sizes 64 × 64 and 128 × 128 had a performance difference of 31.1% and 41.43%, respectively. The performance results for the smallest block size of 8 × 8 were 210 μs for 8TPB, 200 μs for 16TPB, 70 μs for 32TPB, and 64 μs for 64TPB. The performance results for the largest block size of 128 × 128 were 1400 μs for 8TPB, 820 μs for 16TPB, 570 μs for 32TPB, and 560 μs for 64TPB (Fig. 3).

Finally, tests were run on PC #2 to determine the effects of changing the number of TPB, as seen in Fig. 4. These tests utilized a volumetric dragon model of various sizes and a source VEG (3D volumetric mesh) file [6]. The model had 959 vertices and 2,591 tetrahedral mesh elements, the counts were kept the same for all calculations.

The results indicate that the processing time decreases as the number of TPB increases. One exception is the 128 TPB case (except for VEG File), where the processing time increases. This is due to the overhead of managing a large number of threads. For the VEG file, 128 TPB had the fastest performance at 16,000 μs, while 64 TPB was the slowest at 30,500 μs.

It is also worth noting that the processing time increases as the block size increases. This is likely because larger blocks require more processing power to handle a more significant number of data points. For the model block size of 70 × 42 × 42, the fastest TPB was 32 with 26,100 μs, while the slowest was the CPU with 253,000 μs.

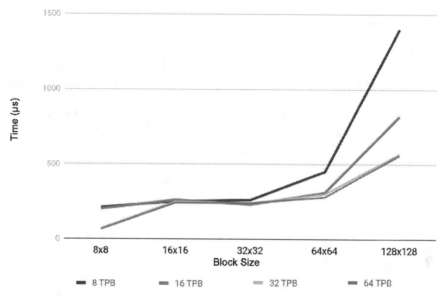

Fig. 3. PC #2 performance for different block sizes and number of threads per block

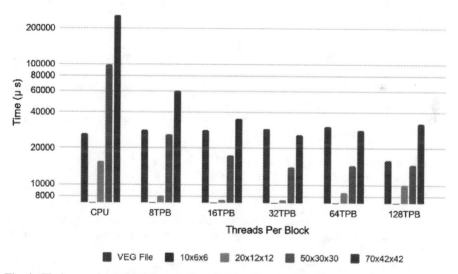

Fig. 4. Timing results (PC #2) from testing showing increased performance when using CUDA.

4 Conclusion

Volume rendering with linear deformation times is another challenge in virtual scenes. PBD is the most popular approach for simulating dynamic systems in computer graphics. We implemented GPU-based PBD to iMSTK, an open-source toolkit for rapid prototyping interactive multi-modal surgical simulation, and compared it with available GPU-based PBD solvers. We successfully showed that utilizing the GPU is 10x faster than using the CPU for the PBD calculations, as the GPU is optimized for highly multithreaded workloads.

Acknowledgments. This project was supported by grants from the National Institutes of Health (NIH)/ NIBIB 1R01EB033674-01A1, 5R01EB025241–04, 3R01EB005807-09A1S1, and 5R01EB005807–10.

References

1. Bender, J., Müller, M., Macklin, M.: A survey on position-based dynamics 2017. In: Proceedings Eurographics Association Computer Graphics Tutors, pp. 1–31 (2017)
2. Müller, M., Heidelberger, B., Hennix, M., Ratcliff, J.: Position based dynamics. J. Vis. Commun. Image Represent. **18**(2), 109–118 (2007)
3. Fratarcangeli, M., Pellacini, F.: A GPU-based implementation of position based dynamics for interactive deformable bodies. J. Graph. Tools **17**(3), 59–66 (2013)
4. Yan, J., Arikatla, S., Wilson, A.: Fast deformation dynamics using model order reduction in iMSTK (2020)
5. Macklin, M., Müller, M., Chentanez, N., Kim, T.-Y.: Unified particle physics for real-time applications. ACM Trans. Graph. TOG **33**(4), 1–12 (2014)
6. Sin, F.S., Schroeder, D., Barbič, J.: Vega: non-linear FEM deformable object simulator. Comput. Graph. Forum **32**(1), 36–48 (2013)
7. Pan, J., et al.: Real-time VR simulation of laparoscopic cholecystectomy based on parallel position-based dynamics in GPU. In: 2020 IEEE Conference on Virtual Reality and 3D User Interfaces (VR), pp. 548–556 (2020)
8. Berndt, I., Torchelsen, R., Maciel, A.: Efficient surgical cutting with position-based dynamics. IEEE Comput. Graph. Appl. **37**(3), 24–31 (2017)
9. Pan, J., Bai, J., Zhao, X., Hao, A., Qin, H.: Real-time haptic manipulation and cutting of hybrid soft tissue models by extended position-based dynamics. Comput. Animat. Virtual Worlds **26**(3–4), 321–335 (2015)
10. Milaszewicz, J.P.: Improving jacobi and gauss-seidel iterations. Linear Algebra Its Appl. **93**, 161–170 (1987)
11. Fratarcangeli, M., Tibaldo, V., Pellacini, F.: Vivace: a practical gauss-seidel method for stable soft body dynamics. ACM Trans. Graph. TOG **35**(6), 1–9 (2016)
12. Cetinaslan, O.: Position-based simulation of elastic models on the GPU with energy aware gauss-seidel algorithm. Comput. Graph. Forum **38**(8), 41–52 (2019)
13. Fatica, M.: CUDA toolkit and libraries. In: 2008 IEEE hot chips 20 symposium (HCS), pp. 1–22 (2008)

Innovative Thinking About Human-Computer Interaction in Interactive Narrative Games

Xintong Gao and Wei Yu(✉)

School of Art Design and Media, East China University of Science and Technology,
No. 130, Meilong Road, Xuhui District, Shanghai, People's Republic of China
yuwei@ecust.edu.cn

Abstract. Research on game interaction has been popular in recent years. Interactive narrative games are a branch of role-playing game games. In order to give interactive narrative games a stronger sense of immersion and a more diverse experience, the study of their interaction methods is essential. In this paper, we start from the development experience of interactive narrative games and categorize the existing game interaction methods into eight types: visual, auditory, tactile, gesture, expression, virtual reality, augmented reality, and intentional interaction according to the existing applications. And on this basis, based on the interaction design principles proposed by Donald Norman and the acceptance aesthetics theory proposed by Hans Robert Jauss, the interaction methods of future interactive narrative games are explored. Finally, the trend of interaction development and innovation of interactive narrative games is summarized as five points: the compounding of interaction medium, the naturalization of interaction behavior, the receptive innovation of interactive aesthetics, the warning innovation of interaction ethics, and the development of dual-universe integration of interaction experience.

Keywords: interactive narrative games · game interaction · interaction innovation

1 Introduction

In recent years, the video game industry has become an important contributor to the global entertainment economy. According to the ***Global Game Market Report 2021*** released by Newzoo: the global game market size will exceed 200 billion USD in 2024, with a total of 3.3 billion players [1]. Video games can not only attract the youth group represented by Generation Z, according to the 2021 Tencent ***Game Industry Development Research Report***, the prime age and even the old age group will also play video games. In Japan, the United States, and other countries with more fertile soil for console games, nearly 20% of game users are over 50 years old [2].

In addition, the new crown epidemic since 2019 has caused people to be confined and compressed into small spaces for long periods, and games are rapidly evolving into a more important role than the usual entertainment media.

Today, the game world has become somewhat of an extension of our real world: it can be a major destination for social gatherings, and a venue for singers to hold concerts. More and more developers are realizing that the metaverse may be moving from science fiction stories to the real world. People will imitate the behavior in reality through various personal information terminals, or VR devices. As the Internet can cross physical barriers in the cyber scene and enable the use of virtual images, the forms of games are becoming more and more diverse, and can even carry more diverse and narrative interactive experiences than in reality.

Interactive narrative games are a branch of role-playing game (RPG) games. Through a variety of interactive methods (such as visual, auditory, haptic, and virtual reality), users can immerse themselves in the characters and feel the charm of the plot and story. Most of these games tend to emphasize plot rather than gameplay, but there are a few games such as *Disco Elysium* that combine gameplay and plot very well.

In this paper, we start from the main development history of interactive narrative games and explore the trends of interaction innovation in future interactive narrative games based on existing applications.

2 The Development Process of Interactive Narrative Games

The origin of interactive narrative games is generally considered to be the short film *Kinoautomat* that appeared at the Montreal World's Fair in Canada in 1967 [3]. The director of the film designed to install two red and green buttons in each of the 127 seats in the cinema, and there were nine plot choices in the film, requiring the audience to vote for the next plot direction by clicking on the buttons. The audience thought they could decide the ending of the film's protagonist through their own choices, but their votes were meaningless, and no matter how they chose to vote, the film would eventually lead to the same ending. The audience will only find themselves being played in the end. This satirical black comedy became the world's first interactive movie game.

The world's first text adventure game, *ADVENT*, was designed by programmer William Crowther in 1975. Subsequently, a series of text adventure games, represented by *Adventure International* designed by Scott Adams, and *Zork* designed and produced by members of the MIT Power Modeling Group, were developed like a spring. Due to the low development threshold of text adventure games, they became the representative of interactive narrative games for a long time when 3D technology was not mature.

In 1997, Nintendo Gunpei Yokoi, former head of the first development department, developed the world's first physical interactive game using an arcade as a vehicle. Users took on the role of a western cowboy, holding a revolver model in their hands and dueling to the death with an on-screen opponent. The interactive narrative game really attracted attention in the game industry from the development of *Heavy Rain* by Quantitative Dream. Since then, developers have focused on interactive narrative games, such as *The Walking Dead*, *Life Is Strange*, *A Way Out*, and *The Invisible Guardian* and other games as representative of the interactive narrative game have become a common game genre.

3 Existing Interactions and Applications

Looking at existing applications of game interaction, this paper argues that they have been or are being used in the following ways.

3.1 Visual Interaction

Visual interaction is the most basic game interaction method and the most effective way for humans to receive information. From the design of the basic interactive interface to the use of visual illusions in games such as **Monument Valley** and **Moncage** to narrate and decipher, visual interaction can give users information and interactive feedback in the simplest way.

3.2 Auditory Interaction

Music and sound effects throughout the user's entire game, Mario Top Bricks 8bit sound effects are still many players' memories. In the **FINAL FANTASY XIV** 6.0 expansion pack, which was supervised by Masayoshi Soken, every time the user completes the plot and reaches a bond with a NPC (Non-player character), a track will be added to the background music, achieving effective interaction between the background music and the game narrative.

In addition, there are also many games whose narrative or gameplay is directly structured on top of music and sound effects. For example, In **Voice notes** [4] uses voice-activated input, where the user controls the forward jumping motion of the notes by emitting different volumes of sound. In **Verbis Virtus**, users chant spells, release magic, and explore lost temples through voice interaction.

Auditory interaction can also take good care of the visually impaired group. As of December 2021, the game **Hearing of the world** [5] has served 120,000 visually impaired people in total. This game has no graphics, only a simple black background, and by identifying the type of sound, location, and other information, users can interact with the game by sound alone.

3.3 Tactile Interaction

Four main types of haptic interaction are widely used, namely vibration feedback and tension and tension feedback.

Vibration feedback is a common way of interaction in console games as well as mobile games. Whenever the user controls the character for hitting action, a car driving out of the road, or horror thriller games appear in scary scenes, the handle or phone itself will prompt the user through vibration. In addition, it is also commonly used to increase the sense of combat action.

Tension feedback is mainly found in physical games. Nintendo's **Ring Fit Adventure**, its external device Ring-Con, a built-in tension sensor, by applying an external force to the Ring-Con, can test the user's strength level, and in the screen will give the user equivalent feedback.

Tension feedback to the DualSense wireless controller developed by Sony, for example, Sony designers in the controller's L2 and R2 keys to add adaptive triggers to allow users to better experience the tension of actions such as drawing a bow, or shooting an arrow.

3.4 Natural Gesture Interaction

Gesture Recognition, is the topic of recognizing human gestures through mathematical algorithms. Gesture recognition generally refers to recognizing the movement of a person's face and hands, but it can also recognize the movement of various body parts. Current gesture recognition is mainly concerned with recognizing human emotions by the gestures of the human face and hands.

Since Oculus first introduced gesture recognition on Quest at the end of 2019, many developers have released small test samples of gestural VR (Virtual Reality) games on platforms such as SideQuest and continue to test multiple directions for VR gestures. Currently, users can interact with gestures in the world of VR or through their home computers with peripheral controllers such as Leap Motion and Kinect.

For example, Thomas Van Bouwel, a Belgian independent developer, developed a VR game with gesture interaction 3D virtual blocks, where users use gestures to grab and drop blocks and fill the puzzle. Students from Fuzhou University developed a computer game *True Words* [6] that is completely free from keyboard and mouse. Through Leap motion's gesture recognition function, users can use gestures to fight, talk with NPCs, and read secret books to learn new sign language skills. In the course of the game, users can also learn about sign language, reflecting the care for the deaf community.

3.5 Expression Interaction

Human expressions are important social signals that reflect the emotional intent of both parties interacting with each other, and they can convey many subtle messages through expressions that cannot be conveyed by other interaction methods. However, this type of interaction also involves a series of security concerns regarding user privacy.

In the game *Who's Lila?*, the developers keenly captured this and made modifying the character's expressions through mouse clicks the core of the gameplay. But nowadays, facial capture technology is so advanced that it is already possible to interact directly by capturing the user's facial expressions, such as the game *Dream Chaser: the Showbiz*, which is a game simulating female entertainers in the entertainment industry and can provide the immersion of the user's script by capturing the user's delicate micro-expressions and feeding them to the virtual character.

3.6 Virtual Reality Interaction

Virtual reality games based on head display and physical interaction devices, such as HTC Vive, oculus rift, gear VR, etc., for the user to simulate a three-dimensional space of the virtual world, providing users with the simulation of the visual, auditory, tactile and other senses, so that users feel the immersive experience while being able to freely interact with things in the space.

In fact, virtual reality interaction often combines motion capture, sensors, eye tracking, myoelectric simulation, and other basic interaction methods mentioned in Sects. 3.1–3.4. For example, in the narrative puzzle game *Red Matter 2*, a world where almost all elements are interactive, the player takes on the role of an agent who uses a jetpack, hacking tools, and other props to infiltrate a base in space and stop the spread of Red

Matter. The game is filled with physics puzzles, and by interacting with the gamepad, the weight of objects responds realistically to the user - picking up a book is light, and lifting a box is heavy.

In addition, the 360° free view allows virtual reality to also give the user a greater impact in terms of spatial and volumetric sensation. For example, in *Red Matter 2*, in the episode of visiting Saturn's moons, walking down the long outdoor ramp, the planet overhead and the huge gas giant below can most visually tell the user—in the measure of the universe, how small humans are.

3.7 Augmented Reality Interaction

Augmented Reality (AR) is a new technology developed from virtual reality technology, which presents corresponding text, images, 3D objects, and other multimedia information through camera equipment and angle position discrimination, presenting virtual space images and the real world together on the same screen to achieve a seamless connection between the virtual world and the real world [7].

AR games have the advantages of moving and operating in three-dimensional space, panoramic interface interaction, and realistic fusion effects, combined with geographic location and other multi-player interactions than traditional game forms, so AR games can make the game based on reality while transcending reality.

In July 2016, PokémonGo [8], an augmented reality RPG jointly produced and developed by Nintendo, Pokémon, and Google NianticLabs, was released, making the AR game a hot topic of attention. However, after that, there are not many interactive narrative games using AR technology, and AR technology is mainly used in science education games or public welfare games. For example, in the game *Haze Ambush* [9], users can choose different travel methods according to carbon emissions, and open the cell phone camera to identify the haze monsters in the surrounding air and fight with them on the way out, and the rewards and game mechanisms in the prize game are connected with the offline environmental protection behavior, which is intended to guide users' green It is intended to guide users' green travel and environmental behavior utilizing "behavioral design".

The multi-platform game *Five Nights at Freddy's AR: Special Delivery* is a good case of combining horror narrative with AR technology. When users interact in a dimly lit room using AR-enabled devices such as cell phones, scary dolls, or other frightening elements will be hidden in your familiar room.

3.8 Intentional Interaction

Ideational interaction is also known as brain-computer interaction or brain-computer interface (BCI). It is the use of Electroencephalogram (EEG) signals to achieve direct communication and control between the human brain and computers or other electronic devices [10]. BCI technology combines the latest achievements in the fields of neuroscience, psycho-cognitive science, and intelligent information processing.

BCI is divided into two forms: invasive and non-invasive. The non-invasive BCI does not require surgical implantation of electrodes into the skin, which is more acceptable to consumers and more likely to land in the gaming field. However, this method still suffers from the problems of poor signal reception accuracy and low carrying capacity of information.

There are no interactive narrative games that use mental interaction yet, and most of the games developed using this interaction method are puzzle games with only one or two simple mechanics. Such as Neurable launched the brain machine VR game *Awakening*.

4   Trends of Interaction Innovation in Interactive Narrative Games

This paper argues that the global epidemic has accelerated the arrival of the metaverse era. Even without relying on VR devices such as head monitors, people can get a good gaming experience just through cell phones, computers, game consoles, and other carriers. The following will discuss the trend of interaction innovation of interactive narrative games based on the analysis of three main factor levels or perspectives: current social demand, technical development, and user psychology.

At the level of realistic demand for social activities, games serve as an important vehicle that enables users to gradually move towards participating in a simulated world with fewer restrictions than the real world through virtual and digital worlds. Whether it is the creation of Vtubers(Virtual YouTubers), virtual online concerts, or the explosion of games such as *VRChat* that allow people to make friends through virtual images, the demand for a more realistic virtual world is evident.

Technology development support level, Leap motion, Kinect and other affordable external devices have made somatosensory interaction, and gesture interaction on the computer side of the game has become possible. Through software such as FaceRig and LiveLinkFace, even an ordinary cell phone camera can capture the user's delicate expression changes. In the development of VR equipment, the 6DoF (six degrees of freedom) head display has developed quite mature. Hardware facilities are no longer a means of constraining diverse interaction methods.

From the perspective of user psychology, users with different personalities have different demands on interaction methods, and the interaction methods in the information age should be more delicate, more diverse, and closer to the real emotional needs of people. It is difficult to bring a different psychological experience to users by simply clicking different windows with the mouse.

In addition, the dual-universe fusion of interactive experience is becoming an important trend in the development of game interaction in the future. The so-called "dual-universe" fusion refers to the breakthrough of the original VR game framework and the migration of human social identity and social relationship to the meta-universe world. In other words, the dual-universe fusion of the real world and the meta-universe world. The future interactive narrative game may not only be role-playing in the virtual world but also doing realistic self in the virtual or augmented reality world.

Summarizing the above, the trend of interaction development innovation of interactive narrative games can be summarized as five points: compounding of interaction medium, naturalization of interaction behavior, acceptability of interaction aesthetics, early warning innovation of interaction ethics, and dual universe integration development of interaction experience.

4.1 Compounding Innovation of Interaction Medium

Today's interactive narrative games tend to interact simply/individually, with the simple operation of the mouse or handle. For example, the walking simulation game *Edith Finch*, only uses the keyboard and mouse to interact, although the inclusion of many mini-games within the game, the sense of immersion there is still a lot of room for optimization.

With the continuous strengthening of cell phones, tablets, and other smart terminal hardware, as well as the continued development of VR devices, games similar to *Beat Saber* and *Red Matter 2* with multiple interaction compound will become more and more common.

4.2 Naturalized Innovation of Interaction Behavior

Natural interaction not only gives users a stronger sense of immersion and presence, allowing them to better immerse themselves in the inner world of the story and characters but also reduces their learning costs.

Good games often have no tutorials for newcomers, and Nintendo's classic *Mario* series is widely praised for having no tutorials for newcomers. Natural interaction allows users to transfer their real-life habits to the virtual world without realizing it.

4.3 Receptive Innovation of Interactive Aesthetics

Games are a new art form created in the information age, through which a unique interactive experience can be brought to the user. In his book *Les jeux video*, French scholar Jean-Jacques Annaud states, "Video games have always been the future of cinema [11]." The immersion of cinema, the storytelling of theater, and the concerto of theater can all be presented in a good interactive narrative game.

Enhancing the aesthetics of interactive narrative game interaction can be started from Hans Robert Jauss' theory of receptive aesthetics, which is generally used in the field of literature, while interactive narrative games have a strong literary aspect due to their plot-heavy nature, which is compatible with them. The position of the reader in the theory of receptive aesthetics will be transformed into the position of the player (participant) in interactive narrative games, which emphasizes the importance of the interaction between the user and the system more than traditional design thinking.

Deconstruction of the Traditional Narrative Style. Deconstructing and critiquing traditional narratives is a classic theme of interactive narrative games. In a traditional narrative, the author is the prophet, the guide, the preacher, and the reader is left to passively listen, learn, and accept. The *Stanley Parable* breaks with this, as the traditional author is similar to the narrator in this game, who guides the player to the next step through language. For traditional games, it seems logical to follow the instructions of the guide or tutorial to play the game. But in this game, the "good" player will only get to the normal ending, and the truth of the story will still be covered up. Only by not following the narrator's instructions and exploring freely will it be possible to find the truth and reach the true ending. Similar approach are also used in the game *Disco Elysium*.

Today, AI text generation and the popularity of random events allow this structure to perhaps go deeper. Games with strong random events, such as *The Scroll Of Taiwu* and *Wildermyth*, are based on a large library of random events and a few fixed events, amplifying the "butterfly effect" of reality in the sandbox of the game, where every move of the user Every action of the user will greatly and randomly change the pattern and development of the game world.

Further, AI's real-time generation can customize unique stories based on each user's specific actions and choices, truly transforming the "reader" from a passive recipient to an active "author". This requires further development of next-generation AI.

Aesthetic Experience and Experience Design. At a later stage of Jauss's research, the concept of "aesthetic experience" was introduced, which means that readers recreate the text in reading and thinking, and relate the content of the text to reality, thus creating a deeper sense of identification and emotional resonance with the text itself. When the reader reads, the content of the text in the present evokes memories of the past, and the aesthetic experience takes on meaning through the medium of memories. Recollection breaks the bonds of time and space between the reader and the author, blending past and present, traditional and modern, etc., rationalizing the text in the present and allowing the reader to find an aesthetic experience appropriate to the self [12]. This concept actually has great similarity with the reflective layer design mentioned in Donald Norman's Emotional Design, both of which are based on the user's original social perception, breaking the bondage of time and giving the user a deeper experience. This experience may be a clearer understanding and reflection on past experiences, or it may be some revelation for future life.

In *NEEDY GIRL OVERDOSE*, the player plays the role of the manager of the online anchor "Sugar". Sugar is a depressed person; she depends on the attention of the network to survive. On the surface, the game is to help Sugar get 2 million followers and fulfill her wish. But after passing several endings, players can easily find that the best ending of this game is to take Sugar to the hospital to treat her mental illness at the beginning of the game, instead of allowing her to continue to rely on the Internet, which will only aggravate her condition.

The above examples only give the user reflections on the level of narrative, while the aesthetics of the specific interaction can be sought from the design of interactive installation art. For example, *Dare to Dream* by Ouchhh, an independent creative new media studio in Istanbul, is a virtual projection using real-time face tracking, where images composed by artificial intelligence algorithms are combined with sound effects, and the virtual projection is activated when the experiencer and the artist smile at the same time, and the face breaks up when they start making sounds. The work expects to enhance human communication through the interaction of each other's smiles, and it satisfies the aesthetic and emotional needs of users to participate in the creation of artwork [13].

Assuming that the imagination of interaction in installation art can be transferred to game design, it can give more meaning and reflection to the game and give it an aesthetic connotation.

4.4   Early Warning Innovation of Interaction Ethics

Game ethics is the rule of interaction and connection between players and players, game makers, and the game itself. Although the virtual world generated by games is independent of the real world, its real immersion and immersion characteristics make the border between virtual and reality more and more blurred due to the development of technology. The social interactions generated by players in games also overlap and intertwine with real-world life, and various information and behaviors in games will inevitably affect the ethical construction of players' real and incarnate selves, so the production and circulation of games need a

The ethical code of ethics is regulated by [14].

The ethical connection between virtual characters and their manipulators has been explored in many movies (e.g., *Ghost In The Shell*, *The Matrix*) and writings. While it is true that complete adherence to realistic morality and law can make many games seem tasteless, it is undeniable that to design game interactions that completely ignore the basic moral norms of reality is to ignore the fact that the act of play is a symbolically mediated interaction that has ethical relevance as an act of social interaction.

Since the actions made are only those of the game character, the user does not have to bear the responsibility of realistic ethics, so the low ethical norms in the game world are frequent. In addition, the safety of human-computer interaction in AR games and VR games is also a topic worth discussing. In traditional games, users are often guided to interact through "utilitarian moral game mechanics", i.e., direct punishment or incentives are given to encourage users to follow realistic ethical norms.

For example, in *Assassin's Creed*, once you attack or mistakenly injure a passerby it will cause the user to lose sync. In the vast majority of RPGs, the more people you help, the more they will come to your aid at the end of the game or when the big event comes. A utilitarian morality game mechanic makes you think: despite the moral reality of what I do, do I really mean it or do I want to accomplish what the game sets out to do?

Interactive narrative games often give users a dilemma due to the plot-heavy nature of the genre. In *My Child: Lebensborn*, the user takes on the role of the adoptive parent of a "war orphan" who is not accepted by the locals because of his or her Nazi heritage and helps him or her to integrate into the life of the town through a series of choices. The game is based on the real-life story of the orphans born under the Fountain of Life program, and just like in the real world, it is difficult for the user to change the prejudice and discrimination against his/her adopted son as a resident of a town invaded by the Nazis. Therefore, no matter how one chooses, one can only change the time and form of the discrimination received by the child, but not stop it from occurring. The end of the game is destined from the beginning to be a move away from the town.

This dilemma is like the reflective layer of design mentioned in *Donald Norman*'s *Emotional Design*. After experiencing the game, it is hard not to think, is it right to label innocent children based on birth? Is it right to label innocent children based on birth? Even if their parents are evil and commit unforgivable crimes, do their children deserve to receive some "ostracism" from society? Are the people of the town bad people? Why did the ordinary people who were invaded become the perpetrators after the war? People are so complex and multi-faceted. This is the reflection brought to people through the plot, the reflection of the game's ethics mapped to reality.

From the perspective of human factors engineering, ethical guidance feedback to users from several aspects can be provided through the violent vibration of the handle, the strongly colored prompt window, and the harsh sound effects. For AR games, such as using AR glasses and other carriers, care should be taken so that the user interface and other information should not obscure too much of the user's view and cause safety accidents. For games that require map exploration, attention should also be paid to avoiding the interaction points from the real places with potential safety hazards such as roads, high places, riversides, etc. At the same time, the user should not be too addicted to the game and pay attention to the safety of nearby vehicles.

4.5 Dual-Universe Integration of Interactive Experiences

Video games provide interactive content for the meta-universe and are one of the keys to its content development. The interactive narrative games of the future use the identity, skills, and knowledge possessed by the users themselves as a part of the game content to provide a more immersive, or more educational, experience.

Such as the integration of games and theme park design dual universe virtual reality. The entire theme park can participate in a game where each visitor has both a personalized interactive exploration journey and a social experience of collective celebration in the main street and plaza. Thus, whether we are in the park, or at home experience, the metaverse brings us a fresh experience of the integration of physical space and the digital world [15]. In this regard, The Walt Disney Company has begun work on the development of the Disney theme park metaverse.

5 Summary

The era of the metaverse is coming, and interactive narrative games will play a more and more important role. In the future, the interaction trend of interactive narrative games will evolve in terms of the compounding of interaction medium, the naturalization of interaction behavior, the acceptability of interaction aesthetics, the warning of interaction ethics, and the development of dual-universe integration of interaction experience.

References

1. Global Game Market Report 2021. https://newzoo.com/insights/trend-reports/newzoo-glo bal-games-market-report-2021-free-version. Accessed 17 Feb 2023
2. Game Industry Development Research Report. https://newzoo.com/insights/trend-reports/ newzoo-global-games-market-report-2021-free-version. Accessed 17 Feb 2023
3. Department of Science and Technology, State Administration of Radio and Television of the People's Republic of China. 5G High-tech Video—Interactive Video Technology White Paper. http://www.lincang.gov.cn/__local/C/FE/A8/468AC31BA2C842523A506403 C22_8806EDBF_28FAB9.pdf?e=.pdf. Accessed 17 Feb 2023
4. Voice notes. https://www.taptap.cn/app/78876?hreflang=zh_CN. Accessed 17 Feb 2023

5. Hearing of the world. https://apps.apple.com/cn/app/id1305792802. Accessed 17 Feb 2023
6. True Words. https://www.bilibili.com/video/BV1nS4y1272a/?uid=4256316E5334793132
   373261. Accessed 17 Feb 2023
7. Van Krevelen, D.W.F., Poelman, R.: A survey of augmented reality technologies, applications
   and limitations. Int. J. Virtual Real. **9**(2), 1–20 (2010)
8. Report: 'Pokémon Go' downloads top 15 million. http://www.usatoday.com/story/tech/gam
   ing/2016/07/13/reportpokemon-go-downloads-top-15-million/87022202/. Accessed 17 Feb
   2023
9. Haze Ambush. https://www.bilibili.com/video/av251591768/. Accessed 17 Feb 2023
10. Bernard, G., Montgomery, S., Maes, P.: Brain-computer interfaces, open-source, and
    democratizing the future of augmented consciousness. Front. Comput. Sci. (2021)
11. Nanming, X.: Diction Of Film Art, Revision China Film Press, China (2005)
12. Wei, Z.: Research on interactive video installation art based on reception aesthetics. Jiangnan
    University (2020)
13. Yijie, S.: Research on the interactivity of virtual art. Northwest University (2020)
14. Shuping, S., Yuning, Y.: Design strategy of anti-addiction mode for minors under the guidance
    of game ethics. Sci. Technol. Inf. **20**(12), 212–215 (2022)
15. Theme Park Metaverse: The Future Has Come, Decoding the Fusion Experience of Virtual
    and Real Symbiosis. http://www.our-themepark.com/web/article?id=401. Accessed 17 Feb
    2023

Visual Guidance in Game Level Design

Gang Guo$^{(\boxtimes)}$

Digital Hollywood University, Tokyo, Japan
G211TG2013@dhw.ac.jp

Abstract. With the development of game consoles and game computers, the number of players is increasing, and game maps and scenes are becoming larger and larger, allowing players to freely engage in activities within the map, which in today's game industry is called an open world. We are going to study visual guidance in game level design, with the focus on how players should follow the path envisioned by the level designer when they enter the actual game map. We will also study the method and flow when designing game levels.

Keywords: Visual guidance · Level design · Game Design

1 Aim

In today, vide006F games are becoming more and more common, but the level design in video games has become very complex and difficult, and there are two type of games, open-world games and linear games. Open-World games are not the same as traditional linear games. In open-world games players can explore the whole world in the order and way they like, while traditional linear games follow a strictly controlled process to advance. As an important part of video games, level design is an important criterion for many media to evaluate the merits of video games. An example of this is GameSpot, a games review website, who evaluates level design as part of rating. However, the research on the level design of open world games is very scarce, and the reason is that to a large extent, the expressions and level composition involved in level design are very complex and the knowledge structure required and the disciplines involved are also complicated. By analyzing several game cases, we try to analyze the game level design and provide some basic elements for level design in video games.

2 Background

With the continuous iterations of game development technology and updates, the open world type of games are gradually increasing in the game market nowadays. In 2021, a total of 86 AAA games were released, 40 of which were open-world games, compared to about 100 AAA games released a decade ago, but only 32 open-world games [19]. In open-world games, unlike traditional linear games, players are free to explore the entire map as they like, so how designers can guide players in this type of game becomes a

X. Fang (Ed.): HCII 2023, LNCS 14046, pp. 100–113, 2023.
https://doi.org/10.1007/978-3-031-35930-9_8

topic worth studying. It becomes a challenge on how to guide the player to go in the right direction to correctly advance the game. This requires the level designer to use a variety of elements to guide the player.

In recent years, partly because of the impact of the COVID-19, the number of game players is increasing, according to Newzoo's [18] game market analysis report in 2022. According to Newzoo's [17] forecast, there will be 3.2 billion game players worldwide in 2022, with an estimated growth of 2.1% per year. Each year will launch a large number of games across a wide variety of genres is released. An release list by Metacritic [19] indicates that the majority games released were 3D RPG games.

The goal of this paper is to research visual guidance used in video game level design. This is done through observation of recurring game elements and their workings in levels.

3 Method

First, we analyze the games that have been released, and select commonly occurring visual guidance techniques used in the level design. We will then, analyze the techniques, and report the results (Table 1).

Table 1. Selection of analyzed games

	Open world	Linear
Title	The legend of Zelda Breath of the wild The division 1 Red dead redemption 2 Assassin's creed 2 Ghost of Tsushima	A Plague Tale Innocence A Plague Tale Requiem It takes two Shadow of the Tomb raider Call of duty Modern warfare Journey Mirror's edge

4 Level Design

Level is a video game term used to describe the virtual visual divisions or stages of a video game challenge. The term level design and the profession of level designer were originally created in the mid to late 1990s with the popularity of 3D space shooters. And now, MOBA games and 2D games will also need level designers to design effective levels for players to experience. "The Level Design Book" [1] refers to game level design as the practice of planning and building space within a video game. According to Phil Co: "A room or space of the game starts like an empty box, but an empty box is boring, and the level designer is the one responsible for making these empty boxes interesting to design" [2]. Levels are important to games, and their importance is mainly reflected in how they can control the rhythm of the game, difficulty ladder, etc. According to Wikipedia's summary of level design, "A level contains a variety of challenges, with obstacles arranged in two- or three-dimensional space in the shape and height of the presentation." This concept is useful for games similar to "Super Mario Bros" and while it is still somewhat applicable to game level design for modern games, the variety and richness of modern day games make it so this definition is simply not sufficient for all game types in the current market. Different games offer different kind of achievements, leading to different types of challenges. Some games instead rely on multiplayer modes where the challenge comes from fellow players.

5   The Need for Visual Guidance

The visual guidance design in the game level is to guide the player through the hints or clues set in the level. This is a necessary ability that every level designer needs to master to accurately guide the player through the level to experience the game completely and to mobilize the player's emotion during the game. Visual guidance can help with this and it is for that reason we believe the research into it is necessary.

We have analyzed different styles of games and divided the main ways and means of visual guidance into four categories, namely color, affordance, moving objects, and targets. The techniques are generally liberally used together to design a level.

5.1   Color

Color is divided into two categories; color and light. Light serves well to attract the players' attention. Color also plays a role in setting the atmosphere of the space.

Light
Light is used within the game to guide the player, generally using means like electrical lights, light sources born through fire as well as other light emitting elements in the game scene to guide the player, through the aforementioned attracting the player's attention. For instance, in the game "A Plague Tale Innocence" [9] there are a wide variety of dark environments where the player's path is visualized through light sources. Since the

Fig. 1. A Plague Tale Innocence scene

contrast between light and dark is significant, the player's eyes are immediately attracted towards the light sources.

Due to the game's setting of plague infested Europe, there is also a constant threat from feral rats who will devour the player in the event the rats manage to get to the player. To escape from the rats, light is used, as the rats are afraid of fire. This gives further significance to the importance of light in this game, as the fire doesn't just highlight a potential path, it highlights the safe path (see Fig. 1 and Fig. 2). The same method of guidance is also used in the sequel. "A Plague Tale Requiem" [10].

Fig. 2. A Plague Tale Requiem scenes

Figure 2 also shows the rats' behavior when the player is carrying a torch, swarming around the player but staying out of reach of the light. While this game uses light as an important gameplay mechanic on top of guiding the player, the "A Plague Tale" series is far from the only game series using light to guide players. Another example of a game that does this is "Shadow of the Tomb Raider" [13].

Figure 3 shows a scene from "Shadow of the Tomb Raider." From this screenshot, despite the relatively empty square, a fountain has been set in the center. The movable range of the venue is limited to a circle. A large number of relatively bright cool lights dot the background, whereas the lights in the red range are comparatively dark. The warm colored lights mark the player's goal, with the game taking advantage of players being attracted to more illuminated areas. In this area, the warm colored lights are used for guidance, with the cool lighting being used as additional support, while making sure the players don't hang around in the blue areas for too long. Through this, designers have mapped out a clear route for the player to travel.

Color

Colors are an effective tool to guide players. Using highly saturated colors, designers can guide players using those colors as those colors more readily catch the player's attention. In the game "Mirror's Edge" [16], the player uses parkour to get around the game world. To highlight the objects that can be used for parkour, the developers decided to highlight all of those objects with a saturated red color. Because the main color scheme of the rest of the environment is white and blue hues, it's easy to focus the player's attention on the parkour objects this way. This way of color coding the parkour objects is used from the start until the end of the game.

Fig. 3. Shadow of Tomb Raider scenes

Fig. 4. Mirror's Edge scenes

As can be seen in Fig. 4. Parkour objects are color coded with the color red. Orange hues are also visible, and are primarily used to visualize the areas the player can access. The rest of the scene adopts a more cool color scheme, using mostly white and blue hues, meaning that both the red and orange color coding is easy to make out. It should be noted that color coding can still work without relying on extreme contrast variation like those found in Mirror's Edge.

Fig. 5. A Plague Tale Requiem scenes

In "A Plague Tale Requiem" (see Fig. 5), there are some objects and environments that the player can interact with. Sometimes the designers of the game add some colors that are more prominent compared with the environment, to guide the player's sight. After the player understands the mechanic, the player needs to pay close attention to the color guidance in order to play the game correctly (Fig. 6).

Fig. 6. Shadow of Tomb Raider scenes

The same approach can be seen in "Shadow of the Tomb Raider", a game where the designers used a way to give the player a certain degree of guidance in the level design without affecting the player's gaming experience. The color used will change according to the surrounding environment and scene. For instance, in "A Plague Tale Requiem" and "Shadow of the Tomb Raider" low saturation whites are used, while in the "The Division 2" [6] brighter yellow colors are used (see Fig. 7). Although the color is different, the effect and function of guiding the player's line of sight is completely the same.

Fig. 7. The Division 2 scenes

5.2 Affordance

Usually consisting of objects or environments in the game scene. The term was originally coined by American psychologist James J. Gibson in his 1966 book "The Senses Considered as Perceptual System" [29], the term is widely utilized in a variety of fields. Gibson expresses affordance as "the affordance of the environment to the animal is what he can supply or provide to the animal, whether good or bad". After this, Donald Arthur Norman [29] introduced the concept of affordance into the field of design. He defines it as "Affordance is derived from the spiritual interpretation of things, based on past experiences and knowledge that people use to perceive things around them." It can be seen that there is a big difference between Norman's idea and Gibson's idea, because the concept has appeared in various fields so far, resulting in no complete definition, but there is a preference for the meaning of "perception". So when affordance appears in the game's level design, it also focuses more on player's perception and guiding the player. Whenever this method is used, it generally takes into account the feelings and perceptions of the players when they see the scene, the environment, and the objects. This will require the game designer to use the shape of certain objects or the player's psychological perception, for example, a door can provide the function of "opening and closing", while a chair can provide the function of "sitting". In this way, players will understand which objects or environments in the game scene the player can interact with, which cannot be interacted with, and what kind of interaction will take place (Fig. 8).

Fig. 8. It Takes Two scenes

This is liberally utilized in the game "It Takes Two" [11], For example, when the player first encounters a level where both left and right walls can be jumped back and forth to climb it, the game designer did not give any text based instructions, but instead placed the arrows shown above on the background wall. When the player sees these arrows pointing to the left and right plus their placement on top of each other, experienced players will naturally understand what has to be done. This game is a cooperative game, so even inexperienced players can easily progress as long as their partner has some experience playing games. This not only to enhance the experience of the game, but serves as a communication method as well. Many more examples exist throughout the game.

Of course, "It Takes Two" is not the only game that uses this method. In The Shadow of the Tomb Raider (see Fig. 9) the scene has flooded. The player is quickly taught that water is a dead zone (the blue area), and that to progress the player has to use objects floating around on or sticking out of the water (the yellow area).

Fig. 9. Shadow of Tomb Raider scenes (Color figure online)

5.3 Moving Objects

Moveable objects, characters, NPCs, etc. can be set up in the scene to guide the player forward in the right direction. An upside of this method to guide players is that it directly uses the game world itself to guide the player, thus upping immersion. Furthermore, in the case of an NPC doing the guiding, it may also provide a sense of security to the player. This is due to the game world still being alien to the player, and therefore any hazards are still unknown. This uncertainty of when danger could appear can result in stress for the player. However, when being guided by an NPC or something else, the player's focus point will be on that object, and therefore the unknowns of the rest of the game world will be of lesser importance.

Fig. 10. Call of Duty Modern Warfare scenes

In the game "Call of Duty Modern Warfare" [14] (see Fig. 10), the player is guided by NPCs in a number of scenes. The NPC provides explanations while directly leading the player towards the goal. Further visual effects are used to focus on the NPC doing the leading.

Fig. 11. A Plague Tale Requiem scenes

The same method is used in "A Plague Tale Requiem." In the opening moments of the game, the player finds themselves on a beach, where the goal is not directly made clear. Instead, a magical red bird (see Fig. 11) will form the primary guide, constantly moving towards the goal and showing the player where the player needs to go. The bird will match progression with the player, meaning that if the player stops, so does the bird.

5.4 Targets

Specifically established targets can be used to guide players within the game. Sometimes these targets show the final goal of the game, or sometimes they serve as a focal point.

Landmark

Landmarks are usually relatively large structures, creatures, etc. made to serve specifically as visual guides. To properly guide the player, these objects tend to have a unique design, especially compared to the environment which they inhabit. This is meant to guide the player, to give the player a reference point in the map in case the player gets lost. For instance, in Assassin's Creed [12] (see Fig. 12), players are encouraged to find the highest building whenever they enter a new environment, to get information about the area as a whole.

Fig. 12. Assassin's Creed 2 scenes

Mission Objectives

When players enter the game environment, sometimes objects within the game (NPCs, readily visible objects, etcetera) will serve to highlight the road towards the goal of the environment. This is done to inform the player of the road to take, without explicitly telling the player what to do.

In the game "Journey" [15], players will see a giant shining mountain from the moment they start playing (see Fig. 13). Since the game doesn't offer anything in the form of a map, the mountain is one of the few guidelines the player will get. Since it stands out compared to the rest of the environment, players are therefore encouraged to seek out this mountain.

"A Plague Tale Requiem" employs a similar technique. As can be seen in Fig. 14, the blue area shows the navigable area, whereas the yellow area shows a castle that clearly stands out in comparison to the rest of the scene, as the lone building in the entire scene. Due to this building being unique, players are more likely to make this building their goal whole navigating this environment.

Other environments in the same game use the same approach in a variety of forms. Supported with NPC dialogue, one environment has a huge monolith in the background that clearly stands out. Another area required the player to reach the highest point, to find out more about the target and the environment.

Fig. 13. Journey scenes

Fig. 14. A Plague Tale Requiem scenes (Color figure online)

6 Conclusion

We analyzed visual guidance methods in game design, and classified the guidance methods into four categories: color, affordance, moving objects, and the target. However, it should be noted that our study focused on a subset of games, and this list is by no means exhaustive. In the process of studying and analyzing these four types of visual guidance, we found that the knowledge framework involved in visual guides is very complex and requires game level designers to have a certain degree of cognitive psychology, logical thinking, programming ability and aesthetic ability in addition to basic level design skills. This is crucial to level design, and it is a very complicated and difficult task to consider the rhythm and balance of the level while thinking about the game content. In the future, we will continue to study level design, and we aim to further contribute to level design methodology.

References

1. "What is level design", The Level Design Book. https://book.leveldesignbook.com/introduction. Accessed 15 Oct 2022
2. Phil, C.: Level Design for Games: Creating Compelling Game Experiences. New Riders Games, USA (2006)
3. Jiujiechangpu: Four Point for game level designer (2015). https://youxiputao.com/articles/6965. Accessed 30 Sept 2022
4. GamerSky: Game list (2022). https://ku.gamersky.com/release/pc_202112/. Accessed 28 Oct 2022
5. Nintendo, E.P.D.: The Legend of Zelda Breath of the Wild (Software), Nintendo, Japan (2015)
6. Massive Entertainment: Tom Clancy's The Division2 (Software), Ubisoft, France(2019)
7. Rocket Star: Red Dead Redemption 2 (Software), Take-Two Interactive, America (2018)
8. Sucker Punch Productions: Ghost of Tsushima (Software), Sony Interactive Entertainment LLC, Japan (2020)
9. Asobo Studio: A Plague Tale Innocence (Software), Focus Home Interactive, France (2019)
10. Asobo Studio: A Plague Tale Requiem (Software), Focus Home Interactive, France (2022)
11. Hazelight Studios: It Takes Two (Software), Electronic Arts, America (2021)
12. Ubisoft Montreal: Assassin's Creed 2 (Software), Ubisoft, France (2008)
13. Crystal Dynamics: Shadow of the Tomb Raider (Software), Square Enix, Japan (2019)
14. Ward, I.: Call of Duty Modern Warfare (Software). Activision Publishing Inc, America (2020)
15. Thatgamecompany: Journey (Software), Sony Interactive Entertainment LLC, Japan (2012)
16. EA DICE: Mirror's Edge (Software), Electronic Arts, America (2008)
17. Tom, W.: The game market's bright future: player numbers will soar past 3 billion towards 2024 as yearly revenues exceed $200 billion. https://newzoo.com/insights/articles/the-games-markets-bright-future-player-numbers-will-soar-past-3-billion-towards-2024-as-yearly-revenues-exceed-200-billion. Accessed 10 Nov 2022
18. Tom, W.: The game market will show strong resilience in 2022, Growing by 2.1% to reach $196.8 billion. https://newzoo.com/insights/articles/the-games-market-will-show-strong-resilence-in-2022. Accessed 10 Nov 2022
19. Metacritic: Game releases list, https://www.metacritic.com/browse/games/score/metascore/year/all/filtered?year_selected=2021&distribution=&sort=desc&view=detailed/   Accessed 10 Nov 2022

20. Wikipedia. Game Level. https://zh.m.wikipedia.org/zh-hans/%E9%97%9C%E5%8D%A1_ (%E9%9B%BB%E5%AD%90%E9%81%8A%E6%88%B2. Accessed 10 Dec 2022
21. PUBG Studio, PlayerUnknown: BattleGrounds (Software). https://guide.pubg.com/en-na/ gameinfo/maps. Accessed 23 Dec 2022
22. "How to make a level" Level Design Book, https://book.leveldesignbook.com/process/ove rview. Accessed 15 Dec 2022
23. Riot Games, League of Legends. https://www.leagueoflegends.com/en-us/. Accessed 20 Dec 2022
24. Valve, Counter-Strike. https://blog.counter-strike.net/. Accessed 23 Dec 2022
25. Wikipedia, Cognitive psychology. https://zh.wikipedia.org/zh-cn/%E8%AA%8D%E7%9F% A5%E5%BF%83%E7%90%86%E5%AD%B8. Accessed 15 Dec 2022
26. Wikipedia, Skinner Box. https://zh.m.wikipedia.org/zh-hans/%E6%96%AF%E9%87%91% E7%BA%B3%E7%AE%B1. Accessed 26 Dec 2022
27. MBA, Logical Thinking. https://wiki.mbalib.com/wiki/%E9%80%BB%E8%BE%91%E6% 80%9D%E7%BB%B4. Accessed 27 Dec 2022
28. Baidu, Programming. https://baike.baidu.com/item/%E7%BC%96%E7%A8%8B/139828. Accessed 27 Dec 2022
29. Wikipedia, Affordance. https://en.wikipedia.org/wiki/Affordance. Accessed 27 Dec 2022–12–27

Toward a Toolkit for Co-designing Collaborative Play Tool with and for Autistic Children

Mohamad Hassan Fadi Hijab[1]([✉]) [iD], Dena Al-Thani[1] [iD], Joselia Neves[2] [iD],
Nahwan Al Aswadi[2] [iD], and Shaza Khatab[1] [iD]

[1] Information and Computing Technology Division, College of Science and Engineering,
Hamad Bin Khalifa University, Doha, Qatar
{mhhijab,dalthani,shkh41443}@hbku.edu.qa
[2] College of Humanities and Social Sciences, Hamad Bin Khalifa University, Doha, Qatar
{jneves,nalaswadi}@hbku.edu.qa

Abstract. The prevalence of autism is currently on the rise around the world. Autism is often associated with challenges in social communication, which could impact children's ability to play and integrate with their surroundings. Despite this, there is a lack of studies on that explore collaborative play for autistic children. To address this deficiency, a contextual inquiry was conducted which comprised of a semi-structured interviews with teachers, specialists, and parents, as well as observation sessions of nine autistic children engaged in play-based activities. The purpose of this study is to investigate the interaction between autistic children and play tools during play sessions and to make recommendations for the development of toolkits for co-designing collaborative play with autistic children. The analysis phase includes evaluating the play tools based on the level of interaction, targeted skills, and employed senses. According to the findings, autistic children mostly explore the tools, while their teachers focus on enhancing their motor abilities. Also, the sense of touch was employed most frequently during play sessions. This study contributes to the development of future toolkits supporting co-design of collaborative play experiences for autistic children.

Keywords: Autism · Collaborative Play · Child-tool interaction analysis · Co-design · Multisensory

1 Introduction

Studying the human-interaction is the core to the field of computing. This body of knowledge encompasses fields of Human-Computer Interaction, Interaction Design, and a variety of areas and theories that explore the complex relationship between the human and machines. Numerous studies have attempted to clarify the interaction concept, describe its application, and relate it to other notions in the field of Human-Computer Interaction, social science, and psychology [1–3]. Child-computer interaction has gained attention in the past two decades [4, 5]. The interactions with objects including toys and tools have also been thoroughly studied as well [6, 7]. This interaction evolves from primarily exploratory to incorporating functional and symbolic actions [8]. Moreover, object

X. Fang (Ed.): HCII 2023, LNCS 14046, pp. 114–132, 2023.
https://doi.org/10.1007/978-3-031-35930-9_9

manipulation is a critical component in children's development as it provides a wide range of information on physical characteristics and functions [9]. In the subsequent stages, children learn to develop and refine their motor and cognitive skills, including bimanual coordination [10], small rotational wrist movements, and mental rotation [11]. Through object manipulation, children also acquire linguistic, social-cognitive, and narrative skills [12]. In this paper, the interaction between the autistic children and play tools was explored. The aim is to build a foundation of knowledge toward co-designing play and explore tools and objects that may be employed in co-designing collaborative play with autistic children.

Play is characterized by pleasure, voluntary involvement, intrinsic motivation, flexibility, non-literal orientation, active involvement, and a focus on the process rather than the outcome [13]. Play is crucial for children's socioemotional and cognitive growth, learning, and teaching [14]. Collaborative and social play require interactions between two or more children [15]. In collaborative play, the players work together to achieve a common objective. This form of play can enable the children to improve their ability to empathize with each other's perspectives, develop their negotiation skills, and gain experience with alternative conflict resolution methods. Additionally, to be able to collaborate, role-taking skills must be honed [15].

There is still continuous disagreement regarding the interpretation and definition of autism. The American Psychiatric Association defines it as a neurodevelopmental condition in individuals with difficulties with social interaction and communication, in addition to restricted and repetitive behaviors, activities, and interests [16]. There is an increasing number of autistic individuals worldwide, with one in 54 children in the United States [17], approximately 1% of the British population [18], and one in 87 children in Qatar [19] being diagnosed with autism. Since the term has not been fully defined, it is difficult to choose the appropriate language and terms for referring to autistic individuals [20]. Many studies have discussed the different viewpoints of the various autism communities. In this study, "autism" refers to the clinical diagnosis of autism spectrum disorder. Further, to respect the preferences of most autistic individuals [20], the identity-first language "autistic person" is used throughout this paper.

There has been a shift in the field of HCI toward a more democratic approach in technology design. In the context of HCI, co-design was adopted to build and assess interactive technologies in which users are integral members of the design team. In the recent decade, HCI design processes have shifted from being methodical and closely aligned with engineering to taking into account the users' and researchers' social and cultural background and skills [21, 22]. Participation of the user in the design process is at the heart of the third wave of HCI. This has bolstered the significance of the Participatory design (PD) method, which emerged in Scandinavia to back the labor movement and the right to participate in the design process of computer programs in the workplace. PD is now a widespread method in HCI, in which the target audience is included at every stage from initial concept to final assessment. Despite the difficulties, several researchers are considering utilizing PD with children, this approach is now commonly seen in research and often yield promising results. Research has shown that co-designing with children can be challenging, particularly when cultural, language, and situational barriers exist [23]. This difficulty is further compounded when working with individuals with disabilities, including autistic children. Autistic children, especially those with co-occurring learning difficulties and communication differences, face additional barriers in the technology design process due to societal perceptions of their difficulties with social communication [24]. Unfortunately, when incorporating autistic children into the design process, researchers often reinforce a deficit-oriented approach by creating technologies aimed at reducing social and communication deficits [25]. This results in limited opportunities for autistic children to be recognized as experts and to contribute their unique experiences, skills, and interests. However, some researchers have taken a strengths-based approach and actively involve autistic children in the design process [26]. This approach provides more than just a voice to these children and young people; it also enables them to participate in designing and developing products and services specifically for them. According to [27], children can be involved in the technology research and development process in four ways: as users, testers, informants, or design partners. With the inclusion of children's input, this framework has been applied in the context of autism to develop interactive technology interfaces. The children's roles have varied from testers to design partners, although in cases where the end-users have limited communication abilities, the involvement of indirect stakeholders such as caregivers and teachers was deemed necessary.

Studies had shown that play is often challenging for autistic children in their early development [28], especially social and collaborative play [29]. According to the Diagnostic and Statistical Manual [16], autistic children play in a stereotyped and repetitive manner, with an emphasis on the sensory qualities of the objects. Several studies [30, 31] have indicated that autistic children have difficulty engaging in more complex situations that require imagination and play. Additionally, Chamberlain et al. [32] suggested that autistic children can participate in some forms of play; however, they lack a degree of complexity. For instance, autistic children face delayed social competencies, and, as a result, they may engage in inappropriate behavior [31]. It has been suggested by Petrina et al. [33] that social engagement and play interactions among autistic children could be diminished due to social obstacles that may arise through peer interactions. While most of the studies on autism and play had a deficit-focused view, there is an existing thread of research that stresses that autistic children do engage in play in various forms that may often be different than their neurotypical peers. Mitchell and Lashewicz [34] stated that their actions consist of the fundamental elements of play, such as fun and joy.

Toys are commonly thought of as being essential to play. The role of toys is to stimulate children's feelings and senses enrich the child imagination, and support their physical, cognitive, social, and emotional development [35]. A toy can be described as an artifact which purpose is to facilitate play and encourage positive effects [36]. It is a physical object that a child can interact with, and all toys have purposes. For example, a plush toy is for cuddling and love, a doll is for talking and dressing, and a robot is for carrying out tasks. The functionality of these toys is determined by their intended use. Such toys may have varying degrees of smart responses and interaction capabilities. For example, toys can be designed as tangible sets that promote the development of different skills, focusing on narrative and social skills [37]. In contrast, toys can also be designed as interactive toys that integrate technology to support play [35]. Autistic children might have difficulty initiating social interactions for a variety of reasons. These reasons may include a lack of motivation, attention to relevant environmental stimuli, and unclear expectations. Autistic children who do not initiate a social interaction may miss out the opportunity to learn from their environment [38]. It is also possible that they may not ask for assistance or support when it is truly needed. Moreover, those who do not initiate social interactions do not receive the responses that normally follow such statements and are limited to receiving only the information provided to them by others. As such, teaching autistic children how to initiate spontaneous interactions with others can also be a goal on its own [39]. According to Belchic and Harris [40], providing autistic children with the opportunity to initiate and maintain play with their peers is crucial to overcome their lack of relatedness and increase engagement.

The aim of the work reported in this paper is to identify tools and objects to support co-designing a tool for collaborative play with autistic children. To the best of our knowledge, there has yet to be a study that has analyzed the interaction between autistic children and tools used for collaborative play. This study is part of a larger project that aims to co-design a collaborative play tool with and for autistic children [41]. A contextual inquiry was conducted as part of the larger project, which included semi-structured interviews and observation sessions. This study examined the interaction between autistic children and the tools they played with during the observation sessions. Therefore, this study aimed to recommend a toolkit. A toolkit is a group of resources, and suggestions for a particular topic or activity, or a set of tools made to be used together for a specific purpose [42]. The remainder of this paper is organized as follows: Sect. 2 describes the research methodology and analysis; Sect. 3 highlights the results and findings; Sect. 4 provides the discussion, and Sect. 5 concludes and offers recommendations for the toolkit.

2   Methods

2.1   Study Design

To fully understand collaborative play in the realm of autism, a contextual inquiry was carried out in a local center for children with disabilities. 80% of the children in this center are diagnosed with autism. Contextual inquiry is a user-centered research method that entails observing and interviewing users in their natural environment to learn about their goals, tasks, and challenges. It is frequently used in design and development processes to gain insights into how users interact with products, services, or systems, as well as to identify areas for improvement [43]. This study consisted of two phases; the first phase which includes 22 semi-structured interviews that were conducted in person at the center with specialists, teachers, and therapists, while eight were conducted over the phone with parents and the second phase which involves 20 observation sessions of nine autistic children in their regular schedule. The interviews were transcribed and analyzed along with the observation videos using thematic analysis by two researchers. Subsequently, observation sessions were conducted with the presence of three researchers during regular class time of the children at the center. A total of 20 sessions were recorded on video and analyzed by the same researchers. Prior to the start of the contextual inquiry, an ethical approval was obtained from the Research Board of the Qatar Biomedical Research Institute.

2.2   Participant Recruitment and Data Collection

Prior to starting the contextual inquiry, the researchers met with therapists and teachers of the center and presented the project aim and contextual inquiry process. The teachers then identified ten autistic children to participate in this study. Following that, the parents' consent was obtained. Table 1 summarizes the demographic information of the children participating in this study.

Table 1. The information of the autistic children that participated in this study.

Child	Gender	Age	Form of communication
C1	M	12	Verbal
C2	F	7	Verbal
C3	M	11	Non-verbal
C4	M	11	Verbal
C5	M	9	Verbal
C6	M	7	Non-verbal
C7	M	10	Verbal
C8	M	11	Verbal
C9	M	11	Verbal
C10	M	10	Verbal
Min		7	
Max		12	
Average		9.9	

The observation sessions were held at the center with the absence of one child. These sessions included sports, interactive floor projection, reading, and music activities. The children were also observed during their lunch break. The sessions were identified by the center as the ones including play. Sports session included a warmup followed by different activities. The reading session included a visit to the library and storytelling activities with the teachers. The interactive floor projection session included different games that are projected on the floor. The children could interact with the projected image where their movements are detected through motion sensors. The children typically have their meals while seated at the dining table during the lunch break. The music session included watching their teacher while playing a musical instrument. The session will also include a teacher encouraging the children to use some musical instruments. Each session will consist of a teacher or specialist and a teaching assistant. In addition to the formal sessions at the center, two free play sessions were observed in which all the included autistic children were involved without any adult supervision. During all observation sessions, both a fixed and a moving camera were used to film the children, while two researchers took notes.

2.3 Interaction Analysis

The analysis of this study consisted of three parts: the interaction between the tools and the autistic children, the relationship between the interaction's level with tools and the targeted skills during the session, and the relationship between the interaction's level with tools and the senses employed. Baranek et al. [6] Object Play Coding Scale was adapted to understand the children's interaction levels with the tool. To provide a measure of playability, Baranek et al. [6] developed unified definitions for four distinct categories of play: exploratory, relational, and functional play. These categories were used for the object play coding scale. The term exploratory play refers to any action performed by children, guided by their eyes, and focusing on a specific location to provide information about the object or environment. In relational play, two or more objects are used together regardless of their attributes or functions. In contrast, functional play refers to the use of an object based on its cultural properties and the act of pretending to play with the object. Extracted from the general coding scale developed by Baranek et al. [6], a set of four main categories was used to code the interaction with the tools observed during the session. The main categories and their different levels of interaction are presented in Table 2. The child's interaction with each tool during the session, is then classified according to this coding scheme. In Table 3, examples of the tools observed in the sessions are mentioned as well.

Table 2. The elementary levels of object play with canonical examples.

Theme (Category)	Sub-theme (Level)	Example
Exploration	L1: Indiscriminate actions	Rub; Shake; Bang; Mouth
	L2: Simple Manipulation of single objects	Rolling toys; Pushing buttons; Spin; Rock
Relational	L3: Takes combinations of objects apart	Pull apart assembled toys
	L4: Presentation/ general combinations	Assemble
Functional	L5: Object-directed	Placing lid on a pot; Dumping objects from a truck
	L6: Self-directed	Drinking from an empty cup; Raising phone to ear and vocalizing
No tool interaction		Walking and crawling; Observing an object; Being pushed on a swing

After analyzing the child-tool interactions, the skills and senses targeted when using each tool are studied. The analysis of the targeted skills was comprehensive and addressed the significant skills of human functioning, such as social, motor, language, play, and academic skills [44]. Individuals acquire social skills to become aware of their social environment and social contingencies, solve social problems and engage in other appropriate behaviors during their developmental stages [45]. Some examples of social skills include social initiations, greetings, communication rules, proper use of toys and other materials, social communication, showing empathy, and symbolic and imaginary play. Motor skills refer to the ability to perform complex movements with muscles and nerves [46]. Communication and language skills refer to the ability to use a language to communicate and interact with others. Some examples of these skills are listening, speaking, reading, and writing [47]. Play skills refer to voluntary engagement in self-motivated activities usually associated with pleasure and enjoyment [48]. In contrast, academic skills refer to the skills pertaining to a subject area related to the academic curriculum [49]. Then, cognitive skills are associated with knowledge and abilities and the motivation to apply them. Cognitive skills are thinking, learning, remembering, and paying attention [50]. All these skills work together to process the incoming information and integrate it into the knowledge that individuals rely on in their daily lives, either at school, work, or personal lives [50]. The analysis of the senses was used to categorize the senses as either distal or proximal. Distal senses include sighting and hearing, whereas proximal senses include touching, smelling, and tasting [51]. The categorization of the senses was based on the way the children use the tool in the recorded videos.

3   Results

Ten tools were observed during the sessions. The interaction with these tools were analyzed according to their level of interaction, targeted skills, and the senses employed. Figure 1 shows these tools.

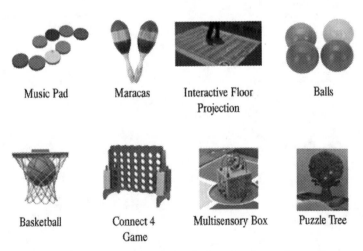

| Music Pad | Maracas | Interactive Floor Projection | Balls |
| Basketball | Connect 4 Game | Multisensory Box | Puzzle Tree |

Fig. 1. Example of the extracted tools from the observation sessions.

3.1   Levels of Interaction

In this section, the results are presented according to the sessions in which the tools were employed. Figure 2 illustrates a summary of the outcome. Before doing the interaction analysis, it was determined whether the interaction was self-initiated or prompted by a teacher or therapist. It is clear that children explore all the tools except the interactive floor projection. The children primarily explored the tools during the music session (maracas and music pad), as evidenced by their manipulation of the tools (L1–L2). During the sport and free play sessions, however, the children were more likely to investigate the tools (L1–L2) and assess its relational (L3 and L4) and functional (L5) uses. This section includes a full overview of the various degrees of interaction between the children and the tools.

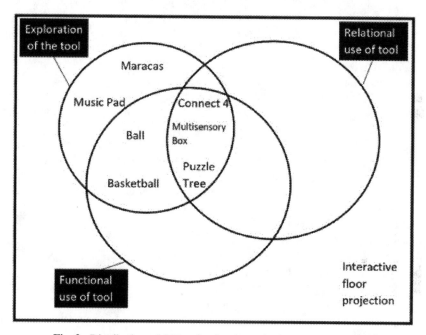

Fig. 2. Distribution of the levels of tools on the interaction category.

Music Session

Two tools were observed during the music sessions: the maraca and the music pad. The maraca is a musical instrument composed of a hollowed gourd with a handle, which is filled with either seeds, beans, or stones. When provided with maracas, the children began to shake and explore them. The children were then encouraged to shake their maracas in time with the teacher's rhythm. The teacher instructed the children on how to play the maracas by showing them how to shake their hands forward and backward. Because the autistic children typically interacted with the maracas by shaking, beating, and stroking (L1), it was classified as exploration category. At the end of the music session, the teacher led the autistic children together to the music pads, where they stepped on. The round music pads were set on the ground and produced sound when stepped on. The is can be categorized as an exploration in which the children were rubbing (L1), pushing, and spinning the instrument (L2).

Sport Session
Three tools were observed during the sports sessions: the ball, the basketball, and the Connect 4 game. The teacher gave instructions regarding the utilization of all three tools. For instance, autistic children were instructed to catch the ball and place it in the corresponding containers. The children explored the ball by holding, shaking (L1), and rolling it towards the pot as requested (L2). In addition, the children were directed to take the balls from the box, which is categorized as Object-directed level (L5) and represents functional use of a tool category. Similarly, when playing basketball, the teacher directed the students to catch and return the ball. The children shook (L1), rolled (L2), and eventually place the ball into the net (L5). Hence the basketball game is classified as exploration, relational, and functional. The Connect 4 game was also utilized regularly. Connect 4 is a classic strategy game in which two opponents compete to line up four discs of their respective color. As players drop the discs into the grid, they stack them vertically, horizontally, or diagonally (Nasa et al., 2018). The teacher did not exactly follow to the Connect 4 guidelines with the autistic children, but instead separated them into two groups and instructed them to catch a random disc, run towards the grid, and place it anywhere within the grid. In the beginning of the game, the children assisted the teacher in clearing the grid of discs (L5), then grasping the disc, shaking it (L1), spinning it (L2), and placing it in the correct location on the grid (L3) (L4). The relationship between Connect 4 and the children was therefore categorized as exploring, relational, and functional.

Interactive Floor Projection Session
The autistic children engaged with the projected image on the floor during the interactive floor projection session. Once the autistic children selected the preferred activity, the teacher commenced it on the interactive floor projection, and the autistic child began interacting with the activity. Hence, the choice of the activity was self-initiated by the children. The interactive floor projection sessions included projected games such as blowing bubbles, chasing chickens, scoring goals, and plucking leaves from the water. Yet, several portions of the video recording were omitted due to insufficient lighting that caused fuzziness. No instances of shaking, rubbing, rolling, or assembly were noted throughout the session. The children were simply walking on the projected images and observe its graphics.

Free Play Session
During the free play sessions, the individuals interacting with the autistic children in the center, such as teachers or specialists, refrained from interfering with the children's play in any way. Consequently, the selection of play tools was self-initiated by the children, including items such as balls, a puzzle tree, and a multisensory box. It was noted that the selected tools displayed a spectrum of interaction levels. The autistic children utilized the ball pit for activities such as throwing balls at one another and leaping into the pit. In addition to shaking (L1) and rolling (L2) the ball, either on themselves or toward others, the children also placed and threw (L5) the ball into the ball pit. The puzzle tree, a plastic

tree with detachable plastic apples, showed three interaction types as children removed an apple (L3), shook it (L1), and sought to attach it to the tree (L4). These actions fell under the categories of exploration and relational use of tool. The multisensory box, like the puzzle tree, represented all three interaction categories. The multisensory box is a six-sided wooden box holding various activities, such as a bean maze, a tiny xylophone, a puzzle, and a shape-matching game. During the free play session, the exploration category was determined when the autistic child shook and pounded the xylophone stick or the puzzle pieces (L1). In addition, the kid participated in the multisensory box activity by hitting the corresponding buttons (L2) and removing, then placing the associated puzzle piece in the correct spot (L3–L4–L5).

3.2 Relation Between the Skills and Interactions

Throughout the observed sessions, a wide variety of skills were apparent while using the tools. As shown in Fig. 3, the distribution of these tools within their respective categories is shown. Motor, social, play, cognitive, and communication and language skills were observed in exploration, relational, and functional use of tool categories. Academic skills were only noticed in the exploration category.

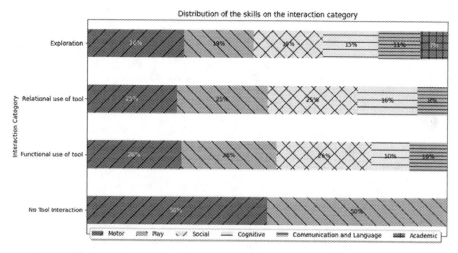

Fig. 3. Distribution of the level of interaction of the targeted skills.

Upon examination of the tools used during observation sessions, it became clear that motor and play abilities were the primary focus. The exploration category emerged as the most prevalent observed form of interaction. Academic skills, in contrast, were found to be the least represented. This is due to the observation sessions' emphasis on collaborative play, with only maracas and music pads incorporating academic, motor, and cognitive skills. To improve these skills, the teacher taught the students to follow the rhythm and shake the maracas (L1), as well as press the music pads (L2). In addition, the multisensory box and puzzle tree were used to improve the cognitive, motor, social, and play skills of autistic children; this interaction is characterized as relational use of tool. During observation sessions, basketball and balls were used to target motor, social, communication, and play skills through exploration and functional use of tools. Motor and play skills were visible during interaction floor projection despite the absence of interaction.

3.3   Relation Between the Senses and Interactions

Throughout the recorded sessions, there was no indication of the use of the taste and smell senses, so we focused our analysis on the three remaining senses. Figure 4 illustrate the distribution of the tools in relation to the three senses.

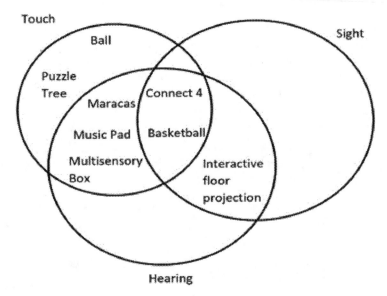

Fig. 4. Distribution of the toys on the used senses.

In the observed videos, it was found that the touch sense was utilized in all tools except for interactive floor projection. During the free play sessions, the children interacted with the puzzle tree by detaching (L3–L4) and reattaching (L5) apples, discovering its pieces by touch, and feeling its texture (L1–L2). During the sport and free play sessions, touch was also noticed when playing with the balls, which were rolled (L2), shook (L1), and placed in a bin (L5). During the music session, the children were given maracas and music pads. This engaged both the tactile and auditory senses. The children could touch and shake the maracas (L1) to provide auditory feedback, and similarly, they could bang and rub their feet on the pad (L1) while pressing on it to generate sound (L2). In the multisensory box, children shook and bang the stick (L1) to play the xylophone and listened to the resulting tone.

In contrast, the interactive floor projection did not entail touch, but rather solely sight and hearing. The basketball and connect 4 tools required the use of the three senses. The children could feel the texture, weight, and shape of the basketball and hear its sound while bouncing toward the teacher before shooting it into the net (L1–L2–L5). During playing the connect 4 game, the children similarly started by dropping the discs outside the grid (L5), then grabbed and shook the discs (L1), rolled and pushed them into the grid (L2), and assembled the discs into the grid (L4). Consequently, it can be argued that the various instruments used in the study were designed to stimulate the senses. This can result in a more immersive and effective learning environment for children.

4 Discussion

In this study, nine children with autism are observed as they played with various tools. In the sessions, eight tools were observed (ball, multisensory box, puzzle tree, interactive floor projection activities, maraca, music pad, connect 4, and basketball). The levels of interaction with the tools were divided into three categories: object exploration, relational use of tool, and functional use of tool. The children in the interactive floor projection session did not interact with any objects as they merely walked on images projected onto the floor. Table 3 provides an overview of tools noted during the observations.

Table 3. Overview of tools appeared in the sessions.

Tool	Shape	Color	Texture	Feedback
Ball	Spherical	Multi-colored	Soft	Catching and throwing the ball
Multisensory Box	Cubical	brown and colorful activities' components	Soft and rough (based on the activity on it)	Visual and audio feedback
Puzzle tree	Plastic Tree shape	Brown branch and green and red apples	Soft	Tactile through feeling the apple and attaching it on the tree
Interactive Floor Projection Activities	rectangle projected image on the floor	Multi-colored (based on the chosen activity)	Using sensors by leg (no texture feeling)	Visual and audio feedback
Maracas	Cylinder	Brown and pink	Soft	Audio when shaking
Music Pad	Circle	Multi-colored	Soft	Audio and feeling pressing on it
Connect 4	Ring	Blue grid with yellow and red rings	Soft	Visual by watching the ring slides in the grid and audio when collapsing the rings together in the grid
Basketball	Circle	Orange	Soft	Audio when bouncing the ball, visual and tactile when catching and throwing the ball

All through the sessions, the children showed curiosity about the various tools available to them. For instance, children typically grasped a ball and regularly hit it during the sport session. Interestingly, shaking and rolling tools were the most common kinds of interaction seen. These exploratory behaviors appear to be initiated by autistic children upon encountering any tool. An example of manual exploration includes shaking, transporting, and turning things [52, 53]. Through employing these techniques of exploration, the child can get a variety of perspectives on items at hand. Supporting these techniques could enhance the experience of autistic children when playing.

The analysis of videos revealed that the interactions with tools involved three senses: touch, sight, and sound. Autistic children utilized these senses to touch, observe, or seek auditory feedback from the tools. As a result of their grabbing instinct, the initial reaction of autistic children when interacting with tools was to look and touch them. Throughout the observation sessions, children attempted to touch the texture of the tools after eagerly inspecting their color and shape. Thus, children frequently shook and banged the tools in search of auditory feedback. These findings are consistent with the existing research, which highlights that children examine toys and tools through oral (i.e., mouthing), manual (i.e., grasping, fingering, shaking, banging, or rotating), and visual (i.e., looking; [54, 55]). Consequently, the inclusion of a multisensory tool might enhance autistic children's interaction with the tool and therefore support their playing experience.

In the sessions, motor skills were the most often addressed skills across all interaction categories. As discussed, autistic children interacted with the tools by shaking, rolling, assembling, and pressing buttons, all of which require the use of muscles and nerves. According to empirical studies, autistic children frequently have gross and fine motor deficits [56]. Thus, to help the development of motor skills in autistic children, professionals such as therapists, teachers, and specialists tend to add tools that involve the use of muscles variety of muscles. The results of this study concur with this tendency, highlighting the need for motor skill-improving aids that can assist the complex motions of autistic children.

4.1 Recommendations Toward a Toolkit

Based on the results of this study, a number of recommendations in terms of tool choice are highlighted in this section. These recommendations contribute to developing a toolkit that can support co-designing social play for children with autism. Co-designing with autistic children who have learning difficulties and communication differences presents various challenges [57]. These challenges are research-related such as difficulties in recruitment [58], to population-related such as communication barriers [59]. Despite these constraints, a number of studies managed to conduct co-design with autistic children [60–62]. As co-design technique provides autistic children with more than just a voice in the technology development through allowing them to participate in the different levels of product and services creation adapted to their needs.

Diversity of Texture
The diversity of textures in toys and tools is an important factor in the play experiences of autistic children. These children often have heightened sensitivity to touch and a preference for specific textures, which can impact their sensory regulation and emotions [26]. The observed tools showed a diversity of texture. This diversity also emphasized the importance touch sense. Hence, to enhance their play experiences and improve sensory processing, it is crucial to consider the diversity of textures in play materials. Providing

a range of textures can help reduce anxiety, improve regulation, and enhance the overall collaborative play experience for autistic children [63].

Multi-colored Tool

A multi-colored tool was inferred from the observation sessions. As autistic children exhibit a heightened sensitivity to colors, often perceiving them with more intensity than they are [64]. The colors present in indoor environments can have a significant impact on their mood, learning, and behavior, making it important to carefully consider the selection of colors. By using autism-friendly color palettes, such as pastel shades, neutral colors, and muted tones, it is possible to create a calming sensory experience in an indoor environment [64]. Thus, the choice of colors can help the children to develop a positive relationship with their toys or any objects. As a result, it is significant to identify the colors that would help to support the play experience.

Audio Feedback

Auditory feedback in toys can play a crucial role in supporting the development of autistic children. This type of feedback provides immediate and clear reinforcement, helping autistic children to understand the cause and effect of their actions [65]. It can also support the development of early listening skills, attention, and memory. Moreover, auditory feedback can assist in improving the child's ability to engage in social interactions and develop communicative abilities [66]. For example, toys that provide auditory feedback when buttons are pressed, or levers are pulled can help to increase the child's motivation to play and participate in activities. In conclusion, auditory feedback in toys can provide numerous benefits for autistic children, helping to support their engagement with the toy and the whole play experience.

4.2 Limitation and Future Work

It is important to acknowledge the limitations of this study which are highlighted in this section. Most of the children that the center recruited were male, hence the tools used may differ if there were equal amounts of children of each gender. Additionally, the observation sessions were only held in the center, restricting the variety of tools that could be found at home or other locations. As a result of increasing the number of observed sessions, more tools will be found to be analyzed and more recommendations for toolkit will be presented. Finally, the observed sessions were guided by the teachers, who selected the tools, not the autistic children. Giving the freedom for autistic children to select the favorite tool could lead to another result.

The purpose of this study is to contribute to a larger project that is intended to co-design a collaborative play tool for autistic children. The findings of this study are considered to be the basis of the co-design sessions. Therefore, in our future work, co-design sessions will be conducted using the recommended toolbox. Several workshops will be conducted with teachers, specialists, and autistic children in order to co-design a final prototype and evaluate it. The results of this study might also help further research on child-objective interaction in play.

5 Conclusion

Autistic children are known to have challenges in social and collaborative play [16]. Several studies in the literature have tried to support social and communication skills for autistic children, but there has been a lack of studies that have focused on collaborative play. This study analyses the tools used in the observation sessions to produce a toolkit that could be used in the co-design sessions. The results of this study were aligned with the literature [52, 53], as the most common theme was exploring an object, which included the first two levels of interaction. Additionally, motor skills were the most targeted skills in addition to the tactile sense. The study recommends the importance of considering the diversity of textures, multi-colored toys, and auditory feedback in the choice of toys for autistic children. Diversity of textures can enhance their play experiences and improve sensory processing, while multi-colored toys can create a calming sensory experience and improve their mood, learning, and behavior. Moreover, auditory feedback in toys can provide immediate reinforcement, support early listening skills, and assist in social interactions and communicative abilities. These recommendations could guide in creating better play experiences for autistic children and support their development.

Acknowledgement. This study was made possible by NPRP grant # NPRP13S-0108-200027 from the Qatar National Research Fund (a member of Qatar Foundation). The findings achieved here are solely the responsibility of the author[s].

References

1. Beaudouin-Lafon, M.: Instrumental interaction: an interaction model for designing post-WIMP user interfaces. In: Proceedings of the SIGCHI Conference on Human Factors in Computing Systems - CHI '00, pp. 446–453 (2000). https://doi.org/10.1145/332040.332473
2. Beaudouin-Lafon, M., Designing interaction, not interfaces. In: Proceedings of the Working Conference on Advanced Visual Interfaces - AVI '04, p. 15 (2004). https://doi.org/10.1145/989863.989865
3. Hornbæk, K., Oulasvirta, A.: What is interaction?. In: Proceedings of the 2017 CHI Conference on Human Factors in Computing Systems, pp. 5040–5052, May 2017. https://doi.org/10.1145/3025453.3025765
4. Antle, A.N., Hourcade, J.P.: Research in child-computer interaction: provocations and envisioning future directions. Int. J. Child-Comput. Interact. **32**, 100374 (2022). https://doi.org/10.1016/j.ijcci.2021.100374
5. Lehnert, F.K., Niess, J., Lallemand, C., Markopoulos, P., Fischbach, A., Koenig, V.: Child–computer interaction: from a systematic review towards an integrated understanding of interaction design methods for children. Int. J. Child-Computer Interact. **32**, 100398 (2022). https://doi.org/10.1016/j.ijcci.2021.100398
6. Baranek, G.T., Barnett, C.R., Adams, E.M., Wolcott, N.A., Watson, L.R., Crais, E.R.: Object play in infants with autism: methodological issues in retrospective video analysis. Am. J. Occup. Ther. **59**(1), 20–30 (2005). https://doi.org/10.5014/ajot.59.1.20
7. Westeyn, T.L., Abowd, G.D., Starner, T.E., Johnson, J.M., Presti, P.W., Weaver, K.A.: Monitoring children's developmental progress using augmented toys and activity recognition. Pers. Ubiquitous Comput. **16**(2), 169–191 (2012). https://doi.org/10.1007/s00779-011-0386-0

8. Rachwani, J., Tamis-LeMonda, C.S., Lockman, J.J., Karasik, L.B., Adolph, K.E.: Learning the designed actions of everyday objects. J. Exp. Psychol. Gen. **149**(1), 67–78 (2020). https://doi.org/10.1037/xge0000631

9. Needham, A.: Improvements in object exploration skills may facilitate the development of object segregation in early infancy. J. Cogn. Dev. **1**(2), 131–156 (2000). https://doi.org/10.1207/S15327647JCD010201

10. Michel, G.F., Campbell, J.M., Marcinowski, E.C., Nelson, E.L., Babik, I.: Infant hand preference and the development of cognitive abilities. Front. Psychol. **7** (2016). https://doi.org/10.3389/fpsyg.2016.00410

11. Örnkloo, H., von Hofsten, C.: Fitting objects into holes: on the development of spatial cognition skills. Dev. Psychol. **43**(2), 404–416 (2007). https://doi.org/10.1037/0012-1649.43.2.404

12. Goldstein, T.R., Lerner, M.D.: Dramatic pretend play games uniquely improve emotional control in young children. Dev. Sci. **21**(4), e12603 (2018). https://doi.org/10.1111/desc.12603

13. Wolfberg, P.J.: Play and imagination in children with autism (1999)

14. Siraj-Blatchford, I.: Conceptualising progression in the pedagogy of play and sustained shared thinking in early childhood education: a Vygotskian perspective. Educ. Child Psychol. **26**(2), 77–89 (2009)

15. Whitman, E.C.: The impact of the social play on young children. Murray State University (2018)

16. Diagnostic and statistical manual of mental disorders: DSM-5TM, 5th ed. Arlington, VA, US: American Psychiatric Publishing, Inc. (2013)

17. Maenner, M.J., et al.: Prevalence and characteristics of autism spectrum disorder among children aged 8 years—autism and developmental disabilities monitoring network, 11 sites, United States, 2018. MMWR Surveill. Summ. **70**(11), 1–16 (2021). https://doi.org/10.15585/MMWR.SS7011A1

18. N. A. Society: "What is autism?"https://www.autism.org.uk/advice-and-guidance/what-is-autism

19. Alshaban, F., et al.: Prevalence and correlates of autism spectrum disorder in Qatar: a national study. J. Child Psychol. Psychiatry **60**(12), 1254–1268 (2019). https://doi.org/10.1111/jcpp.13066

20. Kenny, L., Hattersley, C., Molins, B., Buckley, C., Povey, C., Pellicano, E.: Which terms should be used to describe autism? Perspectives from the UK autism community. Autism **20**(4), 442–462 (2016). https://doi.org/10.1177/1362361315588200

21. Harrison, S., Sengers, P., Tatar, D.: Making epistemological trouble: third-paradigm HCI as successor science. Interact. Comput. **23**(5), 385–392 (2011). https://doi.org/10.1016/j.intcom.2011.03.005

22. Bødker, S.: Third-wave HCI, 10 years later—participation and sharing. Interactions **22**(5), 24–31 (2015). https://doi.org/10.1145/2804405

23. Brown, A.V., Choi, J.H.: Refugee and the post-trauma journeys in the fuzzy front end of co-creative practices, **2**, 1–11 (2018). https://doi.org/10.1145/3210586.3210598

24. Frauenberger, C., Good, J., Alcorn, A., Pain, H.: Conversing through and about technologies: design critique as an opportunity to engage children with autism and broaden research(er) perspectives. Int. J. Child-Comput. Interact. **1**(2), 38–49 (2013). https://doi.org/10.1016/j.ijcci.2013.02.001

25. Gillette, D.R., et al.: Interactive technologies for autism. In: CHI '07 Extended Abstracts on Human Factors in Computing Systems, pp. 2109–2112, April 2007. https://doi.org/10.1145/1240866.1240960

26. Spiel, K., Frauenberger, C., Keyes, O.S., Fitzpatrick, G.: Agency of autistic children in technology research - a critical literature review. ACM Trans. Comput. Interact. **26**(6) (2019). https://doi.org/10.1145/3344919

27. Druin, A.: The role of children in the design of new technology. Behav. Inf. Technol. **21**(1), 1–25 (2002). http://legacydirs.umiacs.umd.edu/~allisond/child_info_tech/Druin-BIT-Paper2 002.pdf
28. Charman, T., Swettenham, J., Baron-Cohen, S., Cox, A., Baird, G., Drew, A.: Infants with autism: an investigation of empathy, pretend play, joint attention, and imitation. Dev. Psychol. **33**(5), 781–789 (1997). https://doi.org/10.1037/0012-1649.33.5.781
29. Jordan, R.: Social play and autistic spectrum disorders. Autism **7**(4), 347–360 (2003). https://doi.org/10.1177/1362361303007004002
30. Bauminger-Zviely, N., Agam-Ben-Artzi, G.: Young friendship in HFASD and typical development: friend versus non-friend comparisons. J. Autism Dev. Disord. **44**(7), 1733–1748 (2014). https://doi.org/10.1007/s10803-014-2052-7
31. Gunn, K.S., Trembath, D., Hudry, K.: An examination of interactions among children with autism and their typically developing peers. Dev. Neurorehabil. **17**(5), 327–338 (2014). https://doi.org/10.3109/17518423.2013.778348
32. Chamberlain, B., Kasari, Æ.C., Rotheram-fuller, E.: Involvement or Isolation ? The Social Networks of Children with Autism in Regular Classrooms, pp. 230–242 (2007). https://doi.org/10.1007/s10803-006-0164-4
33. Petrina, N., Carter, M., Stephenson, J.: The nature of friendship in children with autism spectrum disorders: a systematic review. Res. Autism Spectr. Disord. **8**(2), 111–126 (2014). https://doi.org/10.1016/j.rasd.2013.10.016
34. Mitchell, J., Lashewicz, B.: Quirky kids: fathers' stories of embracing diversity and dismantling expectations for normative play with their children with autism spectrum disorder. Disabil. Soc. **33**(7), 1120–1137 (2018). https://doi.org/10.1080/09687599.2018.1474087
35. Hall, L., et al.: Still looking for new ways to play and learn… Expert perspectives and expectations for interactive toys. Int. J. Child-Comput. Interact. **31**, 100361 (2022). https://doi.org/10.1016/j.ijcci.2021.100361
36. Zagalo, N., Branco, P.: The Creative Revolution That Is Changing the World, pp. 223–243 (2015). https://doi.org/10.1007/978-1-4471-6681-8
37. Sylla, C., Pires Pereira, R.S., Sá, G.: Designing manipulative tools for creative multi and cross-cultural storytelling. In: C C 2019 – Proceedings of 2019 Creative Cognition, pp. 396–406 (2019). https://doi.org/10.1145/3325480.3325501
38. Schadenberg, B.R., Reidsma, D., Heylen, D.K.J., Evers, V.: Differences in spontaneous interactions of autistic children in an interaction with an adult and humanoid robot. Front. Robot. AI **7**(March), 1–19 (2020). https://doi.org/10.3389/frobt.2020.00028
39. Koegel, R.L., Koegel, L.K.: Pivotal response treatments for autism: communication, social, & academic development. Koegel, Robert L.: Koegel Autism Center, Gevirtz Graduate School of Education, University of California, 1110 Phelps, Santa Barbara, CA, US, 93106: Paul H. Brookes Publishing Co. (2006)
40. Belchic, J.K., Harris, S.L.: The use of multiple peer exemplars to enhance the generalization of play skills to the siblings of children with autism. Child Fam. Behav. Ther. **16**(2), 1–25 (1994). https://doi.org/10.1300/J019v16n02_01
41. Hijab, M.H.F., Al-Thani, D.: En route to co-designing inclusive play with and for autistic children. In: 2022 9th International Conference on Behavioural and Social Computing (BESC), pp. 1–4, October 2022. https://doi.org/10.1109/BESC57393.2022.9995240
42. Adolfo, G., Lacayo, A.: Diabetes Guidelines Implementation Toolkit (2011)
43. Holtzblatt, K., Beyer, H.: Contextual Design: Defining Customer-Centered Systems. Elsevier (1997)
44. Gould, E., Dixon, D.R., Najdowski, A.C., Smith, M.N., Tarbox, J.: Research in autism spectrum disorders a review of assessments for determining the content of early intensive behavioral intervention programs for autism spectrum disorders, **5**, 990–1002 (2011). https://doi.org/10.1016/j.rasd.2011.01.012

45. Gillis, J.M., Butler, R.C.: Social skills interventions for preschoolers with autism spectrum disorder: a description of single-subject design studies. J. Early Intensive Behav. Interv. **4**(3), 532–547 (2007). https://doi.org/10.1037/h0100390
46. Chin, Y.J., Lim, W.N., Lee, C.S.: Mobile game for the elderly: bundled bingo game. In: IEEE Region 10 Annual International Conference, Proceedings/TENCON, vol. 2017-Decem, pp. 2262–2267 (2017). https://doi.org/10.1109/TENCON.2017.8228238
47. Richards, J.C.: Longman Language Teaching and Applied Linguistics. Pearson Education (2002)
48. Daryl Niko, L., Cempron, M.A.: Motor, play and self-care skills: an index of childrens pre-indications. Int. J. Adv. Res. **9**(5), 294–305 (2021). https://doi.org/10.21474/ijar01/12835
49. Jordan, R.: Academic skills. In: Volkmar, F.R. (ed.) Encyclopedia of Autism Spectrum Disorders, pp. 19–25. Springer, New York (2013). https://doi.org/10.1007/978-1-4419-1698-3_399
50. Gishin, D.: types of indicators for measuring cognitive skills for a professional career in IT sector, **1**(4), 47–50 (2022)
51. Korsmeyer, C.: A tour of the senses. Br. J. Aesthet. **59**(4), 357–371 (2019). https://doi.org/10.1093/aesthj/ayz026
52. Barrett, T.M., Traupman, E., Needham, A.: Infants' visual anticipation of object structure in grasp planning. Infant Behav. Dev. **31**(1), 1–9 (2008). https://doi.org/10.1016/j.infbeh.2007.05.004
53. Needham, A., Barrett, T., Peterman, K.: A pick-me-up for infants' exploratory skills: early simulated experiences reaching for objects using 'sticky mittens' enhances young infants' object exploration skills. Infant Behav. Dev. **25**(3), 279–295 (2002). https://doi.org/10.1016/S0163-6383(02)00097-8
54. Palmer, C.F.: The discriminating nature of infants' exploratory actions. Dev. Psychol. **25**(6), 885–893 (1989). https://doi.org/10.1037/0012-1649.25.6.885
55. Ruff, H.A.: Infants' manipulative exploration of objects: effects of age and object characteristics. Dev. Psychol. **20**(1), 9–20 (1984). https://doi.org/10.1037/0012-1649.20.1.9
56. Ozonoff, S., Pennington, B.F., Rogers, S.J.: Executive function deficits in high-functioning autistic individuals: relationship to theory of mind. J. Child Psychol. Psychiatry **32**(7), 1081–1105 (1991). https://doi.org/10.1111/j.1469-7610.1991.tb00351.x
57. Frauenberger, C., Good, J., Keay-Bright, W.: Designing technology for children with special needs: bridging perspectives through participatory design. CoDesign **7**(1), 1–28 (2011). https://doi.org/10.1080/15710882.2011.587013
58. Wadhwa, B., Cai, J.: Collaborative tablet applications to enhance language skills of children with Autism Spectrum Disorder. In: ACM International Conference on Proceeding Series, pp. 39–44 (2013). https://doi.org/10.1145/2525194.2525297
59. Adjorlu, A., Serafin, S.: Co-designing a head-mounted display based virtual reality game to teach street-crossing skills to children diagnosed with autism spectrum disorder BT - interactivity, game creation, design, learning, and innovation, pp. 397–405 (2020)
60. Lewis, J.R.: The system usability scale: past, present, and future. Int. J. Hum. Comput. Interact. **34**(7), 577–590 (2018). https://doi.org/10.1080/10447318.2018.1455307
61. Reiter, M.A., Mash, L.E., Linke, A.C., Fong, C.H., Fishman, I., Müller, R.-A.: Distinct patterns of atypical functional connectivity in lower-functioning autism. Biol. Psychiatry Cogn. Neurosci. Neuroimaging **4**(3), 251–259 (2019). https://doi.org/10.1016/j.bpsc.2018.08.009
62. Pauk, J., Zawadzka, N., Wasilewska, A., Godlewski, P.: Gait deviations in children with classic high-functioning autism and low-functioning autism. J. Mech. Med. Biol. **17**(3) (2017). https://doi.org/10.1142/S0219519417500427
63. Nonnis, A., Bryan-Kinns, N., Olly: a tangible for togetherness. Int. J. Hum. Comput. Stud. **153**(June 2020), 102647 (2021). https://doi.org/10.1016/j.ijhcs.2021.102647

64. Nair, A.S., et al.: A case study on the effect of light and colors in the built environment on autistic children's behavior. Front. Psychiatry **13**(November), 1–18 (2022). https://doi.org/10.3389/fpsyt.2022.1042641

65. Russo, N., Larson, C., Kraus, N.: Audio-vocal system regulation in children with autism spectrum disorders. Exp. Brain Res. **188**(1), 111–124 (2008). https://doi.org/10.1007/s00221-008-1348-2

66. Hailpern, J., Karahalios, K., Halle, J.: Creating a spoken impact: encouraging vocalization through audio visual feedback in children with ASD. In: Conference on Human Factors Computer and System Proceedings, pp. 453–462 (2009). https://doi.org/10.1145/1518701.1518774

Visual Summarisations for Computer-Assisted Live Color Casting and Direction in *League of Legends*

George Margetis[1]([✉]), Konstantinos C. Apostolakis[1], Stavroula Ntoa[1],
Ioannis Chatzakis[1], Eirini Sykianaki[1], Ioannis Markopoulos[2],
and Constantine Stephanidis[1,3]

[1] Institute of Computer Science, Foundation for Research and Technology-Hellas (FORTH), 70013 Heraklion, Crete, Greece
{gmarget,kapostol,stant,johnhatz,eirinisi,cs}@ics.forth.gr
[2] NOVA, Athens, Greece
ioannis.markopoulos@nova.gr
[3] Department of Computer Science, University of Crete, Heraklion, Crete, Greece

Abstract. Esports has become a juggernaut in mainstream entertainment. For broadcasting and production stakeholders to establish a foothold in this exploding market, live-streaming broadcasts of matches should become more meaningful for fans, and more attractive to newcomers, ensuring their retention. This work describes an end-to-end solution for enhanced live production and streaming of the popular esport, *League of Legends*. The solution is based on several interconnected dashboards, which are fed by an inference engine reasoning on events transpiring in the game. Its aim is to lend decision support to directorial and color commentary tasks undertaken by the production crew. Hence, it supports the broadcasting director in using data to create shots of rich visual storytelling, while generating automated running commentary for esports casters to adapt the broadcasting script on-the-fly. Deduced knowledge is linked to custom infographics, that can be used to overlay the stream with visual summarisations of the action. The tools comprising our solution integrate with professional-grade broadcasting software, leveraging established workflows, and enabling complex management of multiple scenes and graphics from a single point of access. Our solution's usability has been evaluated by esports experts through a cognitive walkthrough, verifying the approach.

Keywords: Esports · Casting · Color commentary · Data-driven production · Multiplayer Online Battle Arena

1 Introduction

The cultural influence of video games in today's society is no longer under question. After having been an underground niche for decades [33], electronic sports (esports) has become a serious, thriving business. In fact, esports is growing into a popular spectacle, generating worldwide revenues of over a billion USD [6]. The industry's growth shows no signs of slowing down, as, even in the face of the COVID-19 pandemic, esports persevered. While many sports were postponed or cancelled altogether, esports content kept people company during the lockdown and self-isolation periods [8].

In order to keep up with the exponential rise and demand for esports content, many organisations traditionally involved in mainstream sports, including sports-related media programming and broadcasting companies, are beginning to grasp the benefits of diversifying into the esports domain and, as such, broadening their audience [24, 29]. Like traditional mainstream sports broadcasts, esports is heavily dependent on keeping fans engaged and enthusiastic about the content [17]. Hence, in order to fully unlock esports' potential as a broadcasting property, producers of live esports coverage should cater to the preferences and perceptions of consumers regarding their content.

A logical first step is to compare esports audience motives for watching online gaming competitions with those that drive viewership in major televised sports. Recent research into this topic shows that motivational factors behind content consumption in both cases are significantly similar (e.g., showing a genuine interest in the sport, opportunities offered for dramatic match outcomes, and deriving joy from players' confrontation) [25]. However, for people to buy into these concepts, it is important that uninitiated (e.g., non-gamers, or people who do not play a particular esport themselves), or first-time watchers, are in a position to follow and understand what is transpiring on the screen. The complexity of esports is a compromising factor, with some of the more popular games taking place on large maps with several simultaneous objectives for the players (e.g., micro-management of resources, map movement, item purchases, etc.) [32]. Hence, players' strategies and in-game choices may not be as easily discernible as in traditional sports.

Esports broadcasts thus employ a similar coverage approach to traditional sports with one or more casters, who accompany the live footage with compelling storytelling, combining play-by-play announcing with insightful color commentary. Therefore, explainability of the broadcast to newcomers, along with opportunities to experience heightened drama, is dependent on the skills and knowledge of the caster(s), and their ability to break down and contextualise unfolding events and players' accomplishments [10]. Further, to get the most out of the on-air talent, broadcasting teams involve highly skilled virtual camera operators (observers) and/or directors, who must demonstrate lightning-fast reflexes in both capturing high-stakes gameplay moments in real-time, and deciding on the best possible camera shot to use in the final broadcast. Finally, one or more graphics coordinators (or a director) enrich the footage with informative graphics, to address the audience and present interesting facts, as well as aiding casters with stimuli to build narratives around the contents of the graphic [2].

To address challenges in the current workflows of the identified actors in the esports broadcasting ecosystem, this paper presents an end-to-end software solution for producers of live esports content, summarised in Fig. 1. The presented

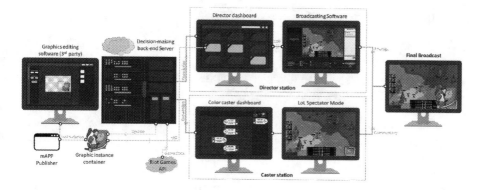

Fig. 1. Proposed solution internal architecture and data flow.

tools are aimed at streamlining tasks both prior and during live coverage by: (i) delivering real-time decision support in the assembly of interesting shots fuelling the live broadcast; (ii) automating on-the-fly creation of insightful, data-enriched graphics; and (iii) assisting casters in their task of coming up with topics for color commentary. To achieve this, we employ automatic analysis of key statistics related to transpiring in-game events, and compare the subsequent players' accomplishments in those events against a broad dataset of past performances, making the information readily available to the broadcast crew. In this way, the final broadcast can be made: (i) more *cinematic*, where a director will be notified in real-time on availability of graphics containing interesting and insightful recounting of match moments, streamlining the process of integrating such graphics into the final broadcast; (ii) more *dramatic*, in enabling casters to more quickly react to out-of-the-ordinary player performances; and (iii) more *explainable*, by means of timely, glanceable graphics, overlaid on top of the broadcast to help audiences (both enthusiasts and first-timers) grasp the significance of individual play-by-play moments. In order to validate the usability of our solutions, our user-facing applications were reviewed by esports production experts by means of a cognitive walkthrough [18]. Our tools focus on one of the most popular esports in the world, *League of Legends* (LoL) [26] but easily apply in other esports settings as well.

The remainder of this paper is organised as follows: Sect. 2 presents an overview of related work, highlighting the unique aspects of our work. It also provides context by presenting LoL, and the rationale behind our in-game events' selection. Section 3 discusses our methodology, fully aligned to Human-Centered Design (HCD) strategies for coming up with efficient designs to meet target stakeholders' needs. Section 4 describes the components of our solution depicted in Fig. 1. Section 5 elaborates on the evaluation of the solution with experts, discussing key findings regarding usability and recommendations for practical use of the system in real settings, while Sect. 6 discusses key takeaways from the evaluation study and limitations. Finally, Sect. 7 wraps up our article with concluding remarks and outlines future work.

2   Background and Context

2.1   Overview and Classification of Related Work

Despite esports' explosion over the past decade, only recently has the topic been placed at the forefront of researchers' attention. Among the various items listed on the esports research agenda [6], the development of digital technologies aimed at enhancing spectators' experiences are among the most interesting in multimedia content creation and information visualisation disciplines. Systems proposed in this topic aim at both facilitating an understanding of the drivers and motivators behind esports spectatorship, and accelerating the growth of the esports viewing audience. The topic is quite novel, and has occupied research concerned with testing hypotheses and formulating design specifications.

We propose a classification of the relevant research work in this area into three distinct categories, based on their purpose and target end-users. Hence, the reported works are classified on the grounds of their utilising the collection and visualisation of in-game data toward (i) *spectator dashboards and companion-like applications*, where the target end-user is a member of the viewing audience; (ii) *data-driven production tools* targeted at professionals in live broadcasting of esports matches; and (iii) *tools for other esports ecosystem actors* (e.g., players and game developers) to visualise facts about in-game performances, toward improving individual skills and/or design aspects related to future game updates. While the related works presented in the following paragraphs make clear mentions of their intended usage and target end-users, most of the conclusions derived can be adapted in support of use cases in the other categories (e.g., using information regarding player motivation in a colour-casting capacity). Hence, while our own work fits within the scope of the second category, we present an overview of the related literature in topics (i) and (iii), so as to cover all aspects of esports information visualisation that should be considered in the development of user-facing, graphic-rich applications, as the ones presented in this work.

Esports Spectator and Companion Applications. In this line of esports information visualisation solutions, the focus is placed on the development of information-rich dashboards for presenting real-time and post-game statistical data about matches, usually via dedicated web or smart surface applications. Emphasis is put on second-screen experiences, i.e., companion applications, which contextualise the main broadcast to the consumer using comprehensive data and visuals.

Charleer et al. [5] were among the first to design and develop such dashboards for popular first-person shooter (FPS) and multiplayer online battle arena (MOBA) games, driven by a strong end-user co-design methodology, to visualise real-time, in-game data, side by side with the final broadcast. Their findings formulated fundamental esports spectator dashboard design objectives, among which *glanceablity* (i.e., the ability to understand the presented information 'at a glance') and *transparency* (i.e., the means to deliver information in an explainable way) were highly sought-after qualities. Kokkinakis et al. [16] explore similar design rationales in the context of a second-screen application for the consumption of esports broadcasts and live event attendance. Their work too discusses important considerations toward the design of similar future data-driven companion experiences. More in-depth research into the esports spectator experience has demonstrated the utility of multimedia (e.g., text, audio, and graphics) dashboard content, aiming at complementing the main broadcast narrative with information that commentators (or even audiences) might not have the time to verbally address, or otherwise focus on, as the game progresses at a rapid pace [28].

While most spectator dashboards deal with information visualisation in terms of facilitating easily readable graphics and information whilst consuming streams in conventional channels and platforms, several other works related to this topic have experimented with novel means to enhance the spectator experience. These include the use of portable augmented reality applications to view interactive game content from practically any desirable angle [1], prototypical systems projecting match elements onto 3D tabletop surfaces [3], and auto-generation of textual coverage using artificial intelligence systems to complement the highlights reel of an event [23]. Surprisingly, virtual reality spectatorship [11] remains unexplored territory research-wise in the esports domain.

Data-Driven Production Tools. The scope of data-driven production is to directly incorporate insightful analytics and (potentially) graphic overlays into the final broadcast itself, consumed by spectators via conventional viewing channels and platforms (e.g., Twitch, YouTube, etc.), i.e., without necessitating the download and use of a companion application. These tools aim at streamlining processes in the production pipeline, and making it easier for broadcasters to captivate audiences by providing more engaging and inclusive coverage.

The work of Block et al. [2] is arguably the first to formulate the topic of data-driven production in esports, developing a tool (*Echo*) for statistically rich, audience-facing graphics that in tandem support audiences' understanding of the unfolding game, and provide opportunities for esports casters to deliver extensive and insightful commentary, particularly with respect to extraordinary player performances. Further work toward supporting live esports casting stems from research into detecting and highlighting player behaviors that deviate significantly from the commonly adopted/accepted strategies (known as the "meta", or "metagame" [15]). Thus, they create opportunities for casters to comment on the more elusive yet peculiar (and hence more interesting) aspects of live matches [30]. Another element explored in support of esports production teams is the capacity to anticipate and react in a timely manner to interesting game events. In [31], such a system is realised using machine learning algorithms for the prediction of team fights in MOBAs. This technology could help an observer to select the proper camera shots based on the likelihood of an event occurring on a particular player's screen, or it could inform casters to build up audience excitement in anticipation of such a cherished event.

Related to the above-mentioned approaches, recent research work has been presented in [35], toward artificially generated audio commentary in accompaniment to the broadcast video. With hours upon hours of gameplay footage making its way onto the world wide web on a daily basis, this technology could deliver low-cost esports casting in non-professional settings, or provide a solution for production companies (or individual streamers), in cases where the employment of human casters might be impractical, or too expensive.

Player Understanding and Self-Improvement Tools. This topic of esports visualisation explores the use of data-driven analysis for uncovering player motivations and decision-making processes behind in-game behaviour. The findings of such an analysis could then be exploited towards: (i) learning from one's own or other players' performances (where the resulting tools are aimed at esports players themselves); or (ii) improving game design choices, whenever esports are to be updated to a newer version (in which case tools are directed at the games' development staff).

With respect to (i), a comprehensive literature review of data-driven efforts used by actual (esports) players, as a means to improve their performance in the game, is presented in [12]. Due to the inherent utility of such tools in the professional esports scene, the same research group attempted to define a new information visualisation taxonomy for the actions of esports players as observed by others, through a spatio-temporal visual representation of their gameplay [13]. In fact, the use of gameplay data together with artificial intelligence toward attaining deepened knowledge of particular gamers' strategies, and using them to achieve learning goals, has recently been positioned as a new area of eXplainable AI (XAI) research, under the term *Open Player Modeling* [36]. Apart from benefiting players, research in this area is expected to also be of significant utility to game developers (ii). In fact, [14] presents evidence of using sequence and interactive behaviour analysis toward understanding MOBA game actions from the players' point of view. The resulting knowledge is mapped onto game design choices, meant to help game developers address shortcomings or fine-tune a particular aspect of their game (e.g., correct imbalances or fix exploits).

2.2   Context of the Proposed Work

Our work is closely related to the works reported in Sect. 2.1, as our goal is to provide esports production crews with online tools for flexibly reacting and adapting their coverage and commentary to live game outcomes. *League of Legends (LoL)* was selected as the vehicle to contextualise the developed solutions. LoL is regarded as one of (if not) the largest and most important esports [9], organised under a global league structure. Competitive events are played on the 'Summoner's Rift' map, where two teams of 5 players ('Summoners') vie to destroy the opposing team's 'Nexus'. Each Summoner selects one of over 150 unique game characters ('Champions'), assuming a role (Top, Jungle, Middle, Bottom and Utility), and a position ('Lane') on the map.

Each Champion has certain abilities and a levelling system. As the player accumulates experience points by defeating other players and non-player characters (NPCs) in the game, their Champion levels up, unlocking new or enhancing already attained abilities, gaining advantage over their Lane opponent. Other ways for players to outperform their adversaries include buying Items that enhance their Champion's skills (e.g., deal more damage to enemy Champions), or slaying 'Epic' monsters scattered throughout the game. To buy Items, a Summoner has to gather in-game currency ('Gold') by completing various objectives around the map, including defeating their opponents in battle (and claiming their 'Bounty').

The above simplistic description already reveals the complexity involved, not only in terms of playing the game and excelling at it (i.e., players having to make decisions regarding several different aspects of the game, such as moving their characters strategically on the map, engaging in battle with other players or NPCs, etc.) but also, from a spectator's perspective, being able to follow the action, which requires familiarity with the game and its mechanics. Furthermore, as important or exciting events (e.g., team fights) may simultaneously occur in several different locations on the map, observers, directors and casters need to stay vigilant at all times to make sure important aspects of the match are captured and communicated to the audience. Therefore, LoL presents an interesting case study for the proposed solution.

3 Designing a Usable Solution

To address pain points in a complex domain, such as the LoL broadcasting ecosystem, understanding the people at whom solutions are directed is key. Hence, we involved representative end-users in the design and development of applications and systems, following the iterative design methodology outlined in the HCD framework [19]: (i) Understanding the context of use; (ii) eliciting and documenting the user requirements; (iii) prototyping and designing solutions; and (iv) evaluating the designs with end-users. We elaborated on step (i) in Sects. 1 and 2 of this paper. This Section outlines the processes involved in step (ii) of the HCD process. Section 4 delivers a detailed overview of the solutions implemented to address the elicited needs of our end-users (Step [iii]), while Sect. 5 elaborates on step (iv).

3.1 Co-design with Esports Experts

We elicited requirements and design ideas for our proposed solution by organising two online co-creation workshops [7], in which 14 people from Greek and Spanish esports production companies participated (Table 1). Both companies specialise in organising and producing media content for several competitive online multiplayer video games (including LoL) in a national and international context. Proper informed consent procedures were put in place to comply with ethical guidelines and regulatory requirements.

Table 1. Demographic Table for co-creation workshop participants

Role	Frequency (N)	Percent (%)
Production/Management	4	28.57%
Director	4	28.57%
Graphics/Live tech. support	6	42.85%

Over the course of two hours, the following structured exercises were conducted with the participants:

- **Introduction**: An overview of the workshop aims and objectives, complemented by general guidelines for participants, was provided.
- **Warm-up**: Participants took turns introducing themselves, followed by a game of 'Two Truths and a Lie', adopting a carefree attitude about sharing their opinions. The activity was short but cultivated a sharing attitude among the group and promoted team bonding.
- **Current practices**: Participants listed software platforms and tools used in esports productions, and discussed favourable, problematic and lacking features in each case. Notes were kept on a shared electronic whiteboard. A second round of discussions toward ealborating on the tools listed on the whiteboard followed, where participants reviewed and grouped items.
- **Features wish-list**: Each participant proposed five essential features to streamline tasks and improve the broadcasting crew's experience. Each list was published on the whiteboard, where it was further elaborated on and re-ranked by all participants in a second round of discussions.
- **Summary and conclusions**: Key takeaways were presented, and a round table discussion took place to comment on findings with participants.

3.2 Elicited End-User Goals and Preferences

The following points were emphasised by participants during workshop activities, providing us with a baseline toward defining specific requirements, as reported in Sect. 3.3:

Direction. Regarding broadcasting direction, participants expressed desire for an integrated production pipeline, alleviating the need of resorting to too many different tools, and instead opting for a single point of access and control for as many of the directorial responsibilities as possible (e.g., scene observation and selection, vision mixing, etc.). Participants underlined the importance of provisioning endpoints (e.g., for graphics visualisation), which would enable seamless and solid integration with third-party broadcasting solutions (i.e., OBS Studio). Automation and ease of use were highlighted as key wish-listed features. Also, participants expressed their desire to leverage simplicity and speed-up during the complex task of managing the live streaming production.

Graphics. In the esports production environment, graphics software should support creation, editing, and publishing into a unified end-to-end solution. The capacity to construct, import, edit, and reuse pre-made graphics templates aimed at specific purposes (e.g., post-match reports and analysis) was highlighted. Participants pointed out the need for graphics playout software to integrate seamlessly with live data and analytics services, thus enabling the harvesting and population of the graphic with live statistics without human intervention, automatically creating informative visual content and enhancing the broadcast (and with it, the spectators' experience).

Live Commentary. Regarding esports casting, our findings were similar to [2]. Esports commentators participating in the co-creation activities emphasised the need for the esports broadcasting script to focus on the players as the protagonists, embellished with facts and statistics important to spectators. To put the spotlight on the players despite the often chaotic nature of the game, casters highlighted the need for having access to near real-time player statistics, preferably contextualised using various filters (e.g., per event, chronologically, etc.), accompanied by explainable graphics. Match color commentary should feature meaningful ways to describe players' actions, not only by focusing on match MVPs and top-tier players but also by providing an in-depth analysis of individual play via access to historical match data and past player performances. This enables casters to adapt the broadcasting script and focus on otherwise inconspicuous players, who might be having an exceptional game, surprising everyone with their performance.

3.3   Requirements and Design Specifications

Key findings were analysed using inductive coding [4], involving two researchers. More specifically, a researcher reviewed the data collected during the workshops and assigned one code for each one of the functionalities identified by participants as features desired by the platform. Then, these codes were shared with the second researcher and both researchers carried out a data classification process, whereby they examined the data in order to assign to each response one of the predefined codes. The outcomes of the two individual analyses were compared, following a consensus-building approach to address inconsistencies in the codes assigned. Following code analysis, key functional requirements were identified. Based on these requirements, high-fidelity design mock-ups were produced, elaborating on specific interaction characteristics, user interface (UI), and core graphical features our user-facing applications should incorporate.

4   Description of the Proposed Solution

Our end-to-end solution for streamlining live esports coverage production consists of front-end, user-facing applications connected to back-end tools and services providing computation-intensive functions. A Cloud-based, flexible microservices architecture is followed. In this Section, we describe these functional blocks and the dashboards implemented to deliver on the key functionalities for the different production roles. This narrative shall introduce the relevant components in sequence, as specified in the internal architecture and data flow diagram presented in Fig. 1.

4.1   Live Graphics Setup and Instantiation

Following the creation of broadcast graphics using commercial editing software, we created a web-based live graphic publisher, which exports live graphics instances in the form of micro-applications (mAPP). These are full-stack applications featuring a UI (where the graphic is displayed) and a back-end component exposing an API for retrieving and updating the information displayed on top of the graphic. Upon creation, each mAPP is automatically containerised and indexed by the graphic provider. A user can then request the deployment of the mAPP container to generate an instance of the graphic. In this case, the graphic provider automatically sets up an appropriate endpoint to make the instance accessible to third-party software (e.g., OBS Studio). In this manner, a single graphic can be simultaneously deployed multiple times by different users, and display match-specific information without interference from the other instances.

4.2   Decision-Making Back-End Server

When LoL matches are being played as part of a tournament broadcast, informative data around the live game can be harvested by the production crew using several official APIs maintained by the game's developer, *Riot Games* [27]. The back-end server component in our architecture aims to: (i) trigger the acquisition of this data; (ii) filter it through an expert system applying Rule-Based Reasoning (RBR); (iii) aggregate discovered knowledge in a comprehensive data structure; and (iv) forward the data object as a JSON message payload to the proper endpoints. To realise its functionality, the server comprises several microservices and a historical matches database, which requires pre-processing of data before the start of the match, in order for the rule-based logic supported by our server to be applicable. Each sub-component is described in more detail in the following sub-chapters.

Player Historical Matches Database. When leagues or tournaments are organised, broadcasters are aware of team rosters and the in-game aliases of the players participating (and the 'Summoner IDs' associated with those players' game accounts). For each Summoner ID, past Match IDs (and from those IDs, the complete log of match data) can be obtained, corresponding to games that the player has played during the elapsed season of ranked competitive play. Hence, important events monitored by the event callback micro-service (see below) can be readily associated with the match data kept internally, limiting calls to the external API service and reducing the delay between an event being triggered and the calculated data being forwarded to the front-end applications.

Event Callback Service. This micro-service implements an inbound interface toward the Live Client Data and Live Events APIs of the LoL official developer tools. The latter enables the callback service to trigger whenever updates on a variety of live-tracked events are relayed by the API. A similar structure is accommodated by the service for past, recorded games, where the list of all events that occurred is obtainable through the corresponding Match ID. In this case, recorded event timestamps on the JSON object are associated with the current video playback timeline by means of a custom script and player (built in Unity). This enables the callback service to trigger at the time the event would have occurred if the game was being played live. The latter functionality is provided for post-match analyses and was used for the cognitive walkthrough evaluation (see Sect. 5).

Rule-Based Reasoner. The rule-based reasoner determines whether an event forwarded by the event callback is worthy of mention, based on rules for recognising the event's significance with respect to the affected players' match histories. The reasoner queries the historical matches database to compare the stats of the Summoner ID triggering the event, against the collected body of past performances where similar events were triggered by the same player or Champion. The core decision-making mechanism employs a rule-based conditional logic scheme, aimed at comparing the player's current output against their average performance for a specific statistical category (e.g., Dragon kills). The query can be further filtered to include games played with the currently selected Champion or Role or to consider a particular range of events in the calculation (e.g., player performance within a specific league or tournament). Consequently, interesting knowledge may be generated for the audience whenever calculations show an out-of-the-ordinary performance. Similarly, the reasoner compares the performances of the current Lane opponents and makes team-based comparisons. The data flow for the reasoner is displayed in Fig. 2. An indicative list of events monitored by the service is presented in Table 2.

As soon as key facts about the players' performances are discovered, they are broadcast via an asynchronous communication protocol through a micro-services message broker into a queue, where they can be consumed by the subscribing front-end dashboards, described in Sects. 4.3 and 4.4.

4.3   Color Caster's Dashboard

This application automatically compiles all noteworthy events relayed by the decision-making back-end server, and displays them in reverse chronological

Table 2. Event types handled by the rule-based reasoner.

Event Type	Description of statistics extracted and converted to graphics
Special Kill: Stats related to a player scoring an *Ace* (i.e., slaying the last man standing in the opposing team), *First Blood* (scoring the first Champion kill of the match), *Multi-kill* (e.g., defeating two or more enemies from the opposing team within 10 s of one another) and *Shutdown* (defeating a player who has acquired a high bounty)	Number of times the player has performed the triggered special kill in the past. Calculations may take into account usage of the currently selected Champion by the Summoner, the overall average performance of the Champion by others, and a specific range of games (e.g., within the tournament) for as long as the Riot Games API serves these statistics
	Maximum amount of games in a row, where the player has triggered this event in the past. Filters may apply to the calculations, as mentioned above
	Number of times the player's Lane opponent has achieved a similar special kill in the past. Filters may apply to the calculations, as mentioned above
	Comparison of the total number of similar special kill occurrences in the current match between the two Lane opponents
Elite Monster Kill: Stats related to a player killing an Epic monster. Such events benefit the entire team, granting a considerable boost to all team Champions	Number of times the player has killed the same Epic monster in the past. Calculations may take into account usage of the currently selected Champion by the Summoner, overall average performance of the Champion by others, and specific range of games (e.g., within tournament) for as long as the Riot Games API serves these statistics
Building Kill: Stats related to a player destroying an enemy Tower or Inhibitor, granting the player a considerable amount of Gold. Destruction of the first Tower grants a Gold bonus to the player and nearby allies	Number of Towers and/or inhibitors that the player has destroyed in the past. Information can include total number, average Tower/Inhibitor kills per game, maximum number of Tower or Inhibitor kills from all games, as well as elaboration of those stats for the chosen Champion
	The number of first Towers that the player has destroyed in the past, juxtaposed with his/her win rate after destroying the first tower in past games (if this statistic is greater than 60-70%, it shows a tendency of the players to dominate their Lane opponent)
Champion Kill: Stats related to a player scoring a kill against an opposing player	Average Champion kills per game (can include the average kill count per game for the chosen Champion)
	Difference between the player's and Lane opponent's kills (e.g., average, maximum, total)
	Difference between the kills (e.g., average, maximum, total) achieved by both teams
Item Purchased: Stats related to a player purchasing an Item for their Champion. Such purchases may impact the game, if, for example, a player has more items than their Lane opponent	Percentage of games where the player has purchased that Item in the past, including total times bought. Information can be fine-grained to include the number of times an Item has been purchased with the chosen Champion. If the statistics show that the player does not purchase the particular Item on a regular basis, insightful casters may comment on the strategy behind the purchase decision (multiple reasons: enemy player's items, enemy champions, etc.)

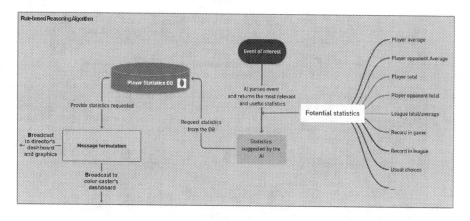

Fig. 2. Rule-based Reasoning Algorithm flowchart.

order, following the presentation style found in typical sports-related live blogging platforms [20]. The dashboard is used side by side with the game's spectator screen, providing an efficient means to signpost content not readily available from the in-game/on-screen statistics output provided by the spectator client. The information is made available to the caster on a need-to-know basis, enabling the casters to maintain their focus on the live gameplay footage, and react to significant player outcomes much faster. Each message broadcast by the back-end server triggers the creation of a new item on the timeline, comprising an icon, and a short and concise textual description of the marked accomplishment and the Summoner triggering it.

Each item can be expanded to reveal additional information about the calculations taking place (in the interest of facilitating explainability and reinforcing trust of the caster in the automated storytelling, as warranted by [5]), along with a more detailed description of the triggered event. Taking into account the dynamic nature of the broadcast, and to support casters in reacting to game events at their own pace, the dashboard enables users to 'pin' items on a separate tab for later use. A screenshot is presented in Fig. 3.

4.4   Director's Dashboard

The director's dashboard is a web-based graphical UI application subscribing for content updates to the decision-making back-end server's messaging queue. It is aimed at supporting the broadcasting director in keeping up with the rapid pace of the match using the continuously updated graphics instances deployed as mAPPs (see Sect. 4.1). To support current workflows and practices, the dashboard seamlessly integrates with OBS Studio, by exposing an API for keeping track and selecting Scenes for display in the main broadcast.

The dashboard enables the director to monitor all graphic mAPP instances deployed prior to the beginning of the broadcast, and correlates them to their corresponding Scenes in OBS Studio, for enabling one-click vision-mixing of the

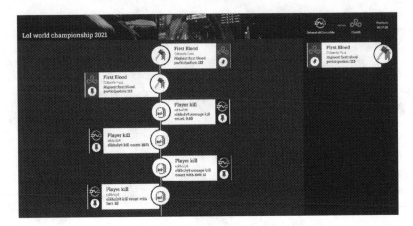

Fig. 3. Screenshot of the color caster's dashboard, showcasing automated reporting of events in reverse chronological order and pinning functionality.

currently displayed Scene and matching graphic overlays. Hence, directors are supported in switching the source ending up in the live broadcast, and enable accelerated compositing with the proper infographic upon receiving an update from the server. In a complex scenario involving player-facing cameras, our tool provides a glanceable interface that could tell the director to switch to a live-action shot of a player, whom the graphic concerns, and craft data-enabled visual storytelling content to accompany remarkable match moments.

The main workspace of this dashboard is shown in Fig. 4, and is composed of several cards, each corresponding to a 'live' graphic mAPP instance summarising the latest update message received by the back-end server. Information on the graphic's content is displayed using a short textual description and a combination of (at the most) three icons:

- The first icon relates to the graphic recounting a Summoner- or Champion-specific event. It hence informs the director which OBS Scene corresponds to the graphic.
- A second, mandatory icon specifies the event type from the list of tracked possibilities defined in Table 2.
- A third (optional) icon may be used to denote the Lane, where the event has taken place.

Upon each update, cards flash in a bright orange colour, notifying the director to react to changes and evaluate their significance to the current broadcasting script. After inspecting the content on the updated cards and setting up the next shot from the list of available sources, the director may elect to mix one of the graphics with the currently displayed Scene, by clicking on the corresponding button on the graphic's card. In this way, timely integration of graphics with the live broadcast becomes a much more streamlined experience for the director.

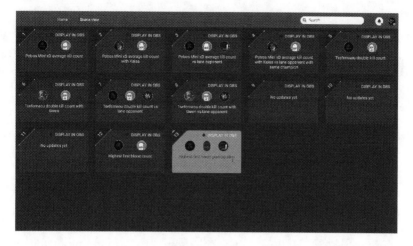

Fig. 4. Screenshot of the director's dashboard interface, showcasing functionality when a new update message is received by the server back-end.

5   Usability Evaluation

To assess usability, explainability and clarity of the proposed solutions, we carried out evaluation of the system with five (5) domain experts (see Table 3) following the Enhanced Cognitive Walkthrough (ECW) approach [37]. We opted to recruit professionals engaged in the live broadcast of LoL, who are specifically targeted by our applications. Participants volunteered for this study, and informed consent was acquired prior to their participation.

Table 3. Demographic Table for cognitive walkthrough participants

Category	Sub-Category	Frequency (N)
Role	Production/Management	2
	Director	1
	Graphics/Live technical support	2

5.1   Methodology

The walkthrough was held virtually. In order for our demo environment to correspond to a typical high-stakes match between accomplished players, pre-recorded footage was used (see Sect. 4.2), while indicative graphics were designed and pre-deployed on standalone mAPP instances as explained in Sect. 4.1.

Evaluation of the system aimed at identifying major issues prior to conducting studies with a larger number of users. The employed ECW methodology involves a total of nine questions being asked for each screen, so as to assess if each system provides adequate clues and feedback, and if users are able to identify and perform intended actions. If evaluators identified an issue, they were further inquired about the origin and causes of this issue, e.g., users' lack of expertise, inadequate system cues and explanations, inappropriate texts or icons, unnatural sequence of functions, or insufficient system feedback. Participants were first explained the aims and objectives of the system, and were guided through the demonstrator. Then, the evaluation focused on each system separately, assessing it on the grounds of clarity and usability.

5.2   Results

Both dashboards received an overall positive rating, with the director's dashboard being rated with an average of 4.26 (SD: 0.73) and the color caster's dashboard with 4.48 (SD: 0.78), on a scale from 1 to 5. More importantly, valuable comments and suggestions were provided in the process of elaborating on the possible causes of the identified problems.

For the director's dashboard, most of the suggested improvements aim to assist directors in being aware of high priority things to do, in ensuring that they are provided with adequate flexibility to support their job tasks, and in avoiding mistakes. A major concern driving most of the suggestions was that directors work in a busy environment and that they usually do not have much time to focus on each screen in front of them, therefore prominent information should stand out. At the same time, it was pointed out that there are periods during a game when events do not occur that often, therefore this time could be used to display past events of importance, even if they are not timely.

For the color caster's dashboard, few improvements were suggested, most motivated by the need to allow casters to easily locate information in a very short time It was indicated that the system provides useful information for casters for all the game events, even the ones that are not captured by the observer, or are not prompted via their headphones. In addition, it was pointed out that the timeline could also be useful for producing post-game articles, serving as an overview and history of the game's noteworthy events.

Positive aspects praised for both systems include the support for the most important game statistics, the usage of appropriate icons and game terms, as well as the clear feedback provided by the system. For both systems, it was pointed out that, as users become more familiar with them (and in combination with their job expertise), both directors and casters will be able to capitalize on them and advance their daily job tasks. In addition, it was stressed that the combination of these two systems would facilitate the job tasks of both directors and casters, allowing them to be in sync without the need for manually transferring statistics from a control room to the casters. An additional functionality for direct communication would also be a valuable future improvement. Furthermore, users suggested exploring alternative setups, which would allow them to operate the system from a distance, such as a large screen accommodating more information operated with gestures.

6   Discussion

Results and feedback gathered from our cognitive walkthrough showed that the proposed systems constitute a useful asset for esports directors and casters, allowing them to capitalise on information and game statistics and employ them in their narrations in the best possible way, either during action-packed moments or after ('idle' time). Concrete suggestions for improvements were raised for both systems, so as to better serve the needs of target users, who often work in busy environments and stressful conditions, with little time to identify noteworthy information, take action on it, and work in close collaboration with one another.

Identified improvements mostly aimed at enhancing the feedback provided by the system, the entailed flexibility in use, the visibility of information and system status, as well as error prevention. Besides specific improvements in the UI suggested by the evaluators, several high-level conclusions came up:

- In current business processes, syncing between directors and casters occurs without the mediation of technology (e.g., by direct communication over the phone or intercom). In this respect, the information exchange and effortless synchronization that can be achieved by the proposed systems is a valuable asset to assist both professionals in better accomplishing their business goals.
- Information overload is a major concern, for all professionals involved in esports production, since game action is rich with events, and hence users should not be overwhelmed by the information that the system produces.
- Information delivered during the live coverage of an event can be valuable for post-processing as well. After the game analysts can delve deep into the produced statistics and provide a meta-analysis of the game, which can augment the storytelling for this event.
- Consistency with the terminology and statistics typically used in the specific game (LoL) is a major requirement for any system, since it capitalizes on professionals' domain knowledge and allows them to easily understand the information delivered by the system and use it during esports casting.

We believe that a similar design and development approach can adapt the context of our solution to the needs of the same actor roles in esports broadcasting teams for such ventures.

We also highlight as a limitation, the lack of female participants in both user studies (indicative of the gender gap present in the esports landscape [34]), which could have implications on the development of gender-informed solutions.

7   Conclusions and Future Work

In this work, we presented an end-to-end solution for streamlining directorial and casting tasks during the broadcasting of a live esports affair. We considered best practices reported in the emerging scientific literature on live esports data visualisation, further grounding the solutions design process in the HCD methodological approach. This has allowed us to come up and implement rich graphical UI applications for lending decision support in each task, based on the outputs of a Cloud-based, rules-driven expert system. Our user-facing applications have been favourably evaluated in terms of their usability by stakeholders in the live esports production environment.

Despite encouraging feedback, our solution leaves room for improvement, which is a prime concern for the authors regarding future work. First off, our director's dashboard allows the director to "steer" the broadcasting script with insightful visualisations regarding player accomplishments, not only for the audience but also in support of the caster, similar to the evidence reported in [2]. However, in both works the focus is on the delivery of *a posteriori* knowledge (i.e., knowledge becomes available *after* the event has transpired in-game). This requires an experienced observer to meticulously follow the on-screen action so as not to miss out on important happenings. Recent research work has made progress with regard to the topic of predicting the probability (and hence, allowing observers to anticipate) exciting events using machine learning methodologies [31]. Furthermore, optical tracking by means of computer vision techniques applied directly on the game footage may generate additional insights into the game in progress, which may not be available in data logs provided by the games' developer tools [21]. Such computational modules can be accommodated by our services-oriented architecture to deliver further insights. Finally, additional setups and interaction modalities can be explored, such as large displays and gesture-based interaction [22], liberating users' hands from interacting with the system and allowing them to control the system from a distance if needed.

Acknowledgement. This work has received funding from the EU's Horizon 2020 innovation action program under Grant agreement No 957059 (COPA EUROPE). This paper reflects only the authors' view and the Commission is not responsible for any use that may be made of the information it contains. The authors also wish to thank all study participants for partaking in our co-creation workshop and increasing our understanding of the esports landscape through their insightful comments.

References

1. Apostolakis, K.C., Zioulis, N., Doumanoglou, A., Alexiadis, D.S., Zarpalas, D., Daras, P.: Beyond online multiplayer: sharing and augmenting tele-immersive 3D game experiences with multiple geographically distributed users. IEEE COMSOC MMTC Commun. - Front. **12**(1), 11–15 (2017)
2. Block, F., et al.: Narrative Bytes: data-driven content production in esports. In: Proceedings of the 2018 ACM International Conference on Interactive Experiences for TV and Online Video, pp. 29–41. Association for Computing Machinery, New York, NY, USA (2018). https://doi.org/10.1145/3210825.3210833
3. van den Broek, W., Wallner, G., Bernhaupt, R.: Modata - improving dota 2 experience and spectatorship through tangible gameplay visualization. In: Extended Abstracts of the Annual Symposium on Computer-Human Interaction in Play Companion Extended Abstracts, pp. 723–730. Association for Computing Machinery, New York, NY, USA (2019). https://doi.org/10.1145/3341215.3356284

4. Chandra, Y., Shang, L.: Inductive Coding. In: Qualitative Research Using R: A Systematic Approach, pp. 91–106. Springer Singapore (2019). https://doi.org/10. 1007/978-981-13-3170-1_8

5. Charleer, S., Gerling, K., Gutiérrez, F., Cauwenbergh, H., Luycx, B., Verbert, K.: Real-time dashboards to support esports spectating. In: Proceedings of the 2018 Annual Symposium on Computer-Human Interaction in Play, pp. 59–71. Association for Computing Machinery, New York, NY, USA (2018). https://doi.org/10. 1145/3242671.3242680

6. Cranmer, E.E., Han, D.I.D., van Gisbergen, M., Jung, T.: Esports matrix: structuring the esports research agenda. Comput. Hum. Behav. **117**, 106671 (2021). https://doi.org/10.1016/j.chb.2020.106671

7. Degen, H., Ntoa, S.: From a workshop to a framework for human-centered artificial intelligence. In: Degen, H., Ntoa, S. (eds.) Artificial Intelligence in HCI, pp. 166–184. Springer International Publishing, Cham (2021). https://doi.org/10. 1007/978-3-030-77772-2_11

8. Grix, J., Brannagan, P.M., Grimes, H., Neville, R.: The impact of COVID-19 on sport. Int. J. Sport Policy Politics **13**(1), 1–12 (2021). https://doi.org/10.1080/ 19406940.2020.1851285

9. Keiper, M.C., Manning, R.D., Jenny, S., Olrich, T., Croft, C.: No reason to LoL at LoL: the addition of esports to intercollegiate athletic departments. J. Study Sports Athletes Educ. **11**(2), 143–160 (2017). https://doi.org/10.1080/19357397. 2017.1316001

10. Kempe-Cook, L., Sher, S.T.H., Su, N.M.: Behind the voices: the practice and challenges of esports casters. In: Proceedings of the 2019 CHI Conference on Human Factors in Computing Systems, pp. 1–12. Association for Computing Machinery, New York, NY, USA (2019)

11. Kim, D., Ko, Y.J.: The impact of virtual reality (VR) technology on sport spectators' flow experience and satisfaction. Comput. Hum. Behav. **93**, 346–356 (2019). https://doi.org/10.1016/j.chb.2018.12.040

12. Kleinman, E., El-Nasr, M.S.: Using data to "Git Gud": a push for a player-centric approach to the use of data in esports. In: EHPHCI: Esports and High-Performance HCI Workshop, 2021 CHI Conference on Human Factors in Computing Systems. OSF Preprints, April 2021. https://doi.org/10.31219/osf.io/v3g79

13. Kleinman, E., Preetham, N., Teng, Z., Bryant, A., Seif El-Nasr, M.: "What Happened Here!?" a taxonomy for user interaction with spatio-temporal game data visualization. Proc. ACM Hum.-Comput. Interact. 5(CHI PLAY) (October 2021). https://doi.org/10.1145/3474687

14. Kleinman, E., et al.: "And Then They Died": using action sequences for data driven, context aware gameplay analysis. In: International Conference on the Foundations of Digital Games. Association for Computing Machinery, New York, NY, USA (2020). https://doi.org/10.1145/3402942.3402962

15. Kokkinakis, A., et al.: Metagaming and metagames in esports. Int. J. Esports **1**(1) (2021)

16. Kokkinakis, A.V., et al.: DAX: data-driven audience experiences in esports. In: ACM International Conference on Interactive Media Experiences, pp. 94–105. Association for Computing Machinery, New York, NY, USA (2020). https://doi. org/10.1145/3391614.3393659

17. Ludwig, S., Lachmann, K., Papenbrock, J., Mesonero, S.: Let's Play! 2021 The European esports market. Report, Deloitte Insights (2021)

18. Mahatody, T., Sagar, M., Kolski, C.: State of the art on the cognitive walkthrough method, its variants and evolutions. Int. J. Hum. -Comput. Interact. **26**(8), 741–785 (2010). https://doi.org/10.1080/10447311003781409
19. Margetis, G., Ntoa, S., Antona, M., Stephanidis, C.: Human-centered design of artificial intelligence. In: Handbook of Human Factors and Ergonomics, Chap. 42, pp. 1085–1106. Wiley. (2021). https://doi.org/10.1002/9781119636113.ch42
20. Matheson, D., Wahl-Jorgensen, K.: The epistemology of live blogging. New Media Soc. **22**(2), 300–316 (2020). https://doi.org/10.1177/1461444819856926
21. Maymin, P.Z.: Smart kills and worthless deaths: esports analytics for league of legends. J.Quant. Anal. Sports **17**(1), 11–27 (2021). https://doi.org/10.1515/jqas-2019-0096
22. Ntoa, S., et al.: UX design of a Big Data visualization application supporting gesture-based interaction with a large display. In: Yamamoto, S. (ed.) HIMI 2017. LNCS, vol. 10273, pp. 248–265. Springer, Cham (2017). https://doi.org/10.1007/978-3-319-58521-5_20
23. Olarewaju, O., et al.: Automatic generation of text for match recaps using esport caster commentaries. In: 6th International Conference on Computer Science, Engineering And Applications, vol. 10. AIRCC Publishing Corporation (2020). https://doi.org/10.5121/csit.2020.101810
24. Pizzo, A.D., Kunkel, T., Jones, G.J., Baker, B.J., Funk, D.C.: The strategic advantage of mature-stage firms: digitalization and the diversification of professional sport into esports. J. Bus. Res. **139**, 257–266 (2022). https://doi.org/10.1016/j.jbusres.2021.09.057
25. Pizzo, A.D., Na, S., Baker, B.J., Lee, M.A., Kim, D., Funk, D.C.: eSport vs Sport: a comparison of spectator motives. Sport Mark. Q. **27**(2), 108–123 (2018). https://doi.org/10.32731/SMQ.272.062018.04
26. Riot Games: League of legends (version 11.23). Video game (2009)
27. Riot Games: Riot developer portal (2013). http://developer.riotgames.com/
28. Robertson, J., et al.: Wait, but why?: assessing behavior explanation strategies for real-time strategy games. In: 26th International Conference on Intelligent User Interfaces, pp. 32–42. Association for Computing Machinery, New York, NY, USA (2021)
29. Scholz, T.M.: Deciphering the world of esports. Int. J. Media Manag. **22**(1), 1–12 (2020). https://doi.org/10.1080/14241277.2020.1757808
30. Sifa, R., et al.: Archetypal analysis based anomaly detection for improved storytelling in multiplayer online battle arena games. In: 2021 Australasian Computer Science Week Multiconference. Association for Computing Machinery, New York, NY, USA (2021). https://doi.org/10.1145/3437378.3442690
31. Tot, M., et al.: What are you looking at? Team fight prediction through player camera. In: 2021 IEEE Conference on Games (CoG), pp. 1–8 (2021). https://doi.org/10.1109/CoG52621.2021.9619038
32. Vinyals, O., et al.: Grandmaster level in Starcraft II using multi-agent reinforcement learning. Nature **575**(7782), 350–354 (2019). https://doi.org/10.1038/s41586-019-1724-z
33. Werder, K.: Esport. business & information. Syst. Eng. **64**(3), 393–399 (2022). https://doi.org/10.1007/s12599-022-00748-w
34. Witkowski, E.: Doing/undoing gender with the girl gamer in high-performance play. In: Gray, K.L., Voorhees, G., Vossen, E. (eds.) Feminism in Play, pp. 185–203. Springer International Publishing, Cham (2018). https://doi.org/10.1007/978-3-319-90539-6_11

35. Xu, J.H., Fang, Z., Chen, Q., Ohno, S., Paliyawan, P.: Fighting game commentator with pitch and loudness adjustment utilizing highlight cues. In: 2021 IEEE 10th Global Conference on Consumer Electronics (GCCE), pp. 366–370 (2021). https://doi.org/10.1109/GCCE53005.2021.9621827
36. Zhu, J., El-Nasr, M.S.: Open player modeling: empowering players through data transparency. arXiv preprint arXiv:2110.05810 (2021). 10.48550/ARXIV.2110.05810
37. Zidianakis, E., et al.: The invisible museum: a user-centric platform for creating virtual 3D exhibitions with VR support. Electronics **10**(3) (2021). https://doi.org/10.3390/electronics10030363

Toward Computationally-Supported Roleplaying for Perspective-Taking

Caglar Yildirim[1]([✉]), Sercan Şengün[2], Pakinam Amer[3], JJ Hawke[3], and D. Fox Harrell[1]

[1] Computer Science and Artificial Intelligence Laboratory (CSAIL), Massachussetts Institute of Technology, Cambridge, MA 02139, USA
{caglary,fox.harrell}@mit.edu
[2] Illinois State University, Normal, IL 61761, USA
ssengun@ilstu.edu
[3] Massachussetts Institute of Technology, Cambridge, MA 02139, USA
{pakinam,jjotto}@mit.edu

Abstract. Designing and studying computationally-supported roleplaying for changing social perspectives of players is a complex and challenging problem. As indispensable components of roleplaying games (RPGs), narratives have the potential to promote successful perspective-taking. In this paper, we first present the design of a visual novel style RPG scenario addressing xenophobia and bullying, using an interactive narrative powered by a computational narrative engine. We then report on a usability evaluation of our interactive narrative system and an empirical evaluation of the RPG's effectiveness in promoting successful perspective-taking through a crowdsourced online experiment.

Keywords: Roleplaying · Roleplaying Games · Narrative Games · Xenophobia · Bullying

1 Introduction

Many issues that stoke conflict, such as bias, discrimination, and xenophobic attitudes about social groups, are rooted in a failure to understand the perspectives of others. Yet, with reflection, it is possible for people's perspectives to change, and roleplaying games (RPGs) have the potential to encourage successful perspective-taking [11]. In fact, such roleplaying systems are now pervasive and have been shown to be powerful means of sparking conceptual and behavioral change for users [1].

This paper presents the design, development, and evaluation of a system that supports perspective-taking and perspective change through the use of computationally-supported narrative style roleplaying games. Drawing on both computer science and social science approaches, our system is aimed at (a) supporting players in perspective change through reflection and (b) modeling social

© The Author(s), under exclusive license to Springer Nature Switzerland AG 2023
X. Fang (Ed.): HCII 2023, LNCS 14046, pp. 154–171, 2023.
https://doi.org/10.1007/978-3-031-35930-9_11

phenomena such that players measurably better understand the perspectives of others with different social identities.

While these social identities may emerge from differences of various factors, such as nationality, ethnicity, gender, and values, the current study focuses on nationality and ethnicity, as they play a key role in individuals' proclivity for xenophobia. As a multidimensional construct, xenophobia refers to apprehensive, prejudiced, and exclusionary views and behaviors against individuals from different groups, countries, or nations [28]. Xenophobic individuals tend to exhibit in-group and out-group biases in terms of assuming that their group members (in-group) are superior to those from different backgrounds (out-group members) and of failing to openly accept out-group members into their perceived in-group community [23]. In addition, xenophobic tendencies usually manifest in the form of bullying and microaggressions directed at individuals perceived to be from an out-group, which can have a profound negative impact on out-group members' sense of belonging in the community into which they are integrating. Therefore, it is important to devise strategies to promote positive perspective-taking through interactive experiences.

In the current study, we address this need by developing and evaluating a visual novel style RPG addressing xenophobia and bullying. Our contributions include (a) the development of a computationally-supported roleplaying narrative game addressing xenophobia and bullying, and (b) empirical evaluation of its usability and effectiveness in promoting successful perspective-taking. In the following sections, we first provide a review of the relevant literature on roleplaying for perspective-taking and on bullying and then present the empirical studies.

2   Literature Review

2.1   Roleplaying for Perspective-Taking

Visual novel style RPGs have been used in previous studies for a variety of purposes. In one such study, Harrell et al. [4] developed an interactive narrative, called *Grayscale*, to encourage reflection on gender discrimination in the workplace. In relation to the potential of RPGs for supporting and promoting perspective-taking, the authors assert that it is possible to better model social identity and interactions in games that *"stands in stark contrast to a large swath of games that do not highly value complex models of identity for non-player characters."* These findings are expanded in a conference paper of the same year [24] and reported that the study *"successfully enabled [...] study participants to critically self-reflect on the themes of our interactive narrative."*

Roleplaying has been suggested as a tool for perspective-taking in different contexts and for different groups (see case studies of [30] for its use with preschool and elementary students; [13] for its effectiveness in adult therapy; [14] for its use in cross-cultural communication training; and [1] for its use in teacher education among others). Downey [7] asserts that for a successful roleplaying for perspective-taking activity, the participants (especially youth) need to be provided with sufficient background and information on the situation. Hughes [13] offers roleplaying games as cultural systems and game characters as personal symbols of reference in their role for therapy and healing. In a recent study in virtual reality (VR), Gupta et al. [27] provide four design principles for transformative roleplaying in virtual environments: (1) explicit and well specified roles to inhabit and enact; (2) coupling the player's body and the character's body when performing actions; (3) high interactional density; and (4) easing players gently into the roleplaying experience.

We base our approach of roleplaying for perspective-taking on previous literature of critical self-reflection [19] and its potential for behavior change (see [29] for an example of personal informatics, [18] for health, and [8] for education). Several other work (see [2,3,9]) present overviews of the work on reflection in relation to the field of human computer interaction (HCI).

2.2   Bullying

Microaggressions have been shown by clinical psychologists to be detrimental to mental and physical health. Many game players and social VR users face microaggressions around social class, gender, race, religion, disability, and so on. For instance, researchers at Columbia University have found that the experience of discrimination can result in traumatic stress [26]. This stress is linked to negative mental health outcomes, such as depression, anger, physical reactions, avoidance, intrusion, hypervigilance, and low self-esteem. Such experiences have significant costs in terms of healthcare, and profound impacts on feelings of societal cohesion and belonging.

Sue et al. [5] describe such microaggressive comments as falling into three categories: microassaults, microinsults, and microinvalidations. Microassaults are *"explicit derogation,"* which are meant to intentionally hurt an intended victim through name-calling or other epithets [5]. They also characterize microassaults as most likely to take place in private situations and with an added degree of subtlety. Microinsults, on the other hand, are characterized by a degree of rudeness, but often take place under the auspices of unaware perpetrators. Finally, a microinvalidation is any communication that *"excludes, negates, or nullifies the psychological thoughts, feelings, or experiential reality"* of the recipient of the microaggression. Sue offers the following example: *"A blind man reports that people often raise their voices when speaking to him. He responds by saying, 'Please don't raise your voice; I can hear you perfectly well.' (Hidden message: A person with a disability is defined as lesser in all aspects of physical and mental functioning)."* Although all of these varieties fall under the umbrella of microaggressions, they also represent a spectrum or continuum of discriminatory behavior, from overt to covert, intentional to unintentional.

Some common types of responses to microaggressions include:

- oblivious (ignoring the microaggression)
- confused (attempting to figure out if a microaggression occurred)

- suspicious (sitting in anger from self-doubt, and
- aggressive (striking back at the microaggression perpetrator)

The latter three types are derived from existing research in microaggressions [5]. To these, we added the *"oblivious"* type to cover cases in which the recipient is simply unaware of the implications of the exchange at hand or perhaps actively ignores or dismisses them.

2.3 Hypotheses

Based on our prior work regarding how to best achieve perspective transformation, we have formulated two main hypotheses regarding the effect of our RPG on players' perspectives:

H1: A computationally-supported RPG can result in reflective thinking that shifts players' perspectives of rival outgroups (negative relationship to the different group) toward seeing them as high affinity outgroups (positive relationship to the different group).

H2: A computationally-supported RPG can result in reflective thinking that shifts players' perspectives on high affinity outgroups toward seeing them as ingroups (members of the same group).

We base these hypotheses on results showing that one of the most efficacious means of supporting perspective change is to engage users in *"reflective think-ing"* [19–21], which we have previously designed systems to support. Particularly effective for perspective change are systems that engender critical self-reflection, the type of reflection characterized by individuals' reexamination of the presuppositions that inform their own beliefs, thoughts, and actions.

3   Computationally Supported Visual Novel

In this section we describe the Chimeria Engine that was mobilized to run our RPG, the development of the script, and how the resulting RPG game was used in an online study.

3.1 Narrative Engine

Chimeria narratives are formed of clauses (specifically orientation, entrance, narrative, decision, branch, evaluation, conclusion, and coda clauses). Each clause type is described by its role in a narrative, identifying its internal name in Chimeria. Note that the clause types correspond to some, but not all, typically recognized components of stories. But, some clause types are specific to the dynamic narrative capabilities of Chimeria. The primary source for many of these clause types is sociolinguist William Labov's [17] seminal empirical work on narratives of personal experience, but others have been added to support the unique interactive needs of Chimeria. Every clause has a type, a unique ID, text contents

```
CreateClause("decision", "step28.2b", "", "Byron").
    AddAction("You give Burnet a small placating smile.").
        AddFallout(IncrementActorFeatureValue("Status", gestureFalloutAmount, "Burnet")).
        AddFallout(IncrementActorFeatureValue("Self-Esteem", -gestureFalloutAmount, "Taran")).
        AddFallout(IncrementActorFeatureValue("Conformity", gestureFalloutAmount, "Byron")).
    AddAction("You do nothing.").
        AddFallout(IncrementActorFeatureValue("Status", (gestureFalloutAmount / 2f), "Burnet")).
        AddFallout(IncrementActorFeatureValue("Self-Esteem", (-gestureFalloutAmount / 2f), "Taran")).
        AddFallout(IncrementActorFeatureValue("Conformity", (gestureFalloutAmount / 2f), "Byron")).
    AddAction("You clap Taran on the shoulder, supportively.").
        AddFallout(IncrementActorFeatureValue("Status", -gestureFalloutAmount, "Burnet")).
        AddFallout(IncrementActorFeatureValue("Self-Esteem", gestureFalloutAmount, "Taran")).
        AddFallout(IncrementActorFeatureValue("Conformity", -gestureFalloutAmount, "Byron"));
```

(a) Sample Decision Clause Declaration

(b) Sample Decision Clause Display

Fig. 1. Chimeria Engine. (a) shows how a decision clause is declared and illustrates how authors can specify the effects of players' choices on characters' attributes. (b) shows how the clause is displayed to players on the graphic novel user interface (UI). Note that the UI is independent of the engine, so it can be customized for each narrative.

(or alternative choices) that are the clause's contribution to the story, and an Actor that is the source of the text. Additional characteristics can be added to most types. See Fig. 1 for an example of how clauses are declared and displayed in Chimeria.

The narrative structure component of Chimeria defines the sequencing of clauses in the narrative in two ways:

- Specific: by specifying particular clause identities; or
- Probabilistic: by specifying clause type, filtered by actor state, then chosen randomly.

The narrative structure is composed of a sequence (or possibly more complex network) of narrative elements, each of which identifies a specific clause or a clause type from which to select. Chimeria supports numerous ways of varying the narrative. The Chimeria narrative structure specifies the overall progression of clauses, while the clauses themselves can provide further variation to the user experience.

The narrative aspect of the Chimeria engine can be described as an Event Structure Machine [10]. Technically it is a *"probabilistic bounded transition stack machine"* in that it can probabilistically vary the details, while respecting a specified structure, when progressing through a narrative [10]. Going beyond presenting a fixed linear narrative, these variations provide a great deal of flexibility. This flexibility, nonetheless, places a higher design burden on the narrative author who needs to ensure that all possible traversals of the dynamic narrative work and make sense to the audience. These example variations are possible in Chimeria:

- variations in narrative structure triggered by player choices, varying the presentation order and details of various clauses.
- variations provided by clauses that are dependent on the state of category membership and naturalization trajectories, and Chimeria automatically choosing the next clause, filtered by clause type, filtered by actor and narrative state, then randomly selected (avoiding unwanted repetition).

When authoring the narrative, each clause can be provided with one or more tests of character narrative state. These author-specified tests, if all pass, qualify their clause for selection based on current character and narrative state. Tests are added to clauses to ensure that the clause instances that are chosen probabilistically are presented coherently within the changeable state of the narrative and its characters. These sources of variation make each traversal of any dynamic narrative fresh and new when experiencing many replays.

3.2   Narrative Script Development

The narrative was designed as an RPG and took place in a local shop in a fictional small country called *Virtualea*. The script was centered around an incident among the three characters of the narrative, as described below:

- **Burnet**, a native of *Virtualea*, is the shopkeeper with xenophobic attitudes toward outsiders. Burnet was the bully in this scenario.
- **Taran**, a member of the *Faraway clan* against whom citizens of *Virtualea* hold some prejudiced views, is the customer who visits the local shop to purchase essential food items for his family. Taran was the victim in this scenario.
- **Byron**, a native of *Virtualea*, is a local resident of the town. Byron was the bystander in this scenario. As part of our RPG, players assumed the role of Byron (bystander) and controlled his reactions to the exchange between Burnet (bully) and Taran (victim).

As shown in Fig. 2, the illustrations of the characters reflected the in-group vs. out-group membership of each character as per their persona. Taran, the victim in the narrative, was dressed ostensibly differently compared to Burnet and Byron. We have a strong concern for diversity, equity, and inclusion, which is represented in our labs work overall. The illustrations in this experience intentionally

Fig. 2. Narrative Characters

do not include characters of obviously different ethnic backgrounds in order to avoid confounding factors based in the biases of our experiment participants.

The narrative begins with a background story regarding *Virtualea* and the *Faraway clan*, describing the views of *Virtualea* citizens against outsiders and how this has led the *Faraway clan* to feeling unwelcome in the country and has forced them to the outskirts of the country. Despite the unwelcoming views of *Virtualea* citizens, members of the *Faraway clan* rely on the local shops in *Virtualea* for essentials, which is how we get to witness a rather unpleasant exchange between a proud *Virtualea* citizen, Burnet, and an outsider, Taran, through the perspective of our bystander, Byron.

The narrative was designed to give players the autonomy to change the direction of the narrative by choosing how their character, Byron (the bystander), should react to the situation. This was done to provide for a better gaming experience for players, as RPGs with branching decisions have been shown to lead to greater game enjoyment compared to RPGs with linear narratives [22]. Throughout the narrative, players made two major choices that determined the branching of the narrative with three possible outcomes (bully-supporting, victim-supporting, or neutral). In addition, players made two other choices that determined what gestures the bystander should make in response to dialog exchanges between the bully and target. These decision clauses led to fallout adjustments, meaning that characters' author-defined features were updated based on the selection made by players. More specifically, the author-defined feature was social status (power and influence over others) for the bully, self-esteem (confidence in one's own worth or abilities) for the victim, and conformity (support for the bully) for the bystander. Based on players' choices, these features were updated. Apart from player-made choices, the Chimeria engine also made automatic clause selections based on the characters' features. These engine-specified clauses portrayed characters' reactions based on their features. For instance, the bully would smile at the bystander if the player made a choice that supported her, and the victim would sigh in frustration. At the end of the narrative, players were presented with a coda corresponding to their standing in the game (i.e., the extent to which they supported the bully). This coda clause provided more context on how players' choices affected the bully, the victim, and the bystander.

3.3 Pilot Study

We performed a small-scale pilot study that aimed to test the usability of our system, as well as to elicit reactions to our bullying scenario. In the flow of the research, the participants first experienced the bullying scenario at least once and, then, as much as the user wanted through a Unity-based web app. Afterward, they went through three surveys on Qualtrics: (1) custom open-ended questions about the scenario; (2) System Usability Scale (SUS); and (3) User Demographics.

The pilot study had 23 participants with the mean of age 40 (R=60-22=38) who were 47.62% female and 52.38% male; almost 100% USA born & raised (1 in Canada); self-defined White (71.4%), with others mixed, and/or Asian, Black, Hispanic, and Pacific Islander. Our participants had high experiences with games (rated 3.05 out of 4) and roleplaying (rated 2.67 out of 4) in general.

For SUS, the participants rated our system as 4.3 (out of 5) for all positive responses (easy to use 4.9; sparks confidence 4.7; easy to learn 4.5; well-integrated 4; replayable 3.3) and 1.2 (out of 5) for all negative responses (inconsistent 1.4; complex 1.3; cumbersome 1.3; needs scaffolding 1.1; needs support to be used 1). The average SUS score was 85.6 (SD = 11.4). Given the industry standard of an average of 68 on the SUS, the perceived usability of our narrative system was considerably high.

Participants used similar words to describe the experience of the scenario (*discrimination* with 13 mentions, *intervention* with 6, *bullying* with 4, etc.) and what it was trying to achieve (*teach or train* with 8 mentions, *understanding* with 4, *encourage action* with 4, etc.). The majority (65.2%) did not see raising this issue as a game as being less comfortable. The majority (69.9%) also agreed that raising this issue as a game felt more engaging than seeing it in another kind of format. We also collected open ended responses. Representative responses include:

- *"This was designed to create an experience that is different enough from the participants' own world that they can separate themselves, but also similar enough that real life world issues can be simulated."*
- *"As a game, with fantasy characters especially, it does feel slightly separated from 'reality' and easier to 'tackle'. I wonder by raising this issue as a game, whether people would answer it honestly as 'themselves' or the character they are portraying."*
- *"I'd be curious for more ambiguous answers."*

4   Main Study

4.1   Experimental Design

Having established the usability of our system, we sought out to examine its effectiveness in affecting players' responses. For this purpose, we conducted a large-scale online experiment on Amazon Mechanical Turk (MTurk) to investigate whether the positioning of the protagonist as in-group vs. out-group affected players' responses, including both their in-game choices and perceptions of characters (the bully and the target). The independent variable of the experiment was the orientation type and was manipulated between-subjects, with each participant being assigned to one of the four orientation conditions. Specifically, the orientation types used in this study were as follows (see Table 1 for actual orientation clauses):

- **In-group connection:** the protagonist was positioned as a member of the same group as the bully, and the target was depicted as an outsider.
- **Out-group connection:** the protagonist was positioned as a member of the same group as the target and thus was depicted as an outsider to the bully's community.
- **Neutral connection:** the protagonist was positioned as a member of neither group; the orientation specified no in-group or out-group alignment and provided a neutral orientation clause.
- **No orientation:** no orientation clause was presented.

As for the dependent variables, Bystander Conformity (BC) and Transformative Reflection were measured in each condition. BC is an in-game metric that indicates the player's affinity with either the bully or the target. As mentioned before, throughout the narrative, players' choices resulted in fallout adjustments to their conformity feature. At the end of the gameplay, the greater the BC value was, the more bully-aligned the player was throughout the game. The Learning Activities Survey (LAS) instrument was administered as a measure of the extent to which the game was effective in promoting transformative reflection [16].

4.2   Sample

The sample included 211 MTurk workers with an average age of 37.6 ($SD = 9.95$). Some 39.3% of the sample reported identifying with female gender ($n = 83$), 59.7% with male gender (n = 126), and 0.47% with nonbinary (n = 1).

4.3   Visual Novel

Participants interacted with the same online visual novel as used in the previous pilot study. The major difference was the orientation clause used to position the protagonist differently as a function of the experimental condition. This resulted in four different version of the same visual novel, with each using one of the

Table 1. Orientation Clauses

Orientation Type	Orientation Clause
In-group connection	You are Byron, proudly born and raised in Virtualea. You need to buy bread and milk before the storm as thunderclouds are on the horizon. You decide to go to a well-known local shop owned by another Virtualea native for food. You've just entered your local shop and found Burnet, the shopkeeper, having an argument with Taran, a member of the Faraway clan. What will you do?
Out-group connection	You are Byron, a newcomer to Virtualea from another group called the Faraway clan. You need to buy bread and milk before the storm as thunderclouds are on the horizon. You decide to go to the nearest local shop for food. You've just entered the shop and found the shopkeeper, whose name you overhear is Burnet, having an argument with Taran, who, like you, is a member of the Faraway clan. What will you do?
Neutral	You are Byron, a person living in Virtualea. You need to buy bread and milk before the storm as thunderclouds are on the horizon. You've just entered your local shop and found the shopkeeper, whose name you overhear is Burnet, having an argument with a member of the Faraway clan whose name you gather is Taran. Will you side with either of them?
No orientation	No orientation clauses was presented

four orientation clauses presented in Table 1. Figure 3 shows an example of how the orientation clause was displayed on the visual novel UI. After completing the visual novel, participants were directed to an online survey where they completed the study measures.

4.4   Procedure

The online study was posted on MTurk. MTurk workers were able to read the description and sign up for the study. The sign-up survey first presented participants with an informed consent form. Participants were then presented with a link to one of the four versions of the visual novel, which was randomly chosen. Participants interacted with the visual novel and made choices throughout the narrative. At the end of the narrative, participants were directed to another online survey containing the study measures. At the end of this second survey, participants were given a confirmation code that they needed to submit on the MTurk page as proof of their completion of the study. The entire study took less than 15 min (with an average completion time of 11 min), and MTurk workers were compensated with $2.00 in exchange for their completion of the study.

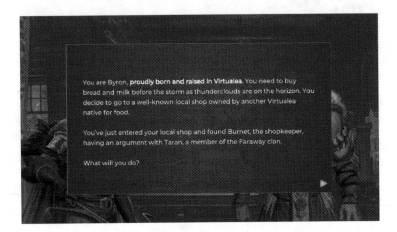

Fig. 3. Orientation Clause

4.5   Results

Bystander Conformity. We were mainly interested in the influence of the positioning of the protagonist on bystander conformity, i.e., the player's affinity with either the bully or the victim. Figure 4 shows the distribution of Bystander Conformity values as a function of the orientation type. A one-way analysis of variance (ANOVA) was conducted to investigate the effect of orientation type on players' affinity with either of the characters. Results revealed no significant differences among the four orientation types, $F(3, 207) = 1.04$, $p = .377$.

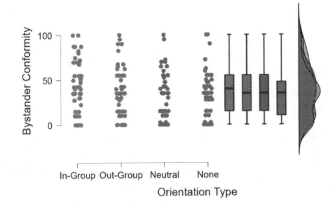

Fig. 4. The Effect of Orientation Type on Bystander Conformity

Transformative Reflection. In relation to the effect of the orientation types on players' engagement in tranformative reflection during the gameplay, we analyzed participants' LAS scores, which are visualized in Fig. 5. Results from one-way ANOVA showed no significant differences among the four orientation types, $F(3, 207) = .125$, $p = .945$.

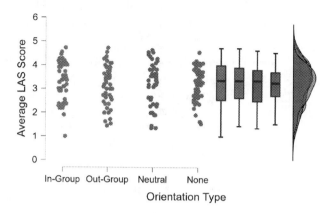

Fig. 5. The Effect of Orientation Type on Transformative Reflection

Qualitative Analysis. The goal of the qualitative analysis was to gain a deeper understanding of the experiences of the participants. To this end we analyzed the answers to three open-ended questions by a combination of lexical analysis [12,25] and codebook [15] methods.

To analyze the answers to question "Briefly describe what happened," we qualitatively determined lexicon groups that could be associated with our research aims and calculated word frequencies by revising the textual data based on the context and semantically-grouped lexicons as needed. This resulted in five categories: (1) personal-only descriptions; (2) a combination of personal and character-name based descriptions; (3) character-name based descriptions; (4) character-status based descriptions; and (5) distant descriptions (see Table 2).

Table 2. Response Analysis to Question "Briefly describe what happened"

Category	Words	Percentage
Personal-only Descriptions	I only	45.1%
Character-name Based	Names only	21.6%
Combined	I, Names	15.7%
Character-status	Shopkeeper, Customer	9.8%
Distant Descriptions	Three, People, Them	7.8%

Personal-only Descriptions: 23 out of 51 responses (45.1%) never mentioned characters in their response and directly described the situation through a personal lens. Some examples are: *"I realized how important it is to not just stay silent, and to speak up when you hear things like happening,"* *"I thought about* *how I don't usually say anything out loud when I see someone treating someone else badly due to a trait that they cannot change,"* and *"I was proactive than I would usually be."* Although this indicates high-empathy toward the situation, we also recognize its distance from the roleplaying aspect of the application.

Combination of Personal and Character-Name Based Descriptions: 8 out of 51 responses (15.7%) used a combination of character names and "I" to describe what happened. Some examples are: *"this has happened to me several times in my life when I have been treated like Taran and someone has stood up for me at times[, there] were also times where I had to stand up for myself,"* *"last month in a grocery shop I was treated like the Taron with shop attender,"* and *"I nodded my head after Taran had spoke."* We see this category at the intersection of high-empathy and successful roleplaying since the comments indicate that they were able to empathize both with the situation and the characters.

Character-Name Based Descriptions: 11 out of 51 responses (21.6%) used only the names of the characters in their descriptions and did not make any personal connections. Some examples are: *"Taran was told to leave the store by the shopowner [...] Byron was silent and didn't do very much [...] The shopowner eventually got what she wanted,"* *"[Byron] is fundamentally influenced by the people,"* and *"The shop owner's behavior was little bad towards Taran."* We see this as an example of moderate empathy since the participants perceive the events through characters without acknowledging that they had a role to play.

Character-Status Based Descriptions: 5 out of 51 responses (9.8%) used words like shopowner, shopkeeper, or customer to describe the situation, never mentioning names or not fore-fronting their personal perspectives strongly. Some examples are: *"It is about the shopping and satisfy the customer need"* and *"I thought the shopkeeper should be a little more lenient especially since the customer had money to pay."*

Distant Descriptions: 4 out of 51 responses (7.8%) used words like *people* or *three* to describe the situation as distantly as possible. Some examples are: *"argument between three [...]"* and *"they [are] just talking and arguing about some problem."* We see the final two categories as the least empathetic responses as well as having the most distance to the effects of roleplaying. The being said, the former category at least acknowledges the roleplaying aspect of the story by relaying character status.

To analyze the answers to question "What influenced this change?," we created a codebook wherein we categorized the answers into four categories: (1) actor behaviors (41.2%), (2) introspection (29.4%), (3) story events (19.6%), and (4) reaction to injustice (9.8%).

Actor Behaviors: 21 out of 51 responses (41.2%) stated that their transformative change was the result of actor behaviors (presented as dialogue in our application). Some examples are: *"[...] when it said that Burnette will likely pause before doing something similar, as she did to that other customer," "I saw Taran being excluded from what should have been an ordinary interaction,"* and *"that customer's politeness."*

Introspection: 15 out of 51 responses (29.4%) mentioned a personal reflection and introspection as the reason for their transformation without mentioning the characters or scenario. Some examples are: *"I think that it was a serious of various interactions and experiences that I have had in the recent past that have helped me in this area," "a previous life situation,"* and *"[...] being bullied for my race is what lead me to understand how discrimination feels like."*

Story Events: 10 out of 51 responses (19.6%) mentioned a story event as their reason for transformative change. Some examples are: *"situation made [an] influence"* and *"reading the narrative at the end."*

Reaction to Injustice: 5 out of 51 responses (9.8%) provided their general reaction to injustices as their reasons for transformation. Some examples are: *"just seeing injustice and bullying," "I think that being fair and nice to others pays back [we] do not have to be mean and discriminate [to others] just because..."* and *"nothing can be judged by one's appearance."*

To analyze the answers to question "What did your experience with our simulation have to do with the experience of change?," we created another codebook wherein we categorized the answers into six categories: (1) learning (35.3%), (2) association (17.6%), (3) conversations (15.7%), (4) roleplaying (9.8%), (5) acting as self (9.8%), and (6) no relation (13.7%).

Learning: 18 out of 51 responses (35.3%) stated that they learned from the experience and articulated what they learned. Some things that were cited as learned were *"respecting people," "how the bully thinks and how we should respond to it,"* and *"to stand up to bullies."* Three responses specifically brought up how reading the coda affected their change.

Association: 9 out of 51 responses (17.6%) associated their change with how the experience related to their own lives. Some examples are: *"the game made me think about that I need to have more courage if I'm ever in a situation that calls for me to act," "many [people] discouraged me a lot [, but I] decided to overcome all the challenges in my life,"* and *"it brought me back to my own experiences [..and...] how it feels like to be discriminated against."*

Conversations: 8 out of 51 responses (15.7%) mentioned that reading and determining the flow of the dialogue was effective in triggering their change. These participants reasoned that *"understanding the conversation"* and the *"meanness"* of the dialogue were what triggered the change.

No Relation: 7 out of 51 responses (13.7%) were not able to articulate or find any relationship between how they changed and the experience (which might mean they did not experience any change or they were not able to pinpoint what initiated their change).

Roleplaying or Not Roleplaying: 5 out of 51 (9.8%) and 4 out of 51 (7.8%) responses reasoned that not roleplaying or roleplaying, respectively, were associated with their change. These participants either stated that roleplaying as a character (e.g., *"it made me realize [that] I was caving and doing something I'm morally against in order to receive goods"*) or going through the experience as themselves made them consider what was happening in a different light (e.g., *"I gave my own perspective [as if I was] there at the situation"*).

5   Discussion and Conclusion

The results from our pilot study provide support for the usability of our interactive, narrative-style RPG. In relation to the empirical evaluation of our RPG, results were ambivalent. On the one hand, the quantitative results were inconsistent with our hypotheses. On the other hand, we have found strong self-reported indicators of perspective change in the qualitative results (based on the data provided by 51 of the 211 participants (24.2%).

For quantitative analyses, we expected that the way the players were positioned in the beginning of the game would influence their in-game choices. For this purpose, we had four different conditions, each with a different orientation (in-group connection, out-group connection, neutral connection, or no orientation). At a more granular level, we expected that players whose orientation clause provided an in-group connection to the bully would be more likely to align with the bully when making branching and gesture choices in our RPG. This would mean greater conformity scores for players in the in-group connection condition. By the same token, players whose orientation clause provided an out-group connection to the victim would be more likely to align with the victim when making branching and gesture choices in our RPG. This would lead to lower conformity scores for players in the out-group connection condition. Results revealed no significant differences among these conditions in relation to players' affinity for the bully or the victim. Similarly, the orientation had no significant effect on the extent to which players engaged in transformative reflection.

Our findings from the quantitative data are inconsistent with the Mimesis Effect, which posits that when players are given an explicit role in an RPG, their in-game actions will reflect their role description [6]. As a possible explanation, we postulate that the manipulation of the orientation clause in our experiment may not have been strong enough to engender changes in players' in-game choices. One implication of the findings is that future studies should employ stronger manipulations. It should be noted, nonetheless, that there may be a small effect that cannot be detected with the sample size of our experiment.

As for our qualitative data, the open-ended responses from the participants contained indicators of self-reported perspective change. First, our lexicon analysis revealed indicators of high situational empathy and the characters: 45.1% of the qualitative responses described the scenario as personal experiences and 82.4% of the total responses (including the previous category) used a combination of personal pronouns (indicating a personal experience) along with character names to describe the events of the story. This is echoed by the responses to our second question, wherein a total of 70.6% of the qualitative responses indicated that their perspective change was triggered by either actor behaviors or personal introspection about the events. Finally, 35.5% of the qualitative responses indicated that they learned more about bullying dynamics through observing actor behaviors.

Taken together, quantitative results and qualitative insights indicate that: (1) our narrative system had high usability; (2) a stronger orientation was needed to encourage roleplaying-the participants did not roleplay their character and chose to omit their character's allegiance; but, despite this shortcoming, (3) they self-reported high situational empathy toward the scenario and characters; as well as (4) perspective change triggered by (learning from) actor behaviors and introspection.

As a future research direction, we plan on replicating the same study with more strongly worded or participant-selected orientations and on investigating whether results would differ in a more immersive environment. For this purpose, we are actively working on developing a 3D version of the same RPG so that it can be played both on desktop platforms and virtual reality platforms. By comparing players' responses to different orientations across these platforms, we hope to better ascertain the confluence of immersion and orientation types on players' in-game choices during RPGs.

References

1. Athanases, S.Z., LSanchez, S.: 'A caesar for our time': toward empathy and perspective-taking in new teachers' drama practices in diverse classrooms. Res. Drama Educ. J. Appl. Theatre Perform. **25**(2), 236–255 (2020)
2. Baumer, E.P.: Reflective informatics: conceptual dimensions for designing technologies of reflection. In: Proceedings of the 33rd Annual ACM Conference on Human Factors in Computing Systems, pp. 585–594 (2015)
3. Baumer, E.P., Khovanskaya, V., Matthews, M., Reynolds, L., Schwanda Sosik, V., Gay, G.: Reviewing reflection: on the use of reflection in interactive system design. In: Proceedings of the 2014 Conference on Designing Interactive Systems, pp. 93–102 (2014)

4. Harrell, D.F., Ortiz, P., Downs, P., Wagoner, M., Carre, E., Wang, A.: Chimeria: Grayscale: an interactive narrative for provoking critical reflection on gender discrimination (2018)
5. Sue, D.W., et al.: Racial microaggressions in everyday life: implications for clinical practice. Am. Psychol. **62**(4), 271 (2007)
6. Domínguez, I.X., Cardona-Rivera, R.E., Vance, J.K., Roberts, D.L.: The mimesis effect: the effect of roles on player choice in interactive narrative role-playing games. In: Proceedings of the 2016 CHI Conference on Human Factors in Computing Systems, pp. 3438–3449 (2016)
7. Downey, M.T.: Doing history in a fifth-grade classroom: Perspective taking and historical thinking. In: American Educational Research Association (AERA) Annual Meeting, San Francisco, pp. 18–22 (1995)
8. O'Rourke, E., Haimovitz, K., Ballweber, C., Dweck, C., Popović, Z.: Brain points: a growth mindset incentive structure boosts persistence in an educational game. In: Proceedings of the SIGCHI Conference on Human Factors in Computing Systems, pp. 3339–3348 (2014)
9. Fleck, R., Fitzpatrick, G.: Reflecting on reflection: framing a design landscape. In: Proceedings of the 22nd Conference of the Computer-Human Interaction Special Interest Group of Australia on Computer-Human Interaction, pp. 216–223 (2010)
10. Harrell, D.F.: Walking blues changes undersea: imaginative narrative in interactive poetry generation with the griot system. In: AAAI 2006 Workshop in Computational Aesthetics: Artificial Intelligence Approaches to Happiness and Beauty, pp. 61–69 (2006)
11. Harrell, D.F., Kao, D., Lim, C.U., Lipshin, J., Sutherland, A.: Stories of stigma and acceptance using the Chimeria platform. In: Proceedings of the Electronic Literature Organization Conference 2014: Hold the Light (ELO 2014) (2014)
12. Freitas, H., Moscarola, J., Jenkins, M.: Content and lexical analysis: a qualitative practical application. ISRC, Merrick School of Business, University of Baltimore (MD, EUA), WP ISRC (070498), 35 (1998)
13. Hughes, J.: Therapy is fantasy: roleplaying, healing and the construction of symbolic order. In: Anthropology IV Honours, Medical Anthropology Seminar, Dept. of Prehistory & Anthropology, Australian National University (1988)
14. Klafehn, J., Inglese, P., Davis, C.A.: Walking a mile in simulated shoes: Development of an assessment of perspective taking. In: Proceedings of the Eleventh annual MODSIM World Conference (2018)
15. DeCuir-Gunby, J.T., Marshall, P.L., McCulloch, A.W.: Developing and using a codebook for the analysis of interview data: an example from a professional development research project. Field Methods **23**(2), 136–155 (2011)
16. King, K.P.: The handbook of the evolving research of transformative learning: based on the Learning Activities Survey. IAP (2009)
17. Labov, W.: Oral narratives of personal experience. Cambridge encyclopedia of the language sciences, pp. 546–548 (2010)
18. Mamykina, L., Mynatt, E.D., Davidson, P., Greenblatt, D.: MAHI: investigation of social scaffolding for reflective thinking in diabetes management. In: Proceedings of the SIGCHI Conference on Human Factors in Computing Systems, pp. 477–486 (2008)
19. Mezirow, J.: Perspective transformation. Adult Educ. **28**(2), 100–110 (1978)
20. Mezirow, J.: Learning as transformation: critical perspectives on a theory in progress. The Jossey-Bass Higher and Adult Education Series, ERIC (2000)
21. Mezirow, J., Marsick, V.: Education for perspective transformation. women's reentry programs in community colleges (1978)

22. Moser, C., Fang, X.: Narrative structure and player experience in role-playing games. Int. J. Hum.-Comput. Inter. **31**(2), 146–156 (2015)
23. Olonisakin, T.T., Adebayo, S.O.: Xenophobia: scale development and validation. J. Contemp. Afr. Stud. **39**(3), 484–496 (2021)
24. Ortiz, P., Harrell, D.F.: Enabling critical self-reflection through roleplay with Chimeria: Grayscale. In: Proceedings of the 2018 Annual Symposium on Computer-Human Interaction in Play, pp. 353–364 (2018)
25. Richard Bolden, J.M.: Bridging the quantitative-qualitative divide: the lexical approach to textual data analysis. Soc. Sci. Comput. Rev. **18**(4), 450–460 (2000)
26. Carter, R.T., et al.: Initial development of the race-based traumatic stress symptom scale: Assessing the emotional impact of racism. Psychol. Trauma: Theory Res. Pract. Policy **5**(1), 1 (2013)
27. Gupta, S., Tanenbaum, T.J., Muralikumar, M.D., Marathe, A.S.: Investigating roleplaying and identity transformation in a virtual reality narrative experience. In: Proceedings of the 2020 CHI Conference on Human Factors in Computing Systems, pp. 1–13 (2020)
28. Soyombo, O.: Xenophobia in contemporary society: a sociological analysis. IFE Psychol. Int. J. **16**(2), 85–104 (2008)
29. Consolvo, S., McDonald, D.W., Landay, J.A.: Theory-driven design strategies for technologies that support behavior change in everyday life. In: Proceedings of the SIGCHI Conference on Human Factors in Computing Systems, pp. 405–414 (2009)
30. Wentink, E.: The effect of a social perspective-taking training on role-taking ability and social interaction in preschool and elementary school children (1975)

Critical Success Factors to Evaluate Startup Success

Stephanie Zhao[1], Lauren Fang[2], Gene Hoyt[3], and Fan Zhao[3]([✉])

[1] University of Florida, Gainesville, FL 32611, USA
[2] Naperville North High School, Naperville, IL 60563, USA
[3] Florida Gulf Coast University, Fort Myers, FL 33965, USA
fzhao@fgcu.edu

Abstract. Startup companies are newly established businesses that are trying to survive and expand. These organizations are typically formed from innovative ideas and aim to grow to be successful. Every year thousands of new startups are established, however, most of them fail within a short period of time. This paper attempts to establish a systematic method to predict the success of a new startup through a case study. We develop a critical success factor framework within the Lifecycle of Startups. The factors within this framework were utilized in the business success prediction. In the case analysis, the results show a positive successful status of DecorDash in Lifecycle Stage 1. Factors from Stage 2 and Stage 3 are also discussed. The paper concludes with some implications of startup success prediction.

Keywords: Critical Success Factors · startup · business success · gamification

1 Introduction

For a company to be characterized as a startup it is not necessary that it works with technology, or obtains investment, or even that it is innovative. The only necessary requirement is scalability (capacity for exponential growth). Every other factor commonly associated with startups is somehow related to growth.

A startup is a company structured to grow quickly and continuously. This is exactly why it is so difficult to succeed in this market. The good side of this is that if there is growth, the whole business tends to work out. To grow fast and relentlessly, startups need a scalable business model and a broad market that is validated. This is the primary difference between a restaurant and a social network, for example. While a restaurant can accommodate up to a maximum number of people due to its own physical structure, a social media like Facebook has the capacity to support billions of users.

To have a successful startup, innovation is the key word. In addition, there are other exponential factors and unique characteristics that make the entrepreneur able to go through all the difficult and inevitable phases that the business goes through. Based on that, this literature review will focus on two important questions: What are the critical success factors for a successful startup business? And how to make a startup business successful? This review will analyze those key factors that are crucial for a startup to be successful in the market.

X. Fang (Ed.): HCII 2023, LNCS 14046, pp. 172–186, 2023.
https://doi.org/10.1007/978-3-031-35930-9_12

2 Literature Review

2.1 Entrepreneurship – Necessity vs Opportunity

When talking about startup, it is also about entrepreneurship. The culture of entrepreneurship is very strong and present in our society. Every day, people with creative and innovative minds put their ideas into practice, make successful businesses and stand out in the market [1].

However, not everyone jumps into the entrepreneurship scenario motivated by their own dreams. Entrepreneurship consists of an initiative to open a business and offer something relevant to people. The motivations behind this act may vary and are often a picture of the degree of incentive and development of entrepreneurial practices in a country. However, there are those who undertake because they see a business opportunity and those who undertake motivated by necessity, because they cannot find alternatives [1].

The entrepreneur by necessity is the one who decides to invest in his own business because the situation in which he finds himself ended up leading him to it. In general, the entrepreneur by necessity is that person who has been unemployed for some time and cannot find a job.

It could also be that professional who stayed away from the job market for many years and is struggling to get a professional replacement. These are the people who find in entrepreneurship a way to earn income and get around their financial problems—or even problems related to self-esteem and a professional career [2].

This type of entrepreneurship often gives entrepreneurs the opportunity to develop talents and new skills that their former careers would not provide in the same way. As the name suggests, entrepreneurship by necessity arises when a person finds himself without other possibilities to guarantee his livelihood. So, it starts with its own initiative, with autonomy, to generate income.

In this modality, entrepreneurs do not have much commercial knowledge or access to significant capital to invest. Often, they are individuals who have lost their jobs and are experiencing a reduction in their family income. With little professional experience, they find in their own business a chance to have more financial stability and also personal fulfillment [2].

Opportunity entrepreneurship, on the other hand, occurs when the entrepreneur identifies a particular need or desire in society. This demand creates the opportunity for this entrepreneur to offer the solution that people ask for in the form of a product or service. In general, this type of entrepreneurship comes from an individual choice, in which the person has skills to be exploited in favor of the market. These are individuals with access to some capital and prior business knowledge. They undertake in a more planned and strategic way, unlike those who undertake out of necessity [2].

Opportunity entrepreneurs are, therefore, extremely observant, and attentive to market demands. Combining their financial reserves and their knowledge, they take the bold step of overcoming the challenges of having a business, but they do it by choice [2].

2.2   Challenges in Entrepreneurship

Entrepreneurs face several challenges during their journey, and some of them are always a constant pain. Every person who undertakes, whether large or small, faces an endless stream of challenges in their business almost daily. Innovation and bureaucracy (legal and regulation) are two of the most common challenges entrepreneurs face on a daily basis. In addition, problems with management of individuals and financial management are also other obstacles that entrepreneurs have to deal with [3].

Within management of individuals, the main difficulty pointed out by entrepreneurs is in training leaders for the company. Training leaders is a fundamental point for any business. Without good leaders, the company cannot move forward and ends up going in circles. For this challenge to be overcome, it will be necessary to invest more in actions aimed at developing leaders [4]. If talking about finances is already complicated, in a year of crisis, managing the company's finances becomes an even greater challenge for entrepreneurs. Perhaps this scenario is a great way to explain the practically equal, and high, marks attributed by the surveyed groups [4].

2.3   Startups in the Current Market

In the current startup market, there is no room for those who settle for less. To grow exponentially, entrepreneurs need to desire, plan and work hard for it. Investors are looking for companies that can scale globally and build a business of great value to society.

Growing a lot is not only a question of financial survival, but it is also part of the very nature of the market in which competition is fierce. If the entrepreneur does not think about scaling, his competitors will, in turn removing him from the market.

A startup is an extremely risky venture because it operates under conditions. Although a lot of study and planning is required, being proactive is even more important. Quick results and quick learnings require quick actions. In a startup, most of the time it is better to make a mistake doing it than to make the mistake of thinking too much, after all, it is always possible to extract knowledge from experiences [5].

In addition, investors are the key for startups to take off. There are aspects that everyone looks for and values in a company, such as the technical execution capacity of the team and their motivation, integrity, and leadership capacity. Investors are looking for startups that have a high potential for scalability, so they will invariably keep an eye on numbers, team performance and market size [5].

2.4   Lean Startup

Created in 2012, Lean Startup is a method for developing companies and products that is based on the principles of lean production, a manufacturing methodology that values the ability of a business to change quickly.

Furthermore, the Lean method, if done well, can shorten product development cycles through the adoption of a combination of experimentation. If entrepreneurs invested time in building products or services repeatedly to meet the needs of initial customers, they would reduce market risks and could circumvent the need for large amounts of initial project funding and expensive, failed product launches [6].

The Lean Startup methodology aims to eliminate wasteful practices and increase value-producing practices during the product development phase, so that startups can increase their chances of success without the need for large amounts of external investment, elaborate deals, or the perfect product. In this methodology, customer feedback during product development is essential for startup development, ensuring that the developer does not waste time designing features or services that consumers do not want. This is done primarily through two processes: the use of performance metrics and a continuous deployment process. [6].

2.5 Startup Life Cycle

As all startup companies have development stages, startups are no different. Startups have stages from their foundation to consolidation in the market as sustainable and profitable. The first phase is "Solving a problem", which consists of the initial research phase regarding the audience and which business models best suit the organization's emerging ideas [7].

Once the company knows the customer profile and their expectations regarding the product, its sales are established without great efforts (viral effect) and if consumer acquisition costs are structured, it is time to move on to the second stage called of "Development". This phase is marked by positive cash flow (revenues cover costs) and restructuring of employees and internal processes [7].

In the "Market-Entry" or "Scaling" phase, the company has already acquired greater liquidity and is growing more steadily. It is the moment when it focuses on Key Performance Indicators (KPIs). For startup business models to be promising, it is essential that these companies analyze their position in the market and the position of other companies, focusing on their critical success factors. The final phase is called "maturity" [7]. This phase is when the company got an established foothold in the market, have a good customer retention rate, are influencing the industry and turning a profit. As soon as the company is giving these types of results, it is a fairly good bet that it is nearing the maturity stage [8].

2.6 Business Model - Startup

To avoid these types of challenges mentioned above, having a well-formulated business model is a key point in the development and growth of the startup. The business model is how a company creates value for customers. From the business model, a company defines the main aspects to be able to put the enterprise into practice. That is, the model allows a macro view of what is essential for the project to work [9].

There are different types of business models for startups. Some of them are more scalable, others are more affordable or faster to release. Even disruptive ideas can give rise to new business models that are not yet used. The four most important types of business models used today are: marketplace, e-commerce, Saas, and franchising [9].

The marketplace format is one of the most scalable today. After all, it is possible to reach a large number of customers without having to increase business costs in the same proportion. Many entrepreneurs, when considering launching a business, immediately think of creating a virtual store. The biggest attraction is that the business is popular, simple, and cheap [10].

Another business model for startups is SaaS (software as a service). This type of solution works as an autonomous software in the cloud and serves to automate processes that would previously be manual. Typically, the SaaS model charges users a monthly fee. That is, the customer does not buy the software source code, but a monthly license to use the service offered [9]. Franchising is also a well-known type of business among those who want to undertake. In it, the franchisor grants the franchisees the right to use its trademark. In return, franchisees pay a percentage of profits to the brand owner [10].

2.7 Pre-startup Planning

The planning phase can be defined in depth and intense research on the problem and the market entrepreneurs want to explore. At this stage, it is very important to put into practice falling in love with the problem, not the solution.

Ideation is not just a time to come up with ideas, but to outline problems and identify solutions capable of easing the client's pain. Therefore, the great challenge is precisely to validate the solutions, products and services that really add value to the target audience, in order to have the potential to become a highly scalable business [11].

Thus, the startup starts with this funding, or even the founders themselves put a certain amount to start. Then, the founders go after investors capable of lending a certain amount of money that makes it possible to run the business: the angel investor [12].

Angel investment is the first round of investments for a startup and aims to test the business thesis, assemble the team capable of executing and developing the idea. So, when focusing on the preliminary growth phase of a startup, it needs investors who are willing to take risks, with the possibility of earning many times the invested capital [11].

2.8 Success Factors for Startups

Critical success factors in startups include aspects such as agility, flexibility, integration, and innovation. The human factor is decisive for the success or failure of most organizational projects. Within the scope of startup-type ventures, they also consider that intellectual capital is one of the factors that contribute to the development of an incubated startup.

The success of startups can be measured through studies carried out among their investors. The items that are most relevant for investors to support a startup and believe that it will bring many benefits are the multidisciplinary training of the team, followed by innovative ideas and the technology available [13].

It is worth noting that investors also prioritize the fact that the product is launched in a timely manner and that startups are aware of the legal aspects involved in the project. There is still a classification from the point of view of the startup founder that analyzes the most relevant factors during the development of his venture [14].

The factors that were most relevant from the entrepreneurs' point of view were the team's expertise in the project's area of activity, hiring the appropriate team, knowledge in the startup's area of activity and planning, in order respectively. From the point of view of startup investors, the only factor that differentiates is planning, in which, although this is important for them, the degree of innovation and scalability are more important. In addition, the number of partners involved, the volume of capital invested and the location where the startup will be installed are key factors that must be considered when designing the company [15].

When talking about starting a startup, innovation becomes crucial because it is the only way to stand out among the competition. The current practice of innovation is related to the longevity of the business. The customer acquisition owes much to their perception of value of what they are presented [16]. Customers buy or adhere to a product that present certain benefits, whether best features beyond those competitors are alternatives with lower price. The main advantages that any startup can include in the innovation of its business idea is to have competitive advantage, more efficiency and productivity, and competition with larger companies [16].

2.9 Indicators for Success

KPIs are the main targets to make the maximum impact on strategic results in startups. KPIs support the company's strategy and help teams focus on what's important.

Using KPIs in startups is the only way to know exactly where the company is going and keep the business on track. After all, this type of company requires quick and accurate decisions, and only performance indicators offer parameters for truly agile management. When well designed, managed and measured, KPIs offer a clear view of the company's situation and detail the progress in each of the essential activities and processes. So, when all employees have access to metrics, it is easy to keep everyone moving in the same direction and focused on what really matters to achieve success [17]. In addition, just check the indicators to understand how close the company is to its goals. Therefore, they are also useful for showing the startup's value to investors, as they are full proof of the company's evolution and detail its performance in strategic areas. For this, KPIs in startups need to be fully aligned with business goals and follow a series of criteria.

There are eight KPIs for startups: total addressable market, customer acquisition cost, customer retention rate, lifetime value, customer acquisition, cost recovery time, monthly burn, runway, and profit margin [17].

Here are some reasons it is important for startup businesses to use all these KPIs: Showing growth - using KPIs can give startup companies insight into their recent progress, which allows them to estimate future growth [17]. They may look at their most recent cash flow statements and monthly burn value to determine the rate at which they may grow in the upcoming sales period; Identify areas of improvement - KPIs allow startup businesses to recognize areas of improvement within their business model. For example, if a company recognizes that it has a low runway, then company staff may conduct fundraisers to increase their workplace's runway and help it sustain growth for a longer period of time; and Give investors insight into sales potential – it is important for startup companies to gain investors to grow their business and expand their budget. KPIs allow investors to identify a startup's financial forecast and determine if they want to invest in it or not [17].

2.10 Failure Factors for Startups

The risks involved in the decision-making process of a startup are exponentially linked to its growth. As the company develops, structural problems arise that can be solved if there is a coherent basis for each strategic action. Therefore, it is important to seek a reproducible and scalable business model.

At this stage, finding a sales channel that meets the customers in terms of cost and perceived quality delivery is essential to start the process of structured growth and scale gains. Additionally, strategic problems involved in the absence and inconsistency of planning as well as incorrect rationalization of costs and other factors may lead to the failure of startups [18].

The reasons for failure of startups can be related to personal or external factors. In personal factors, business planning and management, administrative and financial management are highlighted. As external factors, technical and financial support, taxes, and bureaucracy are highlighted [18].

On the other hand, the failure of startups is more related to the environment in which these companies are inserted and the very structure that was determined at the time of conception, than with the personal characteristics of the entrepreneur himself, such as education level, knowledge, and experiences. in the area of management, networking capacity, among others [19].

2.11 Sustainability in Startups

Sustainable entrepreneurship is characterized by startups that combine the generation of wealth with the responsible addition of the environment. In short, it is the term used to define companies that carry out their activities based on measures that do not harm nature.

The actions that make up a sustainable company range from the simplest, such as reusing office paper, to even the creation of programs and projects for environmental causes. Possessing as fundamental characteristics: investments in sustainable alternatives - it looks for investments that impact in the reduction of the degradation of the environment; understanding of the consumer's need - applying the concept in the business, he seeks ways to soften the impact of resources, such as, for example, packaging; and they promote programs and make people aware - recycling programs are created, energy consumption awareness, habit re-education [20].

However, changing the mental pattern and the way of doing business is the challenge that is imposed on individuals and companies in times of equations with complex solutions. Reconciling population growth and increased consumption with a decrease in natural resources therefore presupposes facing an incredible management challenge [21].

For companies that really want to make a difference and positively impact the sector itself, governments, and society, going beyond palliative measures and focusing on the core of socio-environmental challenges in their processes are decisive attitudes in the quest for sustainability. However, the most relevant issues – both related to products and environmental history and reputation – are often replaced by proposals that are simpler to implement. Maintaining social projects is the classic example of how many believe they collaborate with sustainability [20].

With the dissemination of the concept of sustainability, the act of consuming will never again be something banal – more and more people are thinking twice before buying. In addition to being useful and efficient, products must be in line with the individual's values. Creativity to deliver solutions that add performance and efficiency, practicality and socio-environmental concern has become an imperative for any company. Sustainability means, therefore, a genuine opportunity for the emergence of new business niches [20].

Bringing sustainability to business management strategically is certainly not a simple task. Companies have to be aware of the emerging opportunities of the new economy and act to make business, more and more, transforming agents for society in times of global warming and scarcity of resources. For this evolution to happen, however, a cultural change needs to gain space within organizations [21].

During the production process of a sustainability report, almost all corporations hold so-called "stakeholder panels" in which the interests of different audiences that are related, in some way, with the company are heard. Effectively incorporating these opinions into decision-making, however, represents a much longer path. In addition, if the debate goes beyond specific issues, the suggestions end up getting lost [21].

3 Research Framework

3.1 Lifecycle of the Company

The Lifecycle of a company can be broken down into three separate stages, the Bootstrapping stage, the Seed stage, and the Creation stage [7]. Each of these individual stages corresponds to a company's level of growth and the things that it must pay attention to.

In the Bootstrapping stage, the founder(s) starts the process to transition his or her idea into a working business. This stage's objective is to set up the undertaking for development by demonstrating if a product can be feasibly brought to the market, the cash management ability of the company, team collaboration and management, and customer approval [22]. Within the Bootstrapping stage, angel investors are also more likely to make an investment.

In the Seed stage, founder(s) begin developing their actual product or service. The stage is distinguished by team work, product development, market entry, the value of the venture, as well as investments to further grow the company [7]. The seed stage places emphasis on initial capital used to create the product or service. Many startups tend to fail in this stage due to not being able to find support mechanisms. However, those that do survive tend to have a higher success rate and a better chance at becoming a profit-making business (Fig. 1).

In the Creation stage, the founder(s) begin to enter the market and sell its product or service [7]. This is the stage in which employees are hired and larger investments are poured into the company. This stage is facilitated by venture capitals as they fund the venture that entrepreneurs are pursuing. By the end of the Creation stage, an organization or firm comes to be formed and the main choice for providing finances for the firm is corporate finance.

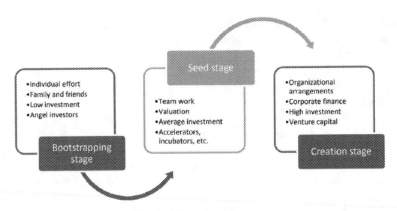

Fig. 1. Lifecycle of Startups

3.2 Research Framework

According to the literature review, we propose a research framework to explain the indicators predicting the success of a startup company in a lifecycle of startups (Fig. 2).

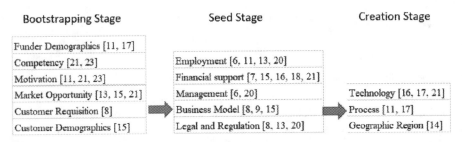

Fig. 2. Research Framework

4 Case Study

4.1 Background of the Company

DecorDash offers services helping home owners/renters put up or take down seasonal decorations both indoors and outdoors. The group of Naperville North High School students aims to revolutionize the process in taking down and putting up decorations for the holidays to make the task less stressful and more accessible to home owners/renters. They conducted a survey containing 114 individuals, 84% of which resided within the DuPage County. 89% of individuals interviewed lived in a house that could be decorated. Within the survey 74% of individuals expressed that they would decorate their home more often if they did not need to worry about putting decorations up and 78% said they would decorate their home more often if they did not need to worry about taking decorations down. 57% of individuals also stated that they tended to leave holiday decorations up for

1–2 weeks after the holiday had passed and 24% stated that it typically took them over 3 weeks. DecorDash would allow for individuals to order services to put up or take down seasonal decorations so that clients would not have to worry about the hassle of doing it themselves. The service could be offered for both indoor and outdoor decorating since 83% of individuals surveyed indicated that they preferred to decorate both indoors and outdoors. High-schoolers involved with DecorDash would go over to clients' houses to put up or take down their decorations upon request.

While this service would make decorating more enjoyable and accessible for many, there are a number of risks involved. Decorating for the holidays often involves hanging up lights and especially for two-story houses, this may be a liability. Students run the risk of injury as well as causing damage to the home. Poor handling of decorations could additionally result in the breaking of property. Clients may also take issue in the organization of their decorations when students are putting them away.

5 Discussion

5.1 Predicting the Success Using Critical Success Factors

According to our framework, we are analyzing the success factors in the lifecycle of startups to predict the success of DecorDash.

Stage 1 of the Lifecycle of Startups, called the Bootstrapping stage, reflects the current status of DecorDash. Factors within this stage including competency, motivation, customer requisition, market opportunity, and customer demographics.

Competency of a company involves how a business differentiates themselves from others. In the case of DecorDash, they are opportunity entrepreneurs that have identified a problem within society and have created a unique service to combat the issue. They have allowed themselves to standout within the market due to there being no other companies with the same niche. Thus, we can predict that DecorDash's future success according to their unique competency.

Motivation within a startup often lies on the shoulders of the founders. In order to help the company to further develop, founders need to be able to push each other to complete their respective tasks, which in turn will help to expand the business. The founders of DecorDash have showed their enthusiasm for the project by coming up with and presenting the idea for their business, as well as creating and conducting a survey to gauge consumer interest. From this we can infer the success of the company if we assume that they will apply this same motivation in the future as their company grows.

Customer requisition is the show of interest received by the company from consumers for their service or product. This can help to show whether or not a startup will be successful by estimating the demand for the service within their targeted market. DecorDash had consumers from the states of Florida and Illinois complete a survey indicating their interest in the company. It can be predicted that DecorDash will be successful based upon their survey results, with 74% of individuals stating that they would decorate their home more often if they did not need to worry about putting decorations up (see Fig. 3) and 78% stating they would decorate their home more often if they did not need to worry about taking decorations down (see Fig. 4).

Would you decorate your home more if you didn't have to worry about putting decorations up?
113 responses

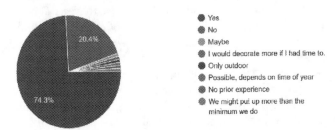

Fig. 3. Percentage of people who like the decoration putting-up service

Would you decorate your home more if you didn't need to worry about taking decorations down?
91 responses

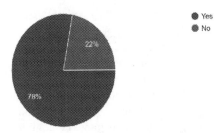

Fig. 4. Percentage of people who like the decoration Taking-down service

Market opportunity is whether or not there is a need or want for a service within a consumer market that is not supplied by rival companies. The previously conducted survey demonstrating consumer interest shows that there is an opportunity for DecorDash to succeed within their market. Figure 5 shows the survey results that 61.5% individual are interested in the services DecorDash is trying to provide. DecorDash is also an innovative business with no known business rivals, meaning that it has a strong market opportunity to succeed. However it will also need to posses unique features to stand out if competitors enter their market in the future [16].

Customer demographics involve understanding which kind of customer to target your goods or services towards. In knowing the target market, new businesses can then start by advertising their products towards the groups of consumers they know would be interested in the product. DecorDash's survey involved individuals from the states of Illinois and Florida from which they received positive results. Therefore, it can be inferred that if DecorDash were to launch its business in Illinois and Florida, it would have a higher chance of success.

According to the analysis of the above factors, the success of the company DecorDash can be predicted. It has fulfilled many of the beginning factors a business needs to be successful.

Stage 2 and 3 are the seed stage and creation stage respectfully. These are the next two stages that the company will reach. They reflect the future status the company will

Please select the services that you would be interested in!
91 responses

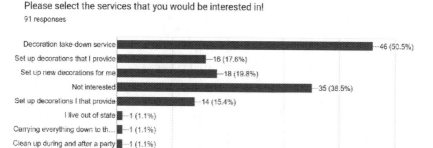

Fig. 5. Service People interested in

need to reach in order to become successful. Factors within this stage include financial factors, technology utilization, employment, and management and process development.

Financial factors are extremely important in the ultimate survival of a business. To fully bring a business to life, a company needs investors to invest into its product and provide financial support for founders to bring a product or service to the market. DecorDash will have to ensure that they can acquire interest from investors into their product and obtain funding from them.

Technology utilization involves whether or not a company can and does utilize technology that can vastly help improve their business in terms of management and process development. In the future, DecorDash should seek technological opportunities to create a more efficient business, which in turn, can help them to further grow and expand. For example DecorDash could possibly adopt a Customer Relationship Managment (CRM) system or Enterprise Resource Planning (ERP) system to help streamline and grow the business.

Employment is also an extremely important factor in determining whether a business will succeed. The employees that are recruited should be qualified and get along well to avoid having personal issues within the company that could endanger it. DecorDash will need to find motivated and responsible employees to help expand their business in the future. Without the right team to further build the company, DecorDash risks failing due to internal issues.

Management and Process development means developing better leadership and management strategies leading to a more defined and efficient business process. This means that DecorDash will have to develop efficient business processes for their daily business to provide better customer service.

Overall, these factors will not be applied until the company progresses in the future so there is no certain way to evaluate whether or not the DecorDash will be successful. However, based upon their current status in Stage 1 they are on the path to successful growth. If they are able to satisfy the factors within Stages 2 and 3, it will be a good indicator of the company's future success.

5.2 Additional Predicting Factors

Failure Factors

There are many factors DecorDash should avoid to better its chances of success. When modeling their business, they should ensure that it is scalable and reproducible in order to avoid structural problems. If faced with strategic problems such as the absence or inconsistency of planning, incorrect cost rationalization or other factors, it can eventually lead to the failure of a startup or new company [18]. It is essential that DecorDash should find a sales channel that reaches the expectations of clients regarding cost and quality in order to continue structured growth as well as scale gains.

Personal or external factors are what can ultimately lead to the failure of a business. When it comes to personal factors, DecorDash should be cautious when planning and managing the business, specifically when it comes to administrative and financial management. When it comes to external factors, DecorDash should be cautious when approaching technical and financial support, specifically taxes and bureaucracy [18]. Without careful management of these factors, DecorDash may find itself facing both internal and external issues such as poor administrative management and incorrectly filed taxes.

Sustainability

Sustainability is an important factor for the success of business especially in the modern environment. Investing in reducing the environmental impact of a business is important in helping consumers to become more conscious of their environmental footprint. With many more businesses spreading the message of sustainability, many customers may also now be more focused upon the ways a company is seeking to soften its effects upon the environment. DecorDash may not have to worry as much about sustainability as much as many other companies since they are mainly utilizing manual work. However, they will have to put into consideration the amount of waste they are contributing to when owners ask them to throw away certain decorations. DecorDash could possibly come up with a system where they donate or sell older working decorations that clients want to throw out to those who may not be able to afford them in order to help lessen the waste they create.

6 Conclusions

Startups are defined as companies that have scalable and replicable types of business as a concept, that is, innovative companies with the capacity for rapid growth. The startup always works in a more projected way, there is a growth plan, making it much faster. This paper develops a research framework to predict success of startups based on critical success factors associated with each lifecycle stage of startups. Through a case study of a startup company idea, we evaluate some indicators in stage 1 and give suggestions of the future with critical success factors in stage 2 & 3.

Overall, in order for DecorDash to become a successful business in the future, they will need to carefully plan their business structure as well as ensure their idea is innovative and unique enough to appeal to their target audience. The company needs to be scalable and have room for rapid growth. DecorDash, as a new business, should also be willing to invest both internally and externally in innovative products or services that can help them to grow and develop faster and more profitably. If DecorDash follows the factors we proposed in the research framework and takes care when managing their business, they will have an overall stronger potential for success.

There are limitations in this study. We only conduct one case and the startup does not compete all three stages yet. In the future, we plans to study more matured startup cases and evaluate our research framework quantitatively. In addition, we are trying to concentrate more on employee training and education in the future success assessment in stage 2 & 3. We suggest adding gamification in both training and education to improve working skills of employees hired by startups.

References

1. Vivarelli, M.: Are all the potential entrepreneurs so good? In: Entry and Post-entry Performance of Newborn Firms, pp. 131–143. Routledge (2007)
2. Fairlie, R.W., Fossen, F.M.: Opportunity versus necessity entrepreneurship: two components of business creation (2018)
3. Bennett, V.M., Chatterji, A.K.: The entrepreneurial process: evidence from a nationally representative survey. Strateg. Manag. J. **44**(1), 86–116 (2023)
4. Molaei, R., Zali, M.R., Mobaraki, M.H., Farsi, J.Y.: The impact of entrepreneurial ideas and cognitive style on students entrepreneurial intention. J. Entrepreneurship Emerg. Econ. **6**(2), 140–162 (2014)
5. Kurode, T., Kurode, A.V., Moitra, K.: A study of critical challenges in startup management. Available at SSRN 3348534 (2016)
6. Lizarelli, F.L., et al.: Critical success factors and challenges for lean startup: a systematic literature review. TQM J. **34**(3), 534–551 (2022)
7. Salamzadeh, A., Kawamorita Kesim, H.: Startup companies: life cycle and challenges. In: 4th International Conference on Employment, Education and Entrepreneurship (EEE), Belgrade, Serbia (2015)
8. Wang, X., Edison, H., Bajwa, S.S., Giardino, C., Abrahamsson, P.: Key challenges in software startups across life cycle stages. In: Sharp, H., Hall, T. (eds.) XP 2016. LNBIP, vol. 251, pp. 169–182. Springer, Cham (2016). https://doi.org/10.1007/978-3-319-33515-5_14
9. Weking, J., Böttcher, T.P., Hermes, S., Hein, A.: Does business model matter for startup success? A quantitative analysis. In: ECIS (2019)
10. Hokkanen, L., Xu, Y., Väänänen, K.: Focusing on user experience and business models in startups: investigation of two-dimensional value creation. In: Proceedings of the 20th International Academic Mindtrek Conference, pp. 59–67 (2016)
11. Gelderen, M.V., Thurik, R., Bosma, N.: Success and risk factors in the pre-startup phase. Small Bus. Econ. **24**, 365–380 (2005)
12. Castrogiovanni, G.J.: Pre-startup planning and the survival of new small businesses: theoretical linkages. J. Manag. **22**(6), 801–822 (1996)
13. Okrah, J., Nepp, A., Agbozo, E.: Exploring the factors of startup success and growth. Bus. Manag. Rev. **9**(3), 229–237 (2018)
14. Díaz-Santamaría, C., Bulchand-Gidumal, J.: Econometric estimation of the factors that influence startup success. Sustainability **13**(4), 2242 (2021)
15. Nalintippayawong, S., Waiyawatpattarakul, N., Chotipant, S.: Examining the critical success factors of startup in Thailand using structural equation model. In: 2018 10th International Conference on Information Technology and Electrical Engineering (ICITEE), pp. 388–393. IEEE (2018)

16. Marullo, C., Casprini, E., Di Minin, A., Piccaluga, A.: 'Ready for take-off': how open innovation influences startup success. Creat. Innov. Manag. **27**(4), 476–488 (2018)
17. Saura, J.R., Palos-Sanchez, P., Grilo, A.: Detecting indicators for startup business success: sentiment analysis using text data mining. Sustainability **11**(3), 917 (2019)
18. Kvedaraitė, N.: Reasons and obstacles to starting a business: experience of students of Lithuanian higher education institutions. Manag. J. Contemp. Manag. Issues **19**(1), 1–16 (2014)
19. Prohorovs, A., Bistrova, J., Ten, D.: Startup success factors in the capital attraction stage: founders' perspective. J. East-West Bus. **25**(1), 26–51 (2019)
20. Petrů, N., Pavlák, M., Polák, J.: Factors impacting startup sustainability in the Czech Republic (2019)
21. Kim, B., Kim, H., Jeon, Y.: Critical success factors of a design startup business. Sustainability **10**(9), 2981 (2018)
22. Brush, C.G., Carter, N.M., Gatewood, E.J., Greene, P.G., Hart, M.M.: The use of bootstrapping by women entrepreneurs in positioning for growth. Venture Capital **8**(1), 15–31 (2006)
23. Lee, S.B.: An analysis on the critical startup success factors in small-sized venture businesses. Asia-Pac. J. Bus. Venturing Entrepreneurship **12**(3), 53–63 (2017)

A More Reasonable Mecha Design Approach in AI – Mecha Characters with Tang Dynasty Elements as an Example

Yubin Zhong and Jing Luo[✉]

College of Art and Design, Shenzhen University, Shenzhen, Guangdong, China
luojng@szu.edu.cn

Abstract. In fields such as virtual reality and video games, with a large number of virtual character design needs, the auxiliary application of AI can enable producers to improve their work efficiency. AI is mainly used for visual generation and procedural modeling. This study discusses a method of AI visual recognition model generation, and constructs a process from AI visual recognition to programmatic model generation. Enable the AI to programmatically generate models that are more reasonable and fit with its design goals. In this study, the development of AI visual recognition and the development and application of game procedural modeling are analyzed, and the difficulties of model character design process and procedural generation modeling are analyzed from the perspective of producers. A model generation method based on AI is proposed to identify the contour, divide the structural plane and segment the model area. This approach allows the model to not stack assets and structures on top of each other, but to meet its design goals. By taking the Tang Dynasty pattern as the initial element, the research preliminarily shows the process of programmatic model generation assisted by AI. In the future, as the demand for visual sensation and virtual reality develops, producers will need to create a large number of complex structural characters. Procedural modeling assisted by AI can help producers reduce a lot of working time and design costs, and at the same time design mecha characters with reasonable structure and in line with design objectives.

Keywords: AI · contour segmentation · model generation · Mecha · Tang Dynasty culture

1 Introduction

The use of VR (virtual reality) has grown exponentially over the past decade, along with the demand for gaming and visual experience, and the rapid growth of the meta-universe. With advantages such as profitability, versatility and practicality, as well as applications spanning all areas of research, this new medium has a place in the market [1]. Whether in gaming or VR, a large number of virtual things need to be created. Things that don't exist in reality, such as the various characters and architectural scenes in games, the huge space fleet and future cities in movies, require 3D modeling to get the job done.

X. Fang (Ed.): HCII 2023, LNCS 14046, pp. 187–201, 2023.
https://doi.org/10.1007/978-3-031-35930-9_13

Modeling characters in these areas is an extremely large and complex task, with a large number of genres having mechanical structures, such as robots, mecha characters, and so on. In the case of humanoid mechanical structure characters, the design is usually made by means of digital engraving technology, which is mainly used to make ultra-realistic 3D models by digital sculpting software such as ZBrush and Mudbox [2]. This process takes a lot of time for the maker to make the design. For the design of the main character objectives, skilled artists can create complex models with fine control using current tools such as Maya or 3DS Max, but they require extensive training [3]. In work projects, detailed design of major objectives is inevitable, which also means a huge amount of work. For some non-key mechanical character design, producers usually adopt asset-based model production. With the further development of artificial intelligence and computer, producers further use AI to assist in completing these huge work requirements, and construct NPC or non-key character designs in games. The complexity of modern computer games has increased dramatically over the past few decades. Along with the demand for realistic games, the demand for complex game AI, especially for non-player characters (NPC), is growing [4]. During this period, AI-assisted game design also experienced rapid development.

Ai-assisted game design refers to the development of AI tools that support the game design and development process. This is perhaps the area of artificial intelligence research that holds the most promise for creating better games [5]. In the construction of role model, different methods are adopted to provide reference for the development of procedural modeling and AI-assisted modeling. At present, the methods to improve the efficiency of modeling are mainly designed by computer image recognition and programmatic model class generation. Among them, the modeling method of computer image recognition effectively improves the modeling efficiency in the work. Through the recognition and reverse derivation of 2D or 3D models by computer neural network, the design of the model is further constructed. The program generation change class needs the producer to design objectives preset, the program optimization asset generation model. Asset model refers to the fact that 3D models are in great demand in the video game industry and film production, and many 3D models have been created and stored [6]. These basic 3D models can be extracted as asset monomers to generate models. AI has been widely applied in the field of visual image recognition and 3D. For example, AI has made great progress in image analysis and generation. For example, in the field of painting, artificial intelligence research and application began to expand rapidly [7]. Artificial intelligence software and applications are developed based on the most advanced machine learning model and technology, and diversified artificial intelligence features and functions are realized through large-scale data training [8]. In the training of visual images by AI, the performance of computer vision tasks is greatly improved after deep learning is applied. This kind of object recognition, object segmentation, object tracking and so on have reached a superhuman level. Most algorithms are trained through the use of supervised learning. Often, the performance of computer vision can be improved by increasing the size of data [9]. This study mainly discusses the method of combining asset programming modeling with computer recognition image modeling by AI. An optimized role modeling method is further discussed.

2   The Transformation of 2D Images and 3D Models

From the modeling process, polygon modeling is the most traditional modeling method of 3D software. It consists of multiple polygons formed between a series of points and different vertices, which then form polygonal components [10]. The 3D modeling process means multiple modeling steps for designing a model. Common manipulation elements in 3D modeling systems include 3D basic geometric objects or 2D contours [11]. Computer vision recognition modeling mainly studies the conversion between 3D and 2D. Currently, image-based 3D reconstruction modeling technology has been developed for decades [12]. Forming models through 3D scanning is a modeling method of computer vision recognition, which is an image reconstruction method based on existing models. As for the method of converting 2D into 3D model, relevant research in Japan proposed a method of semi-automatic creation of 3D model similar to anime from a single illustration. By applying PCA to existing anime like 3D models, we obtain the basic models used to generate natural 3D models and use them to create 3D models that look close to the input illustrations [13]. In the process of image recognition, prediction, description and interpretation are carried out simultaneously, from rough object subparts and class interpretation of an image, to fine distinctions between object subclasses and more accurate three-dimensional quantization of objects [14]. Thus realizing the conversion of images from 2D to 3D. However, there are still many defects in the process from the recognition of the whole image to the formation of the model. In the research of 3D surface reconstruction based on 2D contour, the problems of branching and matching have not been solved [15]. The division of detail and contour depth is the key problem in image conversion to 3D model. AI has great advantages in contour recognition and image recognition generation, but it is difficult to generate models for matching region problems directly through image recognition. In preserving the details of the generation model on the area surface. By calculating the character vector of each vertex of the three-dimensional geometric model; Next, the 3D geometric model is segmented preliminarily based on the self-organizing feature map. Finally, the maximum relativistic rule is used to merge the over-segmented regions and get the final result [16]. Such an approach has good results in segmenting model regions, but it cannot give further adjustment to model generation. To preserve the model optimization details. Export the complex model to a 3D environment or open the model that has been created in the 3D environment, then freeze the entire model [17] to form a grid surface and extract its vertex model. The optimized model is obtained. Make it more reasonable to generate the model. Both approaches focus on how to preserve and optimize the details of the model.

In the process of program asset modeling, producers need to add asset models to the basic model to obtain usable models. Therefore, the advantage of computer image recognition lies in image recognition, extraction and generation, and the lack of details and regional rationality in the generation of models. Program assets need to be adjusted by the creator, the surface of the uncorrected model is chaotic, and the surface model is stacked and repeated in large numbers. Unable to generate models that fit the topic reasonably. Therefore, this study mainly discusses the role models in a large number of mechanical structures, and how to combine the advantages of AI computer image recognition and program assets to generate a more reasonable and regional model with high matching degree.

3   Mecha Modeling Research

The research of mecha model production is divided into two parts. First, from the perspective of relevant practitioners and production personnel, to understand the process of making mecha role models and the steps of the whole process. The second part analyzes the production process, analyzes the process of mecha model generation, and summarizes the characteristics of the model generation process. Explore how to use AI computer image recognition and programmatic model generation two methods to solve problems in different processes. Therefore, the preliminary design method is proposed.

3.1   PEST Analysis

Firstly, the work flow of the producer and relevant practitioners is studied in Fig. 1. In the game or the design of mecha characters in a major project, the design function, design background and design perception are usually taken as the basic role setting. The mechanical shell structure of the characters is set according to the target framework set by it, such as the design of warrior armor in a future era. The design style of the theme target is cyberpunk and doomsday style, or simple style of biological structure. Therefore, the first step of the design process is to set the elements of the direction of the theme and determine the style and background of the design. The second step is to determine the role's use function, such as combat reload type or mobile type. The third

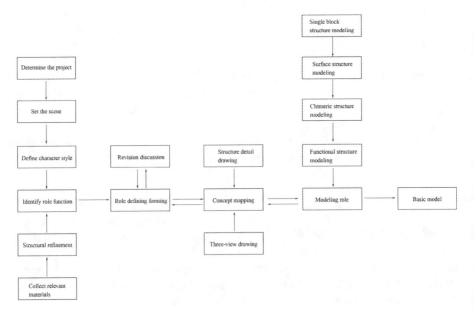

Fig. 1. Design the workflow of making Mecha characters

step is to set the concept drawing of the role. In the concept drawing, the designer draws the front view, side view and top view of the role. The fourth step is for the modeler to model the character on the concept sketch. At each step, the producer needs to discuss and modify according to the theme and set function.

3.2 Production Process Analysis

According to the modeling structure analysis of mecha, its mecha is different from complex biological structures. Its surface is complex and uneven. Most mecha surface structures are formed by flat extrusion, with uniform thickness and smooth surface without complex non-geometric structure. After the shape is determined, the surface is pressed and the overall geometric contour is moved, and the overall surface structure is flat. In the process of mecha design, the outline of the geometric structure of mecha is related to the theme, such as cyberpunk style mecha, whose surface contains a lot of wires, and the structural transition is mostly chamfered transition. Thus the style determined by the theme determines the mecha's geometric style, which is determined by the geometric outline. Most of the mecha surface structure is the overall transition change of surface and line after the extrusion of the basic image, and the overall change is presented logically.The process is shown in Fig. 2.

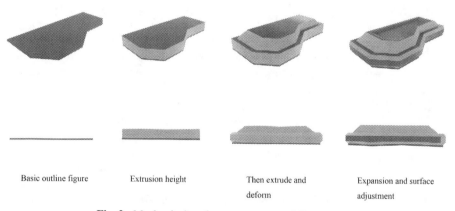

| Basic outline figure | Extrusion height | Then extrude and deform | Expansion and surface adjustment |

Fig. 2. Mechanical surface monomer modeling process

The complex surface structure is composed of several monomers, and the monomer is generated by the basic contour through extrusion, deformation and expansion, so the realization step of the monomer is composed of two stages from graphic to logical deformation. Combining these two stages, a design concept is proposed. The theme elements are extracted graphically through AI computer recognition, and then transformed into new Outlines. Complete the first phase of graphic extraction. In the second stage, the graphics surface is modeled logically by program assets. This ensures the independence and originality of the graphics, and also ensures that the programmatic modeling will not randomly assign the surface. The graphic outline of the surface is automatically generated by AI combined with computer recognition.

4 AI Recognition Segmentation Area Method

In this design objective, the pattern of Tang Dynasty elements is adopted as the design objective, the image with its pattern is taken as the conversion image, and the reference mech image is taken as the source file training image. AI extracts the basic contour by collecting the contour of the source file image, and extracts the geometric contour of the pattern in the transformation image, and divides it into several monomer. Reassemble as the base figure. AI generates new contours through the intersection of basic graphics and basic contours, and then cuts coordinate plane of target model with the contours. AI visually recognizes different regional planes, and then classifies the surface structure, chimeric structure and functional structure of the cut plane, and generates a capital model according to its regional functions. By recognizing images of different mecha types, the structure generated by AI can be more rich, and different types of Mecha characters can be generated according to different design themes.

4.1 Multiple Combination Structure Description

In the whole process of logic generation, computer vision mainly divides the whole structure into regions. This process can be divided into regions by AI visual judgment or manually. The components of complex mechanical structure and hard surface structure are complex, and it is difficult to realize the rational combination and design of surface structure, chimeric structure and functional structure in the replicative program.

For the design of the overall external surface structure, the program divides it into two categories: no structure surface and low structure surface. An unstructured surface is a structure with a smooth surface, consisting of elemental patterns or low-height structures. Usually used as a wrapping part or display part of machinery. While the low structure surface has the function part, but does not have the outline or function influence on the overall design or object function. Therefore, Fig. 3 shows this in the surface structure part, the available adjustment options are pattern filling, low height structure filling and low structure generating.

Chimeric structure refers to the connection structure between different components, which usually exists mostly in the connection part of surface structure and functional structure, as well as the connection part between different functional structures, as well as the connection part of multiple complex bodies in the whole. The whole set contains multiple sub-set parts, and the connection structure of the sub-combined part can be designed as a single structure. Therefore, in the design of the connection structure, the connection structure of the sub-joint part should be designed first or last. Otherwise, the overall connection structure will be unbalanced. The forms of connection structure are diversified. In the design of complex mechanical body, strong structure connection and soft structure connection are usually adopted. Strong structural connection refers to the connection structure of high strength, stiffness, and fixed change. Such as fixed groove rotation structure, hydraulic clamp structure. Soft structures are those with strong flexibility, random changes and strong ductility. Such as spring connector, cable connector. So in the generation of chimeric structures. The order shall be to give priority or delay to the connectors that generate the sub-binding parts, and then to regenerate the connectors within the parts. In the connection option, should provide strong structure connection,

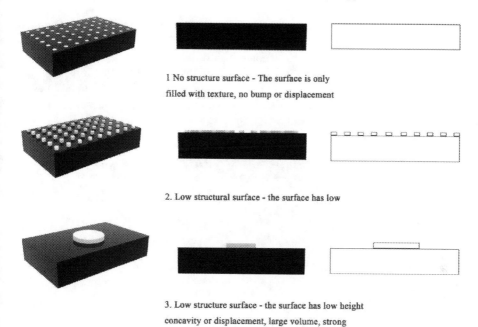

1 No structure surface - The surface is only
filled with texture, no bump or displacement

2. Low structural surface - the surface has low

3. Low structure surface - the surface has low height
concavity or displacement, large volume, strong

Fig. 3. Three different surface structures

and soft structure connection option, according to its division of different areas, as well as the relationship between components, generate different connections, and then through the combination of superposition, make it more random and diversified.

Functional structure refers to the mechanical whole or the structure with independent function and form in the mechanical structure. For example, a naval gun on a warship is a whole that can be applied to other structures without damaging the use. Therefore, its functional structure itself tends to be more asset-oriented. Generate its features on the functional partition area.

4.2   AI Image Geometry Extraction and Mapping Surface Cutting

In the first step, when conducting AI recognition and image training, the producer needs to select the required type of mecha images and transformed images. The purpose of AI recognition of mecha pictures is to recognize the geometric contour of humanoid mecha. AI recognizes basic mecha types and summarizes the regional structure through contrast recognition and linear recognition. Through training and recognition of the mecha pictures put into training, the height and thickness are determined, and the contour is extracted in a closed manner. In contour extraction methods, discrete optimization techniques (such as dynamic programming and graph algorithm) are often used for contour recognition. These algorithms often provide a strong guarantee of the quality of the solutions they find, thus allowing a clear separation between the way the problem is formulated (the choice of the objective function) and the way the problem is solved (the choice of the optimization algorithm). [18] computer vision learning thus corrects to an accurate profile. The type of image to be trained can be single, or it can be modified and diversified according to different needs of the producer. In the process of graphic training, the region after contour extraction is mainly divided. For the contour of chimeric structure and surface structure, it is segmented by polyhedron; for contour recognition, depth recognition is mainly carried out by recognizing the change of normal lines of texture; finally, its contour is simplified and extracted, so that the producer can screen and extract the contour recognized by AI.The process is shown in Fig. 4.

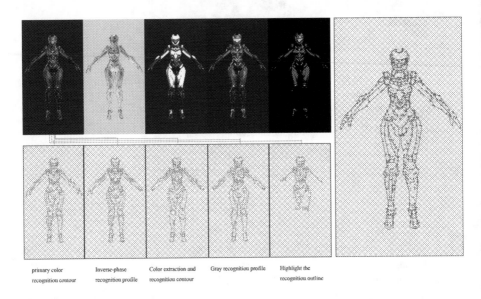

| primary color recognition contour | Inverse-phase recognition profile | Color extraction and recognition contour | Gray recognition profile | Highlight the recognition outline |

The AI uses multiple layers to extract visual contours from the graphics, using a floating-point approach to correct symmetry

Fig. 4. AI recognizes the contour extraction process of the source image

The extraction of transformational materials mainly extracts the graphic features and composition features related to the theme. Usually transformational materials have a large number of graphic features related to the theme, which can clearly train the size, outline, direction of the composition line and the spatial situation of the composition structure. The extraction style takes its vertical and horizontal coordinates as the plane. Here, the plum texture is taken as an example for graphic training. The main feature of transformational image training is to disassemble contour and reassemble contour. Different from the source mech image training, AI converts and recombines the image by disassembling a single piece of the image, rather than identifying and extracting contour through multiple layers at a time. See Fig. 5.

Figure extraction contour

Outline disassembly assembly

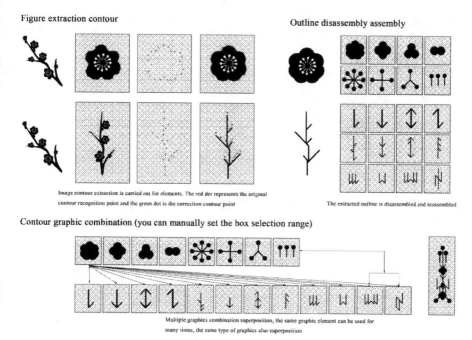

Image contour extraction is carried out for elements. The red dot represents the original
contour recognition point and the green dot is the correction contour point

The extracted outline is disassembled and reassembled

Contour graphic combination (you can manually set the box selection range)

Multiple graphics combination superposition, the same graphic element can be used for
many times, the same type of graphics also superposition

Fig. 5. AI recognition training image extraction monomer and combination process

For its transformational materials, the royal court pattern materials of the Tang Dynasty are taken here as the basic image for AI image recognition and extraction, and also as the design target of its producer. After the transformational images are trained, AI first extracts the main contours of the transformational images, decomposes them into separate geometric contours, and then recombines and connects them. In the process of connecting the re-patterns, the overlapping patterns will be removed and the transition treatment will be carried out, so that the geometric outline after connecting can present the natural state. See Fig. 6.

After extracting the monomer, AI combines and overlaps the contour extracted from the training pattern of the source mech with the element monomer. In order to generate more types of generated contour randomly, AI should combine the misaligned contour at the position of the source mech contour recognition when filling the contour, and the misaligned contour is set between 5%–30%. The overall pattern filling should be scaled and moved according to its density. For example, the hand and chest of the source mecha have a large surface area, so the pattern filling should be enlarged in the area with a large proportion of blank area, while in the area with a small proportion of blank area, the layout density increases and the pattern area shrinks, so the array filling after recognition should be adopted. The overall process is shown in Fig. 7.

Original transformational image - Tang Dynasty element pattern

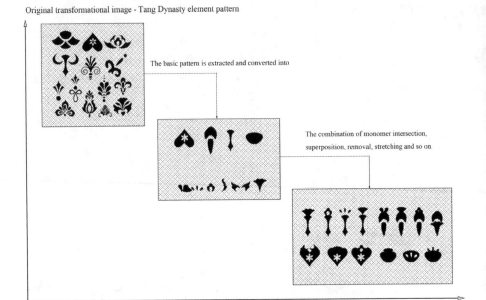

The basic pattern is extracted and converted into

The combination of monomer intersection,
superposition, removal, stretching and so on

Hierarchical disassembly

Fig. 6. To the Tang pattern element graphic extraction combination

After combining contour generation, AI will map the expanded human body model. In order to ensure the correctness of projection from the perspective of model expansion and mapping, TenBo model, a new tension-based three-dimensional human body model (TenBo model), is adopted here. In contrast to the popular SCAPE model, which separates shape and posture deformations, this approach systematically models shape and posture deformations. Experiments show that the performance of TenBo model is better than SCAPE model. Better projection of the human body model after UV expansion [19]. Carry out contour projection from the positive perspective, side perspective and back perspective, and cut the surface of contour projection separately. When the mapping contour of the three perspectives has dislocation and intersection, the random fusion method is adopted for the intersection. Two different surfaces will generate 30%–70% cross-section and 40%–75% fusion. See Fig. 8. The resulting individual faces are the base model for the area separation, which is then functionally divided.

Original transformational image - Tang Dynasty element pattern

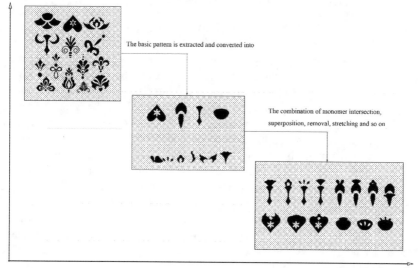

The basic pattern is extracted and converted into

The combination of monomer intersection, superposition, removal, stretching and so on

Hierarchical disassembly

The obtained element monomer is combined and replaced into the mecha contour, and then recognition combination extraction is carried out. In the process of contour combination, filling changes are carried out according to the recognition proportion

A new binding profile is obtained

Fig. 7. AI combines the outline with the image monomer to generate a new outline

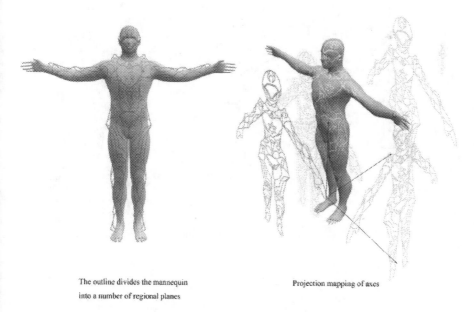

The outline divides the mannequin into a number of regional planes

Projection mapping of axes

Fig. 8. The outline is mapped to the mannequin from three perspectives

4.3 Mapping Surface Area Division and Model Generation

The mapping plane divides the basic human body model into many structural planes, which will be divided by AI recognition. In the method of combining the regional plane with the model, the feature template is deformed into the shape of inserting feature points on the scanning model by using the global warpage function based on the radial basis function (RBF). Then a surface fitting process is used to optimize the feature template to approximate the given model, so as to achieve the coincidence between the region after surface cutting and the human body model [20]. In the design of mecha, its surface structure covering a large range is taken as the basis, while its chimeric structure is usually in part of the structure and joint, and its functional structure will also change with the different design objectives. Therefore, the order of selection of its regions is surface structure area, chimeric structure area and functional structure area. AI recognizes the image, divides the mapping surface, and initially divides the functional area surface. In this process, the producer can further improve the uniqueness of the desiZone extrusion generates the structure of the outer surface of the mechaognizes and divides the area.See Fig. 9. The producer can change the different structural surfaces of the AI classified areas. After the classification of the regions is determined, the program extruded and generated according to the order of surface structure, chimeric structure and functional structure. First, the initial model is generated by basic superposition extruding on the surface structure.

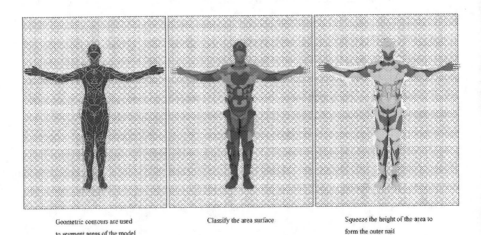

Geometric contours are used   Classify the area surface   Squeeze the height of the area to
to segment areas of the model   form the outer nail

Fig. 9. Zone extrusion generates the structure of the outer surface of the mecha

After the height of the surface structure is generated, the structure is further generated. Firstly, the hard surface structure is generated by the surface structure. Here, displacement mapping is used to simulate the generation of the surface structure. Producers can adjust different assets to suit their design goals.See Fig. 10.

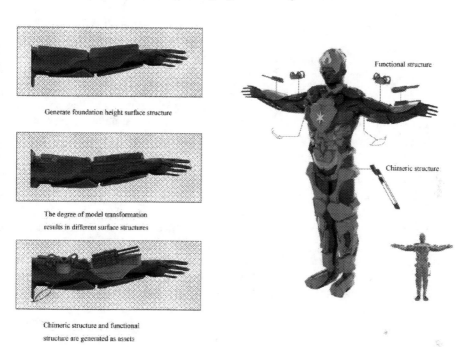

Generate foundation height surface structure

The degree of model transformation results in different surface structures

Chimeric structure and functional structure are generated as assets

Functional structure

Chimeric structure

Fig. 10. The base model surface generates other structures

5   Design Evaluation

This study aims to provide a design method to improve the previous Mecha orange and the design process involving a large number of mechanical structures. Through computer recognition and AI generation, it can generate a large number of mechanical structures with reasonable structure and configuration and in line with its theme design through programming under the condition of logical conditions. It greatly reduces the workload and time of some non-focused mechanical structure things in the aspects of film and television or game development. Meanwhile, it improves the rationality and complexity of the previous asset-based procedural generation model, greatly reduces its repetitive structure and chaotic stacking structure, and enables it to generate mechanical structure products similar to those designed by human beings. At the same time, it can provide designers with sample reference for more in-depth design.

In the process part of AI recognition design, due to the different functions and uses of different structures, it is necessary to make regional division and correction of the output works. Only through more adjustments can a good effect be achieved.

The method of its design process can also guide the thinking order of human in the design of mechanical mechanism, so as to form a logical design method. As a reference for designers to understand topics and make good designs without relying on programs. It can also be used in conventional modeling and scenery software as a way to understand and construct models.

In the case of program model generation, more implementation possibilities will use it as a plug-in, so that it can be easily adapted to a variety of different platforms, while its asset library should be constantly updated, and assets can be added and removed as needed to avoid complex computing processes.

Its disadvantage is that it is not enough to replace the focused and personalized design. More applications and background, non-key model design, as well as computer AI identification and generation process, there will be different structural errors, at the same time, the development of its programmed generation requires a large number of experiments, its generation program has not been implemented.

6 Conclusion

Through the logical design process, the method can reduce repetitive work and make it more diversified. Through the logical design, more complex and reasonable mechanical structures can be generated and the efficiency of model design can be improved. At the same time, it can be programmed to generate a large number of geometric structure extraction, so as to ensure that the generated model retains its original basic visual and proportional feeling, so that it is in line with the direction of the design target. A large number of patterns generated by AI computer vision recognition can generate different models, which increases the creativity of design work. This study shows a model design method in the field of mecha. For more complex model generation methods, further discussion and experiments are needed.

References

1. Siva, P.E., et al.: 3D model optimization workflow for game development. In: 20th Virtual and Augmented Reality (SVR) Workshop 2018, Iguazufus, Brazil, pp. 225–229 (2018). https://doi.org/10.1109/SVR.2018.00041
2. Yue, Z.: Deep learning for digital engraving of 3D high-precision models for the next generation of games based on artificial intelligence. Multimedia Progr. 3 years, article ID 2022, 4683455, 8 years (2022). https://doi.org/10.1155/2022/4683455
3. Jackson, B., Keefe, D.F.: Lift-off: using reference images and freehand sketching to create 3D model in VR. IEEE Trans. Visual. Comput. Graph. 22(4), 1442–1451 (2016). https://doi.org/10.1109/TVCG.2016.2518099
4. Denault, A.K., Vangheluwe, J., HansMcDowell, P.: 2nd International North-American Conference on Intelligent Games and Simulation, 19–20 September 2006
5. Yannakakis, G.N., Togelius, J.: A panorama of artificial intelligence and computational intelligence in games. IEEE Trans. Comput. Intell. AI Games 7(4), 317–335 (2015). https://doi.org/10.1109/TCIAIG.2014.2339221

6. Kaku, K., Okada, Y., Niijima, K.: Similarity measures for 3D model search based on OBBTree. In: Proceedings of International Conference on Computer Graphics, Imaging and Visualization. CGIV 2004, Penang, Malaysia, pp. 46–51 (2004). https://doi.org/10.1109/CGIV.2004. 1323959

7. Stork, D.G., Coddington, J. (eds.) Computer Image Analysis in Art Research; SPIE/IS&T: Bellingham, Washington, USA (2008). [Google Academics]

8. Tao, C., Gao, J., Wang, T.: Testing and quality verification of ai software - perspectives, issues, and practices. IEEE Access **7**, 120164–120175 (2019). https://doi.org/10.1109/ACC ESS.2019.2937107

9. Cho, S., Geun Choi, S., Kim, D., Lee, G., BongSohn, C.: How to generate image data sets based on 3D models and deep learning methods. Int. J. Eng. Technol. **7**(3.34), 221–225 (2018)

10. Yan, T., Yan, C.: Research on the visual design of 3D computer simulation effects in the characterization of science fiction animation. In: 32nd International Conference on Power, Electronics and Computer Applications (ICPECA), Shenyang, China, pp. 2–2022 (2022). 1080.1083/ICPECA10.1109.53709

11. Hu, C.-C., Chi, M.-T., Chang, T.-K.: Design and evaluation of game-based learning modules for 3D modelling. In: 2018 IEEE 18th International Conference on Advanced Learning Technology (ICALT), Mumbai, India, pp. 128–132 (2018). https://doi.org/10.1109/ICALT.2018. 00038

12. Tseng, Y.-L., Chung, S.-L.: Transforming a picture into an outline of a 3D model reminiscent of a 3D printed low relief. In: Proceedings of the 33rd Conference on Control in China, Nanjing, China, pp. 2953–2957 (2014). https://doi.org/10.1109/ChiCC.2014.6897110

13. Niki, T., Komuro, T.: Semi-automatic creation of an anime like 3D face model from a single illustration. In: International Conference on the Internet World 2019 (CW), Kyoto, Japan, pp. 53–56 (2019). https://doi.org/10.1109/Cw.2019.00017

14. Brooks, R.A.: Symbolic reasoning among 3-D models and 2-D images. Artif. Intell. **17**(1–3), 285–348 (1981). ISSN 0004-3702

15. Meng, Y., Wang, S.: A new interactive method for 3D modeling reconstruction from contour. In: International Conference on Computer Applications and Systems Modeling (ICCASM 2010), Taiyuan, China, pp. V2010-6–V496-6 (2010). https://doi.org/10.1109/ICCASM.2010. 5620388

16. Wang, R., Li, J., Liu, G., Li, X.: 3D geometric model region partitioning method. In: The 7th World Intelligent Control and Automation Congress, Chongqing, pp. 7–2008 (2008). 8456.8459/WCICA.10.1109

17. Wang, L., Zhang, J.: A fast and efficient 3D game character modeling method. In: 2008 International Conference on Internet Computing Science and Engineering, Harbin, China, pp. 118–121 (J.:). https://doi.org/10.1109/ICICSE.2008.57

18. Felzenszwalb, P.F., Zabih, R.: Dynamic programming and graphical algorithms in computer vision. IEEE Trans. Pattern Anal. Mach. Intell. **33**(4), 721–740 (2011). https://doi.org/10. 1109/TPAMI.2010.135

19. Chen, Y., Liu, Z., Zhang, Z.: Tensor-based human body modelling. In: 2013 IEEE Conference on Computer Vision and Pattern Recognition, Portland, OR, USA, pp. 105–112 (2013). https:// doi.org/10.1109/CVPR.2013.21

20. Tong, K.-M., Hui, K.-C., Wang, C.C.L.: Mesh fitting based 3D character modeling. In: Pan, Z., Aylett, R., Diener, H., Jin, X., Göbel, S., Li, L. (eds.) Edutainment 2006. LNCS, vol. 3942, pp. 861–872. Springer, Heidelberg (2006). https://doi.org/10.1007/11736639_106

Gamification and Serious Games

Driving Consumer Value Co-creation and Repurchase Intention and e-WOM by Gameful Experience in Gamification

Hassan Alsaggaf[✉]

King Abdulaziz University, Jeddah, Saudi Arabia
hamalsaggaf@kau.edu.sa

Abstract. One of the most significant developments at the start of the twenty-first century is gamification. We create a framework for analyzing the effects of gamification, which is one of the most important developments at the turn of the century. The goal of this study is to use gamification to demonstrate a link between consumer value co-creation and purchase intention. The review of the literature includes independent factors (examined gamification), dependent variables (examined purchase intention and e-WOM), mediating variables (customer value co-creation), gamification contexts, and types of studies conducted on gamified systems. The study collects data from consumers, and the empirical findings show that persuasive knowledge and game design are related to self-reference and, as a result, co-creation value, building on the work of Suh et al. (2017). Finally, our findings suggest that gamification has the potential to increase value co-creation and encourage consumer participation. The review's conclusions provide direction for future research as well as the development of gamified systems. This study is unique in that it introduces a brand-new framework to extend the "dynamics" into the incubation and implementation stages while also creating positive electronic word-of-mouth (e-WOM) to achieve the desired results using the quantitative method and primary data.

Keywords: Gamification · Gameful Experience · Customer value Co-creation · Purchase Intention · eWOM

1 Introduction

Gamification has received a lot of attention in recent years as a way to support user engagement and improve beneficial patterns in service use, such as increasing user activity, social interaction, or the quality and productivity of actions (Deterding and Dixon 2011; Hamari and Lehdonvirta 2010; Hamari, and V. Lehdonvirta 2012). (Hamari 2013). According to Hamari and Lehdonvirta (2012), these desired use patterns are thought to develop as a result of satisfying, intrinsically motivating, and "gameful" experiences brought on by game/motivational affordances integrated into a service. Be a result, gamification is frequently referred to as the next generation of marketing and customer engagement strategies. For example, Gartner (Gartner 2015) predicts that by

2015, more than 50% of businesses managing innovation processes will gamify various areas of their operations. In addition, there are more and more prosperous startups that help more established businesses gamify their current services or whose entire service is focused on adding a gamified layer to a core activity. Academic research on gamification is also becoming more prevalent, reflecting the increased public interest in the topic. It is particularly remarkable that, in this research, instances of the phrase "gamification" have been appearing more frequently than results from broad searches. This shows that academic research on gamification is growing in popularity.

Despite the fact that the issue has had a lot of hits, there is a lack of cogent knowledge regarding the kind of research that have been done using the term "gamification," as well as the methodologies used, the results they produced, and the contexts in which they were conducted.

Another important difficulty from a practical standpoint is determining whether gamification is successful. Investing is being made in gamification-related initiatives, and a startlingly high number of businesses already offer gamification services. Gamification is discussed extensively, for instance, in industry chitchat, most of which is based on anecdotal and intuitive assumptions that can range from extremely unfavorable to extremely positive opinions. Therefore, empirical data on the success of gamification is needed. The introduction of technology innovation has revolutionized how business owners market to and draw clients to their brands. The modern customer is better equipped and situated thanks to their gadgets to actively participate in co-creation processes in business operations as well as actively exhibiting extra-role behaviors that have a direct impact on the company (Kennedy & Guzmán, 2016). Through consumer commitment to a particular brand and brand loyalty, businesses can also obtain a competitive edge. The understanding of the specific marketing content that appeals to or suits the consumer behavior that will enhance their behavior toward the business is thus crucial to developing a business-consumer relationship that will result in a win-win situation where consumers are satisfied and the business is gaining competitive advantage (Sen, Johnson, Bhattacharya, & Wang, 2015). According to Park and Bae (2014), more than 70% of Forbes Global 2000 companies stated that they planned to employ gamification for marketing and customer retention.

As gamification gains popularity and exerts a significant influence on practically every aspect of human endeavor, marketing researchers are eager to explore how it may be used in business marketing to advance academic integrity and encourage successful corporate endeavors. For instance, gamification marketing may be used as a tool for analysis by firms to track consumer perception and take appropriate action to either uphold the status quo or make essential changes that may greatly affect the consumers (Al-Zyoud 2018; Schweidel & Moe 2014). By utilizing game-like techniques (such as scoreboards, points, and personalized fast feedback), gamification aims to create a game-full experience (Sigala 2015a), motivate and direct users' behavior, and increase users' engagement with the "play" tasks (Lee & Hammer 2011). These techniques help people feel more ownership, flow, and purpose when engaging with the "play" tasks (Pavlus 2010). Businesses utilize gamification in consumer-focused websites and mobile applications to motivate users to use e-Commerce tools in order to increase customer loyalty, brand awareness, and efficient marketing engagement (Deterding et al. 2012; Sigala 2015b).

Gamification is the use of game mechanics and game thinking in non-game contexts to help users solve problems on their own, take responsibility for their actions, and improve their subjective acceptance and sense of immersion. Therefore, the primary goal of gamification is to encourage user participation (Deterding et al. 2011; Zichermann and Linder 2013). As a result, gamification design features have been a crucial tool for helping customers behave in a way that aligns with businesses' objectives while also satisfying customer needs (Gatautis et al. 2016). Gamification has been widely applied in a variety of industries, including marketing, education and training, human resource assessment, and information mechanism application, as a powerful tool to encourage individuals to engage in their ideal behaviors (Zichermann and Linder 2013). On how gamification design elements should be composed, there is no agreement. The mechanics-dynamics-aesthetics (MDA) framework of gamification design was put forth by Hunicke et al. in 2004.

2 Literature Review

In essence, gamification of marketing strategies can affect consumer behavior. Even while gamification in marketing has enormous potential (Cramer et al. 2011), there aren't many research looking at how effective it is (Xu et al. 2016), particularly in the Arabian environment. The usefulness of gamification in influencing customers to accept marketing and promotional messages is actually lacking in proof (Xi and Hamari 2020). The ability of marketing managers in the Arab world to adopt gamified services and reap its benefits is limited by a lack of data on consumer reactions. According to Amalgam Insights (2018), despite significant expenditures in gamification, a number of gamified business projects have failed. More specifically, only a small number of academic studies have looked at the positive effects of gamification on brand connections (Berger et al. 2018), brand engagement (Xi and Hamari 2020), digital sales (Eisingerich et al. 2019), hedonic value and utilitarian value (Hsu and Chen 2018), and product adoption (Müller Stewens, Schlager, Häub & Herrmann 2017). Therefore, it is crucial to investigate how gamification platforms and applications may encourage customer loyalty, which in turn may drive repurchase intents and the intentions to communicate positive electronic word-of-mouth (eWOM), which in the Arabian context is a cost-effective advertising technique.

The current study aims to fill a gap in the literature in three different ways. To investigate the effects of I gamification on consumer loyalty, (ii) consumer loyalty on eWOM sharing behavior and repurchase intentions, (iii) consumer loyalty on the mechanism by which gamification mediates the link between gamification and two significant marketing outcomes (i.e., eWOM sharing behavior and repurchase intentions). In conclusion, this paper will provide fresh insight into how businesses may leverage gamified experiences to increase customer loyalty and facilitate customer interactions that in turn drive sales and good e-WOM.

The use of games to inspire, engage, and influence communities, groups, and individuals to drive intentions (behaviors) or generate desired results is illustrated by a variety of systems, methods, and design concepts (Glover 2013; Nicholson 2015). Because of the current trend of gamification, there has been a growth in the popularity and rise of games in marketing activities, which has attracted marketers' attention. The marketing executive is progressively becoming more aware of gamification. Gamification, according to Xu (2011), also provides clients with the chance to receive branding messaging in a fun way. Additionally, it permits reiterating branding statements. As a result, gamification's deep connection can increase people's feelings of identification, loyalty, and belonging to a company, good, service, or brand. Loyalty is more than just wanting to keep a relationship going; it also entails acting in ways that support the connection (such as reinforcement, defense of the relationship and favorable treatment of object of loyalty). Oliver (1999) defined customer loyalty as "a strongly held commitment to consistently re-purchase or patronize a preferred product/service in the future, resulting in repetitive same-brand or same brand-set purchasing, despite situational influences and marketing efforts having the potential to cause switching behavior." According to Aksoy et al. (2015), consumer encounters and relationships with a company, product, service, or brand can shape consumer loyalty. Particularly, gamification communication by businesses increases the likelihood of a favorable brand image and improved perceived service quality, both of which can increase customer loyalty.

Although still relatively new, the concept of "gamification," which first appeared about 2010, has quickly acquired acceptance in both academic and practical circles (K.J, 2017). Gamification, which focuses on user engagement to encourage behavioral changes (Schoech et al. 2013; Tobon et al. 2020), is primarily described as the usage of game features in situations other than games (Deterding et al. 2011.a). It is made up of game mechanics, sometimes referred to as game functional elements, such points and leaderboards, which in turn generate complementary game dynamics, such as rewards and competitiveness, which appeal to players' desires (Zichermann and Cunningham 2011.b). Although card decks and board games can also be used for gamification, modern gamified systems mostly use digital tools like web- and mobile-based applications (Patrício et al. 2018). Nowadays, gamification is frequently used in the business and educational sectors to increase engagement (Petridis et al. 2015; Szendr˝oi et al. 2020), and game elements are progressively included into employees' everyday duties and students' learning processes. Gamification has recently been highlighted as an approach with promise for enhancing staff productivity and student learning, according to a growing body of evidence (Newcomb et al. 2019; Van der Heijden et al. 2020).

Business organizations are gamifying their external marketing initiatives in addition to using it internally in the workplace, with the goal of enhancing both present and potential customers' digital experiences. While "Advergames," "In game advertising," and "social network games" are three sorts of gamified advertisements that fall under the general definition of "gamification" in the marketing context, they do not adhere to the academic definition of this term (Hsu and Chen 2018). They actually use a different model, promoting adverts throughout entertainment games, which is different from the core definition of gamification, which is the application of game features in non-game contexts. According to (Patrício et al. 2018), the main use of gamification in marketing literature is to give mundane tasks a sense of value. Huotari and Hamari further elaborate that gamification is "the process of enhancing a service with affordances for gameful experiences in order to support users' overall value creation."

According to recent empirical data, businesses use gamification largely to increase engagement, positive word-of-mouth, and customer loyalty (Leclercq et al. 2017). Consumers' cognitive, affective, and behavioral involvement were found to be strongly predicted by playful consuming experiences. It was discovered that gamification consumers' engagement behaviors are triggered by informational, amusing, lucrative, and relational material (Dolan et al. 2019). Consumer loyalty seems to increase with system usability and trust, and gamified, entertaining, and interesting apps seem to stimulate good feelings, which in turn boost motivation, interaction, and engagement. This is because highly gamified interactions are likely to increase players' emotional and cognitive attachment to the self-brand (Berger et al. 2018). Previous research found that gamified loyalty programs increased consumer loyalty, which in turn enhanced consumers' participation intention and app download intention more than the conventional loyalty programs. This research theorizes that gamification will serve as a mechanism for increased loyalty (Hwang and Choi 2019).

Customers' participation is frequently influenced by their psychological views of the brand, as emphasized by Brodie et al. (2011). A comprehensive review undertaken by Tobon et al. (2020) that identified five major psychological theories frequently used in evaluating the marketing implications of gamification has been used to support this. Self-determination theory, the technological acceptance model, the theory of planned behavior, the flow theory, and the social influence theory are the five theories. The literature has examined the impact of gamification on customer engagement from additional theoretical angles, but the majority of these reviews were psychological in nature, reflecting the central role that users' psychology plays in mediating the impact of gamification on their behavioral outcomes and value creation experiences. The idea of value creation has historically been shaped by research in the service dominant logic, service logic, and customer-dominant logic. Originally, this idea was thought to refer to the independent perception that consumers have regarding a service's quality, either during or after the consumption process (Hansen 2019).

3 Theoretical Framework and Hypothesis

According to the logic of the service-dominant industry, this can be seen as a collaborative but indirect creation between the businesses and their customers who utilize their expertise to continue the process of marketing, consumption, and value creation. Customers are no longer seen by businesses as passive tar gets as a result of their tendency to demand more active involvement in production and decision-making. Instead, they are allowing consumers to customize their consumption experiences and participate in the development of new products and services by opening their systems and processes. The growth of the internet and the emergence of social media networks have considerably aided this conceptual transition from customer value generation to value co-creation (Rathore et al. 2016). Nambisan and Nambisan (2008) assert that five important role product conceptualiser, product designer, product tester, product support specialist, and product marketer have been linked to customer co-creation in online communities. A more sophisticated variation of this phenomena known as "crowdsourcing" has emerged throughout the rapid spread of this phenomenon, when businesses systematically harness their customers' collective intellect to produce precise and well-constructed assignments.

Thus, we propose the following hypothesis:

H1. Consumer value-creation will benefit from gamification. Repurchase intent and eWOM sharing are complicated, rich behaviors that call for both aptitude and drive.

Consumer value-creation is a crucial marketing indicator that may be evaluated based on attitudes and behaviors, claim Macintosh and Lockshin (1997). Attitudinal value-creation essentially refers to a psychological attitude toward a company, its products, or services in which customers express a desire to advocate and urge others to utilize the company's goods and services. Consumer behavior traits including the frequency of their visits, their propensity to make repeat purchases, and their purchasing intents are all covered under behavioral loyalty. Consumer value-creation, according to Srivastava and Kaul (2016), is defined by purchasing a service, good, or particular brand over time. According to Ngobo (2017), there are three stages of consumer value-creation: no loyalty, latent loyalty, and true commitment. Consumer advocacy, positive word-of-mouth advertising, willingness to suggest, and patronage encouragement are all examples of displaying customer loyalty. Despite having switching options and/or learning about alternative brands, products, and services, loyal customers tend to return and repurchase more frequently. Due to previous dealings and the built-up trust, loyal customers are less inclined to seek for and/or evaluate a company's goods and services.

Thus, we propose the following hypotheses:

H2. Repurchase intents will positive impact from consumer value creation.

H3. Consumer value creation will be positively impacted on behavior of e-WOM Sharing

The usage of gamification marketing approach encourages customers to interact with the brand, reinforces their participation, and builds needs in them that frequently lead to buy intents (Wen, Chang, Lin, Liang, & Yang 2014). A higher rate of referrals on the virtual platform can be obtained from high-quality business-consumer relationships (Abubakar, Ilkan, & Sahin 2016). According to this perspective, consumer value-creation can have a significant impact on both customers and businesses. While value-creation saves customers time, energy, and effort when looking for and comparing competing goods and services, for businesses, loyal customers are a crucial success factor that brings in significant money (Chang & Chen 2009). According to research, interactivity and flow might boost gamers' loyalty (Khang, Kim, & Kim, 2013). Consumer value-creation has been employed as a predictor of referral behavior and tourist propensity to visit (Al-Htibat & Garanti 2019). Others (Gu, Oh, & Wang, 2016; Su, Chiang, Lee, & Chang, 2016) examined consumer value-creation as a response variable and behavior as well as a gamification mediating variable that connects crucial functions to buy behavior and e-WOM communication (Hsiao & Chen 2016; Oliver 1999).

Thus, we propose the following hypotheses:

H4. Gamification will mediate the relationship between consumer value-creation and eWOM sharing behavior (Fig. 1).

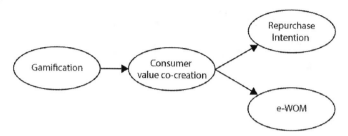

Fig. 1. Conceptual framework

4   Research Method and Data Collect

4.1   Samples and Scales

Businesses frequently work to attract and boost the number of customers. Positive feelings are said to be triggered by gamification, a contemporary marketing and promotional tactic. However, current research has hardly ever looked at how gamification affects consumer value creation and other results. The objectives of the current study are dual. This study looks at how gamification influences co-creation of Customer Value first. Second, this study explores the manifestation of repurchase intention and eWOM sharing behavior in Customer Value co-creation as a result of gamified interactions. A straightforward random sampling technique was used to collect data from 309 respondents who were consumers. A smartr PLS technique was used to examine the data that was obtained. Smart PLS results showed that gamification is a predictor for improved Customer Value co-creation. Customer Value co-creation not only encouraged eWOM sharing behavior and repurchase intention, but it also acted as a mediator in the relationship between gamification and eWOM sharing behavior. Linker scales were also employed to efficiently gather client feedback. By experimentally analyzing its influence on crucial marketing factors, this article adds to the body of knowledge about gamification marketing. Along with limits and future research directions, implications for theory and practice are examined.

4.2   Design/Methodology/Approach

The effect of gamification's reward system on customers value co-creation continuance, customer intention, and eWOM evaluation was investigated using scenario simulation experiments of the between-subjects design.

5   Results

5.1   Structural Model

Data analysis is performed using the most recent version of PLS-SEM, a second-generation multivariate analytic tool (Ringle et al., 2015). PLS-SEM is useful for formulating ideas and generating predictions. It can deal with formative and reflecting measurement models (Hair et al., 2014, 2016). In our investigation, every construct was reflecting (Fig. 2).

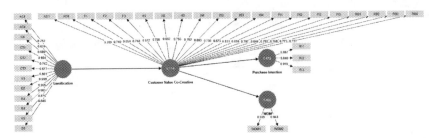

Fig. 2. Structural Model

5.2 Construct Reliability and Validity

First, the measurement model was employed to evaluate the data's reliability and validity. Next, the structural model was used to evaluate the path coefficient and significance. The reflective measurement model's reliability and validity were assessed using the criteria of internal consistency reliability, indicator reliability, convergent validity, and discriminant validity. Second, Cronbach's alpha is used to assess internal consistency. The authors state that for a test to be accepted, Cronbach's alpha must be more than 0.70. Since the values of Cronbach's alpha in Table 1 in our research varied from Customer Value co-creation to 0.957, Gamification to 0.945, Purchase Intention to 0.862, and eWOM to 0.785, the present study effectively met the internal consistency criteria. The authors suggested that the standardized range of the composite reliability coefficient be 0.7 or higher. The current study's composite dependability (CR) coefficient is set at 0.96 for co-creating customer value, 0.999 for gamification, 0.874 for repurchase intention, and 0.868 for word-of-mouth (eWOM), as shown in Table 1. Average variance retrieved was advised by Fornell and Larcker (1981) for convergent validity (AVE). AVE and factor loading for all latent variables were used to establish convergent validity. Convergent validity is the degree to which a measure has a positive connection with other measurements of the same variable. A standardized value of AVE must be higher than 0.50 (Hair et al. 2014). The current study's convergent validity has been demonstrated,

Table 1. Construct Reliability and Validity

	Cronbach's alpha	Composite reliability (rho_a)	Composite reliability (rho_c)	Average variance extracted (AVE)
Customer Value Co-Creation	0.957	0.96	0.961	0.553
Gamification	0.945	0.999	0.945	0.596
Repurchase Intention	0.862	0.874	0.915	0.783
eWOM	0.865	0.868	0.937	0.881

according to recent research results that show all AVE values to be above the acceptable range.

5.3 Discriminant Validity

In the subsequent stage of the measurement model, the concept's validity—which mandates that each latent variable be constructed differently from other constructs—is evaluated (Bagozzi et al. 1991). The Fornell-Larcker test, the heterotrait-monotrait trait (HTMT) ratio, and cross-loadings are used to evaluate it (Hair et al. 2011; Hair et al. 2014). In order for the Fornell-Larcker test (Fornell and Larcker 1981) to assess discriminative validity, the square root of the AVE value must be greater than the correlation between all study variables. The results in Table 2 corroborate this. As a result, this study demonstrated discriminative validity.

Table 2. Fornell-Larcker Criterian

	Customer Value Co-Creation	Gamification	Repurchase Intention	eWOM
Customer Value Co-Creation	0.743			
Gamification	0.338	0.772		
Repurchase Intention	0.688	0.327	0.885	
eWOM	0.657	0.327	0.805	0.839

5.4 Heterotrait-Monotrait (HTMT)

When estimating the correlation between variables, HTML is utilized, and if the HTMT value is less than 1, the constructions are distinct from one another (Haider et al. 2018). Kline (2011) designated .85 as the final cutoff as a result. Table 3 of the study's findings reveal that all values are below 0.85 So, in our investigation, the discriminant validity is demonstrated.

5.5 Outer Loadings

It should be easy to ascertain the factor loading of the different items by looking at the outer loading of each researched variable. The researcher provides a standardized value for maintaining an individual's possessions valued greater than 0.70. All values in the current investigations, with the exception of a few, were higher than 0.70. It has no effect on the analysis, though. It is therefore kept in situ, demonstrating the accuracy of all measures (Table 4).

Table 3. Heterotrait-Monotrait Ratio (HTMT)

	Customer Value Co-Creation	Gamification	Repurchase Intention	eWOM
Customer Value Co-Creation				
Gamification	0.288			
Repurchase Intention	0.742	0.3		
eWOM	0.711	0.354	0.831	

Table 4. Outer Loadings

	Customer Value Co-Creation	Gamification	Repurchase Intention	eWOM
AC1		0.752		
AC4		0.624		
AD1	0.709			
AD3	0.74			
C4		0.68		
CT1		0.604		
CT2		0.742		
CT3		0.677		
E1		0.861		
E2		0.9		
E3		0.905		
E4		0.903		
E5		0.876		
E6		0.64		
F1	0.659			
F2	0.748			
F3	0.672			
H1	0.766			
H2	0.692			
H3	0.783			
H4	0.792			
IS2	0.663			

(continued)

Table 4. (*continued*)

	Customer Value Co-Creation	Gamification	Repurchase Intention	eWOM
IS3	0.73			
IS4	0.673			
PI1	0.831			
PI2	0.816			
PI3	0.797			
PI5	0.644			
RB1	0.792			
RB2	0.768			
RB3	0.773			
RB4	0.777			
RI1			0.887	
RI2			0.848	
RI3			0.918	
WOM1				0.935
WOM2				0.943

5.6 Square

Second, the path coefficient of the fictitious connection is computed using the PLS technique, and significance is achieved using the usual bootstrap error. A significant connection is shown by a t value of larger than 1.96 (p.05). The following step involves deriving the coefficient of determination (R^2). According to Table 6, the value of R^2 reflects how much variation the exogenous variable explains. R^2 values of 0.114, 0.473, and 0.432, respectively, are regarded as moderate and significant (Hair et al., 2014). Recent investigations show that the model can handle a considerable amount of volatility (Table 5).

Table 5. R-square

	R-square	R-square adjusted
Customer Value Co-Creation	0.114	0.111
Repurchase Intention	0.473	0.472
WOM	0.432	0.43

5.7 Hypothesis Testing

P-values in route analysis show a strong relationship between variables. All hypotheses show a positive correlation, and the standard deviation number indicates how much the two variables deviate from their mean. Table 6 shows the p-values, t-values, and threshold levels for each hypothesis. All of the hypotheses were broadly accepted.

Table 6. Path Analysis (Direct Effect)

	Original sample (O)	Sample mean (M)	Standard deviation (STDEV)	T statistics (|O/STDEV|)	P values	Remark
Gamification -> Repurchase Intention	0.281	0.299	0.042	6.635	0.000	Accepted
Gamification -> eWOM	0.27	0.287	0.042	6.416	0.000	Accepted

5.8 Mediation

Since all beta values are positive and show a significant relationship between the p-value variables, all assumptions are accepted. The standard deviation value suggests that the two variables oscillate around the mean. This table demonstrates that the influence of mediation reduces mean and standard deviation values, demonstrating mediation's effectiveness but a reduced direct effect. When both direct and indirect impacts are present, partial arbitration occurs, in accordance with Baron and Kenny's (2010) arbitration criteria. Total mediation, on the other hand, takes place when the indirect influence is significant but the direct effect is not. The variables in this table show how the two structures are somewhat mediated. Table 7 indicates that all hypotheses are true, indicating that co-creation of customer value significantly mediates the positive correlation between gamification, Repurchase intention, and word-of-mouth (WOM).

Table 7. Path Analysis (Indirect Effect)

	Original sample (O)	Sample mean (M)	Standard deviation (STDEV)	T statistics (lO/STDEVl)	P values	Remark
Customer Value Co-Creation -> Repurchase Intention	0.688	0.69	0.041	16.686	0.000	Accepted
Customer Value Co-Creation -> eWOM	0.657	0.659	0.054	12.209	0.000	Accepted
Gamification -> Customer Value Co-Creation	0.338	0.35	0.046	7.35	0.000	Accepted

6 Conclusion

Although businesses are investing more in gamification (more than 50% of businesses will gamify certain areas of their business by 2020), (Gartner 2012). Previous research by Kaya et al. (2019) and Tata, Prashar, and Parsad (2019) revealed that consumers' perceptions of the usefulness of eCommerce sites and items are predictors of satisfaction and propensity to leave favorable reviews. This study emphasized that managers might gamify their business platforms to increase customer value co-creation in order to support this line of argument. For instance, Belanche, Flavián, and Pérez Rueda (2020) stated that social media's interactive capabilities enable users who are interested in disseminating advertisements to do so promptly and directly. Co-creation of consumer value benefits both customers and businesses. Boosts sales volume, decreases uncertainty and search efforts for potential customers, and serves as a cost-effective advertising and marketing medium. In actuality, game-mediated objects have the ability to stimulate cognitive engagement through involvement, presence, arousal, memory, and accomplishment (Abbasi et al. 2019). These types of pleasure frequently elicit routine behavior (such as buying habits) and/or narrative behavior (i.e., eWOM sharing behavior). Managers must therefore carefully examine their gamification and customer value co-creation initiatives in order to modify and utilize the successful strategies for locking in customers in order to foster their intentional inertia and lock-in effects. According to this study, gamified platforms have led highly devoted and engaged users to assume that actual Repurchases, buy intents, and even repeat purchases are natural behavioral acts.

Very few of these studies look at how gamification affects long-term results, despite the fact that it is demonstrably effective at encouraging eWOM and Customers Value co-creation to participate in communities and contribute to the production of brand value. In order to better understand the attitudes and behaviors of active and passive users, demographic characteristics should also be researched, possibly in light of novel marketing theories outside of the mainstream ones. Additionally, we advise further research into the function and effects of gamification in the rapidly expanding sharing economy sector, which is rarely covered in the literature. In addition to considering gamifying additional co-creation activities that were not mentioned in the literature but are typically connected to real-world commercial operations and corporate social responsibilities, we also shed light on the potential inclusion of advanced gaming technologies that could further enliven users' experiences.

References

Huotari, K., Hamari, J.: A definition for gamification: anchoring gamification in the service marketing literature. Electron. Markets **27**, 21–31 (2017)

Schoech, D., Boyas, J.F., Black, B.M., Elias-Lambert, N.: Gamification for behavior change: Lessons from developing a social, multiuser, Web-tablet based prevention game for youths. J. Technol. Hum. Serv. **31**, 197–217 (2013)

Tobon, S., Ruiz-Alba, J.L., García-Madariaga, J.: Gamification and online consumer decisions: Is the game over? Decis. Support Syst. **128**, 113167 (2020)

Deterding, S., Dixon, D., Khaled, R., Nacke, L.: From game design elements to gamefulness: Defining "gamification". In: Proceedings of the 15th International Academic MindTrek Conference: Envisioning Future Media Environments, Tampere, Finland, 28–30 September 2011, pp. 9–15. ACM, New York (2011)

Zichermann, G.; Cunningham, C.: Gamification by Design: Implementing Game Mechanics in Web and Mobile Apps, 1st edn. O'Reilly Media: Sebastopol, CA, USA (2011)

Patrício, R., Moreira, A.C., Zurlo, F.: Gamification approaches to the early stage of innovation. Creat. Innov. Manag. **27**, 499–511 (2018)

Petridis, P., et al.: State-of-the-Art in business games. Int. J. Serious Games **2**, 55–69 (2015)

Szendr˝oi, L., Dhir, K.S., Czakó, K.: Gamification in for-profit organisations: a mapping study. Bus. Theory Pract. **21**, 598–612 (2020)

Newcomb, E.T., Camblin, J.G., Jones, F.D., Wine, B.: On the implementation of a gamified professional development system for direct care staff. J. Organ. Behav. Manag. **39**, 293–307 (2019)

Van der Heijden, B.I.J.M., et al.: Gamification in dutch businesses: an explorative case study. SAGE Open **43**, 729–760 (2020)

Hsu, C.L., Chen, M.: How gamification marketing activities motivate desirable consumer behaviors: focusing on the role of brand love. Comput. Hum. Behav. **88**, 121–133 (2018)

Petridis, P., Hadjicosta, K., et al.: Gamification: Using gaming mechanics to promote a business. In: Proceedings of the Spring Servitization Conference, Birmingham, UK, 2–14 May 2014, pp. 166–172. Aston University, Birmingham (2014)

Deterding, S., Dixon, D., Khaled, R., Nacke, L.: From game design elements to gamefulness: defining gamification. In: Proceedings of the 15th International Academic MindTrek Conference: Envisioning Future Media Environments, September 28–30, 2011, Tampere, Finland, pp. 9–15. ACM (2011)

Hamari, J., Lehdonvirta, V.: Game design as marketing: how game mechanics create demand for virtual goods. Int. J. Bus. Sci. Appl. Manage. **5**(1), 14–29 (2010)

Hamari, K., Lehdonvirta, V.: Defining gamification: a service marketing perspective. In: Proceedings of the 16th International Academic MindTrek Conference, October 3–5, 2012, Tampere, Finland, pp. 17–22. ACM (2012)

Hamari, J.: Transforming homo economicus into homo ludens: a field experiment on gamification in a utilitarian peer-to-peer trading service. Electron. Commer. Res. Appl. **12**(4), 236–245 (2013)

Ryan, R.M., Deci, E.L.: Self-determination theory and the facilitation of intrinsic motivation, social development, and well-being. Am. Psychol. **55**(1), 68–78 (2000)

Gartner: Gartner says by 2015, more than 50 percent of organizations that manage innovation processes will gamify those processes. http://www.gartner.com/newsroom/id/1629214, April 12, 2011

Zichermann, G., Cunningham, C.: Gamification by design: Implementing game mechanics in web and mobile apps, Sebastopol, CA, O'Reilly Media (2011)

Deterding, S., Dixon, D., Khaled, R. and Nacke, L.: From game design elements to gameful-ness: defining 'gamification'. In: Proceedings of the 15th International Academic MindTrek Conference: Envisioning Future Media Environments, Association for Computing Machinery, Tampere, pp. 9–15 (2011)

Zichermann, G., Linder, J.: The Gamification Revolution: How Leaders Leverage Game Mechan-ics to Crush the Competition, ISBN: 9780071808316. McGraw-Hill Education, New York (2013)

Gatautis, R., Vitkauskaite, E., Gadeikiene, A., Piligrimiene, Z.: Gamification as a mean of driving online consumer behavior: SOR model perspective. Eng. Econ. **27**(1), 90–97 (2016)

Hunicke, R., LeBlanc, M., Zubek, R.: MDA: a formal approach to game design and game research. Proceedings of the AAAI Workshop on Challenges in Game AI in Nineteenth National Conference on Artificial Intelligence, San Jose, CA **4**(1), 1722 (2004)

Cramer, H., Ahmet, Z., Rost, M., Holmquist, L.: Gamification and location-sharing: Some emerg-ing social conflicts. Paper presented at Proceedings of the International Conference of the ACM on Computer Human Interaction, May 7–12, 2012, Vancouver, Canada (2011)

Xu, F., Tian, F., Buhalis, D., Weber, J., Zhang, H.: Tourists as mobile gamers: gamification for tourism marketing. J. Travel Tour. Mark. **33**(8), 1124–1142 (2016)

Xi, N., Hamari, J.: Does gamification affect brand engagement and equity? a study in online brand communities. J. Bus. Res. **109**, 449–460 (2020)

Amalgam Insights. Industry analyst: Failed gamification projects, costing U.S. businesses more than $700 million, can be fixed (2018). https://globenewswire.com/news-release/2018/03/19/1442013/0/en/Industry-Analyst-Failed-GamificationProjects-Costing-US-Businesses-More-Than-700-Million-Can-Be-Fixed.htm

Berger, A., Schlager, T., Sprott, D.E., Herrmann, A.: Gamified interactions: whether, when, and how games facilitate self–brand connections. J. Acad. Mark. Sci. **46**(4), 652–673 (2018)

Eisingerich, A.B., Marchand, A., Fritze, M.P., Dong, L.: Hook vs. hope: How to enhance customer engagement through gamification. Int. J. Res. Mark. **36**(2), 200–215 (2019)

Glover, I.: Play as you learn: gamification as a technique for motivating learners. In: Edme-dia+ innovate learning, pp. 1999–2008. Association for the Advancement of Computing in Education (AACE) (2013)

Nicholson, S.: A RECIPE for meaningful gamification. In: Reiners, T., Wood, L.C. (eds.) Gami-fication in Education and Business, pp. 1–20. Springer, Cham (2015). https://doi.org/10.1007/978-3-319-10208-5_1

Xu, Y. (2011). Literature review on web application gamification and analytics, pp. 5–11. Honolulu, HI

Oliver, R.L.: Whence consumer loyalty? J. Mark. **63**, 33–44 (1999)

Aksoy, L., Keiningham, T.L., Buoye, A., Larivière, B., Williams, L., Wilson, I.: Does loyalty span domains? Examining the relationship between consumer loyalty, other loyalties and happiness. J. Bus. Res. **68**(12), 2464–2476 (2015)

Al-Zyoud, M.F.: Does social media marketing enhance impulse purchasing among female cus-tomers case study of Jordanian female shoppers. J. Bus. Retail Manage. Res. **13**(2), 135–151 (2018b)

Dolan, R., Conduit, J., Frethey-Bentham, C., Fahy, J., Goodman, S.: Social media engagement behavior: a framework for engaging customers through social media content. Eur. J. Mark. **53**(10), 2213–2243 (2019). https://doi.org/10.1108/EJM-03-2017-0182

Hwang, J., Choi, L.: Having fun while receiving rewards? exploration of gamification in loyalty programs for consumer loyalty. J. Bus. Res. **106**, 365–376 (2019)

Brodie, R.J., Hollebeek, L.D., Juric, B., Ilic, A.: Customer engagement: conceptual domain, fundamental propositions, and implications for research. J. Serv. Res. **14**, 1–20 (2011)

Leclercq, T., Poncin, I., Hammedi, W.: The engagement process during value co creation: gamification in new product-development platforms. Int. J. Electron. Commer. **21**(4), 454–488 (2017)

Srivastava, M., Kaul, D.: Exploring the link between customer experience loyalty consumer spends. J. Retail. Consum. Serv. **31**, 277–286 (2016)

Rathore, A.K., Ilavarasan, P.V., Dwivedi, Y.K.: Social media content and product co-creation: an emerging paradigm. J. Enterp. Inf. Manag. **29**, 7–18 (2016)

Hansen, A.V.: Value co-creation in service marketing: a critical (re)view. Int. J. Innov. Stud. **3**, 73–83 (2019)

Granic, I., Lobel, A., Engels, R.C.: The benefits of playing video games. Am. Psychol. **69**(1), 66–78 (2014)

Hamari, J., Tuunanen, J.: Player types: a metasynthesis. Trans. Digital Games Res. Assoc. **1**(2), 29–53 (2014)

Yee, N.: Motivations for play in online games. Cyberpsychol. Behav. **9**(6), 772–775 (2006)

Suh, A., Cheung, C.M.K., Ahuja, M., Wagner, C.: Gamification in the workplace: the central role of the aesthetic experience. J. Manag. Inf. Syst. **34**(1), 268–305 (2017). https://doi.org/10.1080/07421222.2017.1297642

Phua, P.J.: Starring in your own Snapchat advertisement: Influence of self-brand congruity, self-referencing and perceived humor on brand attitude and purchase intention of advertised brands. Telematics Inform. **33**(5), 1524–1533 (2018). https://doi.org/10.1016/j.tele.2018.03.020

Kennedy, E., Guzmán, F.: Co-creation of brand identities: consumer and industry influence and motivations. J. Consum. Market. **33**(5), 313–323 (2016)

Sigala, M.: The application and impact of gamification funware on trip planning and experiences: the case of TripAdvisor's funware. Electron. Markets **25**(3), 189–209 (2015a)

Sigala, M.: Applying gamification and assessing its effectiveness in a tourism context. Asia Pac. J. Inf. Syst. **25**(1), 179–210 (2015b)

Pavlus, J.: The game of life. Sci. Am. **303**, 43–44 (2010)

Lee, J., Hammer, J.: Gamification in education: what, how, why bother? Acad. Exch. Q. **15**(2), 1–5 (2011)

Schweidel, D.A., Moe, W.W.: Listening in on social media: a joint model of sentiment and venue format choice. J. Market. Res. **51**(4), 387–402 (2014)

Khan, Z.A., Ullrich, J., Voyiatzis, A.G., Herrmann, P.: A trust-based resilient routing mechanism for the internet of things. In: Proceedings of the 12th International Conference on Availability, Reliability and Security, pp. 1–6, August 2017

Hsiao, K.L., Chen, C.C.: What drives in-app purchase intention for mobile games? An examination of perceived values and loyalty. Electron. Commer. Res. Appl. **16**, 18–29 (2016)

Su, Y.-S., Chiang, W.-L., Lee, C.-T.J., Chang, H.-C.: The effect of flow experience on player loyalty in mobile game application. Comput. Hum. Behav. **63**, 240–248 (2016)

Al-Htibat, A., Garanti, Z.: Impact of interactive eReferral on tourists behavioral intentions. Market. Intell. Plan. **37**(5), 527–541 (2019)

Khang, H., Kim, J.K., Kim, Y.: Self-traits and motivations as antecedents of digital media flow and addiction: the Internet, mobile phones, and video games. Comput. Hum. Behav. **29**(6), 2416–2424 (2013)

Chang, H.H., Chen, S.W.: Consumer perception of interface quality, security, and loyalty in electronic commerce. Inf. Manag. **46**(7), 411–417 (2009)

Abubakar, A.M., Ilkan, M., Sahin, P.: eWOM, eReferral and gender in the virtual community. Market. Intell. Plan. (2016)

Wen, D.M.H., Chang, D.J.W., Lin, Y.T., Liang, C.W., Yang, S.Y.: Gamification design for increasing customer purchase intention in a mobile marketing campaign app. In: Nah, F.F.H. (ed.) HCIB/HCII 2014. LNCS, vol. 8527, pp. 440–448. Springer, Cham (2014). https://doi.org/10.1007/978-3-319-07293-7_43

Hair Jr., J.F., Sarstedt, M., Hopkins, L., Kuppelwieser, V.G.: Partial least squares structural equation modeling (PLS-SEM) an emerging tool in business research. Eur. Bus. Rev. **26**(2), 106–121 (2014)

Ringle, C., Da Silva, D., Bido, D.: Structural equation modeling with the SmartPLS (2015)

Bido, D., da Silva, D., Ringle, C.: Structural equation modeling with the SmartPLS. Braz. J. Market. **13**(2) (2014)

Hair, J.F., Ringle, C.M., Sarstedt, M.: PLS-SEM: indeed a silver bullet. J. Market. Theory Pract. **19**(2), 139–152 (2011)

Kline, R.B.: Principles and Practice of Structural Equation Modeling, 3rd edn. Guilford, New York (2011)

Haider, S., Jabeen, S., Ahmad, J.: Moderated mediation between work life balance and employee job performance: the role of psychological wellbeing and satisfaction with coworkers. Revista de Psicología del Trabajo y de las Organizaciones **34**(1), 29–37 (2018)

Belanche, D., Flavián, C., Pérez-Rueda, A.: Consumer empowerment in interactive advertising and eWOM consequences: the PITRE model. J. Market. Commun. **26**(1), 1–20 (2020)

Gartner: Gamification: engagement strategies for business and IT. Report G00245563 (2012)

"Escapad" Dance Serious Game: Designing a Therapeutic Tool for Elderly with Mild Cognitive Impairment

Sawsen Ayari[1]([✉]), Olivier Gavarry[1], and Alexandre Abellard[2]

[1] IAPS, Université de Toulon, CS60584, 83041 CEDEX 9 Toulon, France
sawsen-ayari@etud.univ-tln.fr
[2] IMSIC, Université de Toulon, CS60584, 83041 CEDEX 9 Toulon, France

Abstract. The care of elderly people with neurodegenerative diseases leading to cognitive disorders and dementia represents a major health issue. In this context, serious games (SGs) can improve cognitive functions efficiently. Exergames can boost cognitive functions such as attention and memory. In this population, negative feelings can be exacerbated by inadapted technological design. The aim of this study is to design and evaluate an adapted exergame named Escapad for older adults suffering from Mild Cognitive Impairment (MCI). As part of preliminary study, two versions of Escapad were used with both therapists and MCI patients, who rated version 2 as more adaptable. Hence, we have implemented Escapad to stimulate several cognitive domains in elderly people with MCI who have a depressive tendency. Our results showed a significant improvement in visuospatial abilities/executive functions ($p = 0.033$), temporo-spatial orientation ($p = 0.048$) and a significant reduction in depression ($p = 0.033$). Technical aspects and game use are discussed in this paper.

Keywords: Serious Game · Dementia · Cognitive Impairment · Rehabilitation

1 Introduction

1.1 Context

Dementia has been characterized as a global public health priority, its impact on individuals, families, and societies has been enormous [1]. In high-income countries, the number of people with dementia is expected to triple by 2050 [2]. There is likely a continuum of function between normal aging (normality) and the early signs of Alzheimer's disease. This transient condition has been termed Mild Cognitive Impairment (MCI) [3].

Neuropsychiatric symptoms (NPS) such as: agitation/aggression, depression, apathy, psychosis, sleep disturbances, and aberrant motor behaviors [4] are common and disabling features of dementia with key impacts on the Quality of Life (QOL) of patients, caregivers, and caretakers and result in significant societal cost [5]. Older adults with MCI with associated NPS are more likely than those without NPS to progress to major neurocognitive impairment [6].

© The Author(s), under exclusive license to Springer Nature Switzerland AG 2023
X. Fang (Ed.): HCII 2023, LNCS 14046, pp. 222–236, 2023.
https://doi.org/10.1007/978-3-031-35930-9_15

Early detection of MCI is a crucial step for a better disease management if the cause of the impairment is a neurodegenerative disease [7]. A number of studies have noted that NPS are associated with accelerated cognitive decline, raising the possibility that effective treatment might not only reduce psychiatric morbidity but also delay cognitive and functional decline [8, 9].

1.2 Cognitive Rehabilitation Using SG

Cognitive rehabilitation is an individualized approach aimed at improving functional capacity of older people with cognitive impairment, helping to reduce caregiver burden [10, 11]. Dance combines physical activity, social and emotional engagement, and cognitive stimulation all programmed to maintain synaptic connections and plasticity [12]. Serious games (SG) can be used in this context to improve cognitive functions in efficient way [13–16]. Exergames can have a particular positive impact on cognitive functions, such as attention and memory [17, 18] and visuospatial abilities [19]. They may also have a positive impact on social life and emotional functions [18, 20] and reduce depression [21].

Nevertheless, most research to date has been conducted using commercial video games and cognitive games (such as Wii Fit and Wii Sport, Lumosity) designed for entertainment purposes, and with a "typical" healthy user [22]. Wargnier et al. [23] stated that few technological systems are specifically designed to population with cognitive impairment who is already subject to frustration and lack of confidence due to their condition. Unsuitable technological designs can fuel additional negative feelings [24]. Technologies aimed at people with cognitive disabilities must consider their needs, preferences, abilities, and limitations. Ignoring their particularities not only affects them, but also their families and the society in general, involving a costly burden for the community [25].

Therefore, a SG called "Escapad" has been designed and tested in two versions with caregivers and patients suffering from (MCI) to provide an adapted tool. In this study, we attempt to describe the different stages of conception and implementation of the SG Escapad taking into consideration the therapists' recommendations and the older person's abilities. This study is part of a larger study about the interest of dance in the cognitive rehabilitation of MCI people.

2 Materials and Methods

2.1 Participants

Five older adults with mild cognitive impairment (MCI) according to Petersen criteria [3] and six caregivers were recruited to test the Escapad serious game. The participants belonged to two different facilities in the south of France:

- "Mas des Senes" nursing home (La Garde)
- Alzheimer's caregivers' day center (Bandol)

The elderly MCI patients were 3 women and 2 men aged between 66 and 91 years. The diagnosis of MCI was established using education-adjusted scores from the Mini-Mental

State Examination (MMSE GRECO version), as in (1):

$$MMSE = rawMMSE - (0.471 \times [education - 12] + (0.131 \times [age - 70]). \quad (1)$$

MMSE score ranges between 0 and 30, 30 being the best score possible. A person suffering from MCI has MMSE ranging between 19 and 26 [26]. These participants were also screened based on MCI designation often supported by an overall Clinical Dementia Rating (CDR) score of 0.5 [27]. (CDR < 0: normal cognition, CDR = 0.5: MCI, CDR > 1: dementia) were included [28].

In addition, the caregivers were 4 women and 2 men between the ages of 23 and 69 years. The caregivers were a doctor, a nurse manager, 3 health care assistants and a medical-psychological assistant (Table 1).

Table 1. Characteristics of MCI patients and caregivers during tests of Escapad versions V1 and V2 (NA: Not Applicable, adjusted MMSE score, GE: game experience, DE: dance experience, ♀ female)

	Escapad V1				Escapad V2			
	MCI patients (n = 2)		Caregivers (n = 3)		MCI patients (n = 3)		Caregivers (n = 3)	
	Mean	SD	Mean	SD	Mean	SD	Mean	SD
Age	85.0	8.5	44.7	18.8	81.7	13.7	48.3	17.9
% ♀	0.0	0.0	100.0	0.0	100.0	0.0	25.0	0.0
IMC	24.8	0.3	24.4	3.0	21.0	1.6	22.7	0.8
Educ	4.0	0.0	12.3	2.5	10.0	7.9	15.3	3.5
MMSE	27.8	2.1	NA	NA	21.0	1.6	NA	NA
CDR	0.5	0.0	NA	NA	0.5	0.0	NA	NA
GE	0.0	0.0	1.7	1.2	0.0	0.0	3.3	2.9
DE	2.0	1.4	2.0	1.0	1.3	0.6	1.7	0.6

Elderly people with MCI were selected in accordance with the following criteria:

- good vision
- good hearing
- good understanding of the instructions
- good hand-eye coordination
- being able to use the mini-bike (see Sect. 2.2) with their hands or use the joystick

We have excluded elderly people with vision problems such as AMD (Age-related Macular Degeneration) or cataracts. We also excluded people with probable dementia according to the National Institute of Neurological and Communicative Disorders and Stroke/Alzheimer's Disease and Related Disorders Association (MINCDS/ADRDA) criteria.

2.2 Escapad

Escapad is a third person exergame consisting of a succession of short game sequences alternating cognitive and functional stimulation (memory games, pedaling exercises, Stroop test, spatial orientation) (see Figs. 1 and 2). The game ends with a musical sequence on a dance floor with a partner chosen by the player. The choice of short duration for game sequences has been done in accordance with rehabilitation sessions as well as elderly people physical and cognitive abilities. Escapad was developed according to the recommendations of a specialized occupational therapist.

Two main interfaces can be used according to the player's choices and abilities: either a joystick or an electronically adapted mini-bike that can be connected to a laptop USB port. This last interface is especially innovative and one of the goals of the experimentation phase was to check its interest for elderly people.

Before a session, participants were asked to write the current date and to draw a 3D figure (like a cube) for 5 min. Then, each participant trained individually on Escapad for approximately 20 min.

Fig. 1. Escapad: spatial orientation and short memory exercise

2.3 Experimentation Phases

Our study was designed following the recommendations for the adaptive use of serious games [29]. This interventional study was approved by the Ethical Committee for research in STAPS- Toulon University (notice number IRB00012476–2021-30–09-127). All participants were informed about the conduct of this study, which we conducted in a therapeutic workshop format. All participants were consenting. Our preliminary study had three phases:

Phase 1 (version 1): testing Escapad first version in "Mas des Senes" with 3 female care staff (nurse manager, caregiver, and medical-psychological assistant; mean age =

Fig. 2. Escapad: pedaling exercise as executive functions training.

44.66 years) and 2 male residents (mean age = 85 years). Each caregiver completed a self-administered questionnaire about the SG and each resident completed a semi-structured questionnaire. Following this test, we realized both residents and nursing staff experienced many difficulties. We therefore called upon the developer of Escapad to improve and adapt the first version while considering the recommendations of the participants and the occupational therapist/PhD student of this study. Once version 2 was ready, we proceeded to phase 2.

Phase 2 (version 2): testing Escapad second (and improved) version in the Alzheimer Caregivers Day care center with 3 caregivers (one doctor and 2 caregivers; both sexes; mean age = 48.33 years) and 3 female residents (mean age = 81.66 years) (see Table 1). Figure 3 shows examples of Escapad sessions.

Fig. 3. Escapad use by an elderly MCI patient (left) and by a caregiver (right), using either joystick or mini-bike.

Phase 3: Designing a methodology for using Escapad. A classic Delphi method [30] was used as well as a questionnaire aimed to the care staff about their feeling on the general framework for using the SG: For whom? Why? When? With whom?

2.4 Evaluation

Phases 1 and 2. The design of the Escapad SG was based on studies that examined cognitive outcomes in dual-task tasks in which, there is naturalistic interactivity as in the cybercycle scenario [31] as well as other interactive modalities such as dance [32–40]. These studies had the objective of achieving cognitive improvement, especially concerning executive functions.

The questionnaires given were designed to evaluate 3 items:

- the technical aspect of the SG
- adaptation to the public
- adaptation to the objectives of cognitive training

Phase 3. The Delphi method we used for this study is inspired by [30]. A list of questions (For whom? For what? Where? …) was addressed to the caregivers. In most cases, the answers were written directly on paper just after the end of a session with Escapad. In other cases, answers were collected by phone in a short time period after an Escapad session.

3 Results

After testing the Escapad serious game, the six caregivers and five residents completed their respective questionnaires. The caregivers responded in a self-administered manner to a questionnaire containing 12 questions on three items:

- technical aspect of the SG
- suitability for the public
- adaptation to the objectives of cognitive training

The residents responded in a semi-structured way to a questionnaire containing 8 questions on two items.

- adaptation to the audience
- technical aspect

The processing of the data from the questionnaires was done in a qualitative way for both the 1st and 2nd phase.

3.1 Results of Phase 1 and Phase 2

The results are summarized in Figs. 4 and 5.

Results for the Healthcare Staff. When we look at the results of the healthcare personnel, we find that the item "adaptation to the public" is the item that most meets the

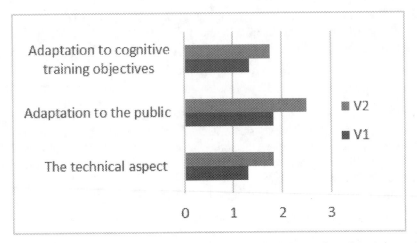

Fig. 4. Results of the caregiver's questionnaire concerning both Escapad versions (min possible score: 0, max possible score: 3).

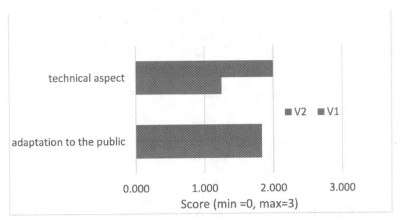

Fig. 5. Results of the MCI patient's questionnaire concerning both Escapad versions

expectations of the healthcare professionals, it represents 43% of the score against 29% for "the technical aspect" and 28% for "adaptation to the cognitive training objectives". These two items continue to meet the experts' expectations to a moderate degree.

Regarding the item "adaptation to cognitive training objectives", the Escapad SG does not seem to be a tool that could be used in full autonomy by MCI elderly people; a caregiver would have to accompany the elderly person each time it was used. Similarly, 33.33% of the caregivers did not answer whether the SG could improve the executive functions, especially the mental flexibility of the MCI elderly, the technical terms used in this question seem to be at the origin of the lack of response. Nevertheless, the caregivers found that SG provided memory training and therefore met the expected cognitive objectives.

As for the "technical aspect" item, the caregivers were satisfied with the sound ambiance of the SG, which has a playful aspect for the elderly MCI and is adapted to this target population.

Outcomes for MCI Seniors. Regarding the item "technical aspect", the elderly appreciated the graphic design of the SG, 100% of the residents are very satisfied with the graphic design, which is now a strong point of the Escapad SG. However, the use of the pedalboard (minibike) remains a difficult task for the MCI elderly because of the degraded state of their shoulder joints. This is a real weakness of the SG, as it was designed to provide both physical stimulation (pedaling) and cognitive stimulation.

As for the item "adaptation to the public", the concept of the SG in general as well as the change of atmosphere are strong points of the tool in version 2, 34% declare to be very satisfied with the concept and 67% declare to feel immersed in another environment and cut off from their environment, this aspect makes them very satisfied. Nevertheless, the SG was not considered as a fun and entertaining tool, 33% were not at all satisfied with this fun aspect and 33% were moderately satisfied.

To summarize and considering the feedback from the elderly and the nursing staff, the SG has strong points:

- the graphics
- the sound environment
- the adaptation to the target audience
- the stimulation of the memory
- the immersion in a virtual world

and weak points:

- the use of the minibike
- the inability of the residents to play independently.

3.2   Delphi Results

The Delphi analysis show the following scores on nursing staff recommendation on the use of "Escapad" (Fig. 5).

This Delphi study enabled us to precise in what conditions Escapad should be used by elderly MCI people. "Once a week" seems largely favored use frequency, in a medical context ("day center" or "hospital"), with the help of a therapist or a caregiver. Escapad is also acknowledged as a tool for cognition rehabilitation and stimulation [45].

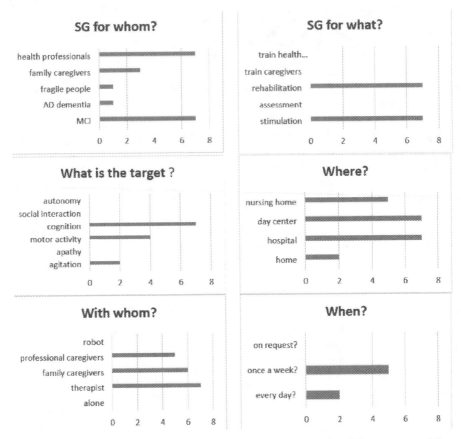

Fig. 6. Results of the Delphi study on "Escapad" use recommendation (Max. score possible on each item = 7)

4 Implementation and Testing of Escapad in Rehabilitation

4.1 Participants

Five new MCI seniors were recruited to train with the Escapad SG (version 2). These seniors had never seen or tried the tool. Participants were 3 women and 3 men aged between 74 and 90 years old. The diagnosis of MCI was established using education-adjusted scores considering their MMSE score (cf. Section 2.1) in addition with an overall Clinical Dementia Rating (CDR) score of 0.5 [27]. Depressive diagnosis was established using the Geriatric Depression Scale-15 (GDS-15) [41], scores superior to 3 were inclusive. Participants characteristics are described in Table 2.

We also used Montreal Cognitive Assessment (MoCA) to assess cognitive functions before and after the training [42].

4.2 Assessment Protocol

Cognitive Measures. The MoCA was developed for the detection of mild cognitive impairment (MCI) by health professionals. The assessment consists of a 30-point test and can be administered in 10min. A score of 26 or above is considered normal [43]. The MoCA assesses several cognitive domains. These are Visuospatial/Executive, Naming, Memory, Attention, Language, Abstraction, Delayed Recall and Orientation (to time and place). Visuospatial abilities are assessed using a clock-drawing task and a trail-making task which is said to be useful in assessing fitness to drive [44].

Psychological Measures. The Geriatric Depression Scale-15 (GDS-15) is a short 15 items instrument specifically designed to assess depression in geriatric populations. Its items require a yes/no response. According to conventional GDS-15 theory, a score of five positive items indicates mild depression, while a score of 10 positive items indicates moderate to severe depression, and so it is recommended to follow-up with a clinical examination to confirm diagnosis [45]. As the GDS-15 is a self-report scale, it requires patients to be capable of self-administrating. In addition, GDS-15 can detect depression among elderly people with mild to moderate dementia and physical illness [46]. Thus, GDS-15 (Geriatric Depression Scale-15) is a reliable and valid tool for measuring depression among elderly patients.

4.3 Intervention

We conducted 4 individual training sessions. The training was carried out by a medical and psychological assistant and a teacher in adapted physical activities. Session duration per person was approximately 25 min as described in Sect. 2.2. Outcomes were measured at baseline and after 4 training sessions with Escapad V2. Two clinical evaluations were carried out before and after the training with these participants. These evaluations were conducted by an occupational therapist who did not know the residents and who did not attend the training sessions. Medication intake was controlled and remained stable throughout the procedure.

4.4 Data Analysis

To determine the group difference for the cognitive and psychological function, several tests exist. Student's t-test is first performed with Shapiro-Wilk normality test. Wilcoxon test is subsequently used in case previous results are abnormal [47]. Descriptive statistics were calculated to demonstrate the groups' baseline sociodemographic characteristics. A significance level was set at 5% for all statistical analyses. All values in the text and tables are presented as the mean $\pm$ Standard Deviation (SD).

4.5 Results

Table 2 summarizes the sociodemographic outcomes of the participants, all suffering from both MCI and depressive tendencies.

Table 2. Clinical and sociodemographic outcomes at baseline. Data presented as mean ± SD. BMI: Body Mass Index (F: female)

Characteristics	MCI participants (n = 5)
Age (years)	82 ± 6.5
Sex (frequencies)	3F/5
BMI (kg.m^{-2})	25.1 ± 1.4
Schooling (years)	7 ± 3.7
MMSE adjusted (score/30)	25.1 ± 1.2
GDS-15 (score/15)	6.2 ± 4.1
CDR	0.5
Experience in SG (frequencies)	1/5
Experience in years of dance	2/5

Table 3 draws the comparison of GDS-15 and MoCa scores before and after the 4 training sessions. Each MoCa item is detailed with its score as well as the whole MoCa score. $p \leq 0.050$ means a significant effect measured by MoCa. $p \leq 0.033$ means a significant effect measured by GDS-15.

As it can be seen, improvements measured by either MoCa in two cognitive domains, namely visuo-spatial/executive functions and orientation. A signification psychological state improvement has also been measured with GDS-15.

Table 3. Effects of 4 sessions of SG training on cognitive functions and psychological states for Escapad intervention group (NS : Not Significant, * : significant effect measured by MoCa or GDS-15).

Clinical evaluations	Pre	Post	P
GDS-15	6.2 ± 4.1	3.6 ± 3.7	0.033*
MoCa	17.8 ± 2.6	22.2 ± 3.8	0.004*
Visuo spatial/ executive	2.2 ± 1.5	3.4 ± 1.1	0.033*
Naming	3 ± 0	3 ± 0	NS
Attention	4.4 ± 1.1	5.2 ± 0.8	0.072
Language	2 ± 0	2 ± 0	NS
Abstraction	1.2 ± 0.4	1.4 ± 0.5	0.621
Delayed recall	1 ± 1.2	2 ± 1.4	0.142
Orientation	3.2 ± 1.8	4.6 ± 1.9	0.048*

5 Discussion and Conclusions

The goals of this study were to prove whether taking into consideration different therapist recommendations and patients' abilities are important in designing a successful SG with good cognitive and psychological results. We evaluated three important domains: the technical aspect of the SG, suitability for the public and adaptation to the objectives of cognitive training.

Concerning the first point, Escapad seems technically adapted to both caregivers and elderly MCI patients. Joystick was largely favored compared to the minibike that was hard to use for people suffering from physical weaknesses, like arthrosis. Patients especially appreciated the graphics and the immersion into the game environment.

Caregivers give a good point to the sound ambiance and to the memory training given by the SG.

According to the caregivers, Escapad seems adapted to elderly MCI people with some restrictions. For example, it cannot be used in autonomy or at home, but these were not aims we had in mind when conceiving this SG. Escapad can have a positive effect with a therapist, nurse or caregiver staying near the patient to explain and motivate him to play the game.

Our results showed that the V2 of SG Escapad is most adapted to the MCI older adults compared to V1. V2 takes better in consideration the physical and cognitive limitations of MCI elderly people so that their game experience is improved and more comfortable.

Our findings showed that ecological individual training is effective to enhance cognition (MoCA) especially visuo spatial abilities, executive functions, orientation and reduce depression (GDS). Executive functions results are consistent with the findings of Ben-Sadoun et al. [48].

Finally, we observed significant improvements on some cognitive items, especially visuo-spatial abilities, executive functions, and orientation. Escapad seems to show efficiency as a rehabilitation tool in these specific areas.

Despite these positive results, we must acknowledge the following limitations. To begin with, our study is at a preliminary step, with a limited number of patients. Healthcare centers aimed at elderly MCI persons are difficult to access for scientific experiments, since elder people are fragile, administrative process is long and regulations are restrictive. Covid-19 confinements complicated furthermore the possibilities of experimentation for a long time.

Moreover, the use of a mini-bike by hand proved to be very difficult to use, while we thought this interface would be innovative and useful for upper-limb members rehabilitation by game. The pedalboard presented a big mechanical resistance for elderly people suffering from arthrosis, and the arms movements were too large and repetitive. However, since cognitive training was the priority of Escapad sessions, this is not be a big issue. If we want to use a similar interface in the future, it will have to be specifically studied, in terms of mechanical resistance and lower movement amplitude.

Finally, Escapad version 1 showed major flaws since medical staff and caregivers were not involved enough in the design phase. A co-design approach including programmer, occupational therapist, medical staff and caregivers should be systematically performed for the design of a new software adapted to a specific audience.

234   S. Ayari et al.

References

1. World Health Organization: Global patient safety action plan 2021–2030: towards eliminating avoidable harm in health care. World Health Organization, Geneva (2021)
2. Schmachtenberg, T., Monsees, J., Hoffmann, W., van den Berg, N., Stentzel, U., Thyrian, J.R.: Comparing national dementia plans and strategies in Europe – is there a focus of care for people with dementia from a migration background? BMC Public Health **20**, 784 (2020). https://doi.org/10.1186/s12889-020-08938-5
3. Petersen, R.C.: Mild cognitive impairment as a diagnostic entity. J Intern Med. **256**, 183–194 (2004). https://doi.org/10.1111/j.1365-2796.2004.01388.x
4. Lyketsos, C.G., et al.: Neuropsychiatric symptoms in Alzheimer's disease. Alzheimer's & Dementia. **7**, 532–539 (2011). https://doi.org/10.1016/j.jalz.2011.05.2410
5. Bradfield, N.I., Ames, D.: Mild cognitive impairment: narrative review of taxonomies and systematic review of their prediction of incident Alzheimer's disease dementia. B. J. Psych. Bull. **44**, 67–74 (2019). https://doi.org/10.1192/bjb.2019.77
6. Teri, L., Gibbons, L.E., McCurry, S.M., Logsdon, R.G., Buchner, D.M., Barlow, W.E., et al.: Exercise plus behavioral management in patients with Alzheimer disease: a randomized controlled trial. JAMA **290**(15), 2015 (2003). https://doi.org/10.1001/jama.290.15.2015
7. Porsteinsson, A.P., Isaacson, R.S., Knox, S., Sabbagh, M.N., Rubino, I.: Diagnosis of early Alzheimer's disease: clinical practice in 2021. J. Prev. Alzheimer's Dis. **8**(3), 371–386 (2021). https://doi.org/10.14283/jpad.2021.23
8. Modrego, P.J., Ferrández, J.: Depression in patients with mild cognitive impairment increases the risk of developing dementia of Alzheimer type: a prospective cohort study. Arch. Neurol. **61**, 1290–1293 (2004). https://doi.org/10.1001/archneur.61.8.1290
9. Rosenberg, P.B., Mielke, M.M., Appleby, B.S., Oh, E.S., Geda, Y.E., Lyketsos, C.G.: The association of neuropsychiatric symptoms in MCI with incident dementia and Alzheimer disease. Am. J. Geriatr. Psychiatry. **21**, 685–695 (2013). https://doi.org/10.1016/j.jagp.2013.01.006
10. Germain, S., et al.: Efficacy of cognitive rehabilitation in Alzheimer disease: a 1-year follow-up study. J. Geriatr. Psychiatry Neurol. **32**, 16–23 (2019). https://doi.org/10.1177/0891988718813724
11. Oltra-Cucarella, J., Pérez-Elvira, R., Espert, R., Sohn McCormick, A.: Are cognitive interventions effective in Alzheimer's disease? a controlled meta-analysis of the effects of bias. Neuropsychology **30**, 631–652 (2016). https://doi.org/10.1037/neu0000283
12. Dominguez, J.C., et al.: Improving cognition through dance in older filipinos with mild cognitive impairment. Curr. Alzheimer Res. **15**, 1136–1141 (2018). https://doi.org/10.2174/1567205015666180801112428
13. Golliot, J.: Towards a cognitive and conceptual rupture in the orientation of the therapeutic dimension in cognitive functional rehabilitation: introduction of a therapeutic Serious Game as a mediation device. https://hal.science/tel-03169009 (2020)
14. Rego, P., Moreira, P.M., Reis, L.P.: Serious games for rehabilitation: A survey and a classification towards a taxonomy. In: 5th Iberian conference on information systems and technologies, pp. 1–6. IEEE (2010)
15. Robert, P.H., et al.: Recommendations for the use of serious games in people with Alzheimer's disease, related disorders and frailty. Front. aging neurosci. **6**, 54 (2014)
16. Wattanasoontorn, V., Hernández, R.J.G., Sbert, M.: Serious games for e-health care. In: Cai, Y., Goei, S.L. (eds.) Simulations, Serious Games and Their Applications. GMSE, pp. 127–146. Springer, Singapore (2014). https://doi.org/10.1007/978-981-4560-32-0_9

17. Stavros, Z., Fotini, K., Magda, T.: Computer based cognitive training for patients with mild cognitive impairment (MCI). In: Proceedings of the 3rd International Conference on PErvasive Technologies Related to Assistive Environments, pp. 1–3. Association for Computing Machinery, New York, NY, USA (2010). https://doi.org/10.1145/1839294.1839319

18. Weybright, E., Dattilo, J., Rusch, F.: Effects of an interactive video game (Nintendo Wii) on older women with mild cognitive impairment. Ther. Recreation J. **44**, 271 (2010)

19. Yamaguchi, H., Maki, Y., Takahashi, K.: Rehabilitation for dementia using enjoyable video-sports games. Int. Psychogeriatr. **23**, 674–676 (2011). https://doi.org/10.1017/S1041610210000 01912

20. Boulay, M., Benveniste, S., Boespflug, S., Jouvelot, P., Rigaud, A.-S.: A pilot usability study of MINWii, a music therapy game for demented patients. Technol Health Care. **19**, 233–246 (2011). https://doi.org/10.3233/THC-2011-0628

21. Fernández-Calvo, B., Rodríguez-Pérez, R., Contador, I., Rubio-Santorum, A., Ramos, F.: Efficacy of cognitive training programs based on new software technologies in patients with Alzheimer-type dementia. Psicothema **23**, 44–50 (2011)

22. McCallum, S., Boletsis, C.: Dementia Games: A Literature Review of Dementia-Related Serious Games. In: Ma, M., Oliveira, M.F., Petersen, S., Hauge, J.B. (eds.) SGDA 2013. LNCS, vol. 8101, pp. 15–27. Springer, Heidelberg (2013). https://doi.org/10.1007/978-3-642-40790-1_2

23. Wargnier, P., Benveniste, S., Jouvelot, P., Rigaud, A.-S.: Usability assessment of interaction management support in LOUISE, an ECA-based user interface for elders with cognitive impairment. Technol. Disabil. **30**, 105–126 (2018). https://doi.org/10.3233/TAD-180189

24. Smeenk, W., Sturm, J., Eggen, B.: A comparison of existing frameworks leading to an empathic formation compass for co-design. Int. J. Design **13**, 17 (2019)

25. Czaja, S.J., Lee, C.C., Schulz, R.: Quality of life technologies in supporting family caregivers. Quality of life technology handbook, pp. 245–260. Routledge Taylor & Francis Group, England, UK (2013)

26. Mungas, D., Marshall, S.C., Weldon, M., Haan, M., Reed, B.R.: Age and education correction of Mini-Mental state examination for English and Spanish-speaking elderly. Neurology **46**, 700–706 (1996). https://doi.org/10.1212/wnl.46.3.700

27. Hughes, C.P., Berg, L., Danziger, W.L., Coben, L.A., Martin, R.L.: A new clinical scale for the staging of dementia. Br. J. Psychiatry. **140**, 566–572 (1982). https://doi.org/10.1192/bjp. 140.6.566

28. Khan, T.K.: Chapter 2 - Clinical Diagnosis of Alzheimer's Disease. In: Khan, T.K. (ed.) Biomarkers in Alzheimer's Disease, pp. 27–48. Academic Press (2016). https://doi.org/10. 1016/B978-0-12-804832-0.00002-X

29. Robert, P.H., et al.: Recommendations for ICT use in Alzheimer's disease assessment: monaco CTAD expert meeting. J. Nutr. Health Aging **17**(8), 653–660 (2013). https://doi.org/10.1007/ s12603-013-0046-3

30. Linstone, H.A., Turoff, M.: The delphi method. Addison-Wesley Reading, MA (1975)

31. Anderson-Hanley, C., et al.: The aerobic and cognitive exercise study (ACES) for community-dwelling older adults with or at-risk for mild cognitive impairment (MCI): Neuropsychological, Neurobiological and Neuroimaging outcomes of a randomized clinical trial. Front. Aging Neurosci. **10**, 76 (2018). https://doi.org/10.3389/fnagi.2018.00076

32. Burzynska, A.Z., et al.: White matter integrity declined over 6-months, but dance intervention improved integrity of the fornix of older adults. Front. Aging Neurosci. **9**, 59 (2017). https:// doi.org/10.3389/fnagi.2017.00059

33. Dhami, P., Moreno, S., DeSouza, J.F.X.: New framework for rehabilitation–fusion of cognitive and physical rehabilitation: the hope for dancing. Front. Psychol. **5**, 1478 (2015). https://doi. org/10.3389/fpsyg.2014.01478

34. Foster, P.P.: How does dancing promote brain reconditioning in the elderly? Front. Aging Neurosci. **5**, 4 (2013). https://doi.org/10.3389/fnagi.2013.00004
35. Kattenstroth, J.-C., Kalisch, T., Holt, S., Tegenthoff, M., Dinse, H.R.: Six months of dance intervention enhances postural, sensorimotor, and cognitive performance in elderly without affecting cardio-respiratory functions. Front. Aging Neurosci. **5**, 5 (2013). https://doi.org/10.3389/fnagi.2013.00005
36. Marquez, D.X., et al.: Regular latin dancing and health education may improve cognition of late middle-aged and older Latinos. J. Aging Phys. Act. **25**, 482–489 (2017). https://doi.org/10.1123/japa.2016-0049
37. Müller, P., Rehfeld, K., Schmicker, M., Hökelmann, A., Dordevic, M., Lessmann, V., et al.: Evolution of Neuroplasticity in response to physical activity in old age: the case for dancing. Front. Aging Neurosci. **9**, 56 (2017). https://doi.org/10.3389/fnagi.2017.00056
38. Osoba, M.Y., Rao, A.K., Agrawal, S.K., Lalwani, A.K.: Balance and gait in the elderly: a contemporary review. Laryngoscope Investig. Otolaryngol. **4**, 143–153 (2019). https://doi.org/10.1002/lio2.252
39. Rehfeld, K., Müller, P., Aye, N., Schmicker, M., Dordevic, M., Kaufmann, J., et al.: Dancing or fitness sport? the effects of two training programs on hippocampal plasticity and balance abilities in healthy seniors. Front. Hum. Neurosci. **11**, 305 (2017). https://doi.org/10.3389/fnhum.2017.00305
40. Schoene, D., et al.: Interactive cognitive-motor step training improves cognitive risk factors of falling in older adults – a randomized controlled trial. PLoS ONE **10**, e0145161 (2015). https://doi.org/10.1371/journal.pone.0145161
41. Acosta Quiroz, C.O., García-Flores, R., Echeverría-Castro, S.B.: The geriatric depression scale (GDS-15): validation in Mexico and disorder in the state of knowledge. Int. J. Aging Hum. Dev. **93**, 854–863 (2021). https://doi.org/10.1177/0091415020957387
42. Gauthier, S., et al.: Mild cognitive impairment. Lancet **367**, 1262–1270 (2006)
43. Ciesielska, N., Sokołowski, R., Mazur, E., Podhorecka, M., Polak-Szabela, A., Kędziora-Kornatowska, K.: Is the Montreal Cognitive Assessment (MoCA) test better suited than the mini-mental state examination (MMSE) in mild cognitive impairment (MCI) detection among people aged over 60? meta-analysis. Psychiatr Pol. **50**, 1039–1052 (2016). https://doi.org/10.12740/PP/45368
44. Hobson, J.: The montreal cognitive assessment (MoCA). Occup. Med. **65**, 764–765 (2015). https://doi.org/10.1093/occmed/kqv078
45. Ştefan, A.M., Băban, A.: The romanian version of the geriatric depression scale: reliability and validity. Cogn. Brain Behav. Interdisc. J. **21**(3), 175–187 (2017). https://doi.org/10.24193/cbb.2017.21.10
46. Sheikh, J.I., Yesavage, J.A.: Geriatric depression scale (GDS): recent evidence and development of a shorter version. Clin. Gerontologist: J. Aging Ment. Health. **5**, 165–173 (1986). https://doi.org/10.1300/J018v05n01_09
47. van den Brink, W.P., van den Brink, S.G.J.: A comparison of the power of the t test, Wilcoxon's test, and the approximate permutation test for the two-sample location problem. Br. J. Math. Stat. Psychol. **42**, 183–189 (1989). https://doi.org/10.1111/j.2044-8317.1989.tb00907.x
48. Ben-Sadoun, G.: Développement d'un serious game portant sur l'activité physique et les fonctions exécutives pour l'évaluation et la stimulation des patients présentant une maladie d'Alzheimer ou une pathologie associée. https://www.theses.fr/2016AZUR4073 (2016)

Using MediaPipe Machine Learning to Design Casual Exertion Games to Interrupt Prolonged Sedentary Lifestyle

Erik Berglund[✉] [iD], Izabella Jedel[iD], and Aseel Berglund[iD]

Department of Computer and Information Science, Linköping University, Linköping, Sweden
`aseel.berglund@liu.se`

Abstract. Casual exergames have shown potential in providing sufficient levels of exertion to decrease sedentary behavior. However, previous casual exergame implementations do not follow the guidelines of allowing for shorter (2–3 min) active breaks during more regular increments. To evaluate if casual exergames could be applied following the guidelines of shorter more regular increments we designed and developed a casual exergame using MediaPipe. The resulting game, Balloon Pump, was evaluated at a game and cosplay festival with 60 participants playing the game. After game play, perceived exertion, control and immersion, and overall experience of the game, was measured and the performance and number of movements were noted. The results from the evaluation study showed that the game was perceived as controllable, had produced sufficient levels of exertion, and was perceived as fun. The immersive experience of the game was low and the participants commented on several ways in which this aspect could be improved, such as adding more incentives and variation in the game.

Keywords: Casual exergames · MediaPipe · Exertion · Perceived Immersion · Perceived Control

1 Introduction

Prolonged sedentary lifestyle is associated with several health risks and diseases e.g., diabetes and heart disease [1–3], regardless of a person's level of physical activity [4]. Regular short active microbreaks (2–3 min light intensity exercises) every 30 min can improve the physical and mental health of sedentary people [5]. To encourage active microbreaks, causal exergames have shown potential [6]. Casual exergames combine the concept of exergames and casual games [7]. Exergames are games that require physical exertion or movement while playing [8], whereas casual games are games with low entry points played during shorter time periods [9]. By combining both concepts, casual exergames are games played during short duration with moderate physical intensity [7]. Previous research has demonstrated that casual exergames can generate appropriate levels of exertion for combating sedentary behavior [10] as well as increasing cognitive performance [11, 12]. Introducing casual exergames into a work [13, 14] or school [10, 15] setting could therefore offer potential both for the health and productivity of the workers or students.

Despite the promise of casual exergames being demonstrated in previous studies [6, 7, 16], most studies on causal exergames study the specific exergame GrabApple based on ten minutes increments of game play. To allow for shorter more regular breaks as has been recommended by previous research [5] we wanted to design, develop and evaluate an exergame designed to be played during shorter increments (2 min) at regular intervals during the day (every 30 min [17, 18]). The aim of the present study was therefore to design, develop and investigate a casual exergame as a tool to interrupt prolonged sedentary lifestyle. In evaluating the game, we wanted to ensure that moderate to high levels of exertion were reached, that the exergame was perceived as controllable and immersive, and understand the players' overall perception of the game. Furthermore, we wanted to explore the relationship between game performance, number of movements, perceived control, perceived immersion, and perceived exertion.

2 Related Work

2.1 Interrupted Prolonged Sedentary Lifestyle

Regular short-duration walking breaks prevent reduction of cerebral blood caused by prolong sitting with no interruption [19]. Interrupting prolonged sitting is associated with positive health benefits [20, 21]. For example, Peddie et al. [18] found that taking regular active breaks (1 min 40 s) is more effective than single continuous physical activity (30 min) to reduce postprandial glycemia and insulin concentrations. Furthermore, three minutes of activity every half hour can improve the health of sedentary people [22]. To have positive health effects in the short term when playing exergames sufficient levels of exertion must be encouraged during play sessions [23]. One way to measure sufficient levels of exertion is through the Borg scale of perceived exertion [24]. The Borg scale ranges between 6 - no exertion at all, and 20 - maximum exertion, with a rating of 10–11 representing low intensity, 12–13 representing moderate intensity and 14–16 representing high intensity [25]. Previous studies on casual exergames have followed the guideline of producing perceived exertion level of moderate to high intensity [7], since these levels have been associated with improved aerobic capacity [26].

2.2 Exergames

Exergames are games that require physical activity of movement, that goes beyond sedentary behavior, in order to play [8]. The term is often used through related concepts such as exertion games, highlighting the physical effort required to reach the game's goal [9], or movement-based games, highlighting that movements are used to control the game [27]. For exergames to be designed successfully it is critical to consider the effectiveness of the tool in producing appropriate levels of exertion, and the attractiveness of the tool in producing a motivational experience [28]. Isbister and Mueller [27] defined the following guidelines for exergame design, based on expert interviews and prior research:

Movement Requires Special Feedback: exergame designers should embrace the ambiguity of the players movements by not being to sticks in movement precision; include real time feedback about how players move; consider that additional cognitive load is introduced when moving while playing; and allow players to focus on feedback from their bodies by not drawing to much attention to the screen.

Movements Leads to Bodily Challenges: exergame designers should consider that fatigue becomes part of the game challenge and include it strategically as a part of the challenge of the game; exploit that movements imply physical risk that can be included as thrilling part of the game; and map movements to the game in imaginative ways that are not necessarily possible in real life.

Movements Emphasizes Certain Kind of Fun: exergame designers should help players identify rhythm in their movements; support players in expressing themselves by using their bodies; and facilitate social fun by making movement a social experiment..

Apart from following specific guidelines about the movement-based nature of exergames it is also necessary for exergames to facilitate a positive in game experience. Two aspects that are related to the game experience in exergames is the sense of control of the game as well as the immersive experience. The sense of control over a game is about players perceiving that they are able to control a game [29]. Perceiving a game as controllable is an important part of the enjoyment [29] as well as immersive experience of a game [30, 31]. Immersion in a game context is defined as a sense of presence or involvement with a game to the extent that the player loses tracks of their surroundings and are fully focused on the game [32]. Previous research has shown that immersion plays an important role in a positive exergame experience [33] and that the movement-based nature of exergames can enable a more immersive experience [34].

2.3 Casual Games

Casual games are defined by the Casual Games SIG of the International Game Developer's Association (IGDA) as "*games with a low barrier to entry that can be enjoyed in short increments*" [9] Casual games have the following criteria [9, 35]:

Easy to Learn: Casual games should be easy to learn, have limited instructions, provide rules that are easy to learn, and guide players.

Simple Controls: Casual games should use controls that are simple.

Play in a Relatively Short Play Period: Casual games should be able to be played in short time sessions.

Forgiving, Non-punishing Game Play: The game should avoid large and complex set of actions.

Speak to a Player's Desire for Fun: Casual games should avoid adrenaline stimulation.

Inclusive, Rather than Exclusive: Casual games should not contain objectionable content, such as overt violence, or sexuality.

2.4 Casual Exergames

Casual exergames are games that are easily learned, can be accessed quickly, and have simple game mechanics, intended to motivate a game play that is short in duration and moderate in physical intensity [7]. Previous research demonstrates several examples of casual exergames being developed to encourage regular physical activity [6, 7, 16] and to enhance cognitive performance [11]. The concept of casual exergames emerged from combining the field of casual games with exergames and was first introduced in a study in which the casual exergame GrabApple was developed and evaluated [7]. GrabApple was designed based on the principles of casual game design [9] and to encourage movement, elevated heart rates and exercise intensity, and developed through Microsoft Kinect motion detection sensors [7]. The game was a computer-based game played during a time period of ten minutes and included a game theme of grabbing apples and avoiding bombs. The results of the study indicated that the game had produced sufficient levels of maximum heart rate (72%) and sufficient levels of perceived exertions (12.38). Compared to a mouse-based version of the game, more participants had reported that the movement-based version of the game was perceived as more fun, exciting, and challenging, whereas there was not difference in terms of ease to learn nor frustration [11]. Overall, the initial study highlighted that casual exergames offer promise in producing moderate-intensity aerobic activity and a fun game play. A follow-up study, conducted with pre-adolescents in a school setting playing GrabApple, showed that the game produced perceived exertion values within recommended intensity levels (12–16), and that the game was perceived as more fun compared to traditional exercise [6]. At the same time, while some students mentioned positive impacts on concentration while playing exergames, others mentioned that it could have a negative impact on concentration due to fatigue and interrupted workflow [6]. The casual exergame GrabApple was also evaluated with adult university participants in terms of exertion, affective experience, and cognitive benefits [11]. The study showed that recommended levels of exertion had been reached (12.5), that the movement-based version of the game had higher arousal compared to a mouse-based version and traditional exercise and that the game produced cognitive benefits equivalent to traditional exercise [11]. Another study showed that casual exergames could also be implemented to increase enjoyment and provide physical activity for children, in two new versions of casual exergames designed specifically to be played in wheelchairs [16]. Overall, the previous studies conducted on casual exergames show that casual exergames can be successful in producing both enjoyment and exertion, offering a promising avenue to decrease sedentary behavior.

3 Methods

3.1 Design and Development of the Casual Exergame

User-Centered Design approach [36, 37] is applied for the design and development of the casual exergame. Developing the exergame is done iteratively within four main components: understand context of use, specify requirements, create design solutions, and evaluation until the exergame is ready for deployment (Fig. 1). The focus in the context analysis is to understand the context where the exergame will be played. Defining the requirements is focused on defining the desired exercise movement, the exergame guidelines, the causal guidelines, and the technology possibilities and challenges. The exergame design contains six components:

1. Exertion interaction design – the focus is on identifying a stable a stabile interaction. The design is conducted iterativly by prototyping different body interactions and then testing with different user (with long and short hair and different clothes) under different lighting conditions. This is conducted iteratively until a stable interaction that works for many conditions is identified. Since different interactions work for different persons in different contexts it is important to test with different persons and in different contexts.

2. Exergame concept generation and ideation – exergame concepts are generated when an extertion design is identified. The concept is then tested with users to identify how well it works with the extertion game design.

3. Core exergame mechanics design - Once the exergame concept has been determined the design is focused on the core game mechanic so the exergame rules work well together with the mechanics. By prototyping and testing with users to better understand the extertion interaction design since so the game mechanic is adjusted to the time needed to move the body during the interaction.

4. Scoring design - Once the game mechanics is in place, the focus is on designing the scoring. The scoring rules will impact the players' movement pace and therefore the scoring rules has to support the desired exertion. The applied scoresing rule in the exergame is that desired exertion give a better scoring but less movement provide input and action. This has ben prototyped and tested with users iteratively.

5. Progression design – when the scoring is in place the progression design is in focus. How to make the game interesting for longer play times. This is dependent of the level of exertion of the game. For high levels of exertion, the game is designed for a collection of resources – e.g., balloons - as proof of physical ability such as reaching a high score. In the long run, collecting balloons of different types as proof of continuously having reached very high scores is a better way to make the exergame relevant to play for longer periods of time.

6. Art assets production – finally, the art assets for the game are produced and integrated in the game.

The exergame is evaluated continuously together with different users in different contexts. Observations, usability testing, and expert evaluations are applied during the evaluations. The exergames is even distributed to test users for long term testing. Finally, the game is deployed on a webpage.

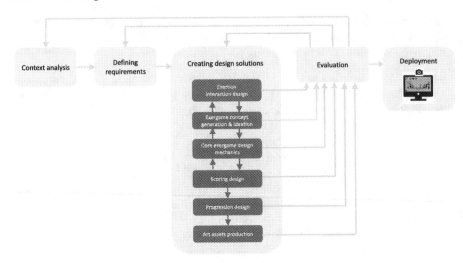

Fig. 1. The exergame design and development process

3.2 Technical Setup

MediaPipe is a cross-platform pipeline framework to build custom machine learning (ML) solutions [38]. In this project we use human pose estimation data from the MediaPipe [38] framework and its premade Pose-estimation solution, using the the BlazePose ML-model [39]. MediaPipe uses a detector and a tracker in its framework to detect human skeletal main points.

The MediaPipe Pose Estimation is high-fidelity body pose tracking that provides a set of 33 skeletal points (for instance, nose, shoulders, wrists and so forth) (Fig. 2). Mediapipe is an open-source framework using open-source ML- models and can be

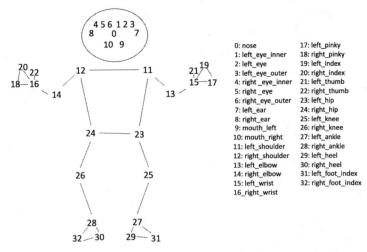

Fig. 2. 33-joint human skeleton model of 3D Human Pose Estimation

used in varying platforms, including the web and running the sensor in JavaScript. This makes the Pose Estimation very accessible, possible from common hardware like a laptop computer or a mobile phone. Mediapipe's strength is in its runtime abilities of providing relatively good frame-per-second data such as above 30 on many modern hardware platforms.

The development of the games was conducted using the Godot Engine, a C++ -based graphical open-source game engine suitable for development of 2D and 3D games for desktop, mobile, and web. Godot Engine has in recent years become very popular platform and grown into a mature and stable game engine (Godot games can be developed using C++, and C# and its own python-like GDScript).

3.3 Evaluation Setting, Participants, and Method

To initially evaluate the Balloon Pump game, a study was conducted at the NärCon 2022 Summer event, Scandinavia's largest game and cosplay festival. The game was set up on two 24-inch monitor screens in a room in which attendees could try different games in early stages of development. The attendees of the festival who walked past were asked if they wanted to participate in a study about exergames, and those who were interested got to read through a consent form including information about the study set up, that their participation would be treated anonymously and was voluntary, and about how data was handled in the study. Those who consented to participate signed the consent form (participants under 18 had their guardian sign the consent form on their behalf) and were thereafter instructed to stand 1.5 m from the screen. The participants were instructed about the movements of the game (squatting), the goal of the game (pumping as many balloons as possible during the 2-min game session) and were shown a visual instruction about the movements to use in the game (Fig. 3). The participants were asked if they had understood the game and got additional explanations if needed. When the game session started, the authors of the study counted the number of squats done during game play. When the game session ended the authors of the study wrote down the performance in the game. The participants were asked to sit down after they had finished playing and answered a survey consisting of a demographic survey, the Borg Scale of Perceived exertion [25], the perceived immersion and perceived control scale from the Swedish version of the Exergame Enjoyment Questionnaire [40], and the following voluntary open ended question: "Is there anything additional you want to add about your experience of the game". Sixty participants were included in the study in total with 21 participants answering the last open-ended question. The participants ranged in age from 9 years old to 57 years old with a mean age of 26 (SD = 8,13), 16 of the participants identified as women, one reported that they were usure of their gender, three identified as un-binary, three did not want to report their gender, and 37 participants identified as men. Eight participants had no previous experience of exergames, 22 participants had experience of exergames but only on some occasion, and 30 participants had played exergames several times or during a longer time. Descriptive statistics were used to understand the levels of exertion, immersion, and control experienced, a correlation matrix was produced to understand the relationship between performance, movements, exertion control and immersion, and the last open ended question was analyzed using thematic analysis [41].

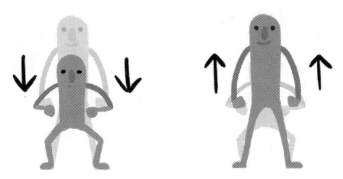

Fig. 3. Movement instructions Balloon Pump

4   Results

4.1   Balloon Pump – A Casual Exertion Game

Game Concept. In Balloon Pump (Fig. 4), the goal is for the player to pump as many balloons as possible during the 2-min plays session. Balloons are pumped. Each pumped balloon adds one point to the player's total score. The game is controlled by knee bending or squats made by the player. The user bend knees or do squats to pump balloons in two minutes.

Designing for Casual Interaction. The Balloon pump game is designed according to the principles of casual game design in the following ways:

1. Easy to learn – The pump balloon game is easy to learn. Each time the user interaction is detected the user gets feedback in means of pressing the pump handle, pushing more air in the balloon so it expands, and the releasing the pump handle the balloon.
2. Simple controls – uses the player's body as the game controller. The game controller is very easy to use and the player have good control. The game is playable at a close distance from the camera and therefore only require seeing the upper part of the body. The game does not require calibration of the player body.
3. Play in a relatively short play period. Each play session takes 2 min to play. The player sees a video feed showing where the player body is located and how much of the body is captured in the video feed.
4. Forgiving, non-punishing game play. Balloon pump has simple game mechanics and controls. Players can't lose the game, but they can compete for a higher score.
5. Speak to a player's desire for fun. The pumped balloons have different shapes and appearances.
6. Inclusive, rather than exclusive. Balloon pump has no objectionable, violent, or sexual content.

Designing for Exertion. The Balloon pump game is designed to encourage physical activity.

1. The game facilitate player making varying deep knee bending from relatively light to deep squat.

2. The game is designed for all and enable different types of large body movements and combinations of these such as knee bending, back, bending and jumping or moving back and forth. Some people may not be able to bend their knees.
3. The game gives higher scores for faster and deeper bending to motivate more exertion. Beating the high score requires large physical exertion. A natural break is also part of the game when a new balloon is loaded and this gives players some rhythm, variation, and rest which is particularly appreciated at the second of the two of a game round.
4. The game focuses on a physical competes where strength or stamina would be required to play the game.

Fig. 4. Balloon pump game interface

Game Implementation. The user interaction is detected by analyzing the skeletal data using machine learning estimating the body pose by means of a webcam. The game tracks the body movements and detects downward movement per frame, using a threshold to filter out small movement. Air is pressed into the balloon on downward movement, but the player gets the most out of pressing the pump handle fully down before lifting it up since this should theoretically give the minimal movement per balloon. However, speed of input could also impact the movement and a combination of movements such as bending the knees and bending the back or bending and then jumping all give input to the sensor since it's not detecting a knee-vs-hip bend angle and instead uses downward movement of shoulders.

An initial design for the controller was that the pump handle would first only move down until it reached the bottom and then move only up until it reached the top. This would increase competence in the game because it puts further focus on finding the optimal movement that will go all the way down and all the ways in nonmovement. This should be more fun, but it also makes the game less easy to understand and in our design testing we also found that the most interesting aspect of the game is to really push yourself and this finer skill dimensions is much less clear for most players. This, however, would also make the game less easy to understand and for to ease the use we designed against this and made all downward movement provide air.

During play a trained observer can see that the handled sometimes gets a little misaligned but since the game is so straight forward the player will compensate for this by themselves according from our observations because of the straightforward input.

At the current state we have not addressed any more motivational aspects of the game and deeper game play in order to facilitate ease of play and multiple movement. In a longer game play perspective, we would like to focus on collection and clearing a game board as a motivations design, by uncovering new balloons, getting to a new level and looking at high score but also score average. For this game type, we think motivating players but aspects outside the interaction, while requiring some higher scores should be more motivating than allowing players to progress with relatively low scores.

A challenge when developing the controller was finding a control design that works well for different physical abilities and movements without calibration. The ML-agent doesn't really track the body distance to the camera so movement will be different for different body sizes. Also, the ML-agent data is much less exact for movements towards the camera than to the sides, in our experience.

The control is working well because of the combination of tracking only the relative shoulder down-up-movement. This means that squatting, but also bending your back or moving back and forth works to drive the pump handle. In our design-time testing, we still found that the game works well for different players and distances to the camera and that scores are correlated to amount of exertion. Also, we found that squatting in combination with jumping is the optimum and fast bending of the back is not as good an alternative since it may create dizziness. Moving back and forth is not a good strategy.

4.2   Evaluation of the Casual Exertion Game

The results from the initial evaluation study highlight that the game was in general perceived as controllable and that the players had been physical active and experienced exertion (Table 1). Simultaneously, the level of immersion was relatively low. The mean exertion corresponded to high intensity [25] and exceeded exertion levels Borg ratings measured in the ten minute long casual exergame [11], supporting the notion that short duration casual exergames can produce adequate levels of exertion for health related benefits. The perceived control scale was above average, corresponding to the players on average agreeing to the game being perceived as controllable, indicating that MediaPipe could successfully be used to detect the movements in the game and that the feedback provided to players about their movements had been sufficient. The perceived immersion scale was, however, lower than average, corresponding to the players on average not agreeing to the game being perceived as immersive. This result could derive from the game having a simple game theme but could also be due to the short duration of game play.

The thematic analysis of the open-ended responses offers more detail about the players perception of the game. Five themes emerged from the thematic analysis: fun game experience, lack of variation, delayed response, lack of incentives, and too high exertion:

Table 1. Perceived control, immersion, and exertion, number of movements and performance in Balloon Pump

Measurement	Mean	SD
EEQ Perceived Immersion scale: measured on 1–5-point Likert-scale	2.63	0.87
EEQ Perceived Control scale: measured on 1–5-point Likert-scale	3.82	0.73
Borg Perceived Exertion scale: measured on a 6–20 scale	15	2.27
Number of movements: number of squats during 2-min game play	96	37.69
Performance: number of balloons pumped during 2-min game play	8.35	1.38

Fun game experience: players had commented on perceiving the game as fun and one mentioned not being aware of the movements due to the game being perceived positively: *"It was fun to keep on going because you did not think about it hurting, but instead thought about continuing pumping the balloons"*.

Lack of variation: players had commented on perceiving that the game lacked variation and game specific suggestions on improving the game such as balloons not repeating, including more colors, and having different difficulty levels: *"More and different actions needed. Good start, even if a bit too tough for me. Maybe allow difficulty levels.*

Delayed response: players commented on feeling like there was a delay in the movements and that the game did not respond to their actions in a way to let them know how to adjust their movements: *"It felt a bit hard to know if it was good to squat slowly or faster to make the game respond to your inputs. Otherwise fun!*

Lack of incentives: one player commented on wanting more incentives in the game to want to play the game: *"Without for example statistics, point or incentives (leaderboard, personal challenges, points to unlock new things in the game and so on…) I did not feel like I had any motivation to play the game actually"*.

Too high exertion: players commented on becoming sweaty, not being able to continue playing, and feeling like they were too old or untrained for the game: *"need to train more, I'm too fat for this game!"*.

The correlation matrix showed a significant positive relationship between movements and performance (Table 2) but not between the other variables. The positive relationship between movements and performance indicated that exertion could be used strategically to increase the performance of the game, aligned with the guideline of movements leads to bodily challenges [27]. There was no correlation between immersion and control, indicating that other aspects were important in creating the immersive experience, such as the themes presented above from the thematic analysis.

Table 2. Correlation matrix between variables *significant at p < 0.05

	Performance	Movements	Exertion	Immersion	Control
Performance		0.281*	0.005	0.102	−0.112
Movements	0.281*		0.103	−0.012	0.194
Exertion	0.005	0.103		−0.033	0.001
Immersion	0.102	−0.012	−0.033		0.108
Control	−0.112	0.194	0.001	0.108	

5 Discussion

5.1 Contributions and Findings

The present study demonstrated that MediaPipe could successfully be used to detect movements in casual exergames in which the controllers of the game are perceived as controllable. Optimization could be done to the game controllers and their feedback, as some players perceived delay in response. As recommended by Isbister and Mueller [27], more feedback about how the players move could be provided in the game. For example, highlighting the pump movement clearer in relation to the players movements.

Similar to previous studies on casual exergames [6, 7, 16], the present study showed that casual exergames could produce sufficient levels of exertion. The present work also showed that this holds true for casual exergames played during shorter intervals of game play (2 min). At the same time, the level of exertion might have been too high for some players mentioning that the level of exertion did not correspond to their fitness levels. Allowing for a game play in which the exertion level could be adapted to the players current fitness level would therefore be an avenue for further development and research.

Immersion was, on average, perceived as low in the game. Casual exergames, played during shorter increments with simple game mechanics [7], might not be appropriate in enhancing immersion which requires full focus on the game [32]. Instead, more complex game mechanics and longer game play might be needed. The thematic analysis indicated that this might hold true. Players had commented on a lack of variation and lack of incentives. An avenue for further development and research would be how to introduce more variation and incentives in the game, balanced with simple enough game mechanics required for casual games [9, 35]. At the same time players had commented on having a fun game experience. The aim of casual exergames might therefore be more focused on creating enjoyment rather than immersion. The present study did not include any measures on enjoyment and can therefore not shed light on this issue, but this could also be an avenue for further research.

There was a positive correlation between the performance and movements in the game, indicating that exertion had been part of creating the game challenge (as recommended by previous exergame guidelines [27]). This was implemented by having a point system that was linked to both the number of movements the player had done and the extent of the movement.

5.2 Limitations and Further Research

As suggested by previous research, implementing casual exergames in a controlled environment does not offer the full picture in terms of how casual exergames will actually be used in a field setting, and does not address long term effects [6, 7]. Further research should therefore study the implementation of causal exergames in a field setting over longer time periods to determine if casual exergames can successfully be used to decrease sedentary behavior. As has been recommended by previous research, further research should also investigate the inclusion of socially based motivational elements such as leader boards [6]. This could easily be implemented with the current exergame as the point system leads to a comparative measure of players performance in the game. Finally, the nature of the study is explorative, conducted with relatively few participants, which limits the generalizability of the study and more studies should be implement with different types of participants, different types of casual exergame implementations and in different contexts (e.g., casual exergames in work compared to study settings).

6 Conclusion

The present study showed that casual exertion games designed for activities using larger muscles in the body detected by webcam and interpreted with MediaPipe ML can provide a controllable 2-min play with high levels of movement and exertion. The game can be played using different body movements which support players of different physical abilities. We are encouraged to continue developing the game for deeper level of immersion, which the result of the study showed is needed.

References

1. Chau, J.Y., et al.: Daily sitting time and all-cause mortality: a meta-analysis. PloS One **8**(11), e80000 (2013)
2. Patel, A.V., et al.: Leisure time spent sitting in relation to total mortality in a prospective cohort of US adults. Am. J. Epidemiol. **172**(4), 419–429 (2010)
3. Young, D.R., et al.: Sedentary behavior and cardiovascular morbidity and mortality: a science advisory from the American Heart Association. Circulation **134**(13), e262–e279 (2016)
4. Patel, A.V., et al.: Prolonged leisure time spent sitting in relation to cause-specific mortality in a large US cohort. Am. J. Epidemiol. **187**(10), 2151–2158 (2018)
5. Radwan, A., et al.: Effects of active microbreaks on the physical and mental well-being of office workers: a systematic review. Cogent Eng. **9**(1), 2026206 (2022)
6. Gao, Y., et al.: Decreasing sedentary behaviours in pre-adolescents using casual exergames at school. In: CHI PLAY 2014 - Proceedings of the 2014 Annual Symposium on Computer-Human Interaction in Play (2014)
7. Gao, Y., Mandryk, R.L.: GrabApple: the design of a casual exergame. In: Entertainment Computing - Icec 2011, 6972, p. 35–46 (2011)
8. Oh, Y., Yang, S.: Defining exergames & exergaming. Proc. Meaningful Play **2010**, 21–23 (2010)
9. IGDA 2008–2009 Casual Games White Paper (2009)

10. Gao, Y., et al.: Decreasing sedentary behaviours in pre-adolescents using casual exergames at school. In: Proceedings of the First ACM SIGCHI Annual Symposium on Computer-Human Interaction in Play (2014)
11. Gao, Y., Mandryk, R.L.: The acute cognitive benefits of casual exergame play. In: Conference on Human Factors in Computing Systems - Proceedings (2012)
12. Chandrasekaran, B., et al.: Does breaking up prolonged sitting improve cognitive functions in sedentary adults? a mapping review and hypothesis formulation on the potential physiological mechanisms. BMC Musculoskelet. Disord. 22(1), 1–16 (2021)
13. Ren, X., et al.: Step-by-step: exploring a social exergame to encourage physical activity and social dynamics among office workers. In: Extended Abstracts of the 2019 CHI Conference on Human Factors in Computing Systems (2019)
14. Neil, D., et al.: Limber: exploring motivation in a workplace exergame. In: Proceedings of the 2013 Conference on Computer Supported Cooperative Work Companion (2013)
15. Azevedo, L.B., et al.: The effect of dance mat exergaming systems on physical activity and health–related outcomes in secondary schools: results from a natural experiment. BMC Public Health 14(1), 1–13 (2014)
16. Hicks, K., Gerling, K.: Exploring casual exergames with kids using wheelchairs. In: Proceedings of the 2015 Annual Symposium on Computer-Human Interaction in Play (2015)
17. Liebenson, C.: Micro-breaks. J. Bodyw. Mov. Ther. 6(3), 154–155 (2002)
18. Peddie, M.C., et al.: Breaking prolonged sitting reduces postprandial glycemia in healthy, normal-weight adults: a randomized crossover trial. Am. J. Clin. Nutr. 98(2), 358–366 (2013)
19. Carter, S.E., et al.: Regular walking breaks prevent the decline in cerebral blood flow associated with prolonged sitting. J. Appl. Physiol. (2018)
20. Healy, G.N., et al.: Breaks in sedentary time: beneficial associations with metabolic risk. Diabetes Care 31(4), 661–666 (2008)
21. Healy, G.N., et al.: Sedentary time and cardio-metabolic biomarkers in US adults: NHANES 2003–06. Eur. Heart J. 32(5), 590–597 (2011)
22. Smith, J.A., et al.: Three weeks of interrupting sitting lowers fasting glucose and glycemic variability, but not glucose tolerance, in free-living women and men with obesity. Am. J. Physiol.-Endocrinology Metabolism 321(2), E203–E216 (2021)
23. Dutta, N., Pereira, M.A.: Effects of active video games on energy expenditure in adults: a systematic literature review. J. Phys. Act. Health 12(6), 890–899 (2015)
24. Borg, G.A.V.: Psychophysical bases of perceived exertion. Med. Sci. Sports Exerc. 14(5), 377–381 (1982)
25. Mackinnon, L.T., et al.: Exercise management: concepts and professional practice. 2003: Human Kinetics
26. Borg, G.: Borg's perceived exertion and pain scales. Human kinetics (1998)
27. Isbister, K., Mueller, F.: Guidelines for the design of movement-based games and their relevance to HCI. Hum.-Comput. Interaction 30(3–4), 366–399 (2015)
28. Sinclair, J., Hingston, P., Masek, M.: Exergame development using the dual flow model. In: Proceedings of the Sixth Australasian Conference on Interactive Entertainment (2009)
29. Klimmt, C., Hartmann, T., Frey, A.: Effectance and control as determinants of video game enjoyment. Cyberpsychol. Behav. 10(6), 845–847 (2007)
30. Brown, E., Cairns, P.: A grounded investigation of game immersion. In: CHI'04 Extended Abstracts on Human Factors in Computing Systems (2004)
31. Mortazavi, B., Lee, S.I., Sarrafzadeh, M.: User-centric exergaming with fine-grain activity recognition: a dynamic optimization approach. In: Proceedings of the 2014 ACM International Joint Conference on Pervasive and Ubiquitous Computing: Adjunct Publication (2014)
32. Jennett, C., et al.: Measuring and defining the experience of immersion in games. Int. J. Hum Comput Stud. 66(9), 641–661 (2008)

33. Ho, S.S., et al.: Escaping through exergames: Presence, enjoyment, and mood experience in predicting children's attitude toward exergames. Comput. Hum. Behav. **72**, 381–389 (2017)
34. Lee, J.Y., Woo, T.: A novel method for natural motion mapping as a strategy of game immediacy. KSII Trans. Internet Inf. Syst. **12**(5), 2313–2326 (2018)
35. Gao, Y., Mandryk, R.L.: GrabApple: the design of a casual exergame. In: International Conference on Entertainment Computing. Springer (2011)
36. Bevan, N., Curson, I.: Planning and implementing user-centred design. In: CHI 98 Conference Summary on Human Factors in Computing Systems (1998)
37. Pagulayan, R.J., et al.: User-centered design in games. In: The human-computer interaction handbook, pp. 915–938. CRC Press (2002)
38. Lugaresi, C., et al.: Mediapipe: a framework for perceiving and processing reality. In: Third Workshop on Computer Vision for AR/VR at IEEE Computer Vision and Pattern Recognition (CVPR) (2019)
39. Bazarevsky, V., et al.: Blazepose: on-device real-time body pose tracking. arXiv preprint arXiv:2006.10204 (2020)
40. Fitzgerald, A., et al.: The exergame enjoyment questionnaire (eeq): An instrument for measuring exergame enjoyment (2020)
41. Braun, V., Clarke, V.: Thematic analysis. 2012: American Psychological Association

Rethinking Gamification Through Artificial Intelligence

Stephen Bezzina[✉] and Alexiei Dingli

University of Malta, Msida 2080, MSD, Malta
{stephen.bezzina,alexiei.dingli}@um.edu.mt

Abstract. The concept of gamification was introduced in the early twenty-first century, but it didn't gain traction in academic communities until the second half of 2010. Whilst gamified approaches have the potential to motivate and engage users, some argue that gamification's one-size-fits-all approach is neither personalized nor adaptive. This impersonal and static nature of gamification has fueled the interest of researchers and designers to explore a more personalized and adaptive form of gamification, which caters for individual user differences and can potentially leverage a more intrinsic form of motivation. In this sense, Artificial Intelligence (AI) presents itself as an interesting technology for the successful implementation of such an approach to gamification through its autonomous, adaptive and personalized characteristics. This paper seeks to extend the conceptual basis of the term 'AI-enabled gamification' by examining the views of two game designers and two AI scientists through two focus groups. The results suggest that there is a positive understanding amongst the four experts of the potential application of AI to gamification. This includes the adoption of dynamic difficulty adjustment, dynamic reward computation, provision of personalized feedback and prediction of potential user failure/success. On the other hand, access to the right datasets in terms of both quantity and quality and the necessary privacy and ethical considerations were identified as possible challenges. Consequently, the findings suggest that AI has the potential to play a significant role in enhancing gamification; however, this requires the need for more research and further development of AI-enabled gamified systems.

Keywords: gamification · artificial intelligence · adaptive · personalized

1 Introduction

The concept of gamification was introduced in the early twenty-first century, but it didn't gain traction in academic communities until the second half of 2010 [1]. A number of psychology and learning theories, most prominently behaviourism and cognitivism, support the applications and perceived benefits of gamification, which can lead to an increased feeling of motivation and engagement [2, 3]. However, gamification has been criticized by a wide range of academics on several fronts, including philosophical and practical ones [4–6]. Some argue that gamification's one-size-fits-all approach is neither personalized nor adaptive [7]. As a result, the end-users' freedom of choice, agency, and ownership become constrained [8].

X. Fang (Ed.): HCII 2023, LNCS 14046, pp. 252–263, 2023.
https://doi.org/10.1007/978-3-031-35930-9_17

This impersonal and static nature of gamification has fueled the interest of researchers and designers to explore a more personalized and adaptive form of gamification [9, 10], which caters for individual user differences and can potentially leverage a more intrinsic form of motivation in the end-user. In this sense, Artificial Intelligence (AI) presents itself as an interesting technology for the successful implementation of such an approach to gamification. In addition to being able to act autonomously, AI-powered systems are also adaptive [11], which in turn makes such systems capable of learning from experience and, in turn, improving their performance.

2 Gamification

Gamification is defined as "the use of game design elements in non-game contexts" [12]. These elements are deployed in settings other than those in which games are played in order to engage and motivate users in pursuit of goals. It commonly employs game mechanics such as points, levels, leaderboards, badges, rewards, challenges and competition to contexts such as work, education, health and marketing [13].

Gamification has its roots in the field of psychology, particularly in the areas of motivation and engagement. The philosophical underpinnings of gamification are rooted in Self-Determination Theory (SDT) [14] and the concept of flow [15]. SDT posits that humans have three innate psychological needs. These are autonomy, competence, and relatedness, which are crucial for well-being and optimal functioning. Gamification can fulfil these needs by providing people with a sense of autonomy and agency in the choice of tasks and goals, a sense of competence through clear feedback and opportunities for skill building, and a sense of relatedness through social connections and shared experiences [16]. The concept of flow involves a state of engagement, where the individual is so engrossed in an activity that they lose track of time and self-consciousness. This state refers to the complete immersion in an activity characterized by a sense of effortless action, full engagement, and complete absorption [15].

Furthermore, a number of learning theories, most prominently behaviourism and cognitivism, support the applications and perceived benefits of gamification [2, 3]. Behaviourism posits that learning occurs through the manipulation of external rewards and consequences [17]. In the context of gamification, behaviorist principles can be applied through the use of tangible rewards and immediate feedback, such as points and badges, to reinforce desired behaviors and increase engagement [18]. This approach aligns with behaviorism's focus on shaping behavior through reinforcement and consequences. On the other hand, cognitivism places emphasis on the mental processes involved in learning, such as perception, attention, and memory [19]. According to cognitivist theory, learning is an active process in which the learner actively processes and integrates new information. In the context of gamification, cognitivist principles can be applied through the use of challenging tasks and problem-solving elements, which engage the user's cognitive processes and facilitate deeper learning [20].

2.1 Game Design Elements

Points, badges, progress tracking, challenges, competition, collaboration, and fantasy are the most commonly used game design elements in implementing gamification [21].

In addition to providing immediate feedback in the form of points or badges as well as a sense of accomplishment when goals are met, these elements also encourage users to engage with their tasks on a deeper level [22]. Progress tracking allows users to see their progress and set new goals, which in turn gives a sense of purpose and direction. Challenging tasks and problem-solving encourage deeper learning by engaging the user's cognitive processes, while competition and collaboration between players create a social dimension, which provides further motivation [23]. Fantasy elements such as backstories and character development make for an overall more immersive experience [24]. By leveraging these game design elements, gamification can effectively engage and motivate users to learn and develop new skills. For instance, points, badges, and other tangible rewards can increase intrinsic motivation by providing immediate feedback on progress while underpinning further achievement/s. This can encourage users to continue their development efforts in pursuit of goals [25]. Moreover, the use of challenges and problem-solving elements requires active participation and cognitive effort from the user. This can lead to the acquisition of new knowledge and skills [20]. Leaderboards and multiplayer options have the potential to encourage collaborative learning by promoting interdependence and a sense of community among users [23]. Moreover, the use of immersive environments and story-based elements can facilitate the active processing and integration of information by engaging the users in a more meaningful and relatable experience [26].

2.2 Benefits and Challenges of Gamification

Literature suggests that gamification has the potential to increase engagement, motivation, and performance in a wide range of contexts, including work, education, health and marketing [27]. For instance, gamification has been shown to positively affect engagement and motivation at the workplace, leading to improved job satisfaction and increased productivity [3]. In the field of education, gamification has been used to increase engagement and motivation in students, resulting in improved learning outcomes [28]. Health-related applications which utilize gamification reveal an increased level of motivation and accomplishment in users [29]. Furthermore, gamification has been used to increase engagement with customers and drive sales in the marketing industry, for example, through loyalty programs and promotional campaigns [30]. Thus, it is clear that gamification can be an effective tool for engaging and motivating users and potentially promoting achievement.

However, gamification also faces several challenges, particularly in terms of design and implementation. One of the main challenges is the risk of reducing intrinsic motivation if the game design elements are perceived as controlling or externally imposed [4]. Another challenge is the risk of devaluing the rewards and recognition if these are perceived as meaningless or arbitrary [31]. Additionally, gamification can be perceived as manipulative, and if not implemented in an ethical and transparent manner, it can have negative consequences for the users and the organization [32]. Consequently, gamification has been criticized by a wide range of academics on several fronts, including philosophical and practical ones [4–6]. Some argue that gamification's one-size-fits-all approach is neither personalized nor adaptive [7]. As a result, the end-users' freedom of choice, agency, and ownership are constrained [8]. This can lead to a decrease in intrinsic motivation, where users become less interested in the activity itself and more focused on the rewards that are associated with it [33]. In reality, the over-reliance on extrinsic motivators may be the outcome of classic gamified settings that provide the same material and challenges at the same fixed level/s of difficulty and acknowledge the same accomplishment using the same metrics for all end-users. This may not adequately cater to the diverse needs and abilities of individual users and can lead to demotivation, as users may feel that the challenges are too easy or too difficult or that the rewards are not meaningful to them.

2.3 Towards Personalized and Adaptive Gamification

To avoid these potential negative outcomes, gamified settings should be designed to strike a balance between extrinsic and intrinsic motivators and to provide a personalized experience that takes into account the unique needs and abilities of individual users. In this regard, the impersonal and static nature of gamification has fueled the interest of researchers and designers to explore a more personalized and adaptive form of gamification [9, 10] which caters for individual user differences and can potentially leverage a more intrinsic motivation in the end-user. In this sense, AI presents itself as an interesting technology for the successful implementation of such an approach to gamification. Defined as the "science and engineering of making intelligent machines, especially intelligent computer programs" [34], AI can be used to automatically adapt the game experience based on the user's preferences and performance. By leveraging AI technologies such as machine learning or natural language processing, gamified systems can analyze and anticipate users' behavior and offer them a uniquely tailored gaming experience that is adapted to their profiles and abilities [35]. This implies that in addition to being able to act autonomously, AI-powered systems are also adaptive, which can be defined as "the ability to modify an internal representation of the environment through sensing of the environment in order to change future sensing, acting, and reacting for the purpose of determining user intent and improving assistance" [36]. In conjunction with autonomy, this means that such systems are capable of learning from experience and, in turn, improving their performance.

3   Research Question

The objective of this paper is to extend the conceptual basis of the term "AI-enabled gamification" [37] by examining the views of two game designers and two AI scientists on the rethinking of gamification through AI. To this end, the following research question has been posed: How can AI enable more personalized and adaptive gamification?

As such, this paper seeks to explore the potential and limitations of AI-enabled gamification through a conceptual discussion with experts in the fields while also providing practical insights into the design and development of AI-enabled gamified settings. By examining their views and opinions, the paper aims to shed light on the potential of AI to rethink gamification and provide new and innovative solutions for personalization and adaptivity. This will enable a better understanding of the opportunities and implications of AI-enabled gamification whilst also informing future research and design initiatives.

Consequently, the research question which guides this study is of interest to researchers, practitioners, and educators in the fields of AI, gamification, and human-computer interaction. Its outcomes will contribute to the development of best practices and guidelines for designing and implementing AI-enabled gamification systems that are both effective and ethical.

4 Methodology

In order to accomplish the research goal, two focus groups with professionals in the fields of gamification and AI were conducted. The first one included two game designers, and the second one comprised two AI scientists. Table 1 illustrates the gender and respective background (including the number of years in the role) of the respective participants. Both focus groups were conducted online using a semi-structured format with open-ended questions and moderated by the first author for a duration of ninety minutes. A purposive sample design was used to select the four participants who had at least three years of experience in their respective fields.

Table 1. Focus groups participants

Professional	Background	Gender
Game Designer (GD-1)	Lead game designer (7 years)	male
Game Designer (GD-2)	Level designer (4 years)	female
AI Scientist (AIS-1)	Machine learning engineer (4 years)	female
AI Scientist (AIS-2)	AI research scientist (3 years)	male

The moderator began the discussion by introducing the research topic and briefly explaining the purpose of the focus group before inviting participants to share their viewpoints and experiences. Apart from the specific elements of AI that could potentially transform gamification by essentially rethinking its static and one-size-fits-all nature, the focus groups delved deeper into the participants' underlying perceptions, potential benefits, and challenges posed by the integration of AI and gamification.

The qualitative approach underpinning this paper utilizes thematic analysis to identify, analyze and interpret patterns of meaning within the data resulting from the two focus groups. Audio recordings of each session were transcribed verbatim and then analyzed through thematic analysis in NVivo to uncover key themes [38]. This method of qualitative research provides insights into a research question by examining emerging themes from a data set [39]. This process involved reviewing each segment individually and generating codes, followed by analyzing these codes to identify commonalities or differences between participant perspectives. After the analysis was completed, the codes were refined and grouped together into a number of distinct thematic categories, which are discussed in the sections that follow.

5 Results

The thematic analysis revealed four key themes related to the potential benefits of the integration of AI with gamification. These are the dynamic difficulty adjustment of the levelling up and progression procedures, the dynamic reward computation based on individual preferences and needs, the provision of personalized feedback and the prediction of potential user failure and/or success within the gamified system. On the other hand, two central themes surrounding the perceived challenges in this regard were identified. These include access to the right datasets in terms of both quantity and quality and the necessary privacy and ethical considerations underpinning such systems. The following sub-sections provide a deeper understanding of these findings.

5.1 Dynamic Difficulty Adjustment

Dynamic Difficulty Adjustment (DDA) is a game design technique in which the difficulty of the game changes in real time based on the player's performance. GD-1 explained how this enables games to scale their challenge and accordingly adjust various elements, such as enemy stats, item availability and level pacing, to match each skill level. All focus group participants have agreed that one of the prime benefits of the application of AI to gamification is its ability to offer DDA to phenomena which are normally static in gamified environments. These include levelling and progression, which are normally hardcoded within gamified systems and consequently offer limited flexibility or adaptivity. GD-2 suggested that DDA could also be applied to narrative and storytelling, allowing AI-enabled gamified systems to customize the storyline based on the user's choices in order to create more engaging experiences. AIS-2 argued that this could be done through various AI techniques such as machine learning, natural language processing and computer vision, which would allow for wider and more accurate predictions of user behavior. The application of AI in DDA can be accomplished through algorithms that monitor and analyze the user's generated data, such as their completion time, textual inputs and facial expressions. Based on this information, the AI can adjust the difficulty level in real-time, ensuring that it is always appropriate for the user's current level of skill and knowledge. Moreover, GD-3 suggested that AI could be used to create adaptive gamified content, which is generated based on a user's current situation or state of mind to ensure a more personal and engaging experience. This could be achieved by analyzing the player's activity, progress and interactions to dynamically tailor the gamified experience, resulting in a more immersive and meaningful user journey.

5.2 Dynamic Reward Computation

Another theme that emerged throughout both focus groups, which is also underpinned by the non-static and autonomous capabilities of AI, is the dynamic reward computation. This involves utilizing AI algorithms to compute points and rewards, including badges and transaction values, based on users' actions or progress in real-time. AIS-1 explained how AI algorithms could be designed to track users' behavior and continuously adjust the reward computation accordingly. GD-2 argued that this could be used to personalize user rewards, as different types of rewards are more suitable for different users. Similarly, AIS-2 suggested that AI systems can detect when a user is struggling with certain tasks or objectives and offer extra incentives, such as in-game bonuses or higher points, for completing the task successfully. This ensures that such a gamified system remains dynamic and engaging by making the computation of rewards more unpredictable and customized to the individual user's preferences and behaviors. Furthermore, GD-2 discussed how AI could be used to compute rewards within the game which are more meaningful, personalized and thus more relevant to the different users. For instance, virtual goods can become 'unlockable' based on the user's current experience (which includes progression, struggles, preferences, etc.) and are not hardcoded for all users alike. GD-1 argued that such an approach could help to balance game difficulty and make it easier for gamification designers to keep users focused on long-term goals as opposed to short-term reward seeking. GD-2 confirmed that by implementing dynamic reward computation with AI, game designers could develop gamified systems which incentivize skill mastery over luck or chance while allowing different kinds of users (from beginners to experts) access a gamified environment which is tailored specifically to their level of engagement.

5.3 Personalized Feedforward

Personalized information on the user's actions was deemed as another potential benefit of the application of AI to gamification. AIS-2 explained that this involves using AI algorithms to track users' preferences and behaviors and consequently provide real-time, personalized information, which is not just about past actions but naturally assumes a forward-looking nature due to its adaptivity. This includes machine learning algorithms that can detect patterns and correlations in user data and consequently infer user preferences and optimize the feedforward accordingly. Therefore, personalized feedforward is relevant to gamification because it can engage and motivate users by providing real-time information that is aligned with their individual goals, interests, needs and motivations with a focus on their future actions. By offering both on-demand and also just-in-time personalized feedforward, GD-1 argued that this could help take the guesswork out of gamification design. GD-2 further explained that this type of information would be particularly useful in educational and training contexts, as it helps reinforce learning by providing positive reinforcement whenever the player progresses or succeeds, as well as constructive criticism, which is forward-oriented and an enabler for further learning when a user fails or has difficulty with a certain task. GD-2 also argued that this type of feedforward could help to build user confidence, as it is based on specific actions and not on the generalized ability or lack thereof. AIS-1 also commented on how AI can be used to tailor such information to the player's preferred communication style, including textual, visual and/or audio formats. Consequently, the personalization of information presented to the user has the potential to guide the latter towards mastery by offering insights into effective strategies for completing tasks whilst keeping them focused on reaching long-term objectives.

5.4 Prediction

The predictive capabilities of AI have been mentioned as a critical attribute of the application of AI to gamification. AIS-1 explained how algorithms powered by AI could use users' data and behavior to predict future actions and performance. This information can be used to offer users with more targeted feedforward, which is generated in view of predicted failures and/or successes. GD-2 commented on how these predictive capabilities have the potential to enhance the personalized goal-setting and motivation of AI-enabled gamified systems, whereas AI algorithms can predict the player's motivations and preferences and use that information to set achievable goals that align with the player's interests. GD-1 then argued that this could be used to offer proactive guidance and advice to the users, which would enable them to achieve their objectives more effectively while also enhancing engagement and motivation within the gamified environment. Such an approach facilitates the design of game elements that are tailored to individual progress and, as GD-2 suggested, produce not just dynamic reward computations and level adjustments but also predict the kind of reward or challenge the user might respond best to and consequently adjust the difficulty level and/or reward accordingly. AIS-2 opined that this could also lead to the design of more proactive game elements that anticipate users' needs and consequently adjust their behavior in order to better align with users' preferences. AIS-2 further commented on the ability of AI algorithms to predict failure/s within a system and thus provide the user with warnings and alternative strategies for progress when such information still matters. This further boosts the forward-looking nature of the personalized information generated by the gamified system.

5.5 Quantity and Quality of Data

AI algorithms are dependent on the amount and quality of data available. All four participants concurred that this presents a challenge for the successful implementation of AI-enabled gamification. AIS-1 argued that poor-quality data or insufficient amounts of it could lead to less accurate results or even incorrect outputs. AIS-2 added that these data sets are just difficult and expensive to obtain when working on smaller-budget gamification projects. Furthermore, a lack of human oversight into how algorithms construct and interpret data can also cause challenges, as without proper and enough data, incorrect scenarios or variables could negatively affect game mechanics. GD-1 further observed that this implied that an initial data 'threshold' is required in gamified systems until enough quality data is available and properly monitored in order to achieve desired outcomes. This means that the early user experience within such systems would lack the level of adaptivity and personalization that an AI-enabled approach could bring and thus potentially impact the overall user journey. This is further exacerbated by the data noise that is common in data collection, as confirmed by AIS-1, hence further accentuating the need for carefully designed and tested collection methods. Moreover, AIS-2 foresees another possible challenge in this regard, whereas it might not always be possible to collect enough good data from individual users in order to build accurate user profiles. This limits the provision of personalized information and experiences within the gamified system, thus diminishing its effectiveness in terms of user engagement and motivation.

GD-2 added that this might also be the case for gamified systems having a small user base, thus making it very difficult to collect enough data to reach the 'threshold' mentioned by GD-1.

5.6 Privacy and Ethical Considerations

Having a large quantity of high-quality data is essential for an AI-enabled gamified system to provide dynamic difficulty levels and reward computations, offer user-based personalized feedforward and predict successes and failures within the system. However, privacy issues in collecting such data can be another key challenge. AIS-2 commented on the privacy considerations that must be in place when designing such environments. GD-1 observed that users might not consent to provide their personal information, preferences and gameplay data for these AI-enabled gamified systems. AIS-2 suggested that data can be anonymized or aggregated in order to protect users' privacy but cautioned that this could also lead to an inaccurate representation of user preferences. Furthermore, the ethical dimension also poses another challenge for designers and developers. As explained by AIS-2, AI algorithms can have biases that developers must be aware of and take into account. Data collected may not be representative of all users and their experiences and could lead to unfair outcomes or preferential treatment in certain instances. For instance, AIS-1 argued that a common ethical concern across all AI-powered systems is the potential to reinforce discrimination which is a reflection of existing biases in society and could be perpetuated in the personalized feedforward and rewards provided by the algorithms. Additionally, there is the potential for misuse of sensitive player data or information given by user interactions within gamified systems, which could be unsettling and thus discourage user participation. AIS-2 recommended that in order to ensure the ethical implementation of AI in gamification, developers need to be transparent about how their algorithm works and how data is collected from users. Safeguards within the gamified environment must also be provided in order to protect users' privacy.

6 Conclusion

The impersonal and static nature of gamification has fueled the interest of researchers and designers to explore a more personalized and adaptive form of gamification [9, 10], which caters for individual user differences and can potentially leverage a more intrinsic motivation in the end-user. The potential of AI for the personalization and adaptation of gamification has been recognized by a number of researchers and practitioners in the field. Consequently, the aim of this paper was to extend the conceptual basis of the term "AI-enabled gamification" [37] through two focus groups with experts in game design and AI. The findings suggest that there is a positive understanding among the focus group participants about the application of AI to gamification. The two game designers and two AI scientists have highlighted both the expected benefits, as well as some potential challenges that should be taken into account when developing AI-enabled gamified systems. In this regard, AI can be used to dynamically adjust the level of difficulty in gamified systems according to the individual user's preferences, needs and abilities. This would allow for a more personalized gaming experience in which users are challenged at their own level, thus increasing their sense of accomplishment and engagement. Similarly, AI-powered systems can be used to offer personalized rewards that are tailored to the end user. This could result in an increased sense of ownership over the gamified experience and, consequently, a higher level of engagement. The personalized feedforward afforded by AI could potentially lead to a more emotionally and intrinsically driven engagement for users whilst guiding the latter towards mastery by offering insights into effective strategies for completing tasks and keeping focused on reaching long-term objectives. Moreover, the predictive capabilities of AI enable designers to anticipate user behaviors and adjust goals accordingly. On the other hand, participants commented that the quantity and quality of data required to achieve personalization and adaptation is a challenge for developers. Additionally, ethical considerations such as algorithmic bias, data privacy, and misuse of sensitive information were identified and are to be addressed in order for AI-powered gamified systems to be successful. Whilst these findings shed light on the potential of AI-enabled gamification and the challenges that should be taken into account, there is still much to explore in terms of understanding user interaction with such systems as well as their effectiveness. As this field is still in its infancy, further empirical research is needed to assess the potential of AI-powered gamified systems and uncover new applications and strategies.

References

1. Walz, S.P., Deterding, S.: The gameful world: approaches, issues, applications. MIT Press, Cambridge (2014)
2. Saleem, A.N., Noori, N.M., Ozdamli, F.: Gamification applications in e-learning: a literature review. Technol. Knowl. Learn. **27**, 1–21 (2021)
3. Silic, M., Marzi, G., Caputo, A., Bal, P.M.: The effects of a gamified human resource management system on job satisfaction and engagement. Hum. Resour. Manag. J. **30**(2), 260–277 (2020)
4. Bogost, I.: Why gamification is bullshit. In: Walz, S.P., Deterding, S. (eds.) The Gameful World: Approaches, Issues, Applications, pp. 65–80. MIT Press, Cambridge (2015)
5. Chee, C.M., Wong, D.H.: Affluent gaming experience could fail gamification in education: a review. IETE Tech. Rev. **34**, 593–597 (2017)
6. Hung, A.C.: A Critique and Defense of Gamification. J. Interact. Online Learn. **15**, 57–72 (2017)
7. Nacke, L.E., Deterding, C.S.: The maturing of gamification research. Comput. Hum. Behav. **71**, 450–454 (2017)
8. Li, K.C., Wong, B.T.M.: Features and trends of personalised learning: a review of journal publications from 2001 to 2018. Interact. Learn. Environ. **29**(2), 182–195 (2021)
9. Ayastuy, M.D., Torres, D., Fernández, A.: Adaptive gamification in Collaborative systems, a systematic mapping study. Comput. Sci. Rev. **39**, 100333 (2021)
10. Carlier, S., Coppens, D., De Backere, F., De Turck, F.: Investigating the influence of personalised gamification on mobile survey user experience. Sustainability **13**(18), 10434 (2021)
11. Brown, S. M., Santos Jr, E., Banks, S. B., Oxley, M. E.: Using explicit requirements and metrics for interface agent user model correction. In: Proceedings of the Second International Conference on Autonomous Agents, pp. 1–7 (1998)

12. Deterding, S., Dixon, D., Khaled, R., Nacke, L.E.: From game design elements to gamefulness: defining "gamification". MindTrek'11. Tampere, Finland (2011)
13. Oktaviati, R., Jaharadak, A.A.: The impact of using gamification in learning computer science for students in university. Int. J. Eng. Technol. **7**(4), 121–125 (2018)
14. Ryan, R.M., Deci, E.L.: Self-determination theory and the facilitation of intrinsic motivation, social development, and well-being. Am. Psychol. **55**(1), 68–78 (2000)
15. Csikszentmihalyi, M.: Flow: The psychology of optimal experience. Harper & Row (1990)
16. Deci, E.L., Koestner, R., Ryan, R.M: A meta-analytic review of experiments examining the effects of extrinsic rewards on intrinsic motivation. Psychol. Bullet. **125**(6), 627 (1999)
17. Skinner, B.F.: Superstition' in the pigeon. J. Exp. Psychol. **38**(2), 168–172 (1948)
18. Kapp, K. M.: The gamification of learning and instruction: game-based methods and strategies for training and education. John Wiley & Sons (2012)
19. Bruner, J.S.: Toward a theory of instruction. Harvard University Press (1966)
20. Gee, J.P.: What video games have to teach us about learning and literacy. Comput. Entertain. **1**(1), 20 (2003)
21. Nah, F., Eschenbrenner, B., Claybaugh, C.C., Koob, P.B.: Gamification of enterprise systems. Systems **7**(1), 13 (2019)
22. Balci, S., Secaur, J.M., Morris, B.J.: Comparing the effectiveness of badges and leaderboards on academic performance and motivation of students in fully versus partially gamified online physics classes. Educ. Inf. Technol. **27**(6), 8669–8704 (2022)
23. Morschheuser, B., Maedche, A., Walter, D.: Designing cooperative gamification: conceptualization and prototypical implementation. In: Proceedings of the 2017 ACM Conference on Computer Supported Cooperative Work and Social Computing, pp. 2410–2421 (2017)
24. Tanouri, A., Kennedy, A., Veer, E.: A conceptual framework for transformative gamification services. J. Serv. Mark. **36**(2), 185–200 (2022)
25. Deterding, S., Sicart, M., Nacke, L., O'Hara, K., Dixon, D.: Gamification - using game-design elements in non-gaming contexts. In: CHI 2011 Extended Abstracts on Human Factors in Computing Systems, pp. 2425–2428 (2011)
26. Westenhaver, Z.K., Africa, R.E., Zimmerer, R.E., McKinnon, B.J.: Gamification in otolaryngology: a narrative review. Laryngoscope Invest. Otolaryngol. **7**(1), 291–298 (2022)
27. Zichermann, G., Cunningham, C.: Gamification by design: implementing game mechanics in web and mobile apps. O'Reilly Media, Inc. (2011)
28. Hamari, J., Koivisto, J., Sarsa, H.: Does gamification work? A literature review of empirical studies on gamification. In: 2014 47th Hawaii International Conference on System Sciences, pp. 3025–3034. IEEE (2014)
29. Sardi, L., Idri, A., Fernández-Alemán, J.L.: A systematic review of gamification in e-Health. J. Biomed. Inform. **71**, 31–48 (2017)
30. Hofacker, C.F., De Ruyter, K., Lurie, N.H., Manchanda, P., Donaldson, J.: Gamification and mobile marketing effectiveness. J. Interact. Mark. **34**(1), 25–36 (2016)
31. Nicholson, S.: A recipe for meaningful gamification. Gamification in Education and Business, pp. 1–20 (2015)
32. AlMadi, N., AlBalawi, W.: Proposed framework for measuring enterprise gamification impact on employees' performance: ABANA enterprises group company case study. J. Manag. Strategy **6**(4), 50–74 (2015)
33. Deci, E.L., Koestner, R., Ryan, R.M.: A meta-analytic review of experiments examining the effects of extrinsic rewards on intrinsic motivation. Psychol. Bull. **125**(6), 627 (1999)
34. McCarthy, J.: What is artificial intelligence? Stanford University (2004)
35. Ponce, P., Meier, A., Méndez, J.I., Peffer, T., Molina, A., Mata, O.: Tailored gamification and serious game framework based on fuzzy logic for saving energy in connected thermostats. J. Clean. Prod. **262**, 121167 (2020)

36. Brown, S.M., Santos, E., Banks, S.B., Oxley, M.E.: Using explicit requirements and metrics for interface agent user model correction. In: Proceedings of the second International Conference on Autonomous Agents, pp. 1–7 (1998)
37. Bezzina, S., Pfeiffer, A., Dingli, A.: AI-enabled gamification for learning and assessment. In: International Conferences Mobile Learning 2021, pp. 189–193 (2021)
38. Leech, N.L., Onwuegbuzie, A.J.: Beyond constant comparison qualitative data analysis: using NVivo. Sch. Psychol. Q. **26**, 70–84 (2011)
39. Braun, V., Clarke, V.: Using thematic analysis in psychology. Qual. Res. Psychol. **3**, 77–101 (2006)

Serious Game Design for High-Risk Training – The Case of Offshore Wind Turbine Maintenance Personnel Training

Shin-Mei Chen[1]([✉]), Meng-Dar Shieh[1] [ID], and Shun-Yuan Cheng[1,2]

[1] National Cheng Kung University, Tainan City 70142, Taiwan (R.O.C.)
p36104136@gs.ncku.edu.tw
[2] Metal Industries Research and Development Centre, Kaohsiung 811, Taiwan (R.O.C.)

Abstract. Offshore wind turbine maintenance personnel work in high-risk environments and must undergo repeated training prior to work to ensure work safety and improve serviceability. However, the cost of training operation and maintenance personnel is considerable. To increase the efficiency of training and reduce training costs, offshore wind power company have been actively seeking efficient training aids, especially in relation to online training method.

Therefore, this research develops a serious game of offshore wind turbine power system maintenance, which is develop for maintenance simulation training used by maintenance personnel. It was difficult for them to be trained in the real place due to safety, money, and time cost factors, but serious games can be used for simulated training. This way is suitable as a training path for high-cost and high-risk fields of wind turbine operation and maintenance training.

Since serious game development focuses on specialized fields and special target users, it is important to emphasize the opinions of all the stakeholders. Therefore, we use the concept of participatory design to include all the stakeholders in our design process and incorporate the theory of gamification and educational design into our design.

The process of developing this power maintenance game will target user testing as a basis for the advancement of the next generation of prototypes, and we will evaluate it with usability and learning performance. This research will document the process of organizing iterations as design recommendations for subsequent serious game development.

Keywords: Offshore Wind Turbine · Serious Game · Participatory Design · High Risk Skill Training

1 Introduction

1.1 Background

Driven by the global commitment to the development of sustainable energy, and by the decline in the cost of wind power units and batteries, wind power development is particularly rapid, and it is estimated that it will grow further in the next 30 years. The

X. Fang (Ed.): HCII 2023, LNCS 14046, pp. 264–282, 2023.
https://doi.org/10.1007/978-3-031-35930-9_18

growth rate of global wind power is 24% by 2040, making it the fastest growing energy industry. The Renewable Energy Statistics Report indicates that the installed capacity of wind turbines has grown 2.3 times over the past decade, from 267 GW in 2012 to 823 GW in 2021. And the EU, as a major pioneer in wind power development, aims to become a major source of wind power after 2030 [2].

As for the economic and employment opportunities generated by wind power development, according to the statistics [1], the number of people employed in the global wind power industry increased from 1.25 million in 2020 to 1.4 million in 2021. The development of wind power has created more employment opportunities, and offshore wind power requires human capital investment because the construction, installation and maintenance technologies are more complex and dangerous. Due to the high risk and of the work, there is also a serious demand for qualified labor.

Wind Turbine Maintenance Work Risk. Offshore wind power operation and maintenance personnel must work in high-risk environments, including dangerous conditions at high altitudes, high pressures and uncertain sea winds, and they often face the risk of death or serious injury. According to statistics, the number of accidents in recent years has increased significantly compared to a decade ago, with an average of 104 accidents per year in the UK from 2002 to 2011 and 197 accidents per year from 2012 to 2021 [9]. In the statistics of fatalities and injuries, the on-site workers are the main groups of casualties, such as operation and maintenance personnel, installation workers, and crews [9].

In order to ensure safety at work and avoid accidents, operation and maintenance personnel must be trained to understand their relevant standards and safety norms for high-voltage and high-risk work at sea, to protect themselves and to learn contingency measures in the event of accidents, in order to reduce injuries caused by accidents.

Offshore Wind Power Operation and Maintenance Cost. According to the offshore wind turbine failure cost analysis, the resources required for offshore wind turbine maintenance may account for about 30% of the total energy cost [3]. Depending on the scale of each repair, the wind turbine must be shut down for at least eight hours to three days, and three to five operation and maintenance personnel are required each time. Compared with the impact of the failure of the housing, blade and gearbox on the availability of wind turbines, the maintenance of gearboxes and generators has a greater impact because the failure rate is higher and the repair time is longer during major replacement. The basic maintenance time of the offshore wind turbine model currently in use is 60 h per year. During the normal power generation period, it is necessary to continuously monitor whether the wind turbine has any abnormal conditions that need to be checked and repaired. The downtime required for each repair to eliminate errors affects the power generation rate of the wind turbine. Therefore, the detection and debugging ability of the operation and maintenance personnel is also the key to affecting the power generation cost.

In order to have more qualified technical personnel to meet work demands, offshore wind power operators must train local operation and maintenance personnel, and the time and monetary costs involved in training operation and maintenance personnel are considerable. According to the statistics, on average, it takes more than 11,000 euros and at least 24 full working days to train an offshore wind maintenance and operation personnel during the first four years of work.

1.2 Research Purpose

The past research related to the digitization of offshore wind power personnel courses and the research and development of serious games were mainly based on virtual reality simulation auxiliary high-altitude work courses. This research cooperates with the Marine Science and Technology Industry Innovation Zone of the Metal Center in Taiwan to take the power system maintenance and practical course in the content of the BTT course as the main content, to train the safety protection concept, high-voltage power distribution and maintenance of operation and maintenance personnel. We develop a serious game of computer-assisted training, and to verify their learning effect and usability through testing and data analysis, and to record and organize the development process as the development proposal of relevant games.

This research is the first stage of planned development of the game. In the future, based on our research, the wind turbine maintenance database will be combined to serve as a portable maintenance simulation database for future operation and maintenance personnel during simulation exercises and maintenance before wind power maintenance.

2 Literature

2.1 Serious Games

Serious games are defined as "video games for purposes other than entertainment, [29]" and are used in a wide range of applications such as military, education, corporate training, healthcare. Serious games leverage features such as games and simulated environments to allow learners to experience situations that are rare or difficult to find in the real world for reasons such as safety, cost, and time [5, 26].

Serious games help learning by adding gamification features to the purpose of learning, and more and more employees are familiar with computer games or mobile games in recent years than in the past, and are more familiar with and interested in learning course content in the form of video games. Research suggests that gamification promotes learning and improves learners' internal motivation for learning [21, 27, 31], and Mitchell and Savill-Smith discuss that games can help develop many different abilities: Analytical and spatial ability, strategic ability and insight, learning and memory, visual selective attention, etc. [18].

As pointed out by Chen and Michael, serious games are also becoming increasingly important in the global education and training market [4]. The use of serious game-assisted training allows the company to reduce the cost of trainers, special equipment, venues, etc., so its development is actively supported by the owners. In the field of talent training, there have been many studies that gamification is significantly helpful for training learning results. Using the gamification process can increase the motivation and participation of independent learning of tasks, and provide entertainment effects in the process, such as competitive scoring in games, increasingly difficult levels, role-playing and other game elements have proved to be very effective in enterprise talent training.

2.2   Serious Games for High-Risk Technology Training

In the field of special working ability of professional talent training, the simulation of serious games as a training technology in high-risk industries is quite helpful. The simulation of serious games allows trainees to learn by making mistakes without any safety consequences. In the simulation training, users are given knowledge, novice learning skills, improved professional skills and they can pre-model the rare situations they may encounter. In the Nisansala, Weerasinghe research, it was stated that serious games in the fields of pilots, astronauts, military, fire rescue and medical surgery are well suited as training tools [20], and the Federal Aviation Administration also announced that the human factor includes mental and physical factors that have a significant impact on aviation safety, and that this is a reality common to all high-risk areas, and that accidents are mostly caused by these factors. Serious games provide a low-cost way to simulate real environments, including the handling of crisis situations that rarely occur in real life.

Serious games have also been verified in the past literature in different fields. These research [11] indicate that the application of serious games to train medical professionals is on the rise, and serious games form a training tool that provides a challenging simulation environment, ideal for future surgical training. Using serious games to train these doctors can be effective in making them safer for patients. Due to the dangers and expertise of surgery, it is important for game designers and educators to work together to design and validate serious games that target specific educational issues. Only in close cooperation with experts will serious games be included in the medical training curriculum as a teaching tool.

Graafland, Schraagen [11] also make reference to the high initial development costs of serious games. But when a basic game structure has been developed, it can serve as a platform for different institutions and departments to provide relevant professional content. This allows the game to be used more extensively in training, thus keeping the additional development costs relatively low.

2.3   Serious Games for Wind Power Maintenance Personnel Training

In recent years, for Global Wind Organization (GWO) training courses, the literature on operation and maintenance personnel has been mainly for high-altitude work courses, and most studies have shown that the purpose of serious game development is to enable wind power industry personnel to have low-cost and low-risk training methods.

In the Joghee [12] research, he introduced the high-altitude work course in the GWO certification course, introduced the new technology of virtual reality to develop a serious game, and gave suggestions for the development of relevant games in the research conclusion. The research suggests not only cooperating with domain experts in the process, but designers should actually participate in the training course, and enhance the game for the professional background and the course details. Due to the complexity and high-risk characteristics of the learning content, not all training sessions are suitable for serious game training. Errors in the specialty field may lead to unexpected consequences. Therefore, in the early stage of game development, it should be confirmed whether the learning content is suitable for replacing the actual course with games.

2.4 Serious Game Design

In terms of serious game design, Mildner and Mueller put forward several design guidelines and suggestions in the Design of Serious Games [17]. The book proposes that the development of serious games is similar to that of general entertainment games. The biggest difference is that the learning content of serious games is a professional field, so domain experts play an important role in the design process, and most serious games need to be designed with specific target users in mind. Games should be designed according to the special needs and preferences of these users, so that the purpose of serious games can be effectively achieved.

Since serious games are good designs that require many stakeholders to work together, the difficulty with game design is how to make appropriate decisions with different perspectives. Mildner and Mueller suggest that all parties should work together from the beginning of the game design process, and most games are designed with iterative loop frames, and games will continue to improve iteratively as they are discussed and tested. It includes recommendations from experts and operators, as well as modifications and improvements tested by target users. And like user-centric design, participatory design is a design that helps to make serious games more effective and practical [17].

2.5 Gamification for Serious Games

Serious games, unlike general e-learning applications, must provide entertainment in the learning process. If the learner does not find it interesting in the process, it will not help to promote the actual serious game goals. Therefore, effective gamification of the original learning content is the key to enable the learner to learn actively and help the learning effect.

Gamification refers to the use of game design elements in non-game environments, and gamification can facilitate the start or continuation of goal-oriented behavior. In past research, several authors have proposed game design elements. Reeves and Read [22] proposed "ten elements of great games," which include expressing oneself through avatar, narrative context, feedback, competition, and team. Werbach and Hunter [32] 15 important gamification elements, including avatar, badge, leaderboard, points and team, and the interaction of points, badge and leaderboard is emphasized, which is viewed by them as features of gamification applications. The use of gamification elements to help serious games has also been confirmed by research. Sailer, Hense et al. [24] conducted research on the seven elements including points, badge, leaderboard, performance chart, meaningful story, avatar and teammates, matching psychological needs and elements and verifying that gamification elements have a positive impact on learning effect and motivation.

There are many case studies on the application of gamification elements in serious games, which mainly discuss the elements by means of literature review analysis. According to the literature analysis of gamification-related review [15, 25], the research analyzes the use of gamification in different fields. The gamification elements including points, badge, awards, leaderboard, challenges, status, progress, achievements, avatar, small games, characters, narratives, time pressure, and feedback are counted. Points, badge, leaderboard and achievements in the field of education are repeatedly used elements, while in the field of computer, points and badge are often used to achieve continuous behavioral effects through games. Besides points, badge and leaderboard, avatar, achievements and narratives are often used. Many research and case studies on skills training gamification focus on the use of points, and badge, which are among the simplest game elements, mainly as external motivators.

2.6   Gagne Teaching Events in Serious Games

In his book, The conditions of Learning [10], Gagne proposes nine teaching events in teaching that promote learning and are widely adopted design foundations in the course of instructional design, which can help to develop an effective and comprehensive curriculum.

In the past research, Gagne's nine teaching events are often used in the transformation of teaching methods or the introduction of new technologies into the design of teaching. In the Neo and Mai research [19], in the traditional teaching curriculum, new technologies are introduced into the classroom by adding multimedia. They design and develop their learning with Gagne's theoretical framework, use these events as curriculum elements to promote effective learning, and verify that the students' understanding of the content of the curriculum has increased, and also effectively increase the students' learning motivation, transforming students from passive learning roles to active, and teachers become important learning facilitators.

Mancia, Saavedra Filho [16] also use their educational events for high-risk personnel training games, they believe that teaching events provide a useful method for game training of hazardous activities. When using the nine teaching events, trainees can fully understand and remember knowledge. They use a single transformer replacement task as the game content, demonstrating that the game content uses its pedagogical theory as a game to help the operator's knowledge of tasks, skills, attitudes and decisions during risky activities in the work environment.

In the game development model proposed by Tang, Hanneghan [28], reference is made to how nine teaching events using Gagne are used in serious game design as an indicator to confirm whether the design is designed for a full or partial learning experience. They indicate that game parts can be associated with one or more teaching events during the design of the game, that these teaching events are tagged to each part of the game during development, and that the design team thinks about embedding learning content and activities into the game based on the tags to correspond to the type of teaching event.

Gene also mention that the exact forms of these events are not generalizable for all courses, but must be used for different learning objectives. Tang, Hanneghan [28] mention that whether all nine teaching events are included in a serious game depends on the learning environment in which it is used. If games are used as part of the course exercise, only three kinds of teaching events may be provided: learning guidance, stimulation and feedback. The remaining teaching activities are also conducted through lectures and course assignments. The teaching content other than serious games can be mapped to the nine teaching events as a whole, confirming that the teaching of physical courses has a complete learning experience, while serious games designed for complete learning need to meet all nine teaching events. This can be an indicator to check if the game is designed for a full or partial learning experience.

2.7 Capability Decay

Lawani, Hare et al. [13] conducted research on the retention of skills and knowledge acquired by GWO-trained wind power maintenance workers emphasizing the importance of the training course proficiency for the safety of maintenance personnel, but due to little or no training of operation and maintenance personnel during the non-working period and the fact that these acquired skills and knowledge may be forgotten over time, the capability tests on the day of training, one month after training and three months after training confirm the rapid decay of high-altitude safety and rescue skills within four weeks of acquisition, followed by gradual decay. Upon confirmation of the results, Lawani et al. also suggest that due to the emergence of new technologies and the reduction of costs, medical procedures could be practiced in the past in aviation for pilot training, Formula 1 racing, and by surgeons using model-based simulators. In the future, electronic simulation scenarios or virtual reality could be used for training in dangerous or emergency situations, the operation and behavior of equipment could be simulated, and equipment or systems could be reconstructed for training purposes.

3 Method

3.1 Participatory Design

Participatory design is a collaborative design that involves all stakeholders in the design process and emphasizes a power parity approach to design. It contains user-centered design concepts that bring stakeholders such as users and experts into the design process. Through participation, users can learn from each other in different roles, and help them express their ideas with simple tools (such as paper models, Lego), so that important stakeholders can truly participate in the design process, and help design outputs reflect the positions and expectations of various stakeholders [23].

Participatory design can be seen to be used in general interactive system designs, but may be subject to cost constraints or the development team and player conditions are highly repetitive and not often used in game design. However, user engagement should go beyond testing at the end of the development to give users the opportunity to participate in the creative part of the game design process, which is particularly helpful for serious games, as the gap between the target audience and the game designer will be larger for traditional entertainment games.

The development of serious games in the past is usually dominated by the owner, experts and designers, while the users are usually considered in the process of developing the final test, the users' voice cannot be heard in the process due to technical gaps. When the participatory design method is applied in the development of serious games, the power of users is increased. During the participation process, experts and the stakeholders can understand the users' needs and pain points, while the users can understand the development limitations, and after mutual learning process, the stakeholders of serious games can put forward more effective ideas and suggestions in this process, promoting the development of more user-friendly and feasible products.

Software Technology for Evolutionary Participatory Systems Development (STEPS) is a participatory design method that does not require the use of other tools. It is a design method that focuses on product development team and user participation as core concepts for iterative design, emphasizing that the design process needs to be decided jointly. Its basic architecture emphasizes mutual learning between stakeholders and designers [8].

The core philosophy of STEPS is to promote use and co-development of products as a co-design and exploratory learning process. Technology and system need to be considered during the R&D phase, the development prototype will enter the actual field for testing, and the quality of the developed product will be tested in actual use. The development process is a circular iterative process in which the core outputs of the evolutionary prototypes of their products learn from each other and are adapted to changing needs (Fig. 1).

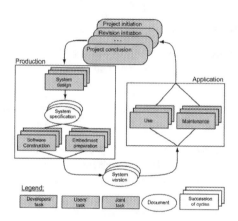

Fig. 1. STEPS method flow chart.

3.2 Gamification

In the process of designing serious games, gamification elements are effectively inserted into serious games. Dozens of gamification elements have been used by different research institutes in gamification literature, and we would use elements that are highly repetitive and theoretically proven in past cases, including Points, and Badges [23]. Besides this, because of hoping to be attractive and continuous in training behavior, Avatars and Meaningful Stories are also suitable for this research. In addition to the above four elements, the research will also use more gamification elements that have appeared in the past literature in the design process, but the following discussion will focus on important elements.

Points. Points are a fundamental element of gamification. They are often rewarded for successfully completing a specific activity or task, and represent the player's progress digitally. The most important purpose of points is to provide feedback, which can measure the player's behavior in the game.

Badges. Badges are visualizations of achievements that can be obtained and collected in the game. Players can have players show off and confirm achievements, such as the player's virtual identity, and badges provide feedback like points.

Avatars. Avatars are visual representations of players in gaming or gamification environments. Players can distinguish themselves from others and become part of the game by selecting or creating their own characters.

Meaningful Stories. Narrative is independent of player performance. Serious games can include narrative contexts to contextualize activities and characters in the game and give them meaning beyond the mere pursuit of points and achievements. Typical complicated storyline of a video game can be role-played.

3.3   Gagne Teaching Events

Gagne's book The conditions of Learning [10] creates a nine-step process called teaching events, which is linked to learning conditions and solves problems. Teaching events and related psychological processes are in order described below.

Gaining Learners' Attention. In order for any learning to occur, it is first necessary to attract the attention of the students.

Informed Learners of Objectives. At the beginning of the course, students should be informed of the learning objectives. This process inspires internal expectations and helps motivate learners to complete the course. These objectives should also form the basis for assessment and possible accreditation. Typically, learning objectives are presented in the form of "You will be able to…" after completing this lesson.

Stimulate Recall of Prior Learning. Linking new content to previous experience and knowledge can facilitate the learning process. Learners are more likely to store information in long-term memory when linked to personal experience and knowledge. A simple way to stimulate recollection is to ask questions about previous experiences, understanding of previous concepts, or content.

Present the Stimulus. This is the part where the new content is actually presented to the learner. The content should be structured with explanations and then demonstrated. To attract different ways of learning, various media can be used, including text, graphics, audio narratives and films.

Provide Learning Guidance. To help learners encode information for long-term memory, additional guidance should be provided while presenting new content. Guidance strategies include the use of demonstrations, case studies, graphical representations, mnemonic symbols, and simulations.

Elicit Performance. Learners need to practice new skills or behaviors, excitement presents learners with an opportunity to confirm their correct understanding, and repetition further enhances retention.

Provide Learning Feedback. When learners are practicing new behaviors, it is important to provide specific and real-time feedback on their performance. Unlike post-test questions, the exercises in the tutorial should be used for understanding purposes rather than for formal scoring. Other guidance and answers provided at this stage are called feedback.

Assess Performance. Upon completion of teaching, students should be given the opportunity to participate in post-testing or assessment. This assessment should be done without additional guidance, feedback, or prompting. Material mastery or certification is usually awarded after a certain score or percentage has been reached. The generally accepted level of mastery is between 80 and 90% correct.

Enhance Retention and Transfer. Skills learned from training programs need to be internalized and applied to the job, combining media that help retain and transfer learning content to the job. Repeating what they've learned is a proven way to help them remember.

3.4 Observational Survey

The observation survey is a research method that systematically observes phenomena or individual behaviors in a natural or controlled situation according to the purpose of the research, and then makes objective explanations and interpretations according to the observation records. The use of observation helps to understand and predict target behavior patterns. By observing the occurrence of events without adding personal opinions, we can get more accurate and objective information.

Interview Survey

Interview survey is a common way to obtain qualitative information, mainly to obtain the personal feelings and life experience statements of the interviewees. In this research we use semi-structured interview survey.

The interviewer and the interviewee use dialogue to exchange ideas and communicate [30]. When the interviewer collects the interviewee's statement, the interviewee can also discover the interviewer's motivation, opinions, etc., it is a two-way interactive process. The semi-structured interview can have both qualitative orientation and quantitative orientation. The main reason is that the interviewer uses the loose but not completely uncontrollable interview structure basis to guide the interview. Usually, the interview program is designed before the interview, but the wording and the order of questions do not need to be too restrictive, and the type or discussion method during the interview can be carried out in a more flexible way.

3.5   Think Aloud

Think aloud is a design method often used in usability testing of interface design [14]. When using Think aloud method in the interface usability test, the testers need to operate the specified task and at the same time speak out the thoughts in their minds, telling what they saw, what they thought, and how they felt. Researchers can collect insights and information from the process. When the test users interact with the test product and speak out at the same time, it allows the researchers to better understand the feelings of the test users, their immediate thoughts, whether there is a problem, and their expectations outside ideas. The process will be recorded by video, and video analysis will be carried out after testing multiple users [6].

The Think aloud method can help designers observe the process of real interaction between users and products. Users who have not received design training can use this method to allow designers to observe various thoughts in addition to the external performance during use, so that designers can understand Intuitive idea of use. Misuses and misconceptions are also presented truthfully, and these misconceptions often turn into design suggestions.

3.6   Protocol Analysis

Protocol analysis is a way to understand the cognitive process or state of the object through the oral narration of the individual. Ericsson and Simon [7] mention that the protocol analysis is divided into three steps:

1. Record oral information: the first step is to record the oral process with electronic equipment.
2. Oral data extraction: Transcribing the audio recordings into verbatim transcripts. Distinguish which parts of the verbatim draft content are related to the theme and which are different, and classify them according to the relationship between the theme and the content according to space, time, repetition, etc.
3. Coding of oral data: Coding the segmented data. The coding is usually classified and coded according to the theoretical framework, and each category is independent and non-overlapping. After integrating the classified and coded data, through the answers of the interviewees, think about the relationship between the content and the research topic and the meaning it represents. At the same time, record the impressions and comments at the coding place and mark the key points expressed by the interviewees and keywords, then assign different classification codes to the content of the verbatim draft.

4   Process and Result

4.1   Research Flow

This research divides the process into three parts: preliminary research, content development, and analysis of results. In the preliminary research phase, we first worked with training company to confirm the development of serious games for power system maintenance in the training of GWO courses. In the literature review phase, we collected literature related to offshore wind power maintenance, and learned relevant background knowledge. In addition, we especially organized the literature for the development of serious games as a reference for the subsequent serious content games.

The research first conducted in-depth research on the users and the teaching situation, and the design team observed the course process of the participants in a non-participatory natural observation way. Subsequently, we conducted interviews on the maintenance personnel, coaches, partition managers, etc. According to the contents learned and observed by the researchers in the classroom, the use of semi-structured interviews is to obtain the qualitative data of the preliminary research, and this part of the data serves as an important design reference for the primary prototype.

The process of game development is based on the STEPS framework of participatory design. In the early stage of development, the design team uses the data of the preliminary research as the design basis to design the primary prototype. The experts are involved in the design process and decision-making, so that the content of the output is not mistaken because it is transformed into a serious game, and they can also give advice on the professional content. In the previous iterations, we used expert usage tests for rapid improvement. The game test in the middle and late stages will be located in the Marine Science and Technology Innovation Zone for users to use in the actual field to conduct the test with think aloud method, and the oral data analysis method will be used for coding analysis. The collected data will enter the improvement basis of the next iteration cycle. The test results will also be reviewed by the standard formulated by the expert as the basis for whether to enter the next iteration (Fig. 2).

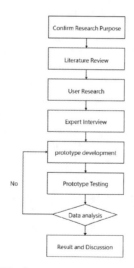

Fig. 2. Research flow chart.

4.2 Preliminary Research

The research team first use the non-participant observation method, we conducted observations in the BTT class teaching in marine innovation and technology zone. We observed the trainees' learning context, interaction with the coach, the class status of the practical course, and how they solve the problems encountered in the course.

There are about 3–12 students participating in a course, and all the students are employees of offshore wind power companies. The practical part started with simple component measurement, followed by wearing protective equipment and practical operation teaching. During the course, the instructor would demonstrate how to look at the circuit diagram for power distribution work. Students could ask questions at any time, and the instructor would give corresponding guidance. After the students complete the circuit, they would do trouble shooting. If there were errors, they would search for them. The instructor would help them at this stage. We list the observed insights below.

- The experience of different student electricians varies greatly, and there will be obvious performance when operating.
- They spend the most time at the stage of wiring.
- The correspondence between the distribution diagram and the panel needs to be explained repeatedly.
- Some students need to check with the coach from time to time whether they are doing the right thing.
- The coach repeatedly emphasized the importance of high-voltage protection measures, operating standard procedures and safety during the course.
- The instructor will prevent students from wiring according to their own ideas, and they need to follow the wiring diagram.
- Trouble Shooting is a difficult part and may not be completed during class.
- The student preform actively wants to finish the mission in the class.

After observing the BTT courses, we conducted interviews with the instructors. When designing a serious game, the expert's opinions are one of the keys to the design, so we adopted semi-structured in-depth interviews. The researchers conducted interviews based on relevant background information and observations. This interview mainly increases our understanding of the key points of course learning, test standards, mistakes that students are prone to make, possible actual maintenance situations, and background profiles of students, and gives us opinions after explaining our design goals. In addition, the focus of our interviews with users includes the user's background, motivation to participate in the course, and expected content. We recorded the interviews during the interviews and coded and organized them afterwards. Doing the protocol analysis which helped the design team understand the interrelationships between the focus and content of the interviews.

According to the coded data, the experts mentioned the most frequently in the category of safety protection, where the tags include "zero energy", "power", "protective equipment", "do not touch", and words such as "important" and "dangerous" appear in the sentences. After analyzing the coded tags, it can be sorted out that the game's safety teaching part may be important and indispensable in the game. The second is the actual field category, where the tags include "teamwork", "emergency response", and "working together", which shows that the part of the situational simulation can be modified in the direction of multi-person cooperation. These data and suggestions will be discussed in the next development stage.

4.3   Content Development

First Generation Prototype Development. In the framework of STEPS, in addition to designers, experts also enter the design process at a very early stage. The first step is the development of the first-generation prototype. This approach emphasizes a mutual learning process, with designers discussing with experts at every stage of development. Experts participate in understanding designers' ideas, technical difficulties, etc., and give design and professional opinions. Experts also teach in professional fields during the process, such as wind power operation and maintenance systems, electrical components, and maintenance processes. In the process of learning from each other, the products produced can not ignore the opinions of any party, and reduce the situation that the products have professional mistakes or are too ideal. At this stage, the design team confirms the content and requirements to be learned with domain experts, and discusses the overall structure of the game with experts. Design teams use design tools like paper prototypes and mockups to make the discussion easier (Figs. 3, 4 and 5).

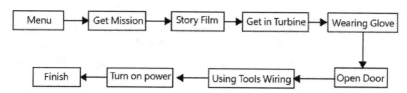

Fig. 3. Game flow of first generation prototype development.

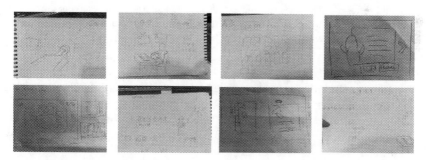

Fig. 4. Paper prototype used in first generation prototype development.

In the process of designing game content, gamification elements are used as an important reference to transform learning content into serious games. In this way, the improvement of the entertainment of the game can be carried out in a well-founded manner, and it can help improve the inner motivation of the user to play the game (Table 1).

The design team uses Gagne's nine teaching events to verify the integrity of learning. Since this serious game is mainly based on auxiliary training after the course is completed, the purpose is to improve the learning effect. Therefore, in the teaching event, it is informed that the learning objectives will be implemented in the classroom and

Fig. 5. Mock up prototype used in first generation prototype development.

Table 1. Gamification elements used in the serious game.

Gamification Element	Game Content
Point	Player would get the point after completing the mission
Badge	After completing multiple missions, players will get different levels of certification
Avatar	Players could become maintenance workers in the game, doing the tasks from the first perspective, and can freely choose the equipment to wear
Meaningful Stories	The player would experience the game story of receiving the company's assigned task and carrying out the task on the wind turbine with his colleagues

the evaluation results will need to be verified by coach. This part of the high-risk work training is considered irreplaceable by the game after expert evaluation and must be evaluated by experienced senior workers. Therefore, these two events were not used in this serious game design. We mark the game part corresponding to the teaching event on the flow chart.

Design Iteration. After the research team produces an interactive first-generation prototype, it will go through about 5 iterations with the participation of 3–5 designers, 1–2 experts and 0–1 offshore wind turbine maintenance company representatives. The steps are for quickly iterate and produce prototypes that can be used and meet the expectations of experts and industry players before being formally used for testing. The discussion is conducted in the form of a workshop. The designer first shows the entire game process, explains the modified parts of the previous generation prototype, and then discusses the content of the game. All participants will put forward suggestions or solutions during the discussion. During the process, participants with non-design backgrounds will be encouraged to use the game framework to simply draw pictures, so that they can communicate more effectively during discussions. The design team will use the collated information after the discussion to make corrections and propose it in the next workshop. The frequency of the workshop is once a week.

Then we took our game to the actual field to do user testing and used Think Aloud method to collect feedback from them. We recruited five students for the user testing of the first iteration, and three students for the user testing of the second iteration. They are all employees of offshore wind power companies who came to study. First, we explain the purpose of the research to the users and conduct a demonstration teaching of Think Aloud method. Before the test, we will ask them to do a short exercise, and then start after confirming that the subjects can do the Think Aloud method in right way. The researcher will assist if they need during the process. After the users finished, the user will be asked to give additional explanations on the thoughts that were not expressed during use. At this time, the user will be allowed to freely operate the game to help recall the memory. After the test, the collected audio recordings and observation records will be analyzed and used as the basis for revision.

We recorded the results of the test for oral data analysis, coded the verbatim transcripts to obtain feedback from experts and different users on the game, and combined the data observed during the test for analysis and sorting (Table 2).

Table 2. Important finding in user testing.

1st user testing
In some pages they can't jump out to end the game
Icon of the distribution diagrams can be misleading
When selecting the tool, it is hard to think that you can scroll down to select other tools
Names and descriptions of tools and components are necessary for students with no experience in electrical maintenance
The instructional part is too short so it is easy to forget the steps, and it will be difficult to practice without prompts
2nd user testing
The text description is so long that they will want to skip it.
The dialogue words of the characters in the game are unnatural
Buttons are sometimes expressed in icons and sometimes in words, which makes people feel strange
Inconspicuous prompts when selecting wire connectors
It is recommended to increase the sound effect during maintenance

In the process of the STEPS method, after the user testing phase is over, it will return to the development stage again, and carry out rapid iterative development with experts, and these encoded data will be used as discussion materials in development, and the next stage of development will be over. Afterwards, user testing and data analysis will be performed again, and this process will be cycled to make the output of the research closer to the expectations of all participants (Table 3).

Table 3. The Evolution of the Three Generations of the Prototype.

	1st Generation	2nd Generation	3rd Generation
Game Flow			
Story Dia-log			
Wir-ing			
Wear-ing Glove			
Zero En-ergy Chec k			

5   Conclusion

During the development of this study, we can draw the following conclusions through the collected data and test results. First, participatory design is suitable for the development of serious games with high-risk training. Participatory design allows participants from different positions to learn from each other. During the design process, the design team needs in-depth study in the field of wind turbine maintenance, and the design team can have more advanced knowledge than previous research cases. At the same time, for experts, we can observe that they can better combine their professional knowledge to express their ideas about the game in the design process and can also use design tools such as paper models for discussion. Users can also actively put forward ideas and suggestions for the game after understanding the game development process. After learning from each other, all participants can communicate more efficiently and find a solution acceptable to everyone from different positions.

The learning content of serious games must be rigorously verified; thus, it is necessary to confirm whether there are errors or missing parts in the content. In each iteration, because the design team may correct the teaching content in the process of modifying the game content and must carefully judge whether or not each teaching content can be replaced by the game in the process of game design, using the STEP method of participatory design can effectively as well as quickly check and prevent errors.

This research also records the problems and solutions encountered in serious game design, which can be used as a reference for future similar game design. For example, in user research, we found that users have considerable differences in electrical degree and experience, and in prototype testing, users of different degrees will put forward conflicting opinions. In the study, we therefore paid more attention to the safety part of the upper fan, because all users have no experience in. There is also a problem that users will skip the teaching content quickly because the text description is too long. In combination with the situation that the actual maintenance will be led by senior operating and maintenance personnel, we will present it in a dialogue way to shorten the length of continuous reading for users.

This research developed a serious game for offshore wind turbine maintenance training, and the developed game framework and interface can serve as the basis for the development of subsequent online training system. It also records the problems met in the development process and our solutions, which can be used as a reference for serious game design in the future. Moreover, this study also proposes an effective research and development method based on participatory design, which can be used as the follow-up development of this research and the development of similar high-risk simulation training games.

References

1. Renewable energy and jobs: Annual review 2022. 2022, International Renewable Energy Agency, International Labour Organization Abu Dhabi, Geneva (2022)
2. Renewable Energy Statistics 2022. 2022, International Renewable Energy Agency: Abu Dhab (2022)
3. Carroll, J., McDonald, A., McMillan, D.: Failure rate, repair time and unscheduled O&M cost analysis of offshore wind turbines. Wind Energy **19**(6), 1107–1119 (2016)
4. Chen, S., Michael, D.: Proof of learning: Assessment in serious games. Retrieved October, **17**, p. 2008 (2005)
5. Corti, K.: Games-based Learning; a serious business application. Informe de PixelLearning **34**(6), 1–20 (2006)
6. Ericsson, K.A., Simon, H.A.: How to study thinking in everyday life: Contrasting think-aloud protocols with descriptions and explanations of thinking. Mind Cult. Act. **5**(3), 178–186 (1998)
7. Ericsson, K.A., Simon, H.A.: Verbal reports as data. Psychol. Rev. **87**(3), 215 (1980)
8. Floyd, C.: Software development as reality construction. In: Software development and reality construction, pp. 86–100. Springer (1992)
9. Forum, C.W.I.: Summary of Wind Turbine Accident data to 30 September 2022 (2021). https://scotlandagainstspin.org/turbine-accident-statistics/
10. Gagne, R.M.: The conditions of learning. Holt, Rinehart and Winston (1970)

11. Graafland, M., Schraagen, J.M., Schijven, M.P.: Systematic review of serious games for medical education and surgical skills training. J. British Surg. **99**(10), 1322–1330 (2012)
12. Joghee, S.C.: Mixed Reality Applications for Safety Trainings in Wind Energy Sector: A Case Study (2021)
13. Lawani, K., Hare, B., Cameron, I.: Integrating early refresher practice in height safety and rescue training. Saf. Sci. **110**, 411–417 (2018)
14. Lewis, C., Rieman, J.: Task-centered user interface design. A practical introduction (1993)
15. Majuri, J., Koivisto, J., Hamari, J.: Gamification of education and learning: a review of empirical literature. In: Proceedings of the 2nd International GamiFIN Conference, GamiFIN 2018. CEUR-WS (2018)
16. Mancia, L.B., et al.: Applying Gagne" s nine events of instruction in development of a serious game for training maintenance activity on power live-lines (2018)
17. Mildner, P., 'Floyd' Mueller, F.: Design of Serious Games, pp. 57–82. Springer, Cham (2016)
18. Mitchell, A., Savill-Smith, C.: The use of computer and video games for learning. A review of the literature (2004)
19. Neo, T.-K., Mai, N.: Note for editor: assessing the effects of using gagne's events of instructions in a multimedia student-centred environment: a Malaysian experience. Turkish Online J. Distance Educ. **11**(1), 20–34 (2010)
20. Nisansala, A., et al.: Flight Simulator for Serious Gaming, pp. 267–277. Springer, Heidelberg (2015)
21. Randel, J.M., et al.: The effectiveness of games for educational purposes: a review of recent research. Simul. Gaming **23**(3), 261–276 (1992)
22. Reeves, B., Read, J.L.: Total engagement: How games and virtual worlds are changing the way people work and businesses compete. Harvard Business Press (2009)
23. Robertson, T., Simonsen, J.: Participatory Design: an introduction. In: Routledge international handbook of participatory design, pp. 1–17. Routledge (2012)
24. Sailer, M., et al.: How gamification motivates: An experimental study of the effects of specific game design elements on psychological need satisfaction. Comput. Hum. Behav. **69**, 371–380 (2017)
25. Seaborn, K., Fels, D.I.: Gamification in theory and action: a survey. Int. J. Hum. Comput. Stud. **74**, 14–31 (2015)
26. Squire, K., Jenkins, H.: Harnessing the power of games in education. Insight **3**(1), 5–33 (2003)
27. Szczurek, M.: Meta-analysis of simulation games effectiveness for cognitive learning. Indiana University (1982)
28. Tang, S., Hanneghan, M., El Rhalibi, A.: Introduction to games-based learning. In: Games-Based Learning Advancements for Multi-sensory Human Computer Interfaces: Techniques and effective practices, pp. 1–17. IGI Global (2009)
29. Tarja Susi, M.J., Per Backlund Serious Games – An Overview. Technical Report, 2007. **HS-IKI-TR-07-001**
30. Taylor, S.J., Bogdan, R., DeVault, M.: Introduction to qualitative research methods: A guidebook and resource. 2015: John Wiley & Sons
31. van Eck, N.J., et al.: Visualizing the computational intelligence field [Application Notes]. IEEE Comput. Intell. Mag. **1**(4), 6–10 (2006)
32. Werbach, K., Hunter, D.: For the Win, Revised and Updated Edition: The Power of Gamification and Game Thinking in Business, Education, Government, and Social Impact. 2020: University of Pennsylvania Press

Fits Like a Game: A Multi-criteria Adaptive Gamification for Collaborative Location-Based Collecting Systems

María Dalponte Ayastuy[1,2]([✉]) [iD], Alejandro Fernández[2] [iD],
and Diego Torres[1,2] [iD]

[1] Depto CyT, Universidad Nacional de Quilmes, R. Saenz Peña 352, Bernal,
Buenos Aires, Argentina
mdalponte@unq.edu.ar

[2] LIFIA, CICPBA-Facultad de Informática, Universidad Nacional de La Plata,
50 y 120, La Plata, Buenos Aires, Argentina
{alejandro.fernandez,diego.torres}@lifia.info.unlp.edu.ar

Abstract. This article proposes an adaptive gamification approach based on a Multi-Criteria Recommendation System (MCRS) for Collaborative Location-based Collecting Systems, adapting the gamification to each user, taking into account her preferences and the project's objectives as a multi-criteria scenario. Specifically, the potentially recommended items are dynamically generated gamification elements, and the recommendation criteria are defined considering two points of view: user preferences and project objectives. Finally, the article includes an evaluation of the proposal and then a discussion of the results.

Keywords: Adaptive Gamification · Multi-criteria Recommender Systems · Clustering-based Collaborative Filtering

1 Introduction

Citizen science encompasses a range of methodologies that encourage and support the contributions of the volunteers to the advancement of research and monitoring. Contributions may include co-identifying research questions; co-designing/ conducting investigations; co-designing, building, and testing low-cost sensors; co-collecting and analyzing data; co-developing data applications; and collaboratively solving complex problems [22]

Gamification is a widely used strategy to engage, retain users and direct their participation. It is about using game elements and mechanics in systems and domains that are not naturally games. Despite the rapid growth of the gameful design research area and the current level of success in user engagement, these findings cannot be generalized to all domains and all users. The one-size-fits-all approach presents several limitations because of the users' different motivations, personalities, needs, and playing styles [3,4,11]. Currently, the research stream on adaptive gamification is considering how to dynamically adapt the game elements and mechanics each user needs in each context. Citizen science projects may apply adaptive gamification to have greater participation from the general public and reach a higher project efficiency. The gamification approach could be adapted to the community members and the project's objectives to achieve better participation and sustained user engagement.

The research on adaptive gamification reveals two main adaptation strategies of game elements. On the one hand, the adaptation approach can recommend at different moments gamification elements corresponding to different types, depending on the estimated user preferences. On the other hand, the gamified system can adapt by adjusting a single gamification aspect according to the player's performance or behavior. Adapting a game element is a change in the features or traits of the specific gamification element. Adapting the game mechanic is an adaptation of the game that generates a rule change, mainly related to difficulty adaptation (i.e., adjusting the time factor, the reward, or enabling an action) [8].

Collaborative location-based collecting systems (CLCS) are collaborative systems where the community of users collects timestamped, geotagged data; this is usually done by using a mobile application [9]. CLCS are found in citizen science projects, such as the AppEar project [5], GeoVin [6], or iNaturalist [17]. In these CLCS-supported projects, volunteers carry out survey tasks (frequently known as *check-ins*) using mobile technologies that allow images, timestamps, and spatial coordinates to be associated with the reports. Usually, CLCS have specific space-time coverage objectives. For example a project may look to maximize coverage of a certain area, or making sure that samples are collected at all hours [9]. A possible approach to specify the needed coverage is to divide the territory into static areas and define a set of time restrictions, indicating how many samples are needed in each area and time. Any attempt to gamify a CLCS should have it's objectives in mind.

To implement an adaptive gamification approach, a strategy for the dynamic generation of game elements considering the user's profile and the current project's coverage objectives is needed. If the user profile is made up of, among other data, user preferences, these can be considered a set of criteria. Similarly, the objectives of the citizen science project can derive another set of criteria. In this way, the adaptation can be addressed through a multi-criteria recommendation system. Although there have been advances on the subject, such as the one presented in [1,16], they do not consider either the spatial-temporal aspect that affects the user's profiling or the project's objectives.

This article proposes an adaptive gamification approach based on a Multi-Criteria Recommendation System (MCRS) for CLCS-supported projects, applying clustered-based collaborative filtering [2] technique. It adapts the gamification to each user, taking into account her preferences and the project's objectives as a multi-criteria scenario. Specifically, the potentially recommended items are dynamically generated gamification elements, and the recommendation criteria are defined considering two points of view: user space-time behavior and project objectives. Finally, the article includes an evaluation of the proposal and then a discussion of the results.

2   Related Work

Since it has been observed that users do not like repetition or uniformity, research has been conducted on the adaptation of gamification elements to users. Particularly, there are approaches of dynamic content generation to adapt the gaming experience based on the profile of the users' characteristics [10], but they still lack a strategy to incorporate user feedback.

One possible strategy could be the use of recommender systems, which takes from a repository of gamified items the one that the person might like the most -using explicit or implicit information about the user-, and there have already been scientific progress on this, such as the general framework for designing adaptive systems in [20] or the proposal in [23] that personalizes activity recommendations by a player model based on activity tracking. Nevertheless, these approaches do not fully meet the needs of citizen science projects as mentioned above, related to modeling spatial and temporal collaborative activities or project objectives.

On the other hand, the application of multiple criteria during the recommendation task has been explored in [16]. However, the application of a multi-criteria recommender system requires its adaptation to the dynamics of gamification, considering aspects such as reward and difficulty level in order to maintain the flow and the user's engagement [24].

From another point of analysis, one of the most used game elements in gamified collaborative systems is game challenges [8], wich is a task or problem in which difficulty depends on the user's skills, abilities, motivation, and knowledge and count toward progress and outcomes [13]. While there is a wide range of types of challenges detailed in the literature [21], to present a gamified application for CLCS, those challenges that require endurance faculties or those that require sustaining a temporality and rhythm must be considered. To develop challenges of this type in a personalized way, it is necessary to model users based on how they interact with the CLCS in terms of how they behave spatially and temporally [9].

3   Space-Time Game Challenges Domain

An example domain is used in the following sections to explain this approach, where a CLCS is gamified through game challenges generation and recommendation.

The space-time game challenges are actions a user must fulfill within an area and a time restriction. Particularly to CLCS, these actions are the previously mentioned sampling tasks, which are registered with a geographically referenced location and a timestamp. For instance, a possible game challenge is to gather two samples in area a_1 on a weekend morning. Additionally, the game challenge is also described with a difficulty estimation and a reward that can influence user preference.

Therefore, the following criteria set C_u describes user preferences using 5 aspects of the game element:

$$C_u = \{area, time\_restriction, difficulty, reward,$$

$$sample\_number\}$$

On the other hand, project priorities can be described through the game challenge's area and time restriction.

$$C_p = \{area, time\_restriction\}$$

The criteria set C_p allows prioritization of challenges associated with specific areas or time restrictions, thus approximating the project's objectives.

An example of a scoring matrix is shown in Table 1, where it can be seen, for example, that the game element ge_0 has been rated by users u_0 and u_2. User u_0 scores 2 points for the challenge's area, 3 points for its time restriction, and 2 points for difficulty, reward, and sample number. According to the project's objectives, both the area and the time restriction of game element ge_0 received a score of 5 points, meaning that it has a great priority.

Table 1. Multi criteria ratings with 5 user criteria and 2 project (global) criteria

	u_0	u_1	u_2	Global
ge_0	(2 3 2 2 2)	?	(3 3 4 5 2)	(5 5)
ge_1	(1 1 2 1 1)	(5 5 4 4 3)	?	(3 5)
ge_2	?	(2 3 3 4 4)	?	(1 4)
ge_3	(0 1 3 0 0)	?	(5 5 4 2 2)	(3 4)

The scoring in C_u may include explicit user preferences, e.g., multi-criteria scoring for game challenges, or implicit user preferences, such as selecting a game challenge from an ordered list recommended to the user. The values in C_p (global column in Fig. 1) may describe the project's criteria in terms of priority sampling areas and time restrictions.

4   Problem Statement and Approach

Recommendation systems are software tools and techniques providing suggestions for items that are most likely to be interesting to the user or to be relevant to her needs. In computing these item suggestions, recommendation systems try to predict what the most suitable items are, based on the user's preferences. The system collects information from users regarding their preferences which are either explicitly expressed or are inferred by interpreting the actions of the user [18]. One possible approach is collaborative filtering, which is based on the fact that if the active user matched in the past with certain users, then the new recommendations coming from these similar users should be relevant and of interest to the active user.

The problem of adapting game elements in the context of collaborative location-based collecting systems is presented in terms of a Multi-Criteria Recommendation System (MCRS) where the recommended items are game elements, such as the game challenges that were presented in Sect. 3. MCRS are systems that use multiple criteria to support recommendation [2]. The performance of alternatives in the game elements set is analyzed upon a set of criteria that may refer to the multiple dimensions upon with the item is being evaluated. These criteria can be related to the game element's attributes but also to other aspects that may be interesting to the user or the project. This work considers two subsets of criteria: the one that expresses the (implicit or explicit) preferences of the user, namely C_u, and the one that expresses the project's criteria, namely C_p.

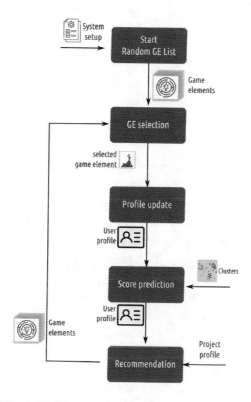

Fig. 1. Multi-criteria recommendation approach

This article presents a multi-criteria recommendation system based on a clustering based collaborative filtering technique with an item selection scoring, which is a less intrusive technique with respect to multi-criteria rating -where the user is asked to rate an item on multiple criteria-. The approach consists of 3 main steps. First, the scores of those elements that the user has not yet rated (unscored game elements) are predicted, calculating also a confidence level for each estimate that gives an idea about the quality and quantity of the available information was used to estimate. Secondly, a recommendation of the N best-scored elements is made, considering (or not) the confidence level. Finally, the user's opinion is incorporated, which is implicitly expressed by the selection of one of the recommended game elements. These steps are depicted through *score prediction, recommendation* and *profile update* boxes in Fig. 1. Notice that in the figure, the workflow begins with a random selection of game elements to present to the user a first recommendation.

The score prediction step is based on a clustering-based collaborative filtering, with space-time clusters. The recommendation step considers the previously estimated criteria scores and applies an aggregation function to have an unique overall score of each element for the target user and be able to build a game element ordered list. The profile update step uses a pairwise computation technique to update the predicted overall score given the user's opinion that is expressed by a game element selection from the ordered list.

This steps are further detailed in following sections.

4.1   Preliminar Definitions

Definition 1 (Criteria score). *The score for an specific criteria c_i (for $c_i \in C_u$) in game element ge_j given by the user u_x is denoted as $r_{ijx} \in [0..5]$.*

Definition 2 (Game element score). *The score tuple for a game element ge_j given by the user u_x is defined as*

$$R_{jx} =< r_{1jx}, .., r_{kjx} >$$

where k is the size of set C_u.

To include multi-criteria rating information in the calculation of the similarity between two different users, k different similarity values are obtained by using a variation of the Manhattan distance. The overall similarity then can be computed by aggregating the individual similarities into an average function, as is explained in Definitions 3, 4 and 5.

Definition 3 (Scoring similarity). *The similarity between scoring R_{yx} and R_{yv} is defined as follows:*

$$sdist(R_{yx}, R_{yv}) = \frac{1}{k} \times \sum_{c=1}^{k} |r_{cyu} - r_{cyv}|$$

Definition 4 (Users distance). *The distance between users u and v is defined as follows:*

$$udist(u, v) = \frac{1}{|C(u, v)|} \times \sum_{g \in C(u,v)} sdist(R_{gu}, R_{gv})$$

where $C(u, v)$ is the set of common game elements between users u and v. This are the game elements that both u and v have rated.

Definition 5 (Users similarity). *The similarity between users u and v is a transformation over the notion of distance:*

$$usim(u, v) = \frac{1}{1 + udist(u, v)}$$

Definition 6 (Overall score). *The overall score of a game element given by a user is a value:*

$$O(u_x, ge_j) = f(R_{jx})$$

where f is a linear function, R_{jx} is the score for the game element ge_j given by user u_x.

It is well known that recommender systems exhibit significant user or item bias, which is explained by some users' tendency to give higher scores than others and some items to be rated higher than others [15]. Mathematically, the average rating per user can be expressed as the summation of nonzero ratings given by the user divided by the user's number of ratings. However, this formula does not consider the number of game elements the user rated. It puts on the same page users who have rated hundreds of game elements and users who rated only one game element. To correct this bias and give statistical significance, a C term is added to the denominator. The C term is called *shrimp term*, and it is a constant value chosen depending on the properties of the data.

Definition 7 (User bias). *The user bias is a description of how the user tends to score the game elements. It is computed as follows:*

$$\bar{u} = \frac{\sum_{ge \in R_u} O(u, ge)}{|R_u| + C}$$

where $O(u, ge)$ is the overall score of game element ge given by user u, R_u is the set of game elements rated by user u, C is the shrimp term.

Finally, in relation to the modeling of the user's space-time behavior, the last two definitions are needed. To synthesize the user activity within the time frame in a single value and thus be able to shape historical activity as a time series, a K-means clustering was executed in order to detect behavioral atoms [7]. The aforementioned behavioral atoms are generated from aggregating a set. of sampling events in a given time interval.

Definition 8 (Behavioural Atom). *A behavioral atom is a categorical value that describes the user's space-time activity within a time frame. They are discovered through a clustering process over a sample task-derived data set.*

With these elements, the UTB (User Traveling Behaviour) series are composed, as described in the following definition.

Definition 9 (UTB). *The User Traveling Behaviour series for a user u is a sequence*

$$UTB_u = \{a_1, .., a_n\}$$

where each a_i is a behavioral atom corresponding to the timeframe i.

These UTB time series can be grouped to give a notion of similarity between people based on their spatial and temporal behavior [9].

4.2 Game Elements Score Prediction

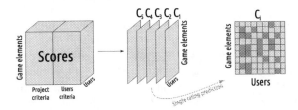

Fig. 2. Score prediction. Dark squares are the predicted scores

This multi-criteria score prediction problem can be approached as multiple predictions by taking each criterion as an independent dimension of estimation and then aggregating this data into an overall score per game element [1]. Considering the criteria in isolation allows the estimation of missing data using any one-dimensional approach (see Fig. 2) and then integrating all the score matrices related to the different criteria using an aggregation strategy, as will be discussed in the recommendation step.

Using a **clustering-based collaborative filtering** approach, to estimate the score of an unknown item (here, game element) for a given user, the neighbors' scores must be considered. These neighbors are users belonging to the same cluster, which is computed based on their space-time behavior (the UTB time series introduced in Definition 9).

The Definition 10 presents the function $S()$, that estimates the individual criterium score in game element g for user u as a weighted average of the known scores of the k nearest neighbors in the cluster. The users' similarity -as defined in 5- is used to weigh the score of each of the other users.

Definition 10 (Adjusted weighted sum). *The adjusted weighted sum S is defined as follows*

$$S(u, i, g) = \overline{u} + \left[\sum_{v \in K} (r_{vig} - \overline{v}) \times usim(u, v) \right] \times \frac{1}{\Sigma_{v \in K} |sim(u, v)|}$$

where K is the set of k nearest neighbors in the cluster, $usim(u, v)$ is a value of similarity between users u and v, $\overline{u}$ is the user bias, and r_{vig} is the known score or criteria c_i in the game element g for user v.

Table 2. Sample scenario

Similarity matrix				User biases	
	u_0	u_1	u_2	User	$\overline{u}$
u_0	1	0.8	0.5	u_0	0.75
u_1		1	0.7	u_1	1,76
u_2			1	u_2	1,56

For instance, assume the user similarities and user biases described in the Table 2, and that K set is composed by u_1 and u_2. Then, the estimation of the score for criterion c_0 in the game element ge_0 for user u_0 is as follows:

$$sum = (r_{100} - \overline{u_1}) \times 0.8 + (r_{200} - \overline{u_2}) \times 0.5$$
$$S(u_0, c_0, ge_0) = \overline{u_0} + \frac{sum}{0.8 + 0.5}$$

Notice that r_{100} and r_{200} are the scores given by user u_1 and u_2 to criterium c_0 in game element ge_0, respectively.

In addition, the score corresponding to the other criteria of set C_u must be estimated. Once all the individual scores are estimated, it is possible to carry out the recommendation stage, as is described in the next section.

4.3   Game Elements Recommendation

Fig. 3. Recommendation

When providing a recommendation for user u, it is necessary to estimate the value of the utility function R_{jx} for every game element ge_j for which it is undefined, and to choose game element ge_i that maximizes R_{ix}, or otherwise, to build an ordered list with top-scored game elements [14].

For this purpose, it is necessary to have an overall score from the individual scores assigned to the different criteria, which allows the establishment of a total order among the game elements. The aggregation function is the relationship between the overall rating and the underlying criteria scores $r_{0jx} = f(r_{1jx}, .., r_{kjx})$. Figure 3 highlights in dark blue color the score given by a player to each criterion within a game element.

There are many approaches to this, but in this work, the $O()$ function defined in 11 is used. It aggregates the values of the individual criteria into a linear function whose weights are approximated by linear regression. Each weight w_i is associated with criterion i and can be interpreted as the importance of this criterion in determining the overall rating.

Definition 11 (Aggregation Function).

$$O(u_x, ge_j) = [\Sigma_{i=1}^{k} w_i \times r_{ijx}] + c$$

where r_{ijx} is the score of the criteria i in the game element ge_j, given by the user u_x.

The weights w_i and constant c are estimated based on the set of known ratings through a linear regression in a batch process that is executed offline, according to the system configurations. The system could consider users who have had a certain load of participation to mark their weights outdated or 'dirty'. See Sect. 4.5 for further details.

The output of this recommendation step is presented to the user as a descending score list of game elements, as defined below.

Definition 12 (Recommendation list).

$$L_u = [l_0..l_n]$$

where l_i are game elements and $O(u, l_i) > O(u, l_j)$ for every $i > j$.

The user has then the opportunity to choose one of them, thus expressing her preference and giving feedback to the system. The impact of this interaction is explained in the next section.

4.4   User Feedback

Once the recommendation of game elements for a user has been resolved, the user can choose an element from the ordered list to express her preferences. The underlying idea is to derive the user's preferences by having her choose a game element from a list sorted by overall score in a descending order. This action makes it possible to correct if needed the estimates that established the order in the list of the recommended game elements. Since the chosen element may not be the best scored, it is possible to adjust the user's profile by considering that

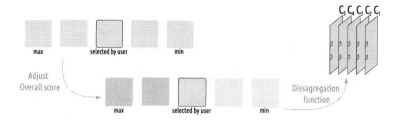

Fig. 4. User feedback: game element selection

by such a choice the user is indicating that the previous items in the list (i.e., for which a higher score had been estimated) should be adjusted to have a lower score than the selected item. Formally, let be l_p the selected element at position p in the list. If $p > 0$ then there is a subset of elements $L' = [l_0..l_{p-1}]$ with the elements that are previous to l_p. The scores of the game elements in L' should be updated according to their relative position with respect to the selected item.

In this approach, a pairwise computation with non-transitive decomposition by difference is applied [16]. The main idea is to update the rating of the items in L' and finally disaggregating these changes into individual criteria preferences.

Asuming that the preference between an object **a** and an object **b** does not depend on the attributes in common of **a** and **b** (principle of preferential independence), the non-discriminating criteria between the selected object and an object above must be removed. The discriminating criteria (i.e. equally scored criteria) is the set defined in Eq. 1

$$\theta_{uij} = \{c \in C_u : r_{ciu} \neq r_{cju}\} \tag{1}$$

Listing 1.1. Pairwise computation

```
1   For prev: 0 to p
2       dcSet = discCriteria(gt, prev)
3       cNum = len(dcSet)
4       lpScore = partialScore(gt, dcSet)
5       prevScore = partialScore(prev, dcSet)
6       delta = prevScore - lpScore
7       critDelta = delta/cNum
8       alpha = 1/p
9       update_profile(prev, alpha, critDelta)
```

To update the overall score of elements in L' their distance to l_p must be computed, but only considering the discriminating criteria set (see line 2 in algorithm detailed in Listing 1.1).

With this set, a partial game element score can be computed through function O_θ defined in Eq. 2 and implemented in line 4 of Listing 1.1.

$$O_\theta(u, i) = \frac{\Sigma_{c \in \theta} r_{ciu}}{\#(\theta)} \tag{2}$$

In Eq. 3 the function $\Delta(u, i, g)$ is defined as the difference between the partial scores of game elements g_i and g_t. Notice that $\Delta(u, i, g)$ is positive in any case, given that g_i is first in the game element list than g_t.

$$\Delta(u, i, g) = O_\theta(u, i) - O_\theta(u, g) \tag{3}$$

Thus, Delta is used to obtain the score of each criterion composing the temporary vector, through the *delta*() function defined in Eq. 4 (these are implemented in lines 6 and 7 of Listing 1.1).

$$\delta(u, i, g) = \frac{\Delta(u, i, g)}{\#(C_u)} \tag{4}$$

Finally, the user profile is updated as is described in Eq. 5. In order to maintain an efficient system -with a balanced impact- the number of pairwise computations that have been done need to be taken account. For this aim, the variable $\alpha = 1/pos(g)$ is used (lines 8 and 9 in Listing 1.1).

$$r'_{ciu} = r_{ciu} + 0, 1 \times log(1 + \alpha \times \delta(u, i, g)) \tag{5}$$

Notice that α relativizes the change in the score according to the position of the chosen element. The more distant the element g_t is from the first element (which has a higher score), the smaller the *alpha* value. Indeed, a logarithmic function is used to reduce the impact of high values. A coefficient of 0.1 is used to control the impact of the new data on the system. Lastly, in order to avoid the negative values obtained with the logarithm, the value of 1 is added.

With this profile update, the system is able to make more suitable scoring predictions.

4.5   Batch Processes

It is well known that the computation of user clusters as well as the distance between all users in each cluster is computationally demanding. That is why this processing must be able to be done offline to the workflow described in the Fig. 1 and that this does not compromise the usability of the recommender system. The same policy is applied in the calculation of the weights that are part of the score estimation, as indicated in the Definition 11.

The situation that triggers the execution of each of these processes is an orthogonal configuration to the system that we propose here. For the case of clusters, in particular, a quality parameter such as mean square error or intra-cluster cohesion can be used.

5   Evaluation and Results

In this preliminary version, while lacking a dataset with the needed characteristics related to playing behaviour and space-time information, the evaluation of this proposal had to focus on the collaborative filtering aspect. This was done using an existing dataset, for which a single cluster is considered, with the expectation that the current implementation behaves adequately according to the literature in evaluation of collaborative filtering recommender systems.

Examples of decision support metrics are **precision at k** and **recall**. The first one is the proportion of recommended items in the top-k set that are relevant, and the last one is the proportion of relevant items found in the top-k recommendations. Moreover, the F1-score measure is a harmonic mean of precision and recall.

Definition 13 (Precision at k).

$$P_k = \frac{(L_u \cap R_u)}{\#(L_u)}$$

Where L_u is the set of recommended game elements for active user u and R_u is the set of relevant game elements.

Definition 14 (Recall at k).

$$R_k = \frac{(L_u \cap R_u)}{\#(R_u)}$$

Where L_u is the set of recommended game elements for active user u and R_u is the set of relevant game elements.

Definition 15 (F1 score).

$$F1 = \frac{2 \times R_k \times P_k}{R_k + P_k}$$

Where R_k is the recall at k and P_k is the precision at k.

In the computation of precision at k, as the divisor can be a zero value, because the recommendation list can be empty, in that case the precision at k must be set to 1 [12,19]. Similarly, when computing recall at k a similar situation can occur when the total number of relevant items is zero. In this case the recall at k is set to value 1.

Given that the development progress of this proposal is preliminary, the aspects to be evaluated are those related to accuracy and recall through offline tests using datasets with historical scoring information. The possibility of using synthetic data was discarded as it presents a significant risk of being biased to favor the algorithms and it is only recommended to use them in the performance tests of the tools [14].

To evaluate this approach, a set of test scenarios were developed, and for all of them, an adaptation of the MovieLens data set was carried out, which contains the scoring of 10681 movies given by 71567 users. The multi-criteria suitability was done replicating the score given by the user in each of the criteria of the set C_u. Relevant elements were also marked, this is, their score exceeds a certain threshold, to then separate 20% of the relevant records in a test set. The test scenarios are described below.

- Scenario A: For this test, N = 10 iterations were performed where each time a user was taken at random and the score prediction and recommendation were performed considering k = 6 neighbors within the cluster. The project criteria were not considered, i.e. the values are set to zero.
- Scenario B: Similar to A, but with random project's criteria scores.

The maximum precision at k obtained was 0.75 in scenario A and 0.9 in scenario B. The maximum recall value obtained was 0.2 in A, and 0.15 in B. The recall value can be seen as too low but is related to the evaluation parameters. As long as the size of the recommendation is limited to a few elements, it will always be much smaller than the full set of relevant game elements.

Recommendation systems have a variety of properties that may affect user experience, such as accuracy, robustness, scalability, and so forth, but the task of evaluating a recommender system must be based on the set of relevant properties for the application [19]. Particularly, numerous strategies have been proposed and used in the literature to evaluate the accuracy, including statistical accuracy metrics (e.g., mean absolute error and mean square error), as well as decision support system metrics that determine how well the recommender algorithm can predict high-relevance items (i.e., items that the user would rate highly) [12].

6   Conclusions and Future Work

This article presented a framework to adapt the gamification of a CLCS-supported project through a multi-criteria recommending system, with awareness of user's and project preferences/priorities. The proposed system satisfies the objective of this work, as it incorporates elements of gamification, the criteria of the CLCS project, and the possibility of incorporating space-time behavior in the prediction of preferences.

The evaluation of the approach, as was mentioned, is limited to offline test scenarios, focused in collaborative filtering performance metrics. To carry out evaluations with real users, it is necessary in the first place to implement this proposal in a citizen science project that will allow to collect space-time data.

The disaggregation function approach supports the implicit formulation of the user's preference model based on the selection of a game element from a list of recommended. This is a less intrusive technique concerning multi-criteria rating, where the user is asked to rate an item on multiple criteria. Nevertheless, the possibility of multi-criteria scoring is a future work, to allow users to provide the feedback about the game element on specific criteria. Finally, another pending but very promising work is to improve the gamification strategy, incorporating the increase of difficulty and reward as part of the project's objectives based on the user's progress on the selected challenge.

References

1. Adomavicius, G., Kwon, Y.O.: Multi-criteria recommender systems. In: Ricci, F., Rokach, L., Shapira, B. (eds.) Recommender Systems Handbook, pp. 847–880. Springer, Boston, MA (2015). https://doi.org/10.1007/978-1-4899-7637-6_25

2. Adomavicius, G., Manouselis, N., Kwon, Y.O.: Multi-criteria recommender systems. In: Ricci, F., Rokach, L., Shapira, B., Kantor, P.B. (eds.) Recommender Systems Handbook, pp. 769–803. Springer, Boston, MA (2011). https://doi.org/10.1007/978-0-387-85820-3_24

3. Böckle, M., Novak, J., Bick, M.: Towards adaptive gamification: a synthesis of current developments. Research Papers (2017). https://aisel.aisnet.org/ecis2017_rp/11/

4. Busch, M., et al.: Using player type models for personalized game design - an empirical investigation. Interact. Design Architect. J.**28**, 145–163 (2016)

5. Cochero, J.: Appear: a citizen science mobile app to map the habitat quality of continental waterbodies. Ecologia Austral. **28**, 467–479 (2018)

6. Cochero, J., Pattori, L., Balsalobre, A., Ceccarelli, S., Marti, G.: A convolutional neural network to recognize Chagas disease vectors using mobile phone images. Eco. Inform. **68**, 101587 (2022)

7. Dalponte Ayastuy, M., Torres, D.: Adaptive gamification in collaborative location collecting systems: a case of traveling behavior detection. J. Comput. Sci. Technol. **22**(1), e05 (2022). https://doi.org/10.24215/16666038.22.e05. https://journal.info.unlp.edu.arjcst/article/view/1943

8. Dalponte Ayastuy, M., Torres, D., Fernández, A.: Adaptive gamification in Collaborative systems, a systematic mapping study. Comput. Sci. Rev. **39**, 100333 (2021). https://doi.org/10.1016/j.cosrev.2020.100333. https://www.sciencedirect.com/science/article/pii/S1574013720304330

9. Dalponte Ayastuy, M., Torres, D.: Relevance of non-activity representation in traveling user behavior profiling for adaptive gamification. In: Proceedings of the XXI International Conference on Human Computer Interaction. Interacción 2021, Association for Computing Machinery, New York, NY, USA (2021). https://doi.org/10.1145/3471391.3471431

10. Dalponte Ayastuy, M., Torres, D., Fernández, A.: A model of adaptive gamification in collaborative location-based collecting systems. In: Degen, H., Ntoa, S. (eds.) Artificial Intelligence in HCI. HCII 2022. Lecture Notes in Computer Science, vol. 13336, pp. 201–216. Springer, Cham (2022). https://doi.org/10.1007/978-3-031-05643-7_13

11. Heeter, C., Magerko, B., Medler, B., Lee, Y.H.: Impacts of forced serious game play on vulnerable subgroups. Int. J. Gaming Comput. Mediat. Simul. **3**(3), 34–53 (2011). https://doi.org/10.4018/jgcms.2011070103

12. Herlocker, J.L., Konstan, J.A., Terveen, L.G., Riedl, J.T.: Evaluating collaborative filtering recommender systems. ACM Trans. Inf. Syst. (TOIS) **22**(1), 5–53 (2004)

13. Iversen, S.: In the double grip of the game: Challenge and Fallout 3. Game Studies 12 (2012). https://www.gamestudies.org/1202/articles/in_the_double_grip_of_the_game

14. Jannach, D., Zanker, M., Felfernig, A., Friedrich, G.: Recommender systems: an introduction. Cambridge University Press (2010)

15. Koren, Y., Rendle, S., Bell, R.: Advances in collaborative filtering. Recommender Systems Handbook, pp. 91–142 (2021)

16. Martin, A., Zarate, P., Camillieri, G.: A multi-criteria recommender system based on users' profile management. In: Zopounidis, C., Doumpos, M. (eds.) Multiple Criteria Decision Making. MCDM, pp. 83–98. Springer, Cham (2017). https://doi.org/10.1007/978-3-319-39292-9_5

17. Nugent, J.: Inaturalist. Science Scope **41**(7), 12–13 (2018)

18. Ricci, F., Rokach, L., Shapira, B.: Recommender systems: introduction and challenges. Recommender Systems Handbook, pp. 1–34 (2015)

19. Shani, G., Gunawardana, A.: Evaluating recommendation systems. Recommender Systems Handbook, pp. 257–297 (2011)
20. Tondello, G.F., Orji, R., Nacke, L.E.: Recommender systems for personalized gamification. In: Adjunct publication of the 25th Conference on User Modeling, Adaptation and Personalization, pp. 425–430 (2017)
21. Vahlo, J., Karhulahti, V.M.: Challenge types in gaming validation of video game challenge inventory (CHA). Int. J. Hum.-Comput. Stud. **143**, 102473 (2020). https://doi.org/10.1016/j.ijhcs.2020.102473. https://www.sciencedirect.com/science/article/pii/S1071581920300756
22. Vohland, K., et al.: The Science of Citizen Science. Springer, Cham (2021). https://doi.org/10.1007/978-3-030-58278-4
23. Zhao, Z., Arya, A., Orji, R., Chan, G.: Effects of a personalized fitness recommender system using gamification and continuous player modeling: System design and long-term validation study. JMIR Ser. Games **8**(4), e19968 (2020). https://doi.org/10.2196/19968. https://games.jmir.org/2020/4/e19968/
24. Zichermann, G., Cunningham, C.: Gamification by design: implementing game mechanics in web and mobile apps. O'Reilly Media, Inc. (2011)

Student's View on Hate Speech: Gamified Annotation for Educational Use

Jan Fillies[1(✉)], Raimi Solorzano Niederhausen[1,2], Silvio Peikert[3], and Adrian Paschke[1,2,3]

[1] Institut für Angewandte Informatik, Goerdelerring 9, 04109 Leipzig, Germany
fillies@infai.org
[2] Freie Universität Berlin, Kaiserswerther Str. 16-18, 14195 Berlin, Germany
[3] Fraunhofer-Institut für Offene Kommunikationssysteme FOKUS,
Kaiserin-Augusta-Allee 31, 10589 Berlin, Germany

Abstract. Online hate speech gains growing attention by educators and scientific researchers. Adolescents are highly active social media users and the majority of them experience or witness online hate speech. Therefore, educators are facing the challenge of how to handle the topic in an engaging and modern way. In prior work it has been shown that the understanding of hate speech varies depending on time, language, and topic. Another challenge is the small number of available data sets. This research addresses the problem of obtaining information to understand hate speech from the perspective of adolescents. Due to the difficulties of working with adolescents (e.g. data protection), it is challenging to create data sets for this specific subgroup. This research closes the gap by presenting a gamified annotation tool to be used in educational workshops within schools. Students are enabled to perform hate speech annotations in a controlled gamified environment. The gamified solution supplies schools with a live and realistic setting for a modern and motivational way to interact with the topic. This research demonstrates how to use the setting of educating students on the topic of hate speech in a safe space while understanding their perspective on hate speech.

Keywords: Hate Speech · e-Learning · Annotation · Gamification · Natural Language Processing · Education

1 Introduction

There are differences between language used by adolescents and language used by adults online [31]. In 2018, 95% of American youth (between 13–17 years of age) either had access to or possessed their own smartphone [1]. About 90% of young adults in the United States use social media, most of them daily [34]. Between January and March 2020 Facebook removed 9.6 million posts containing hate speech [22]. As shown, social media is widely used among young adults, and hate speech is an important topic for social media outlets. Following the data

X. Fang (Ed.): HCII 2023, LNCS 14046, pp. 299–312, 2023.
https://doi.org/10.1007/978-3-031-35930-9_20

supporting the harm of hate speech [12,15,21,29] most platforms e.g., Facebook[1] and YouTube[2] have hate speech detection algorithms in place or are working on understanding the issue. The definition of hate speech varies and changes based on region, platform, media, community, time, and topic. This is reflected in the many different applied definitions found in scientific research papers.

Considering the finding that there is a difference in language, time, and topic in conversations between adolescents [31], it is important to understand further what implications and effects are caused for the field of algorithmic hate speech detection. Due to the difficulties of working with minors regarding data protection and ethical concerns, a supervised setting needs to be established to ensure the safety and wellbeing of the adolescents.

Markogiannaki et al. [19] states that her findings of a sample group of Greek adolescents supports "the need for prevention strategies in the school environment" regarding educational programs for adolescents to understand and counter online and offline hate speech. Even though there are many serious games publicly available regarding online hate speech (e.g. playyourrole[3]), no gamification solution for educational purpose in the field of annotation and education was found.

This research wants to close the gap by introducing a gamified annotation tool to be used in educational workshops within schools. The gamified solution supplies schools with a live and realistic setting for a modern and motivational way to interact with the topic. The tool uses already annotated data regarding hate speech and collects and understands the student's views on given statements, all in a supervised gamified learning environment. This therefore protects the privacy of the students and ensures their mental wellbeing.

The paper is organized as followed: Sect. 2 displays the related work. Section 3 describes the concept and design of the application, including the chosen dataset and gamification elements. Section 4 explains the system design. Section 5 lays out the data protection. Section 6 provides the evaluation of the application thought a demonstration and interviews. Section 7 is a discussion of the results. Section 8 draws the conclusion of the research and identifies future work.

2   Related Work

Current research constructs a variety of hate speech data sets (e.g., [11,13]), while using different definitions of hate speech and annotation schemas [8,26]. The research is often focused on one language, but multilingual data sets exist [8]. Regarding hate speech of adolescents, the research is mostly focused on cyberbullying, a phenomenon partially overlapping with hate speech [35]. In 2018, Sprugnoli et al. [33] created a data set containing annotated hate speech chat conversations between Italian high school students. The data set was created

---

[1] https://ai.facebook.com/blog/how-facebook-uses-super-efficient-ai-models-to-detect-hate-speech.

[2] https://blog.youtube/news-and-events/make-youtube-more-inclusive-platform/.

[3] www.playyourrole.eu.

in an experimental setting to foster a safe and controlled environment. In 2019, Menini et al. [20] presented a monitoring system for cyberbullying. They identified a network of multiple high schools, their students and their friends in the United Kingdom's Instagram community. In 2020, Wijesiriwardene et al. published a multimodal data set containing Tweets labeled for toxic social media interactions. The data set was created focusing on American high school students. Bayzick [3] published in 2011 a data set containing of messages from MySpace.com. The messages are organized into groups of ten and annotated if cyberbullying is contained. The data set also consists of self-provided information about the age of the author. The research of Dadvar et al. [9] found that user context including attributes such as age, gender, and cyberbullying history of the user improves the algorithmic detection of cyberbullying. Chen et al. [6] takes the personal writing style and other user specific attributes into account to identify the potential of the author spreading hate speech.

No work in the field could be identified that consults the teenagers as to their understanding of hate speech during data annotation. The presented research is based on and in connection to the findings and developments in [32].

3   Concept and Design of the Application

The research follows the Design Science Research methodology according to Hevner et al. [14]. Therefore, the research went through three phases, influencing each other and the solution fields. After identifying the problem, a fitting existing annotation guideline for hate speech was chosen and adapted. Next, based on the first cycle, a concept for gamified annotation was developed and implemented in a functional prototype. The prototype was evaluated by experts in a real-world educational environment for its usability.

A central objective of the application is to provide a gamified annotation environment to be used in workshops within German schools. These workshops provide a safe and supervised environment to teach the students about online hate speech. During the workshop, the students are asked to annotate given statements for the hateful content based on a chosen annotation schema. In order to make the workshop stimulating and interesting, a gamification element is introduced: students receive points that can then be used in a following educational game. The collected information about the student's views on the received hateful language provides insights for the research community regarding the difference in hate speech definition based on age group. In the following, the selected data set for the prototype and the used annotation schema is described, which is followed by a description of the application and gamification concept.

3.1   Data Set and Annotation Scheme

This research identified multiple key aspects that are important for the selection of a data set used in the initial study of the application. Firstly, due to the evaluation within a German school, the data set needs to be in German. Further, does the data set need to be available for research, annotated for and in the domain of hate speech. Lastly, it is important to have a well-documented and not from degeneration impacted data sets.

These criteria limit the scope of choices down to 7 possible data sets. These data sets were considered: Ruiter et al. (2022) [28], Yiyi Chen (2022) [7], Assenmacher et al. (2021) [2], Mandl et al. (2019) [18], Wiegand, Siegel und Ruppenhofer (2018) [36], Ross et al. (2017) [27], Bretschneider und Peters (2017) [4]. The final selection of the data set provided by Assenmacher et al. [2] with the title "RP-Mod & RPCrowd" fulfills all the required aspects. The data set was constructed out of comment sections from newspaper articles with the focus of creating a German hate speech data set. It was collected in cooperation with a German newspaper and consists of 85,000 German comments published in the comment section of 22,499 articles. The comments were collected between 2018–2020 and have 5235 authors. The comments are limited to a length of 500 characters and include 7141 comments flagged by community managers as abusive comments. The annotation of the data set is binary and was done by the community mangers of the newspaper. Furthermore, five crowd workers were tasked with annotating the data set, following the annotation schema from Niemann et al. [23]. The Schema developed by Niemann et al. [23] focuses mainly on five classes of hate speech sexism, racism, threats, insults, profane language based on community guidelines, laws and scientific standards. Another factor that contributed to the selection of the data set was the detailed and available datasheet which was published following research guidelines. This document gives a closer view into the demographics of the annotators, which is important for further research.

As annotation schema to be used by the students during the workshop, Zufall et al. [37] was chosen instead of the schema provided with the data set by Niemann et al. [23]. The base for this educational application differentiates from the schema used to annotate the chosen dataset. The data schema introduced by Zufall et al. [37] is due to it defined classes more specific to the topic of hate speech, usable for a multilayer questions based classification, and applicable for non-experts. The framework by Niemann et al. [23] is more general in its core and therefore not suited for this use case. Zufall et al. [37] used European Legislature regarding hate speech and translated it into an annotation framework for identifying if hate speech is punishable by law. They define if the statement was directed against a group or person of a group, define possible group attributes as e.g. race and ask if hatred or violence is incited in connection with specific conduct. To fit local country law, the schema has an optional part asking if the hateful conduct was done in connection to factors like e.g. disrupting the public order.

To fit the framework to the use case, it had to be modified. The goal was to establish a general schema that is simple to use for the students and that can be applied by adolescents without extra training. The main part of the work was therefore reducing complexity. This was archived by removing the optional part of the base schema and reformulating the question into single choice questions. Due to the complex underlying differences, the classes of race and color were combined to increase answer consistency and eliminate a possible hurdle of understanding for the adolescents. Finally, a question asking for readability of the statement was added to the questioner. This question gathers information on the student's ability to read and understand the displayed information. Hereby ensuring that the students have the option to signal a problematic statement that they were not able to evaluate. The Fig. 1 describes the full process of question based annotation.

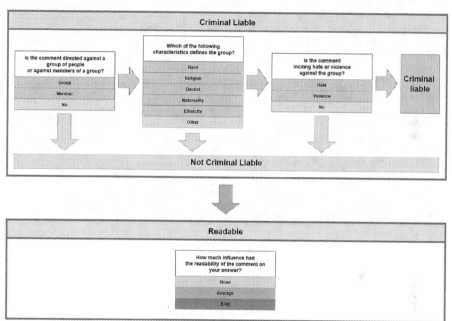

Fig. 1. A figure of the updated annotation schema based on Zufall et al. (2020) [37]. A Legal Approach to Hate Speech: Operationalizing the EU's Legal Framework against the Expression of Hatred as an NLP Task. doi:10.48550/ARXIV.2004.03422.

3.2 Application and Gamification Concepts

The application is designed for the use within an educational workshop. While playing, the students are involved in the field of hate speech. They partake in an observing role and see firsthand what it means to encounter hate speech in the known and commonly used environment of Discord. They learn that it is difficult and challenging to identify hate speech and, in group discussion, realize that they have different views on the definition of hate speech within their peers. During the debate with the teacher, the concepts must be explained and further developed. During the game, the students learn strategies on how to handle hate speech online. All in a save and controlled environment.

The gamification concepts are based on Schöbel and Söllner [30], as the game implements elements such as rewards and collection of points to further motivate but not directly influence the students. Further, a commonly known game and chat interface is used to reduce initial difficulties. This, in combination with the feature of reminders where the teacher can ask the students to participate, is increasing motivation and ensuring a voluntary communal participation without endangering the quality of the results.

Fig. 2. An image displaying the welcome screen of the application.

During the educational workshop, the students are paired into groups and asked to join a discord server with provided anonymized Discord accounts and classify provided statements. The entry screen can be seen in Fig. 2. The statements can contain hateful content. If the students classify a message as hateful, further questions are asked to specify, according to the schema displayed in Fig. 1. Here, the students can use a provided drop-down menu to directly choose the possible answers to the classification task (see Fig. 3), in comparison to asking for written answers this minimizes errors and increases consistency in the responses. As the students classify messages, they receive points for their work as rewards. These points are then pooled collectively into groups of 2–4 players and can be used to play a simplistic game of "Hangman", a game where the participants are guessing certain words. The to be guessed words were taken out of the article, "What to do against hate posts?"[4] If the students are able to correctly solve the riddle within the number of guesses given by the collected amount of points, they receive a reward in the form of information about how to handle online hate speech provided by the same article.

---

[4] "Was kann ich gegen hasspostings tun?", Saferinternet.at 2021, https://www.saferinternet.at/faq/problematische-inhalte/was-kann-ich-gegen-hasspostings-tun/.

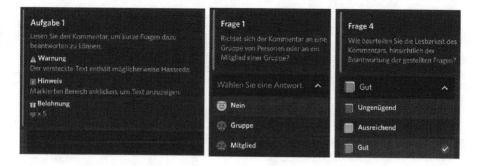

Fig. 3. An image displaying the questions ask in the annotation process.

4 System Design

The application developed is an extension of the Discord application. The extension is categorized as a bot. In the context of Discord, bots are applications that enable automated interaction within communication servers with users. Discord was chosen due to the young user demographic, 64.2% of the users being under 35 [5] and the requirement to make the application relatable to the daily lives of high school students. The use of Discord allows even non-participating individuals to join remotely.

The implemented functions can be classified into three modules: participation, quiz and hangman. The Annotation, the game and the provided rewards are displayed within Discord as chat messages from the bot, e.g. Fig. 3. The use of the application is enabled by two forms of user input: commands and interactions. Communication via commands is relevant for all main components of the application, while interactive elements were used exclusively for annotation.

A permission scheme was designed that includes servers, roles, channels, and users. Protection of participants was the main concern during the design phase. There are three roles within the game, the teachers', the students, and the bots, with all three groups having different permissions and possibilities. Student permissions are kept to a minimum to avoid abuse. Additional permissions for teachers allow for session-specific moderation.

The chat interactions were implemented as Discord bots using python and its library *discord.py*. The bot processes commands sent by teachers or students via chat messages. The bot follows the permission model described above, depending on the role assigned to the user sending the command.

There are different channels for the annotation, the game, a general discussion channel for students and teacher, a welcome channel, a channel for students to talk to all the other students, a reminder or updates channel, and a private teacher discussion channel. The general channel is also a space for general discussion at any given point. This setup is deployed as a preconfigured Discord server.

All data generated during annotation is stored in a database using the object-relational mapping framework *SQLAlchemy*. The used database schema was kept minimal. It allows for the storage of annotations that students create within the application. To increase the potential value of the annotations, contextual information such as session number and the user ID of the anonymized Discord accounts are also stored. Information about whether an annotation is complete is also modeled by the schema.

5 Data Protection

Working with minors requires a high standard regarding data protection and safety concerns. To minimize risks while working in the field of hate speech with students, Derczynski et al. [10] recommendations on structuring the process were used, as described in the following. To "Brief", a pre-up presentation and explanation of the project and the prototype were given. A "Check in", during the experiment, with direct communication about the content was possible and archived. To "Limit", the provided hate speech comments were limited and pre-approved with the teacher. Also, the amount of hate speech to be classified was limited to one comment. To "Support", not just open communication but also personal support, was provided by the present teacher. A "Debrief", was done after the experiment and the interviews.

To reduce privacy issues and following the recommendation of Längsfeld et al. [17], anonymized Discord accounts were provided for the students and the feature enabled to block direct messages with inappropriate content. The consent of the guardians was GDPR conform ensured and the voluntary participation stated.

6 Evaluation

The evaluation follows the concept introduced by Lindner [16]. An evaluation with a group of 22 students and one teacher has been conducted. The evaluation had two phases. Firstly, the demonstration phase, where the developed prototype was live tested in a workshop setting. Secondly, expert interviews with 4 students and the teacher. The goal of the evaluation was to establish user experience, usability in educational context and user well-being. The data security and safety of the students were ensured during the evaluation.

6.1 Demonstration

The demonstration was oriented around the steps drawn from Derczynski et al. [10] described in Sect. 5 Data Protection. There were five main components. First internal technical setup followed by a short introduction. Secondly, a longer technical setup with the students, during which they became familiar with the application. Thirdly, the start of the simulation. Here the teacher, assisted by a research personnel, assigned the roles to the students within discord and started the annotation exercise. All groups annotated the given task while asking questions when they arose. After, the reward-game was played with the collected points. In the final step, a short debrief was done and the devices collected.

6.2   Interviews

Based on Pfeiffer [24] an interview guideline has been developed. The guideline is structured with entry and exit questions. Based on the two different groups, the teacher and the students' different questions were established. The questions for students were rather focused on the experience and the simulation, while the teacher was asked for an evaluation regarding usability within the classroom. Overall, 5 in depth interviews were conducted. The interviews were conducted and transcribed in German.

In the following, for the five topics, the most relevant statements were selected and displayed here. Together, 13 statements are displayed in this paper out of the 142 answers collected during the interviews. In the following, a general evaluation of the answers is given. The student and teachers' names have been anonymized B1-B4 are students, B5 is the teacher.

Hate Speech, regarding the topic of hate speech, all students and the teacher expressed interest in the topic and some addressed the need for further education in schools. One student had personal experience with hate speech online, and all were aware of the problem.

"Yes, because of course I see that it is mainly schoolchildren who are affected. In general, everyone who is younger, uh the generation that is on the net, and the preliminary stages of hate speech are also a problem" (B5, translated from German by DeepL).
"I think, um, it's just such an important topic, but often no one talks about it" (B2, translated by DeepL).

Discord, all students knew and have used discord. The teacher never interacted with it.

"We used to have a class discord. Um we had, um in the lockdown time for example we were often there, helped each other" (B2, translated by DeepL).
"Seen for the first time today" (B5, translated by DeepL).

Simulation, the interviewees were asked about their user experience with the application. It can be summarized that overall, all students and the teachers had a positive experience participating in the demonstration. The teacher explicitly highlighted the positive factor of using an already known tool that is part of the everyday life of the students.

"I found it interesting" (B1, translated by DeepL)
"it was definitely very easy for me to deal with" (B2, translated by DeepL)
"I also enjoyed it because it was something different" (B2, translated by DeepL)
"has been fun with these games" (B4, translated by DeepL)
"I like it then already if the students know that, if they also use that in their reality, [...]" (B5, translated by DeepL)

Regarding negative experience the student mostly mentioned technical difficulties or the need for more additional information on how to use the application.

> "there was one group where it didn't work so well or so in this second game, for example, you had to wait a relatively long time" (B1, translated by DeepL)
> "I [was] a bit disoriented" (B5, translated by DeepL).

For further improvement, the students and the teacher asked for more instruction and information on how to use the application in general.

Annotation, during this part, students were asked to give insights regarding the difficulty of the annotation question and their personal experience during the task. All students stated that the actual task of solving the annotation problem was not challenging, one stated that a group discussion was involved in finding a fitting solution.

> "But [the other game, the quiz task] I thought was very clear and good." (B1, translated by DeepL)

Most students had emotional reactions to the hateful content. Among the most common of reactions were anger, worry and disbelieve.

> "Mixed. So you just know that, so if you reflect on it now, you just know that it's not so true, so you because of your own opinion. But you also have a little bit so um, you are a little bit angry that there are people who think something like that and yes that annoys me then." (B3, translated by DeepL)

> "It worried me." (B4, translated by DeepL)

Usage, in a classroom setting, the questions were only asked to the teacher. No opinion was stated on adequacy of hate speech annotation in classrooms themselves, but it was stated that all technical requirements needed to use the application in a classroom were fulfilled. Explicitly as an introduction to the topic, the application could be of use.

> "There used to be mountains of paper copied for these things, and of course that's then easy and always appeals to them right away." (B5, translated by DeepL)
> "I don't know of any medium right now where you could also do that, ne, with this interconnection and then the interaction among each other." (B5, translated by DeepL)

7 Discussion

The interviews identified an interest in the topic of hate speech. The expressed need for further education within school settings supports the base assumption of the need for more educational tools in the field. All students knew the chat application Discord, which solidified it as the chosen platform for a modern and realistic game play, making the application relatable and easy to use for the young target audience. Other platforms need to be considered, but the accessibility for technical development combined with the young audience makes Discord a good choice. This research did not focus on identifying if Discord is the best suitable platform for the learning environment, therefor further research on the risks and possibilities of different platforms is necessary.

The limited test group did not provide enough data to evaluate the difference to existing annotated data sets. The full annotation process, based on Pustejovsky and Stubbs [25], was not implemented. For example, the interactive annotation aspect is missing.

The positive feedback regarding the experience during the simulation highlights the contribution this application brings to the educational setting, even though more extensive trials with more active usage of the application are necessary. The gamified annotation tasks fit regarding their difficulty and the provided content. It is clear that the goal of the application was reached by involving the students in discussion and showing the multifaceted aspects of online hate speech. The tested approaches could include other educational concepts such as an annotator discussion to improve educational and scientific value. Here, Schöbel and Söllner [30] recommend the direct involvement of the users in designing the gamified application.

To benefit the classroom setting, a guideline and more material needs to be created on how to integrate the application best into a learning concept on the topic of hate speech. The emotional reaction of the participants during the exposure to hateful content needs to be observed and further evaluated with experts to guarantee a safe learning environment. Considering the results of the interviews, the application is a valuable tool to start the debate about hate speech in a gamified educational setting.

8   Conclusion and Future Work

The research introduced a gamified annotation tool that can be used withing educational workshops. It generates scientific insights towards student's understanding of hate speech, while protecting the privacy of the students and ensures their wellbeing.

To quantify student's view on hate speech, a simplistic single choice questioner was developed, that builds upon the annotation schema provided by Zufall et al. [37]. It can be used by a class of untrained students to annotate the hate speech found within a statement. It assesses a general understanding of the perception of the hate character within a text message.

Based on this, a gamified concept was developed in which the students classify given text statements introducing their own view of hate speech. An already existing messaging service was used to create a realistic environment for the students. The students were rewarded with points, which are used to play a simplistic game. The goal of the game is to guess a specific word and afterward information on how to counter online hate speech is presented as a reward.

The implemented prototype was evaluated regarding user experience, usability in educational context and user well-being. For this purpose, a practical test and interviews were conducted in an example lesson within a German school. The concept and annotation process were evaluated by a teacher and multiple students to be relevant for the purpose and received positive user feedback.

Further examination is possible and necessary in different fields of this research. First, more trials need to be conducted to collect scientifically significant data to evaluate the annotations done by adolescent regarding hate speech. Here it is from interest how these annotations differ from the annotations done by trained or untrained experts. Furthermore, other gamification approaches can be tested and evaluated towards their effect on motivation or the overall learning effect for the students. And lastly, it is of interest how the newly created annotations can be used to further benefit automated detection of hate speech.

Acknowledgements. This research was supported by the Citizens, Equality, Rights and Values (CERV) Programme under Grand Agreement No. 101049342.

References

1. Anderson, M., Jiang, J.: Teens, social media & technology (2018)
2. Assenmacher, D., Niemann, M., Müller, K., Seiler, M.V., Riehle, D.M., Trautmann, H.: Rp-mod & rp-crowd: moderator-and crowd-annotated German news comment datasets supplementary material (2021)
3. Bayzick, J.: Detecting the presence of cyberbullying using computer software submitted to the faculty of ursinus college in fulfillment of the requirements for distinguished honors in computer science (2011)
4. Bretschneider, U., Peters, R.: Detecting offensive statements towards foreigners in social media. In: Hawaii International Conference on System Sciences (2017)
5. Ceci, L.: Discord users by age 2022 — statista (2022). https://www.statista.com/statistics/1327674/discord-user-age-worldwide/
6. Chen, Y., Zhou, Y., Zhu, S., Xu, H.: Detecting offensive language in social media to protect adolescent online safety. In: 2012 ASE/IEEE International Conference on Social Computing, SocialCom 2012, pp. 71–80 (2012). https://doi.org/10.1109/SocialCom-PASSAT.2012.55
7. Chen, Y.: Multilingual MigrationsKB: A Mulitlingual Knowledge Base of Migration related annotated Tweets (2022). https://doi.org/10.5281/zenodo.5918508
8. Chung, Y.L., Kuzmenko, E., Tekiroglu, S.S., Guerini, M.: Conan - counter narratives through nichesourcing: a multilingual dataset of responses to fight online hate speech (2019). https://doi.org/10.18653/v1/P19-1271, http://arxiv.org/abs/1910.03270, http://dx.doi.org/10.18653/v1/P19-1271
9. Dadvar, M., Trieschnigg, D., Ordelman, R., de Jong, F.: Improving cyberbullying detection with user context, pp. pp 693–696 (2013). https://doi.org/10.1007/978-3-642-36973-5_62
10. Derczynski, L., Kirk, H., Birhane, A., Vidgen, B.: Handling and presenting harmful text (2022)
11. ElSherief, M., Kulkarni, V., Nguyen, D., Wang, W.Y., Belding, E.: Hate lingo: a target-based linguistic analysis of hate speech in social media (2018). http://arxiv.org/abs/1804.04257

12. Gelber, K., McNamara, L.: Evidencing the harms of hate speech. Soc. Identities **22**, 324–341 (2016). https://doi.org/10.1080/13504630.2015.1128810

13. de Gibert, O., Perez, N., García-Pablos, A., Cuadros, M.: Hate speech dataset from a white supremacy forum (2018). http://arxiv.org/abs/1809.04444'

14. Hevner, A., Park, J.: Design science in information systems research (2004). http://www.researchgate.net/publication/201168946

15. Kovács, G., Alonso, P., Saini, R.: Challenges of hate speech detection in social media. SN Comput. Sci. **2**(2), 1–15 (2021). https://doi.org/10.1007/s42979-021-00457-3

16. Lindner, D.: Forschungsdesigns der wirtschaftsinformatik, empfehlungen für die bachelor- und masterarbeit (2020). https://doi.org/10.1007/978-3-658-31140-7

17. Längsfeld, L., et al.: Warum ist discord interessant für die kinder-und jugendarbeit? (2020)

18. Mandl, T., et al.: Overview of the hasoc track at fire 2019: hate speech and offensive content identification in Indo-European languages. In: Proceedings of the 11th Annual Meeting of the Forum for Information Retrieval Evaluation. FIRE '19, pp. 14–17. Association for Computing Machinery, New York, NY, USA (2019). https://doi.org/10.1145/3368567.3368584

19. Markogiannaki, M., et al.: Adolescent perspectives about online hate speech: qualitative analysis in the selma project. Original Article Acta Medica Academica 50 (2021). https://doi.org/10.5644/ama2006-124.XX

20. Menini, S., et al.: A system to monitor cyberbullying based on message classification and social network analysis (2019). https://fasttext.cc/docs/en/

21. Müller, K., et al.: Fanning the flames of hate: social media and hate crime fanning the flames of hate: social media and hate crime * (2018)

22. Niall, M.: Facebook removes record number of hate speech posts [infographic] (2020). https://www.forbes.com/sites/niallmccarthy/2020/05/13/facebookremoves-record-number-of-hate-speech-posts-infographic/?sh=20c0ef983035

23. Niemann, M., Riehle, D.M., Brunk, J., Becker, J.: What is abusive language? In: Grimme, C., Preuss, M., Takes, F.W., Waldherr, A. (eds.) MISDOOM 2019. LNCS, vol. 12021, pp. 59–73. Springer, Cham (2020). https://doi.org/10.1007/978-3-030-39627-5_6

24. Pfeiffer, F.: Interviewleitfaden für deine experten erstellen mit beispiel (2021). https://www.scribbr.de/methodik/interviewleitfaden/

25. Pustejovsky, J., Stubbs, A.: Natural Language Annotation for Machine Learning, vol. 1. O'Reilly (2012)

26. Ranasinghe, T., Zampieri, M.: Multilingual offensive language identification with cross-lingual embeddings (2020). http://arxiv.org/abs/2010.05324

27. Roß, B., Rist, M., Carbonell, G., Cabrera, B., Kurowsky, N., Wojatzki, M.: Measuring the reliability of hate speech annotations: the case of the European refugee crisis (2016). doi:https://doi.org/10.17185/DUEPUBLICO/42132

28. Ruiter, D., et al.: Placing M-phasis on the plurality of hate: a feature-based corpus of hate online. In: Proceedings of the Thirteenth Language Resources and Evaluation Conference, pp. 791–804. European Language Resources Association, Marseille, France (2022). https://aclanthology.org/2022.lrec-1.84

29. Saha, K., Chandrasekharan, E., Choudhury, M.D.: Prevalence and psychological effects of hateful speech in online college communities (2019). https://dl.acm.org/citation.cfm?id=3326032

30. Schöbel, S., Söllner, M.: Leitfaden für die identifikation, auswahl und kombination von gamification-elementen am beispiel des lernkontextes, pp. 143–161. Springer, Cham (2019). http://www.alexandria.unisg.ch/257617/
31. Schwartz, H.A., et al.: Personality, gender, and age in the language of social media: the open-vocabulary approach. PLoS ONE **8** (2013). https://doi.org/10. 1371/journal.pone.0073791
32. Solorzano Niederhausen, R.: Gamifizierung von Hassredeannotationsprozessen. Master's thesis (2022)
33. Sprugnoli, R., Menini, S., Tonelli, S., Oncini, F., Piras, E.M., Kessler, F.B.: Creating a Whatsapp dataset to study pre-teen cyberbullying (2018). http:// creepproject.eu/
34. Thapa, R., Subedi, S.: Social media and depression. J. Psychiatrists' Assoc. Nepal **7**(2), 1–4 (2018). https://doi.org/10.3126/jpan.v7i2.24607, www.nepjol.info/index. php/JPAN/article/view/24607
35. Tontodimamma, A., Nissi, E., Sarra, A., Fontanella, L.: Thirty years of research into hate speech: topics of interest and their evolution. Scientometrics **126**(1), 157–179 (2020). https://doi.org/10.1007/s11192-020-03737-6
36. Wiegand, M., Siegel, M., Ruppenhofer, J.: Overview of the germeval 2018 shared task on the identification of offensive language, pp. 1–10. Proceedings of GermEval 2018, 14th Conference on Natural Language Processing (KONVENS 2018), Vienna, Austria - 21 September 2018. Austrian Academy of Sciences, Vienna, Austria (2019). https://nbn-resolving.org/urn:nbn:de:bsz:mh39-84935
37. Zufall, F., Hamacher, M., Kloppenborg, K., Zesch, T.: A legal approach to hate speech: operationalizing the EU's legal framework against the expression of hatred as an NLP task (2020). http://arxiv.org/abs/2004.03422

Verification of Repetition of Playing a Game for Activity Selection in a Group

Satoki Fujimoto, Masayuki Ando, Kouyou Otsu, and Tomoko Izumi[✉]

Ritsumeikan University, Kusatsu 525-8557, Shiga, Japan
is0473hr@ed.ritsumei.ac.jp, {mandou,k-otsu,
izumi-t}@fc.ritsumei.ac.jp

Abstract. When a group of people is traveling or gathering to participate in activities, they need to decide on what to do next or where to go. However, occasionally, they lack strong preferences for certain activities, and they do not insist on their preferences. Thus, when members of the group refrain from insisting on their own opinions, deciding upon an activity becomes difficult. In our previous study, we proposed a game mechanism based on the commercial card game, called Hol's der Geier, to realize casual activity selection. The mechanism ensures playful interaction and satisfaction with the selection process among a group, which we verified experimentally. However, familiarity with the game rules helps participants understand their opponents' game strategies and express their own opinions. Therefore, it may affect their satisfaction with the final decision and selection process. In this study, we verify changes in the effectiveness of the game after repeated gameplay from experiments with multiple activity selection sessions. In the experiment, we compared two decision-making methods: 1) free discussion and 2) the proposed game, to make decisions about one food item to eat, one beverage to drink, and one game to play among 6 available candidates. The results show that by repeating the game, participants can strategically modify their requests and better understand other's requests.

Keywords: game design · communication support · activity selection · agreement

1 Introduction

When groups travel or gather for activities, they often need to participate in a form of casual activity selection to decide upon what to do next, which tourist attractions to visit, which restaurants to visit, and so on. In such situations, there are some cases where participants rarely insist on their preferences in terms of which activities to do or which shops to visit. Typically, methods such as majority voting and dice-roll help in arriving at a final decision. However, these methods focus on the efficiency of decision, and thus, do not consider participants' hidden preferences or support enjoyable interactions among participants in the selection process.

Casual activity selection, such as deciding which places or restaurants to visit in a tourist spot, is a common occurrence. In group activity selections, arriving at the final decision is difficult because of the difference in preferences between participants. Accordingly, several group recommendation systems have been proposed. Most of them construct group preferences from individual preference data to provide optimal recommendations [2–4]. Inma Garcia et al. proposed a recommendation system for tourism based on user preferences, their demographic classification, and the places they visited on former trips [2]. The system can offer recommendations for a single user or a group of users. The group recommendation is elicited out of the individual personal recommendations through the application of mechanisms such as aggregation and intersection. However, these studies did not focus on the process of discussion, and ignored the fact that the decision-making process could potentially be enjoyable. Moreover, no study has considered both mechanisms to help participants express their preferences in the decision-making process and arrive at a final decision.

Therefore, in our previous study [1], we proposed a game mechanism based on the commercial card game, called Hol's der Geier, to ensure playful interaction and satisfaction with the selection process within a group. In addition, we developed an iOS application that enables users to play the proposed game on a personal device. This game is for multiple players: each member plays their own numbered cards for a shown scoring card, and the player who plays the highest-numbered card wins the scoring card. The scoring card corresponds to the specific candidate in the activity selection, and the winner of the game decides their next activity from his/her own scoring cards. That is, the numbers with played cards by players represent the degree of their preferences for the candidate assigned to the scoring cards. The participants naturally talk about their requests for the candidates while enjoying the game's tactics, and all of them can grasp the process of arriving at their final decision. In the previous experiment, the results indicated significant differences in the enjoyment and satisfaction with the selection process between the proposed game and the method of majority voting.

From previous experiment, we confirmed that the rules of this game are user-friendly. However, for a candidate in the game, understanding the rules and actually expressing their preferences are quite different. Thus, participants may not openly indicate their requests or express them verbally to other participants the first time they play. That is, a participant's familiarity with the game rule helps them understand their opponents' game strategies and to express their own opinions. Thus, it may affect their satisfaction with the final decision and selection process. In this study, we verify changes in the effectiveness of the game during repeated game play using experiments with multiple activity selection sessions.

If multiple games are to be played, an efficient system for gameplay is essential. In the previous study, the iOS application developed for evaluation was applied as an interface that progresses the game by cycling a single device through multiple players. In addition, the number of turns required to determine the winner was set higher. Thus, gameplay was unnecessarily long owing to the time lost on hand-offs when the participants took turns on a single tablet PC to play their cards. Therefore, in this study, we consider the parameters of the game and develop a new game application to shorten the playing time. This paper provides the results and discussion of the experiments conducted using a new application that enables users to play decision-making games with the reconsidered parameters.

2 Proposed Game for Activity Selection in a Group

2.1 Requirements for Casual Activity Selection Games

Here, we explain our proposed game for casual activity selection. The game design is modified from that proposed in [1]. In Sect. 2.4, we describe the changes to reduce game play time.

This paper deals with situations in which a group cannot choose from candidate activities because group members lack strong preferences for certain activities or do not insist on their preferences. To support their decision, we consider the following four design requirements for casual activity selection games.

1. Only one candidate is selected at the end of the game, playing according to game rule.
2. Participants can make and present ambiguous evaluations for candidates.
3. Participants can understand the process until selecting a candidate.
4. Winning or losing the game provides a unique enjoyment.

2.2 Design of the Proposed Game

The game is based on a card game called Hol's der Geier, which was sold by the company Ravensburger in 1988. The primary rule is simple: each member plays their own numbered cards for a shown scoring card, and the player who plays the highest-numbered card wins the scoring card. The player who has the highest total score of the scoring cards obtained is the winner.

We apply this game for the casual activity selection. The game flow is shown in Fig. 1. The scoring cards correspond to candidate activities in the activity selection. For example, when deciding which restaurant to go, candidate restaurants are assigned to the scoring cards. For this assignment, in this study, each participant votes for candidates in advance, and the candidates are assigned to scoring cards according to the votes. Subsequently, the participants play the game according to the rules of Hol's der Geier, and the winner of the game decides their next activity from their own scoring cards.

The details of our proposed game are as follows: At the beginning, participants receive cards numbered 1–9. Subsequently, a scoring card with a number of points between 1 and 6 is picked from the deck and shown to the players. The scoring card corresponds to the specific candidate in the activity selection. Then, each participant plays their card (see Fig. 2-A), and the participant with the highest-numbered card wins the scoring card (see Fig. 2-B). This process is repeated, and the participant with the most total points of the scoring cards obtained is the winner (see Fig. 2-C). The winner chooses the activity from the candidates of the scoring cards that he/she won (see Fig. 2-D).

Moreover, the game has the following additional rules. By incorporating these elements, the game encourages each user to strategically place card bets to achieve their goals.

1. If more than one participant plays the same numbered card, none of them obtains the scoring card. In this case, the participant with the next highest-numbered card wins the scoring card (see Fig. 3-A).

Arrangement

- Participants receive cards numbered from 1 to 9
- The cards included in the deck are as follows:
  - Six scoring cards with positive points 1-6 and corresponding candidate activities.
  - Three negative cards with negative points (from −3 to −1)

Rules

1. A scoring card is shown from the deck.
2. Each participant plays one of the numbered cards in his/her hand.
   - If more than one participant plays the same numbered card, none of them obtains the scoring card.
   - In a case that the scoring card has a positive point,
     a participant with the highest-numbered card wins the scoring card.
   - In a case that the scoring card is a negative card with a negative point,
     a participant with the lowest-numbered card wins the negative card.
3. The number cards played are not returned to the participants, but are collected. Subsequently, steps 1 to 2 are repeated until all the scoring cards are removed from the deck.
4. The participant with the highest total points is the winner.
5. The winner selects one of the candidates from the scoring cards he/she won.

Fig. 1. Gameplay summary of the proposed game.

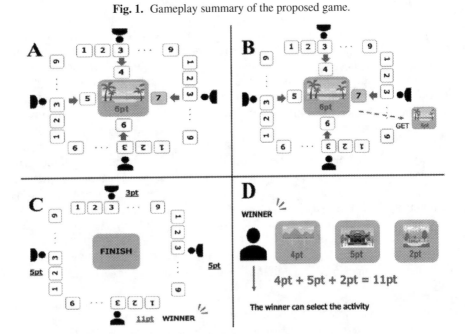

Fig. 2. Illustration of the flow of turn progression in the proposed game.

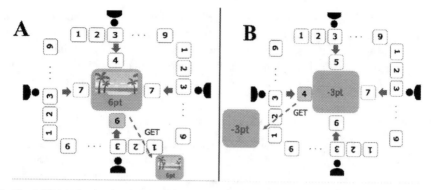

Fig. 3. Additional rules for the cases where more than one participant play the same numbered cards (A) and where a negative card is shown (B).

2. Three negative cards (from −3 to −1) are present in the deck. For these negative cards, the participant who played the lowest-numbered card has a corresponding point deduction (see Fig. 3-B). To avoid the deduction, participants need to play a numbered card with a high value on the negative card.

In short, the playing deck has a total of 9 cards, including scoring cards and negative cards. The game is played for 9 turns, i.e., until all the scoring cards are removed from the deck.

2.3 Correspondence Between Actions in the Activity Selection Process and in the Game

In this section, we explain the how the actions in the activity selection process correspond to those in the game. In this game, since the winner decides the final activity, only one of candidate activities is selected at the end of the game (Requirement 1).

To win the game and decide on an activity, a participant must obtain a scoring card assigned to the activity and scoring cards with high points. To get the scoring card assigned to the activity, the participant must play a high-numbered card on the scoring card. That is, the numbered cards played by a participant represents the strength of the request (i.e., the evaluation value) for the candidate activity. Because the winner knows the numbered cards played by the other participants, he/she knows their evaluation values for the candidate and can select the final decision considering their evaluation values (Requirement 2). Moreover, at the end of each turn, all participants can check the numbered cards played by each participant and the candidates that have been acquired by them. That is, participants can understand the process of selecting a candidate (Requirement 3).

However, negative cards play a different role in the game. To avoid getting a negative card, the participants must play a high-numbered card on the negative card. Considering that the value of the numbered card represents the evaluation value of the participant, this rule appears to be inconsistent with our intentions. However, by forcing participants to purposely obtain negative cards, this rule aids participants to help another participant who owns the desired candidate win or to remove a candidate he/she got. Furthermore, if more than one participant plays the same numbered card, none of them obtains the scoring card. Thus, even if participants play high-numbered cards, they do not know whether they will win that scoring card or not. In other words, any candidate activity can be selected as the final decision. Since the winners and the candidate activities to be decided are not unique, the game has a unique enjoyment (Requirement 4).

2.4   Changes to Reduce Time to Play the Game

Furthermore, we changed the game settings from our previous study [1] to shorten the playing time. Previously, we set the number of scoring cards and negative cards to 10 and 5 respectively, as per the Hol's der Geier game. Because the game turns are determined by the total number of the scoring cards and negative cards it had 15 turns. To shorten the playing time, we reduced the number of cards, i.e., the number of the game turns, considering the game balance. Specifically, the number of the scoring cards was reduced from 10 to 6 and the number of the negative cards was reduced from 5 to 3, keeping the ratio of scoring cards to negative cards unchanged. Thus, the new game setting has six scoring cards with points from 1 to 6 and three negative cards with points from −3 to − 1. Consequently, the game turns reduced to 9.

As mentioned earlier, in our previous study [1], participants played the game by taking turns on one tablet PC, which resulted in lengthy playing times. In this study, we developed a new application for the modified game, in which each participant can join via his/her own smartphone via on-line connection. Figure 4 shows an example of the game application screen. The screen shows the game status for one turn, which displays a scoring card corresponding to the candidate activities and the numbered cards in the user's hand. The Participant selects one of the white numbered cards to bet on the scoring card by tapping the card (the blue cards have already been bet on and are not in user's hand). Subsequently, when the participant presses the "Decide" button, the numbered card is bet. To cancel the selection of the number card, the participant can press the "Reset" button. The system calculates which participant will get the scoring card and displays the result on each participant's game screen. In the game situation field, the app displays the results of that turn, i.e., who got the scoring card with the

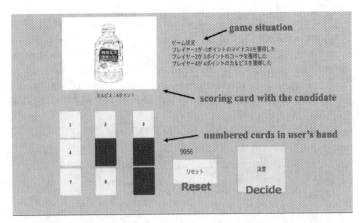

Fig. 4. Game Screen of our application. (Color figure online)

candidate (In Fig. 4, for example, player 4 obtained the scoring card with 4 points which was assigned to "calpico.").

3 Evaluation Experiment

3.1 Experimental Purpose

To evaluate the effectiveness of playing the proposed game multiple times in activity selections, we verified the change in the ease of expressing opinions about candidates through the game process and in the satisfaction with final decisions. In the experiment, we compared the game mechanism (Game condition) with the free discussion (Discussion condition) method, and conducted activity selection three times in each condition. In this experiment, we considered a situation where a group of four participants decided on one food item to eat, one beverage to drink, and one game to play among 6 available candidates. The six candidates for each experiment were selected from those considered familiar to the participants to ensure that none of the candidates was particularly popular and that the candidates included some variety. Moreover, categories such as snacks, candy, and ice cream were displayed as candidates instead of specific product names.

This experiment tests the following hypotheses:

- H1: In the Game condition, on playing the game repeatedly, participants can more easily indicate their requests to others and understand other participant's requests.
- H2: In the Game condition, on playing the game repeatedly, participants experience increased satisfaction with the activity selection process and the final decision.
- H3: In the Game condition, compared to the Discussion condition, participants find the process of activity selection enjoyable even when repeating the game.

H1 was set because we consider that participants will understand the rules of the game through repetition and, consequently, indicate their requests and understand other participant's requests. If H1 is supported, the participants are considered to be more satisfied with the activity selection process and the final decision; thus, we set H2. In addition, since the proposed game has a unique enjoyment, participants will enjoy the process of activity selection more compared to free discussion; thus, we set H3.

3.2 Experimental Procedure

Twenty university students (Male:14, Female:6) participated in the experiment. The experiment was conducted in five groups of four participants each. Each group performed three activity selections, selecting one food item to eat in the first session, one beverage to drink in the second session, and one game to play in the third session. In each session, the participants selected one of the candidates following two different methods in a set order: free discussion followed by the proposed game. Therefore, participants repeated the selection of candidates six times. The final candidate selected in the Discussion condition and Game condition may be different.

In the proposed game, a scoring card needs to be assigned to each candidate in advance. To assign the scoring cards for the game to the candidates, the participants were asked in advance about their preferred candidates using a Google form. Scoring cards were assigned based on the number of those votes. On another day, the four participants from each group assembled in one room.

The flow of the experiment was as follows: First, the experimental procedures were explained to the participants, all of whom provided informed consent. To get the participants to take the selection seriously, before the experiment began, we explained to the participants that they would have to follow through on their decisions and actually eat, drink, and play the selected candidate. Participants were allowed to talk freely during the experiment and were recorded.

In the Discussion condition, we explained to the participants that they could decide on the candidates in any way such as discussion, majority voting, or dice-roll. After the selection in the Discussion condition, the participants were asked to answer a questionnaire regarding the enjoyment and satisfaction they experienced during the discussion.

In the Game condition, the participants used the original app for the game that implemented our proposed method. We explained the rules of the game and the precautions and intent of the special rules such as the one where players can help another player who owns the desired scoring card win by purposely obtaining negative cards. After playing the game, the winners selected one of the candidates according to rules of the game. We subsequently asked the participants to answer the same questionnaire that was given to them after the Discussion condition. In the game condition, the participants were additionally asked to complete a questionnaire regarding their strategies in the game. Finally, according to the questionnaire results, group interviews were conducted to discuss their strategies and thoughts on the game.

4   Experimental Results

4.1   Questionnaire Results on Game Repetition

Participants were asked to complete a questionnaire after the free discussion and the game to verify changes in the effectiveness of the game after repeated game play. Table 1 presents the results of the questionnaire. In the questionnaire, a visual analog scale ranging from 0 to 100 was used to answer the question. The right end of the scale is 100 (Strongly agree) and the left end of the scale is 0 (Strongly disagree), and the position of the answer is scored as a numerical value. The table shows the average scores of the answers for all the participants and the results of a 5% level t-test between Discussion and Game conditions for the same experimental session.

For Q1, which asked about the enjoyment of the activity selection process, the results of the two conditions differ significantly, and the average scores of the Game condition are higher than those of the Discussion condition for all the experimental rounds. Q3 and Q4 asked whether participants expressed their own preferences and understood the preferences of the other players. For these questions, the average scores in the Game condition are higher than those of the Discussion condition except for the first session, for Q3. Moreover, in the Game condition, the average scores increase with the number of repetitions. For the third session, for Q4, the two conditions differ significantly. In contrast, for Q5 and Q6, which asked about the players' consensus and satisfaction with the selection, the two conditions do not different significantly in any of the sessions.

However, for Q2, which asked about the satisfaction of the activity selection process, the Game condition has higher average scores, and has a significant trend ($p = 0.07$) for the third session. In short, the results did not confirm that the repetition of the proposed game increased player satisfaction with the final result. However, it confirmed that, with repetition, players tended to be more satisfied with the selection process.

Table 1. The questionnaire and the average values of the user's responses for each selection task.

Question	Free discussion			Game		
	1st	2nd	3rd	1st	2nd	3rd
Q1. I enjoyed activity selection process in the task	60.1	69.0	76.2	88.9**	91.4**	89.0**
Q2. I satisfied activity selection process in the task	79.8	71.7	82.7	86.3	76.4	88.4*
Q3. I was able to express my preference to other participants	72.5	79.2	78.1	71.8	82.0	84.2**
Q4. I was able to grasp the preferences of the other participants	69.1	80.2	74.8	75.6	81.8	84.8
Q5. I could agree with the final result of the game	84.0	75.2	84.4	82.8	74.7	84.6
Q6. I was satisfied with the final result of the game	86.7	75.8	84.1	83.1	79.3	89.4

The * in the table indicates that a significant difference between the two conditions in same session $p < 0.1$; **: $p < 0.05$

Table 2. Number of Yes/No answers in the questionnaire on the game strategies

Question	1st		2nd		3rd	
	Yes	No	Yes	No	Yes	No
Q7. Did you always try to win this game?	14	6	15	5	11	9
Q8. Did you purposely get the negative cards in this game?	5	15	5	15	4	16

4.2 Questionnaire Results on the Game Strategies

Table 2 shows the results of the questionnaire on game strategy. Q7 and Q8 asked whether participants always tried to win in games and used negative cards strategically.

Participants were asked to answer either "yes" or "no" for these questions. The results for Q7 indicate that more participants gave up on winning the game in the third session than in the first and second sessions. According to the interviews, the reasons they provided for this reduced motivation to win were that they did not care about the

S. Fujimoto et al.

final candidate selected because they did not have strong preferences for any of the candidates, or that they did not think they could win considering their obtained scoring cards.

The results of Q8 indicate that approximately 25% of all participants intentionally got negative cards in all sessions. According to the interviews, the reasons provided for this strategy were that they wanted to help the participant with the preferred candidate win, or eliminate candidates they did not prefer. These reasons were obtained also in our previous study [1]. The results indicate that a few of the participants transferred the selection right to others or lose the right on purpose by obtaining negative cards.

4.3 Discussion

In this section, we discuss the experimental results for the hypotheses shown in Sect. 3.1. As shown Table 1, for Q3 and Q4, which asked whether participants expressed their own preferences and understood the preferences of the other participants, the average scores for the game are higher than those of the discussion method except for the first session of Q3. Moreover, the average scores for the game condition increase with repetition. The results of the questionnaire on game strategy also indicated that the participants adopted various strategies such as transferring or losing the selection right on purpose or giving up on winning strategically. These results indicate that by repeating the game, the participants could understand the game rules and consequently indicate their requests and understand other participant's requests in the game. Therefore, H1 is supported.

For Q2, which asked about how satisfied the participants were with the selected activity, the game method received higher scores than the discussion method and had a significant trend in the third session. However, for all sessions of Q5 and Q6, the results do not differ significantly between the two methods. From these results, the hypothesis H2 is rejected. For Q2, Q5, and Q6, the scores in the second session is lower than those in the first and third ones. This result can be attributed to the type of candidates used in the experiment. In the experiment, the participants had to select one food item to eat in the first session, one beverage to drink in the second session, and one game to play in the last session. For instance, people have strong preferences for a certain beverage. Thus, they may not be satisfied with the selected candidate in the case of beverages. Consequently, the scores for Q5 and Q6 were low.

For Q1, which asked about the enjoyment of the activity selection process, the scores of the game are significantly higher than those of the discussion method. Thus, by using our game, the participants continue to enjoy the selection process even after repeating the game. Therefore, H3 is supported.

5 Conclusions

We introduced a game for casual activity selection among people in a group. To verify changes in the effectiveness of the game when it is repeated played, we compared it with the free discussion method. The results indicated that, with repetition, the participants understand the game rules and can indicate their preferences and understand those of other participants during the game. However, in this experiment, the hypothesis that repetition of the game increases satisfaction with the selection process and the final decision increase was not supported.

Furthermore, satisfaction with the final decision in this game can vary depending on the targets of the selection. For example, in the experiment, the participants had strong preferences for beverages, but not for snacks. In future work, we plan to evaluate the impact of the strength of the preferences for activity selection on satisfaction with the final decision when using our game method.

References

1. Fujimoto, S., Otsu, K., Izumi, T.: Introducing a game to generate a sense of enjoyment and acceptance in the process of decision-making. In: The 13th International Conference on Applied Human Factors and Ergonomics. Affective and Pleasurable Design, vol. 41, pp. 14–20, Springer, Heidelberg (2022)
2. Garcia, I., Sebastia, L., Onaindia, E.: On the design of individual and group recommender systems for tourism. Expert Syst. Appl. **38**(6), 7683–7692 (2011)
3. Ardissono, L., Goy, A., Petrone, G., Segnan, M., Torasso, P.: Intrigue: personalized recommendation of tourist attractions for desktop and hand held devices. Appl. Artif. Intell. **17**(8), 687–714 (2003)
4. Huang, Y., Bian, L.: A Bayesian network and analytic hierarchy process based personalized recommendations for tourist attractions over the Internet. Expert Syst. Appl. **36**(1), 933–943 (2009)

Systematic Review: Incorporating Serious Games into Public Environmental Education on Urban Wildlife Issues

Keyi Gu[1] , Zhifeng Jin[2] , Xinghui Chen[1] , Jingyu Zhou[1] , Jialin Ma[1] ,
and Zhejun Liu[1]([⊠])

[1] Tongji University, 1239 Siping Road, Shanghai, China
{2133707,wingeddreamer}@tongji.edu.cn
[2] No. 808, Institute of Shanghai Academy of Spaceflight Technology, Shanghai, China

Abstract. Urbanization has altered the urban environment, raising concerns among management experts and the general public about the survival of urban wildlife. On the other hand, the application of serious games in the fields of environmental education and biodiversity conservation has gradually improved over the past few years with the development of XR technology, data processing, and sensing technology. It has demonstrated the ability of the serious game to intervene in a number of fields, including formal and informal education, ecology-related conservation, and scientific research, as an appealing and functionally diversified medium. This study, mainly focusing on the issues of urban wildlife, presents the current state of serious game-related applications to intervene in this field through an analysis of examples and studies in the literature. Our intention is to understand the relevance of the intervention mechanisms, game elements and other factors to the goals of the intervention, to gain insights into the opportunities, risks and challenges, and hopefully to guide the direction of future research on the design of the intervention.

Keywords: Serious game · Environmental education · Urban wildlife

1 Introduction

As an engaging and functional medium for the masses, serious games show great potential for educating the public, especially teenagers and young adults. It offers embodied experiences, interaction and feedback as the practice ground, and it is even a good social learning platform that can support autonomous, exploratory, context-based learning, in contrast to the conventional one-way output paradigm of education.

Numerous research show how serious games and gamified applications can be used in the field of environmental education. Given the severe ecological difficulties we face today, environmental education is a multidisciplinary subject with important implications. Its goals include raising public knowledge of environmental issues (such as biodiversity conservation) [1], encouraging environmental friendly attitudes and behaviours [2], and developing public systems thinking to assist sustainable development [3]. It

X. Fang (Ed.): HCII 2023, LNCS 14046, pp. 324–342, 2023.
https://doi.org/10.1007/978-3-031-35930-9_22

has been demonstrated that using games to influence people's cognition, emotions, intentions, attitudes, and behaviours can help implement environmental education [4].

This study examines the state of research on serious games for environmental education, but mainly focus on issues relating to urban wildlife, which is a subject important to biodiversity. Urban, as a particular scenario illustrates the complexity of human-species relationships. Especially in cities with rapidly changing landscapes, the survival of wildlife can be extremely challenging [5, 6]. On the other hand, animal-based digital avatars and nature-themed game scenarios are fairly common in the public's perception (e.g., Animal Samurais, Alba wildlife adventure, etc.), where the relationship between humans and nature is still closely linked in the virtual world and where conflicts that might be disregarded in reality may surface in the game world. This study is therefore relevant in exploring the application of serious games under such a theme.

2   Background

2.1   Serious Game and Gamified Application

Unlike entertainment games, serious games address actual concerns and are created for training, teaching, learning, and behaviour modification in a variety of contexts [1, 7]. Digital games are used to create learning environments where players have the opportunity to learn specific content or topics, according to Prensky's theory of Digital Games Based Learning (DGBL), which has been shown to improve learning performance, higher motivation and interest in learning, and better retention of acquired knowledge. [8] Similarly, it has been demonstrated that using serious games in the context of environmental education and sustainable education helps to increase public knowledge, reflection, empathy, and pro-environmental behaviour.

In addition to serious games, applications that support the environment, especially those developed for mobile devices, are increasingly being used. Along with formal parallels to serious games, these applications might also adopt a "gamification" method. Although a gamification intervention may not be a full game experience, it does involve game components like in-game incentives. Deterding et al. define gamification as "the employment of game design principles in a non-game setting" [9]. Serious games are complete video games with customary gaming mechanics that also induce some sort of targeted behavioural change [10]. Both attempt to utilise games or game elements to educate and transform experiences or behavioural patterns, while they are unavoidably distinct from one another.

2.2   Research on Games Related to Environmental Education

The study by Boncu et al. makes it obvious that although serious games may affect public environmental education at three levels of depth (cognitive, attitude formation, and behavioural motivation) [4], their main objective is to promote behavioural-level change. It highlights the fact that while young people may not necessarily lack information, pro-environmental behaviours might be challenging to initiate and influence. In this review, it is clear that many studies are more interested in interventions at the 'behavioural' level. De Salas et al. cited the concept of Intervention Functions in a behavioural and technical design evaluation of games related to environmental issues [10], stating that behaviour can be influenced by nine core activities: modelling, environmental restriction, training, education, enablement, persuasion, restriction, coercion and incentivisation. According to intervention design experts Michie et al., the selection of these intervention features needs to be based on APEASE (Acceptability, Practicability, Effectiveness/Cost-Effectiveness, Affordability, Safety/Side-Effects and Equity) criteria [11].

From the level of the user and then extending to the level of the practical need to address environmental issues, Sandbrook et al. specifically summarise three main mechanisms through which games can play a role in the field of biodiversity conservation: education and behavioural change, fundraising, and the promotion of research, monitoring, and planning [1].

2.3 Issues About Urban Wildlife

This paper focuses on how serious games can intervene in environmental education related to urban wildlife.

The public believes that animals are often found in non-urban places such as nature reserves, farmland, and woods because of the Nature Deficit Disorder caused by urbanization and information technology. Nevertheless, the role of urban wildlife in the ecosystem cannot be ignored. Urban wildlife management, which addresses the interaction between animal populations and human civilization, is a crucial aspect of biodiversity protection. Although some conflicts between wildlife and human has been revealed, a lot more effort has to be made for public to understand the challenges in this relationship.

On the one hand, the urban environment and wildlife are changing drastically in the rapidly evolving 21st century. It was noted during the epidemic that some wild animals were adapting to the urban environment and were more likely to be found in cities when there was a decrease in human activity. However, several researches have revealed that the general population has a negative opinion of this, which is related to issues with resource appropriation, disease transmission, and conflicts on territory [5, 6]. On the other hand, it may not be widely understood that the process of urbanization itself has resulted in the destruction of natural habitats. The hard-shell liked cities, which are not favorable habitats for some of the native species, have put them in danger, while supported the survival of highly adaptable invasive species. Thus, it is necessary to reconsider how the urban environment could be more friendly to the urban wildlife and how human should interact with those species. Relevant environmental education has to be encouraged and supported.

Based on the advice of experts and prior experience with environmental education interventions, the primary methods of interventions related to the issue of urban wildlife in environmental education can be summarised as follows: 1) the promotion of science to stimulate empathy and provoke public reflection and discussion on related issues; 2) the promotion of species data collection in citizen science; 3) the simulation of wildlife-friendly urban planning and conservation [1].

2.4 Research Questions

We want to concentrate on a cross-cutting topic in this review, which is the use of serious games in environmental education, particularly in relation to urban wildlife. The goal of this study is to determine the applicability of their design objectives to intervention strategies, game mechanics, technology advancements, etc. We insist that the problem of "urban wildlife" is not only related to the practical preservation of species diversity, but also to the question of the inclusiveness of contemporary urban environmental change, the reflection on the relationship between human and nature, both in reality and virtual world. At the same time, this question is also relevant to other content within the field of environmental education, with common features that can be distilled, so by examining serious games and applications related to environmental education that include reflections on urban wildlife, species diversity, and ecological relationships, we hope to answer questions such as:

1) *Can serious games and related digital technology applications promote environmental education, particularly when it comes to examining issues relating to urban wildlife and biodiversity? What features do they have to support the goals? (e.g. strategies, methods, theories, techniques, experiences, etc.)*
2) *How can serious games and related digital technology applications be designed to intervene in environmental education?*

3 Method

3.1 Search Strategy

We adopted a robust and comprehensive approach to systematic review, which is the Preferred Reporting Items for Systematic Reviews and Meta-Analyses [12]. Prior to searching for journal articles, we developed a set of inclusion and exclusion criteria that were essential for assessing the validity and applicability of articles.

We searched for journal and conference articles using keyword combinations based on criteria contained in the Web of Science research database. WoS covers the field of science and arts/humanities, and it is a reputable resource including only journals that meet strict evaluation criteria and demonstrate adequate editorial rigor and quality.

Simple keyword searches for environmental education, urban wildlife, and serious games were used to begin the search. We broadened the search and added synonyms and related words because we were unable to find enough relevant literature in the initial round of searches. As previously noted, we believed that the conservation of endangered species, biodiversity, and habitat management were all relevant to the theme of urban wildlife and could be studied jointly. As a result, we adjusted the search terms and ran another round of searches, which led us to the following selection criteria.

Inclusion Criteria (IC)

IC-1. The manuscript has in the abstract, title or keywords the following phrases: "species" OR "animal" OR "bird" OR "marine" OR "insect" OR "plant", and "education application" OR "education technology" OR "game strategy" OR "game design"

OR "serious game" OR "media technology" OR "virtual reality" OR "augmented reality" OR "game-based learning";

IC-2. The manuscript was published in a conference or journal;

IC-3. The research should include an empirical study either as application research or methodology research. The application can be a none-digital or a digital game, or other applications of digital technology.

Exclusion Criteria (EC)

EC-1. Not publicly available;

EC-2. The manuscript does not have an empirical study;

EC-3. Not related to games, gamification strategies or digital technology;

EC-4. Not directly or indirectly related to urban wildlife issues.

3.2 Study Selection

The retrieved articles were read by two researchers individually for title, abstract and keywords and compared to eligibility criteria in an unblinded standardized manner. When consensus could not be reached in the researchers' assessment of the article, the article was retained for further screening in the full text reading session.

3.3 Data Collection Process

We separated the papers that met the criteria into two categories based on the research questions posed and the types of articles we found: 1) research examples of games or applied forms that serve environmental education, particularly in relation to biodiversity and wildlife, and 2) studies that make a theoretical contribution and methodological guidance to the field of serious game interventions on topics related to biodiversity and wildlife through empirical research.

To address research questions, we decided to conduct a mixed quantitative and qualitative analysis of the first category of articles. To do this, we presented a table of pertinent cases and examined the dimensions of the themes (what they are specifically concerned with), the groups targeted, the technologies, theories, and methods used, the intervention's goals, the play elements used in the intervention, etc.

For the second category of articles, we have used mainly narrative analysis, focusing on their research objectives and conclusions.

4   Results

After the search, we collected 2230 articles, excluding inaccessible articles(). Then we read the first round of titles, abstracts and keywords of the 2230 articles, and removed articles not related to the fields of human-computer interaction, education and ecology, leaving 131 articles to be read through in full. A total of 66 articles were excluded according to the Exclusion Criteria (EC), leaving 65 articles. As mentioned earlier, the literature was divided into two categories: application focused and research focused, with 48 articles in the first category and 17 articles in the second. (See Fig. 1).

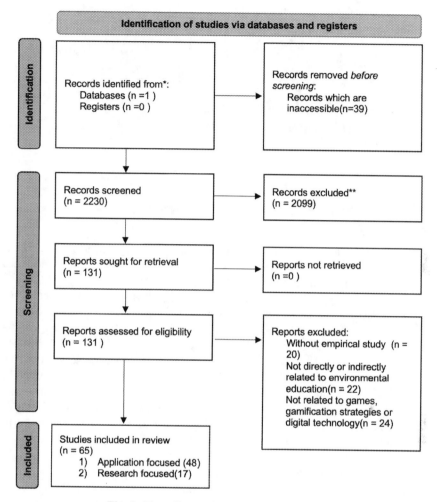

Fig. 1. Flow diagram of the literature selected.

4.1 Results of the 1) Application Focused Studies

Type of application. Four categories were represented among the 48 application instances in total: the greatest percentage was taken by Digital Application (41.67%) with 20 papers included, followed by Digital Game (35.42%), which had 17. The categories of None Digital Game (18.75%) and Media Art (4.17%) had 9 and 2 papers respectively (See Fig. 2).

Background and Theme. In cases collected, the ones related to biodiversity and species were divided into group(A) with (n = 27), of which two were directly related to urban

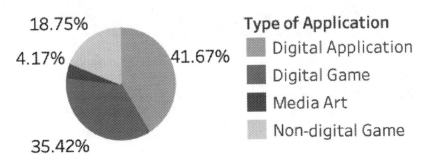

18.75%

4.17% 41.67%

35.42%

Type of Application
- Digital Application
- Digital Game
- Media Art
- Non-digital Game

Fig. 2. Type of application

wildlife issues. And in the other group (B), 19 cases were contained which related to other topics in environmental education. (See Fig. 3).

Urban Wildlife (n = 2, [13, 14]) in category A is a directly pertinent category that has two games with urban birds and discusses the situations that urban birds must deal with in order to thrive in an environment that mixes the artificial and the natural.

The category of Species & Ecosystem (n = 14, [15–28]) focuses on the interaction between species and their ecosystems in general: some offer the platforms for observing real species and engaging in outdoor natural education, and some can be explored as the popularisation of particular species. The Species Conservation (n = 7, [29–35]) category involves a focus on species that are endangered, or whose survival is challenged, and some projects provide citizen science platforms for species data collection to better observe and conserve species, or encourage public participation in some stages of conservation through games. While Museum Education (n = 3, [36–38]) is based on the educational environment of museums, providing information on species to the general public, or using digital tools to make specimens and information about species interactive and interesting, Invaded Species (n = 1, [39]) focuses on the issue of invasive species and deals with the ability to correctly identify invasive species. Critical thinking is emphasised in the theme of "BioBIased & Anthropocene" (n = 2, [40, 41]), which challenges listeners to reconsider how humans and nature interact with each other.

Environmental Management (n = 7, [20, 42–47]), a category we believe having some relevance to the theme of urban wildlife management is included in the Category B. In the related games and apps, the user or player assumes the role of the manager in simulated negotiations and decisions, weighing the interests of the various stakeholders in management and the impact of these decisions on nature. Category B contains some other themes in Environmental Education, including climate change (n = 4, [47–49]), Ocean Related Problem (n = 2, [50, 51]), Waste Sorting (n = 2, [52, 53]), Sustainable Behaviour & Education (n = 3, [54–56]), which refers to content that leads to (broad) sustainable behaviour, or knowledge about it. Besides, Mountain Recognition (n = 1, [57]) is a special group which includes only a win-win image recognition and capture platform benefiting both outdoor enthusiasts and environmental research.

Users or Players. The age and precise user types were not mentioned in 28 researches. A total of 13 studies were explicitly directed towards students, with three studies specifically targeting older students, three targeting primary school students, and three targeting

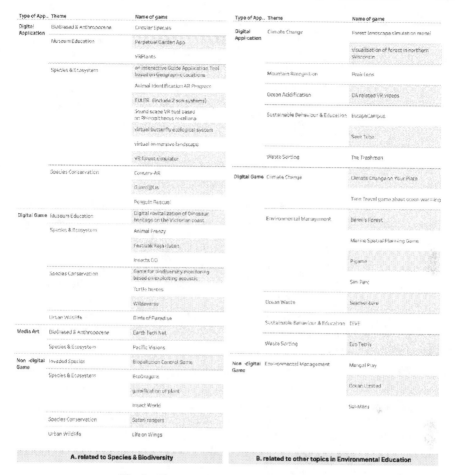

Type of App..	Theme	Name of game
Digital Application	Biobased & Anthropocene	Circular Species
	Museum Education	Perpetual Garden App
		VRPlants
	Species & Ecosystem	an interactive Guide Application Tool based on Geographic Locations
		Animal Identification AR Program
		EULER (include 2 sub-systems)
		Sound scape VR tool based on Rhinopithecus roxellana
		virtual butterfly ecological system
		virtual immersive landscape
		VR forest simulator
	Species Conservation	Conservy-AR
		Guardizcos
		Penguin Rescue!
Digital Game	Museum Education	Digital revitalization of Dinosaur heritage on the Victorian coast
	Species & Ecosystem	Animal Frenzy
		Festival Raja Rusas
		Insects GO
	Species Conservation	Game for biodiversity monitoring based on exploiting acoustic
		Turtle heroes
		Wildeverse
	Urban Wildlife	Birds of Paradise
Media Art	Biobased & Anthropocene	Earth-Tech Net
	Species & Ecosystem	Pacific Visions
Non -digital Game	Invaded Species	Biopolution Control Game
	Species & Ecosystem	Ecodragons
		gamification of plant
		Insect World
	Species Conservation	Safari rangers
	Urban Wildlife	Life on Wings

Type of App..	Theme	Name of game
Digital Application	Climate Change	Forest landscape simulation model
		visualisation of forest in northern Wisconsin
	Mountain Recognition	Peak Lens
	Ocean Acidification	OA related VR videos
	Sustainable Behaviour & Education	EscapeCampus
		Save Tuba
	Waste Sorting	The Trashman
Digital Game	Climate Change	Climate Change on Your Plate
		Time Travel game about ocean warming
	Environmental Management	Benni's Forest
		Marine Spatial Planning Game
		P-game
		Sim Parc
	Ocean Waste	Seadventure
	Sustainable Behaviour & Education	DIVE
	Waste Sorting	Eco Tetris
Non -digital Game	Environmental Management	Mangal Play
		Ocean Limited
		Sui-Mon

A. related to Species & Biodiversity   **B. related to other topics in Environmental Education**

Fig. 3. Themes of group A(left) and B(right)

younger students. Besides, five studies were directed towards both experts and public with 1 targeting only at experts. One game was exploited for the elderlys, with the goal of the study emphasising ease of use (Fig. 4).

Technology Applied. We noticed the wide usage of XR technology took up more than half of the cases, including 15 of applications of AR, 11 applications of VR, and 2 applications of MR. Another technology mentioned as being used more frequently was the GPS, often combined with AR, facilitating outdoor information gathering and ubiquitous learning. The keywords also recorded sensory and motion tracking technologies, which are often applied in interactive design. In addition to this, there are cases where technology is applied to generate immersive environments through natural data. Nine cases were not mentioned or did not use digital technology.

Theory and Methods. Different pedagogical frameworks and learning theories may be used in serious games design and development related to environmental education: for

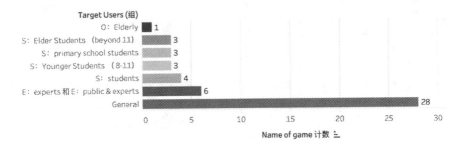

Fig. 4. Target users

example the ARCS model in DGBL, contextual approaches and self-directed learning. The goal of these theories is to provide context for learners and create opportunities for them to practice the skills they have learned. Additionally, there are also theories related to the game design and user experience including MDA framework [58], Flow Theory and so on. The results of the data count showed that 28 items did not explicitly refer to methods and theories in their design process. There are 2 studies referred to the MDA game design framework [14, 34], GBL(Game based learning) [13, 16] and M-learning (Mobile Learning) respectively [15, 23]. Others are mentioned only once including U-learning (Ubiquitous learning) [15], learning based on context, CogInfoCom theories [46] and Contemporary constructivism [47].

Goals and Intervention Strategies. According to previous researches, cognitive, attitudinal and behavioural goals are among the most studied. However, we do not claim that they are achieved in any particular order of priority. Furthermore, the goals of the project may be broken down into multiple levels, for example, to change players' cognition and behaviour by stimulating emotional experiences and developing empathy in the game. In the process of categorisation, we have mainly followed the narrative of the literature to assess its main objectives (Fig. 5).

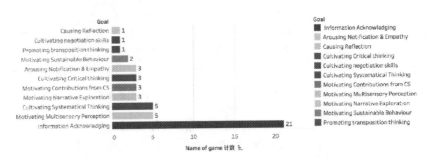

Fig. 5. Goals of intervention

Cognitive Goals. Nearly half of the cases' objectives involved facilitating users' information acquisition, which can be categorised as Information Acknowledging (n = 21). Such goals may be met by 1) utilising a variety of game strategies to accommodate information, such as Escape Rooms (where clues can be organised in space in the form of secret rooms to embed knowledge in sequence [55]), puzzle games (such as Tetris to practice classification [52]), quiz games (organising information in the form of quiz questions and fix mistakes through the game cycle [16]), and card games (reflecting relationships in ecosystems [14, 18, 21, 22, 33]), etc. On the other hand, games and applications may also be used by 2) interactive learning environments that promote user interaction and explorational learning. The related cases including some learning systems based on AR mobile platforms [19, 26], and data visualization in VR environment [27, 38, 48].

Part of the objectives focus on training at the level of thinking skills,

The achievement of some objectives may depend on more complicated structures (for example, simulated negotiations and decision games), as they include training for thinking abilities including simulated choice analysis, systematic thinking, critical thinking, and transposition thinking. The aim of "transposition thinking" may also be related to "empathy," where the player attempts to think beyond the box by adopting the perspective and experiences of other people through emotional empathy. This type of thinking is dialectical rather than monolithic. An example of this is life on wings [14], a paper-based board game that presents a bird's-eye view of the map, reflecting the scenarios and survival challenges that birds in the city may encounter as the seasons change. Indeed players don't have the experience of "bird migration" in reality, they can understand the challenges through the game when find the shelters in urban habitats at different times of the year. Circular species, an application aimed at 'critical thinking', uses a special strategy combining the biodegradable mammoth toy and the AR application to help understand the concept of cycle in the context of the Anthropocene [41].

Attitudinal Goals. We believe that objectives such as Arousing Notification & Empathy, Causing reflection are more likely to be categorised as prompting attitudinal and emotional change. The AR filter Penguin rescue! [32] and the FPS game Turtle Heroes [34] focuses on depicting aspects of animal crises, in which the penguins are contaminated with oil and turtles may lost their way towards ocean or blocked by enemies. In addition, the AR game Wildeverse guides the players to follow and understand the process of wildlife conservation in order to inspire empathy [29]. Probably due to the small sample size, we do not see here any relevant games with animal characters as avatars, which is rather unfortunate, as we understand that embodied cognition may evoke strong empathy [59], while contributing to people's attention and understanding of animals. However, one study in the literature we reviewed discussed the potential user experience of using animals as avatars, particularly in combination with virtual reality technology, which has the potential to create an experience beyond the human experience [60]. Controlling the animal's body or using a different perspective for observation may bring novelty, but may also present some challenges.

There are also some process-oriented goals, such as Motivating Narrative Exploration, which aims to advance our understanding of narrative. In one study, a climate change related game was supported by a time-travel game mode, and the study's main body investigated the use of AI in non-linear narrative [49]. Multisensory Perception category focuses on perceptual stimuli that can eventually lead to cognitive or attitudinal-emotional shifts. It includes games and applications that use MR or VR interventions to present immersive natural environments using rich perceptual cues (visual, sound scape, touch, smell, etc.). It also has similarities to a range of educational applications in the "cognitive goal" category, but these applications do not emphasise the intellectual orientation, but rather give the users more scope for exploration.

Behavioural Goals. Finally, a few of the objectives are directly related to behaviour modification. Finally, a few of the objectives are directly related to behaviour modification. Several apps offer citizen science engagement opportunities that fall under the category of Motivating Contributions for CS. For example, Guard@Lis [31] collects identification data primarily by encouraging users to perform species identification. It provides users with specific routes for bird observation, awarding points for combining audiovisual scientific information in interaction with the AR app. Peak-Lens [57], while offering mountain identification, also collects identification data by encouraging users to perform audiovisual scientific information[]. Additionally, a game that uses sound sensing to monitor biodiversity allows users to participate in yet another way of aiding in biodiversity conservation by detecting and tagging species through sound [30]. Its story takes place in a future where catastrophic climate change and nuclear war have destroyed habitats and caused a mass extinction of animal species. The core mechanic of the game's "DNA collection" reflect on the interaction of "sound recognition", and the player's job as an advanced human is to gather DNA data in order to recreate species from the past.

There are also two other research statements that aim to 'change users' behaviour', categorised as Motivating sustainable behaviours, and their mechanics tend towards simulation. DIVE simulates diving scenarios to allow players to learn more sustainable diving practices, which in turn guide their subsequent behaviour when diving [54]. Another game attempts to train citizen scientists to 'check for invasive species' and thereby increase citizen participation in marine conservation, with the main mechanic of the game being trial and error in determining invasive and non-invasive species [39]. We argue that it actually leads indirectly to citizen engagement through cognitive enhancement, so the assessment of the objectives here can be multi-dimensional.

Game Elements. In terms of mechanics, there is a diversity of intervention elements and mechanisms depending on the objectives set, and it is possible to combine multiple mechanisms to achieve objectives in a single game or applications.

Incentive: Points, Badges, and Leaderboards. Rewards like points, badges, and leaderboards are frequently utilised in educational systems to enhance learning [61], and we have seen from case studies that many games that focus on cognitive learning as well as gamified learning systems frequently incorporate these types of incentives. One study explored the impact of these elements on learning through controlled experiments, addressing their motivational effect, but putting more emphasis on the fact that the most effective gamification efforts should not only include these elements. Instead, those incentives ought to support the game or program's narrative, level of difficulty, and high level of involvement [62]. In addition, the study mentioned that leaderboards are a double-edged sword and that the competition they generate may promote user engagement and may also create pressure for some users.

Senario: Avatar, Narrative, NPCs. Games typically set a specific worldview, a storyline, and define the characters' tendencies to act in order to further immerse the player in the situation. We are concerned that the majority of games use their intellectual setting as the backdrop for their narrative. For instance, games with an animal conservation subject set the game in the environment of the species and highlight the difficulties that they must overcome to survive. While some of these worldviews tend to be presented in an intuitive audio-visual language, such as the case of VR immersive scientific media [28], or simulated escape rooms and debate rooms [63], which give the user an experience that helps them understand the context of the game. Others tend to be presented in a more abstract manner, requiring the user to develop a more concrete understanding as they play, such as life on wings in the form of a board game. Generally speaking, it is more attractive to use a storytelling style of description in serious applications. For example, he backdrop of a story of habitat destruction is depicted in Tuba [56] to interest its target users, a gamification application whose main purpose is to spread the "serious" sustainable knowledge.

In some games, we also discover that the concept of time is influential. In one instance, the player can foresee the extinction of particular species while the story is set in the future [30]. Another game introduces the idea of the changing seasons and encourages the player to consider how various creatures behave differently depending on the season [14]. In another case, the narrative is framed by the paradigm of 'time travel', which allows the player to move across the past and the future and learn about the importance of 'choices' at a certain point, thus provoking reflection on the consequences of environmental issues [49].

In terms of perspective, we learned that board games and video games usually use a bird's eye view, which enables the user to think systematically and comprehend the game. To generate a sense of immersion, games using VR, MR, and AR typically opt for a first-person (more intense immersion) or third-person (more emphasis on the character's movements) perspective. As mentioned earlier, we did not observe any games that used animal avatars or presented the perspective of an animal, even though this could have been an interesting attempt. Instead, the player usually appears as a rescuer of the animal, performing tasks related to rescue, scientific research, etc.

Interaction: Feedback, Work with Others. By altering behaviours and cognition continuously, feedbacks play an important role in the use of games and applications, improving the users' experience over time. The systems' feedbacks are the primary driving force in enabling users to learn new information in some outdoor game-based learning systems [15, 19, 26, 29] where users identify species and acquire new knowledge. In the instance of circular species, the user relies on feedback from the toy and augmented reality (AR) throughout each stage of the life cycle to comprehend the idea of circularity [41].

Additionally, we noticed that some games, such as those that simulate discussion and decision-making, place a strong premium on teamwork [43, 44, 63]. Since players must speak and work with stakeholders to comprehend the positions of their characters, the game's purpose is to encourage the development of collaborative and systemic thinking. This illustrates the point that environmental management problems must be resolved through collaboration. The 'werewolf' model-based game Biocollution Control, in which players check the answers based on genuine species and select to play as 'foreign' and 'native' species, also encourages learning through cooperative play. The game is based on a 'werewolf' model, in which players should check and examine their own identities as "foreign" and "native" species base on their knowledge about invaded species checking. They had to work with other players to make arguments in favour of and against identification during the game rounds according to the researchers' prompts [39].

Obstacle: Challenge, Task, Dashboard, Punishment, Fear. Games frequently contain stressful and motivating features like challenges and tasks. Owing to this factor, the game makes for a richer and more interesting experience. Participants must overcome them, which may result in punishment or the sense of fear due to some of the challenges. Although the theme of *Turtle rescue!* [34] itself does not necessarily require an intense mode, the game is designed to set challenges for the players and to enhance engagement through body movement recognition mechanics. The player will face different difficulty modes in the two levels, and the design of the task is based on real life scenarios. In addition, *escape rooms* [55], as confined and mysterious environments, inherently set players the challenge of 'breaking through' and 'solving puzzles', where they experience the excitement of gradually solving clues and possibly the fear of the unknown. Mello, Gisela's research on escape room games shows that the immersive and active learning environment provided by escape rooms can be a powerful tool for environmental education. The design of puzzles and challenges, hands-on experiences, immersion factors and interactions provided through activities, are influencing changes in knowledge, values and attitudes towards environmental behaviour and sustainability.

Space for Thinking: Choice, Puzzle/Strategy, Knowledge Check. The effectiveness of knowledge acquisition and the playing experience are important factors to take into account while developing many serious games involving environmental education or educationally focused games that support cognition. The major portion of the game, or modules, uses elements like puzzles, strategies, choices, and knowledge viewing to give players time to reflect and make judgements. Players can more clearly understand the relationships within the game system by making decisions that may affect the narrative's conclusion. For instance, a VR game that teaches sustainable diving enables the player to understand the "consequences of non-sustainable diving" as a source of their earlier decisions.

4.2   Results of the 2) Research Focused Studies

In our analysis of the second group of literatures, we wanted to answer the question of how to design serious games to intervene in environmental education related to urban wildlife. Through an empirical investigation, the articles we examined were presented in terms of numerous game design features, user experiences, ethical bias, and other factors. As a result, we have broken down their views into various sets of terms.

Natural Facts and Virtual Worlds. There are a number of relevant studies that look at possible opportunities and problems faced from both a real and virtual perspective. One case that showed the augmented reality (AR) games may change how people engage with nature is the famous character-collecting game, Pokemon Go [64]. Users are drawn to the game's dynamics, which encourage them to go outside and find as many Pokemon as possible. The "collect pokemon" concept, outdoor exploration, and character scanning and collection are all very motivating for users. In addition, several researchers have demonstrated its potential for use in biodiversity monitoring since players provide ecological data due to the ability of interacting with real wildlife while playing the game. Experts have also noted that because the search is restricted to cities, it is needed to expand the available gaming space for users to collect more useful data for scientific research.

Secondly, people's conceptions of nature are also being influenced by virtual nature. According to one study, players' behaviour in-game may be favourably connected with their attitudes towards the environment, although even environmentally conscious players (those with low anthropocentric inclinations) may act unethically in the game depending on the rules (e.g. cutting down trees to collect bugs, island rating systems) [65, 66]. The player's identification with human relationships with natural resources and species may therefore be influenced by the game mechanics, hence the worldview setting should be carefully considered when designing the game. Another XR study contends that it might be simple for some virtual animals to enter a person's environment in situations when there is a blend of the virtual and the real worlds [67]. However, this may result in a reconfiguration of how people, spatial contexts, and species interact. This is because, as shown by place attachment research, our emotional attachment to places shapes our emotional and cognitive responses there. As a result, people may develop negative or positive perceptions of animals as a result of an artificial environment. Additionally, the way we perceive these animals in the virtual world may exacerbate our prejudice towards different species because they may be programmed to behave in a manner that is "out of the wild" [68].

Bias in Experience. Some games have narratives or immersive experiences that use evoking empathy as a strategy [69]. It may be an experience that makes them feel sad, while a moderate amount of sadness may inspire them to behave in a friendly way towards the environment and animals. However, research indicates that experiencing animal pain firsthand, especially when using VR technology, has the potential to be traumatising. VR is considered as a tool for evoking empathy, and through illusory body ownership(a way of taking physical control of another person or species), users can literally connect with the avatar. One study demonstrated the potential of VR to produce beyond human experiences through [] the sense of bodily transference (BT) and the illusion of virtual body ownership (IVBO) by analysing three animal avatars [60]. However, other studies have indicated that VR may not always fulfil the goal of empathy and instead has the potential to reinforce negative views (such as racial prejudice) of the user towards the group they are portraying in unfavourable situations or with an overemphasis on negative messages [70].

Another study examined the effects of two factors, visual immersion and freedom of movement, both separately and in combination, on the intention to change the environment. It came to the counter-intuitive conclusion that the combined effect of intense visual immersion and flexible freedom may not be having the most significant impact [71]. This is just one example of the many factors that interact in virtual reality to skew people's experiences and perceptions. A study of VR interventions affecting donations to endangered species [72], on the other hand, mentions the significance of the multifactorial role and claims that VR is more than just a visually multidimensional medium, with technical elements that allow users to experience remote presence and engage with content. To significantly affect attitudes towards giving, all of the mediating variables (empathy, enjoyment, remote presence, and usability) must be present.

We also studied several psychological issues, such as how empathy wanes when one witnesses a large number of casualties [70]. The prejudice that "bigger species" are more likely to get attention is another. However, one study disproved the idea that "larger attracts more attention" by proving, through a comparative test, that small penguins are more likely than giant penguins to elicit protective behaviour because they are more likely to be viewed as cute [73].

5   Discussion and Conclusion

In the context of serious games for environmental education, we concentrated on the current state of affairs of serious games and applications relevant to urban wildlife. We distiled a number of dimensions to assist the analysis in order to address two primary research questions by combining past studies of the state of the art in the fields of serious games-related theory and environmental education.

The studies reviewed generally show a positive attitude towards theories related to "game-based learning," and they firstly acknowledge the existence of serious game interventions in environmental education. They also suggest that digital technology can be used rationally to support environmental education in multiple ways and from multiple perspectives. Examining validity, however, is outside the purview of this research because different studies have outlined various goals and intervention components, as well as various methods for experimentation and evaluation, some of which may not be adequately reassuring.

However, there are also drawbacks to this literature review, including sample selection issues that might necessitate the use of additional data sets or the inclusion of media analysis from other sources, such as data on for-profit games, online videos, articles, and other items accessible via online platforms. The issue of urban wildlife is not only of research value ecologically, but also has research implications for the social dimension, and a broad collection of information may allow us to see more possibilities for serious gaming interventions.

References

1. Sandbrook, C., Adams, W.M., Monteferri, B.: Digital games and biodiversity conservation. Conserv. Lett. **8**, 118–124 (2015)
2. Janakiraman, S., Watson, S.L., Watson, W.R., Newby, T.: Effectiveness of digital games in producing environmentally friendly attitudes and behaviors: a mixed methods study. Comput. Educ. **160**, 104043 (2021). https://doi.org/10.1016/j.compedu.2020.104043
3. Sajjadi, P., et al.: Promoting systems thinking and pro-environmental policy support through serious games. Front. Environ. Sci. **10** (2022)
4. Ştefan, B., Candel, O.-S., Popa, N.L.: Gameful green: a systematic review on the use of serious computer games and gamified mobile apps to foster pro-environmental information, attitudes and behaviors. Sustainability **14** (2022). https://doi.org/10.3390/su141610400
5. Coman, I.A., Cooper-Norris, C.E., Longing, S., Perry, G.: It Is a wild world in the city: urban wildlife conservation and communication in the age of COVID-19. Diversity **14**, 539 (2022)
6. Collins, M.K., Magle, S.B., Gallo, T.: Global trends in urban wildlife ecology and conservation. Biol. Conserv. **261**, 109236 (2021)
7. Annetta, L.A.: The 'I's' have it: A framework for serious educational game design: Correction to Annetta (2010)
8. Tay, J., Goh, Y.M., Safiena, S., Bound, H.: Designing digital game-based learning for professional upskilling: A systematic literature review. Comput. Educ. 104518 (2022)
9. Deterding, S., Dixon, D., Khaled, R., Nacke, L.: From game design elements to gamefulness: defining "gamification" pp. 9–15 (2011)
10. de Salas, K., et al.: Improving environmental outcomes with games: an exploration of behavioural and technological design and evaluation approaches. Simul. Gaming **53**, 470–512 (2022)
11. Michie, S., Van Stralen, M.M., West, R.: The behaviour change wheel: a new method for characterising and designing behaviour change interventions. Implement. Sci. **6**, 1–12 (2011)
12. Page, M.J., et al.: The PRISMA 2020 statement: an updated guideline for reporting systematic reviews. Int. J. Surg. **88**, 105906 (2021)
13. Cuartero, J., Lee, P., Villanueva, J.: Birds of paradise: a game on urban bird biodiversity conservation. In: Rodrigo, M., Iyer, S., Mitrovic, A. (eds.), pp. 481–483 (2021)
14. Sandbhor, P., Bangal, P., Aggarwal, D., Khot, R.A.: Life on wings: relating to a bird's life in a city through a board game. Proc. ACM Hum.-Comput. Interact. **5**, 1–28 (2021)
15. Lo, J., Lai, Y., Hsu, T.: The Study of AR-Based Learning for Natural Science Inquiry Activities in Taiwan's Elementary School from the Perspective of Sustainable Development. Sustainability **13** (2021). https://doi.org/10.3390/su13116283
16. Ajie, G., Marpaung, M., Kurniawan, A., Suryan,i M., Suryana, I., Paulus, E.: The development and usability testing of game-based learning as a medium to introduce zoology to young learners. In: Riza, L., et al. (eds.), pp. 541–545 (2017)
17. Savitri, N., Aris, M., Supianto. A., IEEE: Augmented reality application for science education on animal classification, pp. 270–275 (2019)
18. Khelifa, R., Mahdjoub, H.: EcoDragons: a game for environmental education and public outreach. Insects **12**, 776 (2021)
19. Liu, T., Tan, T., Chu, Y.: outdoor natural science learning with an RFID-supported immersive ubiquitous learning environment. Educ. Technol. Soc. **12**, 161–175 (2009)
20. Safrodin, M., Bagar, F.N.C., Pralista, F.Y.: The development of digital board game to introduce Indonesian wildlife using AR technology and NFC, pp. 277–282. IEEE (2019)
21. Borsos, E.: The gamification of elementary school biology: a case study on increasing understanding of plants. J. Biol. Educ. **53**, 492–505 (2019)

22. Cosme, L., Turchen, L., Guedes, R.: Insect world: game-based learning as a strategy for teaching entomology. Am. Biol. Teach. **82**, 210–215 (2020). https://doi.org/10.1525/abt.2020.82.4.210

23. Wommer, F., Sepel, L., Loreto, E., Insects, G.O.: A gaming activity for entomology teaching in middle school. Res. Sci. Technol. Educ. https://doi.org/10.1080/02635143.2021.1921724

24. Schubel, J., et al.: Pacific Visions: A Bold Departure for an Aquarium to Enhance Ocean Education (2019)

25. Zhong, Z., Chen, W., Zhang, Y., Yang, J., Dai, Z.: Developing an online VR tool for participatory evaluation of animal vocal behaviours. Interact. Learn. Environ. **30**, 1325–1337 (2022). https://doi.org/10.1080/10494820.2020.1722711

26. Tarng, W., Ou, K.-L., Yu, C.-S., Liou, F.-L., Liou, H.-H.: Development of a virtual butterfly ecological system based on augmented reality and mobile learning technologies. Virtual Real. **19**(3–4), 253–266 (2015). https://doi.org/10.1007/s10055-015-0265-5

27. Chandler, T., et al.: Immersive landscapes: modelling ecosystem reference conditions in virtual reality. Landscape Ecol. **37**, 1293–1309 (2021). https://doi.org/10.1007/s10980-021-01313-8

28. Gil, O., Cardozo, V.: Development of virtual reality (VR) as an affordable learning method with species of nature. In: Zaphiris, P., Ioannou, A. (eds.), pp. 137–144 (2016)

29. Phipps, L., Alvarez, V., de Freitas, S., Wong, K., Baker, M., Pettit, J.: Conserv-AR: a virtual and augmented reality mobile game to enhance students' awareness of wildlife conservation in Western Australia. Mob Learn Futur Qual Res Pract Mob Learn 214: (2016)

30. Loureiro, P., Prandi, C., Nisi, V., Nunes, N., IEEE: On exploiting acoustic sensing and citizen science in a game for biodiversity monitoring and awareness, pp. 572–577 (2019)

31. Venancio, J., Marto, A., Goncalves, A, Rodrigues, N., Ascenso, R., IEEE: Guard@Lis: a new augmented reality mobile application for birdwatching (2019)

32. Pimentel, D.: Saving species in a snap: On the feasibility and efficacy of augmented reality-based wildlife interactions for conservation. J. Nat. Conserv. **66**, 126151 (2022). https://doi.org/10.1016/j.jnc.2022.126151

33. Wulandari, S.: Safari rangers board game as a campaign media for endangered animal conservation, pp. 1–6. IEEE (2016)

34. Theodoropoulos, A., Roinioti, E., Dejonai, M., Aggelakos, Y., Lepouras, G.: Turtle heroes: designing a serious game for a VR interactive tunnel. In: Kiili, K., et al. (eds.) KALA 2022. LNCS, pp. 3–10. Springer, Cham (2022). https://doi.org/10.1007/978-3-031-22124-8_1

35. Dunn, M., Shah, G., Verissimo, D.: Stepping into the Wildeverse: evaluating the impact of augmented reality mobile gaming on pro-conservation behaviours. PEOPLE Nat **3**, 1205–1217 (2021). https://doi.org/10.1002/pan3.10273

36. Antlej, K., et al.: Mixed reality for museum experiences: a co-creative tactile-immersive virtual coloring serious game. In: Addison, A., Thwaites, H. (eds.), pp. 128–134 (2018)

37. Harrington, M.: Connecting user experience to learning in an evaluation of an immersive, interactive, multimodal augmented reality virtual diorama in a natural history museum & the importance of story. In: Economou, D., et al. (eds.), pp. 70–77 (2020)

38. Keenan, C., et al.: The naturalist's workshop: virtual reality interaction with a natural science educational collection. In: Economou, D., et al. (eds.), pp. 199–204 (2020)

39. Miralles, L., Garcia-Vazquez, E., Dopico, E.: Game-based learning for engaging citizens in biopollution control. Interdiscip. Sci. Rev. **46**, 677–688 (2021). https://doi.org/10.1080/03080188.2021.1891684

40. Litman-Cleper, J.: Earth-centered communication technology lichen as a model interface. Leonardo **54**, 483–486 (2021). https://doi.org/10.1162/leon_a_02059

41. Fernanda, D., Vali, L., Assoc Comp Machinery: Circular species designing critical thinking into children's science education through biomaterials and augmented reality, pp. 8–17 (2021)

42. Bolijn, H., Li, M., Reurink, A., van Rijn, C., Bidarra, R.: Benni's Forest–a serious game on the challenges of reforestation, pp. 245–252. IEEE (2022)

43. Dahdouh-Guebas, F., et al.: The Mangal Play: A serious game to experience multi-stakeholder decision-making in complex mangrove social-ecological systems. Front. Mar. Sci. **9** (2022). https://doi.org/10.3389/fmars.2022.909793

44. Mayer, I., Zhou, Q., Keijser, X., Abspoel, L.: Gaming the future of the ocean: the marine spatial planning challenge 2050. In: Ma, M., Oliveira, M., Hauge, J. (eds.), pp. 150–162 (2014)

45. Koenigstein, S., Hentschel, L., Heel, L., Drinkorn, C.: A game-based education approach for sustainable ocean development. ICES J. Mar. Sci. **77**, 1629–1638 (2020). https://doi.org/10.1093/icesjms/fsaa035

46. Gyetvai, L., et al.: Development of a negotiation-based serious game in virtual reality to help teach responsible consumption and production, pp. 000021–000026. IEEE (2022)

47. Pimentel, D., Amaya, R., Halan, S., Kalyanaraman, S., Bailenson, J., IEEE: Climate change on your plate: a VR seafood buffet experience, pp. 1120–1121 (2019)

48. Huang, J., Lucash, M., Scheller, R., Klippel, A.: Walking through the forests of the future: using data-driven virtual reality to visualize forests under climate change. Int. J. Geogr. Inf. Sci. **35**, 1155–1178 (2021). https://doi.org/10.1080/13658816.2020.1830997

49. Arnold, O., Jantke, K.P.: The time travel exploratory games approach: an artificial intelligence perspective. In: Csapó, B., Uhomoibhi, J. (eds.) CSEDU 2021. LNCS, pp. 40–54. Springer, Cham (2022). https://doi.org/10.1007/978-3-031-14756-2_3

50. Fauville, G., Queiroz, A., Hambrick, L., Brown, B., Bailenson, J.: Participatory research on using virtual reality to teach ocean acidification: a study in the marine education community. Environ. Educ. Res. **27**, 254–278 (2021). https://doi.org/10.1080/13504622.2020.1803797

51. Rossano, V., Roselli, T., Calvano, G.: Multimedia technologies to foster ecological skills. In: Chang, M., Chen, N., Huang, R., Kinshuk, S.D., Vasiu, R. (eds.), pp. 128–130 (2017)

52. de Sá Escudeiro, P.E.M., Campos, M., Escudeiro, N.: Eco Tetris: A Serious game on Sustainability. ECGBL **16**, 684–692 (2022)

53. Phatarametravorakul, W., Cheevanantaporn, S., Jamsri, P.: The waste separation game to promote computational thinking through mixed reality technology, pp. 148–153. IEEE (2022)

54. Calvi, L., et al.: A VR game to teach underwater sustainability while diving, pp. 114–117 (2017)

55. Ceccarini, C., Prandi, C.: EscapeCampus: exploiting a Game-based Learning tool to increase the sustainability knowledge of students, pp. 390–396 (2022)

56. Santana, A.F., et al.: Save tuba: a gamified app for children to explore environmental issues and develop sustainable behaviors, pp. 299–306. IEEE (2022)

57. Frajberg, D., Fraternali, P., Torres, R., IEEE: Heterogeneous information integration for mountain augmented reality mobile apps, pp. 313–322 (2017)

58. Hunicke, R., LeBlanc, M., Zubek, R.: MDA: A Formal Approach to Game Design and Game Research, p. 1722. CA, San Jose (2004)

59. Shin, D.: Empathy and embodied experience in virtual environment: to what extent can virtual reality stimulate empathy and embodied experience? Comput. Hum. Behav. **78**, 64–73 (2018)

60. Krekhov, A., Cmentowski, S., Emmerich, K., Kruger, J., Assoc Comp Machinery: Beyond human: animals as an escape from stereotype avatars in virtual reality games, pp. 439–451 (2019)

61. Warmelink, H., Koivisto, J., Mayer, I., Vesa, M., Hamari, J.: Gamification of production and logistics operations: Status quo and future directions. J. Bus. Res. **106**, 331–340 (2020)

62. Leitão, R., Maguire, M., Turner, S., Arenas, F., Guimarães, L.: Ocean literacy gamified: a systematic evaluation of the effect of game elements on students' learning experience. Environ. Educ. Res. **28**, 276–294 (2022)

63. Briot, J.-P., et al.: A serious game and artificial agents to support intercultural participatory management of protected areas for biodiversity conservation and social inclusion, pp. 15–20. IEEE (2011)
64. Dorward, L., Mittermeier, J., Sandbrook, C., Spooner, F.: Pokemon go: benefits, costs, and lessons for the conservation movement. Conserv Lett **10**, 160–165 (2017). https://doi.org/10.1111/conl.12326
65. Ho, M., Nguyen, T., Nguyen, M., La, V., Vuong, Q.: Good ethics cannot stop me from exploiting: the good and bad of anthropocentric attitudes in a game environment. Ambio **51**, 2294–2307 (2022). https://doi.org/10.1007/s13280-022-01742-y
66. Vuong, Q., et al.: On the environment-destructive probabilistic trends: a perceptual and behavioral study on video game players. Technol. Soc. 65 (2021). https://doi.org/10.1016/j.techsoc.2021.101530
67. Pimentel, D., ACM: The Peril and Potential of XR-based Interactions with Wildlife (2021)
68. Carter, M., Webber, S., Rawson, S., Smith, W., Purdam, J., McLeod, E.: Virtual reality in the zoo: a qualitative evaluation of a stereoscopic virtual reality video encounter with little penguins Eudyptula minor. J. ZOO. Aquar. Res. **8**, 239–245 (2020). https://doi.org/10.19227/jzar.v8i4.500
69. Hofman, K., Hughes, K., Walters, G.: The effectiveness of virtual vs real-life marine tourism experiences in encouraging conservation behaviour. J. Sustain. Tour. **30**, 742–766 (2022). https://doi.org/10.1080/09669582.2021.1884690
70. Pimentel, D., Kalyanaraman, S.: The effects of embodying wildlife in virtual reality on conservation behaviors. Sci. Rep. **12** (2022). https://doi.org/10.1038/s41598-022-10268-y
71. Cepok J, et al.: Effects of VR on intentions to change environmental behavior, pp. 874–875 (2019)
72. Moriuchi, E., Murdy, S.: Increasing donation intentions toward endangered species: an empirical study on the mediating role of psychological and technological elements of VR. Psychol. Mark. **39**, 1302–1321 (2022). https://doi.org/10.1002/mar.21650
73. Pimentel, D., Kalyanaraman, S., Halan, S., IEEE: bigger is better: a VR penguin rehabilitation simulation to study animal conservation behaviors, pp. 519–522 (2018)
74. Wang, X., Yao, X.: Fueling pro-environmental behaviors with gamification design: identifying key elements in ant forest with the kano model. Sustainability **12** (2020). https://doi.org/10.3390/su12062213

Using Gamification to Activate University Library Use

Takahiro Kitamura and Yasuyuki Sumi[✉]

Future University Hakodate, Hakodate, Hokkaido 0418655, Japan
t-kitamura@sumilab.org, sumi@acm.org

Abstract. This paper proposes a territory building game to activate library use. Each bookshelf becomes the territory of the player who spends the longest time in front of it, and players compete to win more territories. The time spent in front of each bookshelf was calculated by matching an image taken every 0.5 s by a camera attached to the chest with an image of each bookshelf taken beforehand. According to the questionnaire, players who were more enthusiastic about the game visited the library more frequently and stayed longer, and explored bookshelves they would not normally visit. We present an example of the experimental use of the proposed game in a university library. Fifteen university students were recruited as players of the game, and an eight-week experiment was conducted. The results of the experiment showed that players were divided into four types according to the degree of immersion in the game, with more active players tending to visit the library more often and stay longer, and an interest in new areas of books was also observed.

Keywords: Gamification · University library · Territory building game · First-person view image

1 Introduction

This paper proposes a territory building game as a means of activating library users. Gamification is used to increase the number of times players use the library and the time spent there. It is also expected to broaden players' interest in books by encouraging them to stop by bookshelves they would not normally stop by.

University libraries are responsible for supporting the collection, accumulation, and provision of academic information related to education and research. They are also expected to support students in recognizing the importance of their own active learning. Therefore, libraries are required not only to provide information but also to function as a place for students to learn and share information. To fulfill these functions, libraries have made various efforts, including the development of learning spaces and distinctive collections by theme.

Meanwhile, the widespread use of the Internet has enabled library users to search for information on the Web and easily access a variety of information resources. Online libraries and academic information retrieval services allow users to search for more information by keywords and browse information without having to search the library. Students can now easily find the information they need online without having to physically visit the library or search through bookshelves.

However, there is also information that can be obtained by actually visiting a library. It is a chance encounter with a book in a field the user would not normally see. In the real library, the user would actually go to the bookshelf where the book she/he wants to borrow is located. On the way to the bookshelf, there will be many different types of books. Libraries offer the possibility of encountering books that arouse the user's potential interests.

In order to gain such experiences, we have to reach the real-world library. In the present situation where information can be gathered on the Internet, some motivation is needed to take the trouble to go to the library. Therefore, we thought that using gamification as a motivation would encourage the use of libraries. Gamification is a technique for enhancing user's motivation and royalty by incorporating gaming elements in fields other than games [8,9]. By using this game for library use, we first use the library to participate in the game, but gradually borrow books and use the library as a place of learning.

In order to obtain such an experience, we must visit a real library. With the current situation where information can be gathered on the Internet, some motivation is needed to go all the way to the library. Therefore, we thought that we could promote the use of libraries by arousing motivation through gamification. Gamification is a method of increasing users' motivation and incentives by incorporating game elements into non-game areas [8,9]. By using a game for library use, we aim to encourage users to use the library to participate in the game, and then gradually borrow books and use the library as a place for active learning.

In this paper, we propose a territory building game for the purpose of activating the use of libraries. As a technology to realize the game, we introduce a method to automatically estimate the time spent at each bookshelf from first-person view images in the library. The game encourages users to visit bookshelves they do not usually visit. We examine whether these changes in player behavior have an impact on the expansion of the field of interest in books.

2   Related Work

2.1   Gamification

Gamification is a method of improving user motivation and incentives by incorporating game elements into non-game areas. It has already been adopted in various fields and studied from various viewpoints [13], e.g., e-learning, marketing, system development and so on [10,14,23].

Studies verifying the effectiveness of gamification have also been studied from various viewpoints, and there are various studies such as the efficient design of gamification [7], influence of game design [22], focusing on usability [12], etc. [20]. Especially in the field of learning, effects such as using the system voluntarily by using gamification for student motivation have been obtained [3,15,26]. In these studies, the purpose is mainly to continue or improve motivation, and many studies have continued or improved motivation of subjects [4,16,19]. GamiCAD conducted by Li et al. gave higher achievement and speed than usual by using gamification for AutoCAD's tutorial [17].

In those studies, they use gamification to achieve a specific objective, such as improvement scores. Our study seeks to revitalize library use by using gamification in library use. By using gamification, we aim to increase the number of library visits and the time spent in the library, and focus on how users changed their behavior through the game. We are also examining the impact of user behavior changes on active learning through library use.

2.2 Promoting Behavior Change with Simple Game Rules

Our study aims to activate library use by gamification. There are several similar studies targeting libraries and museums [24,28]. The study by Vandecasteele et al. [27] uses a maze-search type game LIBRARINTH to estimate users' interest in the library. Another study developped a game-like user interface in a library to connect information with the real-world [5].

This paper aims to increase the number of library visits and the time spent in the library by using simple game rules. We expect a change in players' behavior specific to the territory-building game and a consequent accidental broadening of their field of interest. The broadening of the field of interest takes place through encounters with new books.

Thudt et al.'s study [25] also aimed at serendipitous encounters with books in the library by devising visual representations. Our game does not directly produce the encounter with the book itself, but focuses on the effect of leading to an indirect encounter with a new book from the immersion in the game.

2.3 Activity Recognition Using First-Person View Images

In the study of gamification, there are ones that developed games for the purpose of extending research and databases that collected information for feedback to game players by adding game elements to physical activity [1,21].

In these games, a variety of technologies are used in game design. Library-based research includes the development of mobile games using smartphones and QR codes and research using RFID and Bluetooth [11,18]. Similarly, some studies have gamified museum tours by using exhibits as game contents [24,24].

In contrast, our research tracks player behavior in the library and reflects it in game information without the use of devices that require player manipulation in the field. We use a wearable camera as a device to track user behavior and collect first-person images of player behavior.

To feed back game information to players, a badge system or a virtual space with user avatars are often used [2,6]. In our research, we propose a territory building game in which players compete to take bookshelves in a library by mapping the game space to the library space.

3   Proposed System

This paper proposes a territory building game as a gamification system to activate university students' use of the library. Figure 1 shows the conceptual diagram of our territory building game in the library.

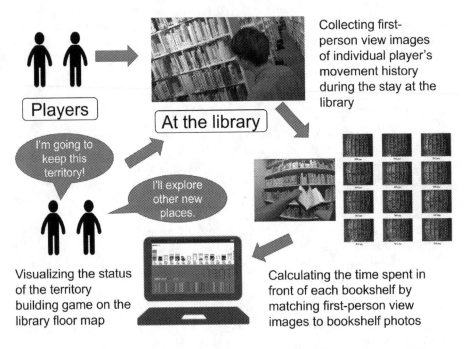

Fig. 1. Conceptual diagram of the proposed territory building game in the library

This paper uses the library as the field for a territory building game. We expect that this will result in an increase in the number of library visits and time spent by players. Furthermore, we hope to broaden the interests of players by using this territory building game. As a side effect of participation in the game, we expect an increase in the number of books borrowed from the library and an expansion of the field of books borrowed. The purpose of this study is to observe whether participation in the game leads to active learning.

The territories in the game are associated with the bookshelves in the library, and the time spent in front of the bookshelves is credited as points for gaining territory. To win in this game, players must increase their territory, and to do so they must visit the library and stay in front of many different types of bookshelves. In other words, the game score will be higher if players visit a variety of bookshelves instead of staying only on the same bookshelf. We hope that such rules of the game will encourage players to encounter new books and help them broaden their interests.

4   Territory Building Game in the Library

4.1   Design of Territory Building Game

This paper proposes a territory building game that encourages library use. In this game, players can expand their territory by increasing the amount of time they spend in the library. The time spent in front of each bookshelf is counted as a point, and that bookshelf becomes the territory of the player who currently has the most points (Figs. 2 and 3).

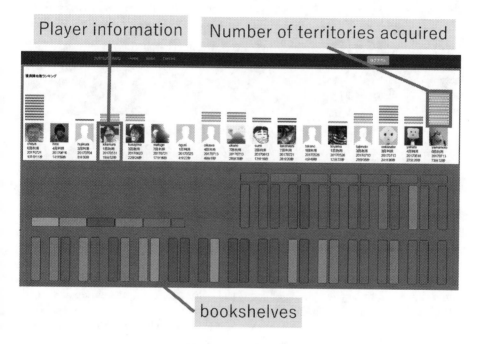

Fig. 2. Display of the number of territories acquired by each player

Players in our game visit libraries to earn points. To automate the calculation of points obtained by staying in the library, players are asked to wear a camera capable of interval photography in front of their chest, and their activities in the library are collected as multiple footprint images. After using the library, the collected first-person images are matched with marker images previously taken of bookshelves in the library to link the player's first-person images to each bookshelf. SURF (Speed-Up Robust Features) was used for matching between images.

The number of first-person images for which the correspondence was confirmed was considered as the time spent, and the game screen reflected points for how long the player spent on the bookshelf. A website was constructed so that the game screen could be easily viewed at any time. The game was played

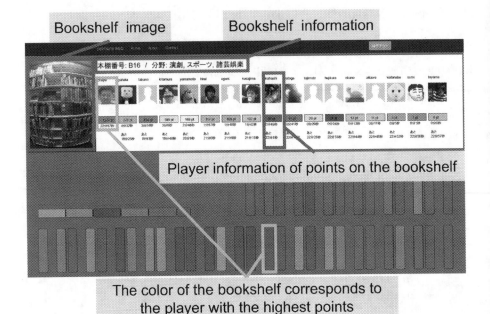

Fig. 3. Number of points earned by each user on a bookshelf

at Future University Hakodate, to which the authors belong, and a floor plan of the university's library was displayed on the game screen.

Each bookshelf was painted with a color associated with each player to indicate which player currently occupies the bookshelf. The number of points was counted according to the time spent and the color intensity was changed accordingly. In other words, a bookshelf painted in a darker color indicates that it is firmly protected by a particular player, while a bookshelf painted in a lighter color indicates that it is temporarily in someone's territory but can be taken over quickly.

The game screen displays the points required for each bookshelf to be taken by the player viewing it. This was intended to encourage players to browse this screen prior to visiting the library and to aim for the bookshelves that can be taken efficiently. The ranking of all players according to the number of territories acquired was also displayed to stimulate competition among players.

4.2 Behavior Record of User by First-Person View Image

We used GoPro Hero 4 which is a camera capable of interval shooting to record the behavior of players in the library. Our game players wear the camera on their chest during visiting the library (Fig. 4).

The camera was set to take one interval shot every 0.5 s and recorded the player's behavior as a first-person viewpoint image. The recorded first-person

Fig. 4. Walking through the library with a camera attached to the chest

viewpoint image of the player was compared with marker images obtained by
shooting each bookshelf in advance, and the feature values were compared.

The system compares the feature points of the two images using SURF,
and if the feature values exceed a certain threshold, the system considers that
the player stayed in front of the bookshelf corresponding to the marker image
with the most features (Fig. 5). Our system matches all first-person images taken
during the player's visit to the library to create a record of the player's bookshelf
stay (Fig. 6).

Fig. 5. Matching bookshelf and first-person view images using SURF

The reason for using first-person view images is that data on stay records for
each bookshelf can be collected with a single wearable camera, without the use
of complicated equipment. First-person images were also used for more detailed
analysis of user behavior in the library.

Fig. 6. Classification of first-person view images to bookshelves

5   Experimental Use of Our Game in a University Library

5.1   Outline of Experiment

We applied our game to a university library and examined what effects the game would have. During the experimental period, participants were asked to wear a camera on their chest to record their behavior when visiting the library, and to view the game page on the web when they wished. The library usage history and the browsing history of the game page were collected.

5.2   Method of Experiment

Participants

Fifteen university students were recruited.

Instructions

The experiment was conducted for about two months. When using the library, participants were asked to walk freely around the library as usual without worrying about the time. No restrictions were placed on the frequency of use, and the participants were asked to use the library whenever they wished.

Accumulated data

Participants were asked to wear a camera (GoPro) capable of interval shooting on their chest to acquire first-person images in the library every 0.5 s. After using the library, participants were asked to report the camera number on the communication tool Slack, and the experimenter promptly collected the data and reflected the data in the game. Participants were asked to cooperate with a subjective questionnaire regarding changes in behavior before and at the end of the experiment. They were also asked to provide a record of their book borrowing during the period.

Hypothesis

We expected that participation in the game would increase the number of visits to the library and the time spent in the library. We also expected that participation in the game would broaden the range of books borrowed.

5.3   Result of Experiment

Five players clearly increased the frequency of library use compared to the frequency of use answered in the questionnaire conducted before the experiment. The other 10 players showed no particular change in the frequency of library use. Figure 7 shows the time spent per library visit for all players. Figure 8 shows the change in the average time spent in the library over time during the experiment. Interestingly, the duration of stay tended to decrease with the number of times. Among the players who used the library more frequently, many of them

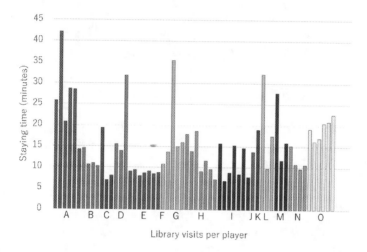

Fig. 7. Time spent per library visit for all players

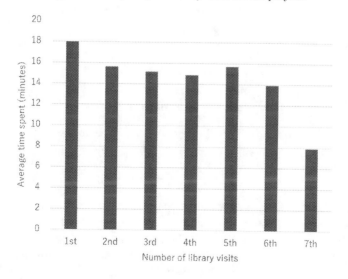

Fig. 8. Change in the average time spent in the library over time

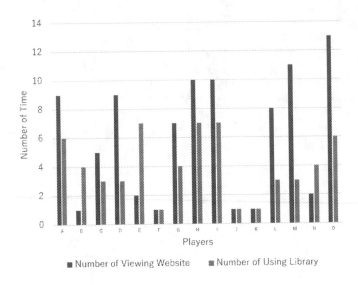

Fig. 9. Numbers of library use and game web browsing per player

were absorbed in our territory building game. They stayed at the shelves that corresponded to the territories they strategically aimed to acquire, which may have resulted in a shorter time spent in the library.

Figure 9 shows numbers of library use and game web browsing per player. The overall correlation between the number of library visits and the number of game web views is low and appears to depend on the individuality of each player. Basically, players with a high number of web browsing are considered to be more enthusiastic about games, and they use the library more frequently. On the other hand, there were some players who used the library frequently regardless of their enthusiasm for games. Some players were found to have a high number of game web browsing but low frequency of library use. However, the results of the questionnaire confirmed that they actually used the library but skipped wearing the camera.

We observed the following four types of game players.

1. Player who continues to defend territory already acquired
2. Player who explores new territory that is not popular
3. Player who tries to take territory that could be taken from others
4. Player who visits the library regardless of the game

Figure 10 shows the behavior by the player who continues to defend territory already acquired. He acted to protect the bookshelves he had acquired during his first library visit from other players. Therefore, there was not much behavior to develop new bookshelves. In addition, he had many accesses to the web to defend his territory. He did not borrow many books. He was often observed browsing for a while looking for new books while staying in front of the bookshelf that was his territory.

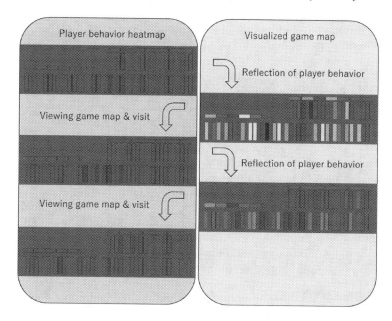

Fig. 10. Behavior that continues to defend territory already acquired

The behavior of players who actively explored the unpopular bookshelves was shown in Fig. 11. This player's strategy is reasonable because an unpopular bookshelf can be easily made into his/her own territory even during a short stay. The player often browsed the game screen and checked the unpopular bookshelves on the game before going to the library. In addition, this player used the library on a daily basis and borrowed many books, and by walking around in new areas, he expanded the field of books he borrowed.

Figure 12 shows the behavior of a player who strategically tries to seize other players' territories that he can take. The player frequently browsed the web site and always tried to keep track of other players' actions. He tended to choose to take bookshelves that were not much maintained by other players, while avoiding the positions defended by type 1 player (who defend the positions they have acquired). As a result, the time spent in the library was gradually increasing.

Figure 13 shows the behavior of a type of player who goes to the library to borrow the desired book, regardless of the game. This player browsed the Web site, but less frequently. In the post-experiment questionnaire, the player answered that the game had little effect on his behavior in the library. In reality, however, the player was interested in visiting bookshelves that were acquired by other players, and his book borrowing record showed that he had developed new areas of interest.

Figure 14 represents the field of books borrowed from the library by experiment participants. The fields enclosed by the inner circle are those obtained from the borrowing record prior to the start of the experiment. Since the par-

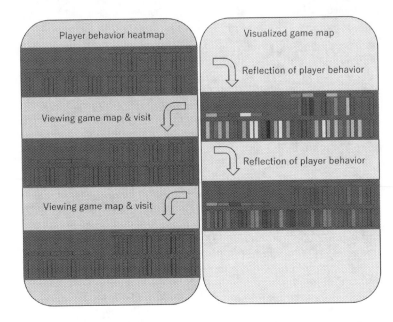

Fig. 11. Behavior that explores new territory that is not popular

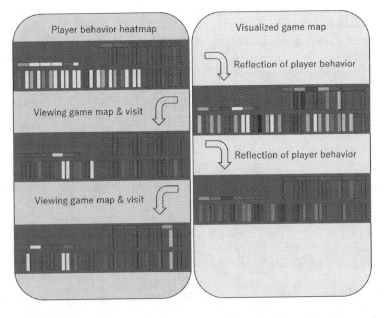

Fig. 12. Behavior that tries to take territory that could be taken from others

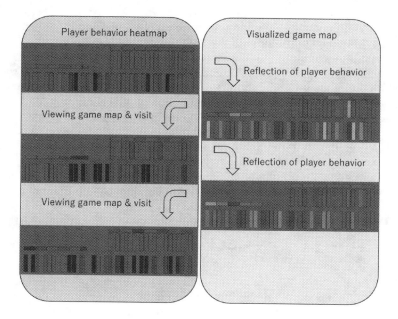

Fig. 13. Behavior that visits the library regardless of the game

ticipants in the experiment were university students in the fields of computer engineering, many of the books were related to their fields of specialization. The fields of books borrowed during the two months of the experiment were extended outside the circle. These included books in fields such as art, literature, urban engineering, and aerospace engineering, which are different from their fields of specialization.

5.4 Discussion

In this experiment, some players increased their time spent in the game by participating in the game. On the other hand, there were a certain number of players whose time spent in the game decreased as a result of participating in the game. A detailed examination based on the first-person view images and points gained suggests that the time spent in the library rather decreased due to actions taken to efficiently acquire territories. We found that changes in the number of library visits and time spent in the library due to the territory building game varied greatly from individual to individual. Although the rules of the game were simple, the immersion in the game was confirmed to be diverse.

The field of books borrowed was confirmed to have been extended during the experimental period. This result is interesting given that they do not need to borrow books in order to gain a position. The fact that the participants followed

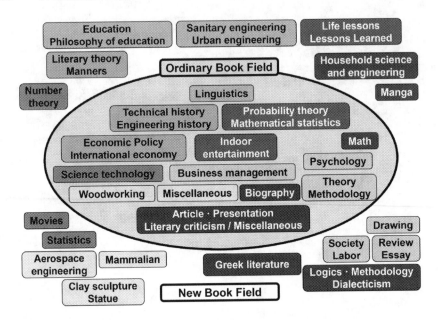

Fig. 14. Expansion of the field of books borrowed by experiment participants

the rules of the game, which were not directly related to their learning objectives, and thus attended the library, increased the chances that they would stay for some time in front of bookshelves that they would not normally stop by. This probably increased the probability that they would be lucky enough to come across a book that caught their interest. It can be said that the game stimulated the habit of going to the library even if the rules were meaningless at first, and this led to active learning. This is the value of gamification, which indirectly achieves the original goal by immersing oneself in rules that have nothing to do with the original goal.

6   Conclusions

A territory building game was proposed to activate the use of the library. The experimental use of the game in a university library increased students' opportunities to use the library and, as a result, the fields of books they borrowed expanded.

The way the game affected each player was different, and in some cases the library's behavior became monotonous for some participants. It will be necessary to find out the characteristics of each player from the game history and use different ways of evoking active learning according to individual characteristics.

References

1. von Ahn, L., Liu, R., Blum, M.: Peekaboom: a game for locating objects in images. In: Proceedings of the SIGCHI Conference on Human Factors in Computing Systems (CHI 2006), pp. 55–64. ACM, NY (2006). https://doi.org/10.1145/1124772.1124782

2. Barata, G., Gama, S., Fonseca, M.J., Gonçalves, D.: Improving student creativity with gamification and virtual worlds. In: Proceedings of the First International Conference on Gameful Design, Research, and Applications (Gamification 2013), pp. 95–98. ACM, NY (2013). http://doi.acm.org/10.1145/2583008.2583023

3. Barrio, C.M., Muñoz-Organero, M., Soriano, J.S.: Can gamification improve the benefits of student response systems in learning? an experimental study. IEEE Trans. Emerg. Top. Comput. 4(3), 429–438 (2016)

4. Brewer, R., Anthony, L., Brown, Q., Irwin, G., Nias, J., Tate, B.: Using gamification to motivate children to complete empirical studies in lab environments. In: Proceedings of the 12th International Conference on Interaction Design and Children (IDC 2013), pp. 388–391. ACM, NY (2013). http://doi.acm.org/10.1145/2485760.2485816

5. Christoffel, M., Schmitt, B.: Accessing libraries as easy as a game. In: Börner, K., Chen, C. (eds.) Visual Interfaces to Digital Libraries. LNCS, vol. 2539, pp. 25–38. Springer, Heidelberg (2002). https://doi.org/10.1007/3-540-36222-3_3

6. Denny, P.: The effect of virtual achievements on student engagement. In: Proceedings of the SIGCHI Conference on Human Factors in Computing Systems (CHI 2013), pp. 763–772. ACM, NY (2013). http://doi.acm.org/10.1145/2470654.2470763'

7. Deterding, S., Björk, S.L., Nacke, L.E., Dixon, D., Lawley, E.: Designing gamification: creating gameful and playful experiences. In: CHI '13 Extended Abstracts on Human Factors in Computing Systems, pp. 3263–3266. ACM, NY (2013). http://doi.acm.org/10.1145/2468356.2479662

8. Deterding, S., Dixon, D., Khaled, R., Nacke, L.: From game design elements to gamefulness: defining "gamification". In: Proceedings of the 15th International Academic MindTrek Conference: Envisioning Future Media Environments (MindTrek 2011), pp. 9–15. ACM, NY (2011). http://doi.acm.org/10.1145/2181037.2181040

9. Deterding, S., Sicart, M., Nacke, L., O'Hara, K., Dixon, D.: Gamification. Using game-design elements in non-gaming contexts. In: CHI 2011 Extended Abstracts on Human Factors in Computing Systems, pp. 2425–2428. ACM, NY (2011). http://doi.acm.org/10.1145/1979742.1979575

10. Dubois, D.J., Tamburrelli, G.: Understanding gamification mechanisms for software development. In: Proceedings of the 2013 9th Joint Meeting on Foundations of Software Engineering (ESEC/FSE 2013), pp. 659–662. ACM, NY (2013). http://doi.acm.org/10.1145/2491411.2494589

11. Fitz-Walter, Z., Tjondronegoro, D., Koh, D., Zrobok, M.: Mystery at the library: encouraging library exploration using a pervasive mobile game. In: Proceedings of the 24th Australian Computer-Human Interaction Conference (OzCHI 2012), pp. 142–145. ACM, NY (2012). http://doi.acm.org/10.1145/2414536.2414561

12. Yáñez-Gómez, R., Cascado-Caballero, D., Sevillano, J.L.: Academic methods for usability evaluation of serious games: a systematic review. Multimed. Tools Appl. 76(4), 5755–5784 (2017). http://doi.acm.org/10.1007/s11042-016-3845-9

13. Hamari, J., Koivisto, J., Sarsa, H.: Does gamification work? - A literature review of empirical studies on gamification. In: Proceedings of the 2014 47th Hawaii International Conference on System Sciences (HICSS 2014), pp. 3025–3034. IEEE Computer Society, Washington, DC (2014). http://doi.acm.org/10.1109/HICSS.2014.377

14. Huotari, K., Hamari, J.: Defining gamification: a service marketing perspective. In: Proceeding of the 16th International Academic MindTrek Conference (MindTrek 2012), pp. 17–22. ACM, NY (2012). http://doi.acm.org/10.1145/2393132.2393137

15. Iosup, A., Epema, D.: An experience report on using gamification in technical higher education. In: Proceedings of the 45th ACM Technical Symposium on Computer Science Education (SIGCSE 2014), pp. 27–32. ACM, NY (2014). http://doi.acm.org/10.1145/2538862.2538899

16. Krause, M., Mogalle, M., Pohl, H., Williams, J.J.: A playful game changer: fostering student retention in online education with social gamification. In: Proceedings of the Second (2015) ACM Conference on Learning @ Scale (L@S 2015), pp. 95–102. ACM, NY (2015). http://doi.acm.org/10.1145/2724660.2724665

17. Li, W., Grossman, T., Fitzmaurice, G.: GamiCAD: a gamified tutorial system for first time autocad users. In: Proceedings of the 25th Annual ACM Symposium on User Interface Software and Technology (UIST 2012), pp. 103–112. ACM, NY (2012). http://doi.acm.org/10.1145/2380116.2380131

18. Lykke-Olesen, A., Nielsen, J.: bibphone: adding sound to the children's library. In: Proceedings of the 6th International Conference on Interaction Design and Children (IDC 2007), pp. 145–148, ACM, NY (2007). http://doi.acm.org/10.1145/1297277.1297307

19. Martin, C., Martinez, R.: Games in classroom and practice in library and information science education. On the Horizon **24**(1), 82–87 (2016). http://doi.org/10.1108/OTH-08-2015-0051

20. Mekler, E.D., Brühlmann, F., Opwis, K., Tuch, A.N.: Disassembling gamification: the effects of points and meaning on user motivation and performance. In: CHI '13 Extended Abstracts on Human Factors in Computing Systems, pp. 1137–1142. ACM, NY (2013). http://doi.acm.org/10.1145/2468356.2468559

21. Payton, J., Powell, E., Nickel, A., Doran, K., Barnes, T.: Gamechanger: a middleware for social exergames. In: Proceedings of the 1st International Workshop on Games and Software Engineering (GAS 2011), pp. 36–39. ACM, NY (2011). http://doi.acm.org/10.1145/1984674.1984688

22. Ramnarine-Rieks, A.: Learning through game design: an investigation on the effects in library instruction sessions. In: Proceedings of the 2012 iConference (iConference 2012), pp. 606–607. ACM, NY (2012). http://doi.acm.org/10.1145/2132176.2132307

23. Raymer, R.: Gamification: using game mechanics to enhance elearning. eLearn **2011**(9) (September 2011). http://doi.acm.org/10.1145/2025356.2031772

24. Rojas, S.L., Oppermann, L., Blum, L., Wolpers, M.: Natural europe educational games suite: Using structured museum-data for creating mobile educational games. In: Proceedings of the 11th Conference on Advances in Computer Entertainment Technology (ACE 2014), pp. 6:1–6:6. ACM, NY (2014). http://doi.acm.org/10.1145/2663806.2663841

25. Thudt, A., Hinrichs, U., Carpendale, S.: The bohemian bookshelf: supporting serendipitous book discoveries through information visualization. In: Proceedings of the SIGCHI Conference on Human Factors in Computing Systems (CHI 2012), pp. 1461–1470. ACM, New York (2012). http://doi.acm.org/10.1145/2207676.2208607

26. Toda, A.M., do Carmo, R.S., Silva, A.L., Brancher, J.D.: Project SIGMA - an online tool to aid students in math lessons with gamification concepts. In: 2014 33rd International Conference of the Chilean Computer Science Society (SCCC), pp. 50–53 (November 2014)
27. Vandecasteele, F., Vanbeselaere, E., Vandemaele, L., Saldien, J., Verstockt, S.: LIBRARINTH interactive game to explore the library of the future. In: Proceedings of the 7th ACM SIGCHI Symposium on Engineering Interactive Computing Systems (EICS 2015), pp. 94–99. ACM, NY (2015). http://doi.acm.org/10.1145/2774225.2775074
28. Yiannoutsou, N., Avouris, N.: Mobile games in museums: from learning through game play to learning through game design. ICOM Education **23**, 79–86 (2012)

Orpheus' Journey

David A. Plecher[⊠], Leonie Wargitsch, Christian Eichhorn,
and Gudrun Klinker

FAR - The Technical University of Munich, Munich, Germany
{plecher,klinker}@in.tum.de,
{leonie.wargitsch,christian.eichhorn}@tum.de

Abstract. Informing oneself about the content of an opera is essential before visiting a performance. For this reason the Serious Game *Orpheus' Journey* was developed as an preparation tool for watching Monteverdi's opera *l'Orfeo*, offering an alternative to more traditional methods of preparation like text or video summaries. The game features both adventure scenes and music sequences. It teaches the player main musical themes as well as the story and characters of the opera. The story is centered around the myth of Orpheus, a musician who wants to rescue his deceased wife from the underworld. He succeeds in reaching Hades, the god of the underworld by playing a lyre. This means that the music acts not only as means to convey the story but is an integral part of the plot. This provides an In-game justification of the inclusion of music sequences in the gameplay and creates a bridge between gameplay and story. This way gaming world and serious content can reasonable be combined via fitting gaming elements, which is an important factor for user acceptance and therefore knowledge transfer. In a small user study the game's effectiveness as a preparation tool and the impact it had on the players' opera experience were investigated.

Keywords: Serious Game · Opera · Cultural Heritage · Orpheus

1 Introduction

Preparing for an opera is an essential part when one is looking for ways to enhance the opera watching experience. Records of opera pamphlets show that methods for opera preparation have existed since the middle of the fifteenth century [5], implicating that preparing before watching an opera has been relevant for centuries. Milak [19] showed that students that received an extra curriculum next to listening to similar concerts before watching a performance indicated an overall improvement in attitude towards the music of the opera after the visit. The attitude of those who did not receive the same preparation didn't improve or worsened. This shows that the amount of preparation influences the opera viewing experience.

A study in which elders participated showed that a university program, which offered a great variety of extensive preparation material, greatly improved the opera experience of every participant. Not only did this course have a positive

X. Fang (Ed.): HCII 2023, LNCS 14046, pp. 360–369, 2023.
https://doi.org/10.1007/978-3-031-35930-9_24

impact on the duration, but also on the intensity of the opera experience. There was also an increased interest in attending more opera performances as well as more open-mindedness toward attending smaller productions [2].

Through the rising popularity of the internet, new ways of preparing for an opera emerged. Video summaries, text summaries and recordings of past performances of operas are more accessible than ever. At the same time, video games became increasingly relevant and with that, the first "Serious Games" emerged. This raises the question whether a serious game would be able to serve as a sufficient preparation tool when compared with more traditional means of preparation like texts or videos. Furthermore it is relevant to ask the question whether playing the game can enhance the opera watching experience and whether such a game can be engaging in itself.

To test these research questions, the Serious Game *Orpheus' Journey* was developed as an preparation tool for watching Monteverdi's opera *l'Orfeo*. After playing the game, they should be sufficiently prepared for watching the opera and have enough background knowledge about Greek mythology to have a similar level of understanding of the myths as past audiences were expected to have. This opera was chosen as the subject of the game for multiple reasons. Being one of the first operas and the earliest work that is still performed regularly, *l'Orfeo* can be considered genre defining [8].

The story is centered around the myth of Orpheus, a musician who wants to rescue his deceased wife from the underworld. He succeeds in reaching Hades, the god of the underworld by playing a lyre. This means that the music acts not only as means to convey the story but is a integral part of the plot. This provides an In-game justification of the inclusion of music sequences in the gameplay and creates a bridge between gameplay and story. This way gaming world and serious content can reasonable be combined via fitting gaming elements, which is an important factor for user acceptance and therefore knowledge transfer [10,18].

2   Related Work

2.1   Serious Games and Cultural Heritage

According to Mortara et al. [9], serious games can be classified differently in terms of tangible and intangible cultural heritage. *Orpheus Journey* is in the area of cultural awareness. Here, the game serves to preserve and communicate intangible cultural heritage. In this case, this concerns music, mythology and opera in general. Other games that are similarly classified are, for example, games that deal with languages. These include *HieroQuest* [14], which teaches ancient Egyptian hieroglyphs, or *Ludus Magnus* [13], which provides insights into the everyday life of a Roman gladiator in Carnuntum (today's Austria) and also includes exercises regarding the Latin language. The same applies to serious games that teach languages such as English [4] or Japanese (Kanji) [11].

History is also a part of cultural awareness. The serious game *Oppidum* [12] uses augmented reality to convey historically accurate information about life in a Celtic village. *LegionARius* [17] similarly transfers knowledge about the processes in a Roman camp near the Germanic Limes to the players.

Regarding greek mythology, Chintiadis et al. [1] made a serious game called *Trials of Acropolis*, where players learn about ancient Greek mythology. It uses virtual and augmented reality to provide an immersive environment and teaches players five different Greek myths presented as trials. In *Myths Troubles* [3], another serious game about Greek mythology, the player helps a farmer in ancient Greece to find Zeus, the king of the gods of Olympus, to beg him to send rain to save his fields from a drought.

2.2   Serious Games and Opera

A nameless serious game for opera or music classes was developed by Kim et al. [6]. The goal of the serious game is to teach students the characters of the opera *The Magic Flute* by Mozart. For this purpose, an RGB-D camera is used to detect the students' movement and gestures. There are multiple activities the player has to complete in order to progress, including acting, role playing, singing, dancing, doing art and speaking. The game consists of multiple levels, each focusing on a different activity. The player assumes the role of Tamino, who is the opera's main character.

3   The Story of l'Orfeo

It is essential to obtain an overview of the plot of Monteverdi's opera *l'Orfeo* in order to decide the content relevant for the game. The opera is split into five acts and a prologue [20].

1. act: Wedding of Orfeo and Euridice (Fig. 1)
2. act: Euridice dies due to a snakebite. Orfeo sets off to the underworld to retrieve his wife (Fig. 2)
3. act: Orfeo enters the Underworld, he is confronted by the ferryman Caronte (Charon). Charon does not want to bring Orfeo to the other side of the river Styx. By playing his lyre, Orfeo gets Charon to fall asleep. Orfeo takes the boat and crosses the river on his own (Fig. 3).
4. act: Proserpina (Persephone) asks her husband Plutone (Hades), who is god of the Underworld, to give Euridice back to Orfeo. Plutone accepts his wife's request under the condition that Orfeo may not turn back and look at Euridice on his way out. Orfeo is overjoyed and confident that he will get his wife back. However, doubts creep in as he sings: "Who will assure me that she is following?". When he hears a load noise, he turns around to look at Euridice. However, this action disobeys Plutone's orders and consequently, he loses his wife forever.
5. act: Orfeo falls into deep desperation because of his loss. Apollo, who is the Greek god of light, music and the sun and also Orfeo's father, descends on a cloud. He offers Orfeo to take him with him to Heaven, where he will become immortal. Even though Apollo explains that he will never see Euridice again, Orfeo accepts the offer (Fig. 4).

Fig. 1. Orpheus and Eurydice at their wedding

Fig. 2. Gateway to the Underworld

4 Game Design

In *Orpheus' Journey*, the player takes on the role of the opera's protagonist Orpheus. The game is a 2D adventure game, in which the player can walk around in the different scenes of the opera, interact with the characters and inspect

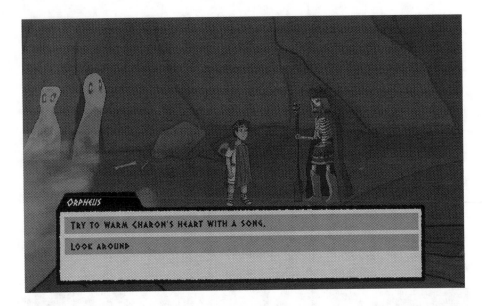

Fig. 3. Dialogue with Charon

Fig. 4. Dialogue with Apollo

important environment elements. It was developed with the Unity Game Engine and is composed of multiple music and adventure sequences. A change of scene happens whenever there is a new act in the opera or the scenery of the opera changes.

Approaching the characters opens up a dialogue box which displays the conversations. Talking to characters can trigger small cutscenes or music sequences. Some conversations also allow the player to decide on the next course of action, by providing them the option to further explore the world (as opposed to continuing the story) or allows them to gain more knowledge about the world and other characters, if they choose the correct dialogue option. The content of the dialogue is mostly pulled directly from the opera, with a few alterations in order to fit the dialogue to the context of the game and/or to provide the player with background information of Greek mythology and ancient Greek culture.

While this gameplay style is similar to the genre of point-and-click adventures, the genre-defining puzzles are not yet implemented. The adventure scenes are accompanied by the corresponding music pieces from the opera as well background sounds that suit the current context, such as the rushing water of a river, water dripping underground or birds when the player is outside.

4.1 Music Sequences

The music sequences during important parts of the story feature gameplay that is similar to the music game *Guitar Hero* and other music games [7]. These sections of the game are triggered by conversing with certain characters and are required to be completed in order to progress. During these sequences, a lyre is illustrated in the background and music from the opera is playing. There are musical notes that move in time with the music from the top side of the screen to the bottom.

When the note reaches a certain part of the lyre, the player has to press the key in the right position and hold it for as long as the note goes. When they do so with accurate timing, they obtain a perfect score. There are points subtracted if the key is pressed either too early, too late or if it was not held long enough. If the player misses a note completely, it counts as missed and they receive no points and lose one of three hearts. When all hearts are lost, a "Game Over" screen is shown and the player has the option to either try again or go back to the main menu (Fig. 5).

At the end of the music sequence, the player receives a rank based on their performance and overall score. This is to keep competitive players, who enjoy the more challenging parts of the game, engaged in the story and music, as they have the ability to try again to improve their score, while more casual players can move on with the story. This ensures that players can choose how to play the game according to their play style and have an overall better experience.

5   Small User Study

For the study, 14 participants (9 male, 5 female) were invited to partake. The majority of the participants were in the age group between 19 and 35, with only two participants being older. They were then split into two even groups of 7. Half of the group that played Orpheus' Journey stated that they usually

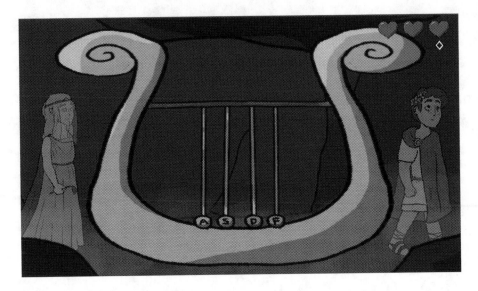

Fig. 5. Orpheus and Eurydice walk through the underworld

don't play video games, one participant stated that they play for more than 8 h a week and the rest were ranging between 1 and 8 h. Only two participants in this group had experience with serious games prior to this study. Their playing time for *Orpheus' Journey* ranged between 20 to 45 min. Across both groups, the majority had at least some past experiences with opera visits.

5.1 Reception of the Game

The game was found to be neither too long (Mean = 1.7; Standard Deviation = 0.75) nor too short (M = 2.28; SD = 1.38). The participants stated that it was easy to learn (M = 5,71; SD = 0.48) and they rarely felt lost while playing (M = 2.00; SD = 1). They furthermore found *Orpheus' Journey* to be engaging (M = 5.43; SD = 0.78) and fun to play (M = 5.00; SD = 0.81). While the majority stated that the music sequences of the game were slightly too hard (M = 4.2; SD = 0.95), many strongly agreed with them being enjoyable (M = 5.86; SD = 0.37). They thought that the music sequences were fitting for the game concept of an opera serious game (M = 5.00; SD = 1.15) as were the adventure scenes (M = 5.14; SD = 0.69). The majority of the participants stated that they would prefer playing a game over other preparation methods (M = 5.29; SD = 1.25).

5.2 Opera Preparation

Group B mainly relied on text summaries of the opera as their method of preparation. Only one participant didn't choose this method and chose to prepare by conversing with others as their sole preparation method. It is of notice that

42% of Group A stated that they usually wouldn't prepare at all before visiting an opera while all participants in Group B stated they would use some way of preparation outside of the study scenario. However, this could have been influenced by asking all groups after they had already prepared for watching the opera. Four of the participants in Group B stated that they didn't prepare for more than 10 min while the rest spend 30 to 60 min preparing.

Out of all the participants of both groups those who had visited at least one opera rated the importance of preparation slightly higher on a scale from 1 (not important at all) to 5 (very important) prior to the study with (M = 3.87, SD = 1.36) compared to those who didn't have any experience (M = 3.2, SD = 0.75). Reasons that were stated for preparation being able to follow the storyline better (100%), greater appreciation for the music and getting to know important motives beforehand (57.1%) and recognizing the characters (50%). Only one person stated that they would prepare to learn about the historical and cultural importance of the opera. Some participants stated that only reason why they would not prepare is a lack of time (42.86%) or the desire to be surprised by the story (35.71%).

In Group A, most people agreed to feeling prepared (M = 4.14; SD = 0.69) on a scale of 1 (I don't feel prepared) to 5 (I feel very prepared) after playing the game. In Group B this number was lower (M = 3.57; SD = 1.13) regarding their feeling about the effectiveness of their own preparation. It is of notice that those in Group B that spend 30 to 60 min preparing did not feel significantly better prepared (M = 3.67) than those who invested less than 10 min (M = 3.50).

After watching the opera, most of Group A disagreed with the statement that they spend too much time preparing (M = 1.57; SD = 0.79), and also slightly disagreed with spending too little time preparing (M = 2.43; SD = 1.40) although the opinions varied on this. Group B produced similar results and also mostly disagreed with investing too much time (M = 1.71; SD = 0.75), although they had contrasting opinions on spending too little time (M = 3.14; SD = 1.34).

5.3   Opera Experience

In order to evaluate the results from the character recognition test, the participants' answers were put into separate categories. If they couldn't recall the name, but provided enough context in which the character appeared or the role the character had in the story, they received a point for context. Incidentally, both groups received the exact number of answers in each category.

Participants of Group A, however, felt slightly more confident that they were able to recognize the characters than Group B. They also agreed more with the statement that they could follow the storyline while watching the opera and recognize the locations. However, these differences were not significant.

A by far greater indicator for a better result in the characters recognition test was the question, whether watching the opera was engaging for the participant. If a participant found the opera enjoyable was indicated when they mostly agreed with the statement that they enjoyed watching the opera and mostly disagreed with finding the opera boring. Seven of the fourteen participants found the opera to be engaging.

If the participant had played the game had no significant impact on whether they enjoyed the music or not, but the opinions on that were more divided in Group A (M = 4.43; SD = 1.81) than in Group B (M= 4.57; SD = 0.98). The participants of Group B did on average enjoy watching the opera more (M = 4.00; SD = 0.58) than those in Group A (M = 3.86; SD = 1.57). Both groups agreed that their preparation made them enjoy watching the opera more (M = 5.28 for Group A, M = 5.43 for Group B) and disagreed with the statement that preparing somewhat ruined their opera experience (M = 1.14 for both groups).

6 Conclusion and Future Work

A protoype of the Serious Game *Orpheus' Journey*, which functions as a method of opera preparation, was successfully created. The game features both adventure scenes as well as music sequences. The player assumes the role of Orpheus and navigates through the story by talking to the opera's key characters and solving music challenges. In a user study players tested different preparation methods before watching the opera *l'Orfeo*. It was shown that the game could prepare players sufficiently for watching the opera while also being engaging on it's own. Therefore, *Orpheus' Journey* is fulfilling its dual purpose as a Serious Game of achieving its serious goal while at the same time being entertaining and engaging. After watching the opera there was no significant difference in knowledge about the opera and the quality of the opera experience when comparing players of the game to those who prepared using conventional methods. As we have already had good experience with the use of mixed reality combined with cultural heritage [15,16] and especially in combination with serious games [11,12,17], *Orpheus' Journey* will also be "extended". To immerse the player even more in the game, an augmented reality mode is currently being developed in which it will be possible to play a virtual lyre using hand gestures.

A follow-up study about *Orpheus' Journey* should be conducted once the testers' feedback is implemented to identify the effect on the players' opera experience of watching *l'Orfeo*.

References

1. Chintiadis, Pantelis, Kazanidis, Ioannis, Tsinakos, Avgoustos: Trials of the acropolis: teaching Greek mythology using virtual reality and game based learning. In: Auer, Michael E.., Tsiatsos, Thrasyvoulos (eds.) IMCL 2017. AISC, vol. 725, pp. 247–257. Springer, Cham (2018). https://doi.org/10.1007/978-3-319-75175-7_26
2. Cuenca-Amigo, M.: Audience engagement through university programmes. A case study of opera in bilbao. Revista Subjetividades 19(1), 6587 (2019)
3. Evangelopoulou, O., Xinogalos, S.: Myth troubles: an open-source educational game in scratch for Greek mythology. Simul. Gaming 49(1), 71–91 (2018)
4. Guillén-Nieto, V., Aleson-Carbonell, M.: Serious games and learning effectiveness: the case of it's a deal! Comput. Educ. 58(1), 435–448 (2012)

5. Haskamp, F.: Das programmheft der oper (1989)
6. Kim, Hyung Sook, Oh, Su Hak, Park, Yong Hyun: Developing an educational game for art education - gesture recognition-based performance guidance for Mozart's opera magic flute. In: Zaphiris, Panayiotis, Ioannou, Andri (eds.) LCT 2015. LNCS, vol. 9192, pp. 573–582. Springer, Cham (2015). https://doi.org/10.1007/978-3-319-20609-7_54
7. LoPiccolo, G.: Harmonix, RedOctane: Guitar hero. Game [PlayStation 2]
8. Monteverdi, C.Z.A.: Claudio Monteverdi: Orfeo. Cambridge University Press, Cambridge (1986)
9. Mortara, M., Catalano, C.E., Bellotti, F., Fiucci, G., Houry-Panchetti, M., Petridis, P.: Learning cultural heritage by serious games. J. Cult. Heritage 15(3), 318–325 (2014)
10. Orji, R., Vassileva, J., Mandryk, R.L.: Modeling the efficacy of persuasive strategies for different gamer types in serious games for health. User Model. User-Adap. Inter. 24(5), 453–498 (2014). https://doi.org/10.1007/s11257-014-9149-8
11. Plecher, D.A., Eichhorn, C., Kindl, J., Kreisig, S., Wintergerst, M., Klinker, G.: Dragon tale-a serious game for learning Japanese kanji. In: Proceedings of the 2018 Annual Symposium on Computer-Human Interaction in Play Companion Extended Abstracts, pp. 577–583 (2018)
12. Plecher, D.A., Eichhorn, C., Köhler, A., Klinker, G.: Oppidum-a serious-ar-game about celtic life and history. In: International Conference on Games and Learning Alliance, pp. 550–559. Springer (2019)
13. Plecher, David A.., Eichhorn, Christian, Naser, Moritz, Klinker, Gudrun: Ludus magnus - a serious game for learning the Latin language. In: Fang, Xiaowen (ed.) HCII 2021. LNCS, vol. 12790, pp. 51–61. Springer, Cham (2021). https://doi.org/10.1007/978-3-030-77414-1_5
14. Plecher, D.A., Herber, F., Eichhorn, C., Pongratz, A., Tanson, G., Klinker, G.: Hieroquest-a serious game for learning Egyptian hieroglyphs. J. Comput. Cult. Heritage (JOCCH) 13(4), 1–20 (2020)
15. Plecher, D.A., Keil, L., Kost, G., Fiederling, M., Eichhorn, C., Klinker, G.: Exploring underwater archaeology findings with a diving simulator in virtual reality. Front. Virt. Real. 3 (2022). https://doi.org/10.3389/frvir.2022.901335, https://www.frontiersin.org/articles/10.3389/frvir.2022.901335
16. Plecher, D.A., Wandinger, M., Klinker, G.: Mixed reality for cultural heritage. In: 2019 IEEE Conference on Virtual Reality and 3D User Interfaces (VR), pp. 1618–1622. IEEE (2019)
17. Plecher, D.A., Wohlschlager, A., Eichhorn, C., Klinker, G.: Legionarius-beyond limes. In: Fang, X. (eds.) HCI in Games. HCII 2022. LNCS, vol. 13334, pp. 618–636. Springer, Cham (2022). https://doi.org/10.1007/978-3-031-05637-6_40
18. Plecher, D.A.: Impacts of Serious Games for Cultural Heritage. Dissertation, Technische Universität München, München (2021)
19. Sims, W.L.: Effects of attending an in-school opera performance on attitudes of fourth-, fifth-, and sixth-grade students. Bull. Council Res. Music Educ. 5–41 (1992)
20. Zentner, W., Würz, A.: Reclams Opern- und Operettenführer. Reclam (1988)

Prototyping Gamification Apps Using Board Games: A Case Study of Muscle Stretching App

Meng-Dar Shieh[1]([✉]), Yi-Lin Tsai[1], Fang-Chen Hsu[2], and Chih-Chieh Yang[2]

[1] National Cheng Kung University, Tainan 701, Taiwan ROC
mdshieh@gmail.com
[2] Southern Taiwan University of Science and Technology, Tainan 71005, Taiwan ROC

Abstract. This study uses a self-development gamified health-related app, "Work? Out!" as an example. To set up two experimental devices: the App prototype (Hi-Fi prototype) and the Board game prototype (Lo-Fi prototype), and to test them respectively. This research is intended to measure the differences between the two devices in game experience and the satisfaction of game elements. Also, it analyzes the demand attribute of the user to game elements, the optimal order of game elements, and the correspondence between game elements and game experience. The research results show that the "board game prototype" can help the "App prototype" usability test to verify the gamification strategy in the early stage of design. In the "game experience" measurement, the performance of the two groups was very similar, and there was no significant difference in the six measurement factors (P value > 0.05). "Game Element Satisfaction" shows that "App Prototype" is generally better than "Board Game Prototype". According to the Analysis of variance (ANOVA), only two game elements have significant differences, which need to be paid special attention to. Although there are obvious differences in the "demand attributes of game elements for users" and the " "optimized ranking of game elements", there is still a similarity of nearly 60%. This study found 6 elements with the same attributes in the two groups, which can be used for the optimization of "App Prototype".

Keywords: Gamification · Game Experience · Game Elements · Mobile Application · Board Game

1 Introduction

1.1 Construction of the Experimental Device

This research used a gamified health APP: gamified muscle soothing app named "Work? Out!" and was developed with the "coding prototype" and "board game prototype" set as experimental devices, which allow participants to operate and compare the game experience and game elements differences between two devices.

"Work? Out!" was divided into exercise and muscle soothing. Referring to the office workers' relaxing training designed by the Health Promotion Administration, Ministry

© The Author(s), under exclusive license to Springer Nature Switzerland AG 2023
X. Fang (Ed.): HCII 2023, LNCS 14046, pp. 370–385, 2023.
https://doi.org/10.1007/978-3-031-35930-9_25

of Health and Welfare from Taiwan, the primary users were office workers. The app provided users with goals, challenges, and missions (game elements of progression paths). Users will gain points after they achieve the aims and accomplish the final intent: exercise. In addition, other functions, including competition, ranking, and communication (social-related game elements) could support users to continue using the app to achieve their goals.

1.2 Background and Concept

Design Background. "Work? Out!" was designed for office workers who work for an extended period. According to the Health Promotion Administration, Ministry of Health and Welfare, sitting at work for over six hours a day can harm the body. Fixed postures can cause poor blood circulation and damage bones or muscles. Due to the symptoms from the long period of working and fixed postures, according to the Health Promotion Administration, Ministry of Health and Welfare, "Work? Out!" provided preventive exercise guidance for the following three symptoms: Carpal tunnel syndrome, Lateral Epicondylitis, neck and shoulder pain. These symptoms are chronic inflammation and cannot be cured easily. Nevertheless, prevention only requires regular relaxation and superficial muscle soothing exercises, which can be done effectively in a few steps. It is easy to forget to get up to rest and relax in a busy office. Therefore, gamification could increase users' motivation for soothing.

After the set goals and challenges have been achieved, users can get points or rewards. Although the app did not provide a complete game for playing, it used equivalent game elements to help users increase their engagement in things called gamification. The "Work? Out!" app provides users with exercise projects, users will be rewarded with local food recommendations after the users complete the exercise. The link with food could be a reminder when users are hungry or preparing to eat. Not only could it effectively remind users to work out, but the recommendation could offer users solutions since they generally had trouble deciding what to get for lunch and dinner. Therefore, this study believes that these themes combined with gamification could bring good user engagement for office workers.

Design Concepts. Design concepts of "Work? Out!" were from a few well-known apps in the market, such as FortuneCity, To-Do Adventure, Walkr, and Plant nanny. These apps conducted gamification to help users engage in goals, the games were not playable but added in game elements to attract users and they all belong to the cumulative achievement elements. Take FortuneCity and To-Do Adventure as examples, they both support users to track their finances or make a memorandum. In FortuneCity, users can get houses and build a city after accounting. In To-Do Adventure, users can collect island maps and develop their own islands. On the other hand, Walkr and Plant nanny are health-related apps. Walkr is a step counter app, users' spaceships in the app can go further to visit different planets if they walk more. Plant nanny is about drinking water, inspired by the connection that both human beings and plants need water. The plant will grow if the user drinks, adding feeding elements to the app.

The apps mentioned previously do not have an integral gaming environment, not even adding many gaming functions but just letting users gather accomplishments by simply achieving daily goals. The app "Work? Out!" was designed under this concept, to connect office health gamification with daily delicious food.

Game Elements and Mechanism. "Work? Out!" design referred to thirteen game elements that are commonly used in health apps from the research of Neupane et al. (2021), displayed as follows: Social influences, Challenges, Competition, Real-life Incentives, Goals, High scores, Narrative, Plot, Unlockable content, Points, Levels, Badges and Collaboration. This study did not apply to all of the items, but a few indicated more importance in the research of Neupane et al. (2021): goals, challenges, social influences, competition, and real-life incentives. Badges and real-life incentives were examined as the most favorable items. The least favored plot and collaboration will not be included in this research.

Even though a few items were excluded, too many game elements existed simultaneously, as the seven-game elements in a project would be considered too many (Neupane et al. 2021). Therefore, this study made some adjustments to the game elements to match the game mechanics. High scores merged with points, levels with badges, and real-life incentives with narrative. In this case, the researchers did not remove any elements but combined them into the same single item. For instance, real-life incentives are included in unlock-required items or badges with level mechanisms. On one hand, the competition element from different points of view from several studies. Some believe that the competition element can be used to drive users into more intention (Sepehr and Head 2013; Mokadam et al. 2015), but others think it might decrease users' engagement (Goh and Razikin, 2015; Morschheuser et al., 2019). Thus, the rank element will replace

Table 1. Work? Out! Game elements

13 commonly used game elements	Game elements applied in Work? Out!
Goals	Emerged into goals
Challenges	
Competition	Replaced by rank
Social Influences	Communicate
Points	Emerged into points
High Scores	
Unlockable Content	Emerged into real-life incentives
Real-life Incentives	
Narrative	
Levels	Emerged into badges
Badges	
Plot	Excluded
Collaboration	Excluded

competition as a more indirect contest. Finally, challenges will emerge with goals in this study due to the lower difficulty of exercise in the app (Table 1).

The explanations of game mechanics and game elements are as follows. Game elements are in the brackets: "Work? Out!" provides users with soothing exercise tasks (missions) and after users finish the exercise (goals) they will gain points (points). Points can be exchanged for prizes (unlockable content) and rewards (real-life incentives). The prizes allow users to build restaurants on the gaming map and reward them with the recommendation of local food that is close to reality incentives. Rewards that were accumulated on the map provided users with accomplishment (achievement). When users achieve a certain number of goals, users can get badges (badges and levels). Users can also check friends' gaming maps and rankings (social influences and rank). The overall game elements boost users' engagement with goals.

Gamification Motivations and Theories: The Gamification Octalysis theory was proposed by Chou (2019) and published in the book: Actionable Gamification: Beyond Points, Badges, and Leaderboard. Gamification design extracts the interesting elements in a game to motivate users' intentions toward goals. Chou (2019) believes that motivation is required before action. Octalysis theory described the eight core motivations and was all categorized from several pieces of research about games. The Octalysis theory could be the framework of gamification, Table 2 displays the description of the Octalysis theory for gamification.

Table 2. The Gamification Octalysis theory (Chou 2019)

Core motivations	Descriptions
Epic Meaning & Calling	Make users feel obligated to accomplish a mission, thereby attracting long-term commitment
Development & Accomplishment	Give users a sense of progress, such as scores, badges, and rankings
Empowerment of Creative thinking & Feedback	Allow users to create their elements in the process of using the product
Ownership & Possession	Users are driven by something and have a desire to "improve" and "get more"
Social Influence & Relatedness	Allow users to have a sense of belonging, friends, or team mechanism so that they feel close to other users, which makes them more difficult to leave
Scarcity & Impatience	You might often feel that something is not easy to get in life, but it will stimulate the motivation to fight for it

(continued)

Table 2. (*continued*)

Core motivations	Descriptions
Unpredictability & Curiosity	People are curious and want to know things they do not understand, which people cannot stop thinking about because they are unpredictable
Loss & Avoidance	This comes from our fear of loss, in which anxiety is a higher motivation than the pursuit of profit

2   Research Procedures

This study sets up a self-developed gamified health app, "Work! Out?" as an example, which includes the coding prototype "Work! Out? -APP" and the board game prototype "Work! Out? -Board game (BG)" experimental devices. There are three sessions, as follows.

Session One: Experiment Design

At this stage, the experiments were designed into two groups: APP and BG. Participants were recruited to perform the experiments. Participants operated the experimental devices "Work? Out! -APP" and "Work? Out! -Board game" respectively and filled out the questionnaire after the experiments. Finally, the game experience, game element satisfaction, and system usability of the two experimental devices are measured.

Session Two: Data Analysis

At this stage, the two groups of experimental data were analyzed for basic data statistics, game experience analysis, game element satisfaction analysis, system usability scoring, and correlation analysis between the game experience and game elements.

Session Three: Results and Discussion

Based on the data results in the second stage and the assumptions in the literature review, the research discussed and verified whether the board game prototype can help the usability test in the gamified app. Ultimately, it can prove gamification strategies and optimization recommendations at an earlier stage.

2.1   APP Group Experiment

APP group operated "Work? Out! -APP" (website app) through computers, tablets, and mobile phones. The experiment was conducted online, and the participant's willingness to experiment increased through the online method. The moderated remote usability test proposed by Sherwin et al. (2022) mainly used Google meet to call and screen share (Fig. 1 and Fig. 2). The researcher could directly guide the participant and see the real-time operation status of the participants in the "Work? Out! -APP" through screen sharing. The operating carrier was mainly a computer for the experiment's consistency and the experimental device's optimization and integrity.

Experiment Process. The first stage was to contact the participant in Google meet, introduce the "Work? Out! -APP", and explain the experiment. The second stage was to describe the experimental task and inform the game content. The third stage was to carry out the practical tasks and the participants operated according to the task contents. The fourth stage was to conduct the survey. After the experiment was completed, a questionnaire was given which mainly included game experience, game element satisfaction, and system usability. The APP Group Experiment Process.

1. Open the Google Meet conference room to contact the respondents, explain the experiment, and confirm that the respondents have the experimental equipment (computers) and that the environment is not disturbed.
2. Give the "Work? Out! -APP" URL link, briefly introduce it to the subjects. Ask them to open the URL link and share the screen to confirm that the "Work? Out! -APP" is running without errors on the subject's side.
3. The participants were given time to explore "Work? Out!-APP" freely. The researchers observed the participants' operations at the same time. The experiment adopted the method of thinking aloud, in which the subjects could share ideas or ask questions at any time.
4. Make sure that the participants are familiar with the interface, informed about the experiment tasks, and start operating the APP as soon as the participants understand the entire process.
5. Observe the participants to achieve tasks and interface operations. Record the issues that the participants face.
6. After finishing the tasks, the subjects were asked whether they wanted to continue using the "Work? Out! -APP". If the participant refused, the experiment was concluded. The subjects were asked to fill out the questionnaire.

Missions

1. Conduct the three soothing exercises in "Work? Out! -APP". The order was not limited, but each item must be completed at least once. The points were rewarded after completion.
2. Spend the point on exchanging rewards (building a house) and feedback (food recommendations) in the APP game.
3. Confirm viewing badges and rankings (other participants' results).

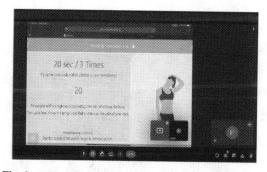

Fig. 1. APP group experiments (exercise circumstances)

Fig. 2. APP group experiments (gaming circumstances)

2.2 BG Group Experiment

The operating device for the BG group was "Work? Out! -Board game". "Work? Out! -Board game" was a paper card board game, which required physical experiments. However, due to the severe epidemic COVID-19 at that time, it was difficult to recruit subjects. "Work? Out! -Board game" can be played by two to four players simultaneously. For consistency of the experiment, it was carried out by two participants in each experiment (Fig. 3 and Fig. 4).

Experiment Process. The first stage was to introduce "Work? Out! -Board game" and to explain the experiment. The second stage was to conduct the experiment, make sure the participants were prepared, then start. The researcher could observe the game status at this stage. The third stage was to conduct the survey. After a player won, the experiment ended and a questionnaire, which mainly included game experience, game element satisfaction, and system usability, was given.

The BG Group Experiment Process:

1. Introduce "Work? Out! -Board game" to two subjects, explain the mechanism and gameplay, and give a simple demonstration. Time was given for the participants to ask any questions.
2. After confirming that there were no problems with the test, let the two participants play the game.

Fig. 3. BG group experiment (exercise circumstances)

3. Observe and record the participants' interactions, questions, and thoughts during the game.
4. When one of them won, the game and the experiment were over. The questionnaire was filled out.

Fig. 4. BG group experiments (gaming circumstances)

3   Experiment Questionnaire

The questionnaire was divided into two versions, which were respectively applicable to the experiment APP and BG groups. The APP group was to operate "Work? Out! -APP" and the BG group was to operate "Work? Out! -Board game". The APP group questionnaire had four parts: the first part was the personal information, and the second part was the GAMEX game experience scale (a total of twenty-seven questions). The third part was the satisfaction questionnaire (eleven questions - positive and negative). The fourth part was the SUS usability scale (ten items).

The BG group questionnaire had only three parts: the first part was the personal information, the second part was the GAMEX game experience scale (a total of twenty-seven questions) and the third part was the satisfaction questionnaire (eleven questions - positive and negative). The BG group lacked the usability scale because "Work? Out! -Board game" was a board game and was not suitable for the system usability scale. Moreover, it would not be meaningful in terms of comparing their usability. The usability test of the APP group was only used to confirm that the user interface of "Work? Out! -APP" does not give too many negative experiences, which would affect the game experience. In addition, there was also an item difference in the element satisfaction part. "Work? Out! -APP" had a ranking element but no competition element. "Work? Out! -Board game" had competitive elements but no ranking elements. The differences between the two groups of questionnaires are compared in Table 3.

Table 3. Survey of two experiments

	APP	BG
Experimental device	"Work? Out! -APP"	"Work? Out! -Board game"
First stage	Personal details (3 items)	Personal details (3 items)
Second stage	GAMEX game experience scale (27 items)	GAMEX game experience scale (27 items)
Third stage	Satisfaction of game element surveys Difference "ranking" element (11 items, 22questions)	Satisfaction of game element surveys Difference "competition" element (11 items, 22 questions)
Fourth stage	SUS system usability test (10questions)	SUS system usability test (10 questions)

3.1 Descriptive Analysis

The experiments were separated into the APP group and BG group to employ. Due to the rising epidemic, the APP group designed the experiment to be conducted online after considering factors such as experimental needs and the recruitment of subjects. However, since online communication and guidance were still less clear than in-person, remote experiments were also time-consuming. Only thirty experiments were conducted, and thirty questionnaires were collected for analysis. Due to the paper nature of the board game, the BG group maintained physical activity. Two participants were required to join the experiment simultaneously, which led to difficulty in recruiting subjects during the epidemic. The physical experiment took a long time to collect but only returned fifteen surveys, which was only half of the APP group's. Although there was a significant difference between the two groups, the analysis was carried out on average or percentage. Statistical analysis was performed on a total of forty-five questionnaires.

The first part was the demographics, this section had a sample of forty-five surveys overall. Respectively, we collected thirty questionnaires from the APP group and fifteen questionnaires from the BG group for descriptive statistics. There were gender, age, and daily sedentary office hours. The statistical results of the APP group were summarized in Table 4 and the statistical results of the BG group were shown in Table 5.

There were thirty valid questionnaires in the APP group. The gender percentage was nearly equal between males and females, with sixteen females (53.5%) and fourteen males (46.7%). The age distribution was mostly between 20–24 years old (96.6%), followed by 25–29 years old (30%) and the least 30–39 years old with only about three percent in only one person.

The demographics also investigated the daily sedentary office hours of the respondents. According to the Ministry of Health and Welfare standards in Taiwan, more than six hours a day is considered sedentary for a long time, as 73% of the respondents in this study had more than six hours. More than eight hours accounted for 40%, six to eight hours accounted for 33.3%, followed by four to six hours was 20% and the rest were the lowest for two to four hours and under two hours accounted for 3.3%. Since the

Table 4. APP group demographics

APP			
Background		N (30)	%
Gender	male	14	46.7%
	female	16	53.3%
Age	20–24	20	66.6%
	25–29	9	30%
	35–39	1	3.3%
Sedentary time of office work	less than 2 h	1	3.3%
	2–4 h	1	3.3%
	4–6 h	6	20%
	6–8 h	10	33.3%
	more than 8 h	12	40%

experiment was based on the method of thinking aloud, several participants indicated in the experiment that the sedentary time in front of the computer even reached ten to twelve hours, which has far exceeded the health standard of 6 h by the Ministry of Health and Welfare. It was confirmed that 73.3% of the samples had a demand for the device, which was the target group set by the device.

Table 5. BG group demographics

BG			
Background		N (15)	%
Gender	male	7	46.7%
	female	8	53.3%
Age	20–24	11	73.3%
	25–29	4	26.6%
Sedentary time of office work	less than 2 h	0	0
	2–4 h	2	13.3%
	4–6 h	3	20%
	6–8 h	5	33.3%
	more than 8 h	6	40%

The BG group had fifteen valid surveys and the gender distribution was close to the balance between males and females, with eight females (63.3%) and seven males (46.7%). The age distribution was mostly 20–24 years old (73.3%) and the rest was 25–29 (26.6%).

The daily sedentary working time of the participants reached 73% in the BG group exceeded six hours, the distribution was at most 40% in eight hours or more, 33.3% in six to eight hours, followed by four to six hours in 20%, the minimum was two to four hours in 13.3% and there were no participants selecting for less than two hours. The distribution of daily sedentary working time in the APP group was similar to the BG group.

Table 6. Demographics comparison of two groups

Background		APP (N/%)				BG (N/%)			
Gender		male		female		male		female	
Age	20–24	9		11		4		7	
	25–29	5		4		3		1	
	35–39	0		1		0		0	
Sedentary time of office work	less than 2 h	0	0%	1	6.3%	0	0.0%	0	0.0%
	2–4 h	1	7.1%	0	0.0%	0	0.0%	1	12.5%
	4–6 h	3	21.4%	3	18.8%	1	14.3%	2	25.0%
	6–8 h	4	28.6%	6	37.5%	2	28.6%	3	37.5%
	more than 8 h	6	42.9%	5	31.3%	4	57.1%	2	25.0%

The comparison of basic information from the two groups is displayed in Table 6. The gender distribution of the APP and BG groups was close to the average. In terms of daily sedentary time, the highest percentage of males was "above eight hours", while the APP and BG groups were 42.9% and 57.1% respectively, followed by "six to eight hours" which both had 28.6%. For females, the highest rate was 37.5% for "six to eight hours", followed by "more than eight hours" with 31.3% and 25% separately. "Four to six hours" was about 14–25%, the rest two to four hours and under two hours were close to none.

In the sampling of this study, the results indicated that the sedentary time of males was higher than that of females. Most of the sedentary time of men was "above eight hours", while women were mainly "six to eight hours". However, the standard of the Ministry of Health and Welfare is six hours and both males and females exceeded close to 70%, which had little difference. The participants were all the target groups set by the experimental device in this study, but men might be the target group with higher usage needs.

3.2   Game Experience Analysis

The second session introduces the analysis results of the GAMEX game experience scale. In this section, the scores of the items in GAMEX were statistically analyzed to calculate the mean (M) and standard deviation (SD). Therefore, the six measurement items and the scores of each question were compared between the two groups in GAMEX. GAMEX is a game experience scale for gamification environments. This study conducted a seven-point Likert scale for scoring.

The Game Experience of the APP Group and the BG Group: In the GAMEX game experience, the measurement results of the six items were displayed in Table 7 and Fig. 5. In comparison, it indicated similar results in both the APP and BG groups in six factors (enjoyment, Absorption, Creative thinking, Activation, non-negativity, and autonomy). The detailed outcomes were illustrated in Table 7, the APP group results were on the left-hand side and the BG group results were on the right-hand side. The APP group gained higher scores in the former three items: enjoyment (M = 5.01; SD = 0.13; M = 4.70; SD = 0.21), Absorption (M = 4.12; SD = 0.06; M = 4.03; SD = 0.13), and Creative thinking (M = 4.78; SD = 0.21; M = 4.53; SD = 0.09). On the one hand, the BG group yielded higher scores in the latter three items: Activation (M = 3.54; SD = 0.22; M = 3.85; SD = 0.18), non-negativity (M = 1.78; SD = 0.18; M = 2.33; SD = 0.26) and autonomy (M = 4.17; SD = 0.21; M = 4.65; SD = 0.11). Although the BG group achieved a higher score in the non-negativity item, the APP group with low scores still performed better considering the question was described negatively.

Table 7. The game experience results of both groups

	APP		BG	
	M	SD	M	SD
Enjoyment	5.01	0.13	4.70	0.21
Absorption	4.12	0.06	4.03	0.13
Creative thinking	4.78	0.21	4.53	0.09
Activation	3.54	0.22	3.85	0.18
Absence of negative effect	1.78	0.18	2.33	0.26
Dominance	4.17	0.07	4.60	0.11
M=Mean ; SD= Standard Deviation				

ANOVA analysis was applied to examine whether the results had a significant difference in both APP and BG groups, due to the outcomes of the six items being alike. Firstly, the Levene variance equality test was applied to examine the differences between the two groups with no significant difference, indicating a homogeneity (P value > 0.05). After the homogeneity was confirmed, an ANOVA analysis was conducted and the results were illustrated in Table 8. Enjoyment (p = 0.30), Absorption (p = 0.85), Creative thinking (p = 0.44), Activation (p = 0.33), non-negativity (p = 0.08), and autonomy (p = 0.21)

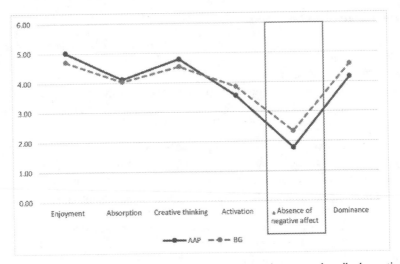

Fig. 5. Line chart comparison of both groups (Note: The questions were described negatively, in which the lower score performed better)

indicated no significant difference (p-value > 0.05). Therefore, it is important to note that the game experience in both the APP and BG groups was similar.

Table 8. Game experience ANOVA analysis results

ANOVA	Enjoyment	Absorption	Creative thinking	Activation	Absence of negative effect	Dominance
F	1.08	0.04	0.62	0.96	3.21	1.61
P Value	0.30	0.85	0.44	0.33	0.08	0.21

After the Levene variance equality test, the homogeneity was confirmed (p-value > 0.05)

The Scoring for Each Question in the Game Experience Scale: The results were displayed in Table 9 and illustrated line chart (Fig. 6) based on six factors. The report indicated that the questions that were significantly different between the two groups were: Enj6, Act2, ANA2, and ANA3. The scores in the bracket were displayed on the left-hand side belonging to the APP group and the right-hand side belonging to the BG group. Enj6 (M = 4.63; M = 3.53), Act2 (M = 2.20; M = 3.47), ANA2 (M = 1.50; M = 2.40) and ANA3 (M = 1.57; M = 2.40). Besides Enj6, the BG group scored higher in the other three questions.

Therefore, the applied ANOVA analysis was due to the different outcomes (see p-value in Fig. 6). Enj6 (p = 0.018), Act2 (p = 0.005), ANA2 (p = 0.008), and ANA3 (p = 0.032) were all lower than 0.05, which indicated that there were significant differences between the two groups in these four questions.

Table 9. The comprehensive results of the game experience for both groups

	Items	APP		BG		P Value
		M	SD	M	SD	
Enj1	Playing the game was fun.	4.97	1.30	5.13	0.99	0.665
Enj2	I liked playing the game.	5.23	1.19	5.40	1.24	0.665
Enj3	I enjoyed playing the game very much.	4.80	1.37	4.47	0.83	0.394
Enj4	My game experience was a pleasure.	5.27	1.23	5.13	1.36	0.742
Enj5	I think playing the game is very entertaining.	5.13	1.11	4.53	1.06	0.089
Enj6	I would play this game for its own sake, not only when asked to.	4.63	1.45	3.53	1.36	**0.018***
Ab1	Playing the game made me forget where I am.	4.03	1.59	4.07	1.75	0.949
Ab2	I forgot about my immediate surroundings while I played the game.	4.03	1.73	4.13	1.73	0.856
Ab3	After playing the game, I felt like coming back to the "real world" after a journey.	4.33	1.69	3.80	1.61	0.316
Ab4	Playing the game "got me away from it all."	4.13	1.70	3.87	1.64	0.618
Ab5	While playing the game, I was completely oblivious to everything around me.	3.97	1.71	3.67	1.40	0.560
Ab6	While playing the game, I lost track of time.	4.20	1.58	4.67	1.54	0.353
CT1	Playing the game sparked my imagination.	4.37	1.40	4.60	1.40	0.601
CT2	While playing the game, I felt creative.	4.87	1.33	4.27	1.44	0.172
CT3	While playing the game, I felt that I could explore things.	5.57	1.38	5.33	1.35	0.593
CT4	While playing the game, I felt adventurous.	4.33	1.79	3.93	1.22	0.441
Act1	While playing the game, I felt activated.	4.63	1.73	4.73	0.96	0.837
Act2	While playing the game, I felt jittery.	2.20	1.37	3.47	1.36	**0.005***
Act3	While playing the game, I felt frenzied.	3.00	1.84	3.07	1.28	0.901
Act4	While playing the game, I felt excited.	4.33	1.47	4.13	1.30	0.658
ANA1	While playing the game, I felt upset.	2.27	1.28	2.20	1.08	0.864
ANA2	While playing the game, I felt hostile.	1.50	0.97	2.40	1.12	**0.008***
ANA3	While playing the game, I felt frustrated.	1.57	0.97	2.40	1.55	**0.032***
Dom1	While playing the game, I felt dominant/I had the feeling of being in charge.	4.20	1.54	4.40	1.35	0.672
Dom2	While playing the game, I felt influential.	3.57	1.48	4.33	1.29	0.095
Dom3	While playing the game, I felt Dominance.	4.47	1.41	5.07	1.10	0.156
Dom4	While playing the game, I felt confident.	4.43	1.57	4.60	1.18	0.719

M=Mean; SD= Standard Deviation; ∗. P value > 0.05

After the Levene variance equality test, the homogeneity was confirmed (p-value> 0.05)

The four questions with significant differences were: "Enj6: I would play this game for its own sake, not only when being asked to.", "Act2: While playing the game I felt jittery.", "ANA2: While playing the game I felt hostile.", "ANA3: While playing the game I felt frustrated.".

Regarding the distinct query according to the description, this study assumed: Enj6 indicated that the gamification of the coding prototype was sufficiently complete and attractive to users, while the board game prototype was more similar to an exercise game; The remaining "Act2, ANA2, ANA3" were speculated to be the differences caused by the "competition" element of the BG group.

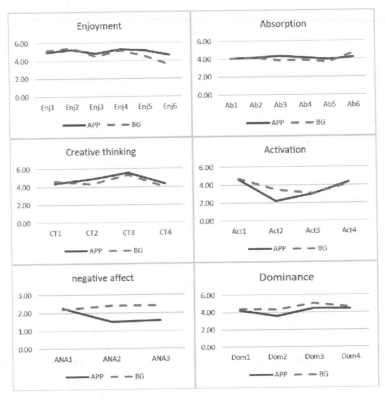

Fig. 6. Game experience detailed line charts

4 Conclusions

This study aimed to compare the game experience and satisfaction of game elements between a high-fidelity prototype (an app) and a low-fidelity prototype (a board game) of a self-development-gamified health app called "Work? Out!" The research found that using the board game prototype helped to test and verify the gamification strategy in the early stage of design. The performance of the two groups in terms of game experience was similar, but the app prototype was generally better in terms of game element satisfaction. The study identified two game elements with significant differences that need to be addressed. Although there were differences in the demand attributes of game elements and the optimized ranking of game elements, there were still similarities between the two groups, which can be used to optimize the app prototype.

References

Chou, Y.K.: Actionable gamification: Beyond points, badges, and leaderboards. Packt Publishing Ltd. (2019)

Goh, D.-L., Razikin, K.: Is gamification effective in motivating exercise? In: Kurosu, M. (ed.) HCI 2015. LNCS, vol. 9170, pp. 608–617. Springer, Cham (2015). https://doi.org/10.1007/978-3-319-20916-6_56

Mokadam, N.A., et al.: Gamification in thoracic surgical education: Using competition to fuel performance. J. Thorac. Cardiovasc. Surg. **150**(5), 1052–1058 (2015)

Morschheuser, B., Hamari, J., Maedche, A.: Cooperation or competition–when do people contribute more? A field experiment on gamification of crowdsourcing. Int. J. Hum Comput Stud. **127**, 7–24 (2019)

Neupane, A., Hansen, D., Fails, J.A., Sharma, A.: The role of steps and game elements in gamified fitness tracker apps: a systematic review. Multimodal Technol. Interact. **5**(2), 5 (2021)

Sepehr, S., Head, M.: Competition as an element of gamification for learning: an exploratory longitudinal investigation. In: Proceedings of the First International Conference on Gameful Design, Research, and Applications, pp. 2–9, October 2013

Sherwin, L.B., Yevu-Johnson, J., Matteson-Kome, M., Bechtold, M., Reeder, B.: Remote usability testing to facilitate the continuation of research. Stud. Health Technol. Inform. **290**, 424–427 (2022)

Empathy Game: Using the Game as SPRINT Warm-Up Process in a Cross-Disciplinary Team Co-creation

Chi-Chi Shih[✉], Teng-Wen Chang[✉], Shih-Ting Tsai[✉], Hsiang-Ting Chien[✉], Cheng-Chun Hong[✉], and Pei-Yun Wu[✉]

National Yunlin University of Science and Technology, Douliu 640, Yunlin, Taiwan (ROC)
{m11035005,tengwen,m11035001}@yuntech.edu.tw,
t10930002@gmail.com, gabrielchun336@gmail.com, luna.wpy@gmail.com

Abstract. This study explores the contextual practice of interdisciplinary teams (namely engineering and design) in the co-creation process. And based on the process of the SPRINT working method, the empathy game is developed as a mode of the warm-up game process. The empathy game combines the methods of the SPRINT project, team role theory, serious games, and interaction design. Through gamification and role-playing, participants can experience cross-disciplinary teams, perform SPRINT scenario simulations, and understand team communication, cooperation models, and their own roles. After preliminary research and iterative design, this study proposes six process steps of an empathy game, of which steps two to five are the four-stage framework of an empathy game. This research follows the method of research over the years and summarizes the CARE theory as the mechanism of the empathy game. In addition, this study discusses the use of digital accessibility in the analysis at the end of the thesis. To reduce the burden on personnel, the possibility of quickly generating different scenarios. Finally, a suggestion is put forward to consider the combination mode of digital assistance and sustainable development that can consider the background operation of personnel in the future. So as to expand and update the generation of inter-team situations. The results of this research will help improve the co-creation efficiency of cross-disciplinary teams, and in the future, more digital assistance methods can be explored through the remote assistance of the empathy game.

Keywords: SPRINT warm-up · Empathy game · Serious games · Cognitive psychology · Cross-field co-creation · Digital assistance

1 Introduction

In the project design, SPRINT is a method that is often used for cross-field co-creation. In SPRINT, it was discovered that engineers and designers would encounter problems in the co-creation process. Therefore, a series of warm-up procedures are needed to help them carry out SPRINT smoothly. We have gone through many experiments and workshops on the aforementioned topic and have produced a record of cross-field team co-creation. To iteratively analyze and plan the structure and actual measurement of such a warm-up process. A project using a game as mefaphr namely an "empathy game" is proposed. And the distal assistance for empathy game is discussed at the end of this paper, to discuss the method of digital assistance in the future [1, 2].

1.1 Cross-Disciplinary Team Communication

With the diverse problems of daily life and the schedule of modern society, when team members need to get along for a long time, they must consider and coordinate with each other in communication [3]. In time, a strategic approach is needed, such as the SPRINT five-day working method, to allow cross-disciplinary teams to effectively agree on a co-creation plan [4]. The development begins with the formation of cross-disciplinary (namely engineering and design) teams and a mutual understanding of the roles and situations of team members. Then discuss how to create together as a team. In team consensus and communication, the problem encountered is the formation of a cross-disciplinary team, which needs to be discussed and strengthened [5].

1.2 Cognition and Prerequisites Before Team Formation

Due to previous research and measurement, not all members of the cross-field team have participated in cross-field co-creation activities. It may also be unfamiliar with the ecology of other fields, which may cause team members to not know how to reach a consensus and understand each other. Therefore, before SPRINT and during the formation of the team, it is necessary to design a warm-up process to strengthen role-playing and promote empathy among team members. Through scenario simulation and logical reasoning stories, the chances for members to share and recognize each other can be improved, thereby promoting the cooperation of experts in the field of design and engineering [1, 2]. At the same time, in the empathy game, you can initially understand the thoughts of each team member through cognitive empathy, so as to deepen the tacit understanding of the team [6].

1.3 Empathy Game

The Empathy Game is a board game that enhances team formation across disciplines. It is the first day of the five-day sprint plan combined with the SPRINT method, and iteratively designed with the previous research method. Its process is divided into four game stages: (1) Ice Break stage: getting to know each other initially, associating activities, and bringing them into role-playing situations. (2) Divergent stage: practice association KJ method, logical reasoning, and mutual sharing. (3) Convergence stage: Try consensus cooperation, sharing ideas, and convergence. (4) Reflection stage: Through summarizing and sharing reviews, guide members to empathize, understand, and empathize [1].

1.4 Process Method

Paper's collaborative design tool can enhance the ideation in the user experience design process. Such as emphasizing the motivation and relevance of an idea, and keeping the focus on the purpose of the idea rather than practicality and solutions [7]. Reinforce the idea by creating something that the collaborators on the team want to do. And how, based on their common understanding, it can be confirmed whether what is already being done, it is possible to expand them to better practice planning [7]. Physical Computing and Embedded Development of computer-aided sensing technologies to sense and manage physical objects, as well as the environment. This expansion enables computing technology in a way that people can control virtual and physical objects through physical gestures or direct manipulation [3].

1.5 Summary

Cross-disciplinary co-creation in project design often uses the SPRINT method, but engineers and designers may encounter difficulties. Warm-up processes are necessary to help them conduct the SPRINT smoothly. We proposed the "Empathy Game," a card game to enhance team formation, and divided its process into four stages. Communication and coordination among team members are essential, and warm-up processes strengthen role-playing and promote empathy. We also discussed the use of paper-based collaborative design tools to enhance communication and understanding. A discussion of future digitally assisted methods of empathy games.

2   Literature Review

Based on the research process of the empathy game, this study proposes a digital assistance model for the cognitive empathy game and integrates the cooperation process of cross-disciplinary teams into the team formation stage. According to the methods and research questions described above. The relevant research can be divided into SPRINT five-day work sprint method, promoting team formation warm-up, recognizing team roles, serious games, and interactive design concepts to develop the empathy game, and interactive design presentation.

2.1   Team Formation and Warm-Up Before SPRINT

When people in the design and engineering fields co-create, they will be exposed to background knowledge in different fields. Before reaching a consensus, they need to integrate knowledge in various fields and recognize the team's creative thinking methods to quickly focus on solutions. So, we integrated and applied the idea and method of Sprint working method created by Google. With the five-day planning on the first day of Monday mode, from the first meeting of the members to set the team's project goals as the warm-up content. And from the previous research, six major process steps have been sorted out, of which the second to fifth steps are the four-stage activity mechanism of the empathy game [1, 2, 4].

2.2 Recognize Interdisciplinary Team Roles

The purpose of this study is to assist participants in their self-awareness, the context of their roles, and getting to know other members of the team. Therefore, joining the Belbin team role theory, participants are asked to recognize the habits of the role during the pre-work. The theory is divided into three categories, subdivided into nine roles, such as action orientation: shaper, performer, and completer. Strategic orientation: innovator, inspector, expert. And Interpersonal Orientation: Coordinator, Team Worker, Resource Investigator [8].

2.3 Serious Game Concept

Serious games are a classification guide composed of three standards: G/P/S, which are used to understand the impact of gameplay and the tolerance of variable space. They are G: Gameplay, which provides information about fun dimensions. P: Purpose, provides information about the function. S: sector (market, age...), the test informs the designer of the public market [9]. Empathy game research, the process steps of the actual measurement framework, will add the first and last stages of the empathy game stage to the preparation and compilation of game stage data respectively. And become the six major processes of the cross-disciplinary team formation workshop: (1) Pre-work, (2) Ice Break stage, (3) Divergent stage, (4) Convergence stage, (5) Reflection stage, (6) Assess/collect data [1].

2.4 Presentation and Method of Interaction Design

The core activity of a collaborative tool, based is on the collective creation of designers and those with no design training. Collaborate during the design development process, from the pre-design phase (determining the scope of the problem) to the post-design phase [7]. Preliminary simple exercises with the concept of the KJ method. This method analyzes the interaction, relevance, and consensus between text fragments in a chaotic state conducts prototype testing, and records feedback and ideas [10] In the perception environment, the presentation and collection of data can be divided into physical and virtual interaction methods, which help computers better understand the needs of users and give users more appropriate feedback [3].

2.5 Summary

After discussing the SPRINT five-day sprint work method in the literature, we assist members who cross fields for the first time, have opportunities to recognize cross-field teamwork before co-creation, design team formation, and warm up the game structure. Based on the role orientation of Belbin's team role theory, it assists members in recognizing roles and brings them into the context of playing. Serious games, interactive design research concepts, and methods learn about empathy game research presentation methods.

3   Research Design and Process

Based on the actual test of the physical board game version of the empathy game, this research collects all the process records from the production of the empathy game to the pre-test, post-test, and feedback of the experience. And briefly discusses the project of the digital assistance mode. The empathy game is to achieve team formation and warm-up cognition before SPRINT. Through preliminary research, use workshop experience observation, iteratively design game structure, content, process, and logical reasoning story, and obtain the process of four-stage activities. To optimize the smoothness of the execution context, apply the basis of the previous version, analyze the content that can be strengthened, or added or subtracted in the next version, and then add the pre-work and assess/collect data before and after. Using this method to continuously adjust the empathy game has become the basis for building the framework of this research.

3.1   Workshop Structure and Process Steps

From the previous empathy game test, the integrated analysis of participatory workshops looks for the digital assistance model of the empathy game research process and divides the workshop process of empathy game experience into the following six process steps and purposes, such as (Fig. 1). (1) Pre-work: Ask each participant to recognize the role of the team, choose a role that is similar to themselves, and group them roughly in a way that each group has a different role. (2) Ice Break stage: With the help of questions and examples, participants organize their situations and share them in the group to generate cognitive empathy. (3) Divergent stage: Apply tasks to practice thinking and KJ, promote team discussions, and share any situations that will happen in your field. This way, we can obtain clues and answers after improving our understanding of each other's domain situations. (4) Convergence stage: The tasks extended from the previous stage allow the team to create ideas and converge together, and repeatedly practice the team's co-creation and summary of solutions to problems. (5) Reflection stage: Each team group presents the plan, reviews the experience of team members getting along,

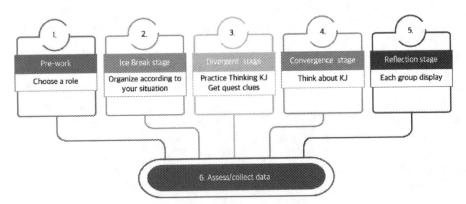

Fig. 1. Empathy game research framework

and looks forward to the possibility of co-creation in the future. (6) Assess/collect data: records and integrates all processes, and can be further improved.

3.2 Research Methods

The empathy game mechanism of this study follows the research framework over the years, from which the CARE theoretical framework is compiled to construct the overall framework steps and game mechanism of empathy game research, as shown in (Fig. 2). They are step 1. Consensus: from the initial acquaintance and conversation, a method of generating associations and consensus in different fields (engineering and design). Assist cross-disciplinary team members to more quickly associate perspectives from different fields when communicating. Step 2. Appreciation: Understand the habits and cooperation modes of cross-disciplinary team members, use creative ideas and activities, and increase conversations among members. This is used to simulate cross-field cooperation, possible problems, and situations where knowledge in different fields occurs. Step 3. Reflection: From the previous step, recognize the situation created by the empathy team, and perform a simulated situation and role-playing again. During the experience process, think repeatedly and find your position in the team. Step 4. Envision: review the overall prior experience, obtain the formation of cross-disciplinary teams, and warm up before the Sprint working method. And look for partners who can create together in the future, and understand your team roles and goals.

Fig. 2. Integrating the theoretical framework of CARE

3.3 Empathy Game Construction

The CARE theory that has been researched and integrated over the years is used as a framework for experimental planning, analyzing the four stages of the empathy game, and adjusting individual items that need to be achieved to find out the mode of digital assistance. The content below is the purpose list that will be carried out at this stage, such as (Fig. 3), which are:

(A) Ice Break stage (Communicate): (1) Review the role positioning of cognitive inter-disciplinary teams. (2) The members recall and associate with each other, and the situational content is in line with their roles and fields. (3) Share the nature of roles similar to yourself, so that team members can have a preliminary understanding and topics.
(B) Divergent stage (Empathy): (1) Use questions to guide team members to discuss and work together to complete tasks. (2) Use logic to deduce the story and bring KJ into the situation. (3) Find keywords and answers from segmented stories and tasks to share anything in your field.
(C) Convergence stage (cognition): (1) After obtaining the answer, reveal the next story and topic. (2) Promote team co-creation through extended tasks, and practice KJ for team creativity. (3) When a consensus solution is reached, members are invited to organize the process into a short briefing according to the specification.
(D) Reflection stage (partnership): (1) Teams share solutions. (2) According to the sharing of each team, ask the team to deliberate on the story sequence tasks, and imagine any moment when the team discovers and solves the problem. (3) Review the teamwork process and confirm your role positioning, partners, and goals.

Fig. 3. Plan base game flow

3.4 Empathy Game Interaction Scenarios

In the actual measurement, the content of the above-mentioned columns will be disassembled into screen presentations, and the experience will be guided to operate with pictures or text, to facilitate the understanding of the task content of this stage, such as (Fig. 4). Picture (A) is the Ice Break stage in the empathy game. Team members are sorting out the most frequently used software and tools by recalling their daily life or field. While (B) is the Divergent stage, team members discuss the keywords related to the answers in the logical reasoning stories during the thinking and sharing tasks, and get more insights after telling anything related to their field. Keywords. Based on the actual measurement results of about 30 people, the iterative analysis of the entire research process, content, steps, assistant operation, and game activity stage design is carried out, and the digital auxiliary structure is planned.

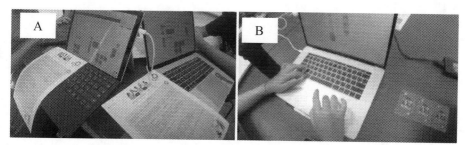

Fig. 4. Empathy game experiment process (A) Ice Break stage, (B) Divergent stage

3.5 Summary

After integrating the CARE theory mentioned in previous studies and the framework of the empathy game relationship method, plan the content of the empathy game test. Combining the user experience of the previous test records and the process of interactive design, a cross-domain cooperative empathy game is proposed, and the possibility of cardboard games and digital assistance integration is explored. And test and analyze the empathy game framework, discuss different technology-oriented solutions, and find out the strategy model that may be more suitable for making digital assistance.

4 Analysis and Discussion

This research builds and integrates to promote the formation of cross-domain teams, and the empathy game of the warm-up game version before Sprint discusses the implementation and testing methods of the digital assistance mode and divides the research analysis and discussion into Lessons learned and test analysis and discussion the proposed three items.

4.1   Lessons Learned

Based on the results of the physical board game workshop, the evaluation of the practical mechanism, and iterative design projects, such as (Table 1). It is expected that the content of manual operation will be added with some digital assistance functions. And make a more diverse and detailed planning of the workshop process steps, and adapt to the situation on the spot. For example, human error is caused by sending the wrong number of keyword cards during the activity stage, and the discussion time of the experiencers needs to be buffered.

Table 1. Brief description of the iterative thinking process

Iterative thought process/ Project Overview	Manual operation	Workshop conducted	Workshop process	Game mechanics
Iteration reason	Time-consuming operation	Personnel execution accident	Consider on-the-spot factors	Not suitable for digital assistance
Reserved Part Game	Process framework	Process/Card	Process/Workshop Framework	Structure/Meaning
Update section	System assistance	Digital mechanism	Process details	digital assistance

4.2   Analysis of Test Experience

Based on sharing stories and exchanges, initially introduce a problem-oriented approach, collect more experiencers and their situations, and create a sustainable situation that enhances consensus with planning, and sets up key points of digitally assisted empathy game mechanisms. The purpose of digital assistance is to (1) reduce the burden of research and staff: manpower, mistakes, time, front-end and back-end operation pressure, and data induction status. Emphasis will also be placed on (2) material from experiencers: Let the experiencer create elements in the game, the possibility of expanding and updating inter-team situations while avoiding the problems found after the experiment and the research process. For example: when people who have experienced it need to cooperate with different people again, they may encounter the same situation in the story stage, and they need to think about whether it is the first experience. Therefore, it is necessary to approach the way of sustainable generation of situations, to study the flexibility that may be suitable for the actual structure of digitally assisted board games, and to discuss records of alternatives and plans.

4.3 Proposals for Discussion

After discussion and analysis, given the direction of research that can be considered in the future, assistant personnel can be selected to perform empathy game and do back-end operations. Or when the participants experience the empathy game, the four-stage assessment is used to explore. List six major process steps: (1) Pre-work: Allow participants to input role and field information to assist each group with a digital system grouped by different roles. (2) Ice Break stage: Assist participants in different fields to organize and create their derivative situations. (3) Divergent stage: build a database based on the original stories and image cards (choose one), and derive more different story images, keywords, or answers. (4) Convergence stage: According to the generated stories, keywords, or answers, relevant topics are extended. (5) Reflection stage: A digital auxiliary tool for recording creative ideas or providing team-sharing solutions. (6) Assess/collect data: digitally assisted to record data at different stages.

5 Conclusion

After empathy game research, use the characteristics of the Monday team forming in the SPRINT method to plan the warm-up content before SPRINT. Apply serious games and interactive design to allow participants to experience gamification to recognize cross-disciplinary team members' roles and cooperation status. Analyze and discuss the feedback from the actual measurement, and construct a digitally assisted model of cross-domain team cognition, to explore the ways of different simulated situations. As well as the direction of future research planning, it can be considered to assist researchers in the operation of the process and quickly generate scenarios for multiple experiencers.

References

1. Shih, C.-C., et al.: Developing an empathy game for cross-disciplinary cooperation. In: Book Developing an Empathy Game for Cross-Disciplinary Cooperation. ICTIK & DMD, pp. 893–902 (2022)
2. Wu, P.-Y., Chang, T.-W., Hung, C.-C.: T-game: a team formation game for enhancing cross-disciplinary cooperation. In: Zaphiris, P., Ioannou, A. (eds.) Learning and Collaboration Technologies. Novel Technological Environments. HCII 2022. LNCS, vol. 13329, pp. 287–300. Springer, Cham (2022). https://doi.org/10.1007/978-3-031-05675-8_22
3. Yu, G.-J., Chang, T.-W., and Wang, Y.-C.: SAM: a spatial interactive platform for studying family communication problem. In: Salvendy, G., Smith, M.J. (eds.) Human Interface 2011. LNCS, vol. 6772, pp. 207–216. Springer, Heidelberg (2011). https://doi.org/10.1007/978-3-642-21669-5_25
4. Knapp, J., Zeratsky, J., Kowitz, B.: Sprint: How to solve big problems and test new ideas in just five days. Simon and Schuster (2016)
5. Fraser, K.: Labour flexibility: impact of functional and localised strategies on team-based product manufacturing. CoDesign 5(3), 143–158 (2009)
6. Hogan, R.: Development of an empathy scale. J. Consult. Clin. Psychol. 33(3), 307 (1969)
7. Olesen, A.R., Holdgaard, N., Løvlie, A.S.: Co-designing a co-design tool to strengthen ideation in digital experience design at museums. CoDesign 1–16 (2020)
8. Belbin, M.: Belbin team roles. Book Belbin Team Roles (2004)

9. Alvarez, J., Djaouti, D.: An introduction to Serious game Definitions and concepts. Serious Games Simul. Risks Manage. **11**(1), 11–15 (2011)
10. Scupin, R.: The KJ method: a technique for analyzing data derived from Japanese ethnology. Hum. Organ. **56**(2), 233–237 (1997)

Research on the Design of Gamified Cervical Spine Exercise APP Based on Octalysis

Qin Yang, Hong Chen(✉), and Xiaoran Zhao

East China University of Science and Technology, No.130 Meilong Road, Shanghai, China
{y81210094,zhaoxiaoran}@mail.ecust.edu.cn, engoy2008@163.com

Abstract. Currently, cervical spine subhealth and even cervical spondylosis are common among young people represented by college students and young white-collar workers, bringing problems to their lives. Current methods to effectively alleviate cervical spine problems focus on exercise, but simple cervical spine exercise is monotonous and boring cannot meet the emotional needs of this group and is less sustainable. The development of mobile application technology and gamification design thinking has created new avenues for cervical spine exercise. Octalysis is a reliable tool for analyzing user behavior drivers in gamification design. This study combines it with player types and different stages of exercise to produce a gamification driver model by summarizing different user types and refining the motivation and needs of each type in the exercise experience, with the aim of improving user experience and making cervical exercise sustainable. Finally, the validity of the model is proved through prototype testing, which provides a reference for the gamification design of sports exercise APP.

Keywords: Gamification design · Octalysis · Mobile application design · Cervical spine exercise

1 Introduction

Cervical spondylosis is a degenerative change of the cervical disc tissue and its secondary pathological changes involving the surrounding tissue structures (nerve roots, spinal cord, carotid artery, sympathetic nerves, etc.) with corresponding clinical manifestations, and is considered to be more common in the middle-aged and elderly population [1]. However, with the increasing pressure of study, further education, employment and work, the lifestyle of young people represented by college students and young white-collar workers has changed, and the bad habits of life, study and work have led to different degrees of injury to the cervical spine of most young people, and the incidence of their cervical spondylosis is increasing. Xie Weixin et al. showed that the prevalence of cervical spine subhealth was as high as 82.3% among the 1397 college students they surveyed [2]. Thse findings of Luo Xiao Yu et al. showed that the incidence of cervical spine subhealth among 958 college students reached 76.2% [3]. The findings of Wu Ji et al. showed that 80% of college students were in a cervical spine subhealth state [4]. The findings of Xu Jie et al. showed that the incidence of cervical spine subhealth among

X. Fang (Ed.): HCII 2023, LNCS 14046, pp. 397–411, 2023.
https://doi.org/10.1007/978-3-031-35930-9_27

966 college students was 66.15% [5]. In addition, according to statistics, the proportion of cervical spine subhealth problems among young white-collar workers in offices is as high as 80% [6]. It is found that most young people are in cervical spine subhesssalth, cervical spine subhealth is not a pathological disease, but will cause symptoms such as neck muscle pain, if timely conditioning and intervention, the body can recover from cervical spine subhealth to a healthy state; on the contrary, it will gradually develop from cervical spine subhealth into cervical spondylosis, affecting its learning, work and quality of life. Current methods to effectively alleviate cervical spine problems focus on exercise, but the youth population's apparent lack of concern for their own health, awareness of disease prevention and care, and self-control, combined with heavy school and workloads, make it difficult for this group to get moderate exercise for the cervical spine and its surrounding muscles. In addition, simple cervical spine exercise is monotonous, does not meet the emotional needs of the youth population, and is less sustainable. At present, the development of mobile application technology has brought great convenience to our life, and also created new ways for sports exercise, especially the gamification thinking and elements are more in line with the preferences of young people, more able to stimulate the group and meet their psychological motivation and needs, for example, Keep, Vitality Street and other sports exercise APP can provide users with fun sports exercise, improve user experience and product user stickiness. The purpose of this study is to explore the design ideas and methods of a gamified cervical spine exercise APP for the youth population in order to alleviate the cervical spine subhealth problems of this group. To this end, it is necessary to focus on the psychological motivation and needs of the youth population in terms of exercise and exercise, so as to develop a more driving design strategy.

2   Gamification in Cervical Exercise APP

2.1 Gamification Design

In 2002, Nick Pelling coined the term "gamification", and around 2010, the idea of using gamification design thinking to improve the Internet product experience became popular. The essence of gamification design is "human-centered design", which means that in a non-game context, gamification thinking and interesting design elements are used to motivate users' behavior and meet their psychological motivation and needs [7]. After the concept of gamification was created, scholars at home and abroad have studied the ideas and methods of its application, for example, Yu-kai Chou [8] proposed the important theory of gamification motivation "Octagonal Behavior Analysis" and systematically developed gamification-driven strategies, which enriched the underlying logic theory of gamification design; Jane [9] proposed the four most important features of gamification design: task goals, participation planning, feedback system and voluntary participation, and introduced the basic methods of gamification design in the book "Games Change the World"; Werbach and Hunter [10] proposed a list of gamification elements and recommended steps; Kumar [11] proposed 5 stages of user-centered gamification design. Although the entry points differ among different scholars, they all revolve around the core of how to make gamification more meaningful, that is, through the way of games, using effective heart guidance and hints, appropriate reward and punishment mechanisms, on the basis of reducing users' negative emotions, using positive emotions such as the sense of achievement and honor of completing game tasks to continuously trigger users' emotional points in order to enhance product stickiness.

2.2 Analysis of the Characteristics of Cervical Spine Exercise APP

Cervical spine problems and their relief fall under the category of fitness and health, so they can be analyzed at three levels: same products, relevant products, and industry products. Based on these three levels, keywords such as "cervical spine", "fitness" and "health" were searched in APP Store and major mobile application markets, and representative products such as "Hello, Cervical Spine", "Moji Fight", "Fitness Ring Adventure", "Vitality Street", "Keep" and "Dr. Ding Xiang" were obtained, and their comparative analysis is shown in Fig. 1. The study found that there are too few similar products for cervical spine problems and the experience is poor; while the gamification design of related products has a good user experience and is more attractive to the youth crowd, but focuses too much on entertainment and lacks professionalism; the industry products are more professional and have medical services, but the content is relatively complicated and poorly targeted. On the whole, there is no more suitable cervical exercise APP in the market, and the unreasonable use of gamification design has also reduced the application of some APPs. In his research, Bai Nan pointed out three reasons for this phenomenon: firstly, the segmentation and positioning of target users are not clear enough, resulting in homogenization of functions and lack of targeted and personalized functions; secondly, most APPs only apply the superficial mechanism of gamification, mainly in the form of point system, rewards and punishments (medals, leaderboards), which are limited to rewards and punishments, ignoring the original purpose of the game; finally, the way to drive users' motivation to exercise is relatively simple, relying excessively on community interaction and tasks, etc. [12].

Products	Functions	diagnosis	planning	guidance	assessment	recording	gamification	reminding	interaction	shopping
Same Products	Hello,Cervical Vertebra	*	*	*	*			*		
	Moji Fight					*	*	*	*	
Relevant Products	Vitality Street			*			*		*	
	Fitness Ring Adventure			*	*		*	*	*	
Industry Products	Keep		*	*		*			*	*
	Clove Doctors	*	*	*	*		*	*		

Fig. 1. Analysis of cervical spine related products

The gamification design of sports exercise APP needs to be controlled within a reasonable range, to distinguish the difference between gamification elements and real games, the core of which is to meet users' needs and curiosity for emotional experience, and to make users have different degrees of emotional experience through interesting interface design, visual style, interaction mode and so on. For this reason, it is necessary to explore the user's driving factors and translate them into the gamification design to stimulate the multi-sensory experience of users, ultimately motivating user behavior and enhancing product stickiness.

3   User Behavior-Driven Analysis of Cervical Spine Exercise APP

3.1   Octalysis

Octalysis is a game attraction model proposed by Yu-kai Chou, in which he summarizes the eight core drivers of game players, which are meaning, accomplishment, empowerment, ownership, social influence, scarcity, unpredictability and avoidance, as shown in Fig. 2, the eight core drivers form the Octagonal Behavior Analysis framework. "Meaning" means that users believe that the meaning of what they do is more important than the thing itself, giving a sense of self-mission; "accomplishment" means the progress and new skills gained by users when they complete things; "empowerment" means providing creative channels for users to take initiative; "ownership" means users' ability to own and control things; "social influence" means users' interconnection with other users; "scarcity" means that some things can be owned by only some users; "unpredictability" means mobilizing users' curiosity by showing limited things; "avoidance" means showing the disadvantages of bad events, and users will choose to avoid losses [13]. Using octagonal behavior analysis method combined with different user types can propose gamification design strategies for different types of users.

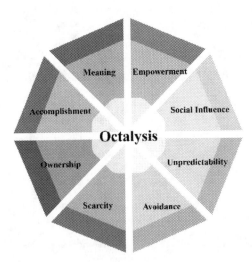

Fig. 2. The Octagonal Behavior Analysis Framework.

3.2 Types of Users of Cervical Exercise APP

In his article "Hearts, Clubs, Diamonds, Spades: MUD Gamer Types" Richard proposes four types of gamers: Achiever, Explorer, Socializer, and Killer. Achiever takes upgrading as the main goal of the game; explorer likes to explore the game, understand the game mechanics and teach others about the game; socializer uses the game as a platform to communicate and interact with other players to build relationships with each other; killer likes to attack other players with the goal of dominating the game and gaining inner satisfaction. Yu-kai Chou analyzes four player types by combining Octalysis: achiever is primarily influenced by "accomplishment" and "scarcity", followed by "ownership" and "empowerment"; explorer is primarily influenced by "unpredictability", followed by "accomplishment", "scarcity" and "empowerment"; socializer is primarily influenced by "social influence", followed by "ownership", "empowerment" and "unpredictability"; killer is mainly influenced by "accomplishment" and "social influence", followed by "empowerment", "ownership" and "avoidance" [14], and the player type analysis is shown in Fig. 3.

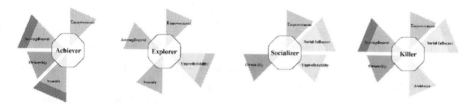

Fig. 3. Player Type Analysis Chart

Based on Richard's classification it is also possible to classify sportsmen into different types. In the process of exercise, there are active and passive sportsmen, active sportsmen are motivated by their own love for sports and exercise, while passive sportsmen are more inclined to accomplish a certain goal; at the same time, they can be divided into interactive sportsmen and action sportsmen, the former are more inclined to enjoy the fun of sports with others, while the latter are focused on their own sports and exercise. Therefore, the sportsmen are classified into four types corresponding to the game player types: relieving sportsmen, exploratory sportsmen, interactive sportsmen, and intensive sportsmen, and the analysis of sportsmen types is shown in Fig. 4.

For different types of exercisers, different behavioral drivers bring diverse game enjoyment, and fun is the aspect of game motivation that is of most concern. Relieving sportsmen are more focused on their state of health, exercising when their bodies need to be exercised or to relieve their mood; exploratory sportsmen who are willing to spend time learning and experiencing different sports and enjoying the fun things that happen during the different sports; interactive sportsmen like to exercise with others and build good social relationships and enjoy each other's company; intensive sportsmen, on the other hand, prioritize winning, and they enjoy more the sense of accomplishment that comes from working hard and being better than other athletes.

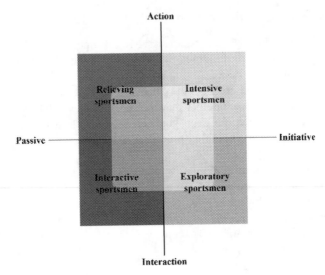

Fig. 4. Sportsmen Type Analysis Chart

3.3 Analysis of Driving Strategies for Different Types of Sportsmen

Human behavior is rooted in internal needs, and only when there are needs will internal motivation be generated, and then driven by internal motivation to take action. The research on the driving force of different types of users needs to capture their core needs and then guide their behavior.

Relieving sportsmen usually have set goals in the process of exercise, and they want to see their improvement after completing the goals, but their exercise is relatively passive, so there should be a function of plan reminder and testing in the cervical spine exercise APP to urge them to exercise according to the set goals on the one hand, and let them understand their condition more clearly through the testing function on the other. Exploratory sportsmen prefer to explore the unknown, and they enjoy the results after experiencing the unknown. Therefore, they need to design a continuous exploration mechanism and game scenarios in the APP to fully attract them. Interactive sportsmen are willing to spend time and effort to share their exercise experience with others and want to build social relationships, so social features and feedback mechanisms can meet their needs. Intensive sportsmen seek higher goals and achievements, they enjoy competition and challenges, and they care about their own achievements, so they need competition and reward mechanisms to motivate them constantly.

4   Cervical Spine Exercise APP Gamification Driven Model Construction

4.1 User Journey Analysis of Sports APP

Yu-kai Chou proposes four stages of the gamer journey based on Octalysis: Discovery (the reason why players want to experience the product), Onboarding (players begin to learn the product's features and operations), Scaffolding (the daily behaviors that players repeat to accomplish their goals), and Endgame (how the product retains its loyal users). At different stages, different core drivers are prioritized differently, and user behavior is influenced by both primary and secondary core drivers. In the discovery phase, users are mainly influenced by the core driver "unpredictability", followed by the core drivers "meaning", "accomplishment", "ownership" and "social influence", and are driven by curiosity to engage with the product, but do not interact with it deeply. The main core driver for users in the onboarding stage is "accomplishment" and the secondary core drivers are "empowerment", "social influence", "scarcity" and "unpredictability". Users in this stage have just started using the product, are capable of performing various tasks, have a strong curiosity about new things and can actively explore them, have a sense of accomplishment for the rewards they get, and will actively share them with the community. The main core drivers of users in the scaffolding phase are "social influence" and "scarcity", while the secondary core drivers are "empowerment", "ownership" and "avoidance". Users in this phase not only interact deeply with the product and have a strong sense of ownership, but also establish some kind of social relationship with other users, which can continue to motivate them to accomplish their goals. The main core driver of the endgame stage is "avoidance", and the secondary core drivers are "meaning", "empowerment", "ownership", "social influence" and "unpredictability". At this time, users will feel a certain dependence on the product, and if they stop using it, they will feel a loss, but the sense of mission and habit will lead them to continue using the product, and the sense of ownership of the product, the maintenance of social relationships and the desire for the unknown will also extend the product life cycle to a certain extent.

The user journey of a campaigner when using the APP consists of 3 phases: early, mid and late, which correspond to the 4 phases of the player's journey, putting the early-exercise in correspondence with the discovery phase, the mid-exercise in correspondence with the onboarding and scaffolding phase, and the late-exercise in correspondence with the endgame phase. Different core drivers need to be used in these 3 stages to motivate user behavior, and also need to combine the 4 types of sportsmen summarized in the previous article, and try to meet the needs of the 4 types of sportsmen in each stage of the user journey, so as to achieve the purpose of driving users.

4.2 Gamification-Driven Model for Cervical Spine Exercise APP

In the design process of cervical exercise APP gamification, targeted design strategies need to be proposed according to different stages of the user journey, while combining the primary and secondary core drivers with the inner needs and behavioral habits of different sportsmen types to jointly establish a gamification driving model.

In the early-exercise period, users lack trust and reliance on the product, and the product needs to get users' attention and attract them to gradually contact and use the product, so it needs to dig deeper into the users' target motivation. In the mid-exercise period, the product needs to give users a good experience, so that different types of users can enjoy it, so the product needs to have the behavioral motivation to let users repeat the experience, but also need to convey information to users, so that users understand their own cervical spine condition, in addition, also need a novel and interesting form of interaction in order to achieve emotional communication. In the later-exercise period, it is necessary to extend the life cycle of the product and to stimulate users' perception of the value of the product, so it is necessary to analyze the motivation of different types of sportsmen to use the product again, simulate the behavior of different types of campaigners, and obtain behavioral feedback.

So far, the gamification driving model of cervical exercise APP can be constructed by combining eight core drivers and four player types, as shown in Fig. 5.

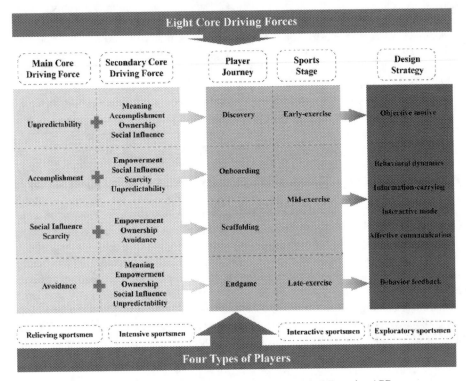

Fig. 5. The Gamification Driving model of Cervical Exercise APP.

5 Cervical Exercise APP Gamification Driven Model Specific Application

C-Rainbow is an APP based on this model, which is designed to help young people with cervical spine problems to alleviate and improve their cervical spine discomfort, and at the same time, based on 6 design strategies, the app can make different types of users feel fun during the exercise process, so that the cervical spine exercise can be persisted for a long time. The specific design strategy transformation process is as follows:

(1) Objective motive. According to the octagonal behavior analysis, the product needs to design different driving strategies for different user types, so the target motivation of the user needs to be mined. In this study, a number of questions were set for the 8

drivers, and the scores were set in the form of a Likert scale (1–5, with higher scores indicating more consistent with the description of the questions), which together formed a research questionnaire (Table 1), and 20 young college students and white-collar workers (10 male and 10 female) with different degrees of cervical spine problems were interviewed, and the 20 target users were classified according to the interview results (Fig. 6, the numbers represent the user's number). For the questionnaire content and different player types, different design ideas are proposed in this study. For relieving sportsmen, functions such as exercise reminder and cervical spine health detection are proposed; for intensive sportsmen, functions such as leaderboard and different difficulty challenges are proposed; for interactive sportsmen, functions such as virtual character interaction and sharing are proposed; for exploratory sportsmen, functions such as scene exploration are proposed.

Table 1. Driving Force Research Questionnaire

Driving Force	Questions
Meaning	You feel that cervical spine exercises are meaningful and necessary for you
Accomplishment	You will have a sense of accomplishment after completing your exercise workout
Ownership	You think a healthy cervical spine will bring you great benefits
Scarcity	You always have expectations in the process of exercise
Avoidance	You feel that if you don't exercise your cervical spine, it will worsen and haunt your life
Unpredictability	You are willing to try new ways in cervical spine exercise and feel that it will give you unexpected pleasure
Social Influence	You expect to participate with others or make certain connections with others during cervical spine exercises
Empowerment	Do you think the freedom and convenience of the cervical spine exercise methods or scenarios, etc. are important to the exercise process?

(2) Behavioral dynamics. From the previous research on the existing cervical spine exercise APPs in the market, it is clear that the key points to attract users of this type of APP are user experience, professionalism and relevance. In terms of user experience, this study focuses on reducing the tedium in simple cervical exercise through an interesting gamification format. A complete cervical spine exercise system should include the detection and evaluation of the health status of the cervical spine and the reasonable design of exercise movements. In the detection of cervical spine health status, we introduced the NPQ pain scale, which is an internationally popular questionnaire for diagnosing cervical spine problems. After the user completes the questionnaire, the system will give the corresponding cervical spine health score according to the content filled in, and give targeted exercising advice and medical advice. In terms of the rationality of exercise movements, we designed the product based on the six standard movements of cervical spine exercise, transformed them into game movements, as shown in Fig. 7,

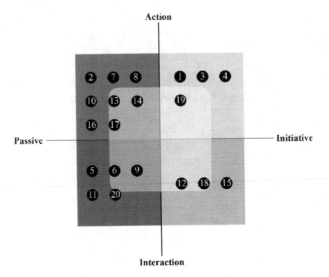

Fig. 6. Classification of research users

and gave guidance on the movements when the user first applied the product. Through the above design ideas, users can be motivated to continue using the product when they are exposed to it.

Fig. 7. Movement Design

(3) Information-carrying. In terms of information transfer, we divided into two parts: information transfer between users and products and information transfer between users and users. First of all, in terms of users and products, in addition to the above-mentioned testing and evaluation functions, we also designed testing records and reminder functions, testing records can convey to the user the stage of cervical spine health status, reminder functions are mainly alarm clocks and desktop widgets, the application of the driver "avoidance" and in the form of status bars designed to motivate users to exercise, as

shown in Fig. 8. In terms of users and users, the leaderboard and sharing functions are designed to motivate users through the drivers "accomplishment" and "social influence", as shown in Fig. 9.

Fig. 8. Desktop Widget Design

Fig. 9. Leaderboard

(4) Interactive mode. In the form of interaction we use technologies such as face recognition and motion capture to achieve real-time feedback of the action, which is also the main aspect of the gamification design of this product. We want users to have more fun when interacting with the avatars they create. In addition, other visual and auditory interactions are also designed in this study. In the visual aspect, it is mainly the color design, we associate the 7 joints of the cervical spine to the 7 colors of the rainbow, so the 7 colors are given different layers and combined with the progress of

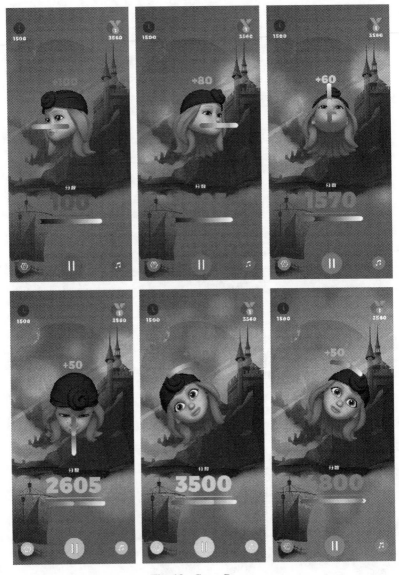

Fig. 10. Game Process

the game and other elements that can represent the degree of development of things, the user can understand their state according to the color change. In addition, we use the illustrator's beautiful design as the scene of the game, as the player score higher and higher, the scene will gradually reveal its original color, at the end of the game, the user can download and save it, we hope that through the drive "accomplishment" and "scarcity" users can get the complete scene picture through their own efforts, and take it as an honor. On the auditory side, we matched different music according to different scenes to try to immerse users in the game scenes (Fig. 10).

(5) Affective communication. Affective communication is the key to enhance the user stickiness of the product, and is the goal we are pursuing. In addition to some of the above design ideas, we also did other research. The first is the function of virtual image, users can create characters according to their own preferences, the virtual character will reproduce the user's movements and expressions in real time during the game, and the length of the user's exercise will also affect the state of the virtual character, through this way we hope to make some kind of emotional connection between the user and the virtual character, rather than simply using the product. Secondly, we also designed the backstory for the game scenes, each of which had a "haze" that the user could dispel by exercising to save each scene, applying the driving force "accomplishment".

(6) Behavioral feedback. In the process of exercise, users can understand the health of their own cervical spine, and through their own efforts to get the scene picture, these can extend the use cycle of the product, the application of the drive "avoidance".

The above design strategy resulted in a total of six main design points: health testing, guidance, exercise reminders, social interaction, avatar, and scenario design, which together form the main functions of the C-Rainbow. To verify the effectiveness of the gamification-driven model in user cervical spine exercise, the prototype was tested again on 20 young volunteers for the six design points mentioned above and scored (1–5) using a Likert scale, and the summary table of scores is shown in Table 2. The prototype testing and scoring revealed that the mean score of each design point was above 3, indicating that the 20 users were satisfied with the functional points of the product design. Therefore, the above gamification-driven model can motivate the behavior of the cervical spine exercise population.

Table 2. Score Summary Table

Design Point	Health testing	Guidance	Exercise reminders	Social interaction	Avatar	Scenario design
①	4	5	5	3	5	5
②	5	4	5	4	5	5
③	4	4	5	3	4	5
④	4	5	5	3	4	4
⑤	4	3	4	5	5	5
⑥	3	3	4	4	5	5
⑦	5	5	4	2	5	5
⑧	5	4	5	3	5	5
⑨	5	4	4	4	4	5
⑩	4	4	4	2	5	4
⑪	4	4	4	4	4	5
⑫	4	3	5	2	5	5
⑬	5	4	4	3	5	4
⑭	4	4	5	3	4	4
⑮	4	5	4	2	4	5
⑯	5	5	4	4	4	5
⑰	4	3	4	3	4	4
⑱	3	4	4	3	5	5
⑲	4	3	4	4	3	5
⑳	5	4	3	5	5	5
Average score	4.25	4	4.3	3.3	4.5	4.75

6 Conclusion

The great abundance of material wealth in the current society makes users put forward new requirements for products, traditional functional products can no longer meet the needs of users. For the design exploration of sports APPs should focus more on user experience and emotional needs, designers need to be more flexible in using drivers to motivate user behavior. This study proves to a certain extent that the gamification-driven model can bring good experience to users and enhance the usage cycle of the product, which provides a reference for the design of sports APPs. Due to the limitation of development cost, the designed APP was not released to the market, so we did not collect extensive user feedback and could only use the prototype to test the results, which is also the shortcoming of this study.

References

1. Sun, Z., Lei, L., Liu, P., Cheng, Q., Shi, J., Li, D.: Analysis of cervical spine health status and influencing factors in college student population. School Health China **40**(04), 631–633 (2019)
2. Xie, W.: Integrated therapy to intervene in the cervical spine subhealth of college students. Shandong University of Traditional Chinese Medicine (2011)
3. Yu, L.X., Jiang, L., Zhang, Y., Zheng, F., Xing, M., Qu, H.: Analysis of the effect of cervical spine exercise therapy intervention on the cervical spine subhealth condition of college students. General Pract. Nurs. **16**(02), 227–228 (2018)
4. Wu, J., et al.: A study on the pain characteristics of neck pain in adolescents. J. Beijing Univ. Tradit. Chin. Med. **37**(09), 633–637 (2014)
5. Xu, J., Zhou, M., Li, Y., Wang, W., Yin, H.: Analysis of cervical spine subhealth and its influencing factors among college students in a school in Zhejiang. China Health Industry **13**(17), 57–60 (2016)
6. Liu, Y.: Interaction design of somatosensory game for cervical spine disease prevention and treatment of white-collar people. Jiangnan University (2016)
7. Deterding, S., Dixon, D., Khaled, R., Nacke, L.E.: From game design elements to gamefulness: defining "gamification". In: International Conference on Entertainment and Media in the Ubiquitous Era, pp. 9–15. Association for Computing Machinery, New York, NY, USA (2011)
8. Chou, Y.-K.: Actionable gamification: Beyond points, badges, and leaderboards. Packt. Publishing Ltd. (2019)
9. Mcgonigal, J.: Reality is broken: Why games make us better and how they can change the world. Penguin (2011)
10. Werbach, K., Hunter, D.: For the win: how game thinking can revolutionize your business. Wharton Digital Press (2012)
11. Kumar, J.: Gamification at work: designing engaging business software. In: Marcus, A. (ed.) Design, User Experience, and Usability. Health, Learning, Playing, Cultural, and Cross-Cultural User Experience. Lecture Notes in Computer Science, vol. 8013, pp. 528–537. Springer, Heidelberg (2013). https://doi.org/10.1007/978-3-642-39241-2_58
12. Bai, N.: Research on the application of gamification design method in college students' sports. Zhejiang University of Technology (2017)
13. Chou, Y.-K.: Actionable Gamification. Wuhan: Huazhong University of Science & Technology Press (2018)
14. Chang, J.H., Zhang, H.X.: Analyzing Online Game-players: from Materialism and Motivation to Attitude. Cyber-Psychol. Behav. **11**(6), 711–714 (2008)

Exploring the Efficacy of Persuasion Strategies for Different User Types in Games that Encourage Environmentally Behavior

Siyu Yue and Yongyan Guo[✉]

East China University of Science and Technology, No.130 Meilong Road, Xuhui District, Shanghai, China

y81210104@mail.ecust.edu.cn, g_gale@163.com

Abstract. With the ubiquitous use of the Internet and mobile technology, game systems are being used in various fields to achieve goals, including the environmental field. Research has shown that persuasion strategies are effective in encouraging people to behave in an environmentally friendly manner, and in order to better facilitate the achievement of goals, environmental persuasion games use a variety of persuasion strategies to change people's behavior and attitudes in order to promote environmental behavior. However, most current gamification systems treat users as a single group, and a one-size-fits-all design approach is likely to reduce the effectiveness of persuasion strategies for different types of users, and personalized environmental gamification systems for different user types are yet to be studied. To bridge this gap, we conducted a quantitative study with a large number of users to investigate the following questions: (1) Are persuasive strategies persuasive in promoting environmental behavior? (2) Are there differences in the effectiveness of different persuasion strategies to promote environmental behavior? (3) Is there a difference in understanding the effectiveness of the same user type when faced with different persuasion strategies to promote environmental behavior? (4) Is there an impact of understanding different user types on the effective-ness of the same persuasion strategy? Our results show that there are significant differences in the effectiveness of different persuasion strategies, and that different user types have different preferences for the same persuasion strategy. Based on our analysis, we provide corresponding personalized design suggestions to develop persuasive environmental applications for different user types.

Keywords: Gamification · User Types · Persuasive technology

1 Introduction

In recent years, rapid economic growth has made environmental problems increasingly serious [1]. Environmental problems not only burden the earth's ecology, but also cause great losses to social health and socio-economics [2]. The developing countries will bear more losses and risks when facing environmental problems [3]. In order to cope with these environmental problems, we have taken many measures and always emphasized

X. Fang (Ed.): HCII 2023, LNCS 14046, pp. 412–431, 2023.
https://doi.org/10.1007/978-3-031-35930-9_28

the need for environmental protection, but the trend of ecological degradation has still not been fundamentally reversed. Because people are concerned about environmental sustainability issues, but often fail to translate this concern into their daily behavior.

Researchers have found that human behavior, no matter how small, has an impact on the environment [4]. Charles and Linda [5] analyzed the long-term environmental impact of human evolution from five perspectives: demographic, affluence, technological, institutional, and cultural. Therefore, it is necessary to change human behavior to reduce the negative impact on the environment. Studies have indicated that gamification can lead people to engage in environmentally friendly behaviors that lead to more efficient use of energy [6]. Orland [7] states that gamification plays a significant role in reducing energy consumption by individuals and is less costly to implement than other energy saving strategies, providing substantial benefits to both the environment and the economy. These studies show that changing human behavior is a key challenge for environmental protection, and that only by effectively filling the gap between people's awareness and behavior can we truly motivate environmental behavior.

Information technology has expanded the concept of environmental behavior and shaped a new daily life for people. Tim [8] have demonstrated the important role of social media in environmental sustainability. Oppong-Tawiah [9] designed a gamified mobile application to encourage the use of sustainable energy in the office. The rapid development of mobile Internet platforms and business model innovations have led to the emergence of a trend to integrate environmental protection actions with Internet technologies. Some platforms use Internet technology to build creative public service environmental booster mechanisms to spread the concept of low-carbon living. Gamification has emerged as a promising approach to implement such future-oriented environmental practices. It can create a relaxing and enjoyable environment for users, satisfy their psychological needs and motivate them intrinsically. In the field of environmental protection, gamification design not only mobilizes the public's initiative to participate, but also transforms the public from passively receiving low-carbon information to actively participating in environmental information to actively participating in environmental practices.

The development process of environment-related game mobile applications uses persuasive persuasion strategies to design relevant system functions. However, a study of the current state of development of persuasion game design reveals that there are still relatively few persuasion design studies applied to the environmental protection field. And they have a one-size-fits-all design behavior, which is counterproductive in motivating users' behavior. Most environmental game applications do not give sufficient consideration to users' individual needs. Existing environmental game designs are too homogeneous and one-sided, and the application of persuasion strategies does not fully consider users' preferences and characteristics. There are no surveys and studies for different user types in the design. The players of different user types in one game may respond differently to persuasion strategies and applications. If we can consider the type of persuasion strategies applied in the game that suits them according to different user types, the intervention of persuasion games will be more effective.

Therefore, this paper investigates the relationship between different user types and the persuasion strategies to inform the design of game systems. Only a few models of several user types from the existing literature are suitable for the design of gamification applications. We chose HEXAD user-type model (philanthropist, socializer, free spirit, achiever, player, and disruptor) proposed by Marczewski [10], which are very focused on game design.

We conducted a large-scale study with 400 participants to investigate existing persuasion strategies commonly used in environmental games in conjunction with user types. To develop models and study possible differences in persuasion strategies faced by different user types. Finally, we propose more convincing environmental game design solutions based on our findings and help optimize the design of environmental game apps.

2 Background

2.1 Persuasion Techniques and Persuasion Strategies

Persuasion technology is an interactive system designed to help and motivate people to adopt favorable behaviors and avoid harmful ones [11].Fogg defines persuasion technology as "a computational system, device, or application that is intentionally designed to change a person's attitude or behavior in a predetermined way [12] and proposes a persuasion system design and 28 persuasion strategies that have been widely applied in a variety of fields such as business, health, education, safety, and environmental protection [12]. Most of the persuasive systems are provided for health promotion, and 25% of them are designed for environmental protection [13]. Gardner and Stern [14] stated that these environmental problems that we will continue to face in the future are due to human behavior. Human behavior must be controlled and changed in order to achieve the purpose of environmental protection. The measures to protect the environment are not as effective as they could be, so we can consider combining persuasive techniques to change people's attitudes and behaviors.

A number of researchers have already applied persuasion strategies to research related to environmental protection. For example, Gabrielli [15] developed an Android prototype for sustainable urban mobility behaviors that uses four behavior change strategies including goal setting, self-monitoring, personalized notification, and sharing. The goal of providing better guidance for developing more effective solutions in the future to support citizens in adopting sustainable mobility behaviors in urban environments. Teulada [16] proposed a voluntary travel behavior change (VTBC) system, a platform that uses a combination of technology and persuasion strategies to encourage individuals to reduce car use and reduce global greenhouse gas emissions. Rahuvaran [17] designed mobile applications for water and electricity consumption saving in Denmark. In addition, Nkwo [18] et al. designed a waste management application that encourages students to adopt clean and sustainable behaviors and thus protect the university environment by providing a variety of personalized persuasion systems.

While the above studies show that the application of persuasion strategies in the environmental field can serve certain purposes, we also found that they screened a large number of persuasion strategies before the study. Because only a limited number of reasonable responses to persuasion strategies could be obtained in the actual research, narrowing down the number of persuasion strategy studies would allow for more accurate and valid conclusions. Therefore, we selected seven persuasion strategies based on the existing literature [19] on persuasion strategies for environmental behaviors. The Table 1 shows these persuasion strategies and their descriptions.

Table 1. Seven persuasive strategies and their descriptions

Persuasive strategies	Description
Competition	Systems with competitive elements aim to stimulate competition among end users
Simulation	This persuades users by providing simulations that emphasize cause-and-effect relationships
Self-monitoring	Systems that help track an individual's performance or status help achieve goals
Suggestion	A system that provides advice in a timely manner is more persuasive
Personalization	Personalize app features, contents, and functionalities to each user to suit their needs
Rewards	Incentivizes users for achieving specific milestones using badges, points etc
Social comparison	Individuals use others as a scale of comparison for self-evaluation in the absence of objective

There is a growing number of applications that use persuasion strategies to motivate sustainable environmental behavior, but no research has investigated whether these persuasion strategies have the same persuasive effect on different users when motivating people to behave in an environmentally friendly manner. This study will categorize users by different user types and suggest individual design ideas to improve the persuasiveness and effectiveness of the persuasion system.

2.2 Gamification Design and Persuasion Strategies

Deterding [20] defined gamification as "the use of game design elements in a non-game environment" and state that it has been widely adopted by the software industry to make products interesting and enjoyable for users. The most research on games has focused on the negative effects of games, but as games have evolved there has been an interest in the positive effects of games [6]. Gamification research has focused more on creating interesting experiences in order to increase overall engagement through the use of game design elements in non-game environments. Gamification has been proven to increase user motivation in a wide range of areas, for example, gamification design in the health field is often used to motivate people to live a more active and healthy lifestyle. And there is also an increasing amount of gamification design in the environmental field, as Guenther [21] experimentally investigated the impact of the average energy consumption of electric vehicles and found that gamification has a significant motivational effect. JouleBug is a gamified mobile application designed to engage users to act in an environmentally friendly way and create a deeper connection between local communities and nature. Divinus et al. [9] developed a system that tracks employees' electricity consumption on computer-related devices that engages them through a gamified mobile application and encourages them to reduce their energy consumption.

Gamification is maturing in applied research, and many designers of persuasive techniques want to use natural or common methods of play among users to deliver their interventions to affect change in end users. As a result, it has become common practice to add persuasive techniques to forms of gamification. The main purpose of persuasive games is to change users' behavior or attitudes using various persuasive strategies. Persuasive games have attracted attention as a new way to promote behavior change. Several persuasive games designed to change user behavior have been developed over the past decade, yet most persuasive games typically take a one-size-fits-all approach rather than tailoring their content and strategies to individual users or groups of users. Several researchers have pointed out the limitations and risks of one-size-fits-all persuasion designs. For example, Orji [22] examined the persuasiveness of ten commonly used healthy eating persuasion strategies and estimated the persuasiveness of these ten strategies for seven game player types using a questionnaire. Orji [23] investigated the differences in persuasiveness of commonly used persuasion strategies in persuasion games based on gender. In the literature, however, no research has been devoted to the study of environmental game design considering differences in attributes based on user type. We will therefore add to the existing research on user type categorization to determine the generalizability of persuasion strategies and develop guidelines to customize a more persuasive gamification system.

2.3 User Type Study

For many years, researchers have been investigating personalized gamification designs so as to improve the problem of ignored user preferences due to the monolithic nature of gamification designs. Research has shown that user personality is an important determinant of motivation and persuasiveness [24]. Halko [25] had further demonstrated a relationship between user personality and the success of different persuasion strategies. Decades of research on game motivation have shown that treating game players as a whole is a poor design approach, because what works for one person may actually have the exact opposite effect on behavior change in another person. This is the reason why gamification can have positive impact effects along with other negative effects [26], which are thought to be due to different perceptions of gamification design as a result of different user types of users [27]. Thus, members of different user types of a game may respond differently to various strategies and applications, and persuasive game interventions would be more effective if the types of persuasive strategies that are appropriate for different user types could be considered for application in the game.

Regarding the study of user types, early researchers have been investigating how certain characteristics affect user engagement when using gamification systems and how to group people into player types [28]. Bartle [29] proposed the first user type model in which he classified players into four user types: (1) Achievers; (2) Explorers; (3) Killers (4) Socializers. Based on Bartle's user type study, Yee [30] collected data from massively multiplayer online role-playing games and proposed an empirical model of player motivation. Another user type model used for research is the BrainHex model, which is based on neurobiological findings and has seven player types: (1) explorer (2) survivalist (3) adventurer; (4) deep thinker; (5) conqueror; (6) socializer; and 7) collector. BrainHex complements research with more diverse user types, but Nacke's [31] study showed that each user type in the BrainHex model is not a psychometric type but a prototype for representing a specific player experience, and that the reliability scores are too low and need further improvement.

In order to create a model specifically designed for gamification, Marczewski [32] proposed HEXAD, a user type model for gamification based on an understanding of human motivation, user types, and practical design experience, in which there are six user types who are motivated differently by intrinsic (e.g., self-actualization) or extrinsic (e.g., reward) motivational factors when interacting with a game system. The division of intrinsically and extrinsically motivated user types is based on Self-Determination Theory (SDT), which states that a task is more likely to be intrinsically enjoyable when it supports three basic human psychological needs: competence - having the skills needed to complete the task at hand; autonomy - the feeling of being in control of the situation; relevance - the feeling of interacting with others. Other work in the field points to the importance of these three basic psychological needs and suggests that they can make a powerful and positive contribution to a person's psychological well-being[33]. Thus, according to Tondello [10], user types driven by intrinsic motivation are (1) socializer; (2) free spirit; (3) achiever; (4) philanthropist; (5) players are motivated by extrinsic motivation and (6) disruptor are not user types from SDT, but from observations of user behavior in online systems [34].

The HEXAD model was chosen for this study, and the Table 2 shows the different user types and their descriptions. It is considered the most suitable user type for custom gamification [27] because it does not categorize users into one specific user type and the model has been empirically validated to be created specifically for gamification [30] and has been successfully used in other recent studies, such as Hallifax et al. [35] who chose the model for use among custom gamification learning, where learner motivation and engagement behavior were significantly impact. In contrast, there is a lack of user-type specific research content in environmental games, so this study will create a more effective environmental gamification persuasion system based on user preferences and experiences.

2.4   Study of the Relationship Between User Type and Persuasion Strategy

To investigate the relationship between different user types and persuasion strategies, this paper develops a model using partial least squares structural equation modeling (PLS-SEM) to investigate the relationship between user types and the persuasiveness of persuasion strategies in the environmental field. PLS-SEM is a popular method for estimating path models to reveal complex interrelationships between observed and latent variables[36]. PLS-SEM is well suited for complex predictive models and has been successfully used by many HCI researchers to estimate the relationship between variables [37], Ndulue et al. [38] used this model to investigate whether the effectiveness of persuasion strategies differs in two different domains because of having different personality traits. It is based on a structural equation model, which consists of two sub-models: a

Table 2. Descriptions of the HEXAD user-type

User Types	Descriptions
Philanthropist	They are altruistic and willing to give without expecting a reward
Socializer	They want to interact with others and create social connections
Free Spirit	They like to create and explore within a system
Achiever	They seek to progress within a system by completing tasks, or prove themselves by tackling difficult challenges
Disruptor	They like to test the system's boundaries and try to push further
Player	They will do whatever to earn a reward within a system, independently of the type of the activity

measurement model and a structural model. The measurement model represents the relationship between the observed data and the latent variables, while the structural model represents the relationship between the latent variables. The iterative algorithm solves the structural equation model and estimates the latent variables using the measurement model and the structural model alternatively.

SmartPLS was chosen for analysis in this paper because it allows testing of theoretically supported linear and additive causal models. SEM can be used to deal with unobservable, difficult-to-measure latent variables. PLS-SEM is a soft modeling approach that does not assume data distribution. It is also recommended when sample sizes are small, applications with little theoretical available theory, when predictive accuracy is critical, and when correct model specification cannot be ensured.

3   Research Questions

The overall research design is shown in Fig. 1. We propose a more effective design for the application of persuasive strategies in environmental games by studying the effect of user types on the effectiveness of commonly used persuasion strategies in existing environmental games, addressing the problem that one-size-fits-all designs of environmental games are counterproductive in the process of motivating user behavior. In order to achieve the above objectives, we propose the following research questions:

RQ1: Are persuasive strategies persuasive in promoting environmental behavior?

RQ2: Are there differences in the effectiveness of different persuasion strategies to promote environmental behavior?

RQ3: Is there a difference in understanding the effectiveness of the same user type when faced with different persuasion strategies to promote environmental behavior?

RQ4: Is there an impact of understanding different user types on the effectiveness of the same persuasion strategy?

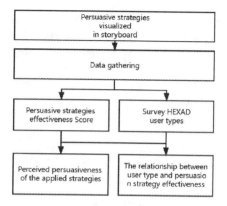

Fig. 1. Research design.

4   Research Methodology

4.1   Measurement Instrument

In this study, our main objective was to investigate whether the effectiveness of commonly used persuasion strategies in environmental games differed in terms of the effectiveness they produced for different user types. We therefore adopted a methodology that has been used in many HCI studies [39]. First we investigated six personality traits among HEXAD user types (Philanthropist; Socialiser; Free Spirit; Achiever; Disruptor; Player), and then we selected seven common persuasion strategies (Competition; Simulation; Self-monitoring; Suggestion; Personalization; Rewards; Social comparison) in environmental games from various types of literature and illustrated each persuasion strategy as a storyboard for explanation. The storyboard images shown are all part of a prototype design of an environmental game system put into use in the real world.

To obtain feedback from participants on the effectiveness of these strategies, we designed a series of surveys to collect users' perceptions of strategy effectiveness. Each prototype had a brief description of the corresponding function in addition to the corresponding storyboard, followed by a validated scale for assessing perceived persuasiveness. The scale, adapted from the study by Thomas[40] et al., is an established scale for assessing the perceived persuasiveness of system features and has been used in other studies related to gamified persuasion [41, 42]. The adapted scale consisted of four questions as follows:

1. The persuasion strategy will affect me.
2. The persuasion strategy will convince me.
3. The persuasion strategy has nothing to do with me.
4. The persuasion strategy will make me rethink my environmental behavior.

For the above questions, we used a 7-point Richter scale ranging from "1 = strongly disagree" to "5 = strongly agree" to measure participants' agreement with these questions. Open-ended response fields were added at the end of each strategy to collect qualitative comments from participants to substantiate their ratings of their preferences for each strategy.

In addition, to identify everyone's user type, we use the HEXAD scale proposed by Tondello [10], which consists of 24 question sets and has been applied in numerous related studies (insert some literature on the use of the hexad user type here). For example, whether a user fits the Socialiser user type is determined by the following four question sets: 1. Interacting with others is important to me; 2. I like being part of a team; 3. Feeling part of a team is important to me; 4. I enjoy group activities. For the above questions, a 7-point Richter scale ranging from "1 = strongly agree" to "7 = strongly disagree" was used to measure participants' level of agreement with the questions. To ensure the accuracy of the study, the questions were presented in a random order to avoid a centralized judgment of four questions for one user type.

4.2   Data Collection and Participant Statistics

In addition, because we chose to collect questionnaires through the Wenjuanxin platform, we ran the risk of automated scripts or bots completing the surveys, which would lead to the mixing of inaccurate data sets. To address this issue, we recruited more than the ideal minimum number of respondents for each survey and screened out invalid questionnaires containing incomplete responses and incorrect responses, as well as those with response times shorter than 3 min. A total of 400 valid responses to the questionnaire were obtained and included in the analysis.

The Fig. 2 shows the demographic information of our participants. 55.5% of our participants were male and 44.5% were female. The highest age range was 26–35 years old (38%) and the lowest was 45 + years old (12.5%). The majority of participants were educated, with 40% having a high school degree, 30.5% having a college degree, 21.5% having a bachelor's degree, and 8% having a master's degree. In addition, we also surveyed the participants' use of environmental game APPs, and the results showed that most 90% of the users had used environmental game type APPs, only 10% had never used them, and 59.5% of the participants used environmental game type software often or even every day, so the participants we counted had some degree of understanding of environmental game APPs.

To determine the suitability of our data for analysis, we performed Kaiser-Meyer-Olkin (KMO) sampling adequacy measures and Bartlett's test for sphericity. Our results show that the KMO was 0.916, well above the recommended value of 0.6. The Bartlett Test of Sphericity was statistically significant ($\chi2 = 7678.546$, $p < 0.0001$). These results show that our data were suitable for further analysis.

5   Results

In this section, we present the results of our analysis, focusing on revealing the preferences of different user types for common persuasion strategies in environmental games. The preferences of older people with different characteristics are also ranked and compared.

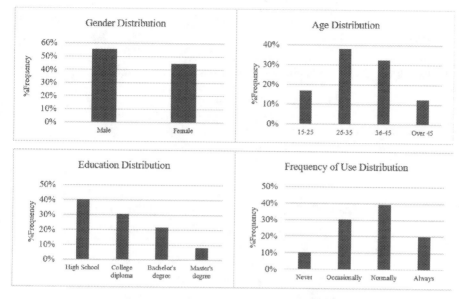

Fig. 2. Participants' demographic information

5.1 Effectiveness of Persuasion Strategies

First, we examined the overall effectiveness of the persuasion strategies. To do so, we calculated the mean value of persuasive power for each of the five strategies in their respective domains. Our results show that all persuasion strategies are effective, as all means are above the midpoint of 3.0.

Table 3. The averaged means of the effectiveness of the persuasive strategies

Persuasive strategies	Mean	SD	Sig
Competition	3.1900	.83472	.000
Simulation	3.2500	.91676	.000
Self-monitoring	3.2088	.93029	.000
Suggestion	3.1438	.89507	.000
Personalization	3.2338	.92497	.000
Rewards	3.2238	.86254	.000
Social comparison	3.2463	.89016	.000

To answer RQ1, the results of the one-sample t-test indicated that all strategies were considered effective in promoting environmental behavior overall, $t(400) = 50.929$, $p = 0.00$ as shown in Table 3, with the mean of the strategies above the midpoint of 3.0.

To answer RQ2, we conducted an RM-ANOVA with strategies as intra-topic factors. The results of the RM-ANOVA revealed the types of strategies ($F = 12.608$, $p < 0.006$).

This implies a significant difference in the overall persuasiveness of these strategies when no other factors are considered.

5.2 The Effect of User Type on the Effectiveness of Persuasion Strategies

We developed structural models for each domain, with personality traits as exogenous structures, as shown in the Fig. 3. Below we present quantitative results (Table 4) from our model and supporting qualitative comments showing the relationship between each of the seven persuasion strategies and user types commonly used in environmental games (RQ3.4).

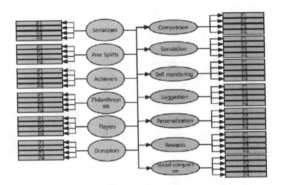

Fig. 3. PLS-SEM model structure.

Table 4. Standardized path coefficients and significance of the models

Factors	Achievers	Disruptor	Free Script	Philanthropist	Player	Socialist
Competition	−0.278	−0.150	−	−0.243	−	0.364
Simulation	−0.254	−	−	**0.298**	−	−
Self-monitoring	−	−0.144	0.241	−	−0.615	−
Suggestion	−	0.166	−	−	−0.346	0.208
Personalization	0.271	−	−	−	−0.412	−
Rewards	−	−0.185	−0.210	−0.184	−	−
Social comparison	−	−	−	−	−	−

p < 0.001 for crude coefficients, p < 0.05 for non-crude coefficients, "-" indicates non-significant coefficients, where negative values indicate negative motivation and positive values indicate positive motivation.

Competition
The competition strategy aims to stimulate competition among users using social influence to motivate their use. The results suggest that the strategy persuades those whose

user type is highly inclined to social home ($\beta = 0.364$, $p < 0.001$). These findings are supported by qualitative comments from the participants, which are sufficient to justify their ratings.

> "This feature is fun for me and will motivate me to use the app more often." "I like to pk with other people, it will make me more engaged in the app and more attractive to me."

The aforementioned review indicated that socializers would be positively affected by the strategy, mainly because it piqued their interest and increased their experience of using it.

The results also indicated that the strategy reduces the behavioral motivation of user types highly inclined to achievers ($\beta = -0.278$, $p < 0.05$), philanthropists ($\beta = -0.243$, $p < 0.05$), and disruptors ($\beta = -0.150$, $p < 0.05$). This suggests that competitive strategies may be counterproductive for those who favor these two user types. This is also well supported by their comments.

> "I don't like competing with others, once I lose more I have no motivation to use the app." "I like to play fun games, not games where I'm competing with others, which can make me tired."

Personalization

The personalization strategy tailors system features and content to user preferences. The results indicate that the strategy persuades those whose user type is highly inclined toward philanthropists ($\beta = 0.298$, $p < 0.001$). This conclusion was equally supported by the participants' qualitative comments, which were sufficient to justify their ratings. They felt that the personalized persuasion strategy it made the system more targeted and was able to automatically provide relevant features without individual action, and that the experience of using it was good.

> "This feature allows me to tailor the software about me to my own situation, and each person's page is individually tailored, which is cool." "Showing content tailored to my own use, and not requiring me to pick my own actions, will automatically be applied to the software, and not wasting time, which I think is great."

On the other hand, the personalized persuasion strategy showed a negative correlation for people whose user type was biased towards the achiever ($\beta = -0.254$, $p < 0.05$). Achievers type people they want to be able to make progress during the task and be able to prove themselves through difficulties. They believe that personalized strategies would break their preference to act according to a plan, and they do not feel the need for personalized strategies, and they would prefer to plan the complete process of use themselves. As stated in their comments.

> "I feel that giving a plan like this will be difficult for me if it doesn't do what I need, and will take time to adjust the plan he gives." "Its personalized application disrupted my original plan of using it."

Rewards

Systems that reward target may have great persuasive powers. Reward strategy attracts user types who tend to be libertarians ($\beta = 0.241$, $p < 0.05$). The reason for preferring rewards is that it gives motivation to users, motivating and encouraging them to use the application, as we can see from the following comments of libertarians.

> "I will stick with this program because he gives me rewards, which allows me to kill two birds with one stone, so that it gives me other achievements besides reaching reaching my original purpose." "Software that has this feature increases my motivation to use it."

Surprisingly, rewards do not have a positive effect on players ($\beta = -0.615$, $p < 0.05$) and spoilers ($\beta = -0.144$, $p < 0.05$) and may instead reduce their motivation to use. They did not perceive the rewards to be very meaningful and they did not choose to use a software because of small rewards.

> "These rewards don't do much for me, maybe it's practical for others, but I don't need it, I don't want something that I don't need as a prize." "Rewards that require me to insist on doing something to get them are like going to work for me, and I don't want to sacrifice time for rest and recreation for these prizes."

Social Comparison

Social comparison is the use of others as a scale of comparison for self-evaluation by individuals lacking objectivity. Social comparison greatly persuaded people who tended to be saboteur ($\beta = 0.166$, $p < 0.05$) and socializer ($\beta = 0.208$, $p < 0.05$) types. They believe that social comparison stimulates their use of software to some extent, and they prefer to use others as evaluation criteria for self-evaluation, and we can see these in the qualitative comments as well.

> "I wish I could get a top ranking on the leaderboard, it gives me a sense of accomplishment." "I can use this feature to determine if I'm currently doing enough or if I'm falling behind others."

However, those who had a strong preference for user-type players ($\beta = -0.346$ $p < 0.05$) were not interested in the social comparison strategy, which they perceived as not leading to a sense of accomplishment and reward, which hardly motivated them to further persist in using the software, as we can see from their evaluations.

> "Simply making ranking comparisons, a format I don't really care about, and I'm not w going to make too much of an effort to compete for first place."

Simulation

The simulation process allows users to quickly observe the connection between cause and effect as a way to convince them. The simulation strategy was highly attractive to those whose user type tended to be an achiever ($\beta = 0.271$, $p < 0.05$). Participants believed that having a first step in the process of the software produced a good help for their mastery of the software and were better able to use the software for their purposes, as can be seen in the comments.

"I think it's great to show the process ahead of time, especially for someone like me who is a slow learner of software, it helps me get up to speed on using a piece of software faster." "Sometimes software has so many features that it's hard to master at once and can consume a lot of unnecessary time and energy."

On the other hand, the simulation strategy significantly reduces the motivation of the user type biased players ($\beta = -0.412, p < 0.001$), who prefer to explore on their own, and it is easy to see in their comments that they do not see much point in this strategy.

"It might be somewhat useful, but it's not very useful to me and I have to keep clicking off the tutorial before using it which can be annoying."

Self-monitoring.
Systems that help track an individual's performance or status help achieve goals. Surprisingly, self-monitoring had a strong negative effect on user types who tended to be liberals ($\beta = -0.210, p < 0.05$), saboteurs ($\beta = -0.185, p < 0.05$), and philanthropists ($\beta = -0.184, p < 0.05$). They perceived that the strategy had no way to motivate them and even turned the heart against.

"I would prefer not to have my usage tracked and recorded, I want to be comfortable using the software." "Telling me my grades doesn't help, because I'm not using it to get good grades."

Suggestion
Systems that provide advice at the right time have more persuasive power. The Suggestion strategy did not yield any particular category of people to whom it appealed or lost momentum in this study, and we collated the ratings of both users who liked the strategy and those who disliked it. Participants who liked the strategy mainly thought that the strategy could give reasonable suggestions at the right time, while those who did not like the strategy thought that giving suggestions that did not impress them enough was meaningless and would disturb their feelings of using it.

"I like that it makes some good points, and I'll take his advice if I have to."

"I don't find it useful, I never browse this content seriously and sometimes he interferes with my experience of using it."

6   Conclusion

Our findings suggest a clear relationship between different user types and the effectiveness of persuasion strategies commonly used in environmental games. In this section, we will compile and summarize our findings in relation to the characteristics of each user type and other extant research findings. And based on the findings, we discuss how our findings can be applied to the development of persuasive environmental game systems to inform design decisions about which persuasive strategies to employ and which strategies to avoid when designing persuasive gamification systems for people with different personalities in different domains.

6.1 Summary of the Relationship Between User Type and Persuasion Strategy

The results on research question (RQ1.2) show that all of these strategies are effective for application in environmental games and can serve to motivate users. And the results of research question (RQ3.4) also demonstrate the extent to which specific participant types respond to different persuasive strategies when these strategies are applied to environmental games.

Philanthropist

Philanthropists have a stronger preference for personalized strategies, whereas competitive and self-monitoring strategies are difficult to motivate them. This may be due to the fact that philanthropists have a willingness to give without reward and they prefer to gain satisfaction by imparting knowledge to others rather than by winning competitions, so they are hardly attracted to strategies with a competitive bias. In contrast, personalized is strongly preferred because it provides more targeted content that is more responsive to the purposes of philanthropist user types [10].

Socialiser

Competitive and social comparison strategies greatly persuade the socialist user types. The reason for this is likely that both competitive and social comparison strategies contain a strong social element that satisfies the socialist's desire to establish social connections with others This finding is consistent with Tondello's findings (cited).

Free Spirit

While rewards are strongly attractive to liberals, self-monitoring is the opposite. The reason for this may be because libertarians, whose goals are more inclined to self-expression and exploration, refuse to receive ties, prefer to set their own goals, and are therefore more resistant to the self-monitoring strategy. The reward strategy, on the other hand, appeals to them to a certain extent, probably because the constant availability of rewards satisfies their desire to unlock content.

Achievers

Achievers have a relatively high preference for simulation strategies and a lesser preference for competition and individualization. It may be because simulation strategies help achievers to complete tasks, cope with difficulties, and thus prove their goals. In contrast, competitive and personalized strategies do not satisfy their characteristics of being more focused on themselves rather than others and preferring exploratory tasks to targeted adjustments (citation).

Disruptor

Disruptors have a strong preference for social comparison strategies and a lesser preference for competition, reward, and self-monitoring strategies. Disruptors tend to reach change by breaking rules, they do not like to follow rules, and have a certain rebellious spirit. Therefore competition, reward, and self-monitoring strategies create a sense of constraint for them and therefore have a negative effect.

Player

Rewards, social comparisons, and simulation strategies do not convince player user types. However, this result differs from the existing findings that player user types usually prefer activities that lead to systematic rewards (citation). The reason for the discrepancy may be that we have differences in drawing the corresponding storyboards as well as in the descriptions, and the reward strategies we present may not match the expectations of the player user types, thus backfiring and making the strategies unpersuasive to them.

In summary, player types may lead to different effects in certain situations, so in the next section we will discuss how our findings can be applied to developing persuasive gamification systems that appeal to specific user types and avoid causing them to resent them.

6.2 Provide Relevant Environmental Game Persuasion Strategies for Different User Types

Customizing persuasive game systems can increase their effectiveness, and based on our study above, we can customize persuasion strategies for user types to further enhance the persuasiveness of environmental games. We eventually organized the most preferred and least persuasive strategies for different user types in Table 5.

Table 5. The most and least preferred persuasion strategies for different user types

Factors	Competition	Simulation	Self-monitoring	Suggestion	Personalization	Rewards	Social comparison
Achievers	✗	✗			✔		
Disruptor	✗		✗	✔		✗	
Free Script			✔			✗	
Philanthropist	✗	✔				✗	
Player			✗	✗	✗		
Socialist	✔		✔				

We can see from the results that although the competitive strategy has strong effectiveness for socialists, it is difficult to work for achievers, disruptors and philanthropists at the same time. The competitive strategy is also the strategies that are difficult to persuade for the most user types, so it should be applied with more caution and preferably used in a targeted manner to avoid the undifferentiated application that makes persuasion less effective. The effectiveness of persuasion is greatly reduced by the indiscriminate application.

The personalization strategy is difficult to work for achievers and can have a stronger persuasive effect for philanthropists. We can consider providing this strategy in a targeted manner, but also consider that most user types do not have a strong correlation with the effectiveness of this strategy, so whether the application of this strategy can play a good persuasion strategy needs to be carefully considered, and the application of this strategy should be more reasonable and attractive to make the persuasion effect further improved.

The reward strategy is highly persuasive for socializers, but at the same time it is difficult to persuade spoilers and players. And we know from the above analysis that the practical application of the reward strategy has a great impact on the effectiveness of persuasion. As one of the most common strategies in persuasion games, designers may consider adopting it in environmental games, but we must realize that if the reward strategy does not meet the real needs of users, it will not motivate their behavior.

The social comparison strategy appeals well to both vandals and socializers, but is difficult to attract player-user types. Therefore, to design persuasive environmental games that promote environmental behavior among people who do not follow the rules, designers can use social comparison strategies. However, these strategies may not work for people with strong social attributes.

The simulation strategy is highly persuasive to achievers, but at the same time it is difficult to convince players. To promote the environmental behavior of people who desire to improve themselves, designers can use the social comparison strategy. The self-monitoring strategy is not persuasive for all three user types: vandals, libertarians and philanthropists, so we can consider reducing or not using this strategy in environmental games.

7   Limitations and Future Research Directions

Our study was based on a prototype implementation that collected self-reports of participants' perceived persuasiveness of these strategies. There are a number of limitations to this. First, testing through screenshots of the prototype is likely to be somewhat guided by participants' understanding, and there may be cases where participants who have not used the software or similar features may be biased in their understanding of the topic, making the results appear less accurate. Such a problem existed in the current study for the reward strategy. Second, the questionnaire was collected online and we knew very little about the participants, and although it met our criteria for returning the questionnaire, there were still a large number of unknowns that we could not determine how much they influenced the conclusions. Finally, there are differences in environmental behavior and environmental awareness in each country and region, so this may also have an impact on the findings.

There has been a lot of research on the effectiveness of implementing persuasion strategies, but there is not enough research in the application of environmental games, especially there is a big gap in the research that combines user types. In the next step, we should build on this research and think further about how we can make judgments about user types during the use of environmental games and apply the proposed targeted designs to them. It is desirable to be able to derive the judgment results during the game use process, so as to provide the corresponding strategy support more naturally.

References

1. Li, G., Lu, S., Shao, S., Yang, L., Zhang, K.: Do environmental regulations hamper small enterprises' market entry? Evidence from China. Bus. Strateg. Environ. **30**, 252–266 (2021)
2. Environmental health inequalities in Europe: second assessment report. https://www.who.int/europe/publications/i/item/9789289054157. Accessed 28 Oct 2022
3. Environmental inequality deepened during the COVID-19 in the developing world | Environmental Science & Technology. https://doi.org/10.1021/acs.est.0c06193. Accessed 28 Oct 2022
4. Li, D., Zhao, L., Ma, S., Shao, S., Zhang, L.: What influences an individual's pro-environmental behavior? A literature review. Resour. Conserv. Recycl. **146**, 28–34 (2019)
5. Vlek, C., Steg, L.: Human behavior and environmental sustainability: problems, driving forces, and research topics. J. Soc. Issues **63**, 1–19 (2007)
6. Morganti, L., Pallavicini, F., Cadel, E., Candelieri, A., Archetti, F., Mantovani, F.: Gaming for earth: serious games and gamification to engage consumers in pro-environmental behaviours for energy efficiency. Energy Res. Soc. Sci. **29**, 95–102 (2017)
7. Orland, B., Ram, N., Lang, D., Houser, K., Kling, N., Coccia, M.: Saving energy in an office environment: a serious game intervention. Energy Build. **74**, 43–52 (2014)
8. Digitally enabled affordances for community-driven environmental movement in rural Malaysia - Tim - 2018 - Information Systems Journal - Wiley Online Library. https://doi.org/10.1111/isj.12140. Accessed 12 Nov 2022
9. Oppong-Tawiah, D., Webster, J., Staples, S., Cameron, A.-F., Ortiz de Guinea, A., Hung, T.Y.: Developing a gamified mobile application to encourage sustainable energy use in the office. J. Business Res. **106**, 388–405 (2020)
10. Tondello, G.F., Wehbe, R.R., Diamond, L., Busch, M., Marczewski, A., Nacke, L.E.: The gamification user types Hexad scale. In: Proceedings of the 2016 Annual Symposium on Computer-Human Interaction in Play, pp. 229–243. Association for Computing Machinery, New York, NY, USA (2016)
11. Orji, R., Moffatt, K.: Persuasive technology for health and wellness: state-of-the-art and emerging trends. Health Informatics J. **24**, 66–91 (2018)
12. Fogg, B.J.: Persuasive technology: using computers to change what we think and do. Ubiquity 2002 **5**,2 (2002)
13. Wiafe I, Nakata K.: Bibliographic analysis of persuasive systems: techniques; methods and domains of application. In: the 7th international conference on persuasive technology, Persuasive technology: Design for health and safety; PERSUASIVE 2012; Linköping; Sweden; 6–8 June Adjunct Proceedings, pp. 61–64. Linköping University Electronic Press, (2012)
14. Gardner, G., Stern, P.: Environmental Problems and Human Behavior, Second Edition. UK (2002)
15. Gabrielli, S., et al.: Design challenges in motivating change for sustainable urban mobility. Comput. Hum. Behav. **41**, 416–423 (2014)
16. Individual Persuasive Eco-travel Technology, a mobile persuasive application for implementing voluntary travel behaviour change programmes - Sanjust di Teulada - 2016 - IET Intelligent Transport Systems - Wiley Online Library. https://doi.org/10.1049/iet-its.2015.0198. Accessed 12 Nov 2022
17. Persuasive Technology to Promote Pro-Environmental Behaviour - Environmental Psychology - Wiley Online Library. https://doi.org/10.1002/9781119241072.ch28. Accessed 12 Nov 2022
18. Nkwo, M., Orji, R., Ugah, J.: Persuasion for promoting clean and sustainable environment. In: Proceedings of the Second African Conference for Human Computer Interaction: Thriving Communities, pp. 1–5. Association for Computing Machinery, New York, NY, USA (2018)

19. Oinas-Kukkonen, H., Harjumaa, M.: Persuasive systems design: key issues, process model, and system features. Commun. Assoc. Inf. Syst. **24**(1), 28 (2009)

20. From game design elements to gamefulness | Proceedings of the 15th International Academic MindTrek Conference: Envisioning Future Media Environments. https://doi.org/10.1145/218 1037.2181040. Accessed 12 Nov 2022

21. Günther, M., Kacperski, C., Krems, J.F.: Can electric vehicle drivers be persuaded to eco-drive? a field study of feedback, gamification and financial rewards in Germany. Energy Res. Soc. Sci. **63**, 101407 (2020)

22. Orji, R., Vassileva, J., Mandryk, R.L.: Modeling the efficacy of persuasive strategies for different gamer types in serious games for health. User Model. User-Adap. Inter. **24**(5), 453–498 (2014). https://doi.org/10.1007/s11257-014-9149-8

23. Orji, R.: Exploring the persuasiveness of behavior change support strategies and possible gender differences. Presented at the Second International Workshop on Behavior Change Support Systems (2014)

24. Hu, R., Pu, P.: A study on user perception of personality-based recommender systems. In: De Bra, P., Kobsa, A., Chin, D. (eds.) User Modeling, Adaptation, and Personalization. Lecture Notes in Computer Science, vol. 6075, pp. 291–302. Springer, Heidelberg (2010). https://doi.org/10.1007/978-3-642-13470-8_27

25. Halko, S., Kientz, J.A.: Personality and persuasive technology: an exploratory study on health-promoting mobile applications. In: Ploug, T., Hasle, P., Oinas-Kukkonen, H. (eds.) Persuasive Technology, pp. 150–161. Springer, Berlin, Heidelberg (2010). https://doi.org/10.1007/978-3-642-13226-1_16

26. Bai, S., Hew, K.F., Huang, B.: Does gamification improve student learning outcome? evidence from a meta-analysis and synthesis of qualitative data in educational contexts. Educ. Res. Rev. **30**, 100322 (2020)

27. Hallifax, S., Serna, A., Marty, J.-C., Lavoué, G., Lavoué, E.: Factors to consider for tailored gamification. In: Proceedings of the Annual Symposium on Computer-Human Interaction in Play, pp. 559–572. Association for Computing Machinery, New York, NY, USA (2019)

28. Ferro, L., Walz, S., Greuter, S.: Towards personalised, gamified systems: an investigation into game design, personality and player typologies (2013)

29. Bartle, R.: Hearts, clubs, diamonds, spades: players who suit MUDs (1996)

30. Yee, N.: Motivations for play in online games. Cyberpsychol Behav. **9**, 772–775 (2006)

31. Nacke, L.E., Bateman, C., Mandryk, R.L.: BrainHex: preliminary results from a neurobiological gamer typology survey. In: Anacleto, J.C., Fels, S., Graham, N., Kapralos, B., Saif El-Nasr, M., Stanley, K. (eds.) Entertainment Computing – ICEC 2011. Lecture Notes in Computer Science, vol. 6972, pp. 288–293. Springer, Heidelberg (2011). https://doi.org/10.1007/978-3-642-24500-8_31

32. Even Ninja Monkeys Like to Play. https://www.gamified.uk/even-ninja-monkeys-like-to-play/amp/. Accessed 12 Nov 2022

33. Ryan, R.M., Deci, E.L., Vansteenkiste, M.: Autonomy and autonomy disturbances in self-development and psychopathology: research on motivation, attachment, and clinical process, pp. 1–54 (2016)

34. Tondello, G.F., Mora, A., Marczewski, A., Nacke, L.E.: Empirical validation of the gamification user types hexad scale in English and Spanish. Int. J. Hum Comput Stud. **127**, 95–111 (2019)

35. Hallifax, S., Lavoué, E., Serna, A.: To tailor or not to tailor gamification? An analysis of the impact of tailored game elements on learners' behaviours and motivation. In: Bittencourt, I.I., Cukurova, M., Muldner, K., Luckin, R., Millán, E. (eds.) Artificial Intelligence in Education. Lecture Notes in Computer Science (Lecture Notes in Artificial Intelligence), vol. 12163, pp. 216–227. Springer, Cham (2020). https://doi.org/10.1007/978-3-030-52237-7_18

36. Partial least squares structural equation modeling using SmartPLS: a software review | SpringerLink. https://doi.org/10.1057/s41270-019-00058-3. Accessed 10 Feb 2023
37. Anagnostopoulou, E., Magoutas, B., Bothos, E., Schrammel, J., Orji, R., Mentzas, G.: Exploring the links between persuasion, personality and mobility types in personalized mobility applications. In: de Vries, P.W., Oinas-Kukkonen, H., Siemons, L., Beerlage-de Jong, N., van Gemert-Pijnen, L. (eds.) Persuasive Technology: Development and Implementation of Personalized Technologies to Change Attitudes and Behaviors. Lecture Notes in Computer Science, vol. 10171, pp. 107–118. Springer, Cham (2017). https://doi.org/10.1007/978-3-319-55134-0_9
38. Ndulue, C., Oyebode, O., Iyer, R.S., Ganesh, A., Ahmed, S.I., Orji, R.: Personality-targeted persuasive gamified systems: exploring the impact of application domain on the effectiveness of behaviour change strategies. User Model User-Adap Inter. **32**, 165–214 (2022)
39. Orji, R., Tondello, G., Nacke, L.: Personalizing persuasive strategies in gameful systems to gamification user types. Presented at the April 21 (2018)
40. Thomas, R.J., Masthoff, J., Oren, N.: Can i influence you? Development of a scale to measure perceived persuasiveness and two studies showing the use of the scale. Front. Artif. Intell. **2**, 24 (2019)
41. Improving the efficacy of games for change using personalization models | ACM Transactions on Computer-Human Interaction. https://doi.org/10.1145/3119929. Accessed 10 Feb 2023
42. Exploring perceived persuasiveness of a behavior change support system: a structural model | SpringerLink. https://doi.org/10.1007/978-3-642-31037-9_14. Accessed 10 Feb 2023

Author Index

Printed in the United States
by Baker & Taylor Publisher Services